VOCAL RITES AND
BROKEN THEOLOGIES

VOCAL RITES AND BROKEN THEOLOGIES

CLEAVING TO VOCABLES IN R. ISRAEL BA'AL SHEM TOV'S MYSTICISM

MOSHE IDEL

A Herder & Herder Book
The Crossroad Publishing Company
New York

A Herder & Herder Book
The Crossroad Publishing Company
www.crossroadpublishing.com

© 2020 by Moshe Idel

The text of this book is set in 12/15 Adobe Garamond Pro.

Composition by Sophie Appel
Cover design by Sophie Appel

Library of Congress Cataloging-in-Publication Data
available upon request from the Library of Congress.

ISBN 978-0-8245-5025-7 paperback
ISBN 978-0-8245-5024-0 cloth
ISBN 978-0-8245-5026-4 ePub
ISBN 978-0-8245-5027-1 mobi

Books published by The Crossroad Publishing Company may be purchased at special quantity discount rates for classes and institutional use. For information, please e-mail sales@crossroadpublishing.com.

[S]ince everything depends on the spiritual force that ascends.

—R. Moshe Cordovero, *Derishot*, p. 56

It is told about the Ba'al Shem Tov, blessed be his memory, since he was hearing speeches from the voice of the violin, [and] he was [transforming] the chirps [into] speeches.

—R. Nahman of Bratzlav, *Liqqutei Moharan*, I, par. 225

This is the issue of the rank of Moses, blessed be his memory, that he elevated and amended his speech, at the beginning they were the flock, which he was shepherding, and afterwards they became his disciples and he gave them the Torah, and studied with them, etc., and the words of the sage are gracious.

—R. Jacob Joseph of Polonnoye, *Ben Porat Yosef*, Koretz, 1781, fol. 99c, quoting the Besht

All the sublime comprehensions that he receives are not so important to him. What is crucial is to introduce an utterance [*dibbur*] into the world since all the supernal and the mundane worlds depend upon each and every utterance which he utters to men.

—R. Nahman of Braslav, as cited by R. Nathan of Nemirov, *Hayyei Moharan*, (Jerusalem, 1985), no. 374 pp. 255–256

The historians who have treated of them [the Hasidim] have been almost exclusively men saturated with Western culture and rationalism.

—Solomon Schechter, "Chassidim"

It is generally true that Western studies of religion have privileged, first, written texts, and second visual images and descriptions. The phenomenology of sound has been largely neglected, much to the detriment of attempts to understand and appreciate spiritual traditions—both Western and Eastern—that have bases, at least in part, in sacred sound as well as in narratives (whether oral or written) and imaginal and iconographic modalities.

—FREDERICK MATTHEWSON DENNY, PREFACE TO BECK, *SONIC THEOLOGY*, P. IX

Experiences of the first order, of the first rank, are never realized through the eye.

—EUGEN ROSENSTOCK-HUESSY

The world of sound is essentially cumulative, culminating. Whereas space has the same cosmic import now as before, sound plays a new and decisive role after the long evolution leading up to man.

—ONG, *THE PRESENCE OF THE WORD*, P. 310

It can scarcely be denied that the supreme goal of all theory is to make the irreducible basic elements as simple and as few as possible without having to surrender the adequate representation of a single datum of experience.

—ALBERT EINSTEIN

Everything should be made as *simple* as possible, *but not simpler.*

—ATTRIBUTED TO ALBERT EINSTEIN

CONTENTS

ACKNOWLEDGMENTS

This study is part of a larger project that intends a reexamination of a central topic in the thought of R. Israel ben Eliezer, known as the master of the good name, Ba'al Shem Tov, whose acronym is the Besht, on the basis of as many available and reliable sources as possible. Conceptually, it started in the late seventies of the twentieth century, when preparing my studies on the magical and Neoplatonic interpretations of Kabbalah in the Renaissance and the magical and theurgical interpretations of music in the Renaissance and Hasidism. Working on these topics was accelerated in 1990, when I prepared papers on "Reification of Language" and "Jewish Magic from the Renaissance to Hasidism," and it continued in 1993 in my lecture for the Eranos conference on "Talismanic Language," in my 1995 book on Hasidism, and more recently in some studies related specifically to the traditions of the Besht written afterward, especially the Hebrew study entitled "The Besht as a Prophet and Talismanic Magician." Much of the results of those studies has been accepted, *mutatis mutandis*, in some studies dedicated to Hasidism by younger students like Jonathan Garb, Tsippi Kauffman, Ron Margolin, Zvi Mark, and Ron Wacks, and to a great extent also more recently by Ariel Evan Mayse.

Here I confine my analyses to some views attributed explicitly to the Besht, whose teachings on cleaving and vocal performance are the main focus of the present study. His views turned out to be decisive starting points of an entire movement, but our concern is not so much with the reverberations of the Besht's thought when his name is not mentioned. My return to these topics is intended not to summarize my previous studies, or just to deepen the analyses of materials that have been dealt with earlier. I am interested here specially to carry forth the earlier line of research by engaging some additional Beshtian traditions, and offer also another, in my opinion profoundly different, picture of the nature of the early Hasidic type of mysticism. This will be done by analyzing the emergence of some of its concepts and practices out of elements transmitted from what Aby Warburg called "Pagan Antiquity" and its Renaissance revival, as well as the later studies of Edgar Wind and Jean Seznec written in this vein.

The major concern here is with questions of transmission and the transformations of late antiquity components of astro-magic that had been relegated to the margin of scholarship in Hasidism in the past and continued to be so also in the present. From this methodological point of view this study continues trends in my earlier book *Saturn's Jews*, where I stipulated the importance of astrological themes that were dominant in Warburg's school, for the perception of Sabbatai Tzevi as a Messiah. In addition I shall deal with the sources and the transmission of the concept of inherent spiritual forces allegedly found within linguistic units, and appropriation of early Hasidism of this view as part of the ideal of a mystical union with them.

It is a much more vocal and dynamic type of mysticism and it is thus divergent from the quietist-contemplative and ocularcentric picture prevailing in the studies of the leading scholars in the field starting with Gershom Scholem and continued rather faithfully by his disciples, a tendency that is quite evident even in the most recent studies in the field.

The paramount importance of the teachings of the Besht, and especially the most vital among them, requires an intense and detailed study. One of those is presented here in order to establish the existence of another, pre-axial type of spirituality, in lieu of the axial approach—to use the terminology of Karl Jaspers—adopted by scholars of Hasidism from Platonic and Christian sources. Hasidism displays a variety of combinations of the two approaches. However, there is no reason to impose the axial axiology upon the pre-axial one, and we shall explore a case of such an imposition that reflects the biases of many scholars of Hasidism who were "saturated with Western culture," as Solomon Schechter already envisioned quite early in the history of the research of this movement in the last decade of the nineteenth century.

I am confident that the amount of material attributed to the Besht that is salient for the topic will be addressed here, and that the details of their analyses, as well as references to their sources, transcend by far any existing scholarly analysis, allowing a different phenomenological and much broader picture of his views on a seminal aspect of his thought. In other words, through focusing on a specific topic of the Besht, the implications of his interpretation of vocal rites, I see in the following analyses a taste-case for the orientations in scholarship of Jewish mysticism in the last two generations, which cultivated the concept of the ocularcentric contemplation as central for Jewish mystics, some form of modern *concupiscentia ocularum*.

Parts of the present studies were written at the Institute of Advanced Studies of The Hebrew University and delivered there at lectures during the academic year 2007–2008, and were also dealt with at seminars at the Department of Jewish Thought at The Hebrew University during the same year and in 2005 and 2011. Time for writing it was part of my fellowship at the Shalom Hartman Institute in Jerusalem. This study should be read as complementing some elements that were discussed in my other recent studies regarding prayer according to the Besht, which will be mentioned in notes 18 and 20 and will be supplemented by discussions on the sources of Hasidic prayer and the study of the Torah as an essentially oral phenomenon in my book *Hasidism*, and in some studies that will follow. I have adduced in many cases the Hebrew originals of the passages under scrutiny in order to allow direct and immediate access to the sources that may facilitate an evaluation or a critique of my translations and analyses.

A small part of this study appeared in *Jewish History* vol. 27 (2013), and it greatly benefited from the careful and wise editorial suggestions of Prof. Ada Rapoport-Albert, for which I am indebted, and another one was printed in my study "The Hasidic Revival," which enjoyed the careful editing of Deborah Greniman from the Israel Academy of Sciences and Humanities. For all the remaining mistakes the responsibility is mine.

INTRODUCTION

After almost two millennia of a gradual development of a culture that was gravitating around written documents—a variety of canonical writings and numerous commentaries on them, and also many supercommentaries—a sudden turn toward various forms of orality took place in the third quarter of the eighteenth century, in what would become a center of Jewry. This turn, starting at the margins of Europe and Asia, left its imprint on growing Jewish audiences in what is called East Europe, producing in the late eighteenth century the Hasidic movement. This unexpected religious phenomenon was not just an attempt to attract less cultivated Jewish masses—none of the early masters of Hasidism deemed to create a movement—but also part of the development of an original type of mysticism that gravitates around instructions to attain mystical union with vocables and speech-acts that were part and parcel of the performance of canonized ritual in Judaism. The valences attributed to the vocal performances attracted both mystical and magical interpretations, and mystical-magical ones, much more than the original meaning of the ancient texts or prayers conveyed, and such developments will be explored in the next chapters.

Though keeping for centuries some forms of ritual activities and customs which changed only slightly, Jews adopted a great variety of theologies, most of them stemming from diverse sources, Orphic, Pythagorean, Platonic, Aristotelian, Hermetic, Christian, astrological, Zurvanic, Sufi, and their medieval reverberations, in addition to some inner developments related to the theories of divine *sefirot*, configurations [*partzufim*], and attributes [*middot*]. In the case of some of the former series of sources, they arrived to the Middle Ages in truncated forms, especially the Orphic,

I

Pythagorean, and Zurvanic theories, as most Jews did not read the language of the original sources. In some cases, especially in the theosophical-theurgical Kabbalah, those theologies or theosophies have been conjugated with the late antiquity Rabbinic rites and new customs shaped in the Middle Ages, in order to create some forms of resonance between belief and practice. In many cases this resonance takes the form of symmetries and correspondences between structures of divine powers and a variety of specific rituals conceived of having an impact on the divine realm; in some others, the consonance is related to some aspects of the human personality that ideally should be elevated to the higher realms and adhere to them. In some other cases, there are different conjugations between the instruction to adhere to, or be united with, the divine world on the one hand, and the impact one's actions have on it on the other hand, while in more complex models, also drawing power from above has been added to the combinations of the two other ideals. In short, my focus is on what is called *via activa*, which includes first an active approach to attaining an experience and in many cases also the drawing powers downward and even distributing them to others.

The belated various forms of Jewish speculations are sometimes more complex conceptually than the earlier ones, and eighteenth-century Hasidism is indubitably a belated stage of Jewish mysticism, and it inherited almost all the range of earlier theosophies, broken into much smaller units. Different figures since the last third of this century struck different balances between the components of earlier speculative panorama and the various models that permeated Kabbalistic literature. Grounded in rather selective and eclectic approaches to sources, the main tone of the following texts to be analyzed does not attempt to display erudition by lengthy quotations in the vein of Renaissance authors, both Christian and Jewish, or interpret canonical texts in this manner, but rather formulate short types of instructions, presented apodictically as part of a technical approach that depends basically on the perfection of human performance.

However, there is a specific propensity in the thought of the early masters that shaped Hasidism: a special interest in the manner in which the rituals were performed, as part of a vision of the supernal world as constituted of sounds and sometimes letters, which is more conspicuous now than it is possible to discern in the earlier stages of Jewish mysticism. Though not an innovation to be sure, this propensity is evident in many writings, but it did not receive the due attention in scholarship of Hasidism. This vision of a transcendental linguistic type of order relates to another important phenomenon I designated as linguistic immanence, namely the presence of the divine within the created worlds by means of letters, basically their utterances. Last but not least: eighteenth-century Hasidism put a strong accent on the performance of vocal rituals. The prominent place of the vocal rites, more than the dianoetic aspects of the recited texts, should be put in relief, especially since their explanations by Hasidic masters involve only different brief theological statements.

The following three factors, the theory of transcendental linguistic ontology or order, linguistic immanence, and the performance of vocal rituals, are sometimes conjugated and should be understood as part of Gestalt-contexture, to use the terminology of Aron Gurwitsch. The first is evident in the various designations of the supernal realm in terms of speech, as, for example, the supernal "world of speech," *'Olam ha-Dibbur*. We may speak about a reorganization of the character and relationship between different elements that already exist separately, in order to resonate with each other and thereby constitute a certain model. By performing the rituals, especially the vocal ones, someone was imagined by Hasidic masters to be able not only to affect the other, more spiritual levels of the linguistic ontology, but also, and more eminently, to change the inner structure of one's psyche and, by adhering to the vocables, to ascend thereby to the higher realms.

In general, Hasidism put a special emphasis on the quality of the performance. According to many of its exponents, it is sufficient to perform a commandment, but it should be done in a specific manner. While in earlier forms of Kabbalah it was the intention of the Kabbalist during his performance that mattered, namely his capacity to keep in mind the supernal structure of the divine world in order to be capable to affect it by his deeds, or later on to extract the divine sparks from the lower worlds, in Hasidism there is a strong propensity to performance out of love and awe, out of enthusiasm, with attachment, or in a devoted manner. The efficacity of the ritual shifted from the knowledge of the details of the supernal world and of the correspondences between those details and the specific commandments, which involve eminent mental operations of the expert Kabbalists, to a view that it is the emotional investment that counts much more, and that the specific details of correspondences are marginal. A more general instruction as to the emotional investment is pertinent for the performance of all the commandments, and in many cases in Hasidism the religious valence has been extended to a long variety of additional non-ritualistic acts, concerning secular activities but conceived now as a religious attitude, designated as worship in corporeality.

Unlike the Rabbinic approach, which insists upon precise manners of observance in the ways of behavior that can be viewed as nomian, here the assumption is that God wishes to be worshipped in a variety of ways. This is not a laxer approach toward worship, but one that is more flexible as to the specifics of performance, while simultaneously it was grounded in putting a strong accent on devotion to God. The early Hasidic masters that were less concerned with the Rabbinic insistence on elaborating on the minutiae of rituals, and with the Kabbalistic concentration of attention upon the metaphysical structures that may inform them, emphasized the emotional dimension of religion, creating a devotional alternative to the basic Rabbinic attitudes to religiosity.

The present study attempts to illustrate the main points made here by concentrating, as much as possible, on teachings attributed explicitly to what scholars envision to be the founder of Hasidism, R. Israel ben Eliezer, known as "the master of the good name," Baʻal Shem Tov, whose acronym is the Besht. Aware as I am of the scholarly controversies as to the authenticity of such attributions, I nevertheless opt here, as I did in the past, for a Besht that was much richer in the spectrum of themes and instructions that he bequested to his followers than regularly assumed in the prevailing scholarship. This multifaceted and conceptually complex figure is one of the major reasons for the diversity of what we can find in the books of his disciples, and of some of the developments in the later generations of Hasidic masters. It is needless to say that diversification in the later phases of this movement owes much also to the different personalities of the disciples of the Ba'al Shem Tov, but it is nevertheless emblematic that they ascribe different teachings to the same master. The conceptual fluidity of the Besht's thought is a major topic in my studies to be referred to in the notes, and it precludes a picture of the Besht as a monotonic figure, namely someone having a message in the singular that can be depicted by some few quotes, while many other discussions that are pertinent to the same topic but differ in content are conveniently ignored by scholars opting for, conceptually speaking, a more simple figure. The question of what is representative of this master's thought or of Hasidism in general is a complex question, since the extant material is diversified, and it should be presented first in detail in order to be capable to make the point of what is more or less representative. To be sure, the occurrence of the same theme in the writings of his main disciples is an important point for deciding what is representative, and the existence of common denominators in many writings may serve as an indication for their origin in the Besht's teachings.

On the other hand, while emphasizing the importance of this figure, I refuse to adopt a Romantic picture of the religious genius, of a hero born with a specific message that is totally new, one having a predestined mission that will transform Jewish life by its dint, as it is possible to see in the more enthusiastic pictures offered by authors like Abraham J. Heschel or Yitzhak Buxbaum, for example. This is the reason that we remain with a much harder and a more pedestrian task. Instead of discovering the one message, now one should collect the dispersed though available and diverse material, propose distinctions between their different aspects and messages, as necessary preliminary steps, before an attempt to propose a much more complex picture, which in my opinion should be seen more as a process than a stable worldview. Not having a theology of himself, as some Hasidic schools did later, the Besht was free to change his mind on this topic and he did so, and I try not to theologize him, since my approach does not allow such an essentialistic attitude, nor harmonize his diverging stances. Even more so since Hasidism built some of its broader worldviews on the basis of concepts and themes that were in the earlier phases of Judaism part of more comprehensive systems, philosophical or theosophical—especially Cordoverian, Lurianic, or Sabbatean—which have been disintegrated, some of those concepts have been selected out of many other alternatives and adopted in much looser structures.

The beginning of this disintegration of vast theosophical systems is evident to a great extent already in the so-called Kabbalistic-ethical writings, most of them emanating from the circle of Cordovero and his followers, who composed much longer treatises that are much less theological and strove basically to instruct people to behave in a certain way. A widespread literature that played an important role in Jewish life since the late sixteenth century, it mediated many Kabbalistic themes—theologumena—to early Hasidism without addressing the complexity of the theological discourses of Safedian Kabbalists, as shown in the pioneering and solid studies of Mendel Piekarz. While some of the Kabbalists who wrote the ethical treatises were well acquainted with the broader theosophical schemes, without however describing them, this is only rarely the situation with early Hasidic masters. They can be described as operating with a series of broken theologies, expressed in the context of instructions concerning vocal rites. When broken away from their context, the theologumena lose much of their earlier valences, and divergences between the broader systems are mitigated.

This fragmentation of earlier forms of speculative systems in Judaism, and the adoption of fragmentary vestiges of earlier Greek or Iranian types of religiosities, still known in the Middle Ages and Renaissance periods, allowed a more flexible understanding of the vocal rites that is much less systematic or dogmatic, emphasizing the more concrete types of religious activity. Elements from earlier modes of thought lose some of their meanings in the comprehensive structures without adopting other, more stable meaning, providing the significant conceptual fluidity of Hasidic thought, an issue to be dealt with as follows. This is the case of the emphasis on vocal rituals and the attachment to the religious leader, the Hasidic *tzaddiq*, both interpreted by means of astro-magical terminology. Just as the emphasis on non-semantic aspects of language allow access, according to the Hasidic theories to be discussed as follows, to mystical experience, the dilution of the role of systems also opened the door to a much more important role of the concrete personality of the leader.

On the other side, the obvious exegetical and homiletical nature of most of early Hasidic literature, and often times the concise type of expression, complicates the emergence of comprehensive Hasidic systems, which appeared only around 1800 in Ḥabad Hasidism in the writings of R. Nahman of Braslav and, to a certain extent, in the writings of R. Hayyim Tyrer of Chernovitz. It is only then that the disparate theologumena used in the various models of thought reported in the name of the Besht by his immediate disciples had been reorganized in a much broader theological structure. These two processes, namely breaking the earlier complex theologies and then the emergence of more systematic writings in Hasidism, are part of the different forms of organizations of Kabbalistic knowledge that generated the conceptual variety of Hasidic schools, a much wider phenomenon than earlier in the history of Kabbalah as an accumulative type of lore.

Though I cannot claim that I have exhausted all the possibly pertinent traditions related to the Besht as to the adherence to the vocables pronounced as part of the rituals—and sometimes even

as part of ordinary discussions—I have nevertheless multiplied
the scope of the primary sources under scrutiny, both Hasidic and
Kabbalistic, in comparison to the other scholarly treatments, a fact
that is represented also by the number and length of the notes. The
accumulative character of Judaism as a religion that combined
many strata of its conceptual developments should be reflected also
in the studies of Hasidism, despite the decline in this movement of
erudition as a major religious value. This decline, however, should
not affect the scholars. Moreover, the necessity to present a broader
picture of the Besht's intellectual panorama, in Jewish and non-
Jewish sources, becomes a challenge that was only rarely addressed.
However, provided the centrality of the topics under scrutiny here
for both the Besht and Hasidism in general, the efforts to document
those issues as much as possible are, in my opinion, quite worthwhile. In any case, my basic assumption is that by paying attention
to the dromenon, namely to what has been done, which means the
nature of the religious performance, one may elicit a better insight
in the overall structure, loose as it may be, than by speculating about
the impact of theology—that is, immanentism—on this movement.
This approach that puts a greater accent on the body, emotions, and
deeds takes in consideration techniques and rituals as much as theologies. In my opinion even more so as the Besht has changed his
mind through his life and adopted a variety of theological stances
which differ from each other, while the details of the performance
of the rituals remained basically the same.

In our specific case, adherence of the soul is imagined to
engage a long, though transitory and elusive, series of vocal entities,
namely the speech-acts of prayer, or of study of the Torah, practices
that differ from excercises of concentration on a fixed subject, as is
the case in a variety of instructions to contemplate or meditate. In
fact, we have an interesting case of the transformation of a preeminently nomian ritual, liturgy, into a mystical technique, a point to
be elaborated as follows. This is, therefore, predominantly a study
of the phenomenology of unusual instructions as to how to attain
a mystical experience, which differs from the classical forms of

ocularcentric concentration and contemplation on stable or fixed subjects, in some cases icons, for example, as part of one technique or another that is related to the graphical nature of the representation of the divine or a simple stable linguistic formula that is repeated orally. To be sure: my purpose here is not to speak about the primacy of vocal versus ocular approaches from a philosophical point of view, or to claim what is more important in Judaism, nor to denigrate one of them at the expense of the other, *à la* Heidegger or *à la* Levinas, but to analyze specific texts and their contexts and their sources and detect the different types of relationships between them. In other Hasidic texts, which will not be addressed here, another attitude can be discerned, an issue that does not concern me in the present study since I do not operate with generalizations about Hasidism. Nor is the present study an attempt to formulate a comprehensive philosophy of language according to Beshtian traditions.

Attempts will be made here to situate early Hasidism also from an historical point of view, not just along the conceptual lines of Lurianism and Sabbateanism/Frankism, as has been done in the dominant line in the analysis of Hasidism, but also of other types of Kabbalah. I shall be concerned here especially with the various forms of the ecstatic one and the Cordoverian corpus and their many reverberations, as well as with the line of a certain type of Jewish astro-magic mediated, especially, by the Cordoverian corpus. The recent studies dedicated to the latter two Kabbalistic corpora, and to Jewish magical literature in general, will be integrated in the exposition of the sources of topics under scrutiny as follows. It should be pointed out, as has been shown in my *Saturn's Jews*, that astral themes were mediated also by other Kabbalistic sources, to Sabbateanism. Therefore, in lieu of a simplistic rectilinear historical explanation imagined to be free of cross-currents, I would like to adopt a much more panoramic picture of starting points, which consists of a variety of vital sources and in more than one important channel of transmission, a fact that contributed also to the polyphonic nature of Hasidism. This proposal concerns the spiritual dimensions of Hasidism, and is not intended to replace historical research.

In short, we should better speak of Cordoverianism as a major presence in the history of Jewish mysticism, just as Lurianism was, and thus allow the emergence of a more complex history of ideas and themes in the field. Here I would like to explore in depth an aspect of the theory of language as quintessential for understanding some of the vital aspects of the thought of the Besht that stem from Cordovero and the Cordoverian tradition—especially the ethical-Kabbalistic literature—and present those aspects as ramifications of the thought of the Safedian Kabbalist. In the notes to this volume and in the last five appendices I will address Cordoverian terminologies that were pivotal for understanding the traditions of the Besht, and which have been neglected in most of the available scholarship about this figure.

However, the general theological context of our discussions is one that assumes an ongoing process of fragmentation of the divine world that started already in Rabbinic theories of the two attributes, in the Kabbalistic theosophies of ten *sefirot* and *sefirot* existing within *sefirot,* the Cordoverian theory of aspects of *sefirot,* and the Lurianic theory of divine sparks fallen in the lower worlds. The more the concept of the divinity was fragmented, the longer the theological discourse became, and R. Ḥayyim Vital's voluminous book *'Etz Ḥayyim* is actually the longest theosophical treatise in Judaism. This explanation assumes a different interpretation of the history of Jewish theologies, and of Hasidism, and to a certain extent of processes endemic to Jewish mysticism. In more general lines, it tells the story of the transformation of an exclusive type of transcendental monotheism into a growingly inclusive one, including immanentism. In immanentism, however, the plurality lost its weight since there was no specific distinction between the presence of the divine in one place or another. Even in the Lurianic theosophy, sparks differ from each other by the dint of their origin and the place they should be returned to by performing the various commandments.

While some of my earlier studies of this issue were dedicated to Hasidism in general, in later studies and especially here the major focus is on a variety of traditions brought in the name of the Besht. Provided the fact that the Besht himself wrote very little, most of the following discussions consist of material cited in his name by his direct disciples, and in some cases, the disciples of his disciples. My assumption is that the more a certain tradition recurs and in more diverse sources, namely in more of his disciples, the greater is the chance that this is an authentic Beshtian teaching. Moreover, the more a certain teaching is consonant with other teachings cited in his name, the greater the chances that they emanate from the shared source of those traditions, the person that was recognized as the master of the disciples.

However, my purpose in general is not to reconstruct a mono-tonic Besht, even less to portray a heroic one but, on the contrary, to highlight the existence of a variety of approaches, in my ter-minology "models" that populate the traditions cited in his name, and to unearth their sources. What had an influence on the history of Hasidism is not only the historical Besht, which certainly did so in a rather modest manner, but also the imagined one by his disciples, and thus, by the dint of the more popular *imaginaire* he became the founder of the movement. This means that when and whether some of the material I cited in the name of the historical Besht may turn spurious, this fact will not diminish its historical impact for the emergence of the movement.

This is a non-Romantic, multilinear type of history and a com-plex methodology that I adopt as follows and elsewhere in my studies, by combining philology, history, and phenomenology, as well as the Warburgian line of research. Though concentrating on one major aspect of the Besht's traditions, namely the place and the role of voice and utterances in vocal rituals as part of a specific form of Jewish mysticism, I shall attempt to characterize also the prevailing scholarly approach to it as reflecting some more general conceptual biases that, in my opinion, are plaguing the study of Kabbalah and Hasidism.

Likewise, another major concern in this study is to illustrate Hasidism in its early phase as exemplifying the last stage of another important historical trajectory of themes stemming from late antiquity magic, Jewish Spanish and Renaissance thought, Cordoverian Kabbalah, and then early Hasidism, a movement that emerged as just one of the possibilities of this trajectory. This explanation is closer to a *longue durée* approach rather than what I call the proximistic approach, grounded in the primacy of Lurianism, Sabbateanism, and Frankism as the necessary background for the emergence of Hasidim. All this does not, however, propose to overlook the possible relevance of some elements in those movements, but the main purpose of the present study is to show continuity in terminology and concepts with Cordoverianism, a task that is much easier to fulfill, with philological tools, as we shall see in most of the appendices.

1

VOCABLES AND *DEVEQUT* IN SCHOLARSHIP OF EARLY HASIDISM

There can be no doubt that the ascent of Israel Ba'al Shem Tov on the scene of Jewish history ushered in a new chapter in the social and spiritual life of many Jews that are described as East European and, later on, also of many Jews elsewhere. Many scholars engaged the few reports of his life and some of the scattered teachings transmitted in his name, and the following pages are one more effort among many to do so. As mentioned in the introduction, this will, however, be done from a quite different point of view. My basic assumption is that the Besht did not have a unified, coherent theory that could become a message, in the singular, intended to create a mass movement, but his thought developed substantially from the conceptual point of view, and a critical approach to the traditions reported in his name should take this assumption in consideration. This means that instead of pursuing the search of a general systemic coherence of those traditions, or one single type of experience deemed to be characteristic to him, it would be better for critical scholars to distinguish between smaller units or clusters of traditions, later on to be called later models that organize some of the materials in a more coherent manner than other models do. This is also the case of models of his experiences. Such an assumption requires a quite different approach not only to the Besht as a polyphonic figure, versus the scholarly assumptions that I call monotonic, namely homogenous, but also to another historical explanation for the emergence of the different trends in early Hasidism that reflect this polyphony.

One of the hallmarks of Baʿal Shem Tovʾs vision of the ideal religious life was his emphasis on a mystical "cleaving to the letters," namely, communing with the presence of godhead as encapsulated in the "letters," namely, the vocables or the sounds of the Hebrew alphabet as found in the sequences of the canonical texts of Judaism. This statement applied especially to the pronunciation of the syllables of the text of prayer, and to those of the Torah study in the sense of studying canonical texts in general—devotional activities which were traditionally performed vocally, some of which, according to many Hasidic sources, were to be performed loudly. It seems quite evident that the practice of vocalizing the texts of prayer and study as shaped in principle by Rabbinic Judaism in late antiquity was intensified in East European Hasidism, at least among some of its constituent groups. In fact, there were two basic and separated Jewish imperatives: to pray vocally on the one hand, and to cleave to God on the other hand, which have been conjugated and explained in an interesting manner by resorting to a terminology stemming from a specific type of magic: the astro-magical or talismanic one.

This oral dimension of both activities, which was self-evident in Rabbinic culture, has been almost entirely overlooked by modern scholarship, notably in the work of the two most important scholars to have focused on the mystical aspects of prayer in early Hasidism, Gershom G. Scholemʾs students, Joseph Weiss and Rivka Schatz-Uffenheimer, and to a great extent they continued an avenue opened by him. This biased reading of Hasidic texts was done under the impact of concepts stemming from Christian Kabbalists, as we shall see more toward the end of this study in chapter 13. This avenue has been used also by some scholars in more recent studies concerning Hasidism, and sometimes also in the case of Kabbalah.

Especially seminal for the entire claim of the present study is the fact that in the discussions of some of the passages to be translated and analyzed as follows, the three eminent scholars mentioned previously have consistently used the term *letter* for rendering the

Hebrew word *'ot*, in the context of a mental type of activity, thus neglecting the obvious sonorous dimension of the linguistic rituals. Their views were shared also by other scholars, as we shall see in some of the following chapters. So, for example, Scholem defines the seminal term *Yiḥud* as follows: "*[y]iḥud* to mean a contemplative act by which man binds himself to the spiritual element by concentrating his mind on the letters of the Torah."[1]

Indubitably, *Yiḥud* is a seminal term in Kabbalah and Hasidism and is a polyvalent, and sometimes, it refers to the uniqueness of God, to his unity—monotheism, to the unification of divine powers and divine names, and finally to the union of the soul with God or the spiritual world. Here, as Scholem duly points out, it stands for the latter sense. Following him, his direct students also emphasized the written dimension and subsequently the contemplative one, as is the case in the studies of Joseph Weiss and Rivka Schatz-Uffenheimer. They resorted to a connection to be found, as they deemed, between the visual aspects of the ritual, the contemplative act as a quintessentially mental event.

The three components of this quote—contemplation, mind, and graphical shapes of letters, or text—are indeed reflecting a Gestalt-contexture that is coloring the core of the modern scholarly understanding of perfection of Hasidic mysticism, defining as they allegedly are the act of cleaving to God. This penchant to emphasize the spiritual aspects of what were in fact vocal performances of rituals—the latter neglected in much of the available accounts of scholars in the field—is part of what can be called a scholarly transfer of categories from Christian mysticism to the academic study of mysticism, to an interpretation of Hasidism, a process that I call Christotropia, and we shall have more to say about this topic in chapter 13. This spiritualized reading amounts to decoding the Hasidic texts—and some Kabbalistic ones—against their conspicuous meaning that follows some earlier traditional modes of ritual activities to be performed orally and sometimes even by loud shouting.

To put it in linguistic terms: the Hebrew word *'ot* that semantically refers to both a graphical sign in the alphabet and a phoneme or a vocable has been understood by scholars of Hasidism as if referring solely to a sign. Needless to say that in Hebrew this phoneme means, in the singular form—though its plural form differs—also a wonder and in some cases also a non-graphical, a sign that is intended to remind something. Provided that the basic academic axiological structure that privileged the graphic sign has been adopted by most of the leading scholars in the field in the past, and also many of their followers in the present, as seen in the list of scholars mentioned in note 1, it is worthwhile to explore in depth the meaning of and the reason for this widespread [mis]interpretation of Hasidism, which radiates also on the more general conception of Hasidic mysticism in prevailing scholarship in the field. The question is indeed what is the reason for the reading of the text by a scholar in the field against their declared intentions both in the past scholarship and, to a great extent, also in the present? In my opinion, the problem is not just a scholarly debate as to the manner of understanding some specific texts, but the much broader topic of the categories that inform scholarship in a certain field as part of resorting to sets of concepts that are not critically examined, and producing results that fit the intellectual ambiance of the scholar, but not the gist of the texts under scrutiny.

My problem is not so much with the scholars' emphasis on the mental communion, which indeed can sometimes be discerned in early Hasidic texts, or with the resort of scholars to the category of contemplation, which is a matter of what senior scholars preferred to put in relief in their analyses, but much more with the exclusive status it has been given, ignoring totally texts that deal with vocal aspects, which are, phenomenologically speaking, quite different. Likewise, as we shall see in the following, the insistent recourse to the category of contemplation represents much less an analytical approach to a specific series of studied texts or to an analysis of the content of systems they represent than the reverberations of earlier scholarly understandings of what Jewish mysticism is as such, which are, in my opinion, quite precarious, an issue whose history will be addressed more at the end of this study.

To be sure, the two main occasions which will concern me most in the following pages, the performance of prayer and the study of the Torah, are not the only moments for cleaving according to early Hasidism, but in Hasidic sources they are dealt with much more emphatically and repeatedly, as we shall see in the following. In general, cleaving was supposed to accompany the performance of each of the commandments and, according to some other statements in Hasidism, actually every human activity in general. Though indubitably a very important mystical value in the long history of Jewish spirituality, *devequt* has indeed been allotted a special place for eighteenth-century Hasidism and its founder, much more than has ever been done earlier in a single school of Jewish mystics, ecstatic Kabbalah aside.[2] In my earlier studies and also in the present one, mysticism is understood as an attempt to establish a contact with what is considered by the mystics to be a higher or more comprehensive power, and *devequt*—especially during prayer—is an appropriate term for designating this pursuit as mysticism.

The centrality of the instruction of cleaving in general, including the cleaving to what has been described in the original texts and in the secondary literature as "letters," did not escape the attention of scholars. Gershom Scholem duly described it as follows:

> This definition of devekut as man's binding himself to the core (*penimiyyut*) of the letters, the Torah, and the commandments, instead of to their external aspects only, seems to be a new point made by the Ba'al Shem.[3]

However, this seminal statement notwithstanding, it seems that to this day there is not a single full-fledged study that has been devoted to this specific issue, important as it was considered to have been by the most respected scholar in the field. What is, someone may ask, the external versus the inner aspect of the letters: the visual aspect or the vocal one? And, what is even more pertinent: is the claim of novelty of the instruction to unite the human soul with "letters" in the Besht indeed true? Moreover, Scholem also surmises that the value of *devequt* was accepted because it is dealing with individual redemption, a view that he claims emerged only around 1750,[4] and this view replaces, in his opinion, the value of *tiqqun* and of collective Messianism. Finally, he asserts that the founder of Hasidism was the first to democratize this mystical ideal.[5]

However, in more recent scholarship on the topic, some specific Kabbalistic sources for the three aspects of *devequt* in the Besht have been pointed out, and thus the assumption that the three approaches to *devequt* are new with the Besht became quite questionable. According to these more recent findings, *devequt* as a way for a personal redemption and as a vital mystical value, sometimes depicted as the starting point of the mystical path, is not a new value at all in Jewish mysticism: It existed already in thirteenth-century Jewish philosophy[6] or in the contemporary ecstatic Kabbalah of Abraham Abulafia.[7] Indeed, its vision as constituting the beginning of the mystical path, and not just as its culmination as in the more standard views of this ideal, is found already in early fourteenth-century Kabbalist R. Isaac of Acre.[8]

The value of *devequt* in Hasidism is pivotal, and I assume that no serious scholar disputes by now this new emphasis. The single notable exception is the claim of Mendel Piekarz, who insisted in many of his writings that the mystical aspects of Hasidism, including *devequt*, should not be taken at their face value as referring to an actual experience, since they are part of a hyperbolic rhetoric which is, according to him, characteristic of the Hasidic style.[9] It is nevertheless an open question what this vision of *devequt* meant in more detail when did it enter the Besht's religious worldview, earlier or later, since it is indubitably not new with him, as we shall see as follows. Given the centrality of this ideal and its multiple ramifications for the thought of the Besht and its detailed reverberations, it is necessary to deal with its various expressions, its concatenations, and the genesis of this topic of the Besht in a more detailed manner than done earlier in scholarship.[10] By mentioning earlier the existence of some few Kabbalistic examples for the instruction to cleave to articulated letters, namely to vocables, I do not attempt, to be sure, to diminish the primacy of this practice for the Besht and his followers, but to contextualize it both historically and systemically. In this case, at least, what is more prominent is not the sheer innovation but the relative new role it played in the economy of Hasidic mysticism.

Moreover, some of the Hasidic teachings to be addressed as follows deal not only with the issue of *devequt* as a value in itself—which is not the single major center of our investigation here—but much more with the effects of this ideal or a state of consciousness, and *devequt* to letters/vocables should, therefore, be seen in many cases in a much broader conceptual context. First, in the following analyses, my point will be that the Besht embraced a view dealing with multiple forms of cleaving to pronounced letters, which can be exemplified in different traditions preserved by his disciples. Then we should speak, at least in some cases, about a syntax that brings together values found in earlier Jewish literatures, especially the loud study of the Torah and vocal prayer, with the value of *devequt*, which are sometimes conjugated in new ways, though the meanings of both have been significantly modified in comparison to earlier understandings of those practices. The proper understanding of each of them in Hasidism is best caught when situated within their wider conceptual contexts in certain systems, or what can be called, following Aron Gurwitsch's concept, Gestalt-contexture.[11] Separating the different phases or modes of cleaving from the next ones, or from a process that succeeds the acts of cleaving, often even ignoring the very existence of a significant sequence to the act of cleaving, simplifies and in fact distorts the more complex positions of the Besht and other Hasidic masters.[12]

On the other hand, it is important to emphasize the need to inspect as many extant traditions as possible before deciding what exactly the Besht's views about a certain topic were. The work of detecting the relevant sources, of discerning the views or the nuances found in each of them, eventually to arrange them in more meaningful conceptual structures I call models, and then to attempt to account for them from the point of view of their place in the Besht's thought, does not allow the very elegant and often unequivocal expositions on the nature of Hasidism as a whole, as found in the influential treatments of Martin Buber and Gershom Scholem, or the essentialist visions of mysticism as a whole as including strong proclivities to passivity, according to Joseph Weiss and Rivka Schatz-Uffenheimer. As we shall see this is true, even when one engages an issue that seems, *prima facie*, to be quite simple, like cleaving to letters/vocables appears to be. Without citing all the relevant material, it is hard to obtain a reliable picture and, for the time being, only a small segment of the traditions reported in the name of the Besht had been addressed seriously by scholars in the field. Collecting the available testimonies allows the emergence of a multifaceted and developmental picture of the Besht's thought.

I shall use in the following the form letter/sound or letter/vocable in singular and letters/sounds-vocables in plural in order to translate those instances when the Hebrew *'ot/'otiyyot* means not just letter/letters but pronounced letters or sounds, to be designated below when translating the Hebrew texts as letters/sounds or vocables. In fact, the *'ot* when translated as "letter" would be almost always a consonant, a graphical, visual, or mental linguistic entity, which cannot be pronounced alone without its accompanying vowel, and thus we have a syllable or a vocable. The double meaning of the Hebrew term *'ot*, referring to both the pictorial and the vocal dimensions, is especially evident in the most important book that contributed to the linguistic speculations in Jewish mysticism, *Sefer Yetziyrah*, where it refers to both a written and a pronounced unit. The latter, which concerns us more here, is evident in chapter 2. It is in this book that an acoustic explanation of the emergence of letters/sounds from the vocal apparatus has been proposed for the first time for the Hebrew language. The views of this book have been appropriated and elaborated by R. Elijah da Vidas, most probably under the deep impact of his teacher Cordovero, and were thus disseminated since the late sixteenth century and reached Hasidism, as we shall see in the next chapter.

The scholarly misunderstanding of this quite simple issue, the double valence of the term *'ot* and the role played by the sonorous or the acoustical aspects in early Hasidism is, however, not just a matter of a mistake of translation; it is related to a corollary and quite influential scholarly approach, one that emphasizes the ocularcentric and contemplative aspects of prayer and more mentalist approaches in general, and in some cases also an unrestricted stress of the scholars on the place of passivity in Hasidic mysticism.

It should be pointed out that though speaking so many times about pronounced letters, the Beshtian teachings do not significantly deal with the Hebrew vowels, which are indispensable for the pronunciation of the Hebrew consonants. Unlike Kabbalists who paid a great amount of energy to explain the meanings of both individual consonants and vowels, including each of their specific shapes and numerical valences, as means to penetrate the details of the divine realm, Hasidic masters were concerned much more with the general categories related to pronunciation, and this form of discourse is much more vague. This shift is related, among other topics, also to the turn to the vernacular Yiddisch as the main language of communication and preaching in the Hasidic audiences, an issue that will be addressed much more in chapter 14. Hebrew was much less a way to comunicate with humans than a way to attract the divine within this world, hardly a matter of dialogue in a Buberian sense.

By dealing with the Beshtian views on the major topic of multiple types of cleaving and their effects, my hope is that we may have also a better understanding of a major model that later on informed many of the main phases of Hasidism. This model has not been mentioned by the scholars who approached Hasidism basically as a contemplative-mystical movement, like Martin Buber, Gershom Scholem, Abraham J. Heschel, Joseph Weiss, Rivka Schatz-Uffenheimer, Louis Jacobs, Joseph Dan, and some of their followers, on the one hand, and even by many of the scholars who wrote extensive monographs and studies about the Besht more recently. In at least one case its pertinence for understanding the Besht has even been questioned, though its cardinal role in the writings of all of his disciples has been accepted.[13] On the other hand, some doubts as to the appropriateness of very resort to the term *magic* in the manner in which I used it when dealing with the mystical-magical model have been expressed.[14] The important contributions of the younger generation of scholars on the Besht's thought should therefore be taken in consideration before expanding upon the content of the Besht's teachings, and I shall try to do so as follows.

With the exception of the monographs of Ron Wacks and Tsippi Kauffman that deal with various early Hasidic topics, which are based upon a rather exhaustive perusal of much of the early Hasidic literature though not focusing only on the Besht but also on all his disciples, the other recent analyses of the first generation of Hasidic masters are much less exhaustive from the point of view of engaging Beshtian traditions. This being the state of the art, the present study requires a concentrated effort to elucidate the Besht's approach on the topic of vocal rites, not by just repeating what has been already discussed, but nevertheless neglected in scholarship, but also by adducing material that escaped the attention of scholars dealing with the magic and the mystical-magical model so far.

My assumption is that the Besht was intellectually richer, namely, including diverse types of thought, than the monotonic picture of his thought that appears from the available studies about him, neglecting as it does the possibility of changes and evolution in his religious attitudes. This is the case with a series of monographs or sustained studies about this seminal figure which were published in the last two decades, for example, M. Rosman, I. Etkes, H. Pedaya, N. Lederberg, R. Elior, Y. Buxbaum, and G. Nigal. In fact I shall try here, as I did in some of my earlier studies of the thought of this figure, to describe the Besht as a polyphonic and fluid thinker, whose complexity should never be transformed into a simple religious message as part of a scholarly, deceptive simplicity. Oscillating between extreme mystical and extreme magical claims and an emphasis on both the importance of modesty and of excessive boasting, he offered, gradually, various syntheses between them, plausibly as part of encountering new forms of religious thought unknown to him earlier in his career. This approach seems to me to be a historical, non-anachronistic one that does not conceive him in a heroic, or dogmatic, manner, neither as someone who consciously acted in order to create a movement.

Methodologically speaking, an attempt will be made in the following to compare several statements attributed to the Besht by different disciples, and by comparing them I shall point out both similarities and differences. Some of these statements have not been addressed yet in scholarship, and by bringing them together, I am confident that a better understanding of the early Hasidic thought in Eastern Europe will emerge, especially its polyphonic, non-dogmatic nature. For a critical understanding of the authenticity of the Besht's teachings, the existence of a common denominator of these statements, which differ from each other both in form and content, is essential: he embraced, relatively early in his career, a view that conjugates the ideal of cleaving to the inner essence of vocables with the assumption that such a cleaving empowers the mystic in different ways.

I propose to see the external dimension of the term *'otiyyot*, namely the vocal aspect as it was conceived by the Besht, as a reference to the concept of a vessel or container that contains its inner aspect that is identical to the concept of *ruḥaniyyut*, a complex and polyvalent term that will be the subject of many of our following discussions. This distinction is part of the complex vision of the Besht that is found already in earlier Kabbalistic sources, what I designate as a mystical-magical model. This model may take two major forms: one that attributes to the utterances of prayer and study of the Torah an inherent cargo of light, luminosity, and spiritual force independent of any human activity, as seems to be the case in the passage dealt with here, and the other one according to which it is the person who activates the letters, that draws these supernal entities or in some cases lights within the letters/sounds, and he is even capable to manipulate them. While this issue has been addressed insofar as many Hasidic texts in general are concerned in the generations following the Besht,[15] the focus of my discussion here is on his thought in particular, though this point has also been made in a tangential manner in my monograph on Hasidism and became even more evident in some studies I published recently, and it will be advanced by some of the following discussions that deal with earlier sources.[16]

It should be stressed that by resorting to the term model, I do not presume that this is the single model found in the Besht, or in Hasidism, but in fact we may speak about the coexistence of several models in teachings attributed to this figure, an issue that will be clarified in the following as it is already the case in my monograph on Hasidism. However, each of those models was adopted from more systematic and wider structures but in a fragmented manner, what I call broken theologies. Both the succinct and the exegetical nature of the Besht's teachings preclude a serious formulation of systematic theologies, though in some cases some forms of theological themes are to be found in the background. To be sure, the term *broken* I propose here does not necessarily mean that for the Hasidic masters there was a broken divinity; it stands solely for my understanding of the cognitive processes that nourished the Hasidic discourse in comparison to many of the Kabbalistic ones, though the Hasidic masters were aware of them.

In several earlier studies focusing on the thought of the Besht, I proposed an approach that surmises that we may discern more than one vision he embraced regarding many important topics. This is part of what I called the cluster-grape approach, which assumes that far from invalidating the reliability of those different approaches, the divergences about a certain issue rather reflect the special importance the Hasidic author or a certain Hasidic school attributed to that topic. This is a Midrashic approach that is part of a broader phenomenon of an ongoing process that becomes more complex in the later forms of Judaism, of organizing religious knowledge.[17] Moreover, when the discussions are not just a matter of an *ad hoc* interpretation but regard some form of more stable instructions for religious behavior, these approaches will be referred to as models.

Thus, we may discern three different models of understanding the Besht's variety of instructions regarding prayer, alien thoughts,[18] or messianism.[19] This is true when we deal even with one quite specific topic like the biblical verse found at the opening of the most important prayer in Judaism, the Eighteen Benedictions.[20]

In those studies I distinguished between three main models in the Beshtian traditions: the agonic model, dealing with the inner struggle, the great *jihad* in the Islamic tradition, or what is known in the Latin West as psychomachia, and this model seems to be the earliest in the Besht's career. Then he operated with a harmonistic model that deals with operations that are intended to induce some form of harmony in the external world, be it by means of theurgical operations that induce a state of union between divine powers, or by the ascent of the soul on high and being united with God and drawing divine powers below. It is this model that will be discussed here in more detail, and it is constituted mainly by the mystical-magical model, to be discussed in detail in chapters 9 and 10. Finally, and last in time in the Besht's career, is the noetic or the acosmic model that assumes some form of divine omnipresence, with the highest human activity as the recognition of this fact. However, even in this model he does not approximate a Spinozistic worldview—though Kabbalists and Hasidic authors resorted many times to the Hebrew formula "God is nature"—*'Elohim hu' ha-Teva'*—since some personalist, or theistic, elements remained part and parcel of the passages that constitute this model. This model will be dealt with shortly in appendix A. Different as those models are, they did not necessarily displace each other but, accumulatively, constitute the variety of Beshtian modes of thought. This variety is reflected also in the writings of his disciples, where those teachings have been preserved and are the main source for the material of the following discussions.

In the vein of the active nature of the harmonistic model, I propose to shift the center of gravity from a contemplative-mentalist scholarly vision of Hasidism as a whole as proposed by many scholars in the field to a more sonorous and active one, understood in positive terms, and attempt to analyze the significance of such an accent for understanding the complexity of the Besht's thought.[21] This does not mean that there were no instructions to contemplate written letters in Kabbalah and in Hasidism at all, or that a more mental cleaving does not exist in traditions related to the Besht, as we shall see as follows, especially in the chapter about R. Moshe Shoham of Dolina's quotations, but it seems that scholars have given to this aspect too exclusive a role in the general economy of early Hasidism, especially in the Beshtian traditions. On the other hand, contemplative elements are indeed evident in the Lubavitch branch of Hasidism, together with the emergence of a more systematic theosophy that invites such an approach.

This disproportionate academic approach that overemphasizes the visual, the contemplative, and the mental alleged dimensions had an impact also on another topic: the scholarly understanding of Hasidism as evincing a strong passive attitude, as it emanates from the studies of Joseph Weiss and, in a more limited manner, in the book of Rivka Schatz-Uffenheimer. The latter was well acquainted also with the activistic dimensions of Hasidism but, nevertheless, she thought that they were mitigated by what she believed was a comprehensive attitude of Hasidism to immanentism. Though we may indeed discern such short treatments of such views in early Hasidic literature, they do not constitute a challenge to my approach, which highlights activist elements, since I do not attempt to reduce the Besht, or Hasidism, to one single theological approach, as for example immanentism. Unlike the passive explanation forwarded by these scholars, which was not compared with the activist elements before generalizing about the nature of the mystical literature under scrutiny, I am content here with putting in relief elements that have been unduly marginalized, despite their prominence in the writings of the main masters of Hasidism and, I presume, also in their practice.

In this context, we should be guided by many Hasidic discussions, and numerous others in Judaism, where the study of the Torah/Talmud is interpreted as pronouncing the letters of the text. Such an expression of the common understanding of the study of the Torah and prayer as paramountly a vocal activity can be learned, for example, from a teaching R. Jacob Joseph of Polonnoye reports that he has heard from the Besht as follows:

> On the way that I heard from my teacher, blessed be his memory, that there are *Yiḥudim* [performed] in speech, either in the speech of Torah and prayer, and in the speech with his friend in the market, when he is capable to link him and elevate him, each one in accordance to his degree, some by means of the speech of holiness and some other by the speech concerning profane issues, since there are within it the twenty-two letters/sounds etc.[22]

Let me point out that the word "speech" that translates the Hebrew *dibbur* is an approximation. In Hebrew the word *dibbur* may refer to both the act of speaking on the one hand, and the result of such an act, the utterance, on the other one. In medieval Hebrew, it may stand also for the capacity of human intellect, *koaḥ ha-dibbur*. When in plural, *dibburim*, it is obvious that it stands for the results of the act of speaking, namely the utterances. What is important for the following discussions is the fact that the Hebrew texts to be cited as follows are less interested in words, which are semantic units that are represented in Hebrew by the terms *davar* and *millah*, but in the linguistic operations and their sonorous results. From this point of view, the utterances are another version of the vocal meaning of *'otiyyot*, which refers in some Kabbalistic and in many Hasidic texts neither to written letters nor to the semantic units they constitute. This is, to use Jacques Derrida's terms though not his approach, a case of phonocentrism without, however, being at the same time a pursuit for logocentrism. Moreover, the vocal aspect of the rites did not invite a creation or a search for metaphysics, as Derrida would claim, but actually a breaking of theologies. The approach that we are dealing with it here assumes a primary reference to be found in the supernal world, and the semiotic process is dislocated by a process understood as activating the ontological connection of the recited letter to its supernal eidos, sometimes by means of the spiritual force, as we shall see in appendices C and D. The "meaning" of the word is conceived in Hasidism to be much less semantic and much more magical: through the attempt to affect the lower world, the technique is imagined to return the vocables to their source or divine origin, and it is this contact that was imagined to be able to establish an impact on entities on the mundane level.

It should be pointed out that the more "dignified" term *ma'amarot*, which can also be translated as speeches or utterances, and is related in Rabbinic literature to the ten divine utterances in the first chapter of Genesis, was much less important in the discussions of cleaving to "letters" according to the Besht's more advanced teachings.

As seen in the previous quote, it is the human speech, even when concerned with mundane or profane affairs, the latter certainly in vernacular, that is eventually the subject of Hasidic teachings regarding cleaving to "letters." Mentioning the market as a possible place for cleaving to God is an interesting assessment that fits other discussions related to the Besht, which widened the scope of acts that are religiously significant, and we shall see in the following other similar examples. This has to do with the popular profile of the Besht and of Hasidism as a movement. The concern with elevating the human utterances is part of a more Neoplatonic mind-set, different from the astro-magic understanding of utterances as capable to bring down supernal powers, which will be examined in many of the following pages.

The switch from the concern with the valences of the written structures to those of the vocal register also created another type of relationship been the mystic and the alleged "letters": it is no more the relatively stable visual objects, the letters of the prayer or the Torah, which matter, but a more mobile and changing object: the pronounced sounds, which do not subsist after their emission and thus do not allow the fixation of attention on one important object alone as is the case in meditation.

I would like to be clear: I do not negate the existence of mental prayer in some few cases in early Hasidism, including some moments in the teachings of the Besht, but I wonder why those rare occurrences lead necessarily to a misinterpretation of other, in my opinion much more numerous, traditions of his if they deal with them or, in some other cases, ignore the other texts altogether. However, notwithstanding the scholars' view, by and large the main concern of the Ba'al Shem Tov is with the oral performance, ritual or in some cases others. Despite the fact that he would mention a series of vocal activities, prayer, study of the Torah, and even profane utterances in ordinary conversations, the actual focus of his interest is prayer, as part of a broader shift that is evident already in sixteenth-century Safed that I call the liturgical turn. In the case of the Besht, this turn is much more evident and emphatic.

On the ground of the quoted passage of the Besht and of the numerous other examples I referred to in note 22, and of many others that can be adduced in addition to them, some few to be discussed as follows, when *Torah*, namely some form of study, and *Tefillah* are mentioned together, one should better try to understand them not as referring just to written texts but to the sonorous metamorphoses of those texts. Subsequently, the term *'otiyyot* occurring in these contexts should be translated in many instances, some to be discussed as follows, as sounds or vocables but not as letters. When the term *'otiyyot* is mentioned, the cleaving is to be understood, as intended, paramount to utterances much more than to written or to other forms of letters, as claimed by scholars, as we shall see immediately. This assessment does not preclude, however, the occurrence of the term *'otiyyot* as referring to graphical signs in some other cases. Neither do the following discussions have too much to do with the ideal of cleaving to the Torah, if it is conceived of as mainly the repository of secrets imagined to be found in its written dimension, as we find in many Kabbalistic sources, especially in the Safedian ones.

Here, and in the many texts to be quoted as follows, the issue is how to produce, vocally, the letters that are inscribed in the text of written Torah and in the prayerbook in such a manner that they will become the locus for the encounter with the divine light or spirituality within them, but also, in many cases, to draw down influxes, light or spirituality, into the units of sonorous performance. This means an intensification of human activity related to both emitting the vocables of the structured texts and to an act of cleaving to them. The assumption is not only that the isolated vocables *qua* vessels have the property to receive the divine spiritual force, but also that their specific combinations of sounds have additional valences by the dint of the specific order of the letters/vocables, even if someone does not understand the meaning of the words or sentences. Let me clarify from the beginning that the term sonority in the context of the Besht does not imply a melodious or harmonic type of sounds—the interest in music in early Hasidism notwithstanding—but points basically to the loud vocal dimension of the rituals.

Though such a shift is evident insofar as the prayer is concerned, which was paramountly an oral event because of the instructions of the late antiquity Rabbis, the study of the Torah as a vocal enterprise is less evident for a reader that is not well-acquainted with Rabbinic ways of study of the Talmud, or with the ritual of reading loudly the Torah or vocal prayer. Indubitably, such a study has a strong oral dimension in traditional Judaism, and this is also characteristic of the Talmudic studies. However, in my opinion in Hasidism, including the "middle" Besht, this dimension is even more central since the term *Torah* means also the sermons delivered by the Hasidic masters, most of them if not all in Yiddisch, which was a major avenue for the dissemination of Hasidism. In any case it should be pointed out that the relatively early testimony related to the Besht's teachings, that of R. Meir Margoliot to be discussed as follows, does speak about Torah study but not about prayer, as in the many other instances to be discussed as follows. It is possible that primacy of prayer became more evident in what can be called the "middle Besht," namely, in the second model described previously, which will be the focus of most of the following discussions.

I propose here, in the vein of some earlier studies of mine in the field of Hasidism, to reshape the understanding of some important aspects of Hasidic practice emphasizing the primacy of the more activist elements, but my focus now is specifically some of the Besht's traditions, though not necessarily Hasidism in general. If the present proposal is adequate, it will illustrate a turn from the scholarly analyses that emphasize the primacy of contemplation or meditation on visual forms of letters to an approach that allows a much greater space to sonorous performance as the starting point of the mystical path as an essential component of Hasidic religiosity, and is part of the most influential legacy of the Besht, even though, as the claim will be later in this article, the role of speech-acts has been attenuated in his later period of activity.

Let me point out that the centrality of the vocal performance of prayer so that each of the vocables is pronounced separately is following a well-known Rabbinic instruction regarding prayer that is expressed by the Hebrew phrase *ḥittukh 'otiyyot*, which obviously refers to the term *'ot* as representing a vocable and not the graphical shape of a letter. To be sure, this approach is reminiscent of another Rabbinic instruction, to design the letters of the scroll of the Torah separately, and that when the letters are touching one another, they invalidate the scroll. In other words, the contemplative interpretation of the Besht's activity in modern scholarship is closer to a Christian type of mysticism rather than to the Rabbinic imperative to pronounce the words of prayer one vocable after another or engage in the vocal study of the Torah. It is the shift from the graphical letters to the pronounced vocables, recited often without looking at a written text at all, that is characteristic of Rabbinic liturgy, a fact that complicates the emphasis on mental prayer in classical forms of Judaism, including Kabbalah and Hasidism, pace the claims of modern scholars. The assumption that each Jew or Hasid in what is commonly called Eastern Europe had in his possession a prayerbook, and that he actually used it while praying, especially the main prayers, is part of an anachronistic picture. More difficult to understand from a scholarly point of view is the process of studying Torah—which may include also the Talmud—by separating the vocables, because of the potential loss of meaning.

Moreover, it is difficult to imagine a study of texts which is not done with books. Nevertheless, this vocal performance permeated many of the instructions of the Besht and his followers.

2

RECONSTRUCTING MULTIPLE MODES OF CLEAVING TO VOCABLES ACCORDING TO THE BESHT

Let me examine the instructions to cleave to "letters," though basically the intention was to vocables, as they have been adduced in the name of the Besht, against this methodological assumption as to the centrality of the vocal performance. A perusal of some of the traditions reported in his name, most of them consisting of relatively short passages preserved mainly in Hebrew, reveals quite an impressive series of references where we find diverse and even diverging discussions to this effect. Nevertheless, the Besht's teachings have not yet been collected systematically by scholars in accordance to their topics and then analyzed in detail, and what is even more surprising, the issue of cleaving to "letters" has not been addressed in an adequate manner in scholarship, despite its wide recurrence and its conspicuous importance. I shall first survey the most comprehensive scheme that addressed the issue of cleaving to "letters/vocables," which deals with a variety of acts of cleaving to different levels of existence of the Hebrew letters, which sometimes are imagined as corresponding to three or four different theosophical or cosmic worlds. Then we shall turn the attention to other models found in the Beshtian traditions.

R. Jacob Joseph ha-Kohen of Polonnoye, the most important and in my opinion also the faithful preserver of Beshtian material, though not exactly his anamuesis, wrote as follows:

The sage has eyes in his head so that he can discern and understand the time that is appropriate to intend his prayer in the secret of the inner [sense] in order to have delight . . . it is good but if someone sees that he is in the secret of *qatenut*,[1] and he cannot direct [his thoughts], because the alien thoughts are overcoming him, let him pray like an one-day-old child who reads the written text, as my teacher [the Besht] testified regarding himself, when he was in another land, he was for a while in this aspect of *qatenut*, and that deserted him,[2] and he was cleaving to the [printed] letters etc., and he said: "When someone prays from the written text [*ketav*] and adheres to the letters, then he elevates the aspect of *'Asiyyah*, because the word *B* is *Binah*." And he [the Besht] commanded to the particular man to do so, until he returns to his high degree, etc., and the words of the wise are replete with grace.[3, 4]

This incident seems to refer to the rather elusive episode of the Besht's short stay in Istanbul[5] sometime at the end of the thirties of the eighteenth century, but not later than the early forties. Perhaps then he was reported to have been in a state of distress that has been interpreted here as the consciousness of the diminished consciousness, designated as *qatenut*.[6] Another possible proposal would be that he refers to one of the Besht's visits in the Northern parts of the Carpathian Mountains in Moldavia or Bukovina. In any case, in such a low spiritual situation, the person is instructed to watch the written letters during his prayer. This practice is indeed described as a form of adherence to printed letters: the Besht was described as himself cleaving in such a manner to the letters, and he recommended this practice for a certain anonymous person, who then succeeded in return to his higher state of consciousness. However, this is an instruction as to how to overcome a certain moment of restricted consciousness in order to reach a peak of experience, and this is the reason why we have here a model that consists of the technique—the performance of a vocal activity, and an ideal to be achieved, the cleaving, and not just one more interpretation of the possible meaning of prayer.

No doubt this approach is depicted as quite a low form of practice, when someone is incapable to direct his thought, *le-kavven*, or concentrate when he is praying. This form of liturgical activity based on looking at written letters corresponds, according to the Besht, to *'Assiyah*. It is quite plausible that the phrase "aspect of *'Assiyah*" refers to the "world of Making," the lowest among the four Kabbalistic worlds, widespread especially since Lurianic Kabbalah. The term *aspect*, however, reflects some form of Cordoverian impact. The Hasidic master recommends elevating this low world to that of *Binah*, which corresponds to the letter *B*. I assume that this is not just the second letter of the Hebrew alphabet, but the first letter of the word *Beriy'ah*, which is the second world of the four cosmological worlds, an issue to which we shall return immediately as follows.

Let me emphasize that the form in which these issues have been formulated is quite enigmatic, and this vagueness is perhaps the result of a fragmentation of an originally longer passage, which has never, to the best of my knowledge, been discovered. Indeed, the occurrence of the tantalizing word *etc.* reflects the truncated nature of the passage. Thus, we may assume that R. Jacob Joseph had in his possession a longer form of the Beshtian teaching, which is for the time being unaccounted. *En passant*, this is not the only instance when the disciple confesses that he shortened the passages he had in his possession, an issue to which we shall return later when dealing with a passage by R. Efrayyim of Sudylkov, the Besht's grandson. Conspicuously, this lower form of activity should be transcended by something more sublime, though from the passage it is not clear how exactly it should be done.

Let me propose that the truncated form of the discourse, which is obviously related to the thought of the mature Besht, both as a practical mystic and as an instructor to others, can be better understood by supplying what seems to me to be the conceptual sequel of that discussion. In an important passage found in an influential collection stemming from R. Dov Baer of Mezerich's teachings entitled *Maggid Devarav le-Ya'aqov*, and in R. Aharon Kohen Perlov of Apta's famous compilation of Beshtian teachings, *Keter Shem Tov* (printed for the first time in 1794), we find the following seminal passage, which does not occur in any other earlier Hasidic source I am acquainted with, in the name of the Besht:

> During prayer he should invest all his strength [with]in the speeches [or utterances] and go from one letter/sound to another so [intensively] that he will forget his corpo-reality, and will think that the letters/vocables combine by themselves and link to each other,[7] and this is a great delight. And provided that in [the realm of] materiality there is a great delight, *a fortiori* in [the realm of] spirituality,[8] which is the world of *Yetziyrah*. Afterwards he should go to the letters of thought [*'Otiyyot ha-Maḥashavah*] and he will not hear what he speaks, and this is [namely means] that he goes to the world of *Beriy'ah*. Afterwards he comes to the attribute of *'Ayin*, since all his material powers have been obliterated, and this is the world of *'Atziylut*, [which is] the attribute of *Ḥokhmah*.[9]

The authorship of the passage is, however, not just a matter of its being included in the Beshtian compilation *Keter Shem Tov*. Such an argument is in my opinion certainly insufficient—if it stands alone—for a critical approach that attempts to reconstruct the Besht's attitude as different from the thought of his students. My assumption is that important aspects of its content are corroborated by other Beshtian teachings, which have been pointed out in the earlier notes in this chapter, despite the fact that it has been preserved without the name of the Besht in the Great Maggid's collection of traditions, but also, as we shall see immediately as follows, by my assumption that it supplements the elliptic statement from *Kutoneth Passim* that has been cited previously. Thus, it seems that while the beginning of the verbal process, either of prayer or of study, consists in an act of attachment to utterances in such an emphatic manner that it necessitates the entire person's powers, the end of the process is closer to what may be described as an ecstatic state of mind. Thus, while in the latter text the lowest world of *'Assiyah* is missing, the passage can be understood as referring to higher forms of cleaving, skipping the lowest one, assumingly related to graphical letters.

This text that deals with controlled investment of power while reciting the utterances, as well as many others, dramatically problematizes the vision of Weiss of early Hasidism as cultivating a *via passiva*, as a "fundamental feature of mystical passivity,"[10] which is hardly discernible either at the beginning or at the end of the process. To return to the passage from *Maggid Devarav le-Ya'aqov* that has been translated previously: This view of ascending during prayer through the different cosmic worlds is, probably, of Lurianic extraction, and it might have had an impact on the more elaborated Ḥabad theory of prayer of the Eighteen Benedictions and the four worlds. It should be pointed out that unlike the content of this passage, according to the Great Maggid, the state of divestment of materiality is some form of preparation that precedes the act of prayer.

Here we have another instruction that teaches how to pray: first to invest all the strength in the acts of speech which, when done in an intense manner, elevate the person over the corporeal state. Thus, the beginning of the process is related to self-control that subsequently weakens, attaining a point when his powers vanish, what I identify as obliteration, which translates the phrase "*nitbattelu . . . kol koḥotav.*"[11] There is no initiated or prepared type of quietist expectation for the intervention of the free divine will or revelation. This is what I call a strong ergetic attitude, namely an approach that emphasizes the necessity of action, here the vocal performance, done with some force, even when some form of dianoetic dimension is not mentioned as accompanying that action. The transcendence of materiality by intense recitation, and the attainment of a more spiritualized state of consciousness, are then described as attaining the world of *Yetziyrah*, the world of formation. This is the third cosmic world according to the Lurianic cosmology, which plausibly corresponds to the vocal activity. Then the passage mentions the ascent to the "letters of thought,"[12] which correspond to the world of Creation, the second of the four cosmic worlds. Here, though dealing with the "letters of thought," there is no sign of stopping the emission of sounds, but the person involved in the ascent simply does not hear what he himself utters. Thus, the vocal is not conceived of as superseded by the mental.

Even higher is the world of *'Atziylut*, the highest of the four cosmic worlds in Kabbalah, which corresponds to a state where the human capacities are obliterated, and is therefore described as *'Ayin*, the divine Nihil, and as corresponding to the attribute of <u>*Hokhmah*</u> in the theosophical system. Interestingly enough, even here the Besht, if we accept the present proposal of his authorship, does not speak about silence or mental prayer, at least not explicitly, and all he mentions is the cessation of the bodily powers. This does not mean, necessarily, that he stops praying but that it is done in an automatic manner. In any case such a cessation is not mentioned. All this seems to be rather clear: we have a sort of ascension though the four worlds by means of referring to different dimensions of letters. However, what is much less clear is how this fourfold process is taking place: does it concern each and every word of the prayer, or is it distributed between the different parts of the prayer, which may become a sort of crescendo? In any case, the end of the passage reflects a connection between the obliteration of the human powers on the one hand, and a contact with the *'Ayin*. This nexus is important since it may reflect a rather introspective type of experience, an immersion in a process that annihilates, temporarily, the identity of the person. Let me point out that in the two passages referred previously, the concept of delight occurs: in the first passage the *qatenut* means that the liturgical performance lacks delight, while in the second one the performance induces a great delight.[13]

Putting the two passages together enables us to reconstruct a more comprehensive Beshtian theory that has been truncated, which may be formulated as follows. There are four modes of prayer:

the first or lowest entails reading from a written prayerbook; the second is the vocalized recitation of prayer that entails the intense emission of sounds into which one draws all one's physical powers; the third is mental prayer, referred to by the phrase "letters of thought," which does not, however, seem to entail a renunciation of sound; and the fourth is para-mental type of prayer, which altogether transcends the letters, but which may still entail some form of vocalization. These modes of prayer relate, in the first instance, to the shapes of the letters, and in the second, considered to be the higher one, to their sounds. They correspond to three of the four cosmological worlds and also to the sefirotic realm, which is represented in the two passages combined by the two *sefirot* that are mentioned in them explicitly, *Binah* and *Hokhmah*, as well as the lowest *sefirah* of *Malkhut*, which is referred to implicitly *qua* the lowest world, *'Asiyyah*.[14]

Although the subject matter of both passages is the ascent through the hierarchy of ontologically distinct worlds, they refer also to correspondingly distinct states of consciousness or awareness during prayer. In addition, we may assume that, when taken together, the two passages reflect two basic and heuristically complementary modes of worship: in the first passage, the mode of worship that is appropriate for the spiritually diminished state of *qatenut*, and in the second passage, three stages of worship that are specific to the expanded state of *gadelut*.

It is appropriate to compare some elements found in the two passages as supplementing each other: in the former a lower form of prayer is described in the context of the lowest world, in the latter three other stages of prayer correspond to the three other higher worlds. In the first the prayer as based on watching the written letters is described, while in the second passage, the sounds and the mental letters are mentioned, as the second and third stage, as well as a fourth, transcendental state of consciousness. This fourth state presumably corresponds to what has been described in Kabbalah and in many Hasidic texts as the divestment of materiality, or corporeality, *hitpashshtetut ha-gashmiyyut*, which corresponds to the ontological level described as *'Ayin*.[15] The Besht capitalizes on a medieval distinction between the three forms of letters: the written, the spoken, and the thought ones,[16] and combines them with a fourth level, the state of mind that transcends the multiplicity of letters and sounds altogether. In the first passage the "world of *Beriy'ah*" corresponds to *Binah*, while in the second passage the higher world of Emanation corresponds to the higher *sefirah* of *Hokhmah*.

Thus, we may summarize, at least tentatively, the relationship between the two passages as supplementing to each other elements that are missing in each of them, allowing the reconstruction of a more complete picture of the Besht's view on this seminal topic. By putting the two passages together, we may reconstruct a more comprehensive Beshtian theory that may be formulated as follows: there are four forms of prayer: the first from a written prayerbook; then an oral one, by emitting sounds in a state of putting one's strength in pronunciation of vocables or sounds; then a mental prayer, by resorting to the phrase "letters of thought" without, however, renouncing at the same time the act of pronunciation of letters; and finally a para-mental prayer. Whether this stage still involves some form of pronunciation is not clear.

Though the topic of the discussions is the ascent to—ontologically speaking—different worlds, the Beshtian passages refer also to the spectrum of different states of consciousness or sorts of awareness that should be attained during prayer. We may presume that the two passages discussed in this chapter also reflect, when taken together, the two basic and heuristically complementary forms of worship: in the first the worship while in the state of *qatenut*, the other three forms of worship in a state of *gadelut*. What is not found in an explicit manner is the instruction to cleave to letters/ sounds in the second passage, when speech and thought are mentioned, an issue that will be addressed in the next chapter. When the two passages are read together, the four worlds are mentioned and so is the existence of the letters on the three levels, as in many other discussions in the Middle Ages.

Let me point out that though the first passage is firmly related to the Besht, the second one is preserved in *Keter Shem Tov*, a book which collects Beshtian traditions and in the Great Maggid's *Maggid Devarav le-Ya'aqov* and in *'Or ha-'Emmet*, but in these cases the passage is not explicitly attributed to the Besht, and I did not find it in any other early Hasidic source. However, given the parallels to the Besht's other traditions, which have been pointed out in the earlier notes, and the complementing nature of the contents of the two passages, I suggest to regard to second passage too as belonging to him, and use it in order to reconstruct a more comprehensive vision of modes of cleaving to letters according to the Besht. In any case, it is hard to understand why someone would invent such a description as found in the second passage, which complements so neatly what has been cited in a fragmentary manner, in the name of the Besht by R. Jacob Joseph of Polonnoye.

The relation between cleaving and ascent via all the four worlds is mentioned again in R. Aharon of Apta Perlov's collection *Keter Shem Tov*, though not explicitly in the context of prayer:

> When he cleaves himself, he should go first to the world of *'Assiyah*, and afterwards he should hover higher and higher and afterwards even higher, in the world of the angels and 'Ofanim, and afterwards to the world of *Beriy'ah*, so that he will feel in his thought that his thoughts hovered very high, to the world of *'Atziylut* . . . and just as someone tours [passing] from one chamber to another, so [also] should he tour in his thought in the supernal worlds.[17]

Interestingly enough, cleaving is mentioned only in an indefinite manner, without indicating what exactly the object of the act of cleaving is. From the context it may well be that cleaving has to do with a mental operation, as only the activities related to thought are referenced. However, it appears only in the context of the phrase "world of creation," just as in the passage we quoted previously from this collection of traditions, where the "letters of thought" have been mentioned, and it is possible that earlier sorts of cleaving took other forms. Thus, it seems that this is an end-experience, concerned as it is with ascension and, in its final phase, with the cleaving to the supernal worlds. According to the Besht the "world of formation," *Yetziyrah*, is, as in earlier descriptions of the four worlds, the world of angels. The reference to the concept of "chambers" is quite interesting, but it should be understood here in metaphorical way, not as referring to chambers in the supernal worlds. As we shall see in the following, the term *ḥadarim*, "chambers," is used in other Beshtian traditions in the context of the utterances emitted during both processes of prayer and study of the Torah or its ritual recitation, as referring to containers. Thus, though it is certainly possible to find in Jewish tradition terms like chambers and palaces that refer to supernal structures, for the Besht their vocal understanding is much more important, as part of what we shall refer to in the following as the architectural *imaginaire* of the sound.

Let me turn to a brief passage that occurs in R. Jacob Joseph, and corroborates in my opinion the Besht's authorship on the passage about the three worlds adduced previously from *Maggid Devarav le-Ya'aqov* and *Keter Shem Tov*:

> From the Besht, blessed be his memory: It is known that the letter *'A*[leph] is in [namely refers to the *sefirah* of] *Hokhmah* and thought . . . since *'A*[leph] enclothed in *B*[et] since *B* is two *Alephs* . . . thus the spiritual force of the Holy One, blessed be He, is within the letter *'A*[leph] and He clothed himself within it and created the light [*'Or*] from the letter *'A*[leph], which is the light of Emanation, and afterwards He clothed with [the letter] *'A*[leph] within the letter *B*[et] and created the world of *Beriy'ah*.[18]

It is obvious that some elements found in the second passage quoted previously occur here, but now they are explicitly attributed to the Besht: the idea that the letter *B* is a shorthand reference to the cosmic world of *Beriyah*, and that *Hokhmah* is both *Mahashavah* and emanation. It should be pointed out that here the written understanding of letters seems to be more pertinent. This short passage offers some form of implied continuous type of cosmology which may serve as the framework for the earlier discussions. In fact, what I described as the linguistic type of order is found in one of the most elaborated and presumably the earliest teaching of the Besht that is extant, which interprets the verse "Your Word Stands in Heaven forever" [Psalms 119:89], which described the heaven, and in a derivative manner also the other creatures not only as having been created by the ten divine utterances, as it is the case already in the classical Rabbinic texts, or by divine names, according to another traditional version, but by letters, which there means sounds, which are also sustained by the creatures thereafter.

In this rather lengthy treatment, the divinity was not described as found within the human produced letters or utterances, as we shall see in the following, but they constitute the divine presence within the firmament alone, as part of the divine speech. This is a view that I proposed to call "linguistic immanence," which should be distinguished from the human verbal phenomena that will occur somewhat later on in the Besht's thought, as discussed here. The latter may be described as a "mystique of pronunciation," grounded in a "mystique of the mouth" that can be discerned in the Besht's family, especially in R. Nahman of Braslav, and in some of his immediate disciples, and more texts to this effect will be adduced as in chapter 14 n. 4 and in appendix F in this volume.

To sum up this chapter: It is quite plausible that the Besht exposed sometime in his career a view of multiple cleaving to letters, understood as existing on three different levels which correspond to three of the cosmological worlds. In order to reconstruct this view, we should take into account material found in the Besht's name in the writings of the direct disciples, but also material found in the next generation in the compilation entitled *Keter Shem Tov*, even when there is no specific source for those passages that R. Aharon Perlov adduced in other Hasidic books available to us today.

The previous discussions dealt with the prayer as the occasion for an ascent from one world to another, without mentioning any effects on either the divinity or on the external world, namely without any theurgical and magical effects, as is the case in the passages to be discussed as follows. We may speak about *devequt* as an end-experience, unlike other Beshtian traditions where we may better speak about means-experiences.[19]

In any case, let me point out that according to a view found in the early nineties of the eighteenth century, R. Issakhar Dov Baer of Zloczow, in a context dealing with prayer and *devequt*, suggests that someone should link himself to the four worlds in order to be able to perform some form of operations, an issue to which we shall return later on.[20] Also in the same period, R. Ze'ev Wolf of Zhitomir claims that the structure of prayer corresponds to the four worlds prominent in Cordovero but especially in the Kabbalah of R. Isaac Luria.[21] However, while the two Safedian Kabbalists devoted space describing the four worlds, this is not the case in the Hasidic instructions, and this is one more instance of broken theology.

A final remark that has to do with the previous passages as well as with the seminal passage to be discussed in the next chapter: there is no mentioning here of divine omnipresence, or general divine immanence, and the centrality of the cosmic fourfold structure testifies as to this absence. In my opinion, divine general immanence or omnipresence is part of the latest phase in the development of the Besht's thought and was reflected in the teachings of many of his direct disciples and colored much of the scholarly, though unqualified, presentation of Hasidism as a whole.

3

R. MEIR MARGOLIOT H̲ARIF
OF OSTROG'S TRADITION

It is hard to know when exactly in his career the Besht had formulated the theory of multiple cleaving to letters/vocables we have proposed previously to reconstruct and to attribute it to him, as was done in the previous chapter. However, it seems that some distinct traces of the view as reflected in the previous passages may be discerned in one of the earliest testimonies about the career of the Besht as a religious figure extant in a book of his acquaintance in his youth, R. Meir H̲arif Margoliot of Ostrog. The partial parallelism we shall discuss in this chapter to the anonymous passage adduced in the previous chapter that dealt with the three levels of prayer strengthens substantially the authorship of the Besht on the views discussed in the previous chapter, and also helps us in situating them as part of quite an early phase of the development of the Besht. One of the earliest references in the name of the Besht is found in a book of Halakhic figure R. Meir Margoliot H̲arif, who was an acquaintance of the Besht already when the former was a youth. The reliability of this tradition has been accepted by all scholars who dealt with it, and the similarity between the issue we are concerned with here and one of the phrases found in it confirms the existence of a multiple type of cleaving. Margoliot uses at the end of paragraph [d]—to be translated later in this chapter—the term *Yalduti*—my youth—a term that is corroborated by another story about him and his brother's acquaintance with the Besht, as found in a collection of stories, which is thought by scholars to be reliable.[1]

Born around 1707, the details of the biography of R. Meir Ḥarif allow an approximation of the dating of the Besht's exposition of the teaching of the twofold cleaving to letters not later than 1727. This means that some years before he became a known figure in the Jewish communities as a spiritual teacher, the Besht already exposed a rather complex theory of cleaving to utterances. Thus, we may assume that around the age of twenty-eight or twenty-nine at the latest, namely several years before his alleged "revelation" in public, which was reported to have taken place around 1733,[2] the Besht taught, or at least was reported by a reliable witness to have done so, a view that remained one of the main cores of his later teachings, and subsisted as a main component of Hasidism as a wider movement. Given therefore the centrality of this teaching for understanding the views embraced by the early Besht, and its misunderstanding related to the translation of *'otiyyot* as "letters," let me address some of its content in some detail:

> [a] whoever prepares himself to study for its own sake,[3] without any alien intention, as I was warned by my great teachers in matters of Torah and Hasidism, included [among them] being my friend, the Hasid and the Rabbi, who is the paragon of the generation, our teacher and Rabbi Israel the Besht, blessed be his memory, [b] let one's desirable intention concerning the study for its own sake, be to cleave himself, in holiness and purity, to the letters/vocables, *in potentia* and *in actu*, in speech and in thought, [so that he will] link part of [his] [lower] soul, spirit, [higher] soul, *Ḥayah* and *Yeḥidah*, to the holiness of "the candle of the commandment, and Torah is light,"[4] [to] "the letters/vocables which are causing [someone] to be wise," and cause the emanation of the influx of lights and vitality, that are true and eternal. [c] And when he deserves to understand and cleave to the letters/vocables, he will be able to understand from the very letters/vocables future [events], because "[the Torah]

is enlightening the eyes"[5] of those who cleave to them [to
the letters/sounds], in holiness and purity, like the *'Urim*
and *Tummim* [d].[6]

Section [a] constitutes the introduction of R. Meir to the
teaching he will adduce in the name of the Besht. Joseph Weiss, in
the article mentioned in n. 6, dealt with the circumstances of the
writing of this passage, sometimes during the eighties of the eighteenth century, in Ostrog, a place where Hasidism became influential, and the new atmosphere could impact the formulations found
in R. Meir's passage.

The main topic of the following part of the passage is the recommendation to cleave to and the effects of the cleaving to the
utterances of the Torah, when it is done in purity. This is a central
topic in the view of the Besht in many other instances, and here
it is articulated twice, in sections [b] and [c]. Though the effects
in each case are different, I assume that we have a significant parallelism between these sections. In any case, the occurrence of a
similar sequence twice, and its articulation in an early testimony,
shows that it is part of the vision of the Besht relatively early in his
career, around 1727. Since then it developed both in his thought
and in the writings of his followers. Here the focus is on the issue of
cleaving to letters/sounds and its more general context as proposed
by the Besht, and I leave for another occasion a more detailed analysis of this passage.

Let me start with the description of the act of cleaving that
appears in the two sections [b] and [c]. In paragraph [b] two different aspects are involved in it: first ritual purity and the linkage of
the unified spiritual faculties of man to the letters/sounds. The state
of purity is most probably related to the pronunciation of the vocables of the study of the Torah by someone who did not defile his
mouth, where the five places of the utterances are found according
to *Sefer Yetziyrah*, chapter 2, a view of R. Moshe Cordovero's as
preserved by R. Elijah da Vidas's *Reshit Hokhmah*. Though quite
consonant to the former's views, I did not find this specific passage

in Cordovero's own writings. Given the importance of this passage for understanding the main topic of our discussion here, namely cleaving to utterances, let me translate this passage:

> And my teacher, let him be in peace, [namely Cordovero] interpreted the words [in *Sefer Yetziyrah*] "Fixed in the mouth" that are said there, to teach us that a great issue that is the existence of the five places [of pronunciation] whose source is found on high in the [divine] head, as it is written in the *Iddra'*, and they descend [by the way of emanation] and reveal themselves from one world to another, according to the aspects of [the four cosmic worlds of] *'ABY'A* and the Holy One, blessed be He, out of His love for man, fixed these letters/sounds in the mouth of man, in order to enable him to cleave to his Creator; by the very pronunciation of the vocables here below, when he studies Torah or prays, he [then] shakes and stirs up the roots above. The meaning of the verb "fixed" is similar to sticking the end of a chain in one place, and the other end in another place; the distance between the places notwithstanding, when a man shakes the end of the chain, which is in his hand, he shakes the whole chain . . . and so we can understand the virtue of our ancestors whose prayers were answered immediately, since they were careful not to defile the twenty-two letters/ vocables that are [pronounced by means of] the five places in the mouth.[7]

This is basically a Cordoverian passage dealing with the linguistic great chain of being, though I am unable to detect yet the precise book of Cordovero's from which it has been copied by da Vidas. What is also important is not just the phenomenological similarity between the claim of the two passages cited previously in this chapter, but also the fact that the latter passage is found in a book with which the Besht has been indubitably acquainted, and this is the reason I see in it, or in its reverberation in Horowitz's classic *ha-Shelah*, the source of the instructions to cleave to utterances according to the Besht. Moreover, da Vidas and the Besht share the assumption that there are multiple forms of cleaving, and they combined them with the stark accent they put on vocal activity. This is indubitably one of the major sources for the emergence of the Hasidic view of linguistic immanence.

A point that is worthwhile to clarify is the fact that in this passage, and in the quotes adduced in the accompanying notes, there are two forms of *devequt* that are discussed together: the first one is to the vocables, the second one to God. The former is indubitably instrumental in achieving the latter. This passage assumes a transition from the lower level, the human mouth, to the higher one by the similarity between the extremities: the lower and higher mouths, and because of the existence of a linguistic continuum that transmits the movement initiated below on high, the human vocal acts may impact the higher dynamics. The lower *devequt* is decribed as a multiple act that takes place by cleaving during the performance of the commandments and speeches, but its result is the *devequt* to God. It should be mentioned that if we presume the centrality of this passage for understanding the thought of the Besht, and there is no doubt that the Besht knew da Vidas' book, the framework of the four cosmic worlds mentioned in the last quote that could inform the thought of the Besht may be Cordoverian as much as it may be Lurianic.

The acts of cleaving as mentioned by Margoliot's tradition are solely "in speech and in thought." No written letters are mentioned here in an explicit manner, though utterances are definitively involved in this act. However, what the meaning is of cleaving in thought is less clear here: is it the mental operation alone that is involved here, or is there also a visual element involved too? If we compare these two forms of cleaving while studying some of the passages analyzed previously, they make perfect sense: indeed cleaving is not to a single type of letters but to more than one type, and in the tradition of Margoliot, explicitly to two. This means that there are two types of cleaving: one to the sounds or utterances, which is not necessarily related to thought, since thought is involved in another type of cleaving. It seems that "speech and thought" is not only a phrase that recurs many times also later in other Hasidic contexts, but it is the most plausible source of the quite widespread expression which recurs in some many cases in the writings related to the Great Maggid: "the world of speech" and "the world of thought."[8] If the two cleavings in R. Meir Margoliot's tradition exclude the clinging to the written letters, the assumption that the divine light exists within them without a human activity is quite problematic, and we must allow a certain impact of such an activity on the presence of the divinity within pronounced language.

Let me point out that just as it is possible to see some consistency between the two passages that I proposed to read together in chapter 2, as reflecting a more general pattern, this may also be the case of the passage from *Kutoneth Passim* and the tradition of R. Meir Margoliot: the two discussions complement each other from the conceptual point of view. Thus, in addition to the Besht's breaking theologies that he uses, as we shall see in the following, also his discussions reached us in a fragmented manner, though sometimes they may be nevertheless reconstructed. Provided the direct contacts of the Besht with his students, and their use of the term *etc.* in some cases, reconstruction is a necessary scholarly effort, especially when fuller, though both earlier and later, formulations of the same topic are available.

Thus, the modest remnants of the teachings of the young Besht turn to be seminal pieces of information for our understanding of some developments in the terminology of early Hasidism, including one of the Great Maggid's most cherished set of terms. Whether the Besht himself, sometime later on in his career, made this transition from the phrase "speech and thought" to the more widespread Hasidic terminology of "world of speech" and "world of thought" is not clear, though it is plausible, as we find in some of his traditions the expression "world of delight," while the expression "world of thought" is found several times also in the writings of R. Jacob Joseph of Polonnoye. Resorting to this expression in the writings of two of the most important students of the Besht, as well as in the book of his grandson, R. Efrayyim, and many times in material collected in R. Aharon of Apta's _Keter Shem Tov_, may serve as proof for its existence in the thought of their teacher, even when his name is not mentioned on a teaching using this phrase.

In my opinion, this is an example of resorting to a reasonable criterion that may be used in order to decide whether a concept is Beshtian or not. The implications of this quite simple methodological assumption for the serious research of the Besht are quite significant, since it is not only a matter of how to work with the writings of the students in a more complex manner in order to reconstruct teachings of their teacher, but in this specific case, we may see that the Great Maggid depends on his teacher even when the latter's name is not mentioned. If we may extrapolate from this example, and there are more like it as mentioned in my notes to it, the figure of the Besht looms more as a decisive factor for the formation of his disciples than assumed in the current scholarship on his thought and character.

Moreover, the entire context of the previous passage points in the direction of an oral activity, at least as the starting point. The study of the Torah for its own sake is certainly not just a simple visual event, or a mental reading, but rather is understood in the way it is practiced in many circles in Judaism, which means that it is eminently an oral operation, which may indeed entail and culminate in a mental operation. Furthermore, my assumption is that the special effects of the letters/sounds are related to a special activity of the purified person, namely pronunciation, and not just his contemplation of the shapes of written letters alone.

Before addressing this major issue related to human activity as a religious act, let me point out the possibility, which seems to me to be the most plausible one in this context, that two different and complementing events are mentioned here: the recitative-oral one and the visual one. The most important one seems to be the recurrence of the motif of light which, at least in a *prima facie* understanding of the passage, may be related to written letters, though, as we shall see later on in this study, actually this is not strictly necessary. However, what may seem to be an evident interpretation may conflict with the way in which some traditions related to the Besht have understood the affinity between lights and letters, and we shall return to this issue in detail as follows.

Though the content of the passage has been adduced expressly in the name of the Besht, the impression is, as it was already duly emphasized by Joseph Weiss, that the Besht was not the only master that taught this view to R. Meir Margoliot, but he was just one of some of his many teachers, though it is hard to find a parallel to its content in the entourage of the Besht. Therefore, he most probably gave expression of an idea that was already known, at least in a small group of masters who were his contemporaries. The ideal of the Hasidic study of Torah is expressed here by the particular interpretation of the phrase Torah *li-shemah*—namely that someone should study Torah for its own sake, which means for the sake of "the letter," though this should, as seen previously, be understood in many cases as for the sake of "the sound" or the utterance.

Two main topics are present in this quote: the idea of the cleaving to the letters/sounds and then to the emanation of the lights and vitality imagined to be found within them, on the one hand in section [b], and the knowledge of the future on the other hand in section [c]. Though the sequence of these two events, found both in [b] and [c], is not specified, on the basis of the order of their presentation, someone may assume that the act of cleaving precedes the descent of the influx.

Let me turn now to the continuation of the previous passage:

> [d] And since my youth, since the day I was acquainted
> with the adherence of love with my master and friend
> the Rabbi, our teacher and Rabbi, the above-mentioned
> Israel [the Besht], let his soul rest in peace, I knew for

> sure that those were his ways of behavior, in holiness
> and in purity, according to the secret of piety and ask-
> esis, [e] since the letters/sounds of our holy Torah are all
> holy, and when a person deserves to cleave to the letters/
> sounds, when he studies for the sake of heaven, he will
> be capable to understand future [events].[9]

This short but quite dense passage is basically a repetition of the Besht's instruction as to the manner of study for the sake of Torah as formulated already in passage [c], but this time the details are attributed to the manner in which the Besht himself behaved, and not just a general instruction. This repetition reinforces, in my opinion, the authenticity of R. Meir Ḥarif Ostrov's passage. If we accept the testimony in paragraph [d], we may assume that early in his career, the Besht not only expounded some form of teaching, but was conceived of as implementing it *de facto*. This means that we may plausibly surmise that the theory and practice described in this passage preceded even the moment of the encounter with the young R. Meir, and that the Besht then was therefore not at the very beginning of the articulation of his teachings.

En passant: the mentioning of the askesis in [e] as a practice of the Besht may point to a form of early behavior of the Besht, who afterward changed his mind on this issue in quite a dramatic manner and even opposed it.[10] On the ground of this analysis, it seems that before the Besht emerged on the public arena as a figure that has some modest form of mystical instructions, he already adopted the theory that will remain the most influential of his teachings in his immediate followers and their disciples.

Last but not least: also in this passage, the concept of divine immanence is missing, divinity being conceived of as dwelling within vocables related to ritual study alone, though not of prayer. This is in accordance with my proposal to see immanence as characteristic solely of the last stage in the Beshtian intellectual career.

4

CLEAVING TO UTTERANCES IN THE BAʿAL SHEM TOV'S HOLY EPISTLE

The lengthiest and most influential document authored by the Besht himself is the famous epistle called in Hasidic sources *The Holy Epistle* or the *Epistle about the Ascent of the Soul*, addressed to his brother-in-law R. Abraham Gershon of Kutov, who had already lived at that time in the Land of Israel for some few years. In the different forms we have of it now, the epistle had been formulated in 1750 or slightly later, though it also contains, according to the Besht's own claim, material which may be a little bit earlier. This is part of what I propose to call the thought representative of the middle Besht. We cannot here enter into the intricacies of the various versions of this epistle, and I assume that the passage dealt with in the following is authored by the Besht himself, despite views of some few scholars to the contrary.

After describing the wondrous mystical experiences and achievements he had accomplished shortly after R. Gershon of Kutov left Podolia for the land of Israel, the Besht recommends to his brother-in-law a special manner of praying and studying the Torah. This is again an instruction addressed to a certain individual, which can be translated as follows:

> But this I announce to you, and God may help you, and your way will be in the presence of God . . . especially in the Holy Land, that during your prayer and your study

[of the Torah] you shall comprehend and unify each and
every speech and you should understand the utterance of
your lips,[1] because in each and every letter/sound there are
worlds and souls and divinity,[2] and they ascend and combine and unify with each other[3] and with the Godhead,
and afterwards they [the vocables] combine and become a
word and they unite in a perfect union with the Godhead,
and [then] the soul[4] will be integrated[5] [into the Godhead]
with them in each and every aspect of them, and all the
worlds are united as one, and they ascend and become joy
and great delight, without an end, when you understand
the joy of bridegroom and bride in *qatenut*, and corporeality, even more so [it is the case] at the high rank.[6]

While in the earlier discussions adduced previously the Besht
referred to either the letters/sounds of prayer, or alternatively to
those of the study of the Torah, here the two forms of vocal activities are adduced together, as it happens numerous times in Hasidic
literature. Moreover, phenomenologically speaking, this passage
reflects a clearly different approach to cleaving than the teachings
we have discussed earlier. It does not assume a series of different
levels of letters to which the mystic cleaves, as in the fourfold discussions we have reconstructed previously, or the double cleaving
in Margoliot's tradition, but just one single type of letters/sounds,
the pronounced ones, to which the mystic cleaves. Then by the dint
of their ascent, also his soul is elevated and thus achieves union
with the divine world.

Let me point out that no other sort of ascent is mentioned here,
by means of lights, for example, for the elevation of the soul. I
assume that the order in which the three dimensions of the utterances were enumerated is significant: the "worlds" constitute the
lower components, then the souls should be regarded as higher,
and then with the highest component being the divinity. Thus,
by cleaving to the lower components, the human soul cleaves
automatically also to divinity. In order to better understand the

significance of the occurrence of the three components, we should resort to the architectural imagery of sound as a parallel to emanation that will be elaborated in chapter 8 in this volume.

This is, therefore, a special version of the ascent of the soul, which is based on the belief that letters/sounds ascend and become vehicles enabling the mystic's ascent or that of his "intention." Here the vocal dimension of the letters, not the written one, is quite obvious. The pronounced letters, namely the utterances, are described as soaring on high, in the vein of R. Moshe Cordovero's approach found in a seminal passage to be discussed as follows, which constitutes also the peak of his *Pardes Rimmonim.*[7] The triad mentioned in the previous passage parallels the concept of the spiritual forces inherent in the utterances.

More implicit is the phase of the cleaving of the soul to the vocables, which are understood as then ascending on high, thus facilitating the ascent of the cleaving soul with them. However, without the assumption that there is some form of cleaving of the soul to the sounds, there is no sense, according to the passage, to the claim that the soul is cleaving to God. This union may be explained in different ways: either according to the views discussed previously, namely that the union is with the emitted sounds, or that the vocables themselves are particles of the soul.

In any case, the theory of language is here much more elaborated than in the earlier discussions. Now there is a *raison d'être* for the cleaving: words are not just part of the vocal ritual, and cleaving to them is part of the concentration on the vocal performance; according to the theory of language here, the sounds are imagined to contain whole universes which have some form of structure; namely, they consist of some form of monads. They constitute, therefore, entities that facilitate the passage of human souls from one world to another, either from the divine to the terrestrial world or *vice versa*, as we shall see also in Cordovero's views to be discussed in appendix C. By its combination of multiple dimensions of reality, this variant is a much more complex theory that transcends the earlier theory of the Ba'al Shem Tov that we have described previously as constituting linguistic immanence. This monadic vision of the vocables is part of a more comprehensive reification of language that started in thirteenth-century Kabbalah and became much more prominent in Hasidic literature.

It should be pointed out that despite the fact that in the *Holy Epistle* the Besht offers the most comprehensive monadic vision of the vocable, he does not mention the inherent dwelling of lights within the utterances, a topic to which we shall turn later on in this study. Let me emphasize that the accent on the separate phonemes is rather widespread, though words or speeches are also mentioned from time to time. However, the accent falls on individual vocables that, when put in practice, are prone, in my opinion, to generate a sharp diminution of the dianoetic valences of the linguistic units under scrutiny. This amounts to a sort of performance of canonical texts as an incantation rather than a communication that has dianoetic valences. This mentioning together of the acts of prayer and the study of the Torah, as two forms of vocal activity that are so widespread in Hasidism, demonstrate the relative indifference toward the semantic cargo as the main aim of verbal activity.

In the Besht's passage discussed here, ecstasy consists of a spiritual state that may be achieved during or after the event of prayer, when the vocables of the recited words to which one cleaves ascend on high, and not as a state of consciousness that precedes the moments of prayer or study. Moreover, the core of this theory is grounded in vocal operations that differ from just a regular recitation of the words of prayer, and they are predicated, on the one hand, upon the extreme atomization of the canonical texts into single letters/sounds, and on the sharp amplification of their ontological status as carriers of one's request and the container of divine vitality or light, on the other hand. Here, we may speak about a synthesis between a theory about linguistic immanence, according to which the letters, in fact their sounds, constitute containers of the highest realities, and by activating them so that they ascend and elevate the soul of the person united with them, and the theory of the possibility to cleave to vocables. This means that the first kind of union is with utterances, basically vocables—not so much entire words—that the divinity is imagined to inhabit, though such an adherence can also be found. The supreme scene of the highest experience, however, is situated in the supernal world, the divinity, where the soul arrives after being elevated by the vocables that serve as her vehicles. Pronounced ritual texts are conceived here to be the conduit of the soul, both because they are the product of the soul, or an externalization of a faculty of the soul, some form of inherent spiritual power, and also because the soul cleaves to them when the person recites those sounds. Thus, there is a deep affinity between the ascent of the utterances and that of the soul on high, as is the case already in Cordovero's final chapter of *Pardes Rimmonim*.

The language used by the Besht is that of an instruction or recommendation, done for his brother-in-law R. Gershon, as the recurring use of the second person shows. While in many other cases in the Besht's teachings, the formulations are resorting to the third person, here the language is quite different. Indeed, this may be the result of the literary genre, namely that an epistle addressed to someone is destined to utilize second person, and this usage is evident also earlier in the *Holy Epistle*. However, the fact that this instruction is not repeated by R. Jacob Joseph or the grandson of the Besht shows that some aspects of it were destined to R. Gershon, in my opinion as part of an earlier dispute between them as to the nature of prayer and ecstasy, which I have analyzed elsewhere.

The approach as formulated in the *Holy Epistle* reflects a some-what later stage in the thought of the Besht, in comparison to Margoliot's tradition, which itself reflects, in my opinion, an early, though perhaps not the earliest available document related to the thought of the Besht.[8] Addressed to R. Gershon as an instruction as to how to pray correctly, this approach was formulated, most plausibly if it is indeed part of the original *Holy Epistle*, as I assume it was, after he left Podolia for the Land of Israel, and the emer-gence of this teaching may be approximated to the mid-forties of the eighteenth century. Is the divergence between the content of the passage adduced previously, the Beshtian traditions adduced earlier, and those to be addressed in the next chapter pointing to a new direction? May we assume that R. Gershon, who most probably was already acquainted with his brother-in-law's instructions regarding the cleaving to utterances, has been informed as to the new development in the thought of the Besht, after he left Podolia?

Indeed, if the basis of his early thought was Cordovero's view and da Vidas's widespread *Reshit Hokhmah*, as I proposed previously, it is hard to assume that a scholar as accomplished as R. Gershon would need this type of instruction from his brother-in-law. At least for the Besht, the ascent of the utterances and the instructions to cleave to them in order to be elevated, though having some sources, was conceived of as a novelty in the manner in which he reformulated it, especially by his addition of the influential monadic perception of the linguistic units. I assume, therefore, that the Besht provided a more complex formulation of the Cordoverian theory of effective ritual, which allowed an even richer role to the pronounced letters as vehicles of the soul and its integration within the divine world, conceived of here as transcendental, than done by anyone beforehand in the history of Jewish mysticism. Its novelty consists of the insertion of the triune formula that is not alluded to in the Margoliot passage. Also in this formulation of cleaving, the theory of general divine immanence—namely omnipresence—is absent, as was the case in the material discussed in the previous two chapters.

In my opinion, the reason for this Cordoverian proposal may be a hidden polemic with his brother-in-law. In a passage that I have analyzed elsewhere in detail, I have shown that there was a controversy between the two as to what is the nature of ideal prayer, which means in my opinion that R. Gershon was in favor of an ecstatic prayer, when the person is possessed by the divine and prays without being conscious, while the Besht recommended a more contained type of ecstasy, related to the moments of verbal rites alone, and I propose to see the recommendation in the epistle as part of that controversy. I would like to reiterate also another, and quite different, proposal, as to the possibility that this recommendation is also part of a controversy with Lurianic types of *Kavvanot* to be performed during prayer. R. Gershon, the addressee of the epistle, served once as a cantor for one of the High Holidays, probably in what was to become the Beit El Yeshivah in Jerusalem, which turned to be a very prominent Lurianic institution. According to the hagiography, the Besht was aware of this event.[9] Thus, it is also plausible that the confrontation between the two Safedian systems of intention during prayer reverberates in the epistle.

Interestingly enough, in the epistle, as well as in many other cases discussed in the present study, the Besht does not invoke an ancient authority for his instructions, and quite rarely an act of evelation, but presents them on the grounds of his own authority alone. More than in some popular writings of Cordovero himself and in those of his many followers, which dealt with Kabbalistic themes and recommendations for behavior, the Besht was ready to offer concise instructions. This is quite an astonishing situation in a type of religion that includes most forms of Judaism in the eighteenth century, especially since he did not enjoy any serious pedigree as a learned individual, he did not write a single book, and did not claim to be a prophet—the views of later figures as to this latter issue notwithstanding.

Let me point out that in the instruction found in the Holy Epistle, the requirement is to understand what one recites, and cause his soul to be included in the utterances. I assume that the Besht was aware of the monadizing effect of the recitation of distinct vocables, and he mentions that the vocables will be reunited when ascending on high, generating thereby the words that disintegrated. It is not new words that emerge out of those combinations, as is the case in many examples in Abraham Abulafia's various types of exegetical practices, but the prior sequences of phonemes that recreate words that have been disintegrated by focusing the attention on their components separately. The importance of the correct canonical text is much more important in the Besht than in Abulafia.

5

R. JACOB JOSEPH OF POLONNOYE'S BESHTIAN TRADITIONS ON CLEAVING TO LETTERS/SOUNDS

Let turn now to other Beshtian traditions quoted in the Hasidic camp, which constitute some parallels of the content of the previous passages, some of them found in the writings of his direct disciples. The importance of cleaving to letters/sounds or utterances is reflected especially in additional traditions reported in his name and preserved by R. Jacob Joseph Katz of Polonnoye, as well as in numerous discussions found in his writings, which are not attributed to any source. In those traditions there is, however, a more complex vision, which assumes that the Besht envisioned an effect that is a sequel to the event of cleaving, and thus the two phases should be seen together as part of what I call the mystical-magical model. In one of them R. Jacob Joseph asserts that he heard from his teacher, which is most plausibly the Besht:

> I heard in the name of my teacher on the issue of prayer
> and its intention, and the *yiḥudim* that one should link
> himself [*le-qashsher 'atzmo*] to them. And it is known
> that [man] is a microcosm and by the lower arousal,
> there is going to be also an arousal on high, and they
> will cause the [process of] emanation downward, until
> the rank of this man who intends this [intention] and he
> receives the influx etc.[1]

There are seminal issues mentioned in this brief quote, which are indispensable for a proper understanding of aspects of the Besht's approach of *devequt*. First, we have here a full-fledged example of the mystical-magical model, which includes the two basic moments of the model: first cleaving to vocables of prayer and to *Yiḥudim*, and then the drawing down of the influx. However, unlike other discussions, here the recipient of the influx is the person who prays, so the magic aspect is more accentuated. Most probably, like in other instances, this teaching as quoted previously is not the full version of the Beshtian tradition, as the occurrence of the form *etc.*, shows. There are three different ontological levels mentioned here: the first, described as the higher ones, in the plural, which is not specifically identified; then the acts of prayer and the intention; and finally, the person in prayer. By his link or attachment to the prayer, he activates the supernal worlds, perhaps a version of the macrocosm, and then draws down the influx upon himself. The verb translated as "they will cause the emanation" is *Yashpiyʻu*. The formulation in a more literal rendering would be "by the lower arousal, they will be aroused on high and they will cause the emanation." Here it is not explicit whether letters/sounds play a role in the descending move, though it is obvious that the supernal unidentified entities are activated by the human arousal. Hierarchy and some form of theurgy are found together, ignoring an immanentist approach.

Here there is a parallel to Margoliot's passage: the act of attachment culminates in some form of operation related to emanation. However, while in the manner Margoliot described the teaching of the Besht there is not the mentioning of a supernal world, and the letters/sounds alone are explicitly mentioned here, it is obvious that such worlds exist and they are affected by the human activity.

If we may read that the two passages are reflecting a similar view, which is not strictly necessary, they will supply a better understanding of each of them. So, for example, the verb *mashpiʻyim*—translated as "they will cause the emanation"—in Margoliot's tradition will be explained by the verb *yashpiyʻu* in R. Jacob

Joseph's passage, and so a better understanding of the former's passage will emerge. Likewise, if we read those two passages together, the explicit linguistic aspects of Margoliot's tradition will become important for understanding the passage adduced by R. Jacob Joseph, as is the case also with the discussions of letters/vocables in the traditions to be adduced immediately as follows. Thus, for example, cleaving to the prayer or to the *Yiḥudim* will be understood as cleaving to the letters/sounds, or more precisely to the sounds of either the prayer or of the *Yiḥudim*.

Despite the fact that such a juxtaposition is not always advisable in reading Beshtian traditions, given the fluidity of his thoughts and their formulations and his recourse to various models, attempts to see the possible implications of one passage for better understanding of another are necessary. Thus, though being aware of this methodological problem and of the possibility that the Besht articulated different opinions about the same topic—as I claim in some cases—it would nevertheless not be wise to atomize his thought in an extreme manner by refusing to compare between similar statements, as we have done previously. The previous juxtaposition assumes that in some cases the teachings of the Besht have been presented in an elliptic manner and that what is missing in some formulations may be filled by turning to the content of other reports. Implied in it is the assumption that fuller forms of instructions were found among the followers of the Besht, but that they did not care always to present all the material they had in full.

On the other hand, this passage constitutes a parallel to a discussion found in the Holy Epistle, where the Besht was told that when he "unifies unifications below by means of the[ir] Holy Torah" there is a great delight on high.2 In both passages the term *Yiḥudim* is mentioned, and an analysis of this parallelism is worthwhile. In both cases, some form supernal powers are involved in the process triggered by human activity. However, while in the Holy Epistle the supernal entities draw delight from the Besht's performance, in the last quoted teaching they also cause emanation of influx upon the person praying. Likewise in the same content in the Holy

Epistle, the joy is triggered by study and prayer as recommended to R. Gershon of Kutov. Is this difference meaningful? I assume it is: in the Holy Epistle we deal with two distinguished spiritual persons, the Besht and his brother-in-law, and the Besht attempts to ensure his superiority over R. Gershon but recommends to him a relatively less sublime way of behavior, which amounts to an ascent on high and causing the delight there by means of vocal activity. In the epistle he describes the joy of the dead people when seeing him on high.

However, the instruction quoted here from Toledot Ya'aqov Yosef is a teaching which is not necessarily intended for a restricted elite and, what is not less important, it involves some form of benefit for the praying person. Thus, we may speak about a spectrum of performances that are recommended by the Besht, some more elitistic than others, but nevertheless the latter are much more representative of what has become the major thrust of Hasidism in the generation of the Besht's followers: the instruction to draw down the divine influx.

Let turn now to a seminal passage that R. Jacob Joseph adduced in the name of the Besht, which reflects to a great extent the mystical-magical model as described previously:

> I heard from my teacher that the great humility of man causes [man] to distance himself from the worship of God, Blessed be He, since because of his [feeling of] lowliness he does not believe that man causes the influx [to descend] on all the worlds by means of his prayer and [study of] the Torah, and that also the angels are nourished by his [study of] Torah and his prayer. Would he believe in it, he would worship God in joy and awe, out of the great [*sic*] and would be careful to pronounce appropriately each letter/vocable and vowel[3] and word, and also pay attention to what Solomon, blessed be his memory, said [Psalm 68:14]:[4] "If you shall lie between the lips" that the Holy One blessed be He, safeguards

and visits the lips of man, to kiss her,⁵ when he says her
[*sic*], during the [study of the] Torah and prayer, out of
awe and love.⁶

Here two out of the three components of the mystical-magical
model are addressed explicitly: the centrality of the liturgical pronunciation of the letters/sounds, and the drawing down of the influx.
Cleaving is not explicit here, though the emphasis on the devotion
that is necessary for an ideal recitation is evident, and it most plausibly constitutes a parallel to the ideal of cleaving. Especially the
last part of the passage, which deals with the presence of the divine
between the lips of man, amounts also to a view that is very close to
cleaving. What is obvious in this passage is that the magical effect
is not attributed to the supernal powers as having been activated by
the lower arousal, as in the first passage quoted in this paragraph,
but to the activity of the humans alone. In the second part of the
passage, however, instead of the impersonal influx we have a much
more personal entity, or entities. Indubitably, the utterances are
crucial for causing the descent of the supernal influx, even if this
influx is not described as specifically descending within the utterances themselves. Since the passage emphasizes the need of precise
pronunciation of each letter, this is compelling evidence for the
descent of the influx within the utterances. The passage is based on
a certain anthropology that attributes an important role to humans
in prayer, and misunderstanding it because of humility constitutes,
according to this text, a religious misbehavior.

The option that there are two different positions, one assuming
that man alone is performing the act of drawing down, and the
other that claims that supernal powers do this is, to a certain extent
at least, a false distinction. I assume that the passages reflect elliptic
formulation. Thus, for example, we read in another Beshtian tradition adduced by R. Jacob Joseph:

The issue of *devequt* to Him, Blessed be He, is by means
of the letters/vocables of Torah and prayer, that he

should cleave his thought and his inner dimension [of
the person in prayer] to the spiritual force found within
the letters/vocables according to the secret [of the verse
from Song of Songs 1:2][7] "He should kiss me by the
kisses of his mouth," the *devequt* of the spirit with the
spirit, as I heard from my teacher:[8] [Psalm 68:14] "If you
shall lie between the lips" etc . . .[9]

The occurrence of the terms mouth and lips points quite plausibly to a vocal activity. The first part of the quote covers a theory of
cleaving to vocables as found in other instances in the name of the
Besht, though his name is invoked only at the end of the citation.
It is obvious that cleaving to the utterances is not an aim in itself
but is conducive to cleaving to the divinity inherent within them.
Though this text may reflect the view that the spiritual force of
the vocables—*ruḥaniyyut ha-'otiyyot*—is always found inherently
within the sounds and someone can then adhere to it, unlike the
concept of causing of the descent of the influx according to the previous text, the theory that letters, basically sounds, are containers
or receptacles of a spiritual force is shared by the last two citations.[10]
This theory and its possible sources—to be discussed in several
instances as follows, especially in appendix D—deals with what I
call the inherent spiritual powers that are not necessarily attracted
by any sort of human activity. Also here, as in the Beshtian tradition mentioned by Margoliot, cleaving is described as related to
speech—reflected by the occurrence of lips—and to thought. In
this case at least, the visual-contemplative dimensions of the letters
are absent here. It should be pointed out that neither here nor in
the other teachings of the Besht adduced by R. Jacob Joseph do the
letters/vocables elevate the soul of the person in prayer, as we have
seen in the passage from the *Holy Epistle*, and this is the reason I
would suggest seeing in this variant an early articulation.

Again, according to another teaching attributed to the Ba'al
Shem Tov by R. Jacob Joseph of Polonnoye, there is a straightfor-
ward description of the purpose of the rituals performed vocally:

> The main purpose of the study of Torah and of prayer is
> to cleave himself to the inwardness of the spiritual force
> [*ruḥaniyyut*] of the light of *'Ein Sof*, which is [found]
> within the letters/vocables of Torah and prayer, and this
> is called a "study for its own sake"[11] about which R. Meir
> said: "Whoever studies Torah for its sake, gains many
> things and he is revealed secrets of the Torah," namely
> that out of the Torah he is revealed future things and
> all the events, and he will know how to behave in mat-
> ters of Torah and worship of God, in addition to seeing
> the supernal worlds, and such things I heard from the
> mouth of my teacher.[12]

R. Jacob Joseph's formulation is rather ambiguous. He does not
quote the Besht but describes some instructions, which are reminiscent of what he heard from his master. Nevertheless, it seems
that the content of this passage indeed reflects faithfully the teaching of the Besht. This is a passage that approximates the tradition of
Margoliot: both teachings commented upon the dictum of R. Meir
from the treatise *'Avot* 6:1, both dealt with the inner cargo of letters/
vocables, both mentioned cleaving, and both describe the possible
effect of that cleaving as a revelation of future things. These affinities indubitably reinforce dramatically the reliability of Margoliot's
tradition. The phrase "all the events" is rather vague, and in my
opinion, it reflects things similar to the capacity to know the future,
or clairvoyance, but also some other extraordinary capacities, as we
shall see also in other passages to be discussed as follows.

What is conspicuous from the content of this last passage is the
fact that within the letters/vocables there is a light which constitutes the divine presence, and the cleaving should be understood,
according to this passage, as related to divine light, an issue that
will be addressed in detail in one of the next chapters. What is also
important in this text is the fact that the Besht was believed to be
capable of seeing more practical issues in such a specific manner,
as we shall see in a passage of R. Menahem Nahum of Chernobyl,

to be discussed as follows. Also here there is not explicit indication
that the sounds and the lights within the vocables are instrumental
in elevating the soul of the person, in the manner mentioned in
the passage from the *Holy Epistle*. It should be pointed out that
according to the end of the quote, R. Jacob Joseph received also
other similar traditions from his master, which he does not quote.

Last but not least: according to a short epistle that the Besht
wrote to R. Jacob Joseph in order to deter him from his intention to practice askesis, the master recommended to his disciple to
cleave to the letters/sounds of the study he studies every morning,
an act that will mitigate the evil decrees that he attempted to obliterate by fasting.

> I advise you, and may God be with you, the strong man:
> in each and every morning, at the time of your study,
> he should cleave to the vocables by an absolute cleaving,
> for the sake of worshipping God, blessed be He and His
> name, and then he will sweeten the judgments in their
> [supernal] root.[13]

From the formulation of the short epistle it is evident that the
Besht wrote it after a long acquaintance with R. Jacob Joseph. Thus,
it seems that the technique of cleaving to utterances, as a limited
form of linguistic immanence, started relatively early, and lasted
for a very significant part of the Besht's career, until he discovered the general immanentist theory, or what I call the third or
the noetic model. Though the limited and the general type of linguistic immanentism are so different from a theological point of
view, for the religious pursuit of early Hasidism, namely a search
for the intimacy with the divine, the difference between them is
not so great.

6

BESHTIAN TRADITIONS ON CLEAVING TO VOCABLES IN THE SCHOOL OF THE GREAT MAGGID

R. Dov Baer Friedmann, better known as the Great Maggid of Miezeritch, is indubitably the most influential disciple of the Besht, especially because of the many disciples he himself had and their great influence. He gave a somewhat more Platonic turn to traditions he received from his master, and he was in some important instances an innovative mystic in comparison to what he received from earlier sources. In his school there are several traditions reported in the name of the Besht, which are unknown from the voluminous writings of R. Jacob Joseph. One such tradition corroborates much of what we found in the two earlier traditions.

In a collection of Hasidic excerpts printed at the beginning of the nineteenth century, we learn about a revelation that stems from the spiritual mentor of the Besht, the biblical Ahijah the Shilonite, who revealed it to the Besht, who at his turn transmitted it to the Great Maggid, and then it was passed over to R. Levi Isaac of Berditchev, who presumably handed it to his student, R. Aharon of Zhitomir. This is, to be sure, quite a legendary pedigree, since the terminology of the passage reflects, in my opinion, much of R. Aharon of Zhitomir's own approach, if someone will mind to study his terminology. Nevertheless, it seems difficult, in my opinion, to assume that the entire content of this passage is an invention of this not very innovative Hasidic figure, even more so since he had access to a formulation reported in the name of the Besht that parallels what we have seen in the traditions reported by R. Jacob Joseph of Polonnoye. This is what he has to say:

> The way of the truth is as follows: In the moment of worship,[1] someone ought to divest himself of [his] corporeality [belonging to] this world, so that he will conceive himself as if he is no [more] in this world at all. [Then] he should pronounce the letters/vocables by voice and simple speech, and cleave and link his thought to the holy letters/vocables and understand the sense of the holy words. Then, by itself, suddenly, the fire of the flame of the blaze of the burning of the supernal awe and love[2] will flame up and become incandescent, in a very strong manner. This is the path that the light is dwelling in so far as the holy and inner worship is concerned.[3]

The imagery here is reminiscent of the theme of descent of the fire upon the sacrifice in the Israelite Temple, which was imagined to consume the sacrificed animal, in accordance to some Rabbinic treatments. Hasidic sources speak indeed about the enthusiasm that should accompany worship, and in Hebrew *hitlahavut* has a clear connotation of fire. In my opinion, here we have an adumbration of an imagery of mystical union as having been eaten by God, which will occur in an explicit manner two generations later in a book of the Ḥabad Hasidism and in that of the follower of the Besht's great-grandson R. Nahman of Braslav, and we shall return to this theme in appendix A.

There are many themes that characterize this passage which are consonant to other Beshtian traditions adduced previously. The divestment of the corporeality is the most obvious of them, and the emphasis on it may reflect also the predilection of the Great Maggid toward such a form of spiritual exercise. What is evident is that the state of divestment should occur only in the moment of worship and not beforehand, or as a general type of ongoing experience, as is the view of the Besht's brother-in-law, R. Gershon of Kutov, which was preserved by the Besht and even adopted eventually in his family.[4] However, a reading of the details of this passage while being aware of the specific style and dominant concepts of R. Aharon of Zhitomir will discern the clear affinity to his thought. Nevertheless, the structure is reminiscent of the mystical-magical model as found in the Besht, and if the source will turn out to be earlier than R. Aharon, we have here the claim that elements that are part of a full-fledged vision of this model in the Besht is not just an impact of earlier Kabbalistic sources, as I assume, but described as the result of a revelation.

As mentioned previously, the entire passage is predicated upon the vision of worship by means of utterances. Just as in the Temple, according to Rabbinic approach, the divine fire descended on the sacrifice and consumed it, so too the fire is described as descending upon the worshiper's pronounced letters. In any case the model that was described here occurs in the writings of R. Aharon of Zhitomir, the author who preserved this tradition from his teacher R. Levi Isaac of Berditchev. He speaks about the causing of the descent of the fire, which causes the inflammation in worship by cleaving to the words of prayer, since in each word there are tens of thousands of lights.[5] Interestingly enough, according to this passage the divestment of corporeality is not an end-experience, but should be complemented by the vocal rite.

Let me adduce now another instance of another tradition in the name of the Besht found in the same Hasidic book, for which I did not find a precise parallel elsewhere. R. Aharon of Zhitomir writes elsewhere:

> It is explicated in the book of the holy and genial R. [Dov] Baer, blessed be his memory, the homilist of the community of Medziretch, and this is belonging to the wisdom of the holy and pure R. Besht, blessed be his memory, that it is essential to speak the speeches of the Torah and prayer with all his strength and then he cleaves himself to the light of the Infinite, Blessed be He, that dwells within the letters/sounds and this [causes to]

subdue all the corporeal powers and he reaches indeed
the divestment of the corporeality, and he arrives to the
supernal worlds and to the new intellectual [entities]
and to luminosity each time.[6]

For the time being, I did not find the precise source of this passage in the writings of the circle of the Great Maggid, a fact that may
strengthen the attribution to the Besht. In any case, the testimony
here is quite fascinating for a number of reasons: the view is indeed
Beshtian, according to R. Aharon, though it is found in a book
from the circle that his teacher, R. Levi Isaac of Berditchev, comes
from there, that of the Great Maggid. What is quoted is indeed
quite consonant to the views of the Besht, as we find them formulated in the writings of R. Jacob Joseph of Polonnoye. Here the
cleaving is not to the utterances, which are indeed important and
should be pronounced, but to the divine light that is found within
them. The two acts that are part of the technique—pronunciation
of nomian texts and cleaving—induce a double experience—sub-
duing the body and then divesting the soul from the body, in a
manner reminiscent of the tradition we have adduced previously in
the first quote from *Maggid Devarav le-Ya'aqov*. Then the mystic is
described as ascending to supernal worlds and receiving some form
of revelations or renewal, which is presumably parallel to what we
shall elaborate upon in chapter 10, as the experience of contact.

In general, let me point out that a perusal of the book of R.
Aharon of Zhitomir shows how much an author belonging to the
fourth generation of Hasidic thinkers is still continuing the Beshtian
traditions, both when he mentions him and when refraining to do
so. In the note I have pointed out a variety of instances where this
author capitalized on the Beshtian traditions, though he does so
anonymously, as it happens in the Great Maggid's school.

According to another Beshtian tradition, the divestment of
corporeality facilitates the cleaving with the divine spark, or the
vitality that is found within the letters, most probably the pronounced one, which is divested of its corporeality.[7] Therefore, in

our case, a spiritualization of man ensures the encounter with the spiritual dimension of language and with that of reality in general.[8]

We have surveyed so far a series of passages that were attributed to the Besht by different authors, some who knew him personally, some of them mentioning his name on the quotes that were referred to. A comparison between them easily shows that none of them is dependent on the others, because of their different terminology and formulation. This means that the Besht formulated a basic idea, or what we call model, in different forms, presumably on different occasions, to different persons. Let me adduce now some later traditions in his name.

R. Issakhar Dov Baer of Zloczow, a minor Hasidic figure, wrote at the end of the eighties or in early nineties (before he left to Safed where he died shortly before 1798), a book entitled *Mevasser Tzedeq*. This is a short treatise rather neglected in the modern scholarship on Hasidism. A perusal of the treatise shows that the author was acquainted with Hasidic traditions from the circle of the Great Maggid, especially those related to R. Levi Isaac of Berditchev.[9] The following passage is, to the best of my knowledge, unparalleled in other sources as a teaching of the Besht, as far as I am acquainted with Hasidic literature, but it is known since the beginning of Hasidism in the context of another master:

> A principle in the name of the Besht, blessed be his memory: vessels to bring down the influx have been made out of the speeches of prayer. Since indeed the Holy One Blessed Be He, knows the thoughts, so why are the speeches needed? [The speeches are needed] only in order to bring down the influx. Behold, sometimes someone wishes to worship and bring down the big and mighty influx, higher than his rank, and the vessels do not contain the greatness of the influx, and the vessels break.[10]

There is no reason in my opinion to doubt the validity of the attribution of this seminal passage as faithfully reflecting a moment in the Besht's thought. It contains all the components of the mystical-magical model as it is formulated in the Cordoverian tradition and in the writings of the disciples of the Besht. The ascent on high is implied in the statement that there are supernal ranks that correspond to the nature of a certain person and any attempt to transcend them will shatter the vessels. Here, the vocal vessels of Cordovero were, *prima facie*, interpreted according to the Lurianic theory of the theosophical breaking of the vessels. This is a point that deserves some special attention: resorting to the phrase does not make the passage into a Lurianic one: the image of broken vessels is found in much earlier Jewish texts, but it receives its specific meaning in a much broader and systematic structure that defines its meaning much more than the words of this phrase. When detached from this system, whether because it is not mentioned here or it is unknown, it is attached to the verbal ritual and receives its different meaning in its new context.

However, the status of the context is not just a matter of dianoetics, but of a theme that is attracted in a major conceptual organizing principle: the Cordoverian theory gravitating around the centrality of the voice and speech that serves as the exegetical grid for understanding the Lurianic theme. As was mentioned in some of my studies, in the encounter between two types of Kabbalah, it is the elements of the Cordoverian one that gives the tone and radically transforms the meaning of the Lurianic ones, which are transposed on a totally different conceptual plane. To put it in more visualist terms: it is not the break of *'Adam Qadmon*'s powers, called vessels or *kelim*, but those of man, namely his utterances. Lurianism is a theology and theurgy of the repair of the broken structure of the divinity, while Hasidism, starting with its founder, tries to do so more eminently with the religiously broken man or his dispersed sparks.

In my opinion, this manner of understanding the emergence of Hasidism transcends the exegesis of a relatively simple passage. It tells a much greater story dealing with the manner in which the sources of the Besht should be understood: the question that is quintessential is not the precise extraction of a certain theme—Cordoverian, ecstatic, Lurianic, Sabbatean, Sufi, or Christian—but the role a certain theme plays in the larger Hasidic conceptually loose structures, and what is even more important, how the earlier meaning of the sources has been understood, subverted, altered, contaminated, or ignored. Attracted in the net of new priorities, often dramatically different or alien from those of the original sources, the dianoetic valence of early terms and themes may be of little relevance for understanding a belated passage, and we may better speak about semantic mutations and contaminations.

The Besht entertained radical semantic interpretations, which differ from the more sustained theosophical interpretations, which are radical too because of his concise types of expositions and the lack of a systematic theology. In many cases, as this is also the situation here, it is the literary context of these terms that imposes a new understanding. However, the literary context may not always the most important one, since it is part of what can be designated as the ritual context, in our case the situation of prayer. Hasidic texts are not just literary or theological treatises but compositions that try to instruct or to inspire a certain type of behavior, and it is the latter that ultimately counts more. In the case of themes that do not strive to shape a certain type of behavior, in Hasidic sources their importance is secondary.

In my opinion, without understanding this type of dynamics of organizing the earlier material, one loses the main intention of a text, looking for hidden messages that subvert the traditional form of Judaism by adopting Sabbatean or Christian terms. Scholars may easily be lost in complex exercises of proving the Lurianic, Sabbatean, or Christian sources while missing the meaning of a certain text or the ideals of a certain Hasidic school that is better supplied by Cordoverianism. Immersed in displays of "erudition," "audacity," "radicality" or comparative insights, looking for relevance of the Hasidic texts for modern life, for a new type of Judaism or Jewish identity, or for an ecumenical discourse—in my opinion important issues for the Jewish society but nevertheless much of them futile purposes from the point of view of scholarship—they read the texts against their declared intention and the manner in which they operated *de facto* in Hasidic societies. Just as in the previous generation of scholars in Jewish mysticism there was a hunt of hidden Sabbateans in order to prove the centrality of this movement, nowadays there is another scholarly hunt for hidden Christian motifs, as if especially relevant for understanding the significance of Hasidic texts. While in the previous generation there was a rebellious attempt to distantiate from Jewish orthodoxy, now there is a propensity to assimilate to the majority culture.

The content of the last quoted passage, though not always its precise terminology, is corroborated by another contemporary author better acquainted to Beshtian traditions, R. Aharon Kohen Perlov of Apta, the author of several books, but more eminently *Keter Shem Tov*, a rather voluminous collection of Beshtian traditions. Because of some historical reasons the two authors, though contemporary, could not know the work of the other, and in any case the formulations of their discussions are independent. R. Aharon printed all his books after R. Issakhar Baer left Podolia, and the latter's book was printed after all the major books of R. Aharon had been printed. I see no reason to presume a conspiracy between so many authors to forge false attributions to the Besht of a model that was known in the past and in any case has been already accepted by all his main followers, though using new formulations. As to what the sources are from which R. Issakhar Dov Baer of Zloczow and R. Aharon of Apta—as we shall discuss his views immediately as follows—drew the statements they attributed to the Besht that are unparalleled in earlier books, this is an important question which I cannot answer here. In any case, from a perusal of the writings of R. Jacob Joseph, it is obvious that he possessed more Beshtian material, especially longer teachings than those he copied in his books, and it seems that he also wrote books in addition to those that are in print. Moreover, in many Hasidic books unidentified "books" or "writings" are mentioned, and they may refer to the circulation of additional material emanating from the circle of the Besht.

Let us turn now to an outstanding formulation of the mode of prayer, adduced—according to the book of R. Aharon Kohen of Apta—in the name of the Besht, and found sometimes without mentioning his name in collections of traditions related to the Great Maggid, while elsewhere it has been quoted in the name of the Great Maggid, who is reported to have received this tradition from the Besht:

> The Besht, may peace be on him, said concerning that which is written in the *Zohar*, that man is judged in each [supernal] palace, this is to be [viewed as dealing with] speeches, which are called palaces, wherein a man is judged, whether he is worthy of entering the letters/sounds of the prayer. If he is [found] unworthy, he is cast out, i.e., an alien thought is sent to him, and he is pushed away.[11]

Here the Zoharic text is understood according to Cordovero's nomenclature. The identification of the utterances or letters/vocables with palaces in a statement attributed explicitly to the Besht, in my opinion correctly, is very important for understanding one of the major sources of his thought, Cordovero's Kabbalistic astro-magic theosophy, which will be discussed in appendix C in this volume. What the precise nature is of the act of entering the palaces, which here are utterances, has been far from clear from the extant discussions. Let me emphasize: the instruction is to enter the vocables, not to contemplate them. In any case, some form of architectural *imaginaire* of the vocables is adumbrated here, and I shall return to this issue in chapter 8 of this volume.

How exactly the Hasidic master imagined that someone is capable of penetrating the utterances he himself emits is quite a difficult question to answer, but it is obvious that some form of spacial imagery occurs not only here, but also in another instance when the Besht was described as teaching that someone should open the sound of the utterance or the word, as we shall see as follows. This special imagery has something to do with the theme of the palace, which has been inherited from Cordoverian Kabbalah and ultimately from the astro-magical Hellenistic and medieval traditions, and the older Jewish images of meeting the king—namely God—within the palace. As we shall see in appendix B, some sort of sonorous garment is known already in the Cordoverian type of Kabbalah. I assume the entrance in the vocables as palaces as something to do with entering the supernal palaces to see the king, but also it has something to do with the notion of being encompassed by a sonorous ambiance during public prayer without losing one's identity, a view to be addressed in appendix A, and in another way in my discussion in chapter 8 in this volume.

Important for understanding the religious phenomenology of early Hasidism is the fact that the late antiquity, medieval, and Renaissance sources, as well as the Safedian ones, do not see the palaces or the utterances as symbols for something higher, but the actual locus for the reception of higher entitites. This concrete, nonsymbolic type of discourse differs from many of the theosophical-theurgical ones, and it made its way to early Hasidism. However, in pre-Hasidic texts, the palaces are astral bodies, or even utterances or words, where the human is not supposed to enter but it is the supernal power that is brought down within them.

Moreover, while the astral-magical sources are grounded in the awareness of the differentiation between the qualities found in each of the astral bodies, namely the seven planets—the palaces—and the specific spiritual force that dwells in each of them—and this is also the case in the Cordoverian discussions of the spiritual forces of the *sefirot*—in Hasidism those essential differences have been obliterated, and thus the main logic of the Hellenistic, medieval, and Kabbalistic sources has been broken, and parts of it ignored. It seems that it is the Hasidic innovation that instructs the mystic to penetrate the sonorous product during prayer or study of the Torah. By assuming both the drawing down of divine power into the palaces and the entrance of the human's soul, or intention, an experience of adherence or union between the two factors is assumed, constituting an interpretation that is novel and reads the magical material in a fresh manner. This may explain at least a part of the importance the Besht and his disciple attributed to the triune structure compound of divinity, souls, and worlds to be found in every vocable, an issue that recurs in several of our discussions in the present study. Moreover, the implication of such a theory is that the Hasidic master by his vocal activity is generating the locus for the encounter with the divinity, and they meet not in an objective site, like nature, divinity, or even the human soul, but in an entity that is temporary and totally dependent on the mystic. It is the contingent nature of this sonorous locus that is characteristic of the Besht's type of mysticism in his second model.

On the other hand, the passage mentions the palaces also in a context that is reminiscent of the much earlier tradition, found in the Heikhalot literature, dealing with supernal palaces where angels are checking the ascenders to see if they are worthy to be allowed to enter these palaces. However, this aspect is also connected in the previous citation to sounds, and from this point of view it differs from the thrust of the Heikhalot treatment. Once again the sonorous elements serve as a grid for interpreting another type of Jewish mysticism.

In another book of R. Aharon Perlov of Apta we read:

> A wonderful sermon from the Besht, blessed be his memory: A Jewish man that stands in prayer or study of the Torah in awe and love[12] is capable of causing [the descent of] influxes and blessings and sustenance [*parnasot*] to the entire world,[13] because all the souls were comprised in first Adam and they are still comprised in the Torah etc.[14]

Unlike the earlier quote that was concerned solely with the impact of prayer on the person who stands in prayer, here the liturgical activity is explicitly envisioned as a way to help all people. Interestingly enough, it is just a Jew who is mentioned here, not a righteous man, who can accomplish such an extraordinary deed. Given the fact that divinity is imagined to dwell within sounds, it is possible to see in this approach a democratic approach that does not privilege the righteous or the leaders of a group, though it necessitates a special effort in order to pronounce the vocable properly and with emotional devotion. This approach that does not insist on the primacy of the righteous as a religious leader but also allows to the simple Jew a role in drawing down of influx by the sonorous activity may reflect indeed a Beshtian attitude, since also in other teachings, the righteous do not play such a special role as it happens in the writings and the praxis of his followers.

Again, in yet another book of the Rabbi of Apta we read:

> This issue is a principle for all the intention of the order [of letters in the prayerbook], and the study of Torah, the psalmodia, the songs, and the praises, since R. Israel Ba'al Shem, blessed be his memory said: when a person has a[n experience of] *devequt* with God blessed be He, he may allow to [his] mouth as if to it speak by the dint of the Holy Spirit, and to use the depth of the intention, that is the voice and the speech, from the depth of the brain and the heart since by means of it he links the speeches to their supernal source, to the Creator, since every speech [act] has a source on high in the *sefirot* of holiness since there is no one that is capable [to perform] any speech [act] or to do any motion without His influx and His vitality, blessed be He, and this is said [Psalm 51:13] "Do not take away your holy spirit from me."[15]

I could not find an earlier source for this quote that illustrates some of my points in this study found together. Nevertheless, despite the doubts as to the reliability of R. Aharon of Apta, the convergence of some issues in the previous passage and treatments of similar themes in traditions related to the Besht point in the direction of validating its attribution to the Besht. Unlike the earlier passage that deals with drawing down influxes, here the central theme is the elevation of the utterances to their supernal source. From the historical point of view, we may discern here once again an impact of R. Moshe Cordovero's interpretation of *kavvanah* as related to the elevation of the utterances on high, though the magical valence of the Safedian Kabbalist does not transpire in the present tradition. This difference notwithstanding, the centrality of voice and speeches in the ritual process is evident, and the passage has been appropriately introduced by its qualification as a principle that underlies a variety of activities related to vocal rituals.

Especially outstanding in this tradition is the identification of the concept of intention, *kavvanah,* with voice and speeches. The latter should stem from the "depth," and this qualification refers, most probably, to the superiority of one type of prayer over the other that is conceived, implicitly, as done in a superficial manner. It is plausible that the *kavvanah* means actually a loud performance, done with all the strength, which may amount to shouting. Though the passage deals with allowing the acts of the limbs to be done as if under the impact of the Holy Spirit, there is hardly a way to interpret this discussion as if an example for quietism. It is not the expectation that the holy spirit will hover over the mystic, but on the contrary the intensification of activity that triggers some form of experience. That everything is done by the dint of the divine vitality does not mean that someone should be passive during the performance of vocal rituals, nor is a reference to an experience of contemplation discernable here.

However, what is also important from my point of view is the affinity between the lower utterances and their sources on high. This observation connects my view as to the transcendental linguistic ontology that is coupled with linguistic immanence in a Beshtian source, though here it is only their presence within man that is hinted at. Interestingly enough, no noetic process is involved in this passage but the activation of ritual language.

According to another late eighteenth-century Hasidic master, R. Reuven ha-Levi Horowitz, who belongs to the school of the Great Maggid, the Besht is reported to have said that:

> The *tzaddiq* comes to worship God, blessed be He, by [means of] Torah and Prayer, and cleaves himself by his

innermost part that is the root of his soul, "he comes home" [Genesis 39:11] refers to his innermost part, "in order to do his work," as I heard in the name of the Besht that "any Torah which is not accompanied by doing"[16] namely that he does not do an action by [means of] the Torah in the supernal worlds, [in order] to elevate the sparks and to draw down the influxes,[17] which is the meaning of doing deeds, and ascends to a higher rank, to a great *devequt*, to the divestment of the materiality.[18]

The subject of the biblical verse to be quoted following is Joseph, who was perceived in classical Jewish sources, especially since the Zoharic literature, as the righteous *par excellence*. The formulation is rather confusing, but it is plausible that we may reconstruct the view of the Besht as reported here as follows: The first part of the passage built on a sequence of actions of the Genesis verse consists in cleaving first— the coming—that is followed by doing the work, which is drawing down the influxes, just as in the Rabbinic dictum that the Torah, first, should be followed according to the sequence of actions in the statement in *'Avot*, by *mela'khto*, doing, afterward. Important in this context is the occurrence of the verb *mamshikh* in the sense of drawing down the influx in a passage attributed explicitly to the Besht, an issue to which we shall revert later on, as well as the occurrence of the ideal of the divestment of materiality, an issue that has been discussed previously. The role of the *tzaddiq* here is worthwhile to be highlighted, since it is this religious type that will become the central figure in the later Hasidic movement. According to this tradition, it is he that embodies the seminal religious acts: cleaving, elevating, and drawing down. However, this figure does not play a role in creating or maintaining a specific group that gravitates around him and for whose members he feels responsible, as is the case in the theory of the Hasidic *tzaddiq* some few decades after the death of Ba'al Shem Tov.

Some of the previous discussions should be compared to the passage cited in the name of the Great Maggid by one of his main followers, R. Levi Isaac of Berditchev:

As I heard from my master, the genius, the pious, our famous teacher and Rabbi Dov Baer, the homilist of Medzeritch, the interpretation of the verse [Genesis 7:1] "Come thou and all thy house into the ark" [*teivah*] which means that a person should put all his powers in the [study of] the Torah and in prayer, so that all his powers will annihilated from all his operations, and by means of the ark, which is the spiritual force of the vocables, he is united and bound to the Creator, blessed be His name. And if he will be worthy because of the persistence of his worship of God, he will be the ruler over the speeches in accordance to the wishes of his pure heart. . . . However at the beginning of his worship the ark/word is ruling over the person in order to cleave to the Creator, blessed be His name, by means of the spiritual force of the vocables, since the vocables are drawn by spiritual force, and they are ruling over the person by the spiritual force. And this is the meaning of the word "speech," namely ruler . . . which means that he is clothed by his speech in the spiritual force and this is the reason why happy is [II Samuel 23:20] "a powerful person, of manifold actions" is linked to the spiritual forces of the speeches which he articulates during the [study of] the Torah of God, day and night, by a strong power, since it is impossible to be linked oneself to God, blessed be His name, but by means of the speech of Torah and prayer.[19]

This is an illuminating concatenation of themes found in the name of the Besht in different sources, including in the Great Maggid's school. First and foremost, the pun on the two meanings of *Teivah*: ark and word, as we shall see in the next chapter. Then the instruction to cleave to vocables of Torah and prayer, and last but not least, the obliterations of one's sense, as seen in the passages discussed beside ch. 2 nn. 9, 11 and ch. 6 n. 3. Here the primacy of vocality is obvious, and it is solely by means of the vocal medium that cleaving to God is conceived to be possible. The distinction that underlies the passage is related to the speeches: a beginner is ruled by his speeches, which means that he attains a sort of union with God by their means. However, an advanced mystic rules over speeches, which means that "wishes of his pure heart" are answered, namely some form of magical operations can be achieved after attaining the cleaving to God. Or, in other terms, is someone led by the ark—the beginner—or is he controlling it—the more expert mystic.

Of great importance for this last point is the resort to the phrase "spiritual force of the vocables," a term that has a long history before the Besht, especially in Cordovero's theory of *Kavvanah* during prayer, as we shall see in appendices C and D. The question is whether this is a "pure" view of the Great Maggid or whether we have another instance of an appropriation of a view of the Besht that is attribtted to the Great Maggid, as I have mentioned in several other instances. The resort to the syntagma "spiritual force of the vocables" is found also in R. Jacob Joseph of Polonnoye, and it has earlier sources, points in my opinion in this direction, as we shall see in appendix D.

Let me turn now to a passage from the so-called *Testament of the Besht*, which has been edited by someone in the circle of the Great Maggid:

> He who uses all the *kavvanot* in prayer knows that he can do no more than use the *kavvanot* which are known to him. But when he says each word with great attachment,[20] all the *kavvanot* are, by that very fact, included, since each and every letter/vocable is an entire world. When he utters the word with great attachment surely those upper worlds are awakened, and thus he thereby accomplishes great actions. Therefore, a man should see to it that he prays with great attachment and enthusiasm. Then he will certainly accomplish great actions in the upper worlds, for each letter/vocable awakens [things which are] above.[21]

This passage differs in its articulation from the earlier formulations that deal with the effect of the cleaving to letters/vocables.

Here the effects are described as affecting the supernal world, but the first part of the model, dealing with devotional performance and cleaving to sounds, is parallel to the Beshtian traditions discussed previously, especially to one adduced by R. Jacob Joseph, as heard in the name of the Besht from another person. What seems to be interesting here is the emphasis on the effect of each and every sound on high. The individuality of the sounds is not only a matter of the atomization of the prayer, but also of the belief in the specificity of the impact of each of the particular vocables.

The overlapping between the different teachings adduced in the name of the Besht concerning the cleaving to letters/sounds is quite considerable, even substantial, and we may say even surprising in an oral culture as early Hasidism was. There is no reason to assume that several Hasidic masters, some belonging to the school of the Great Maggid, would intentionally attribute a teaching stemming from the Great Maggid to the Besht. The fact that in the written collection of his teachings, the Great Maggid himself does not always refer to the Besht in this specific context, as is the case in the collection *Maggid Devarav le-Ya'aqov*, as his source for the view that the utterances are palaces should not, in my opinion, worry us too much since, as it is possible to point out quite clearly, also in other instances, the existence of some sentences found in this book that are verbatim citations of a tradition of the Besht occur in an anonymous manner.[22] This does not mean, let me emphasize, that we may use the views found in the various collections of the Great Maggid's teachings indiscriminately as if constituting, automatically, Beshtian views. However, when an attribution to the Besht is corroborated by an analysis of its context by other sources, or when there is a consensus between the different disciples of the Besht on a certain topic, even a passage found in the teachings of the Great Maggid in an anonymous manner may nevertheless reflect a Beshtian tradition. There is little doubt in my opinion that the Great Maggid had access to a plethora of Beshtian traditions, some of which were known and reported as such by R. Jacob Joseph, but the manner in which they have been dealt with in his school is quite different from R. Jacob Joseph. However, to be sure, this does not mean that some traditions reported in this school in the name of the Besht, some of which will be used here, are not authentic.

Let me reiterate my methodological proposal: if indeed there is an explicit attribution of a teaching to the Besht, and it is also included in the collections of the disciple's traditions in an anonymous manner, I am inclined to accept this attribution after comparing the content with other Beshtian traditions. Thus, if this approach is accepted, another type of relationship between this Hasidic master and Beshtian traditions will emerge, which will confer to the master a greater share in the thought of his disciple than done earlier in the scholarship about the Besht. I am convinced that such a change is necessary on the grounds of the analyses, as I see them now, but we are only at the beginning of tackling the complex editorial situation, since also in the case of the Great Maggid's writings, the more critical analysis is only at the very beginning. In fact we do not have his original sermons but a long series of teachings as preserved by his disciples and edited and printed at least a decade after his death. Let me reiterate: In my opinion, Beshtian traditions are found sometimes verbatim, though anonymously, in those collections.

The easy scholarly approach that disregards many explicit attributions as if problematic, while others are adopted as representative, without giving an account for the criteria for such acceptance, as found in most of the extant scholarship of the Besht, is highly questionable, reducing the scope of the themes he addressed and in fact his spiritual stature. Nor does such an approach explain the variety of treatments of the same themes in early Hasidism.

7

R. MOSHE SHOHAM OF DOLINA'S QUOTE OF THE BESHT

Among the disciples of the Besht who met him only in their youth and late in his career, there are two that are more prominent—not to mention his grandson, R. Ephrayim of Sudylkov. One of them is R. Menahem Nahum of Chernobyl, whose views will be addressed later on in this study, and the other is R. Moshe Shoham of Dolina. The latter is a student of both the Besht and R. Yehiel Mikhal, known as the Preacher of Zlocsow, himself a follower of the Besht, and he cites the latter three times.[1] However, he does not refer to any other disciple of the Besht (except R. Yehiel Mikhal,[2] whose influence on him was quite significant), and we may discern in the discussions to be mentioned as follows an independent source for some few, and probably earlier, views of the Besht. It should be mentioned that R. Moshe is the only student of the Besht who was well-acquainted with Lurianic Kabbalah and even wrote a book in this vein: *Seraf Peri 'Etz Ḥayyim*, which is however not dogmatically Lurianic, but also it does not adopt Cordoverian views.

R. Moshe Shoham dealt with an issue that recurs in his writings following the view of the Besht: the imperative of a continuous cleaving to God, conceived in his writings to be much more a mental act.[3] This approach is quite reminiscent of the general tone of the so-called *Testament of the Besht*, which emphasizes much more the mental cleaving than the sonorous one, which is described as a mere garment for thought, as we shall see as follows.

Needless to say that from the conceptual point of view the ideal of continuous cleaving does not coexist so smoothly with the specific instruction to cleave to the utterances, which are emitted only in relatively restricted moments in time. This is a tension found in Judaism already in the Middle Ages between the mental and the vocal, especially when discussing the ideal prayer, and it is inherent already in some of the Besht's teachings, and it reverberated also later on in the history of Hasidic spirituality. As seen previously, cleaving is sometimes described in the Besht's teachings as related to both speech and thought. Though R. Moshe Shoham differs from the other disciples of the Besht on the nature of causality between the sonorous performance and the drawing down of the influx, his tradition in the name of the Besht nevertheless reflects a twofold vision of religious events. We shall discuss this quote in order to complete a more comprehensive picture of the thought of the Besht concerning the role of the utterances in the experience of *devequt*, and we shall point out the divergences between this quote and the other teachings analyzed previously:

> I heard from the Rabbi, the Holy Lamp the Besht, blessed be his memory, that this is the intention of the Sages, who asserted that "the ordinary conversation of the learned scholars needs a [special] study,"[4] it means that it is necessary to learn how to speak ordinary conversations, but he will not, God forbid, suspend the [state of] *devequt*. And behold there are two benefits: one that he does not suspend the *devequt* . . . and even more so that by its means [of the *devequt*] holiness is drawn onto the thing that he is doing, namely if he buys something or when he speaks about buying something in such a manner, as mentioned above, then he draws holiness[5] to that object. Thus, afterwards, when he uses the object that he bought, it will be easy to use it while being in the state of *devequt*.[6]

Unfortunately, it is hard to know where exactly the citation from the Besht finishes, and my decision is therefore arbitrary. In any case, the assumption is that by being in the state of *devequt* while at the same time speaking ordinary things, someone is drawing holiness down even during his mundane preoccupations, and thus has an impact on the nature of the objects he acquires while he cleaves: he is, to use a modern term, downloading holiness. Someone, the Besht is reported to have said, does not cleave to words he speaks, but to God while he speaks. Or, to be put it differently: someone first cleaves to God, or is supposed to be in a state of mental union with God beforehand, and should maintain this state even after he starts to speak or to perform a commandment. From this point of view there is here a paradigm different from most of the other ones dealt with previously, which assumes a permanent state of cleaving to God, which is reminiscent, to a certain extent, of a view adopted by R. Gershon of Kutov.[7]

Nevertheless, it should be mentioned that according to several discussions found in this book, it is possible to drawn down influxes, especially holiness, though the Besht himself is not mentioned in all these contexts, and one such passage will be quoted immediately as follows. The question of continuous cleaving dealt with here is not, let me emphasize, a theoretical one. The Besht himself experienced, according to the hagiography, a period when he could not speak with people because of being in the state of *devequt*, a state that was considered as problematic, and he was revealed by his angelic mentor a means to cure it by recitation of some specific chapters of the Psalms, which he allegedly recited daily.

According to other reports concerning the Besht, cleaving is not only an instruction for a performance of prayer and study of Torah, but it should also be practiced when someone speaks with people in the marketplace.[8] This means that the Ba'al Shem Tov broadened the nomian performance in a manner that it includes also profane talks, some in vernacular, which are considered in the Rabbinic literature as what I would call anomian. Perhaps in this context we should also understand the admiration of his disciples concerning his smoking the *lulkhe*, the pipe, which is an activity related to the mouth. In any case, the bringing together of Torah and prayer with trivial talks on the market is one more instance when the verbal performance is the only plausible interpretation of the Besht's position. I assume that this development is a relatively late one in the Besht's thought. What should be pointed out is the fact that though some forms of amendments are attributed to the profane talks by means of the *Yiḥudim*, I did not find in the Beshtian traditions the assumption that he drew down the divine influx within the utterances of these talks.

I would say that we may envision a development that starts with the preeminent role of the utterances of prayers and Torah, then adding to them the words of trivial talks, and finally assuming that God is found in every movement of man. This enhancing of the realm of religiously significant deeds has generated an interest in the more omnipresent approach in the realm of theology. In any case, by his attributing such a great importance to continuous cleaving to God, he continues a view of the Besht, though he was not alone in this generation that cultivated this ideal.[9]

Let me adduce one example for the existence of the mystical-magical model in R. Moshe of Dolina, despite his proclivity to mental cleaving and his interest in Lurianic Kabbalah:

> The perfection of the *tzaddiq*—he says—is to purify himself, purification after purification . . . and he should be preoccupied with the Torah and the commandments in a very enthusiastic manner, and with great desire, and insofar as he will multiply them he will be purified more, and he will feel a great delight in their performance, infinitely. Because of this, the good influxes will descend from the supernal worlds.[10]

Though not a view reported in the name of the Besht, it may nevertheless help in understanding the manner in which the Hasidic master understood the words of his master as adduced earlier. In any case they show that also in R. Moshe of Dolina's writings it is possible to discern the existence of a strong nexus between the

acts of cleaving and the descent of the influx.[11] I see in the way this
Hasidic master treats the cleaving of thought, without mentioning
the cleaving to letters or sounds, a later development in the Besht's
thought, when the role of language has been diminished, and the
more omnipresent approach to theology has emerged, what I called
the third, noetic model.[12] If this diagnosis concerning a significant
development in the thought of the Besht is true, then not only the
position of R. Moshe of Dolina as reflecting an authentic trend
in the Besht's thought is important, but in fact the entire attitude
toward the redaction of some of the teachings found in the so-called
Testament of the Besht should be reconsidered, as they presumably
reflect a tendency already found in the Besht himself, though later
in his career, an issue that cannot be dealt with in detail with here.

Without assuming that this so-called "testament" is an authentic
Beshtian treatise as a whole, some passages of this small work may
nevertheless be quite helpful for improving our understanding of
views found in other independent sources, when attributed to the
Besht. As to the reason for such a speculative development in the
later Beshtian thought, which would introduce, at a certain point
in his later career, also the importance of the continuous mental
cleaving that differs phenomenologically from the cleaving to "letters" that is more restricted in time, I have, for the time being,
no answer. Though, as we have seen in the tradition of R. Meir
Margaliot, the cleaving in thought is an early Beshtian approach,
this does not mean that it was conceived of as being a continuous
state of mind. Is this part of the "refinement" of his thought when
moving from a more rural to an urban environment, or just a
change of his mind toward an expansion of the mystical life to
more than the periods of vocal rituals?

We have surveyed previously a variety of formulations of the
meaning of the intention in prayer as a vocal rite. I divided the
variants in accordance to the occurrence in schools that referred
expressly to the Besht in this context. None of those variants is the
result of copying or even paraphrasing any of the others. Especially
interesting is the fact that in the writings of R. Jacob Joseph of

Polonnoye and in R. Efrayyim of Sudylkov's book, the image of the vocal palaces—*heihalot*—is absent, an image that is found in the school of the Great Maggid. On the other hand, the term *ruḥaniyyut*—the spiritual force—is much more characteristic of R. Jacob Joseph's traditions reported in the name of the Besht than in the school of the Great Maggid, though it is also found there. Since the two terms are part of a certain Gestalt-coherence, found, for example, in Cordovero's *Pardes Rimmonim*, Gate XXXII, chapter 2, where the two terms are found together (a larger topic to be discussed in some of the following discussions, especially in appendix C), the question of the possible reconstruction of the Besht's thought as reflecting the Cordoverian structure is quite pertinent.

However, different as they are, these traditions share important features, some of which are indebted to views found in Cordoverian schools, an issue to be discussed also in detail in appendices B–F of this volume. Though none of them is expressly anti-Lurianic, it is hard to discern in those formulations the impact of Lurianic theories of *kavvanot*. Neither are the theories of prayer known among the Hasidei Ashkenaz having any significant impact on those theories.

In fact the previous instructions are somewhat more complex, since they have been read within the framework of the architectural imagery of the sound, part of which has been discussed previously. Let me turn to an additional theme that belongs to this type of imagery.

8

SEEING LIGHTS
WITHIN SPEECHES

As seen previously, the Besht regarded the resort to written letters as a lower form of liturgical activity, in fact the lowest, to be performed only in a state of distress or of diminished consciousness, unlike the view of his disciple, R. Jacob Joseph. In the seminal passage found in some of the versions of the *Holy Epistle* that was discussed earlier, the utterances are regarded as monadic vehicles, which are capable of transporting the soul on high. What is absent in some of the traditions discussed so far is a theme that occurs in several other sources, according to which within the utterances there are lights, and they are allowing not only an ascent of the soul on high but the possibility to enjoy an extraordinary visual experience. Though the presence of the divine light within letters/sounds has been mentioned from time to time in the Beshtian teachings, it was much more a matter of cleaving to the divine light as an expansion of the light of the Infinite within the ritualistic pronunciation rather than seeing it, as we learn from the stories about the Besht. In other words, while we may speak about architectural *imaginaire* of the sound—and the image of the palace that we have seen previously is indicating such an attitude—I am not aware of a parallel architecture of the graphical letters in Hasidism. To a certain extent, this architecture is reminiscent of the sefirotic architecture in Kabbalah, especially in R. Joseph Gikatilla's later writings, but it has been amplified in Safedian Kabbalah, perhaps because of the impact of the astro-magical worldview.

It is in the later form of Kabbalah that internal and external
aspects of the divine powers are often times mentioned, including
a special view that there is a certain realm for each of the sefirot.
So, for example, the inner sefirot or the aspects of the divinity
are described as the light of the Infinite, in a manner reminiscent
of the terminology of the Besht. The external sefirot have been
depicted as vessels of that light. The transposition from the structure of sefirot to the sound, perhaps also influenced by the thought
of R. Moshe Cordovero, is part of the broken theology, since it
adopts a rather minor aspect of a more complex edifice. This spacial imagery is also necessary, provided the monadic perception of
the vocables as containing worlds, souls, and divinity, discussed
previously. This all-inclusive nature of the sounds may well reflect
the architectural imagery.

I wonder whether the Besht envisioned the emission of the
vocables as a parallel to the emanation of the sefirot as vessels in the
Cordoverian theosophy, and the bringing down of the "spiritual
force" within them as the emanation of the divine essence within
the supernal vessels. The entrance of the mystic within the sounds
would be parallel, therefore, to the entrance of the infinite power
within the sefirotic system. As we shall see in the next chapter, in
accordance with a teaching of the Besht, the pronounced Torah is
compared to the secret of emanation. It is in this framework that
the triune monadic vision of sounds as comprising worlds, souls,
and divinity, found in the Besht's Holy Epistle discussed previously, should be understood: the sound below is parallel to the
sefirot on high, which are conceived of as comprising the three
entities. In short, human speeches are conceived of as creative in
a sense similar to the divine creation, as understood in Kabbalah
as emanation, and it constitutes some form of *imitatio dei*. This
is the reason why the importance of the mouth and its purity is
mentioned in several texts discussed earlier and later in this study.

On the other hand we have some traditions according to which
the Besht could, by means of the letters of the Torah or of the *Zohar*,
see from one corner of the world to another, some form of telepathy,

an achievement conceived of as being quite extraordinary. Are the two attitudes to visual contemplation divergent from each other, or can we find an explanation that reduces the discrepancy between them? Indeed, if the contemplation of the visual aspects of letters suffices in order to achieve such an unusual capacity, why would looking at the same letters be considered so low, according to the tradition adduced and discussed previously from *Kutoneth Passim* about the Besht's state of *qatenut*?

According to a tradition preserved, *inter alia*, by R. Ze'ev Wolf of Zhitomir (who died sometime between 1795 to 1798), the Besht interpreted the verse from Genesis 6:16, "Thou shall make a window to the ark" as dealing with the word, since in Hebrew Teivah means both "ark" and "word." Also the word *Tzohar*, window, is interpreted out of its context, as if it is pointing to luminosity illumining the word. This is a well-known Beshtian interpretation of the biblical verse, which recurs in many texts in slightly different forms, but R. Ze'ev Wolf preserved a special formulation of this interpretation:

> [I]n the manner I heard in the name of the Besht . . .
> to make an opening [window] to the word [*teivah*] of
> Torah and Prayer, in order to see by means of it from
> one extremity of the world to another. And this is the
> meaning of [the verse Exodus 15:22][1] "And they exited
> to Midbbar Shur": the sight there, as it is spoken
> [*medubbar*].[2]

The concept that informs the passage is clear: by producing the opening—the window—in the utterance pronounced during prayer and study of the Torah, a couple of activities that we have seen occur together previously in the Besht's instructions, someone sees the light within it and looks thereby from one part of the world to another. This is also the gist of the interpretation of the biblical phrase *Midbbar Shur*: while the plain sense of the phrase is that there is a desert named *Shur*, the Besht interprets *Shur* as referring to looking at, and translated in the passage by the Aramaic noun *'istakkeluta'*, derived from the form *histakkel*, to look at, while *Middbar* was most probably interpreted as *Medubbar*, namely something that is spoken. The verse will therefore mean that they, the Israelites, exited from speech to sight. Thus, according to the Besht, it is not the contemplation of written letters that opens the mystic to the sight of the lights within the letters/sounds, but an operation connected to the act of emission of vocables, which is more dynamic and contingent. This sequence is quite clear also in a passage by R. Efrayyim of Sudylkov, the Besht's grandson, who reports that:

> according to what my grandfather, may he rest in peace, the verse is illumined [namely explained]: the *teivah* points to the word, that is called *teivah*, as it is written "Thou shall make an opening to the word" and he said, blessed be his memory, that you should see over to illumine the word that you utter by your mouth, and he dwelt on this issue at length.[3]

Unfortunately he does not bring anywhere else details of his grandfather's discussion of the topic. It should be pointed out that there are many instances where the disciples of the Besht testify that he elaborated on a certain topic but they did not adduce the whole discussion.

It seems that here, as well as in a statement of R. Barukh, the brother of the author quoted in the note, the illumination of the word, pronounced as well as written, comes from the person, who projects something stemming from himself within the pronounced word. In any case, we have here an example of the vision that when dealing with the Genesis verse, the Besht understood the term *word* as explicitly related to pronunciation. The pun used here resorting to the concept of an ark is indubitably part of the architectural *imaginaire*. Like in the case of the end of the first quote we adduced from R. Jacob Joseph, which ended with the word *etc.*, also here it is rather evident that more teachings of the Besht were available among his followers than we have today. This conclusion can be deduced also from other instances in the writings of R. Jacob Joseph. The basic assumption that explains the phenomenon of clairvoyance is the connection between the light found within utterances and the light without them, which functions like some form of cosmic ether that is imagined to allow the possibility to use the particular manifestation of the light in a certain specific place in order to gain access to the other distant particular event. In any case, the image of the word as an ark is one more example of what I call the Besht's architecture of the sound.

Let me point out that I do not understand exactly the process of entering the structure of the sound. Important as it may be for the Besht, I can hardly imagine how exactly he imagined this event. However, impenetrable as this penetration is for me, there is no reason to belittle its role in the traditions in which it appears. In fact, just as a scholar of Yoga does not have to understand how levitation is attained by the Hindu techniques, or does not believe in it, so too a scholar dealing with the Besht should not neglect the *imaginaire* of entering the vocables he generates. Scholarship should not take the subjective beliefs of a scholar as a criterion for accepting the centrality of traditional treatments as valid or not, and this is especially true in the case of magic.

To turn now to a treatise emanating from the school of the Great Maggid, in the collection of early Hasidic traditions entitled *Liqqutim Yeqarim*, the Besht is reported as saying that:

> a person who [orally] reads the Torah, and sees the lights of the letters/sounds, which are in the Torah, even if he does not properly know the cantillations [of the biblical text], because of his reading with great love and with enthusiasm, God does not deal with him strictly even if he does not properly pronounce them [i.e., the cantillations].[4]

It is hard to decide whether this passage is indeed Beshtian, despite the fact that his name is explicitly invoked on it. In a manner reminiscent of the tradition of R. Meir Margoliot, it does not speak about *devequt*, but only about the experience of the oral reading of the Torah. It seems quite plausible that both the verbs "read" and "pronounce" are related to the subsequent experience that consists of seeing the lights, some form of synaesthesis. Even if someone assumes that the lights are found, in one way or another, already within the written letters of the Torah, as we know from several Rabbinic and Kabbalistic texts, the act of seeing them is predicated upon the existence of utterances, and this is also the case in the next passage. Like in some many other instances discussed in this study, this text also depicts the ritual context, which dictates not only the specifics of performance but also confers a certain meaning to it.

This is also the approach represented in a fascinating passage found in the Great Maggid's collection of traditions, *Maggid Devarav le-Ya'aqov*, and in a longer form, which will be translated as follows, in the version found in *Keter Shem Tov*. It should be pointed out that though in these sources the passage is not reported explicitly in the name of the Besht—though it appears in *Keter Shem Tov* that it is the collection of his teachings—a shorter version of it has indeed been quoted in the name of the Besht by R. Aharon of Apta in one of his books, a fact that has in my opinion a considerable weight for establishing his authorship, especially when it is combined with other affinities to the Besht, to be discussed immediately as follows:

> This is [written] in the name of the Besht, blessed be his memory: The letters/sounds of the Torah are vessels and chambers of God, blessed be He, because by the dint of the intention of man, He draws within them the emanation of His supernal light.[5]

Though an act of drawing related to the letters/sounds is explicitly mentioned here, the descent is done by God and not by the human person in prayer. However, even if we accept this reading as plausible, this divine act is conditioned by the quality of the human intention, and thus an indirect linkage between the mode of activity of the person during prayer, on the one hand, and the dwelling of the divine light within utterances, on the other hand, is nevertheless created, and as such it is the result of the human activity. In general, let me point out that the emphasis I put on the pronounced letters presumes the magic influence of human activity upon the presence of the divine light here following.

It is only in the written forms of letters that someone may assume that there is a permanent presence of the divine light, enduring independently of the presence of a reader. When such written letters are not explicitly mentioned, the assumption should better be that a vocal activity is involved, and it is drawing the supernal presence within the vocables. *Nota bene*: the singular forms used here: it is the divinity or light, namely an undifferentiated approach that is found here, unlike the specificity of the different astral spiritualities in magical texts that inspired Hasidism, a fine example of departure from the astral theology; or in my terms, this is another example of a broken theology. The diversity between the characters of the planets, or even of the seven *sefirot*, lost its centrality and sometimes even disappears, and in lieu the various qualities are comprised in one supernal unit.

However, the point concerning human activity is missing in a longer version of this statement found in the Great Maggid's traditions as well as in *Keter Shem Tov*. Let me translate now the longest version of this teaching, which is an instruction related to religious behavior concerning the utterances related to the Torah, without however mentioning prayer in this context:

> He should put all his thought in the power[6] of the words that he speaks, so that he shall see how the lights [which are] within the words are sparking within one another, and out of them some [other] lights are generated . . . the letters/sounds of the Torah, are chambers of the God [or Name], blessed be He, that He draws within them[7] the emanation of His light [as it is written in the *Zohar*, "The Holy One, blessed be He and the Torah are all one"

and within them should the person put all his intention, which is the soul, since the intention is the soul, and this is the *devequt* between the Holy One, blessed be He, and the Torah and Israel, which are all are one[8]][9] and this is the divestment of materiality, namely he should divest his soul from his body, and his soul will [then] be clothed by those thoughts that he speaks, and will see how many supernal worlds are [found] in man.[10]

I propose to understand the passage as displaying a sexual under-standing of the lights, which by their combinations generate other lights, even more so since according to one of his teachings, the Besht asserts that in each and every word there is an aspect of male and female.[11] This is the single specific image that occurs in a passage that is an instruction, not a legend. Also, the occurrence in this passage of the term *chambers* within which the divine lights are emanated sup-ports such a reading. Indeed, my interpretation should be compared to the commentary of Schatz-Uffenheimer, who elaborates upon an erroneous text, in a manner that does not do justice to the views found in it, resorting to the "contemplative prayer" again. According to her commentary, contemplation, *ha-hitbonenut*, liberates the lights—perhaps of her understanding of lights as Lurianic sparks, quite a questionable one to be sure—and she assumes that the per-son in prayer looks at the written words of prayer. This is just another case of imposing the category of contemplation and the visual activ-ity on a text where there is a clear instance of vocal activity.

The assumption that lights are envisioned to be found within utter-ances may better explain also the passage of Margoliot that has been discussed previously: by dealing with the study of the Torah alone—though prayer is not mentioned as it is in many other cases—which is an oral activity, the cleaving is to sounds, and as we learn from the end of the passage, the Besht is reported there to have believed that lights and vitality are emanated from or by the utterances. Unlike the discussions about the cleaving to the light of the Infinite, according to a tradition adduced previously from R. Jacob Joseph of Polonnoye's

Toledot Ya'aqov Yosef, in the sources analyzed in this chapter, there is no cleaving to the lights as an objective natural entity but some form of pneumatic sight. Thus, to resort to a distinction of Paul Ricoeur, we have here some form of manifestation of a luminous hierophany, dwelling within the oral proclamation, if we may see the prayer as performed by the Besht, a form of proclamation.

Let me be more specific: according to the last passage the person in prayer pronounces utterances, within which there are lights, which are the dwelling places of the divinity. This complexity is reminiscent of the view of the Besht as found in R. Jacob Joseph of Polonnoye's book that was mentioned previously, where the light of the infinite is described as found within or identical with the inner dimension of the utterances. The correspondence between the traditions about the appearance of light[s] within utterances as occuring in some of the Great Maggid traditions without mentioning the name of the Besht, and in R. Jacob Joseph and R. Aharon of Apta who reported them in his name, shows that once again a view found in the Great Maggid's collections of teachings stem from his teacher, even when he does not mention the latter's name.

Let me compare the shorter passage adduced in the name of the Besht to the longer versions. One major addition found in *Maggid Devarav le-Ya'aqov* and in the Jerusalem Ms. in comparison to the shorter version and that found in *Keter Shem Tov* is the reference to the lights found within the letters/sounds. Those lights, which in the manuscript version are referred as ten, are conceived of as the vessels and chambers of God, not the human utterances as in other teachings. I assume that this addition resonates more with the Great Maggid's approach, while the two versions found in the books of R. Aharon of Apta reflect the Besht's teaching better, while in the longer version found in *Keter Shem Tov* there is an accretion, as proposed previously.

Here we witness a strong architectural imagery: the letters, or more precisely the utterances or the words, are chambers—or according to many other texts, palaces—and now it is God who draws His emanation within them, and the human intention/soul leaves the body, or divests itself, in order to enter there and become one with God. According to a discussion found in the Testament of the Besht, one has to enter the sound in his body and strength. Within the pronounced letters, which are conceived of as sonorous palaces, there are to be found also lights, a concept that reflects the concept of the emanation of light, or of the spiritual force, *ruḥani-yyut*, from the Infinite (mentioned in the name of the Besht in two quotes by R. Jacob Joseph adduced previously), and this light is understood as having been seen by the mystic.

It should be mentioned though that while in some cases the light within the utterances is described as being related to the Infinite, this is not always the case, and it is possible that the identification of the lights within utterances with the Kabbalistic concept of "the light of the Infinite" is a later development in his thought. In any case, the pronounced utterances of the Torah are to be seen, there-fore, as constituting a sonorous mesocosm, a space that though cre-ated during the verbal ritual, is entered by either human body or by soul, and the divine emanation described several times as light, in order to be united there. It seems that in the last quoted passage, the person that prays sees not only light but some form of image, which I interpret as being sexually distinct. However, at least insofar as the ritual activity is concerned, the lights within utterances are hardly envisioned as possessing a shape or constituting images.

Let me turn to another passage dealing with the Besht, pre-served by one of his students who met him only in the late years of his life: R. Menahem Nahum of Chernobyl. Following earlier sources, the latter claims that there is a "resplendent light," 'or bahir, by means of which it is possible to see from one part of the world to another, in a manner reminiscent of Shamanic claims.[12] This is known, he claims, from the deeds of people he claims to have seen, and in this context he mentions the Besht:

> who has been reported that when he needed to know a
> certain particular thing, even of issues related to people,
> or a material issue, he was looking in the Torah, and

studied it in awe and love, and cleaved himself, so that
he arrived to the hidden light within it [Torah] and was
indeed seeing the thing that he needed to see . . . and
not everyone deserves this rank.[13]

Here the assumption is that it is not just looking at the visual structure of the Torah letters, but that the Besht was also studying it in awe
and love, and then cleaving—without mentioning to what entity specifically—to allow the magical attainment of telepathy. Though the
oral activity is not explicitly mentioned, I believe that its occurrence is
quite plausible by the dint of the parallels to the other passages related
to the Besht cited in the previous chapters, where Torah study and
prayer were mentioned together as verbal activity, and this is hinted at
also here by the concept of studying the Torah. Here we have the first
two steps of cleaving, to written letters and to sounds, together, and
only as a consequence of these two cleavings is the act of seeing lights
imagined to take place as a third stage. In this passage the light is
seen as some form of ether that permeates the entire reality and allows
the perception of things at distance. In any case, at least here there is
no reason to assume a contemplative act related to the light, since it
serves as just a medium for attaining quite concrete results.

In short, though cleaving is not always mentioned in the process
of seeing lights within the utterances adduced in this chapter, it
occurs nevertheless, as is the case of the tradition of Margoliot. Like
in that tradition, the Besht is described not as the unequaled master,
as is always the case in the hagiography about the Besht, but one of
several extraordinary individuals in his generation. Let me emphasize that this passage is not an instruction, like that from *Keter Shem
Tov*, but a description of the extraordinary individual, similar to
what we found in the hagiography about the Besht. In other words,
it is best that we not impose one later practice on the instructions
of the Besht in order to create some form of coherence in Hasidism.

In this context, we should mention also the tradition preserved in
a collection of Hasidic teachings, which has been edited by R. Levi
Isaac of Berditchev, entitled *Shemu'ah Tovah*. This fascinating text,

which is not explicitly reported in the name of the Besht, speaks indeed about the contemplation of the forms of the letters as found in the mind of the person—some parallel to the concept of the "letters of thought" we have discussed previously—as constituting a means for seeing the distant divinity, like telescopes, as Schatz-Uffenheimer felicitously put it.[14] Here, the lights are not described as dwelling within the mental letters, even less within the sounds, but are understood as transcending them; but it is possible to see them by gazing at these letters. However, interesting as this passage dealing with looking at mental letters is, I am doubtful if the term *contemplation* is the best word to be used in order to describe this approach, it cannot, change the meaning of much more numerous other passages that deal explicitly with sounds. As mentioned previously, it is hard even to know if indeed the Besht is the real author, and it seems that it reflects much more the thought of R. Levi Isaac of Berditchev than anything else I am aware of in the Hasidic camp. This is the reason why this interesting passage should not be considered as representative of the thought of the Besht, and even in the school of the Great Maggid it is hardly paralleled by substantial examples.

It is my hope that the previous interpretations of the texts translated in this chapter solve the problem we formulated at its beginning: just gazing at written letters, or contemplating them, is not opening the possibility to have experiences of telepathy, but this may happen only after those letters have been pronounced. This is also the case with drawing down influx, lights, vitality, or spiritual force. The voice is conceived of as necessary, and in many cases the descent of the higher energies is concerning not only the individual but also the group or larger collectives. In fact, let me emphasize, the Besht, and following him many other leaders of Hasidic groups, have shifted from a more individualistic approach to talismanic magic, to a more communal one predicated also on the collective vocal rites. This turn had been conjugated with an emphasis on the necessity of the prior spiritual achievement, sometimes found also in magical sources, which also mitigated some of the magical aspects of the sources they used.

Let me address an antecedent for some of the themes discussed in this chapter, namely seeing lights within vocables. It is found in R. Moshe Cordovero's commentary on the *Zohar*, a treatise that was extant only in manuscripts until recently, and it is thereby hard to conceive that the Besht could have been acquainted with it:

> Just as there are bones of the body and inmost [aspects] in persons, from which the vapor and breath [stem], so there are in the supernal *sefirot*, the spirit of God, *Tiferet* and *Malkhut* that operate the divine will that is found within them, by means of which the supernal divine will spreads. And the inner will, namely the voice and speech, namely *Tiferet* and *Malkhut*, operates. And when a person prays and studies Torah by means of voice and speech, there are angels that are appointed over that voice and that speech in order to elevate them on high . . . and there is a median one that operate this action and they are the three aspects: one is the vapor, the second the voice that is heard, and the third is speech. And the issue is that voice and speech [refer to] *Tiferet* and *Malkhut*, and the vapor, within which there is the secret of the *kavvanah* and the spiritual force of the letters/vocables. When a person prolongs and enlarges a word, [and] by his *kavvanah* he pays attention to the *hawayyot* and the [divine] names each and every vapor [*hevel*] that exits from his mouth, produces a flame [*lahav*] of fire that ascends on high, *lev H*, namely hints at _Hokhmah_ and *Binah*, namely a similitude of the supernal vapor that is [Psalms 29:7] "The voice of the Lord hews the flames of fire," from the side of *Binah*, so too a person hews flames of fire in accordance to the secret of *kavvanah*, within the voice and the speech, and this is the reason why the flame rides over voice and speech.[15]

The triad of speech, voice, and vapor, quintessential for prayer and study, is interpreted here on two levels: the human and the sefirotic.

The symmetry between the two planes is depicted as the result of the symbolic correspondences between the three components of oral activity, and four of the *sefirot*. Especially interesting is the one related to vapor: the consonants of *hevel* are the same as those of *lahav*, flame, and they also are interpreted as *lev H*, the heart of H or of God. The plural of *lahav*, *lehavot*—flames—is therefore describing an inherent component of the process of speech. The flames are higher than speech and voice, as performed as part of the vocal rites, as it has been expressly articulated in the passage, and they are parallel to the "spirit of God" mentioned at the beginning. Thus, we have here some form of triad that is reminiscent of that found in *Sefer Yetziyrah*: voice, spirit, and speech. No doubt this is a fine illustration of the apotheosis of the oral activity. In fact, the relation between vapor and spiritual force has to do with the meaning of the ancient Greek term that inspired the term *ruḥaniyyut/ ruḥaniyyat*, namely *pneuma*, which means spirit or breath.

However, the importance of this passage transcends this emphasis on the oral components. It contains a seminal phrase, "the spiritual force of the vocables," a term that plays an important role in Cordovero's thought, as we shall see in more detail in appendix D in this volume, and also in some Hasidic traditions, one of which has been dealt with beside ch. 6 n. 19 in this volume. In the framework of the present chapter, I am concerned with the assumption of the creation of flame and fire by means of performing the vocal rites. I propose to see here the impact of another type of magic, that of the rays emanating from every entity, according to a book of the ninth-century Arabic philosopher and astrologer, al-Kindi, an issue to be elaborated as follows in the aforementioned appendix. Here and in some texts referred to in ch. 8 n. 15, the flames, but also the term light, that occur in the content of the emission of sounds are reminiscent of the emission of rays found inherently in the utterances, independent of a theory of drawing down supernal forces in the words.

Moreover, from the point of view of the implied semiology, this passage does not operate with a Platonic theory of surrogationalism, when the word represents some lower, coarse representation of the higher, pure *eidos*, a view that remained influential in Western philosophies of language up to the seventeenth century. Here, in addition to representation, there is a profound ontic connection between the vocables and their corresponding powers in the higher worlds, and there are median powers that activate the higher powers because of the activation of the lower vocables by their pronunciation. This is a vertical type of activation, less concerned with sympathy based on parallelism between two planes of existence, but much more with affinities between different components below and their correponding powers on high, based on an ontic continuum between them and in some cases we may speak even about a linguistic energetic circuit in the cosmos, reminiscent of the circuit of energy related to the role played by sacrifices in archaic religions, according to scholars of religion like Mircea Eliade. As we know already in Rabbinic sources, the prayers have been conceived of as surrogates for sacrifices. There is, therefore, no discernable tension between the ideal and its lower representation, as in Platonism, but some form of synergesis, related to the introduction of the concept of emanation. As such the arbitrariness of language, or the game of language, as philosophers of language assume, is inconceivable in Hasidism insofar as canonical texts are involved. The word is therefore much less the portent or tradent of meaning, though it is understood as a specific type of supernal power that is not cut from the divine realm, and additional texts to this effect are found in Cordovero's writings, some of which will be addressed in appendix C.

The Cordoverian passage supplies therefore both a phenomenological and terminological antecedent for the Beshtian traditions. However, while Cordovero's passage is strongly indebted to the theosophical structure, the Beshtian traditions on this topic are much less concerned with such complex theosophies, as he is reticent in elaborating in detail on the divine structures. Last but not least: the resort to the term *flame* in the context of prayer is interesting in itself, since early Hasidism emphasized the necessity to pray enthusiastically, in Hebrew the term used being *hitlahavut*, a noun stemming from *lahav*, flame.

Let me summarize the findings of this chapter: cleaving to the utterances is not always the ultimate aim of the performance of the verbal rituals. In some cases, there is an additional act that is imagined as viewing or cleaving to lights which appear within the utterances. In some other cases, the vision of the lights is conducive to extraordinary achievements: telepathy and the possibility to draw down supernal powers. The lights are sometimes just supernal presences appearing within vocal entities, sometimes they are described as the immanence of the infinite light of the divinity, and cleaving to it amounts, according to the Besht, to cleaving to the totality. However, let me emphasize that in any case, the very act of generating the utterances contributes to the appearance of the lights, even in the case when the act of drawing lights within them is not explicitly mentioned. Thus, even if the utterances and their lights are conceived of as a unit, and there is no additional act of induction within the vocal medium as container, the act of utterance creates the lights. It is even more so in cases when the Beshtian teachings assume that there are lights belonging to utterances, perhaps in quite a specific manner.

Last but not least: the watching of the luminous *hieros gamos* that may take places within the utterances, which may correspond to the hieros gamos upon the lips of the persons in prayer according to other Beshtian texts, takes the objects of cleaving into a farther dynamic situation. We may regard the gist of some of the previous discussions as moving the locus for some events and entities from the theosophical realm to the realm of language when pronounced, in a rather contigent manner, as part of a ritual in this world. Let me remind the reader that though the order of the Hebrew letters in the canonical texts is stable, their pronunciation in Hebrew depends on the various forms of Ashkenazi vocalization, which differ from one Ashkenazi community to another. The allophones are related to many of the vowels and few consonants. It is within the realm of language as verbally performed that the discussions as found in Cordovero and Luria have now the pregnant significance for the rituals. This move is part of the much more comprehensive Beshtian anthropocentric approach that stresses the importance of the presence of the supernal powers and processes within the human realm: in body, soul, and behavior.

Whether we can suggest a development from one position to another regarding the understanding of the three positions is, in the present state of research, doubtful, and perhaps it will suffice to tentatively propose to see the earlier position, like in R. Meir Margoliot's tradition, as simpler and earlier, and the *hieros gamos* tradition as the latest teaching, while the version in which the light of the Infinite is dwelling within the utterances appears as a middle position. This proposal is based upon the assumption that the more comprehensive view is later. We should remember that in many cases in the Beshtian traditions, the unification of the feminine factor within the divinity with the divine male is conceived of as a theurgical operation performed by means of prayer. Thus, the union of the human soul, or thought, to the divine is conceived as part of a longer and significant series of unions, in which the vocal prayer participates as an indispensable component of the mystical life. The conjugation of the values of *devequt* conceived of as fundamental, with that of causing some forms of sexual union in the divine world (though in other cases only watching them), is another instance of the Besht's bringing together earlier Kabbalistic ideals, which were rarely regarded as coexisting in the same system in earlier forms of Kabbalah, in a new manner. Since this is done in the framework of the utterances, we may add to the ecstatic element related to *devequt*, and to the theosophical-theurgical elements related to the union of sexually distinguished powers, also elements that are found in the talismanic or astro-magical model, concentrated on details of techniques of drawing down supernal power.

In principle, elements found in the three models that constitute in my opinion the three fundamental directions in Kabbalistic literature since the last quarter of the thirteenth century occur together in significant proportions already in Cordovero's Kabbalah. The Besht, however, combined them in a special manner, by emphasizing much more the role of *devequt* to the utterances, and by introducing, in some instances at least, the sight of the lights within the utterances, a combination that I did not find earlier. What is of no small consequence is the fact that Ba'al Shem Tov is the historical personality to whom the effects of the model he forged also had been attributed as an actual achievement in some specific cases, contributing thereby to the contents of some hagiographical tales.

Moreover, if my reading of some of the Beshtian texts as pointing to divine lights as referring to some form of sexual union is correct, we have here for the first time, to the best of my knowledge, the assumption that gazing at this erotic act by a living Kabbalist—not by dead souls—is considered to be part of a mystical path in Jewish mysticism. In any case, it should be pointed out that the watching of the lights is coupled with the instruction to cleave to God, envisioned as a higher stage. Likewise in one of his teachings as adduced in R. Jacob Joseph's *Tzafnat Pa'aneah*, fol. 18b, which has already been discussed, and in a somehow different formulation in the so-called Testament of the Besht, there are famous statements that compare the act of speech in prayer—sometimes described as while making the movements of swaying—to the movements of copulation, and the divine counterpart is the *Shekhinah*, the divine presence or the last *sefirah*, hardly a situation that fits the common use of the term contemplation.

The question may be asked, what is the relationship between the Beshtian teachings where the cleaving to the utterances has been mentioned without referring to lights, and those where lights occur? This is a difficult question, which may be answered in two different ways: one option would be the assumption that there are two different stages in the Besht's thought, with the occurrence of the lights as the later development that supplemented new materials to the earlier stage. The other possible answer would be that what we have called the earlier stage is a case of elliptic formulations, which do not elaborate on issues that were conceived as being evident in a certain group. I am inclined to adopt the second answer given the early date of the tradition adduced by R. Meir Margoliot.

The third possible answer that the discussions related to the divine lights are part of an esoteric tradition seems to me far-fetched in the context of early Hasidic thought. In any case, it should be pointed out that while the vocal substratum of the religious performance discussed previously has an objective existence, namely the sounds were indeed pronounced during the ritual and heard by both the praying persons and by their companions, the luminous phenomena mentioned in the previous teaching are mentioned more rarely, they are much more elusive, and they pertain more to an imaginary perception that is restricted to very few people. This is not just a distinction between an objective and what I would consider to be a subjective dimension of a certain experience, but also one that differentiates between the vocal apparatus that is energized by the efforts of pronunciation and an inner sense of spiritual vision that is necessary for seeing or imagining lights within the vocables.

This complexity of approaches to the lights imagined to dwell within utterances of the rituals goes, in my opinion, far beyond the vision of *devequt* as a popular value to be preached to the simple Jews by Hasidic masters. It is a much more elitist approach, and difficulties in explaining it, much less practicing it, should not be underestimated. However, beyond the question of the social function of the ideal of *devequt*, which is certainly complicated by the sequence of actions that follow the cleaving to the utterances, we must address the fact that the Besht advanced, at least in some later part of his career, quite a complex mystical structure, more complex than most of the forms of mysticism in Judaism that are connected to *devequt*. The previous quotes do not militate in favor of too passive an approach, and neither are they supporting the image of the Besht as a "semi-literate" figure, as Joseph Weiss once estimated his knowledge of Judaism, or elsewhere, his "relative illiteracy," or the view of Hasidism as the revolt of the 'am- ha-'aretz, the ignoramuses, as Buber, following perhaps Solomon Schechter, put it once. As I reiterated in some occasions, in my opinion the Ba'al Shem Tov managed to acquire a much broader knowledge of Jewish texts with time, and he should be envisioned as a "fatter" figure than conceived of by all the scholars that wrote about him in the last generation. This development approach, that does not reduce a person to just one immutable state or situation, is more natural and logical at the same time.

If indeed it is possible to attribute to a figure that emerged from no specific school of learning, without a solid education that we know about in detail, such a complex mystical scheme is a matter that scholarship should seriously ponder over its sources and the possibility that a "semi-literate" figure could indeed generate it. Nevertheless, the testimony of an accomplished legalistic figure like R. Meir Harif Margoliot about the young Besht, as well as of those of his two major students, R. Jacob Joseph and the Great Maggid, also very erudite thinkers—not to speak about stories included in the hagiography—and their respect of the spiritual stature of the Besht tip the balance dramatically in the direction of a positive answer.

Historically speaking, it is hard to account in a reliable manner for any of the details of the Besht's early education and the specific manner in which he acquired, later on, his knowledge in matters of Kabbalah, and in fact of Judaism as a culture in general. Nevertheless, the mainly succinct teachings emanating from him, or attributed to him, testify as to a much better acquaintance with many sources than what is assumed in the dominant scholarship concerning his thought. However, his selective attitude toward sources, which implies also his fragmentation of their more comprehensive theories, and his new combinations between those fragments and rituals or classical texts that are interpreted, differ from the approaches found in the first elite authors.

9

THE BA'AL SHEM TOV AND THE
MYSTICAL-MAGICAL MODEL

Let me turn now to the distinction that has been proposed previously between end-experiences and means-experiences. In the quote from the Rabbi of Chernobyl's *Sefer Me'or 'Einayyim* that was adduced beside ch. 8 n. 14 in this volume, the Besht has been described as initiating a certain sequence of acts in order to know something hidden, by means of an extraordinary manner of cognition, which has nevertheless both specific and material aspects. It reflects, in my opinion, an attempt to answer a question of someone who turned to the Besht as a kind of magician, in a manner we see in several instances in the hagiography *Shivehei ha-Besht, In Praise of the Baal Shem Tov.* The experience of *devequt* was, therefore, part of this series of actions, which culminated in knowing something unknown to others, by means of his clairvoyance or telepathy. The theme of seeing at distance occurs twice in the legends related to him, which were preserved in the famous hagiography. Nevertheless, in the two instances, there is no mentioning of any performance related to the written letters of the Torah or of the book of the *Zohar* alone, but the Besht is described as just looking into the primordial light found within the written letters of printed books after having verbalized them. However, in at least one other case in the hagiography, it is the recitation of the Psalms that generated some form of light that hovered over the Hasidic master.[1]

It seems that only in the passage of R. Menahem Nahum of Chernobyl that was cited previously, which is the earlier testimony in comparison to the hagiography, is there a clear nexus between the instruction of cleaving to utterances on the one hand, and the assumption of the related capacity of achieving telepathy on the other. It is possible that there are two different literary genres that deal with similar issues: the more mystical literature, as represented by the Rabbi of Chernobyl, which is concerned with the technique of inner changes in the individual as a condition for his success: awe and love, *devequt*, study, while the hagiographical literature is concerned much more with the inherent power of the holy man, the *tzaddiq*, a term that is mentioned in the hagiography twice in an explicit manner, though it is absent in R. Menahem Nahum's passage. Though the formulation of the disciple is quite cautious, there is no reason not to describe his passage as reflecting not just the Besht as a popular magician, but also one who puts the instructions related to prayer and study of the Torah in the service of a magical achievement. Thus, we have an explicit example where some forms of mysticism and magic meet.

Let us reflect now on the content of some of the Beshtian teachings adduced in the previous chapters. In some of them the effect of the cleaving is the causing of the descent of the influx on the person who speaks. This is the case especially in a few of the traditions preserved by R. Jacob Joseph and in the circle of the Great Maggid. Unlike the nexus between *devequt* and clairvoyance that describes a quite specific, quite rare, and extraordinary capability that is achieved by *devequt*, the nexus in those traditions, especially as adduced in chapters 5–6, is less clear, and the texts do not specify the details of the outcome of the descent of the influx. I shall try to delve into this issue now.

The effects are achieved by two different components when they come together: the devotional performance on the one hand, and the specific nature of the pronounced canonical texts—the structure of the prayer and the Torah—on the other. The first component is definitively mystical, since it assumes a direct contact with what is considered to be a higher power. The second one has, in my opinion, magical connotations, for two reasons. According to the first one, the original canonical texts have been transformed into vocal entities that are believed to be containers of the divine light or containers within which divine lights are drawn down. This vision draws from magical sources that have been adopted by Kabbalists, especially in the writings of R. Moshe Cordovero, but it was simplified and conjugated by the Besht with the ideal of mystical experience as a necessary condition for causing the descent of the influx for magical purposes.[2]

The second reason is, however, more complex. The issue is now not a matter of magical sources which have inspired Hasidic phenomena, which are significantly different from them, phenomenologically speaking. In Hasidism, just as in Cordovero's thought, the canonical texts as such become a magical formula, effective not because of their dianoetic content to be understood by the reader or prayer, but because of their double nature: the utterances are conceived of as containers of a supernal power that is used in one way or another and, second but not less important, the sequence of the letters in the canonical texts is less important from the semantic point of view, but its efficacy is related to the belief in its special structure, as is the case in a medical formula, which is effective even if not understood. In several cases in the immediate entourage of the Besht, the canonical texts have been envisioned as a series of divine names, and the Torah was once described as even including amulets, as we shall see as follows and in appendix D of this volume. The vision of the sounds as "containers" has something to do with the architectural *imaginaire* that has been discussed in chapter 8.

The recitation of the canonical texts became therefore much more a sort of incantation than a liturgy, a study, or a form of contemplation. Or, to put it differently, it became more a privileged moment for acquiring powers or extraordinary capacities, including healing, than for imploring or contemplating God.[3] At least for some of the participants in prayer in the period of nascent Hasidism, who did not understand much of the Hebrew texts of the liturgy, its recitation became much closer to an incantation of a magical formula. Also, the assumption that the effect of the operation is achieved immediately makes the event closer to the category of magic as I understand it, than to any other category I am acquainted with in the history of religion. Devotional as the Hasidic theories we deal with here are, the results are imagined to be automatic, leaving little space for the role of divine grace. This is the reason why it would be better to designate the Besht's approach as technical, though achieved by means of devotion and enthusiasm.

Let me turn to another instance of what I see as magic use of the state of *devequt*, found in a passage by the Besht's grandson, R. Moshe Hayyim Efrayyim of Sudylkov, though not attributed to the Besht:

> since the Torah and God and Israel all are [constituting] one unity, only when the secret of the divinity is drawn down within the Torah[4] by [means of] the study of the Torah for its own sake [or name]. Then, there is in it [i.e., the Torah] the power of divinity and she becomes the secret of emanation,[5] [in order] to vivify and heal.[6]

I propose to read the passage as dealing first with the mystical event, namely the union of the human soul with the Torah and God, and then with the next step, the causing of the descent of emanation by means of the Torah, and then with a third step, the final effect of the process, which is healing or vivifying. It should be assumed that this power of the Torah does not operate for people who study Torah in general, for example for those who would read it mentally alone, but only for those who engage in some form of mystical union with it. This may well be the meaning of the term *then*. This is not the classical topos of the study of the Torah as possibly healing, or as the elixir of life, as found in several Rabbinic sources, but a much more elaborated view that assumes that there is some form of emanation, or influx, that is related to the achievements of the few who divest themselves from corporeality and are capable to attract the divinity within their vocal activity. The Besht assumed, among other techniques, also a psychosomatic approach to healing that was based on the paramount importance of the healer's utterances, some form of healing by means of words. The assumption that the pronounced Torah is the secret of emanation is reminiscent of the architectural imagery discussed in the previous chapter, as to the similarity between the theosophical emanation and the vocal emanation.

The verb translated in the last passage as "drawing down" is *mamshikhin*, which is a seminal verb in Jewish mysticism since the Middle Ages. Grammatically speaking it is a strong form in medieval Hebrew and it denotes, *inter alia*, the act of causing the emanation to descend into a certain entity. In our case, however, it is not just the influx that is brought down but no less than the divinity, and this is not an exceptional case in Hasidism, though the root *MShKh* is used in many cases as dealing with the descent of the emanation or influxes also in Kabbalistic literature. However, the view of drawing down the divinity is quite rare in Kabbalistic literature, and I am acquainted of such a view only in the most magical of the Kabbalistic corpora, the late fifteenth-century writings related to Sefer ha-Meshiv. This is the case also in few of the traditions previously quoted in the name of the Besht. Also, other forms of the same root, *Mashakh* and *Nimshakh*, may sometimes be understood in such a manner.

In some instances, we may find even stronger formulations when the YRD, in its *huf'al* form, namely *le-horiyd*, is used in order to refer to causing descent of the influx or the spiritual force, *horadat ha-ruḥaniyyut*, a technical term recurring many times in Hebrew medieval and Renaissance astro-magical texts. The term *ruḥaniyyut* recurs, as seen previously, in some few traditions reported in the name of the Besht by R. Jacob Joseph of Polonnoye, though not necessarily related to the assumption that it may be drawn down, as it is nevertheless the case of the *shefa*—the influx—an issue to be discussed in appendix F.

Let me be clear: I certainly do not think that all the Kabbalistic or Hasidic recourses to the verb *MShKh* have magical overtones. Such an assumption would obviously be an exaggeration, since in many instances, starting from the eleventh-century poet R. Solomon ibn Gabirol's famous poem "Keter Malkhut," this verb may point also to the Neoplatonic concept of emanation. This is, indeed, quite a polysemic verb, and the magical aspects of its meaning are informed by the context, which alone can qualify a passage as possessing magical overtones or not. Indeed it is possible to find a variety of Kabbalistic and Hasidic usages of this verb also in a theurgical way, namely as referring to the drawing down of divine powers from a higher level to a lower divine level, and this is also the case of R. Efrayyim. However, in the previous passage—and in some others which cannot be discussed here[7]—I see no better reading than to assume that the healing nature of the divinity operates only when drawn within the vocal performance of the Torah.

In another context, the same Hasidic author describes the "taking" of the divinity within the Torah, since it is constituted, according to many medieval assessments, stemming from magical sources, by a continuum of divine names.[8] In yet another context, the cleaving to the Torah is described as cleaving to the sphere of *Hokhmah*, this high divine manifestation being the source of all the influxes and the emanations that are drawn down [*hamshakhot*], since this supernal realm is a form of hyle, where new forms are given, and from there miracles emerge.[9]

Thus, the basic agreement between various followers of the Besht: R. Jacob Joseph of Polonnoye, the Great Maggid of Medzeritch, R. Efrayyim of Sudylkov, and R. Menahem Nahum of Chernobyl, as to the magical meaning connected, at least in some significant cases, to the root *MShKh*—which indeed follow many earlier similar semantic valences of this verb—points to the existence of a common denominator, to be found actually in some of the teachings reported in the name of the Besht himself. Indeed both the term *hamshakhah* and the verb mamshikh are found in some quotes in the name of the Besht that I consider as authentically Beshtian, as we have seen previously. I would say that the convergence among the views of all the main followers of the Besht should, even without the citations in the name of the Besht, be explained somehow, by scholars that are skeptical as to the authenticity of traditions attributed to the founder of Hasidism. In my opinion the most economic explanation is, however, corroborated by the teachings adduced previously in his name, and that he indeed also was concerned with the process of drawing down influxes, either by utterances or otherwise, like his disciples and some of his contemporaries taught.

The importance of the verbal forms is obvious both in the instruction parts, namely the resort to DBQ, QShR, 'LH (ascend), and in the descriptions of the effects, *MShKh*, YRD, or GRM (both mean "to cause the descent"). Instructions to cleave resort to verbs, and the effects are also actions. This strong emphasis on verbs reflects a much more dynamic and fluid universe, which allows a much greater role to human action, when done on the basis of linguistic performance of canonical texts. The dominance of the verbal forms in the discourse is quintessential for someone like the Besht, who was first and foremost an instructor of a way of behavior, his recommendations consisting in a demand for an intense form of religious action, much more than an exponent of a mystical theory. Likewise, his way of illustrating his instructions by means of parables, some of them borrowing from earlier sources, does not contribute to the emergence of a systematic type of theology.

Moreover, since his instructions do not prescribe, in their vast majority, brand-new forms of religious actions, but some modes of the liturgical performance of the already canonized actions, adverbs also play an important role. Some of the nouns derived from the roots mentioned previously, like *hitqashsherut* and *devequt*, are widely used together with the Hebrew prefix be-, and become thereby adverbial forms that qualify the mode of action rather than the action itself. As has been pointed out in several of my studies, the union with a spiritual realm should be better understood not just by a theological analysis of the identity of that realm, but also by the strength of such a union, according to the reports of the mystics. Since both the details and the more essential structure of theology are changing from time to time even in the writings of the same mystic, and the Besht is, in my opinion, an important example for such a change, what should prevail in a scholarly analysis is to pay the due attention to the insistence upon the necessity of such a union, and to the literary expressions used in order to express it, and less on the details of the theology.

While the resort to the term *contemplation*, as we know from many other mystical traditions, may involve quite intense aspects, the addition of the instructions concerning careful and powerful pronunciation of a series of utterances in Hasidism intensifies dramatically those aspects, and the verbal expressions related to processes evince this approach that differs in its intensity from the more conventional contemplative traditions. As mentioned previously, the Besht himself was reported in the hagiography to have prayed so loudly that the Great Maggid had to leave the synagogue because of the noise, an issue to which we shall revert later on.

Let me be clear: by emphasizing the centrality of the sonorous performance for what I see as the most important period in the career of the Besht, I do not deny the existence of some contemplative approaches in Hasidism, *a fortiori* in medieval Kabbalah or in Jewish philosophy. However, what I intend to do here is to strike another balance than that which is dominant in scholarship about the Besht, and early Hasidism, by claiming that he is certainly more inclined to teach the primacy of powerful pronunciation of words and the divestment of corporeality, namely trance or ecstasy, than to contemplative attitudes which are more connected with stable objects or written letters. Especially important in this context is to emphasize the fact that, unlike the more common contemplative traditions in the history of religion, the Besht is interested not only in the experience of adhering to God, but also in the reception of supernal power that is imagined to be accumulated during the experience of recitation and *devequt*, and in its ensuing magical effects. The accumulation is the result of the intense performance of the rites, and we may speak about an inverse correlation between the role of theology and the intensity of the performance.

The magical element in the Beshtian traditions quoted previously consists of initiating the use of a powerful formula, namely the canonical recited texts whose structure was allegedly designed by the ancient figures who formulated them in order to cause the descent of supernal powers, which are brought to the individual or to the community whose well-being concerns him. On the other hand, it should be pointed out that some of the magical aspects are attenuated by the devotional approach, which has strong mystical components, and this is the reason why I refer to the complex sequence as the mystical-magical model, not just as the magical one, and it corresponds to what Jonathan Garb calls shamanic.

In any case, let me adduce an example of a Beshtian teaching that connected *devequt* to the possibility to also achieve other types of results, even if they are conceived to be inferior. According to a seminal text, which includes an anecdote that seems to me to be quite revealing as to the approach of the Besht, as preserved by R. Ze'ev Wolf of Zhitomir, there are persons:

> who perform ascetic deeds and [ritual] baths and enhance the study of the Torah and pray, and their main intention and aim was to reach the divine spirit and the revelation of [the prophet] Elijah, and similar [attainments]. And I heard that in the days of Besht, blessed be his memory, there was someone like this that made ascetic deeds and went to [ritual] baths in order to attain the divine spirit. And the Besht . . . said as follows: "In the world of the impure powers they are laughing at him and this is the truth. Why should someone pursue this while his heart is vacuous of the cleaving to God, which is the purpose of worship? The purpose of worship is to adhere to His attributes in truth and in a wholesome manner. But after the perfect cleaving, he will be able to attain all the wishes of his heart, and the attainment of the divine spirit, and similar sublime degrees . . . are borne [automatically] from this. But he should not pay attention to this [attainment] while he is worshipping."[10]

The phrase "all the wishes of the heart" is indeed a euphemism, a hyperbolic way to describe the many possibilities opened by the cleaving to God while worshipping. What is important for our claim here is that *devequt* is not just a mental adherence to God, or a contemplative state of mind but, as it appears from so many different traditions reported in the name of the Besht, a much more energetic state, essentially related to spoken words. Eventually those words, which are conceived of as replete with vitality, *Ḥiyyut*, as we learn from many early Hasidic sources, may be used in order to heal, as we learn from the hagiography when the Besht attempted to cure the Great Maggid before the latter became his disciple:

> He wanted to cure him with speeches [*dibburim*]. I heard from Rabbi Gershon of the community of Pavlych that the Besht visited him daily for about two weeks and sat opposite him and recited Psalms. After that the Besht said to him "I wanted to cure you with speeches [*dibburim*] since this is an enduring remedy, [*refu'ah qayyemet*] but now I have to cure you with medication."[11]

This is a precious testimony, as it describes one of the ways in which the Besht was imagined to have acted as a healer. In quite a clear manner he distinguishes here between the linguistic type of magic, that is quite traditional and resorts to the recitation of holy words, the Psalms, and the other one, consisiting in operations by means of medication, namely by using some form of substances, thus a basically non-linguistic approach. The recitation of Psalms is a form of classical Jewish magic, found long before the Besht and related also to the book of magic entitled *Shimmushei Tehilim*. However, it is interesting that the Besht resorts here, at least according to the Hebrew version of the hagiography, to "words" or "speeches," *dibburim*, the same term we have seen in many previous instances, and that occur only in this section of the hagiography, rather than Hebrew terms for verses or Psalms. In any case, we have heard a version of healing that assumes, like the statement we have analyzed previously from his grandson's book *Degel Maḥaneh 'Efrayyim*, the potential capacity of the Torah to cure.

Even if the magical achievements mentioned in the passage of R. Zeev Wolf were conceived of by the Besht as secondary or derivative, in comparison to the primacy and superiority of the state of union with God, the status of these extraordinary effects should not be dismissed. The formulation at the end of the passage is indeed interesting: while worshipping someone should not intend to achieve anything else—namely *devequt* as an end-experience—but, so I understand this statement, he hopes to achieve it only afterward, namely an attitude to *devequt* as a means-experience. The Besht focused his instructions on modes of worship, emphasizing the importance of alacrity, of the investment of all the power, of enthusiasm, of awe and love, and this is the reason why the term worship recurs in many of his teachings, including the assumption that God should be worshipped in all the possible forms, not just by resorting to any one single manner of worshipping.[12] It is plausible that this story reflects a later phase in the Besht's development, since he derides here asceticism, which he himself practiced in his youth for a number of years, and he does not mention—yet?—the cleaving to the utterances.

The emphasis put here on the existence of a two-tiered model related to *devequt* according to the Besht is the most economic strategy to explain why this model occurs in some many forms in all his followers, and why the Besht is indeed the founder of Hasidism: not only because of his more democratic approach, but also because of shaping a way of behavior that informed the concepts of the *tzaddiq* later on: not an exposition of ideals dealing with personal and spiritual perfection alone, but shaping the lives of operators that can also solve problems other than spiritual guidance, using for this aim the special form of the performance of the rituals.

Thus, the present claim is that the Besht was not only a mystic who, at the same time, was moonlighting also as a popular magician and healer, or *vice versa*, two approaches being considered as two different registers, and thus would regard the two dimensions as separated from each other, at least in principle. On the contrary:

I assume that the Besht also proposed a more complex approach, which combines magical with mystical aspects as a religious ideal that he taught, this in addition to his more magical and mystical preoccupations. This does not mean at all that I wish to diminish the more popular magical activities of the future "founder" of Hasidism, but that I propose a reading of some of the instructions he made as a master to disciples, regarding matters of religious behavior, as including also views which are not mystical alone.

Religiously speaking the ascent, either mental or spiritual, to the supernal worlds is not the only spiritual ideal according to the Beshtian teachings, and neither does it stand alone, at least according to some of the teachings. According to some traditions its attainment should be complemented by a descent to the group or community, in order to deal with their more material, economic, or social problems. This is one of the reasons why some of the Hasidic leaders have been conceived of and acted for years as healers and wonder-makers, as it was in the case of the Besht and the two early nineteenth-century prominent personalities in the history of Hasidism in Poland, like R. Jacob Isaac, known as the Seer of Lublin, and R. Israel ben Sabbatai, the Maggid of Kuznitz, or later on in the nineteenth century, to a certain extent, R. 'Izadoq ha-Kohen of Lublin.

The common master of the first two *tzaddiqim* was the famous R. Elimelekh of Lysansk, whose influential book *No'am 'Elimelekh* is replete with discussions about causing the descent of supernal powers by means of the Hasidic righteous man. Numerous discussions to this effect are found also in the early nineteenth-century master R. Levi Isaac of Berditchev's *Qedushat Levi*, and in his disciple R. Aharon of Zhitomir's *Toledot 'Aḥaron*, whose views approximate many teachings of the Besht, as it was pointed out in many of the notes in this study, especially beside ch. 6 n. 19 and in appendix F. Also an important discussion found in R. Qalonimus Qalman Epstein of Krakau contains important assessments as the magical powers of the righteous. In general the hagiographical Hasidic literature has attributed supernatural powers to a long series of Hasidic masters.

Altogether, it is evident that a separation between the magical practices and the teachings of those figures would be too artificial and precarious an approach to understanding both the Besht and some of his followers. However, also in the cases when we do not have external evidence as to the thaumaturgical role of Hasidic masters, the structure of their thought, which is the topic that concerns me here more, should be inspected with the scholar's awareness that the boundaries between the Hasidic mysticism and magic are rather porous, and the former is imagined to empower the mystic that turns into some form of magician. The Besht and his followers were following a path opened by Safedian Kabbalists, who introduced magical elements in the theosophical-theurgical systems. We should distinguish between different forms of magic used by the Besht: the talismanic one, dealing with drawing down the spiritual forces; the other one, dealing with emitting spiritual powers inherent in the vocables, which may ascend and thus create the capability to obtain the answers one requires; then the more Neoplatonic type of magic, based on the possibility to cleave to the supernal power, the universal soul that governs reality, and thereby make changes; and all this in addition to the more traditional Jewish forms of magic, using divine names, Psalms, and amulets. None of them should be identified with what I call theurgy, found in Rabbinic literature and much more in Kabbalah, which deals with inducing changes within the divine realm, unifications of divine powers, or elevating the sparks or the vocables or the words to their supernal source, which the Besht inherited *mutatis mutandis* from various brands of theosophical-theurgical Kabbalah.

It should be pointed out that the Besht and his followers were not concerned with angelic magic that is evident in traditional Jewish magic, in the Renaissance literature, and in Cordovero's writings, though he most probably was aware of the *Book of the Angel Raziel*, in print since the first edition in Amsterdam in 1701. Neither is he using images or effigies *en vogue* in astro-magic since the Middle Ages and in the Renaissance and at the end of the printed version of Sefer Raziel. Though living in a period and location where confluences of many forms of thought were avaible to him, within Judaism and outside it, the Besht was relatively selective in his adoption of earlier material. A question that I cannot answer here, due to the absence of reliable information, is whether also in the case of magical practices, as it is in the case of mystical issues, it is possible to account for a development over years.

In short: a magician by profession, the Besht capitalized also on magical understandings of the power of vocables and words, inherent or induced, found in Cordoverian Kabbalah, and one of his immediate followers, R. Jacob Joseph of Polonnoye, was aware of this affinity and pointed it out explicitly, as we shall see in appendix B.

10

INTENSIFICATION, CONTACT, AND EFFECTS

We may stipulate that the conviction that it is possible to attain extreme mystical achievements caused also an expectation of Hasidic masters for radical forms of empowerment, which culminates in magical effects, imagined to be facilitated by the intimate encounter with and cleaving to the divine power. With the Besht, we have an example of a wonder-maker who adopted from earlier forms of Kabbalah, especially the Cordoverian ones, a model that included already magical components. At the same time, the other so-called masters of the divine names, in many cases healers, worked with traditional magical recipes—and most probably the Besht also did so in many cases—without, however, intensifying at the same time their religious life or attempting to do so for others.[1]

A perusal of the Hebrew magical treatises printed in the lifetime of the Besht, and described in the studies of Immanuel Etkes, Yohanan Petrovsky-Shtern, and Gedalyah Nigal, shows that the Cordoverian elements are almost totally absent there, and only in some few cases are Lurianic Kabbalistic themes addressed. Those magicians used, and I assume also that the Besht did so, traditional popular magic that was basically independent of the various schools of Kabbalah. Neither may we discern in those books of mainly linguistic magic a significant role played by the technical-Hermetic or astral type of magic, though very few references to astronomy may be nevertheless discerned from time to time in those booklets. From this point of view we may see the Besht's approach to magic and to magical healing as a practice reflecting, in some aspects

of his teachings concerning the utterances, one of the last metamorphoses of the complex late antiquity Hermetic approach, as it
was mediated mainly by Safedian Kabbalah, but standing in sharp
distinction from the other contemporary popular Jewish magicians. In this context, let me point out that Jews in the regions
where Hasidism emerged also approached Tatar doctors who used
magical practices in the lifetime of the Besht, as can be seen in the
hagiography about this figure and during many decades later on,
actually until recent times. We cannot exclude the possibility that
he was influenced also by such medical/magical practices, an issue
that deserves more detailed studies.

Indeed, most of the previous teachings that were cited in the
name of the Besht regard the cleaving to letters/vocables not as the
final goal of the religious life, an end-experience, but part of a more
complex sequence of acts, one of which happens after the experience of cleaving and depends essentially on attaining it. However,
either receiving some extraordinary form of knowledge—future
events—or being able to bring down the supernal influx, it is clear
that letters, most probably sounds, are involved in this complex
process.

Let me emphasis the importance of the existence of at least two
major phases in the mystical-magical model: first cleaving to utterances and then emergence of the different effects. We may recast
these two moments as follows: a preliminary intensification of the
manner in which the ritual is performed, by cleaving to the vocables, is conceived of as necessary, and then the contact with the
spiritual world is conceived of as taking place. Those two phases,
namely intensification of the performance of the vocal rites, and
then the attainment of direct contact with a superior world, in
their diverse forms they took in different systems, in my opinion
constitute major components of religious mysticism.[2] Their concatenation takes sometimes the form of causality, namely the drawing
down of the influx, as the resort to the verbs that have been mentioned previously shows. The concatenation mentioned here is
inherited from the Cordoverian tradition, as claimed several times

previously. Its centrality does not have to do with the "depth" of the general theosophical theory of Cordovero, but with the fact that the Safedian Kabbalist and his followers, in many cases less systematic thinkers, offered an easily acceptable interpretation to a central rite. The organizing principle in the Besht is not conceptual coherence, but relevance of one theory or another for an intensified type of worship. This is the reason why he could shift from one type of theology to another, as evident in the three models I mentioned previously.

The strategy used in order to intensify the vocal rituals is based upon an anthropological shift of one of the main meanings of the term *'ot*, as seen previously, from the predominantly written and objective to the predominantly vocal significance and subjective, as well as the interpretation of the term *heikhal*, as witnessed in some Hebrew texts influenced by the Arabic *hayakhal*, since the late Middle Ages. In the medieval astro-magical material pertinent to our discussions, it signifies a supernal palace that is an astral body within which there is the planetary power that can be attracted down, while the noun *heikhal* acquired later on a different magical significance as sound palace, or container of a supernal power, as found already in an explicit manner in the works of R. Moshe Cordovero and his Kabbalistic (and perhaps also in some Hermetic) sources.[3] The two semantic shifts are evident already in the school of Cordovero as exemplified previously.

My insistence on the relevance of the reverberances of Hermetic sources—some of them known in the Middle Ages and Renaissance in Hebrew and Latin—that inspired R. Shlomo ha-Levi Al-Qabetz's and R. Moshe Cordovero's approach to language, magic, and mysticism for an adequate understanding the Besht is not a matter of intellectual archeology of forgotten meanings of terms. It is a strictly necessary corrective to the manner in which some key terms like *heikhal, ruḥaniyyut,* or *hamshakhah* should be understood in many instances in Hasidic literature. Because so many of the scholars of Hasidism have not been acquainted with the history of those terms, these terms have been misunderstood, as is also the case with the translations of some statements of the Besht as dealing with "contemplating letters," as we have seen previously, and we shall have more to say on those topics in appendix C.

Some of the earlier undeniable magical cargo of these terms remained part of their semantic field also after the transformations and fragmentations of their earlier broader contexts as articulated in Safedian Kabbalah, and even after the additional transformations introduced by selections they have undergone in Hasidism. In my opinion, it is surprising to see how reticent most of modern scholarship is to recognize the variety of filiations and the importance of their reverberations in Hasidism. In all those cases, a more dynamic approach is related to an empowered operator, mainly a vocal one. The production of utterances in an emotional and devotional manner is, therefore, one of the main techniques according to the teachings of Besht, intended to enter some form of intensified religious experience and, at the same time, create of the locus where the supernal influx is attracted, according to the mystical-magical model. Speech is, at the same time, the major mode of communication of their teachings, used by early Hasidic masters who, unlike most of the Kabbalists, were less concerned with written forms of communication in general, as a famous story about the demon reading an alleged book written by the Besht, to be adduced in chapter 14 in this volume, shows.[4]

Or, to formulate the previous discussions in different terms: following part of Cordovero's theosophical appropriation of astro-magic, the Besht's conceptualization of the ritual utterances as vessels, palaces, chambers, house, ark, or human body, for the divine spiritual force, light, or the infinite light, is a transposition of the role that the *sefirot* traditionally played in the theosophical-theurgical Kabbalah of the Safedian Kabbalist, as receptacles or vessels for the divine essence or light, to linguistic entities, as the repository of the divinity. The architectural approach is quite evident in this imagery, and its roots are found in the Cordoverian tradition, as we shall show in appendix D. The occurrence of different images for conveying the structure of the sounds relativizes each of them as metaphors for a specific type of relationship: between the container, which is lower, and the contained, that is higher, and invoked to enter the container, where also the human soul enters and can attain some form of extraordinary experience: cleaving to or the ascent by the spiritual force or light.

Now, it is not the objective or theosophical metaphysics that explains where the divinity is dwelling, but the ergetic performance of the vocal ritual that is conceived of as generating the locus for the divine light, which may now be experienced in this world, immediately and directly. Unlike the supernal palaces in the late antiquity Jewish mysticism and in medieval Kabbalah, especially in the *Zohar*, entities that in principle can be contemplated, in Hasidic texts they must be entered. This does not mean that in the Beshtian teachings the divine space is always divorced from a theosophical structure, since indeed there are traditions adduced in his name where the sefirotic structures are found, though in very succinct manner, as part of what I call the broken theology. However, insofar as the model of cleaving to sounds as the vocal rituals is concerned, the pertinent space is situated in the Hasidic texts within the vocables produced by the Hasid in prayer, either as the focus of the encounter or as the vehicle for ascending toward the divine realm.

Another issue that is important for understanding both the Besht and the scholarly discourse we engaged previously is the dynamic nature of the *sefirot*, as vessels or essence altogether, and the transfer of this dynamic to the new level of discussion, namely to the structure of the vocable: They have an external aspect, designated as palaces, and an inner one, the divine power. The references to speeches and vocables/letters as we addressed them previously is to dynamic entities, emitted by the persons who are instructed to adhere to them, not contemplations of fixed theological structures or written letters. This dynamic nature of the utterances is one of the major reasons why I prefer to avoid the resort to the term contemplation, both in the case of the Beshtian treatments discussed previously of the theurgical understanding of the performance of the commandments in the theosophical-theurgical Kabbalah, and of most of Abulafia's anomian techniques in ecstatic Kabbalah. Its centrality is an import of a category pertinent in other forms of mysticism, whose validity is much more limited in Jewish mysticism than scholars imagine.

Let me emphasize the social significance of cleaving to individual letters/sounds rather than to whole words of prayer or of the Torah. By shifting the center of gravity to individual letters/sounds, the Besht, though following some few earlier sources, moves his religious performance toward efforts to produce vocal events, thus marginalizing the centrality of the understanding of the dianoetic meaning of the recited text, not to mention its learned expansion of the oral traditions that constitute the oral law, hinted previously in the concept of the study of the Torah that were so important in many classical forms of Judaism. Loud pronunciation of atomized texts, whose elements function as monads, rather than the fathoming of the dianoetic messages found in them or in the words of prayer, is a much easier operation for the larger audiences to which the Besht addressed some of his sermons.

In a way, sonorous practices intended to allow someone to cleave to the divine light have reinforced sonorous communities, as some of the Hasidic groups are indeed. We may say that, to a certain extent, the vocal medium was, for the Hasidic audience, also the message. Moreover, atomization and monadization of the elements of the recited texts created also a sort of vocal performance that does not necessitate a solid knowledge of the Hebrew language, and this knowledge was indeed quite poor among most of the audiences that were attracted to Hasidism in its earliest phases. When they were performed loudly, stripped of their meaning by the special type of recitation of the monadic sounds, the canonical texts were closer to a magical incantation.

On the other hand, the intensification/contact sequence of acts should not be divorced from the next step, namely the expected effects, and in the cases where the two issues appear together, we may speak not only about the mystical-magical model, but also about an attempt of the Hasidic masters to envision their rituals as efficacious. Then we may speak actually about the Hasidic concepts of ritual efficacy.⁵ What I call the magical dimensions that are found, in my opinion, in some of the previous discussions would then be, from the point of view of the scholar, one particular case of the rationales offered by a traditional author for the efficacy of performing the rituals, for both praying and studying the Torah.

Let me point out that we have analyzed previously several texts that combine instructions and interpretations: instructions that deal with the mode of praxis, and interpretations that point to some form of effects, sometimes involving explanations containing discussions of causalities. Those causalities imply some unsystematic forms of cosmology and theology which are never systematically or analytically elaborated, and which changed, in my opinion, during the intellectual development of the Besht. In most of the cases addressed previously, it seems that the sonorous elements are central, though they do not occur always in an explicit manner. Their centrality in the Hasidic praxis has to do with the multiple roles the Hebrew language played in different areas: in rituals, in what I call linguistic immanence of the divinity within reality by means of the Hebrew letters described as emanated, and even more by divine utterances, in the possibility to encounter the divine within his own utterances, and in the assumption that utterances, as names, are appointed upon external objects and these objects can be manipulated accordingly. It is the role played by vocal rituals that organizes much of the Hasidic approaches since the Besht, which means that modes of performing them, by *devequt*, enthusiastically out of love and awe, with strength, loudly, and so on, are qualifying those performances, as we have seen in some passages cited previously.

The interpretations found in the Beshtian teachings have a double nature: those offered by the Besht himself, and those offered by the disciples to the words of their master. Though quoting his teachings, his disciples and the disciples of his disciples often used them in order to illustrate some views which do not necessarily coincide with the ultimate concern of the quoted teachings. Thus, we should be careful not to project the later interpretations onto the cited Beshtian passages, which are nevertheless quoted, in my opinion, in quite a faithful manner. It is not always clear, as some scholars have pointed out, when the two interpretations differ, since the disciples would hardly disagree with their revered master. In any case, many of the Besht's teachings are short, or at least shortened, and in many cases they appear when embedded within larger and later discussions, an issue that constitutes a challenge for any interpreter trying to separate between the context and the meaning of the brief original teaching. Moreover, in many cases the Besht himself presents his own instructions and reflections as commentaries on Rabbinic or other statements, like commentaries of Rashi, which are themselves commentaries. These strings of interpretations complicate the decoding of the meaning of the Besht's teachings, which disguised late types of spiritualities with unexpected interpretations of earlier texts.

However, there are also many pages at the end of some books of R. Jacob Joseph where Beshtian traditions are adduced together, without any context or commentary, as well as in at least one manuscript. Checking the content of those "dis-embedded" traditions shows that they do not differ substantially from the embedded ones, and I see no reason to hesitate when relying on his quotes in the name of his teacher when they are embedded. However, since my approach is less founded on the assumption that there was a rigid theory that stands alone in clear distinction from other earlier or later theories, all the traditions that have been engaged here represent, despite the differences between them, what I conceived to be authentic Beshtian teachings.

Fluidity, which means changes and vagueness, is the name of the game of traditions stemming from oral teachings, which were passed orally for decades before they were commited to writing. This does not mean, as Moshe Rosman or Ze'ev Gries would assume, that it is impossible to reconstruct historically the views of the Besht, but that the scholarly work of reconstruction, difficult as it is, should take into consideration the basic situation of conceptual fluidity which is, to be sure, as historical a fact as any other historical situation.[6] The guiding hypothesis of our study here is that in the context of the Besht's activity, we deal with a preeminently oral framework which used almost exclusively Yiddisch, namely a vernacular, and this is the reason why the import of some of the strictures addressed by scholars to the question of authenticity or reliability of the Beshtian traditions are attenuated quite dramatically. The fluidity in personal history, namely a life without a relationship with stable educational institutions, of continuous wandering from one place to another, perhaps even from one country to another—perhaps from Podolia to Istanbul and back if it ever took place—and from Walachia to Podolia and sometimes back, is matched by the fluidity in the Beshtian instructions, since I assume that he changed his mind, and what is equally important, those instructions deal with the utterances, which are, unlike written letters, fluid entities too.

However, let me point out that the interpretive stances of the traditions, as related to classical texts and the nature of their aims, namely, to provide instruction as to the ways to perform commandments, provide some form of more stable references that bring together many of the Beshtian traditions. The interpretations of many dicta from the treatise *'Avot*, for example, constitute points of references that recur in the various traditions and create a variety of clusters of interpretations, which despite the differences between them, reflect what his interests were. In some cases, he interprets the commentaries of Rashi.

To sum up our previous discussions, as well as conclusions drawn in some other studies of mine concerning the Besht as to the possible development of his thought: I assume that a linguistic approach to creation, without any specific instructions as to how to behave, constitutes the topic of a relatively lengthy teaching, which presumably constitutes the first documented phase in the Besht's thought. This rather lengthy teaching emphasizes the role of the divine pronounced letters in creation, without mentioning the ideal of *devequt*. Then, in the next hypothetical step of the Besht's thought, we may speak about the centrality of cleaving to the utterances as the main phase in the Besht's career, and in my opinion the most influential one on the religious structure of many phenomena in Hasidism, which is represented by most of the quotes discussed previously. The earliest document that represents this hypothetical second phase would be the tradition of R. Meir Margoliot, as I pointed out in my "Models of Understanding Prayer in Early Hasidism," p. 92.

During this early phase of the Besht's career, he was using a set of terms and concepts that are found in Cordovero's widely read literary corpus and in the wrtings of his many and influential followers. The Safedian Kabbalist, at his turn, had his own sources in some elements found in the Hermetic or astro-magical approach as disseminated in the Middle Ages in Jewish writings in Spain. According to those medieval and Renaissance sources, known in Spain and then in Italy and Safed, there are supernal astral bodies described as palaces, *hayakhal* in Arabic and *heikhalot* in Hebrew, wherein spiritual forces, namely the non-bodily aspects of the planets that confer to the bodies their characteristics, dwell. This sort of magic consists of drawing down the spiritual forces from the astral palaces by means of rituals that correspond in their details to the features of each of those astral bodies.

This dichotomy between palace/spiritual force has already been used by Cordovero in order to propose his complex theosophy built upon the dichotomy of two kinds of *sefirot*: those which are vessels and those which constitute the essence or the light of God. The *sefirot* as vessels or containers of the divine power or of light are a part of a long Kabbalistic tradition, but in Cordovero they also reflect the astral concepts, which speak about "spiritual forces," a concept that is quite rare in pre-Cordoverian classical descriptions of the *sefirot*. By transposing the dichotomy vessel/light from the astral context to what was conceived of as the sefirotic realm, the Safedian Kabbalist opened the way for the manipulation of the sefirotic spiritual forces by the Kabbalists, in some cases, assuming that the Jewish rituals, especially prayer, should be understood in such a manner. It should be pointed out that following Cordovero, his famous student R. Isaac Luria Ashkenazi has also resorted quite repeatedly to the dichotomy vessels/lights in his even more elaborated theosophy. This intra-divine polarity of the nature of the divine powers of container and contained is found also in the Hasidic concept of utterances, and was emphasized there more than beforehand, as we shall see also in appendices C, D, and E.

According to several Safedian Kabbalistic sources, and they are not actually the first articulations of this approach, as examples are also found, for example, in Northern Italy at the end of the fifteenth century, utterances also have their own spiritual force that can be manipulated, this being one of the aims of prayer, and the magical aspects of language in Cordovero are quite explicit. The Besht and his acolytes adopted this dichotomy, but they were much less concerned with the structure of the transcendental theosophy, as the Safedian Kabbalist was, and he preferred instead to deal much more with issues that can help worshipping God in an intense manner. Thus, we find in the discussions about the units of speech as containers or receptacles, and the inherent lights or vitality as the divine essence, views that are also found in Cordovero and his medieval sources, but which are simplified and envisioned as part and parcel of the rituals.

In many Hasidic discussions, the speech is described in quite cosmic terms as the source of vitality, operating like some form of Stoic *logoi spermatikoi*, a vast topic that requires an independent study as part of a larger phenomenon that I called linguistic immanence. Without a better acquaintance with the scholars of Hasidism, with the sources of some aspects of Safedian Kabbalah to be found in medieval astro-magic literature, and the more cosmic understandings of language, it also will be harder to understand some aspects of what is called East European Hasidism, as the mistakes made by the scholarly misunderstandings of the significance of key terms like *heikhal, ruḥaniyyut,* and the meaning of *'otiyyot* demonstrate.[7] These terms deal with the drawing down of the divine powers within the human utterances, as well as with the ascent of utterances on high, but not so much with the incarnation of the divine powers as a word and as part of revelation. It is the temporary aspect of the Hasidic operations that is essential, in opposition to the more metaphysical status of the word in Christianity. It is the ongoing instantiation of the divine presence and adherence to it that counts, much more than an imitation of an ancient drama of a certain unique person. The righteous men, pivotal as they are for many of the groups of Hasidim, have their successors, were married, and were involved in quarrels.

Let me point out that this form of linguistic magic does not exhaust the magical usage of language as found in traditions and teachings attributed to the Besht. They also included more traditional forms of Jewish magic related to the use of divine names as described in some episodes in *In Praise of the Baal Shem Tov*, or to recourse to his name for such purposes, according to two different traditions.

My assumption here is that sometime toward the end of his life, this fascination with the centrality of utterances and sonorous palaces had weakened, and the importance of a mental cleaving to the divine grew, and both moves contributed to diminishing the privileged status given now to language, or even of the canonical verbal rituals, which became more evident. God is found, according to the views formulated in this period, in every thought and movement, not just in ritual speeches, and according to some view even within "alien thoughts" or even within sin or evil.[8] This disparity between the emphasis found in the teachings that were discussed previously that dealt with the pronunciation as a cardinal activity for cleaving, and the other, later approach, which assumes a constant presence of the divine everywhere, which has not been yet put in relief in scholarship, needs some form of explanation. One explanation for this divergence would be that the Besht worked with the two assumptions for most of his career, and no dramatic change took place in his thought and praxis, in the vein of my "clustered" approach, which has been mentioned previously. This is indeed the situation in some later stages of the Besht's thought, when different models most plausibly coexisted with the newer ones. This is certainly the case of his followers, who sometimes offered syntheses between models found in the Beshtian traditions they were acquainted with, as is the case, for example, in the writings of R. Menahem Nahum of Chernobyl.

However, in my opinion it would be more plausible to assume a later development that generated the noetic model in the thought of the Besht, which operates with the seminal assumption that divine omnipresence should be recognized more than experienced. In this model the utterances no longer occupy the main place for the intimate encounter with the divinity, as now the entire reality is conceived of as permeated by the divine light, as is, for example, the case of the famous parable of the king, who created an imaginary palace and walls by means of an illusion, as an allegory for the nature of reality that is misconceived of as not being God.[9] According to the logic of this model, the utterances *qua* palaces have lost their centrality as privileged means for cleaving to God, and now it is God who creates, by illusion, the reality, and the man is supposed to penetrate beyond the veil of illusion and discover His presence everywhere, a special Jewish version of the Hindu concept of Maya.

In a worldview that was conceived of as being saturated by the divine presence, it is difficult to allow to individual utterances, or letters, the same central role they have in the other teachings of his we have previously examined. So, for example, the plural form, namely the reference to linguistic palaces designated as *heikhalot*, disappears, and the singular mode, referring to the palace with the imaginary walls, this time the Hebrew term *'armon*, which is described as some form of an illusion permeated by divine omnipresence, dominates the Beshtian discourse in the seminal parable.[10] In my opinion, the version of the parable and its context as found once in R. Jacob Joseph's book are strongly related to the rituals of Torah and prayer, while in the version of R. Efrayyim of Sudylkov, which is in my opinion later in time, this nexus does not appear.[11] Thus, if this difference is as meaningful as I indeed think it is, in the last phase of his thought the Besht moved from the earlier ergetic attitude to the rituals to a more mental-noetic one. Again, some of the versions of the parable, emphasizing the uniqueness of the son of the king, are much more elitist than the instructions of cleaving to letters/sounds discussed previously that have not been restricted to an elite. It is the third model that was less prone to generate a social movement, and this is an example of the difficulties related in seeing the Besht as possessing a message in the singular, which was intended to inspire a social movement.

I see in this hypothetical shift a move toward a more omnipresent understanding of the divinity on the one hand, and toward a position less concerned with productions of sounds as an avenue for mystical attainments on the other. It is most probably that during this later period the full-fledged formulations of the worship in corporeality or materiality emerged, namely of worshipping God also in non-nomian ways, an approach that is close to what Martin Buber has described as pan-sacramentalism.[12] The critiques addressed to this philosopher's interpretation of Hasidism, emanating from the scholars from the camp of Gershom Scholem's students, especially from Schatz-Uffenheimer, are in large part correct, since Buber indeed attempted to define Hasidism as a whole in such a manner, but they are also inadequate since they ignore other parts of Hasidic literature, where Buber's suggestion may, in my opinion, turn to be correct.

Or, to put a major aspect of the famous polemic between Buber and Scholem in a wider context: the Besht, and to a great extent also Hasidism as a religious movement, inherited two major heritages regarding the nature of the *devequt*: on the one hand the Neoplatonic theory regarding the union of the soul, or of the human thought, as the highest form of human activity, and the soul or the thought were conceived of as the best capacity appropriated to ascent to the spiritual world and to cleave to the source; and, on the other hand, the Hermetic-magical heritage, as transformed especially in Safedian Kabbalah, according to which union is possible within this world, by an attachment to utterances, within which the divine is already found before any additional action is taken, or alternatively, is attracted or caused to descend during or after the pronunciation of the words. Both approaches are found already in some important discussions in R. Moshe Cordovero's Kabbalah and in its many reverberations in his followers' writings.[13] While the Neoplatonic approach is closer to Scholem's understanding of Hasidism, the Hermetic approach is somehow closer to Buber's general vision of this literature.

In my opinion, earlier in his career as a spiritual teacher, though probably not at its very beginning, the Besht became interested in the Hermetic-talismanic oriented interpretations of *devequt* and the centrality of sonorous performance, and then he added the Neoplatonic approach, dealing with the cleaving of the soul, and conjugated the Hermetic approach with the Neoplatonic one. Though later on in his career, as it has been suggested previously, he adopted a more Neoplatonic, interiorized position, in my opinion he never retreated explicitly from the linguistic magical-talismanic aspects of his thought and instructions, and they were preserved by his followers as one of the most important and certainly legitimate among the Beshtian positions. Let me articulate my point even clearer: the Besht's earlier views did not, in my opinion, just linger later on, but remained significant for the Besht to the end of his life. However, in a certain moment, even later than his adoption of some elements found in Hermeticism and in Neoplatonism, another vision, one that emphasizes divine omnipresence, again extracted mainly from Cordoverian sources, moved to the center of the Besht's religious worldview and was conjugated with the primacy of thought as a main mystical organon, and this is the reason why I have designated this development as a noetic-immanentism model.

Indeed the Great Maggid resorts, much more than his teacher, to terms like intellect and intellection as part of his discussions of cleaving to God, an issue that does not concern us here, but should be understood as a continuation of certain later traditions found already in the teachings reported in the name of the Besht. It should be noticed that at least insofar as the issues of cleaving to the utterances, of drawing down the influx on those utterances, of divine omnipresence, and some of the discussions of the cleaving by thought, Lurianic Kabbalah did not contribute anything significant to Hasidism. If we may see the various discussions of cleaving as fundamental for understanding the many instructions of the Besht, we shall better regard them as emerging mainly from the camp of Cordovero and his followers.[14]

The recognition of the omnipresence of divinity as a power or a pervasive vitality that permeates the entire reality not only attenuates the primacy of language, and even more so the canonized specific articulations of language, as the privileged locus of encounter with God, as we have suggested previously, but also of the earlier centrality of the act of cleaving to God by means of language. After all, even if Hasidic prayer is prolonged, as was the case in many instances, that does not facilitate but a temporary contact with divinity. By not recognizing the existence of those diverging spiritual positions, and thus reducing Hasidism to only one of them, the different scholarly analyses elicit sharp polemics that reflect the tensions existing between those Hasidic positions as expressed already by the Besht himself.

Gershom Scholem was less interested in what was described as the noetic-omnipresent model of the latest phase of the Besht's thought, while Buber was more interested in it, in the way he understood it as a sacramental presence within this world. Characteristically enough, Scholem criticized Buber's approach for ignoring some important Hasidic views—some which have not been discussed here[15]—like those dealing with the elevation of the divine sparks, which are sometime described as letters, toward the divine realm, an approach that is more consonant with, though not always derived from, the Lurianic worldview.[16] This is part of Scholem's more general approach that privileged the role of Lurianism, with its complex theosophy and its strenuous mentalistic demands from the Kabbalist as a main source for Hasidism, imagined to be a foil to the Hasidic approach to messianism, or (according to B. Z. Dinur, I. Tishby, and M. Altshuler), as an inspiration for it.

On the other hand, Scholem emphasizes the importance of the divestment of corporeality as related to some form of contemplation rather than to an experience of ecstasy, and indeed this otherworldly ideal runs against Buber's vision of Hasidism as intending to hallow this world. By doing so, Scholem and following him also Joseph Weiss and, to a lesser degree, Schatz-Uffenheimer, have privileged in a dramatic manner the ocularcentric/mental/contemplative/iconic aspects of Hasidism, just as they put in relief the written form of letters over their pronunciation, which is another form of avoiding the centrality of the utterances. Unfortunately, consciously or not, they have sometimes supplied as proof-texts for their theories what I consider to be incorrect understandings of the Hebrew sources or, when writing in English, unclear translations of Hasidic passages dealing with "letters," as has been mentioned previously, thus creating the impression that the Besht preferred the visual-contemplative or the sight experience over the sonorous dimension of language as an instrument of his mystical activity or, alternatively, that he would prefer passivity over action.[17]

The present proposal postulates, however, that the thought of the Besht was far from being a systematic theology, a sort of monotonic approach that can be exemplified by adducing one representative passage that illustrates the message of the Besht, as it is the case in many studies, but it consisted more in instructions whose details contain complex conceptual processes that went through different stages, not necessarily consistent with each other, that may be described by using a theory of models. Elsewhere, I proposed to discern the existence of three different models that may account for the manner in which the Besht dealt with the seminal topic in his thought, the problem of the "alien thoughts" that were believed to distract people while praying: the agonic, the harmonistic, and the noetic/acosmic.[18] The last proposed model corresponds with the noetic model as I discussed it here, and I consider it the latest major form of the Besht's thought, and it represents, at the same time, the most elitist among those three models. The harmonistic model would correspond, from the point of view of timing in the development of the Besht's thought, to the mystical-magical model, concerned with cleaving to utterances, and it may represent the model that contributed most to the emergence of the Hasidic praxis. Those models operated in various phases of the Besht's career and continued to inform Hasidism, and they are the result of adopting theologumena that are part of what I called various broken theologies.

In my opinion, the harmonistic model precedes in time the noetic one. During this second period and as part of the harmonistic model, the instructions to elevate the sounds or letters, or more commonly the divine sparks according to some other teachings, should also be counted as an important component.[19] The instructions to elevate the divine sparks assume a much more dualistic vision of reality than the inner logic of the omnipresent and noetic model. The earliest model I attributed to the Besht in that study, which I designate as the agonic one, deals with the struggle between the two instincts as the main religious event, and it precedes his concern with the mystical-magical model and is widespread in a variety of earlier Jewish texts, and in the immediate vicinity of the Besht in the few texts extant in the name of R. Nahman of Kosov. This model may be connected in some instances with the state of *qatenut*, which implies some form of inner struggle in order to reach a more sublime experience of the divine.

My assumption is that though conceptually different and, historically speaking, emerging in different phases of the Besht's thought, the later models did not supersede or sublate the earlier ones, but were accumulated and functioned in one way or another together, in a non-paradoxical manner, namely without assuming an awareness of the extreme conceptual tensions between them. Such coexistence may be understood as the result, among other reasons, of the fact that each of these models deals mainly with a different religious center of gravitation: The arena of the soul is central in the agonic model, the transcendental divinity indwelling language according to the second model, and the centrality of the omnipresent vision of divinity according to the third, noetic model. This variety is no doubt a reason why someone could use them together or alternatively. In any case, it is undeniable that they have been preserved in the same books of his various followers, without any sense that they reflect different conceptual approaches.

In a way, the three models proposed here reflect three sources, which are, conceptually speaking, quite different: a rather Neoplatonic one, in the case of the agonic model; a more Hermetic/ Cordoverian one in the case of the harmonistic model; and the Hindu approach, dealing with the concept of Maya, in the case of the noetic/immanentist model. Here we have been concerned only with the two later models, and the last of them will be dealt with in appendices A and F.

Those proposals are, to be sure, a tentative attempt at making sense of the existence of the variety of material dealing in different manners with the same themes by forging a narrative regarding the hypothetical intellectual changes in the Besht's thought. They strive to map stages of a religious development, which is based on different materials that are found sometimes together in the very same books of the disciples of the Besht. Unlike the assumption that guides Moshe Rosman's approach, which regarded the discrepancies as problematizing the validity of these passages for understanding the Besht's thought altogether, I assume that we have plenty of reliable material, and the problem is how to deal, methodologically, with the discrepancies found in it. In some of the discussions, they may overlap from the point of view of time, since no doubt the Besht did not intend to distance himself from his earlier views in a significant manner or create any form of conspicuous rupture with his earlier thoughts. When he changed his view, as in the case of his attitude to asceticism, this shift is well-documented.

The coexistence of different ways of thinking, which is found also in the writings of his followers, is the reason why it is not always easy to present clear-cut models, either phenomenologically or historically speaking, as represented by separate systematic writings, of which one of them alone is representative. Perhaps other alternative scholarly narratives will emerge when there is the understanding of the need to inspect carefully the entire available spectrum of his teachings. Such an inspection is strictly necessary in order to clarify what the processes were which generated the emergence of the variety of views, and offer then challenges to the present proposal in general, or to some of its details.[20] Such a development is a *desideratum*, and it may witness the mature phase of the search of the Besht's thought, in comparison to the present presentations that are basically impressionistic ones.

However, without undertaking such a sustained scholarly effort, and by avoiding the risks of the eventual mistakes that are prone to haunt it, the Besht's thought will probably remain a rather rigid theology, and he will turn into an exponent of one basic message which did not develop from the intellectual point of view throughout his life. However, for someone who was so active for a period of more than thirty years, a thinker who did not emerge from a specific school with a precise religious direction, and who scarcely committed something to writing in his earlier career, by reading his teachings it is hard to avoid the impression that in fact he changed his mind more than once.[21] I see in detailed discussions intending to discern the differences between different teachings, and the explanation of the changes from one position to another, a quintessential task for scholars who aspire to understand him, and a necessary condition for understanding him as a historical figure, rather than essentialistic approaches, or the monotonic Besht. Maybe his final position is even more surprising than his earlier positions: The Besht, presumably one of the greatest of the known magicians in Jewish culture, describes, during what I conceive to be the last phase of his religious career as part of his noetic model, God as the great illusionist, by creating the world by means of an illusion.

The quandary that should haunt the critical understanding of the Besht, as well as that of Hasidism as a religious movement, is how to explain, methodologically speaking, the emergence of the diversity of ideas about the same topic at the beginning of the movement and their continuity in later stages of Hasidism, without harmonizing between them or reducing this complexity to what I call a monotonic picture, as is prevalent in the dominant scholarship in the field, though each scholar writing on this figure has his/her peculiar image of the Besht. The attempts to find a comprehensive, fully articulated, and distinct message,[22] or identify a "single" tendency, as proposed by Joseph Weiss;[23] or the one "spiritual message," for example, according to Rivka Schatz-Uffenheimer;[24] or the "ideal" type of "contemplative prayer," according to both Schatz-Uffenheimer and Louis Jacobs;[25] or the more recent portrait of the Besht as predominantly a seer of images, according to Haviva Pedaya;[26] are homogenous pictures, though conceptually they disagree with each other. They are part of what I called in the introduction the scholarly Romantic approach to Hasidism and to the alleged basic message of its heroic "founder." However, the relevance of these one-dimensional pictures is dramatically complicated by the divergences between the findings of the various scholars they depicted in the singular, and by the existence of a variety of approaches extant in the pertinent Hasidic material, which were not addressed by the scholars that conceived of the Besht as a monotonic figure.

These materials include reports stemming from different personalities, active during two generations after the death of the Besht, attributing many and different traditions to the Besht, which though in their origin they stem from the Besht himself, they are quite flexible and sometimes vague in their extant expressions,[27] preserved in poor printing, their chains of transmission are not always reliable,[28] or they have been translated from the vernacular Yiddisch, indubitably the language in which the homilies have been originally delivered, to printed and rather awkward Hebrew. Neither has a simple ideal or compact message become transparent from my perusal of the vast Hasidic literature written after the death of its "founder." Given this conceptual richness, it is no wonder that some scholars dispute between themselves as to the "specific" nature of this message, in the singular, generation after generation.

All these problems, however, do not affect too much the possibility to find out plenty of the necessary texts for proving the existence of a practice of cleaving, which allows to the voice such a creative role, even if this is just a part, important to be sure, of the more complex intellectual structure of the Besht's thought and practice. Historically speaking, the Besht was not a messenger who was delivering one well-structured message, but someone who creatively and continuously recreated some small segments of Jewish mysticism, which were already conjugated with magical approaches before him. This is the reason why I proposed to read the developments in the thought of the Besht mainly against the background of Cordoverian Kabbalah—and of Renaissance magic to a certain extent—which in any case is much more salient than to compare his thought to Christian quietism and ocularcentrism/iconism.[29]

In some of my analyses done previously, and in the studies printed earlier, I was concerned less with the Besht's originality, or with a Romantic approach to his figure or the celebration of the uniqueness of his personality. In principle, the emphasis of a serious scholarship should be also on his panorama of sources; on his selection, restructuring, and reinterpretation of earlier traditions; on how he broke some of them; and on describing the way he organized some of the traditions he inherited in conceptually loose and fluid structures.[30] Let me emphasize: he was not the single individual in his time and place that was acquainted with the Cordoverian traditions discussed here, as is shown in the parallels between his instructions and that of R. Yehudah Leib Pistin and R. Nahman of Kosov as mentioned in ch. 8 n. 5 in this volume. There is no doubt that these two and others, like R. Baruch of Kosov and R. Nathan-Neta' of Siniewa, were also acquainted with other Cordoverian traditions pertinent to our discussions. Thus, at least insofar as the Kabbalistic reverberations of the astral magical worldviews are concerned, there were also other instances of accepting or at least describing them.

This entirely non-heroic agenda clarified, I do not assume that everything available in Jewish mysticism through generations was known by the Besht, or that every type of thought can be found in the Beshtian traditions, or that he would adopt indiscriminately every Kabbalistic idea or others he would encounter. However, at the same time it would be a fallacy to see his thought as represented by a certain homogenous message. Scholars, especially Martin Buber, are accepting the fact that the Besht was a selective mind, but in order to better understand his selective grids we should be aware of what was found on the horizon of his knowledge in both Jewish and non-Jewish sources—*en passant*, what I call the panorama. This problem is not a specifically Beshtian one but is affecting the entire realm of Jewish mysticism, which cannot be reduced to one single conceptual center, whatever it may be, deemed to be representative of many thousands of writings and hundreds of different authors, or of unifying the entire Jewish mystical literature, allegedly developing in an unilinear manner. In my opinion, the concern of early Hasidism, the Besht and his disciples, as well as some authors contemporary to them with ethical Kabbalistic literature is indeed evident, as duly pointed out by Mendel Piekarz. However, there was some form of selective affinities with the Cordoverian elements related to vocal performance, a topic that has not been put in relief in scholarship. Since the ethical literature was much more accessible, it is not necessary to demonstrate direct contact with Cordovero's own books. This does not mean that the Besht was consciously a Cordoverian thinker as, for example, Azulai was, but given the selective affinities discussed in this study, unknowingly he actually was one. Instead of the unilinear approach recommend a panoramic one that allows impact of a variety of sources on nascent Hasidism.

11

BETWEEN LETTERS' SHAPES
AND THEIR SOUNDS

Let me address now an important issue that may be derived from some of the previous discussions: by cleaving to or by entering the vocables, sounds, utterances, or sonorous palaces, one encounters therein the light, which is conceived of as the divine presence within elements of language. According to the Besht it is the spoken language that allows, therefore, the encounter with the divinity in a direct manner, which means an unmediated and non-symbolic understanding of how language functions from the religious point of view, by its external and internal dimensions, as we shall see as follows in chapter 13. Though according to the traditions reported in his name the twenty-two Hebrew letters and sounds differ from each other, deteriorating as they pass from the first letter, 'Aleph, to the last one, Tav, because of their being part of the process of emanation as descent, I did not find, for the time being, an elaborated qualification of the nature of the human encounter with divinity, based on this premise. We may assume that this is not only the case with the Hebrew letters, or their arrangements in canonical texts, but in some rare cases also stories told, most plausibly, in Yiddisch. Nevertheless, the assumption of a story in the hagiography is that the Besht was capable, by listening to the manner in which a certain text was read by a person, namely by intonation, to discern what his problem was.[1]

However, the vocal dimension of the performance raises a problem as to adherence, since both prayer and Torah study were part of a communal practice, and when praying and studying together, it is hard to distinguish between one's own vocables to which he has to cleave and those of his companions. Since it is obvious that it is the specific vocables of a certain person that should be the subject of adherence, and eventually also of one's ascent on high, the distinction between those sounds emitted in a group seems to be paramount. Nevertheless, I have not discerned the existence of any treatment of this problem or an attempt at solving it in early Hasidic literature. Neither could I discern awareness as to a need of a key for the specificity of the pronounced form of each consonant, or the differences between the combinations of those consonants with different vowels. To assume that there were esoteric traditions about those vital questions is most unlikely in Hasidic masters.

Indeed, following the Besht, who himself followed on this point some conceptual lines found in some parts of Cordovero's Kabbalah, Hasidic teachings in general were much less concerned with a symbolic understanding of reality and contemplative practices, and much more with the experience of cleaving to God or the divine lights imagined to dwell or to be drawn within the utterances, and in many cases also exercising an impact on external reality and on the group. It is possible that the passages dealt with in chapter 8 that describe the sight of lights are different from those quoted in the name of the Besht by R. Jacob Joseph when dealing with cleaving to the light of the infinity. The former may be conceived of as more practical-magical, the latter more mystical, though they also may have a sequel that can be described as magical.

By proposing to attribute a much greater importance to the sonorous performances than has has been done earlier in scholarship of early Hasidism, I mean much more than the need to correctly translate some Hebrew passages into the English studies of scholars. What is at stake is, in my opinion, more than some pedantic propensity to correct translations. The difference between the dominant scholarly approach that emphasized the role of written letters on the one hand, and the other one, which I have already proposed in my book on Hasidism and again here, which reinterprets most of the same traditions as dealing in fact with cleaving to sounds or utterances, on the other hand, is not a matter of a negligible semantic nuance. In my opinion, it touches a strong phenomenological chord, making a difference that I would like now to describe in the context of the Beshtian traditions: For the seer or for the recipient of images, the appearance of images is spontaneous, while for the contemplator the printed letters are a stable given, and they are basically consumed, a situation that assumes some form of passivity. From this point of view, the presentation of the Besht as preeminently an alleged ocularcentric contemplator/seer would be closer to the religious phenomenon known as quietism, though certainly not identical to it.

However, according to some of the Besht's teachings discussed previously, the amount of energy that is necessary in order to watch the written letters is much smaller than what happens when the objects of cleaving are utterances in general, and even more so when they are pronounced rather speedily, *bi-zerizut*, namely with alacrity, as the Besht indeed sometimes recommends to pray[2] in order to avoid the intrusion of "alien thoughts," namely the distracting thoughts, even more so when the instruction to see lights, found in a dynamic interaction, is also involved.

An acceleration of inner acts because of hyper-exitation becomes evident if we shift our attention from the scholarly theory emphasizing the alleged "contemplation of letters" to the interpretation of the Beshtian sources as dealing with cleaving to utterances, which have been emitted as part of the act of prayer. This activity is sometimes described as performed better with alacrity. It is more difficult to understand atomization of a written text into its constitutive consonants, which cannot be in principle written letters, while it is much easier to understand how pronunciation of sounds, namely syllables, are distinct units. According to the theory that introduces the concept of contemplation as an important religious act for early Hasidim, we would expect that someone will see entire words, and that their dianoetic cargo would impress the consciousness as such, much more than a preoccupation with the consecutive pronunciations of the monadic and syllabic utterances. Moreover, while the printed letters are a given entity, a kind of predetermined data whose contours have been shaped by someone else beforehand, which the student then "consumes" visually, the utterances require a much more active participation in their creation, and in the case of the Besht's instructions, quite a strong vocal effort is recommended, as we have seen previously. In a way, while the resort to printed letters is more a matter of the present, the pronounced letters are much more dynamic and future-oriented.

This situation allows a much greater degree of freedom, as the performer may choose the pitch, the speed, or the intonation, and a greater degree of participation, or he may do so naturally, according to his capacities, without having to choose. Thus, the question may be asked: how passive and contemplative may someone be when he himself has to produce the sonic objects of cleaving, which are so dynamic by their nature, and have to be both produced and adhered to by the mystic at the same time, not to mention the complexity created by the instruction to watch, or according to other traditions, to cleave to the lights found within the utterances, which sometimes are also depicted to be united sexually?

It is even more so when there is an instruction to discover within the utterances of prayer and Torah the hidden presence of the supernal lights and to cleave to them, or only watch them, this being an operation that further complicates the process of cleaving in comparison to what we find in the still dominant vision in scholarship dealing with devequt in Hasidism. From the point of view of a dynamic versus a static object that is involved in the practice that is conducive to cleaving, the Besht is closer to the techniques of Abraham Abulafia, as Joseph Weiss has already briefly but insightfully pointed out, as a phenomenological remark, insofar as the issue of atomization is concerned.[3] As I have mentioned previously in several instances, a better term for the atomization would be monadization, since the separation between the sounds of a word was accompanied by loading the isolated entities with new and rather extraordinary valences such as, for example, divinity, souls, and worlds. Thus, I assume that atomization in itself would be a meaningless process without the accompanying approach to the linguistic units, namely an amplification of their valences, that I propose to designate as "monadization." I would say also that this phenomenon is paralleled by some Abulafian discussions to this effect. However, by loading the separate linguistic atoms with gigantic valences, what can be called amplification, monads emerge but the meaning of the words compounded of them is, at the same time, dramatically weakened.

However, we should better expand Weiss's interesting phenomenological remark regarding atomization to the fact that in both cases there is a vocal activity that is essential, and that vocables are recited, not just letters contemplated. Thus, another type of activity other than what most of the scholars assume is entailed, and a much more dynamic situation, which may hardly be described as contemplation in the manner this term is commonly used in the history of religion, is referred to in the teachings.[4] Moreover, both in the writings of Abulafia and in the teachings of the Besht, there is an important assumption that the divine spirit can speak through the mouth of the mystic, as well as a privileging of the oral versus the written form of transmission.[5] In the case of the two mystical literatures, the experience of devequt is conceived of as attainable in a relatively short period, without requiring lengthy spiritual preparations. The enunciation of some types of vocables constitutes, therefore, a short type of trigger, part of a technical approach, a practice of a secondary elite figure that attempted also to instruct larger audiences as to how to intensify their vocal rituals, without having to spend much time in casuistic studies.

Last but not least in this context: in both ecstatic Kabbalah and in East European Hasidism, there are some forms of critique of Rabbinism, addressed to their respective contemporaries, done from pneumatic perspectives of what they conceived of as "authentic" Judaism, as part of an attempt at offering an alternative to the more routine approach to religion. These critiques are better known in the case of Hasidism, and they are one of the causes that triggered the famous controversy between Mitnaggedim and Hasidim. In the case of Abulafia, a fierce controversy was ignited between him and R. Shlomo ben Abraham ibn Adret, known as the Rashba', because of the former's claims that he is a prophet and a Messiah, and perhaps also because of his poignant critiques of rabbis, which appear rather late in his career, and these critiques still await a detailed analysis. There is a certain parallelism between R. Elijah, the Gaon of Vilnius's criticism of early Hasidism and that of ibn Adret's attacks on Abulafia, and these two disputes taking place between various forms of Kabbalah deserve a separate comparative scrutiny.

In my opinion, there is a strong affinity between the psychological processes involved in the concentration on utterances in the ecstatic Kabbalah and in early Hasidism, since instead of the contemplative activity, represented by what is known as the Alpha waves, I assume that we may speak about the strong activation of the mind, probably related to the Beta waves. In my opinion, the two Jewish mystics did not resort to rhythmic acoustic stimulation or repetitions of the same simple formulas, but engaged in a strong vocal activity, replete with many small variants, changing all the time. These affinities are not necessarily a matter of direct textual influence of Abulafia's books on the Besht, or the latter's acquaintance with the former's passages about recitations of the combinations of letters as copied verbatim by R. Moshe Cordovero in his *Pardes Rimmonim*.

In my opinion such influences are, historically speaking, not problematic at all. Some years ago, I described several manuscripts of one of Abulafia's most important books, *Sefer Hayyei ha-'Olam ha-Ba'*, which had been copied in Podolia and Poland in the second part of the eighteenth century.[6] Meanwhile, microfilms of two other manuscripts of the same book have arrived to the Institute of Hebrew Microfilms at the National and University Library in Jerusalem. Both manuscripts had been copied toward the end of the eighteenth century in an Ashkenazi hand, and one of them is found in the library of the founder of Ḥabad Hasidism, R. Shneur Zalman of Liady. An analytical survey of the extant manuscripts of Abulafia's other Kabbalistic books, which were copied in Eastern

Europe in the eighteenth century, especially his lengthy book *'Imrei Shefer*, may demonstrate that more manuscripts of his books were available in that region and most probably even quoted in the critical period of the nascent Hasidism, by both an important Hasidic figure, the aforementioned R. Shneur Zalman, and an important author from the camp of the mitnaggedim, R. Menahem Mendel of Shklov, one of the most important students of the Gaon of Vilnius. It is possible that the Gaon himself was aware of this passage and conceived it as fundamental for Kabbalah.[7] Since scholarship about the impact of Abulafia's manuscripts in Eastern Europe is only at its very beginning, I would not like to draw farfetched conclusions at this preliminary stage of research.

However, here I am concerned much more with a phenomenological affinity between the two schools in Jewish mysticism. In both cases recitation of letters/sounds is conceived to be a major component of the path to reach a higher form of religious experiences than the normal ones. Needless to say, many fundamental principles, as well as important details, do distinguish between their two different paths, one of them being the Hasidic recommendation or instruction to watch the lights that are imagined to dwell within sounds, which was presumably one of the peaks of the mystical path according to the Besht, which Abulafia would regard as a relatively inferior form of experience, while for the Besht it is the higher experience.[8]

It seems that in some cases the Besht attempted to offer a synthesis between the vocal dimensions of the ecstatic Kabbalah, which Abulafia regarded to be superior to the sefirotic Kabbalah, as later on such a view reverberated in Safedian Kabbalah, especially Cordovero, on the one hand, and the luminous elements of the sefirotic one, that the ecstatic Kabbalist conceived of as being inferior, as he envisioned them in his famous and seminal epistle entitled *Ve-Zot li-Yhudah*, on the other hand. But now the Besht is also resorting to some astro-magical elements as he found them in the Cordoverianism, which, though they were found in Kabbalah, they were nevertheless quite marginal in the literature belonging to ecstatic Kabbalah and occur only in some few cases in Zoharic Kabbalah.[9] Whether the specific syntheses adduced in his name were already formulated somewhere beforehand is a matter for which I have no simple answer for the time being, an issue to be reiterated in appendix C.

Moreover, the sonorous performance of some of the rituals has a strong collective overtone, since someone is not only emitting sounds, but he is also heard by others who are performing the same sonorous acts, often in a synchronized manner, and together they constitute a kind of sonorous ambiance, each group with its proper psalmody, intonation, and melodies. Contemplation of the shape of written letters that is related to the sense of sight, which is indeed found in some important stages of Jewish mysticism is, however, a much more individualistic enterprise, done in many cases in a state of solitude that hardly can create a community of persons living together for a sustained period of time on the basis of such a central instruction, and is not synchronized with any other member of a group.[10] Someone does not need the quorum in order to read, mentally, any canonical text in a ritual manner.

This scholarly concentration on the ideal of contemplation is, presumably, one of the reasons why the much esteemed R. Nahman of Kosov, the head of a group of pneumatics who was reported as someone who dedicated himself to the contemplation of the written letters of the divine name, did not become the head of a popular movement, as the Besht did. Neither did another contemporary of his, R. Isaac of Drohobitch, who too was acquainted with the Besht and who was reported as practicing contemplation of the Tetragrammaton, create a Hasidic community, though his son, R. Yehiel Mikhal of Zloczow, who became a follower of the Besht, and his own sons, actually did so.[11] They, as well as R. Jacob Joseph of Polonnoye too—another figure who did not attract followers— followed a practice in use earlier in Jewish mysticism, including in R. Elijah da Vida's *Reshit Hokhmah*.

I would say also that the scholarly vision of the Besht as pre-eminently a seer-figure, namely someone who sees images, and as someone who hears voices, as found in H. Pedaya's studies (a description that is indeed in a small part true, but in my opinion much more modest in the material that is available to me), is quite exaggerated if we take into consideration the broader picture of the Besht's personality and the contents of his teachings as I see them. I wonder if this is a quality that could help him promote his capacity to attract persons that would then become a community. They would attract rather a clientele of the magician for a short moment of a special need.[12]

It should be pointed out that putting too strong an accent on the sight experiences of this scholarly approach marginalizes, or even neglects, the sonorous dimensions of the Besht's mysticism, found in some many forms and in so many teachings as we have pointed out previously. Moreover, while the sonorous aspects of the teachings are related to daily religious performances, and thus they are situated at the very center of the Rabbinic and Hasidic life, the extraordinary instances of clairvoyance or the ascents of the soul on high are, indubitably, much more occasional and restricted to the Hasidic elite, and did not become a landmark of Hasidism as a whole. In any case, the vast majority of the Besht's instructions as they have been translated previously refer much more to the utterances during the performance of vocal rites than to experiences related to lights that are seen or to clairvoyance.

This distinction has some relevance also for the possible different audiences: the clairvoyance by the lights is related to the clientele, the instructions regarding utterances to his disciples. The latter scarcely mentioned the Besht as a wonder-maker. For the history of the Besht himself, the distinction between his clientele on the one hand, which was basically interested in his magical performances, and his disciples, who were attracted much more by his spiritual instructions, on the other hand, is not dramatically important as it is, however, for the history of Hasidism as both a spiritual and a social movement. Seers and contemplators, fascinating as some of them may be as ocularcentric mystics, are however much less efficient as founders of religious movements, who are much more connected to watching the more general human condition, and then address the problems of communities at long range, not just helping clienteles, by attempting to solve their momentary problems.

The Besht was, however, remembered by his immediate disciples because of his spreading in wider audiences many religious instructions that strove to shape a mystical way of life, namely for being an instructor with many spiritual messages, much more than for his "successes" as a popular physician, or his attempts to deal in his ascents on high with the pogroms of his times. Between the intransmittable and the idiosyncratic components of the Besht's personality and his specific capacities on the one hand, and the transmittable instructions formulated in so many of his teachings on the other, the understanding of the history of Hasidism should be much more concerned with the latter as formative at long range, though for understanding the historical Besht himself, both aspects are equally important.

The study of the Torah and the liturgical situation, which constitute the two most important vocal rituals in Judaism, are commonly events taking place, however, in the company of other individuals, and in many cases in Hasidism. This is the case, especially in that of the Besht, when the performance was carried out loudly, and thus the devequt-experience is not only a matter of a personal achievement. The plausible role of the loud recitation for the consolidation of communal life (unlike the contemplation of the letters of the divine name), has been addressed in the quite short but nevertheless important observations of Gershom Scholem.[13] However, as pointed out in the previous chapter, it is a quandary for me how the communal vocal performance may allow personal experiences of encountering the divine within someone's vocables.

The Great Maggid, who was a very sensitive person, could not bear the loud voice of his revered master and has been described as sick when the Besht once prayed, and had to leave the schul in order to pray elsewhere, in the study-house, the Beit ha-Midrash.[14]

It seems that this is quite an emblematic moment, since it adumbrates not only a different tendency in early Hasidism, which perhaps appeared already in the later career of the Besht himself, namely some form of domestication of its more uncanny aspects,[15] but also inspired what would happen in the manner in which some aspects of the Besht's praxis would be understood by modern scholarship. The loud noises of the praying voices, sometimes amounting potentially to a cacophony, may be, for the ears of some sensitive persons, too annoying, and this is the reason why the alleged "silent" contemplation of written letters has been preferred indeed in the writings of some Hasidic masters, but even more in the scholarly presentation of the Besht, to the vocal performance of the rituals.[16]

On the grounds of the previous analyses, I can only speculate that also some modern scholars of Hasidism, concerned with the centrality of contemplation and mental prayer, would have gone out together with the Great Maggid from the Besht's schul when he would pray loudly, preferring a much calmer approach, as found indeed in some of the views found in some of the former's Hasidic school. In any case, also the manner in which the Besht has examined, according to the hagiography, the Great Maggid, asking him if he indeed knows Kabbalah, was not part of scrutiny of his erudition concerning the content of some texts but rather a check of the manner in which he is reading—for the Besht in a loud and experiential manner—classical mystical books.[17] It is no wonder that in a religious worldview that preferred sonorous rituals over cultivating states of mental prayer and visual contemplation, the place of music, whatever its ultimate cultural sources may be—Gypsy, Ukrainian, Ruthenian, Old Russian Rite believers, Moldavian, Turkish, Crimean Tatar, or others—as part of religious life was also much greater than ever beforehand in Judaism or in Jewish mysticism, a point that is already reflected in the hagiography of the Besht.

12

THE APOTHEOSIS OF
SPEECH-ACTS

In fact, letters that point to sounds are found in some tension with the voice, since ultimately they refer to individual utterances that divide the sound or the voice and produce some form of melody.[1] Nevertheless, voice and vocal activity played a more substantial role in the teachings of the Besht that dramatically shaped Hasidism, much more than it has been assumed in the available academic portraits of his thought. This is why I proposed to call this vocal practice a "mystique of pronunciation." This "mystique" started, as pointed out previously, with several brief, enigmatic but seminal assertions found in late antiquity in *Sefer Yetziyrah* in discussions about letters, sounds, and their combinations, and it ascended in its formulations and elaborations in many forms of Kabbalah as, for example, in ecstatic Kabbalah, and especially in some of the Safedian Kabbalists, whose books directly or indirectly impacted early Hasidism. As we have pointed out in the material adduced in the notes, and additional examples to this effect are legion, these ritual activities are well represented in the extant material. In any case the vocal performance that refers to adherence to each and every vocable plays a much more important role than the alleged contemplation of written letters, or the role played by his teachings about the seeing of lights and the reception of images, or about his alleged hearing at the distance.

While the utterances mentioned previously are, essentially, part and parcel of the daily ritual, the other experiences of the Besht, especially those related to lights, are in any case rare if not extraordinary. Thus, utterances are, in any case, an incontestable part of his ritual life and, statistically speaking, fill much of his waking life. To what extent the other extraordinary events, such as the seeing of lights and the claims of clairvoyance, indeed took place is a matter of belief, and that central as they certainly were for the self-awareness of the Besht and of his image in the eyes of the others, it is quite difficult to integrate them in a reliable unified picture of the "actual" Besht.

It should be pointed out that despite the major role played by the vocal performance, there is a rather minor place for aural experiences in the extant traditions, which means here that vocal messages that he could receive did not constitute a major avenue for his activity, as we have seen at the end of the previous chapter. On the other hand, there are traditions related to the Besht as being possessed by the *Shekhinah* while praying, and the prayer has been conceived of as the prayer of divinity, or what can be called *oratio infusa*, as discussed in my "Models of Understanding Prayer in Early Hasidism."

In any case, I propose to understand the figure of the Besht as reflecting a second elite type, which was capable of changing not only from the conceptual point of view but also from the behavoristic one, as the shift from practicing some forms of asceticism to a critique of asceticism shows, or from the difficulties to communicate with others, allegedly because of the state of extreme *devequt*, to the possibility to communicate. Also the shifts in his attitudes toward what is called "messianism" may reflect such flexibility. Nevertheless, I have my very great doubts whether the sharp shift from the status of the Besht as a hidden holy figure to a public spiritual leader, as it is claimed in the hagiography *In Praise of the Baal Shem Tov*, and even more in the Habad historiosophy in some few passages preserved in Yiddisch, is indeed a historical fact. I presume that here we have another instance of embellishing history by presuming some period of initiation, hiddenness, as a preparation for revelation. Teleology is a fine tool in traditional hagiography, but quite a poor explanation in a critical type of scholarship. In any case, I assume as more plausible a smoother developmental explanation of the career of the Besht, and my presumption is that we should pay attention to his capacities to adapt himself to new environments and to adopt new conceptual structures, rather than finding a static one predicated on a quite stable personality or a transmitter of a "simple and united" message, as Buber put it, a stance that I see as monotonic, as part of deceptive simplicity. To be sure: I do not deny the potential validity of the stories about the Besht's retreats in the Carpathian Mountains, but at the same time I am very skeptical about perceiving this period as a premeditated preparation for his "heroic" task he was "destined" to fulfill in the future.

I attempted previously to map the conceptual contours of the material found in the teachings reported in the name of the Besht, which I considered to be pertinent for the understanding of the topic of cleaving to utterances, and to put them in their wider contexts in the thought of the Besht. I have dealt previously only succinctly with its possible sources. The main effort was directed to pointing out the existence of significant divergences between these teachings, but also an attempt was made to organize those divergent teachings around more comprehensive paradigms I call models, and then to arrange those models in some hypothetical form of historical sequence that seems to me the most plausible and economic one. The two later steps depend on the first one, since if the Besht was indeed a monotonic thinker, the efforts done as part of the two later phases as hypothetized previously become irrelevant. Thus, the moves I propose here are a necessary effort to offer an account for the existence of conceptual diversity in the teachings of the Besht, and to a certain extent of his followers and Hasidism as a religious movement in general.

These three methodological moves may be relevant for the understanding of more than one topic in early Hasidism. I tried to do so in the case of the Besht's teachings about prayer and messianism, and they should become, in my opinion, a more comprehensive approach to be applied also in other cases when the Besht's thought is analyzed in order to avoid an impressionistic approach. Tentative as this rather complex approach may be, it should, in my opinion, be applied also to other topics in the thought of the Besht, which should be studied in an exhaustive manner, and I am convinced that such an approach will be fruitful, even if my specific theory of models or my proposed explanation of their concatenation will not be accepted in time. Let me repeat what I have already articulated previously in less poignant a manner: It is unfortunate that so many studies about the Besht did not take into serious consideration so many of the Beshtian traditions, neglecting thereby significant parts of the pertinent material, thus choosing to portray his thought in a monotonic manner by ignoring some other pertinent, though diverging traditions adduced in his name. Moreover, this exclusion was done without offering any account for its reason, apparently because the contents of the other teachings would problematize the respective monotonic pictures of the Besht found in various scholars' works.

I would like to emphasize the importance of the second stage in my proposed threefold methodological approach. The wide distribution of the teachings concerning cleaving to letters/sounds in all the different circles in early Hasidism cannot be overestimated, and the reverberation of this approach is even richer than I could adduce in this framework, focused as it is on the Besht's teachings alone. Nevertheless, the conceptual disparity of the Beshtian materials discussed previously is quite visible, and I tried to put those discrepancies in sharp relief, much more than has been done earlier in scholarship, since I presume that this polychromatic approach to different topics is characteristic of the Besht.

However, the major role played by these divergences should not invalidate the authenticity or the reliability of the divergent traditions, as has been claimed by Moshe Rosman, and an attempt is made here to adopt another approach, much more difficult conceptually than refusing to deal with conflicting views. This is one of the main reasons for undertaking my complex approach. The disparity is not dramatically great, and I would not regard the transitions from one model to another as constituting a rupture, as we may see some forms of transition from simpler views to more complex ones and, to a certain extent, also from the centrality of the human voice, as part of an ergetic approach to the ritual, to a greater importance attributed to human thought, with its more comprehensive assumption as to the divine omnipresence in the third model. Such a development is not based, however, upon the premise that later in the Besht's career the earlier models were conceived of as obsolete by the Besht, by his immediate followers, or by the later masters in the third generation of Hasidic leaders.[2] Most of them adopted an accumulative approach, unaware as they were of the development of the thought of their spiritual leader, an approach that assumes the pertinence of all, or almost all, the religious ways of behavior that have been adopted at any point in time by the Besht. To put it in a simple manner: the emergence of the noetic model does not mean that the Besht ceased to pray loudly, and in any case the understanding of prayer is less connected to the third model, but much more with the second one.

Needless to say the specific teachings chosen to be analyzed here, the very attribution of some of them to the Besht—though some of them occur in R. Aharon of Apta Perlov's *Keter Shem Tov* in an anonymous manner—and the nature of the concatenations between them as has been done here involve some degree of selection and even an amount of arbitrariness. This is the case, to be sure, also in other scholarly accounts of the Besht's thought. Nevertheless, the problem created by a specific type of scholars' selectivity can be reduced dramatically by addressing as many extant traditions as possible as being germane for reconstructing the Besht's view, an approach that differs from the dominant type of scholarship that resorts to only few of the available traditions in order to reconstruct the Besht's thought. As to the concatenation between his various teachings, as the one I have proposed in chapter 2 between two texts that were preserved separately in different books that were written by different authors, and as constituting a more comprehensive view that should be understood better as supplementing each other, it is strictly necessary to invest hard and detailed philological work, and I hope that this work has been done here in a proper manner.

In any case, specific claims have been made in the previous analyses as to how to approach the Besht's teachings, which can be accepted or rejected by scholars, either by adducing additional material or by proposing new interpretations of the material already discussed. It should be mentioned that an examination of his teachings alone, essential as it may be for understanding the Hasidic instructions as intellectual alternatives, may not be sufficient for a fuller understanding of the emergence of a social movement as it was; and the personality of the Besht, which galvanized those teachings with his "charisma," was indubitably also crucial for the impact they had, but this is an issue that I cannot address in the present framework.

This approach to the intellectual history of the Besht presumes an accumulative process of conceptual enrichment that not only adopts new modes of understanding the centrality of vocal performance, but also brings the different models together, thus assembling in the course of time different ways of thinking, what I called previously polyphonic, synchronic, and perhaps also diachronic. Such an approach does not generate a simple conceptual picture. I am less concerned with discerning the existence of one profound "message" emanating from the thought of a religious "genius," or with the role played by a "revolutionary" thinker in the history of Jewish mysticism, or with the sociology of a charismatic figure. Each of these claims indeed contains some grain of truth, but when taken alone as a single explanatory cause, they may turn into a Romantic and monotonic vision, to which, as the reader may guess after reading the previous pages, I do not subscribe.

I am concerned here less with a heroic picture that transpires from the hagiographical books and in some more academic Romantic pictures, and much more with the hypothetical moves of someone that will become, postumously, the founder of Hasidism, from one spiritual position to another, though I pointed out previously from time to time what seems to me to be the Beshtian contribution to the earlier sources he resorted to when he built his teachings as well as the possible reasons for his impact.

Following the important distinction of Martin Buber between Jesus of Nazereth, a religious teacher, and the later image of Jesus Christ as the founder of Christianity, my assumption is that it will be better not to impose on the historical Besht the fact that, *a posteriori*, he indeed was considered to be the founder of Hasidism.[3] The latter is an anachronistic picture that assumes a form of telelology that seems to be quite implausible from the historical point of view. Moreover, in order to better understand the two dimensions of the Besht, it would be better to resort to different methodologies, phenomenological in the case of the former and sociological in the case of the latter. In any case, neo-Marxist approaches to Hasidism that attempted to explain Hasidism as mainly a matter of the social and economical situations can hardly explain the emergence and evolution of the Besht's different types of thought, or even one of them alone, or their adoption of views found already in another century and in another center of Jewish culture.

Hypothetical as it is, the developmental proposal to understand the multiplicity of opinions of the Besht that has been formulated previously, and in other studies of mine printed recently, is nevertheless much more historical in its basic approach than any of the other available scholarly accounts of the Besht's thought as the founder of Hasidism, which overlooked the importance of the conceptual discrepancies in his traditions, or did not accord them significance. This approach should be compared to what Erich Auerbach wrote in his *Mimesis*, about the specificity of the biblical style at the end of the first chapter of his book. In both cases, consistency is neither a prescription for historicity nor for a lasting influence. The available scholarly accounts trying to depict his thought are much more homogenous, phenomenologically speaking, and thus leave the impression of a more monotonic thinker, and I would say are also done in a much more impressionistic and selective manner. Never, to the best of my knowledge, have scholars of early Hasidism formulated some criteria, not even tentative ones, that will explain what Beshtian traditions are, in their opinion, reliable or not, and why some of them are considered to be pertinent for their analyses while some others are not, even when they occur in the same books from which other Beshtian traditions had been quoted in academic studies. The arbitrariness of the scholarly decisions is quite evident both in ignoring Beshtian traditions and in selecting among them.

This is the reason why I consider much of the available scholarship which concentrated on the Beshtian traditions as basically being impressionistic, since only a relatively small part of the extant traditions attributed to the Besht have been addressed so far. This does not mean that the extant scholarship is automatically going on the wrong track, but its almost exclusive reliance only on some few excerpts from the vast amount of extant material is hardly a recipe for success, as is demonstrated by the almost general marginalization of the centrality of the sonorous Besht in most of the available academic accounts. Let me formulate my point in a more explicit manner: a homiletic and hagiographical literature in its most important expressions, Hasidic documents should nevertheless be addressed with the same academic rigor as any other texts, but taking in consideration not only the pertinent material that displays a certain idea or series of concepts that are conjugated, but also by discerning and even highlighting the divergences between them, and then striving to deal with the possible development of this figure's thought.

However, my much less elegant picture, with its necessary reliance on massive textual analyses, which strives to be as exhaustive as possible from the point of view of the reliable traditions on the topic, accompanied by long notes that resort to a variety of traditions stemming from multiple Hasidic sources and strive to allow the role of the different voices in the Besht's thought is, hopefully, helpful at least in one domain: it will account more easily for the variety of views found among the Besht's followers. This more complex and inclusive picture of the Besht's thought may also help better explain how some of the different spiritual directions in Hasidism emerged than if we adopt the more homogenous or monotonic understandings of the thought of this movement's "founder" that are prevalent in scholarship. The assumption of an initial conceptual complexity of the nascent phase constitutes a much better formula to explain the possibility to choose between religious alternatives and facilitate the emergence of later conceptual diversity of the movement. Thus, the existence of the more mental attitude to the nature of cleaving in some teachings of the Besht has reverberated and amplified in the thought of Great Maggid, and through his teachings it contributed to the special configurations of the H̲abad version of Hasidism in the third generation of Hasidic masters.

This developmental explanation, which may in my opinion be complemented also by other parallel and similar developments, may contribute greatly to another, quite different explanation of the development of Hasidism in scholarship, which will attribute to the Besht the centrality he has in the traditional image of him as the founder that is recurring in Hasidic literature. Thus, we should discern in the Beshtian teachings not so much a structured message as a complexity of different treatments of a certain theme, and an ensuing variety that emerged as part of the accumulative process. This variety is not the result of a premeditated strategy, but it nevertheless contributed to the emergence of a wide popular movement, which could select one meaning or nuance from a broader gamut. Such popular movement does not emerge and develop solely because of socio-economical reasons, or because of people understanding precisely what a textologist will determine was the authentic textual tradition of the Besht, but because of the meanings expressed in the early traditions, or what was imagined to be found in those traditions. Without denying the importance of historical and textual analyses, they hardly are able to explain the adherence to the nascent movement of so any different persons is such diverse geographical centers in the first century of the development of Hasidism. By overemphasizing historical facts—though overlooking some others as contacts with Altaic tribes for

example—or too bookish an approach to texts, without inter-
rogating their meaning—and their misprisions—many facts are
amassed, which do not engage what the various messages of the
Besht had to say to a certain audience.

On the other hand, the reduction of the contents of Hasidism
to contemplation, passivity or incarnation, or any other single
spiritual "core," which is allegedly consonant to what the scholar
believes is mysticism,—and sometimes what he/she personally
believes—is another quite problematic approach. Without taking
in account aspects of all those different approaches in a more balanced manner, and being aware of the conceptual diversity of the
masters of Hasidism, and more eminently the Besht, sterile scholarship and following them also sterile debates, are prone to haunt
the field.

As mentioned previously, Cordovero's Kabbalah was also far
from being conceptually homogenous, and this is the case also in
many other cases in Kabbalistic literature, most eminently in the
seminal and variegated Zoharic literature.[4] It is perhaps not super-
fluous to mention in this context that the polyphonic (I try to avoid
resorting to the term symphonic) nature of the religious messages
is obvious also in the structure of the two other canonical books
in Judaism, the Hebrew Bible and the Talmud, as they are bodies
of literature generated by groups and not by individuals. This polyphonic attitude is, to be sure, not a conscious decision nor a premeditated approach: It is much more the result of a lack of interest
in systematic theological thought, and a reliance on a variety of,
intellectually speaking, sources that differ conceptually from each
other, on the one hand, and the concentration on the synchronized performance of the rituals, an effort that, consciously or not,
was instrumental in order to create a religious community, what I
call sonorous community, on the other. By their emphasis on the
sonorous performances of transient and changing linguistic units,
Hasidic masters offered an alternative to important elements found
both in the Kabbalistic and in the Rabbinic mentalistic approaches
that shaped Judaism for centuries. In this context the concept of

amending speech, related to both the Biblical Moses and the Besht himself—as I pointed out in ch. 3 n. 8 and and ch. 5 n. 2 in this volume—may reveal also a personal aspect of the development of the Besht himself, from a state when he had problems of communication to one when his entire activity was based on communication.

In the case of Kabbalah, the vocal and the emotional dimensions were less important from the religious point of view, though they were certainly not absent. Also in the manner in which Rabbinic studies were regularly done, the semantic and the mental valences of the studied texts were considered to be more important than their pronounced forms, though vocal reading and arguing were essential for the process of learning. However, they are grounded in resorting to enduring letters in books. However, even in these cases the vocal and the aural aspects of the performance are of utmost importance. Both prayer and study of the Torah are not only vocal events but also aural, since they were performed in a group. Hasidism, following earlier Rabbinic propensities, cultivated the idea of sonorous communities, which means that those vocal rites generated a sonorous ambiance that impacted all the present persons with certain sequences of sounds.

Though continuing these two earlier forms of Jewish religious literature from many points of view, under the aegis of the Besht's teachings East European Hasidism put other accents and offered quite insistently a religious alternative that had been marginal in the earlier forms of Jewish religion, thus being able to attract and inspire the religious lives of other audiences. By shifting the center of gravity from the dianoetic and graphical dimensions to the vocal performance of the canonical texts, a phenomenon that may be designated as the apotheosis of the sonorous activity, the concept of the surplus value of the religious performance has been transferred from the emphasis on secrecy and the mediating role of symbolic dimensions of Kabbalah, sometimes connected to the visual representation, to the direct presence of the divine as light dwelling or attracted within utterances. Even when the concentration of one's thought on God is mentioned, this is less a purely mental act intended to discover His essence or his attributes, to fathom the various contents within a text beyond the visible aspects of nature, to decode symbols or to contemplate systems of divine powers or the drama of suffering and redemption, and more an emotional adherence of someone's consciousness to the certitude of divine omnipresence in all the layers of existence. It is much less an issue of cleaving to a specific content or a revelation of secrets, as in the medieval Jewish literature, and much more a matter of the confidence of the divine presence that matters, an intensification of faith. In short it is more a fideistic propensity than a noetic practice.

In such a manner we should understand also the meaning of mental cleaving in the last phase in the Besht's thought as reflecting much more a matter or faith, as the Besht claimed once that *devequt* is tantamount to *'emunah*. Thus, though sometimes mental, the *devequt* is in the Besht much less noetic in the sense in which Jewish philosophers and some Kabbalists understood most of the forms of *devequt* in Kabbalah, and even in the writings of his follower, the Great Maggid. I surmise that the clinging to the divine, conceived either as transcendental in the vein of Neoplatonism in some cases, or alternatively omnipresent, in my opinion in the later stage of the Besht's development, and in some other cases, the cleaving to the utterances as containers of the divine (a view closer to Hermeticism), was accompanied by an emotional attachment, accentuated more than it has been done beforehand in Judaism in such contexts. The combination between the loud sonorous and the strong emotional performance, both assumed as being less related to mental processes, contributed no doubt to the success of Hasidism in recruiting much larger audiences than Kabbalah did in all its lengthy history, all this in quite a short period, thus becoming in the course of time a popular movement. A movement may emerge not necessarily because of offering new ideas but also because of transforming some old one in new forms as brief instructions.

An issue that has not been addressed in the previous discussions is the relationship between the theory of utterances as a means for cleaving and drawing down influx, and the place of a special type of leadership that emerged in the East European Hasidism. The theories discussed previously that deal with the cleaving to utterances are basically democratic instructions, and the formulations of the Besht's recommendations do not allow an assumption that he restricted their application to a small elite or to any limited Jewish audience. However, as a social movement, and this is obvious already in the writings of his direct students, Hasidism took quite a dramatically different way, turning immediately much less democratic, and its teachings growingly put in sharp relief the fundamental role of the *tzaddiq* as the peak of both the mystical and magical achievements, and as responsible for the well-being of the disciples who could not attain those experiences. From some few points of view, Hasidism as a social phenomenon differs from some of the Besht's more intellectual assumptions, since it has developed much more in the direction that emphasized the primacy of what may be called human mediation of the contact with the divine.[5] As pointed out previously, this vision of the righteous human as drawing down the supernal influx, similar to some of the Besht's teachings quoted previously, ultimately stems from an application of concepts found in late antiquity Hermeticism or medieval astro-magical sources[6] to a Talmudic statement.[7]

Thus, it is better that we speak about an oscillation between the different interpretations of "Hermetic" sources, which informed the specific direction in which the religious structures of Hasidism as a movement went. I resort to the term *oscillation*, which is crucial in my opinion for understanding the phenomenon of Hasidism also after the death of the Besht, when the role of the *tzaddiq* as the leading figure in a certain group or community became well established; many of the teachings of the Besht discussed previously, which are more democratic in their nature and to the best of my knowledge not restricted by the Besht to an elite, were nevertheless preserved in the writings of the Hasidic ideologues of a religious phenomenon that may be called the theory of *tzaddiqism*. Thus, while formulating their influential conception concerning the role of the elite leader of the group, the *tzaddiq*, they at the same time also preserved the much more democratic teachings regarding the emphasis on vocal prayer and *devequt* characteristic of their master. Even in the family of the Besht, most of whose members did not enjoy a special role in the development of this social movement— R. Nahman of Braslav was an exception—the task of the *tzaddiq* became much more prominent than in the teachings of the Besht himself,[8] and this is also the case of R. Jacob Joseph of Polonnoye, a leading figure who did not, however, play the role of *tzaddiq* of a small Hasidic group as his more famous contemporary the Great Maggid did, but nevertheless was a thinker who developed in his writings a sustained elitist approach.[9]

The analysis of one specific theme, though quite an important one, recurrent in the Beshtian traditions as done previously should not, in my opinion, be seen as an exceptional case of perceiving multiple layers and models in the thought of a certain Jewish mystic. It is part of a much more dramatic development in the Kabbalistic literature, what I called the liturgical turn in Safed, and its quite immediate and strong diversification with the emergence of Lurianic Kabbalah, which became more complex as centuries passed and new modes of thinking were adopted by Kabbalists over the years and sometimes substantially adapted to their needs, basically part of their efforts to make sense of their performance of the rituals.

The contribution of the technical-Hermetic or astro-magical approach to the development of Jewish thought, namely to medieval Jewish philosophy and to both Kabbalah and Hasidism, is one important example for such a case, as are the Pythagorean elements. Let me emphasize that I situate the appropriation of the astral-magical model in late medieval Judaism, unlike the theory of Erwin Goodenough, who assumed an impregnation of late antiquity Judaism with Hellenistic mystery religions. The role of the elements belonging to the Hermetic modes of thought in Hasidic spirituality have been either ignored or minimalized by scholars of Hasidism, both in the past and to a great extent also in the present.

It will be difficult to do justice to the spiritual richness of the nascent Hasidism without understanding first the complexity of the Besht's thought, vestiges of Hermeticism being one such significant ingredient, the dynamism of the teachings of the Besht, and their dependence on the rich and variegated intellectual panoramas to which its author has been exposed, both Jewish and non-Jewish.[10] The profound and lasting impact of this seminal figure on so many disciples, independent as some of them intellectually might have been, and on Hasidism in general, for many generations, depends not only on the specific contents of his teachings, but also on their diversity.[11] Some of the figures who wrote the first Hasidic books were interesting personalities in themselves, and each of them has appropriated those teachings of the Besht he was acquainted with, and each has done it in accordance with his own predilections.[12] However, the overwhelming role of the linguistic speculations in so many of the teachings of the direct followers of the Besht, as well as in the Hasidic books written in the generations afterward, especially the writings of R. Menahem Nahum of Chernobyl, R. Aharon ha-Kohen of Apta, R. Ze'ev Wolf of Zhitomir, and then R. Aharon of Zhitomir, for example, convincingly demonstrate that they draw this interest and the details of their discussions from a common source, even when it is not always mentioned explicitly by name. A comparison of Hasidic literature to any other non-Hasidic body of literature—Abraham Abulafia's ecstatic Kabbalah aside— will easily show that it is quite easy to distinguish between them, insofar as the place and the nature of linguistic speculations are concerned. This quite conspicuous trait in Hasidism owes much to the formative role of the teachings of the Besht.

13

ON CONTEMPLATION, SYMBOLISM, AND SCHOLARSHIP OF JEWISH MYSTICISM

As pointed out several times previously, some of the leading scholars in the field have resorted to the category of contemplation in order to describe the approaches that deal with cleaving to the utterances in early Hasidism as well as Kabbalah. This choice is evident also in many of the recent studies in those fields. Such an interpretation is, both philologically and conceptually speaking, in many cases, though not always, quite precarious. One may defend, to be quite generous, such a resort only in the few cases of watching the lights within the vocables, as mentioned in chapter 8 in this volume, or of looking at the written letters of the Tetragrammaton that should not be pronounced, in the case of the Besht or of his contemporaries R. Nahman of Kosov and R. Isaac of Drohovitz. However, the scholars' widespread recourse to contemplation beyond those few instances would require an explanation or a definition of the meaning of this term based on one conceptual tradition or another but, to my best knowledge, such a definition is not found in the studies mentioned previously on early Hasidism, and I am not sure that it is found elsewere insofar as Jewish mysticism is concerned. The scholars' assumption is that the modern reader knows what contemplation is from other accepted, though never mentioned, sources in general scholarship. However, the total absence of such a definition in the description of Jewish mystics is problematic and symptomatic of impositions of conceptual categories as if their meaning is evident to the readers, whereas it is not so sure that it is so for the writers. This scholarly practice is a matter of what I call a transfer of categories from one type of mysticism to another.

Contemplation is a vast spiritual field which changed from one culture to another and was redefined by various practitioners within their different conceptual worldviews, from Plato to the variety of practices in Christian mysticism. A perusal of the various volumes of Bernard McGinn's history of Western Christian mysticism would easily demonstrate the richness and the quite significant changes this term underwent through centuries from Greek philosophers to Christian mystics.[1] While the former is more active, assuming an intellectual effort of the basically unaided human mind, and is connected to some understanding of nature and its sources, the latter assumes a much greater role attributed to some form of revelation or divine intervention in the form of grace. In Christian mysticism contemplation is sometimes related to a higher type of activity than mental prayer, even more so than "crude" oral prayer, conceived to be inferior. In general terms, my opinion is that in Jewish philosophical thought, the tendency is closer to the philosophical type of contemplation.

For the time being, there is no detailed survey of the terms and concepts understood as related to contemplation in Jewish mysticism, a fact that complicates a balanced appreciation of the available scholarly references to the Besht as a contemplative mystic, as part of a wider Jewish tradition. Nevertheless, he was explicitly described as such both by Gershom Scholem and Joseph Weiss, in the context of their discussion of the *devequt*. Let me address some of their discussions that were not addressed previously. In an interesting passage that deals basically with another teaching of the Besht, dealing with the concept of transmigration and the imperative to elevate individual sparks that belong to the soul of a certain *tzaddiq*, Scholem wrote as follows:

> Man's *devekuth* with God (whose significance in Hasidism
> I have analyzed more precisely elsewhere)[2] is a spiritual act

performed through means of concentration and **contemplation.** All spheres of human life, even the most mundane, should be so thoroughly imbued with an awareness of God's presence, that even ordinary and social activities reveal an inward, **contemplative** aspect. This twofold meaning of human actions, as simultaneously visibly external and as carrying a **contemplative** aspect, added an additional tension to religious life. Of course it was likely to arouse a **mental** state that would resemble pure **passivity** to the outside observer. Indeed even the earliest opponents of Hasidism already accused them of a **passive, quietistic** attitude toward life. In many cases the religious tension aroused by the demand for *devekuth* must have been resolved in **passivity**—which, to be sure, was a facile simplification and misinterpretation of this doctrine. But despite its basically **contemplative** character, the ideal of *devekuth* had a strong element of **spiritual activism** for the Baal Shem and his disciples. It is not sufficient for a person to sit lost in **contemplation,** waiting for God's grace to manifest itself. Hasidism emphasizes the special character of **activity** demanded of human beings. The **active** aspect of **contemplative** life finds its finest expression in the Hasidic teaching of the "raising of the holy sparks."[3]

This is indubitably a seminal passage for treating Scholem's understanding of *devequt* in the Besht. As in other cases, the singular mode is prevailing, as if there was one single type of *devequt.* The persistence of the term *contemplation* in this quote is obvious, despite the scholar's feeling that it functions in a manner different from its Christian understandings that are regarded as more passive and more dependent on divine grace. Scholem duly emphasizes also the active aspect of the *devequt,* regarding some of the passive understandings as misinterpretations. In fact, the activism he mentions, the raise of the sparks, is certainly not a novel concept innovated by Hasidism, as it is found already in Lurianic Kabbalah. Aware as he was that the active dimensions of the Besht's thought are fundamental, he resorts to another description of what he called contemplation: "active." Presumably the awareness of the Hasidic mystic that there are sparks within his immediate environment that he should elevate and thus save those components of his one soul, an instruction stemming from Cordoverian and Lurianic Kabbalah, was conceived of as an act of contemplation. Even here, let me emphasize, we speak about a plurality of sparks, and it is hard to assume that we may discern aspects of concentration of one's attention on one spark or another as a sustained effort that may be described as contemplation. Emblematically enough, the acts of contemplation are not conjugated with the vocal rituals, as we have seen previously.

Written in 1957 as part of a lecture at Eranos, for an audience accustomed to concepts like contemplation, this passage precedes his direct students' more emphatic quietistic readings of early Hasidism that have been mentioned previously. Though Scholem understood well the centrality of the activistic aspects of Hasidism, he nevertheless did not deny the presence of moments of passivity and its importance that are connected, at least in some cases, to alleged acts of contemplation, thus opening the possibility that was actually exploited in the subsequent studies of his followers. Indeed, an essentialist understanding of mysticism as a whole as characterized by one major feature, as part of his vision of Hasidism as passivity, has been articulated soon afterward by Joseph Weiss, in some instances in the context of a vision of the Besht as a contemplative figure, though in some cases he points out some important divergences between him and the Great Maggid. So, for example, Weiss wrote:

> We must undersand that the contemplative technique of study involved in *devekuth* is not isolated from the totality of the Baalshem Tov's approach, but is a detail that fits into the complex of the **contemplative system** adopted by the Baalshem Tov during the performance of *mitzwot*, both in physical act, and in Torah study . . .

> the letters of the holy words of the Torah become the
> focal point of the **contemplative** concentration of the
> student.[4]

However, let me point out that it is not the *devequt* by means of
prayer and pronunciation of vocables that is addressed in Scholem's
passage adduced previously, but quite another aspect of the Besht's
teachings, the elevation of the sparks, an important theme stemming mainly from Lurianic Kabbalah. This is the reason why
its claim does not modify our previous discussions dealing with
cleaving to "letters." It is, however, an interesting question if indeed
the elevation of the sparks of the righteous's soul is indeed a matter
of contemplation.[5] This is not only a matter of passivity or activism
that is involved here, but one that deals with the inner reconstitu-
tion of the human soul, which was initially constituted by sparks
that have been spread in the immediate vicinity of the righteous.
This is the personal *tiqqun* of the righteous's soul, a parallel process
to what in Lurianic Kabbalah is the more famous theurgical reparation of the "supernal Adam." According to Scholem's discussions
there, and in several other contexts, the renewed value of *devequt*
was the Hasidic substitute for the Lurianic *tiqqun*, imagined by
him as being rife with strong messianic overtones, which he imagined that Hasidism allegedly neutralized. To what form of contemplation this act of personal reparation corresponds, or what is the
definition of contemplation that allows such a usage, is an issue
that remained in complete darkness.

In fact, the persistence of the category of contemplation in order
to describe the Besht's *devequt* is not an isolated instance in the
history of the study of Jewish mysticism. Also other Jewish mystics
before Hasidism have been described by resorting to an insistent
scholarly category of contemplation, in instances in which, again,
such a term may be quite tenuous. To bring a major example: The
description of Abulafia as a contemplative mystic, whose experience
culminates in an illumination related to divine lights, as offered by
Gershom Scholem already in 1939, is in my opinion an exaggeration,

and I cannot enter here into a detailed analysis of the problematics related to this description.[6] In my opinion the complex anomian techniques proposed by Abulafia and his followers are based on ongoing combinations of letters, their pronounciation according to a certain melodic code, movements of the head and hands, and some form of vocal melody and different rhythms of breathing, most probably influenced by the Yoga breathing technique. These integrated techniques to achieve ecstatic experiences are not based on repetitions, nor are the structures of his techniques resorting to simple formulas or to fixed subjects of concentration in the mind.

My approach to Abulafia's mystical experience suggests a much less conspicuous role to be attributed to acts of contemplation, and this is the reason why I preferred to resort to this term very rarely, in instances when the ecstatic Kabbalist contemplated the three centers of his body.[7] Unlike other Jewish mystics, who contemplated the shape of the letters of the Tetragrammaton, Abulafia combined letters of the divine names with letters of the Hebrew alphabet, or other divine names, and pronounced them, a much more complex and dynamic process that is, in my opinion, far away from what I would call contemplation. Also R. Ḥayyim Vital, another major Kabbalist who was influenced by Abulafia, has been described as articulating contemplative techniques related to recitation.[8]

In fact, according to Scholem, contemplation played quite a central role not only in Hasidism or in ecstatic Kabbalah but in the cognitive formation of Kabbalah in general. According to one of his assessments:

> **All Kabbalistic** systems have their origin in a fundamental distinction regarding the problem of the Divine. In the abstract, it is possible to think of God either as God Himself with reference to His own nature alone or as God in His relation to His creation. However, **all Kabbalists** agree that no religious knowledge of God, even of the most exalted kind, can be gained **except through contemplation** of the relationship of God to creation.[9]

Nota bene: the generalization of the act of contemplation, attributed to all the Kabbalists, and I assume also to Hasidic masters. Elsewhere in a different context, Scholem writes about what he calls "theosophical contemplation," an experience he conceived of as giving birth to Kabbalistic myths.[10] Thus, major aspects of Kabbalah, either ecstatic or theosophical-theurgical, including Lurianism, have been conceived of by Scholem's phenomenology of these literatures as related to some form of contemplative activity. From this point of view, Scholem and his followers' attitude to the Besht too as a contemplative mystic comes as no surprise, as if he was considered to be part of a long tradition of contemplators in Judaism. I consider this overemphasis as part of the new scholarly phenomenon I called Christotropia.

Moreover, in two other brief discussions, Scholem describes also the activity of the Rabbinic scholars as belonging to what he calls the contemplative sphere.[11] In fact Scholem was not the first to understand some forms of Judaism as fraught with a contemplative propensity. An even more comprehensive characterization of the "Jewish mind" as contemplative is found in a statement of an early twentieth-century English theologian and historian of philosophy, Edward Caird.

> The Hebrew mind—he wrote—is intuitive, imaginative, almost incapable of analysis or of systematic connections of ideas. It does not hold its object clearly and steadily before it, or endeavor exactly to measure it; rather it may be said to give itself up to the influence of that which **it contemplates, to identify itself with it and to become possessed by it**. . . . For the most part it expresses its thought **symbolically,** and it constantly confuses the **symbol** with the thing signified, or only corrects the deficiencies of one symbol by setting up another . . . The Greek mind, on the other hand is essentially discursive, analytical, and systematic, governing itself even in its highest flights by the ideas of measure and symmetry, of logical sequence and connection.[12]

I assume that we have here some form of passive contemplation, during which the object of contemplation dominates, according to Caird the thought of the "Hebrews." The affinity between a special type of contemplation[13] characteristic of the "Jewish mind" and the attributing an important role to symbols is especially noteworthy, and we shall revert to this affinity immediately as follows. Like Scholem's confidence that "all Kabbalistic systems" and "all Kabbalists" are related in one way or another to contemplation and symbolism, also Caird's sweeping characterization of the Jews' mind as a separate intellectual entity, as if all Jews were contemplators, are no more than gross totalizing exaggerations. Nonetheless, Caird's characterization of a certain specific type of mystical phenomenon is interesting in itself, though it is hardly specific to the Jewish mystics.

Another well-known scholar of Judaism, Martin Buber, a contemporary of the two aforementioned scholars, had quite an opposite approach, and he distinguished between what he called the "Oriental"—Jews included in this type—and the "Occidental" man, in an interesting manner: the former was described as motor, the latter as sensory; the former more active and expressive, the later more contemplative and inwardly oriented.[14] Thus, given the conflicting approaches of the two giants of twentieth-century scholarship on Judaism to the category of contemplation, it is hardly self-evident that contemplation is indeed central to this religion as a whole, or even for its mystical interpretations.

In fact, there is no need to embrace either of the two approaches in their entirety. A more plausible assumption would be to recognize that in late antiquity Philo of Alexandria can be described as a contemplative thinker. In the early Middle Ages in the so-called Heikhalot Literature, there are some forms of gazing at the divine body, and in some of its later interpretations, also of the divine Glory, though I wonder whether contemplation is the best term for describing those gazings.[15] Later on, in the late Middle Ages, both in Jewish philosophical writings[16] in some early Kabbalistic ones,[17] like in the *Zohar*, for example,[18] and perhaps even in Hasidei

Ashkenaz[19] and in some aspects of Lurianic Kabbalah,[20] we may indeed speak about the presence of some forms of acts that may be described as contemplative.[21] I consider those contemplative moments to play quite a secondary role in the general economy of Judaism, including Jewish mysticism. By and large, in Judaism moments of contemplation are mainly a by-product of the impact of Neoplatonic and Neoaristotelian thought, gravitating around the Platonic *eidos* and the accompanying *theoria* on Jewish philosophy and in some forms of Kabbalah, and in some cases, there are important types of concentration of the mind or of the sense of sight on what may be conceived of as sublime forms, like the structure of the Torah, described as contemplated by either man or God. Scholars have already pointed out that the Rabbinic God's looking to the Torah in order to create the world is reminiscent of Plato's creation by the demiurge that contemplates the world of ideas. On the other hand, let me point out in this context the centrality of the praxis of *theoria* in Orthodox Christianity.

However, insofar as Judaism as a more comprehensive spiritual phenomenon in its long history is concerned, and especially in my opinion also Kabbalah and Hasidism as large bodies of literature, this contemplative scholarly approach is no more than a rare, in my opinion, secondary category of religious life. Religious acts and performances, gestures and sounds, magical and theurgical operations, most of them related to some forms of nomian rituals and techniques to achieve ecstatic or other forms of unusual experiences, are by far more important components of Jewish mysticism. I would say that though not totally incompatible to contemplation, other actions like ritual theurgy, magic, and techniques for achieving experiences—ecstatic, unitive, or other—in many cases related to the centrality of pronunciation of vocables are much more widespread in Kabbalah. They are related to more concrete acts and objects, and at the same time they are less connected to contemplative modes. Even Kabbalistic symbols are much more inviting to action than to contemplation.[22] The attenuation of the dynamic aspects of Jewish mysticism by an overemphasis on the place contemplation occupied, done by scholars consciously or not, represents a neglect of fundamental categories of action that are characteristic of Kabbalah, and to a certain extent also of Hasidism. In terms of Christian thought, in Hasidism *via activa* is indubitably more widespread than *via contemplativa*. An outstanding example of attenuating the magical aspect of Hasidism is the resort to the highly questionable phrase "contemplative magic" as done by Joseph Weiss and, in another context, also by R. J. Z. Werblowsky.[23]

Why, one may ask, has this category moved to the center of the scholarly descriptions of religious phenomena that are, phenomenologically speaking, so different from contemplation? Why are there such unqualified approaches to "contemplation" as if omnipresent in Kabbalah, as if indeed contemplative acts were almost ubiquitous in Jewish mystical literatures? I believe that this is a significant question that can be answered in quite a plausible manner. In my opinion Gershom Scholem, who was the main scholarly promoter of the shift toward a description of Jewish mysticism as contemplative, has adopted it together with the emphasis on the primacy of the symbolic discourse from Christian Kabbalah, more precisely from a seminal statement of Johannes Reuchlin, one of his intellectual heroes. This early sixteenth-century seminal figure contributed much to Scholem's understanding of the phenomenology of Kabbalah, directly and indirectly.

"Kabbalah—Reuchlin wrote—is a matter of divine revelation handed down to [further] the contemplation of God and the separated forms, contemplations bringing salvation. [Kabbalah] is a symbolic reception."[24]

Salvation by contemplation means an individual form of redemption—an issue indeed relevant for some forms of Kabbalah and Hasidism—and I assume that we have here some form of Neoplatonic impact on Reuchlin, who projected it onto Jewish Kabbalah as a whole. Interestingly enough, contemplation and symbolism occur here together just as in the passage of Caird, and in the Scholemian perception of Kabbalah in general. Though the linkage between contemplation and symbolism is not always explicit in scholarship, the recurrence of the two categories is quite substantial and reveals some form of selective affinity of the scholars.

Moreover, elsewhere in the same book Reuchlin distinguishes between the active life of the Talmudists versus the contemplative life of the Kabbalists.[25] In an interesting discussion this major humanist claims that while the Kabbalists elevate the lower things to the world of the intellect by means of their contemplation, the Talmudists relate the higher things to the lower ones, and not *vice versa.*[26] Sabbath is described as the time to be dedicated to contemplation but also as the symbol of the world-to-come. For Reuchlin, there is an important common denominator shared by contemplation and by symbols: like symbols, contemplation was described by the Christian Kabbalist as elevating the soul or the intellect to the supernal world. According to an additional passage in this book, the Kabbalists are removing the material aspects from things, allowing the understanding of their spiritual aspect by means of contemplation, and symbolism is also mentioned in this case.[27] By putting together concepts like symbols, contemplation, and Kabbalah, Reuchlin follows the path opened some few years earlier by a convert to Christianity, the Ashkenazi Kabbalist Paulus Riccius, the former's older contemporary:

> The Kabbalists and those who are called sons of the prophets—he says—proceed from the connection of the human mind with the higher and purer one. They take the **symbols** and the elements that are connected with the higher spirit as far as they can use them for their purpose. They meditate on the holy letters by **contemplating** their numerical value, their form, position, permutation, and combination, by thinking of their genus and referring and bringing them to the holiness of higher and eternal truths. No Kabbalist believes that he has completely exhausted or will completely understand the holy communication of the prophets. He intends only one thing: to convert his soul from earthly matter

through the concentrated and repeated exercise of fan-
tasy, reason, and mind and be transported to the upper
forces in order to join with them.[28]

Though this is a relatively fair description of some aspects of
ecstatic Kabbalah, especially the emphasis on reason and mind,
it hardly helps understanding Kabbalah in general. Riccius combines here elements stemming from different Kabbalistic schools,
as if they display a unified approach. Especially interesting from
our point of view here is the absence of a reference to the vocal
dimensions of letters. Riccius, and following him Reuchlin, were
concerned in forms of contemplation rather than in the actual performance of the rites as envisioned by Kabbalists.

In another seminal discussion Reuchlin regards contemplation
as one of the bases of Pythagorean philosophy, which he alleged
was taken over by Pythagoras from Kabbalah that he conceived of
as an ancient type of philosophy.[29] Though claiming that he recon-
structs the lost Pythagorean philosophy by turning to Kabbalah,
which was in his opinion the alleged source of that philosophy,
all this as part of the more general concept of *prisca theologia*,
Reuchlin in fact instilled in the understanding of this Jewish lore
as a whole much of the Neoplatonism and Pythagoreanism that
were *en vogue* in the Florentine Renaissance, and influenced him.[30]
This unqualified vision of so many forms of Kabbalah as a contemplative form of mysticism has reverberated in many intellectual
circles because of the great influence that *De Arte Cabalistica* had
since its publication. In fact, as I pointed out years ago, modern
scholarship of Kabbalah adopted Renaissance conceptualizations,
in some cases as done by Christian Kabbalists, and those conceptualizations deeply impacted the deep structure of scholarship to
this day. However, for our purpose here, it is only one of these
reverberations that is pertinent.

As I claimed in several instances, Gershom Scholem adopted
a pansymbolic perception of Kabbalah, and a symbolic vision of
mysticism in general,[31] and argued that his resort to this description

of Kabbalah had been deeply influenced by Reuchlin's view.[32] Not that Scholem was totally unaware of the existence of possible differences existing between what he considered to be Jewish versus Christian contemplations, but he was inclined to emphasize the pictorial nature of the latter, while putting in relief the abstract nature of the former.[33] Letters and divine names, most probably their graphical representation, the main objects of contemplation according to his vision of Kabbalah, are conceived of by Scholem as more abstract topics. In fact, this is the adoption of the centrality of the Platonic theory of *theoria*: one ascends from the material to the spiritual archetype.

However, from the phenomenological point of view, written letters as signs are basically similar to any iconic representation of the divine world. They may be, in many cases indeed, but not always, less anthropomorphic. I would, however, not insist so much on the trait of abstraction as reflecting the main difference between the Christian types of contemplation, basically of Platonic origins, and Abraham Abulafia's techniques and some of the Kabbalistic and Hasidic practices. My assumption is that in Jewish mysticism the mobile and changing objects that are part of the dominant techniques, nomian and anomian, played a more important role, including combinations of letters and their pronunciation, and that these objects were much less amenable to the phenomena commonly understood as contemplation. Also, the multiplicity of the objects of adherence, namely the different vocables, marks a dramatic difference in comparison to the more philosophical and Christian approaches to contemplation, including hesychasm, or even the Hindu ones that sometimes gravitate much more around sounds as part of a technique.[34]

Abraham Abulafia was far less concerned with contemplating written letters than manipulating them along with the pronounced and the mental ones. He recommended a technique that has an initial stage of writing letters and then combining them, but the more advanced stages passed to spoken and then to mental letters, which were combined vocally and then mentally, done in a certain

rhythmic manner.[35] This is the case also of the dynamic and rit-
ualist nature of the Kabbalistic theosophy, which invites another
understanding of this type of Kabbalistic intention, different in very
many instances from contemplation. Theosophy, often conjugated
with theurgy, is based on concentration for a longer period on stable
objects or concepts, while the Kabbalistic theosophy has multiple
centers of interest, and there are dynamic relations between them,
and between them and the human ritual activities.[36]

Let me clarify my position once more: I do not attempt to
dissociate the ecstatic Kabbalah, the theosophical-theurgical one,
or Hasidism from cultivating some moments of contemplation,
sometimes influenced by Platonism, but I doubt whether the generalizations used by scholars when resorting to the category of contemplation in so many areas in Jewish mysticism are indeed useful
for understanding the complexity of Hasidism. I assume that the
emphasis on the dromena, namely on forms of activities which
have religious valences, was conceived of as fraught with spiritual
values in themselves. Though one may emphasize the union of the
soul and God found within the vocables as some form of non-
duality, the mentioning of the "worlds" in this context problematizes such an understanding.

In this context the Besht's emphasis on the act of pronunciation—and in other contexts on combinations of letters, a topic that
will be dealt with elsewhere in more detail[37]—represents a continuation of what I would describe as a non-contemplative sort of
spiritual practices found in Judaism. Let me adduce one example,
drawn from R. Aharon of Apta's *Keter Shem Tov*:

> Before he begins to pray, he should reflect [upon the
> fact that] that he is prepared to die while he is praying
> as a result of his [intense] concentration. There are, in
> fact, some [Hasidim] whose concentration in prayer is
> so intense that, were nature left to itself, they would die
> after uttering no more than four or five words in God's
> presence, blessed be He. . . . In reality, it is by God's

> great mercy, Blessed be He, that strength is given to him
> in order to complete his prayer and yet remain alive.[38]

The intensity and the abruptness of the experience related to vocal prayer, which may even become in some cases a lethal effect, differ in my opinion from what is commonly understood as a contemplative mode that is a much more prolonged process. We may speak about a short trigger, consisting in the pronunciation of some few words that suffice in order to induce immediately an experience of divine presence, not a mode of pondering on the meaning of the words of prayer for an extended period of time. The primacy of vocal performance as a pre-axial form of religiosity reflects the lingering of non-contemplative approaches to religious life in Judaism in general and its intensification in Hasidism. The strong accent put in modern scholarship on what can be called the axial aspects of Hasidism was detrimental for the proper understanding of its important pre-axial components, and only when those different kinds of elements are taken into consideration together in proper proportions will a more precise picture of this movement emerge.[39] In order to be clear: I was concerned previously with specific, though in my opinion quite seminal, aspects of the Beshtian theory of prayer and studying Torah as practices that are vocal and thus non-contemplative. This does not mean that in other cases, where the vocal activity is marginal or totally absent, contemplation would not be an appropriate term, even in the case of the Besht. So, for example, this is the case in some few traditions related to gazing at the face of beautiful women in order to attain a sublime experience of the source of beauty, the divine feminine power, an approach that ultimately stems from a Platonic source, as I have elaborated in my study "Female Beauty."

Now it seems quite plausible that the contemplative depiction of Kabbalah as a whole, found in the same passage by the aforementioned Christian Kabbalist, has also reverberated in Scholem's phenomenology of Jewish mysticism in general, including that of early Hasidism and then on scholarship that adopted Scholem's penchant, including some of the most recent studies in the field. A perusal of Hasidic texts, especially those of the Besht, demonstrates that we may detect some important vestiges of Neoplatonism, and this is the reason why the path of contemplation is certainly not alien to some aspects of Hasidism.[40] However, when the category of contemplation is imposed, rather indiscriminately, also on teachings that deal with vocal performances, in many cases performed with alacrity, as the Besht's explicitly recommends, and on the instructions to cleave to utterances, as were discussed previously, it is prone to result in a series of misunderstandings. When seen in the specific social framework of the Hasidic leaders, which includes their communal commitments and performance of rituals—and this is the case also in the mature life of the Besht—in comparison to what we know about the lives of the Christian contemplatives, the scholarly claims for a significant role of the contemplative dimensions in Hasidism turn quite problematic, and in any case, disproportionate. The statistical density of the more concrete, downward vectors in Hasidism are neglected in these Neoplatonic readings of Hasidism.

Though in the case of some Kabbalists, resorting to acts that belong to the category of contemplation would be indeed more pertinent, I doubt whether a general understanding of the Besht, or of Hasidism in general, as if espousing contemplation as a central spiritual activity, is justifiable, as is the view of Schatz-Uffenheimer: "Contemplative prayer became the spiritual message par excellence of Hasidism."[41] Unfortunately, no definition of what contemplation is has been presented by scholars in order to make sense of such an exaggerated conceptualization. The scholarly invocation of the category of contemplation with regard to the activities of certain kabbalists may be more pertinent, but I doubt the validity of understanding the Ba'al Shem Tov, or Hasidism in general, as espousing an act that corresponds to what is commonly regarded as contemplation as a central spiritual activity.

To summarize: What may appear *prima facie* to be a demand for some changes in academic terminology and minor mistakes in

English translations of simple Hasidic terms does, in fact, accumulatively, amount to a totally different picture of the *devequt* to "letters" than the one ventilated in many leading studies conceived to be serious analyses of East European Jewish mysticism. Moreover, by being aware of the archaeology of some of the basic terms used by scholars to describe the field they investigate, in the case of Hasidism "contemplation" and "quietism," their dependence on the Christian understanding of the nature of mysticism, especially in the form of Christian Kabbalah, more precisely that of Riccius's and Reuchlin's, and its reverberations in the nineteenth-century culture in Central Europe, especially via Franz Molitor's book, may become more obvious than it is in any case.[42] In order not to dissolve the stark differences between various forms of Jewish mysticism, between the primary texts and their interpretations, and between these forms of mysticism in Judaism and the various forms of Christian mysticism, a much greater awareness of the significance of the terms used by scholars and their careful definition are strictly necessary.

To be sure: the substantial reliance of the conceptual apparatus dealing with the phenomenology of early Hasidism on two categories like contemplation and quietism in quite an exaggerated manner is not an exception in the field of Jewish mysticism. These categories should be added to resorting to other major categories, used by scholars in order to approach other areas of Jewish mysticism, which have been depicted by using, indiscriminately, the categories of symbolism, of Mariology, or that of incarnation, without a solid philological foundation.[43] By doing so, the specificities of many central dimensions of Jewish mysticism have been ignored, mitigated, and from some points of view even obliterated, especially the performative ones, the theurgical, and the magical altogether and, in our case, the vocal dimension. The previous analyses of the manner in which, in my opinion, scholars misinterpreted some crucial aspects of the Besht's seminal teachings as if they were dealing with cleaving to—namely contemplating—written letters instead of cleaving to speeches constitute just one more fascinating example of reading the texts against their explicit declared intention, but in accordance with the grain of the modern scholars.[44]

My main problem is not only whether resorting to a certain category is good or bad—after all, all categories are approximations—but much more whether the category has been well-defined by the scholar before it has been applied, and even more whether its relative place in the general economy of a certain literature is addressed in an appropriate manner by the scholar and framed in the specific school, without generalizations as to the nature of Jewish mysticism, Hasidism, or Kabbalah, as a whole, and without other exaggerations.

Let me be as clear as possible: in my opinion the misunderstandings mentioned previously are not just the result of the scholars' inability to understand other cultures, or of a strong Eurocentric bias, but much more of their unreflective and inertial resorting to a series of terms and interpretations already used in the studies of founding scholars that could be easily avoided by a critical approach of reading the original texts and their misinterpretations. However, the propensity of scholars to feel Europeans—Western in Schechter's statement, or central Europeans—created the drive to read the texts against their clear intention though they can be understood easily by any reader of Hebrew. However, the Besht and all his immediate followers were figures active in some parts of Eastern Europe or, if someone would like to use this term, in the center of Eurasia, and their impact was felt first mainly there.

On the other side, the terms Europe and Eurocentrism, as they are used by recent writers dealing with what they call Orientalism are, in my opinion, also basically misleading ones, what I call Occidentalist epithets used by Orientalist ideologues, since from the cultural point of view there was more than one—allegedly homogenous—Europe. The Besht was indubitably active in a part of the world which may be described, metaphorically and also geographically, as the middle of Eurasia, and in any case in another "Europe," one of a very complex religious space where a variety of "non-European" elements have been influential, like the Shamanic, the Sufi ones, and the various Altaic tribes: Changos, Turks, or Tatars, all speaking different Altaic languages, and a place where axial and pre-axial approaches were operating together.[45] As I proposed in a recent study, Hasidism emerged in a geographical region that is a crossroad of several European empires and Asian ones, each of them ascending and declining, and the impact of the latter should not be underestimated or totally neglected as part of a Eurocentric approach.[46] The rather idiosyncratic and unusually diversified background from the religious point of view, what I called in my studies the "panorama," has hardly been recognized in scholarship of Hasidism, which preferred simple explanations for the emergence of the earliest stages of this popular movement, be they Orientalist or Occidentalist.[47]

14

ORALITY AND THE EMERGENCE
OF HASIDISM MOVEMENT

The emphasis on speech-acts, both the traditional and the more secular ones, as religiously paramount practices, at least in potence, should be seen in a broader framework than just prayer and vocal study. This is not just a matter of some instructions of the Besht as preserved by his most important followers but also of additional dimensions of orality. In eighteenth-century Hasidism, we may discern an important turn, which reestablished the centrality of the direct oral contact between the religious leader and the members of his group as a main religious moment for instruction and advice. Unlike the contemporary Rabbinic elites and most of the Kabbalists in the past—Isaac Luria aside—who resorted mainly to written forms of communication, books, and epistles mainly in Hebrew in order to formulate their ideas and establish their status in the Jewish society, Hasidic masters since the mid-eighteenth century turned to oral communication in vernacular, namely in Yiddisch, as the main instrument of disseminating Hasidic teachings and for the sake of establishing their privileged role in the new Jewish Hasidic group they shaped, among persons who did not know Hebrew.[1]

Let me adduce a legend that reflects this strong propensity toward orality, which circulated in early Hasidism:

> There was a man who wrote down the torah of the Besht that he heard from him. Once the Besht saw a demon walking and holding a book in his hand. He

said to him: "What is the book that you hold in your hand?" He answered him: "This is the book that you have written." The Besht then understood that there was a person who was writing down his torah. He gathered all his followers and asked them: "Who among you is writing down my torah?" The man admitted it and he brought the manuscript to the Besht. The Besht examined it and said: There is not even a single word [*dibbur*] here that is mine.[2]

The demonic interlocutor of the Besht is a studious and curious reader who attempts to keep himself up to date with any interesting spiritual development in Judaism. It seems that Jewish culture was so imprinted with the concept of the importance of books that even its demons were imagined to be avid readers.[3] In this particular instance, however, involving as it does a story that in my opinion is emblematic of the nature of early Hasidism, the very emergence of a book in the name of the Besht has been regarded as being quite questionable: the "founder" of Hasidism was imagined as trying to preserve the oral form of his teachings as quintessential. In fact, in this case the demon focuses his attention on a composition that the author himself would take to be an extreme falsification of his thought. What went wrong is not a matter of bad intentions or sheer misunderstandings of a disciple: it seems that, as in Plato's famous critique of writing, it is the very nature of the medium that is imagined to be problematic, and not the faulty manner of its performance.

According to this legend, the Besht is allegedly describing his activity as speeches, not as ideas that were distorted. In this context let me turn to a tradition found in the classical book of the great-grandson of the Besht, R. Nahman of Bratzlav. The famous descendant quotes a tradition related to the founder of Hasidism as follows: Also animals and birds have a voice and a chirp, but the basic difference between them and the humans is the speech by means of the five sources in the vocal apparatus, as it has been articulated in *Sefer Yetziyrah*, as we have seen also previously in some cases in Cordovero and da Vidas. Thus, the human is distinct from animals by the capacity to transform the voice and the chirp into utterances or speeches. In this context he indicates that in the Beshtian tradition it is said that "he was hearing speeches from the voice of the violin, since he did [namely transformed] the chirps, [into] speeches."[4] It is, therefore, the vocal—actually the verbal—capacity, not the mental aspect of the term *dibbur*, as is the case in so many texts in medieval Jewish philosophy, which concerns both the Besht and his descendent.

Though adopting technically the Aristotelian definition of man as expressed in Hebrew in Jewish sources, as a living, intelligent, and dying entity, where *medabber* means intelligent, the previous passage avoids this understanding by an emphasis on the capacity of speaking as fraught with mystical and magical valences. This emphasis should be seen in a larger context, of the capacity attributed to the Besht to elevate speeches as part of an ordinary conversation, which we have discussed previously. Such a transformative understanding of the Besht's vocal activity is important also for understanding his magical-linguistic activity and his appropriation of tales from the non-Jewish world and their reworking. Those attitudes are part of what I called the mystique of the mouth, or the mystique of pronunciation, evolving from the brief statements in *Sefer Yetziyrah*, which were interpreted in the light of magical effects of speech, stemming from different intellectual sources.

However, this decisive turn to orality is related to a series of equally important issues. The Besht addressed his audiences basically in the vernacular Yiddisch, and the same seems to have been true of the vast majority of early Hasidic masters, the boundaries of the early Hasidic communities coinciding with the locations where this language was spoken. This turn toward the vernacular is not only a matter of the ordinary personal contacts of the masters of nascent Hasidism with their flock, but also of the sermons they delivered, though the latter have been committed later on to writing in Hebrew.[5] Thus, a popular movement emerged in a geographical area where the Jewish population was using their vernacular, and the major tool of communication was this language, rather than Hebrew. It should be pointed out that according to some stories related to the Besht, he was acquiring his knowledge by listening to what people were reading for him loudly, though in this case the language was Hebrew.[6]

In other words, the tensions found in some medieval forms of Judaism between mental and vocal activities, and to an extent between visual and verbal elements, were resolved in most of the Ba'al Shem Tov's teachings in favor of the verbal and the vocal, without, however, entirely suppressing the eventual presence of mental or visual elements in his experiences, issues that will be more accentuated among his followers.[7] Gaining a better understanding of his teachings demands attention to both aspects in their proper proportions, and that requires a complex scholarly approach emphasizing precise and detailed description of the dominant elements while not ignoring the secondary ones. Thus, for example, an exhaustive inventory and examination of the Besht's traditions reveals that what scholars translated as "letters" in so many cases actually refers to vocables, and to speech-acts, which are more important than the semantic understanding of words, and *devequt*, cleaving, has but little to do with contemplation.

Though a hypostatization of speech is at times discernible in the Ba'al Shem Tov's teachings,[8] to the best of my knowledge those linguistic hypostases are not described as visual objects of contemplation. It is only in the case of the letters of the divine name, which should not be pronounced, that one may discern some elements that one can interpret visually, though I would say that this is related much more to the induction of the feeling of the divine presence.[9] To be sure, Hasidism was not exactly an adumbration of the mid-twentieth-century poetic movement of letterism that flourished in France, nor a Paulinian enchantment with the concept of letters that kill, as found in the second epistle to Corinthians 3:6. It was concerned with vitalizing the vocal Jewish rituals, and this emphasis should be kept in mind when attempting to describe it as a spiritual movement. Unlike the mental, grounded in outstanding individuals, which may divide more than unify as the history of philosophy as a critical enterprise amply shows, the vocal elements in the ritual are serving as a shared denominator, preserving a communal life.

In short, Hasidism as a social movement succeeded for a variety of reasons not dealt with here, including social, economic, and political ones. In drawing upon a spectrum of earlier and newer concepts to shape its spiritual configuration, however, the Ba'al Shem Tov and other early Hasidic masters placed greater emphasis upon vocal activities performed with devotion than upon mental achievements or contemplative practices, and this made Hasidism attractive to a wider and less learned audience. In my opinion, Hasidism rested wholly neither upon a Platonic depreciation of this world, accomplished by contemplating the supernal one, as claimed by Scholem,[10] nor upon the sanctification of this world, as claimed by Buber,[11] but upon a variety of combinations of the two attitudes in different proportions, characterized by the accompanying of human acts with a practice of devotion to and a pursuit of the union with God.[12] Scholarly speaking, none of the two main approaches is better or worse, and it is not my intention here to criticize or to praise Hasidic phenomena, higher or lower, but to try to understand them separately and in their syntheses. Unlike scholars like Schechter and Buber that were judging the relevance of Hasidic literature and life in accordance to some modern conviction, as to what religion is ideally, I try to stay away from passing judgment.

To be sure: the substantial reliance of scholars on the conceptual apparatus transferred from the study of Christianity that deals with the phenomenology of early Hasidism, which puts in relief two categories like contemplation and quietism in quite an exaggerated manner, is not an exception in the field of Jewish mysticism. These categories should be added to the use of another recent major category, utilized by some few scholars in order to approach other areas of Jewish mysticism, which have been depicted by using the term incarnation.[13] By doing so, some of the specificities of many central dimensions of Jewish mysticism have been ignored, sometimes mitigated, and from some points of view even obliterated, especially the centrality of the performative ones, whose meaning may be described as theurgical and magical, and applied in so many cases to the performance of commandments. Early Hasidism, especially the Besht's traditions, has been spiritualized, in my opinion, in modern scholarship much beyond what the salient texts actually point to. Reuchlin's approach, as described in the previous chapter is, however, not an *a priori* Kantian category, but had some definite religious and philosophical intentions in mind, determined by his specific time and place, but it nevertheless inspired modern scholars to an indiscriminate application of categories that were poorly defined and uncritically imposed on texts whose axiology is essentially different. This transfer of categories determined the new interpretation of Kabbalah, and Hasidism as part of it, in terms consonant to the majority culture in Central Europe.

15

CONCLUDING REMARKS

I hope that I have justified my resort to the term *broken* in the title of this study. The Besht used a variety of themes that can be depicted as the result of broken theologies, and he himself adopted elements stemming from more than one single broken theology. However, at the end I would like to address the theological part of the title. What is shared by most of the Beshtian traditions cited and analyzed previously is the conjugation of vocal rites and some theologumena. This conjugation is quintessential for understanding the Besht, and the basic character of his treatment should be understood as such: an attempt to address various theological issues when strengthening the rituals, rather than as an area of systematic discourse that is independent.

Intellectually speaking, I would say that theology is a tragic enterprise. Meticulously mapping the unknown on the basis of ancient texts or on the grounds of reports of experiences of people the theologians never met and whose languages they did not know, the result was deemed as reliable, dogmatic, and often religiously indispensable and implemented by force; theology must also be different from other theologies, which means to be polemical. The confidence with which the unknown has been charted hides, in my opinion, a strong insecurity. After all, in the earliest founding sources of Judaism, Christianity, or Islam, there is nothing like significant theological discourses, but only belated theologizations of scriptures that are hardly consistent with their canonical writings. It is hard to deny the possibility that many of the theologians did not understand at all the absurdity of their arranging in sharp systemic structures the conceptually variegated canonical writings sometimes composed in languages they never knew, in places they never visited, and yet they nevertheless deemed to exhaust their alleged coherent significance.

However, when done out of strong beliefs, or because of religious-political needs, there is some form of *raison d'être* for those tragic efforts. In an age of belief, what may be imagined nowadays as being absurd may have been understood as fraught with a deep meaning. When the historical circumstances of the emergence, the composition, the canonization, and the history of reception of the sacred scriptures become more and more available, their diversity is put more and more in sharper relief, and the document-theory related to the different schools that are represented in the Hebrew Bible is a fine example for diversification.[1]

The ongoing multiplication and diversification of the theologizations since late antiquity, namely the emergence of a variety of comprehensive systems, each claiming to explicate the alleged depth and hidden structure of a religion that developed over centuries, is done in conditions of exegetical, conceptual, polemical, and traditional constraints and pressures. It is certainly not just a matter of the free exercise of one's personal convictions, his private *imaginaire*, or one's idiosyncratic psychology. They are complex and often convoluted constructs attempting to organize the chaos of what is conceived as pertinent, actually selected data. A critical inspection of those belated constructs can easily discern the tensions, the supressions, or the selective grids, the agon with the older traditions. This is one of the reasons why so many great theologians were treated as heretics, from Origen to Luther in Christianity, or the attitude of Jews to Philo of Alexandria and to Maimonides in Judaism, and this is also a part of the tragic dimension of theology.

However, the continuation of the process of theologization done by those believers in the genre of scholarship is not just tragic, but I would describe it as tragicomic. The conceptually artificial constructs of the past should be understood as such, not as conveying some deep coherence or hidden wisdom, whose psychological or philosophical underpinnings should be unearthed. My perusal of the comprehensive theosophies of either Cordovero or Luria shows much of their conceptual fluidity and complexity, which has not been sufficiently noticed in scholarship.[2] A scholar that attempts to find out solely the internal coherence of a certain body of religious writings as if it necessarily consists a system, namely a broader coherence that allegedly unifies several theosophical systems, constitutes a continuation of the theological work of the believers, like the Renaissance authors' concept of *prisca theologia*. From a critical point of view, this is, often times, intellectually futile since it does not help in understanding each of the systems, if systems they are, separatedly, but is prone to confuse or to simplify important discrepancies between them.

As I see the difference between theology and critical scholarship, it consists in the effort of the latter to discern differences, tensions, and the problems created by the analyzed authors' effort to build a system, not by leveling the differences between them, as the former strives to do. A scholar is tragicomic because he works, unnecessarily, as an unbelieving believer or, in the case of Judaism, as a secular Kabbalist or Hasid, and attempts to create a symphony out of cacophonies, but this time with modern conceptual tools.[3] This scholarly theology is an apologetic and artificial enterprise that is prone to generate new theologies, undreamed by the religious theologians of the past under scrutiny, by the dint of homogenization. At least one basic change can be found in the enterprise of building secular theologies: those scholars are not prone to become heretics.

This homogenization is done by modern tools, or a modern conceptual apparatus, like the comparative, philosophical, or psychological, or by the traditional one, the theological. As we have seen in chapter 8 in this volume, Schatz-Uffenheimer has imposed the visualization of letters during prayer, found in a late collection of traditions from the school of the Great Maggid, as if representative for the overall contemplative trend in early Hasidism. Or, more recently, to cite a brief statement from one of Elliot R. Wolfson's discussions of Hasidism:

> "The pietistic ideal is based on perceiving the immanence
> of the divine in all things, but this perception, in turn,
> rests on contemplating the spiritual luminosity clothed
> in the letters."[4]

Here the general immanentism is juxtaposed, actually imposed, on what I called the "mystique of recitation," as if they are identical or part of the same approach, and then an act of contemplation has been imposed on acts related to letters, namely what is considered to be written letters.[5]

However, there is no one single ideal of the pietists, but only if someone is imposing it forcefully on diverse discussions and theories, homogenizing them. As seen previously, letters are rarely in Hasidic instructions the graphical shapes that are contemplated, but actually vocables. The broken theologies, formulated separately and perhaps belonging to different stages of the development of a certain figure, should be left as they are, not be "completed" by a "scholarly" synthesis, creating a comprehensive theology, if the author does not express such a plan or a will, or if there are hints in the different texts that invite a supplemental reading of different texts. It seems much better to let the separate texts speak for themselves without "helping" them to express a fuller or a unified type of theology, and this is the reason for the specific form of treatments that we adopted previously: to separate traditions and analyze them separately before attempting to harmonize or generalize.

Instead of these totalizing tendencies, I would like to pay attention to divergences, which transform more comprehensive theologies in broken types of discourse, or the resort to theologumena from a variety of different theologies. As part of the long-range contest between mental dimensions of human activities, basically stemming from Greek philosophical sources, and the performative aspects related to the commandments, Hasidic masters offered their varying syntheses which preferred the latter to the former, while scholars assessed another type of balance, overemphasizing the visual and the noetic/contemplative dimension. Like other aspects of the investigation of Judaism, Hasidism also suffered from what I call a massive transfer of categories that imposed questions and categories taken from cultures having different conceptual structures, Greek and Christian. Some of those elements were actually alien to the Hasidic masters, but they have been introduced under the impact of fashionable academic jargon, and I have analyzed in some detail elsewhere such an example of introducing negativity in a nonexistent Hasidic statement, which nevertheless had a nice career in recent times.[6]

To resort to a comparison taken from Jewish culture: one may ask questions related to Maimonides's thought as if relevant to Hasidism, and the answers of such questions will be biased by a mental propensity, as indeed happened.[7] However, questions can certainly be asked from adopting another perspective, grounded in a religiosity which was not necessarily known by the Hasidim, an approach that I called perspectivism.[8] A similar approach has been adopted recently by Shaul Magid, without using this term, an attitude that I would call "incarnational perspectivism." This means to inspect Hasidic statements about the *tzaddiq* from the perspective of a theory of incarnation. In principle, there is nothing bad in such an approach. However, the problem with it is that the questions or the perspectives are prone to predetermine the answers, especially if a very large literary corpus is inspected and the criteria for selection of texts and eliciting a significant answer, phenomenological or historical, are not sufficiently articulated, and possible alternative interpretations are not proposed.

However, we should be aware that the problem with perspectivism is that it may represent not just a scholarly tool, emerging out of curiosity to learn another type of culture, but a tool by a scholar that is theologically invested in promoting a certain type of historical process, which is implicitly sustained by a specific form of perspectivist reading that is biased, or a seeker of a personal or communal theology. Needless to say, one scholar may embrace more than one perspective to address the views of the Besht or of Hasidism in general, provided he masters the details of each of the perspectives, their strong and weak points. A multiple type of perspectivism is preferable, since it may correct biases found in one of those perspectives which may amount to a certain type of theologization, exaggeration, or totalization.

However, even more important is to be able to read the Hasidic texts in the original language and against their salient backgrounds. The fallacious manner in which the simple Hebrew term *'otiyyot* or *ruḥaniyyut* have been understood shows that generations of scholars may repeat the same erroneous semantic choice on the one hand, while ignoring the basic ritualistic context of vocal recitation on the other. However, the uncritical repetitions of many mistakes in the past and the present can be detected only when concentrating the effort to a specific question in a specific thinker, before offering totalizing statements in areas where conceptual and linguistic fluidity is so widespread.

Let me summarize some of the findings we reached in the previous chapters: a Christian-like picture of Kabbalah emerged since the late fifteenth century in Christian Kabbalah, especially in the sixteenth century with Johann Reuchlin; it was mediated by the nineteenth-century thinker Franz Molitor, and adopted then by Gershom Scholem, who later on also transferred it to his understanding of Hasidism. Then the contemplative, ocularcentric, and quietist aspects were adopted and elaborated in many details by Scholem's direct students, as mentioned in chapter 1, and finally this picture has been adopted and adapted to an incarnationalist penchant evident in the very recent scholarship of Hasidism in the United States, consonant not with the content of the Hasidic texts but with the hidden agenda of scholars living in the recent ecumenical situation, or even trying to promote it. This historical-phenomenological trajectory can be understood as the result of the scholars' saturation with Western culture, as mentioned previously in the citation from S. Schechter, and I would say also from an effort, conscious or not, to adapt scholarship in the field of Judaica to what may be *en vogue* on the modern intellectual market, and to make it available to Western colleagues in the academy. Unlike

Schechter's predecessors, who were described as saturated, today we may better speak about super-saturation.

On the other hand, my approach puts a strong emphasis on another trajectory that assumes that some significant aspects of Kabbalah relevant for the topics discussed previously should take much more into consideration the magical and astrological components that were added to the extant explanations of the rituals. Inspired by a variety of the Hellenistic and astro-magical Arabic material, flowering since the ninth century in the Near East and North Africa, it was adopted to a certain extent in medieval Kabbalah in Spain, and especially since the late fifteenth century in Florence by R. Yohanan Alemanno, as discussed in my *Kabbalah in Italy* and later on, under Alemanno's impact, by R. Abraham Yagel. In the mid-sixteenth century in Safed, in the writings of Cordovero and his followers **those astro-magical elements** had been even more integrated though in a qualified manner, and so those components reached some eighteenth-century Jewish authors, especially the Besht and early Hasidic figures.[9] However, those specific elements that deal with ritual sonority had not been integrated so much in the Christian understandings of Kabbalah—though some of them had been adopted by Marsilio Ficino—and they did not impact Scholem's picture of the field of Kabbalah or of Hasidism. Especially remarkable is the synthesis between the theories of inherent spiritual powers—stemming probably from al-Kindi—and the more dominant astro-magical texts.

From some points of view my picture is closer to the approach of Aby Warburg's school to understanding culture, which mainly deals with transmission of the Hellenistic modes of thought, especially magic and astrology, to the Middle Ages and the Renaissance.[10] However, while this school had at its disposition many images, in the Jewish culture those are very rare, and the transmission is, as seen previously, basically of terms and conceptual structures. I am much more concerned with elements that resist reduction to modern scholarly categorizations and require another terminology in order to describe them in their idiosyncrasy, as is the case with what I called the mystique of pronunciation as discussed previously.

In a way, the various Hellenistic deviations from the Platonic model, emphasizing what can be called an occult approach, found their ways also in Neoplatonic texts like Jamblichus, for example, or in some aspects of Hermeticism, and created a certain tension between the mental and the concrete performative elements, and this complexity reverberates also in some cases in Kabbalah and Hasidism. To be sure: the Hellenistic material is quite complex, since it includes many philosophical assumptions within the occult material. Moreover, there are clear differences between texts like the Hermetic ones and that of Jamblichus, since the former deals with more material components, as is evident in his *On the Mysteries of the Egyptians*, III: 28–31.

Quite naturally, the ethical-Kabbalistic literature, concerned with modes of behavior, transmitted much of the earlier material adopted by Kabbalists in a more simplified and accessible manner. In this context, the contribution of Mendel Piekarz to unearthing the significant impact of this widespread literature on early Hasidism in his monograph *The Beginning of Hasidism* is a decisive move, which should however be refined by pointing out the sources of the ethical books, mainly in the thought of Cordovero and some pre-Safedian Kabbalistic sources. To his important findings much material can be added, especially the impact of the liturgical literature, like R. Isaiah Horowitz's voluminous commentary on the prayerbook, *Sha'ar ha-Shamayim*, which was an important conduit of Cordoverian views, as well as some earlier Kabbalistic ones, concerning intention during prayer, to Hasidism.

My Warburgian propensity is especially evident from my refusal to adopt a Hegelian approach to history that moves from the concrete to the spiritual, from the hypertrophy of the ritual, implicitly lower, to the mystical experience, as implicitly higher, according to Scholem's historiosophy.[11] The Besht, and I would say most of Hasidism, did not sublate the concrete aspects of earlier forms of Judaism but, on the contrary, enforced their performance. They operated at the same time with a further enchantment of the world, or re-enchantement, especially in the model dealing with immanentism—to be discussed more in the first and last appendices—in a period when disenchantment of the world became more and more widespread in modern European society, which generated a more scientific, cold attitude to reality.

No less important for understanding the critiques addressed to the former approach is the implicit assimilation of Hasidism, and also of Kabbalah, into Christian categories, as part of what I called the "transfers of categories," for three generations of scholars. In my opinion, we may discern an interesting phenomenon of some scholars' assimilation of Judaism to Christianity via their mysticism, while in the earlier generations since the late eighteenth-century Enlightenment, such assimilation took the form of stressing the role of philosophy. This is not a new phenomenon, since from the very beginning of Jewish philosophy, we witness such assimilation, and the specific nature of the writings of Philo of Alexandria, Maimonides, Moses Mendelssohn, and Hermann Cohen are fine examples of this massive adaptation of some Jewish thinkers to what was *en vogue* in their intellectual entourage or in their wider cultural background. Working with broken theologies, just as the Hebrew Bible, early Christianity, or rabbinic literatures did, early Hasidism was less prone to theologize, since it strove to enrich the meaning and the intensity of ritual performances, rather than to build theological systems as such as happened to some Jewish thinkers in Central Europe.

One of the casulties of the Western conceptual trajectory is the diminishing role most of the scholars attributed to pre-axial elements, and in our case of the vocal aspects of Hasidism. In other words, Hasidic texts discussed previously that reflect an intensification of a basic aspect of the Rabbinic rituals, accompanied by fragments of theories extracted from Pythagorean, Orphic, Neoplatonic, astro-magic, and even Aristotelian sources, but put in service of explicating the religious valences of vocal rites, have been either marginalized, misunderstood, or totally ignored. It is the semantic mutations those earlier sources underwent in Hasidism, toward the vocal, that matter much more than their original meanings.

The recognition of the debt of the Hasidic writings to those fragmented sources does not, however, excuse scholars' artificial transfer of categories from the majority culture, West European or American, as discussed previously when describing those writings. Fancy terminologies or complex postmodern theories cannot cover up a weak critical reading of basic Hasidic texts and ignorance of major sources and parallels of seminal discussions in the writings of the same author that can confirm or disconfirm a certain reading.[12] The acid and sometimes exaggerated critiques of the scholarly study of Hasidism, as articulated more than a generation ago by Hayyim Lieberman and Mendel Piekarz, have been hardly internalized in scholarship, which is still quite selective and impressionistic.[13] This situation is evident also in the famous Buber-Scholem controversy over what Hasidism is.[14] Each of the two giant intellectuals chose a different part of the broad Hasidic creativity as if one alone is representative. Buber was confident that it is possible to distinguish the "voice" of the Besht from the views of his disciples, on the grounds of a common denominator. However, I am not sure that the Besht had just one single voice, "simple and united," as Buber thinks, rather romantically.[15]

Let me compare the situation insofar as Jewish studies are concerned to what happened in Hindu studies, where under the impact of English scholarship, the most abstract, noetic, philosophical parts of the Hindu traditions—the Upanishads and the philosophy of Shankara—have been privileged over the more concrete aspects, represented by the Tantric traditions and practices. It took some generations to shift from the former, European-oriented approach, basically Hegelian, to the latter topics. In this case, the role played by Mircea Eliade's book on Yoga as a technique, printed originally in French in 1936, or of his much later book on Shamanism, should be put in relief, for contributing to a less theological approach to religion.[16]

Also, Jewish scholarship in the field of Jewish mysticism still betrays strong theological propensities, minimizing the ritualistic, concrete, and social aspects of Hasidism. It is only recently that the nomian practices used as techniques for reaching what the Hasidic masters would call ideal religious experiences have been investigated.[17] Since I assume that the nature of the techniques has an impact on the ensuing experiences,[18] the present investigation as to the dominant role of the vocal activity should be seen as essential for understanding the Besht and some aspects of later Hasidism.[19]

If seen from the perspective proposed previously, the aspects of early Hasidism related to vocal rites constitute a continuation of a theory and probably also a praxis found in the most articulated manner at the end of R. Moshe Cordovero's classic *Pardes Rimmonim*, as was quoted previously. His disciples and later followers, R. Elijah da Vidas, R. Abraham Galante and his brother Moshe Galante, R. Shabbetai Horowitz, R. Abraham Azulai, R. Aharon Berakhiyah of Modena, R. Yissachar Baer ben Petahyah Moshe, and R. Isaiah Horowitz, copied, sometimes extensively, from Cordovero's writings many passages or just paraphrased his views, and thus disseminated them in larger audiences, and later on they were adopted by the Besht and his disciples. This can be easily demonstrated philologically as done by Piekarz—without discerning the importance of the Cordoverian sources for many of his findings, and again in this study.[20]

For a proper understanding of this process, there is no need to introduce automatically the complex Lurianic Kabbalah, the formative impact of Sabbateanism, or a variety of crises as major factors in shaping Hasidism, as done by scholars.[21] In some important cases it suffices for the scholar to be aware of the content of some basic Kabbalistic texts, some of which were quoted explicitly by the early Hasidic masters. In more precise terms: I am closer to those who confer on what is called the ethical-Kabbalistic literature a formative role in the structure of Hasidism as a conceptual approach, but I assume that this general formulation is not sufficient. In my opinion, we should pay special attention to the Cordoverian stratum in this literature as contributing some key concepts to the spiritual structure of early Hasidism.

In my opinion, this is a systemic development based on reorganizations of easily available theologumena, widespread in the area

of the floruit of early Hasidism, which have been put in relief by
the Besht and adopted by his disciples. I see it as systemic since
Hasidism in most of its major manifestations follows the exoteric
turn so evident in Cordovero and in his followers, though much
less in the politics of esotericism in Lurianic Kabbalah. This, however, does not mean when other topics in Hasidism are discussed
that those specific kinds of influences cannot be discerned, as is
indeed the case of the seminal concept of *tzaddiq* in Hasidism, as
we shall also see later on in this study,[22] but for the time being in
order to ensure a serious scholarly analysis, I propose to operate in
the manner done previously: peruse the pertinent vast bodies of
literature, engage critically the expositions of other scholars, and
refrain from inertial resorting to terms that betray an essentialist
understanding of complex modes of thought, like quietism and
contemplation.

Last but not least: provided the strong vocal/aural propensity of
the Besht and the secondary role of ocular elements in his instructions and experiences, one may ask, was he indeed a phallogocen-
tric figure, in the manner Luce Irigary's essentialist approach would
imagine him as a male? My answer is that essentialism is another
aspect of a theological approach—even when secular scholars subscribe to it,—and that the Besht would not subscribe to any simple
reductionist formula forever. However, quite unexpectedly for her
theory, a male as he was, he nevertheless was not an ocularcentric
figure, nor an anti-ocularcentric one. He was flexible, as reality and
human situations are. He is the first important Jewish figure to
whom was attributed the following statement:

> It is incumbent to worship God, blessed be His name,
> with all his **strength,** since everything is necessary. This
> is because God, blessed be He, wishes that they will
> worship Him in **all the manners.** The intention is that
> sometimes a person **walks** and **speaks with persons,**
> and then he cannot study and it is [nevertheless] incum-
> bent that he will be united to God, blessed be He, and to

> unify unifications. So, when a person **walks on the way,**
> and he cannot pray or study as regular, it is incumbent
> to worship Him in other ways, and he should not be
> sorry because of it, since God, blessed be He, wishes that
> they will worship Him in **all the manners**, sometimes
> in one manner, some other times in other manner, and
> they is the reason that it occurred that he walks on the
> way, or **speaks** with persons, [all this] in order to wor-
> ship Him in such a manner.[23]

This openness toward new ways of worship, consisting of the
most humble types of activities, fits the existence of the three
models mentioned previously on the one hand, and on the possibility to allow a sublime type of experience without even knowing
the content of the pronounced Hebrew texts that were monadized.
Speaking to people, most probably in some form of vernacular, is
mentioned here as a possible occasion for worshipping God, hardly
a matter of contemplating letters, especially when walking or found
in the market, as we have seen in ch. 1 n. 22 in this volume. Again,
this type of worship is depicted as possible even in the most pedestrian activities. There can be little doubt that many conversations
were done in Yiddisch or even in some other forms of vernacular.
It is not the specific content of those conversations that matters
but their vocal aspect when done while one's thought is attached
to God. The importance of sonority is therefore preserved also
beyond the pale of the nomian practices. As already mentioned
previously, phonocentrism does not necessarily also mean logocentrism. The stark emphasis on the oral should be understood
also as part of the importance of language in Jewish mysticism,
though in many cases in Kabbalah it was conjugated with strong
ontological structures. In Hasidism, however, the turn to ritual
and non-ritual languages is more conspicuous provided the weaker
status of the broken theologies. Is this turn related to the reports of
the Besht's early problems of communication with people, as has
been mentioned in the hagiography? Is here an imitation of the

biblical Moses's vocal problems and the fact that he nevertheless became the promulgator of the Torah? The assumption that the Besht received the Torah just as it happened in ancient times recurs in some early Hasidic traditions related to the Besht.[24]

Last but not least: in matters of sonorous activities, it seems that the Besht's positions were adopted by the Great Maggid, even in cases in which he, or the editors of his traditions, did not mention the name of the master. It is interesting, however, that in the writings of Hasidic authors of the third and fourth generations, traditions related to the Besht were preserved, with the authors sometimes mentioning that they received them from the Great Maggid. By resorting to them it is easier to understand the linguistic turn generated by the Besht, which shaped concepts adopted by the nascent movement on the grounds of his emphasis on vocal rites to which he added broken theologies. Interestingly enough, scholarship in the field has attempted at building broader theologies, as if characteristic of early Hasidism, out of those vestiges of the broken ones. While Cordovero, who was one of the main sources for Beshtian traditions, as we shall see much more in some of the appendices as follows, was deeply immersed in a complex theosophical structure, though he also cultivated some linguistic type of magic, the Besht was much freer from the theosophical system and its symbolic valences and concentrated on one of the fragments of the Safedian thinker's system. To be sure: I do not see the Ba'al Shem Tov as an avatar of Cordovero, but someone living intellectually in a very different ambiance, constituted by mixtures of elements derived from a variety of earlier systems. The former selected, intuitively, those components that could serve a more intensified performance of the vocal rites.

Let me mention in this context a similar phenomenon which took place in the twentieth century with the arrival of Yoga exercises in Europe and the United States, when the rich theology and physiology related originally to the various types of Yoga practices have been practically eliminated, and only simple instructions related to mainly body exercises have been preserved. In both cases, as in eighteenth-century Neo-hesychastic renascence, simplification of complex systems should be conceived of as instrumental in the emergence of broader religious movements.

Rites described previously have been performed in the past and can be observed at first hand in the present. The texts pronounced did not change, but in any case their pronunciation is individualized, and it is idiosyncratic to each performer. This is also the case of the emotional and intellectual investments of each of them and also the ensuing effects. Those experiences have been depicted by a variety of terms: *devequt*, divestment of corporeality, self-effacement, annihilation, prophecy, and so forth. The term *experience* that I use covers this variety in Hasidism. The possible denial of the efficacy of the instructions mentioned previously, and of the validity of the rarer subjective descriptions, seem to me an attempt to reduce the discourse of those texts to just literary narratives, whose experiential ideals and praxis are not addressed by scholars.

This is also the result of an implied theological assumption, that there is nothing in common that is shared by some extreme forms of human experiences. Such an implied theology, which is in my opinion another type of *imaginaire*, runs against not just the studies of mysticism, but also of a variety of psychologies, for example the Jungian or the transpersonal ones, of drug experiences, or of findings of modern neurologies, as mentioned in the study referred to in ch. 8 n. 14 in this volume. This does not mean that as a scholar I adopt the ontological implications of the vestiges of the broken theologies as to the existence of spiritual forces, *sefirot*, divine omnipresence, and so on. This would be no more than a ridiculous claim. In my opinion, as expressed often in my studies, those are forms of religious *imaginaire* that populate and were active in a certain culture, and my assumptions do not attempt to confirm or disconfirm their existence. They certainly existed in the *imaginaire* of the Besht and of the early Hasidic masters, and shaped their activities and those of their followers. In other words, I am concerned much more with the belief in the efficacy of the human words when performed as part of a rite than with the so-called word of God that concerns

Western theologians so much, or with conceptual messages imagined to have been innovated by the Besht.

The refusal to take into serious consideration the details of those texts reflects a simplistic attitude to the possible range of human personality. It also constitutes a refusal to deal seriously with the details of texts and interpret them in one way or another. This does not mean that all the Hasidic experiences are the same, and even less, as I emphasized time and again, that they share a common denominator with "mysticism" in general as claimed by other scholars, especially Joseph Weiss, that adopted the quietistic-contemplative theory, as mentioned in chapters 1 and 13 in this volume.

As pointed out, I have a problem with understanding the details of the instruction of cleaving to and entering the vocables one pronounces, especially when the instructions mentioned the need of performing during daily prayer and studies, operations that are done in public and in a relatively speedy manner.[25] My failure to explain them with tools that are available to me should not minimize the necessity to collect and analyze the texts and attempt to give as precise an account as possible of their meaning. After all, they still remained meaningful for a growing audience, even in the present.

Last but not least, one of the main aims of this study is to point out the sources that inspired the Besht's thought concerning much of his theories of prayer and other vocal operations. I believe that this can be done in quite a plausible manner, as seen previously, and much more will be done in appendices B, C, and D in this volume. I believe that this can also be done insofar as another main Hasidic concept, that of *tzaddiq*, is concerned, and also in this case the Besht was instrumental in mediating some truncated Cordoverian traditions to early Hasidism. Those are examples of major dimensions of Beshtian traditions, and hard work is capable, in my opinion, to trace the most plausible sources and quite evident channels that mediated them.

Without a careful perusal of the pertinent Kabbalistic corpora, especially the rather neglected Cordoverian treatises, on the one hand, and the readiness to formulate more modest claims on the alleged general nature of Hasidism, on the other hand, scholars prefer nevertheless to speculate rather than invest spade work in discerning the sources and their phenomenological structure. However, such spade work may contribute to a much more solid picture of the polyphonic Besht as a conceptually "fatter" and interesting figure, though much less heroic and Romantic. Before articulating bombastic generalizations about the nature of Hasidic thought, it would be better to be acquainted with the formative layers of what will later become a movement—the traditions of the Besht and his followers—and be capable to see what is more or less important in the general economy of this vast literature, namely to be able to speak about statistical density as a factor that displays the relative weight of the conceptual centers of gravity.

A much better acquaintance with different layers of Kabbalistic literatures, especially with Cordovero and his followers in the seventeenth century, seems to me also essential, and I would like to illustrate this claim by detailed analyses offered in appendices B–F in this volume. Neither would a significant effort of scholars to study the place of elitist magic, unlike the more popular one that has been discussed previously and again in some of the appendices, as well as astrology, harm the analyses of the Besht, inclined as he was to a Saturnine complex,[26] and of Hasidism as a conceptual and historical phenomenon. From this point of view he is reminiscent also of Marsilio Ficino's alleged Saturnine character, as he is of the combination of the Al-Kindi type of magic with the vestiges of astro-magic, adopted and adapted by him via Cordoverianism.

Indeed, the specific astral magical dimension of the *tzaddiq* in the Besht's teachings has been hardly recognized by scholars and even less accorded what seems to me to be its proper place in the complex and pivotal theories of the *tzaddiq* as we shall elaborate in appendix F.[27] The Buberian repulsion toward magic and the failure of recognizing the various forms of presence of magical elements in Hasidic thought in general, not just in concrete practices, is explicit,[28] and it is found in a more implicit manner also in the presentations of Abraham J. Heschel and Samuel Dresner. More recently this reticence is also evident in much of the modern scholarship in the field, as it is possible to discern such a hesitation toward dealing with magic in a more detailed manner also from the studies of Hillel Zeitlin, Rivka Schatz-Uffenheimer, Joseph Weiss, Shmuel Abba Horodetzki, Arthur I. Green, Norman Lamm, or Shaul Magid, to give some examples. Indeed, without first defining magic, distinguishing between its various manifestations and usages, searching for its sources and also how they were understood in Hasidism, the resort to the term magic remains vague, and it may be as problematic a term as mysticism may be.[29]

Some of these scholars were interested in a kind of Hasidism that is useful and usable for today's democratic approach to religion rather than with tracing the evolution of various aspects of Jewish thought that impacted Hasidism. A rather extreme, modern, and scholarly process of spiritualization of Hasidism, a movement that was conceived of as being founded by a master of the divine name and practiced by some other wonder-makers and many blessings-givers, took place in our generation. This is no doubt part of some writers' search of a spiritual renewal of Judaism, as Buber already openly recognized in connection to his specific representation of this movement,[30] or A. J. Heschel.[31] Some selective affinities between a major dimension of Hasidism indeed found in the written documents, and aspects of modern scholarship: ecumenical, spiritual, and new age, contrived however to neglect other elements that were important and contributed to the emergence, and then to the wide dissemination, of this movement. The complexity of historical Hasidism has been reduced in some forms of scholarship in the field in order to adjust it for the imagined needs of some liberal audiences of today or of tomorrow, seekers for new Jewish identities or of some spiritual experiences.

APPENDIX A

FORLORN UNITIVE VIEWS OF THE BESHT?

The late eighteenth-century Hasidic author R. Aharon ha-Kohen Perlov of Apta has done, without any doubt, a great service to both the dissemination of the teachings of the Besht in traditional circles and to the academic study of early Hasidism.[1] His compilation entitled *Keter Shem Tov* constitutes the first anthology of many Beshtian traditions, most of them embedded in several books, and it still serves as the basis of many scholarly analyses of the thought of the Besht, especially by those who prefer to cite his teachings in an accessible manner, without having to peruse the many books of the Besht's disciples and become acquainted with the contexts of those quotes. Cited many times by modern scholars, the two parts of *Keter Shem Tov* ensured the prominent place of R. Aharon of Apta as a mine of precious information that is easily available, also for some traditions that are not always found in the books of the direct students of the Besht, which served as the main sources for his compilation.

However, in addition to this collection of traditions, this Hasidic writer wrote books of his own that were printed toward the end of the eighteenth century. More eminent for our discussion here is his commentary on the Pentateuch entitled *'Or ha-Ganuz la-Tzaddiqim*, a text that enjoyed a certain popularity and was reprinted several times since its first publication, in an anonymous manner, in 1800. We have referred to this book earlier in this study. In this commentary the Besht is quoted several times, and in some cases it is possible to find the sources in Hasidic books. In some other cases it seems that there is no parallel to his quotations, a fact that provoked accusations as to the adequacy of his citations, or even hints that he forged those quotes. Thus, the first compiler of the Beshtian traditions turned out to be, according to the view of Isaiah Tishby, the first forger of other "Beshtian" passages.[2] Here is not the place to try to solve this interesting quandary, but I am inclined to reject this approach. I would rather like to show how R. Aharon preserved, or perhaps radicalized, the Beshtian vision of what can be called divine omnipresence, inserting in his discussion a brief statement that supports his vision as to the radical omnipresence of the divine. As mentioned previously, such a view does not fit the theory of the existence of the divine spiritual force within vocables, or that it is drawn there by human acts. This discrepancy is the result of the Besht's adoption of a new model, most probably later on in his life, which I described as an acosmic and noetic model that is preserved in quotes of disciples that met him late in his life, like his grandson R. Moshe Hayyim Efrayyim of Sudylkov, who mentions that he heard the parable from his grandfather.

Let me translate a short passage preserved by R. Aharon of Apta and succinctly discuss its content:

> [a] "And God has shown himself" [Genesis 18:1]: the scholar is able to apprehend the innerness, which is the holiness and the *ruḥaniyyut* and the divine name,[3] which maintain everything. In every place that he looks, he sees only the divinity and the divine name even etc. And when is he able to apprehend the above? When he is "at the entrance of the tent" [Genesis 18:1], namely in the moment when he accomplished supernal unification up to *'Eiyn Sof*, that is at the upper window of all the worlds

and of all the heavens and the heavens of the heavens. About them it is said: "He stretched them like a tent" [Jes. 40:22] [b] as it is written in the name of the Besht, blessed be his memory: "Someone should not sit down in the divine but he shall consider himself as if he is entirely stored within the light of the divinity. [c] This is the meaning of [the verse in Genesis 18:1]: "He sits at the entrance of the tent" namely the scholar performs an *Yihud*, up to *'Ein Sof,* which is at the entrance of all the worlds.[4]

The first part of the quote [a] evinces the well-known Beshtian theory that God permeates the entire reality and sustains it, either by the ontological presence, the *ruhaniyyut* in the sense of a spiritual force that is present within the material world, or the holiness, or by the linguistic presence of his name.[5] The act of discerning the omnipresence—I try to avoid here the theological, heavily loaded terms like pantheism or panentheism—should be carried out to the maximum, including the mysterious issue that is hinted at by the phrase "even etc.," which may point either to the divine presence in evil or sin or, in a milder manner, to the beauty of a woman.[6] However, in order to avoid a form of pantheism or panentheism, the Hasidic writer mentions the existence of a hierarchy: the lower existence, though permeated by the divine presence—some form of general immanentism—depends upon a higher entity, *'Eiyn Sof.* The awareness of the connection between the divine realm within the world, and the one outside it, is expressed by the term *Yihud*: it is the attachment of the lower to the higher, including the highest level of the infinite that is necessary, and this is also the case insofar as the human soul is concerned. I assume that this connectiveness is understood as the mystical significance of the Genesis verse "God has shown himself onto him in the terebinths of Mamre." The divinity revealed itself in the terebinths, but He is not identical with the trees. The discovery of the divinity in the world should trigger the process of understanding the transcendental source of the spiritual force that dwells also here below and linkage between the God within and the God without, and this linkage is the unification or the *Yiḥud*.

The cosmic dimension of the discussion so far will help in understanding the other parts of the quote: Abraham [or the scholar], to whom God revealed while he was sitting at the entrance of the tent, is not representing the deeper meaning of the Genesis verse. The material tent is interpreted as a metaphor for the cosmic structure, by resorting to the Isaiah verse: "The heavens were created as a tent." Abraham is sitting therefore not at the entrance of his personal tent here below but, at that of God's one, who embraces everything. In order to reach the Infinity, one should pass through the heavens.

The point made by R. Aharon can be easily understood if the entire discussion ends at the end of paragraph [a]. The short passage in the name of the Besht [b] does not in fact reinforce the point made by the Hasidic author. The most important connection between the quote [b] and the interpretation [a] and [c] consists of the common resort to the verb *YShB*, found in the biblical verse. However, the Besht is quoted as warning not just to sit within divinity but also to feel that he is stored within the divine light. This instruction differs from both the perception of the divine presence, and from the act of unifying the perceived divinity to the infinite divinity. The dictum attributed to the Besht does therefore not reinforce the points made by the interpretation offered by R. Aharon. The Besht is claiming, according to [b], that the mystic should not discover the divine but he should feel himself immersed in the divine light. *Nota bene*: the light is not mentioned in [a], where only holiness, spiritual force, and the divine name are referenced. On the other hand, the statement of the Besht adduced here cannot be found anywhere in the writings of his disciples, insofar as I am acquainted with them. Even more astonishing is the fact that the term *ganuz* appears in a variety of Beshtian texts and earlier ones, concerning the divine presence within the Torah, letters, and utterances, but not in the context we find here: that of the mystic basking within the divine light.

Thus the question may be asked: why should R. Aharon forge a statement that does not serve his commentary on the biblical verse? What may he gain from his forgery if it creates a rather vague statement that hardly contributes to the point he makes? Would it not be much simpler to assume that he found somewhere a statement related to the verse *YShB* and adduced it in the commentary on a verse where the verse is found?

Let me turn now to the verb *ganuz*, translated here as stored, in order to describe the immersion of the mystic within the divine light. In the same book from which we have quoted the previous passage, we find several discussions about the immersion of the mystic within the divinity, and at least in one case the terms used in the name of the Besht as cited previously occur. In one case in this context, the name of the Besht has been mentioned again. After adducing the Aramaic formulas from the Zoharic literature dealing with divine omnipresence, R. Aharon writes:

> [d] From [the mouth of] the Besht, blessed be his memory: "when someone wants that his divinity will dwell onto him it is essential that he will know and understand that there is in him divinity and this is a preparation for the dwelling of the divinity, when he perceives himself as nihil. [e] A parable for it is that someone is roaming in the depths of the sea to gather pearls and gems and then he should be very careful not to suffocate by the water when he holds the breath as it is known. Then he shall quickly gather the gems since if he is lazy and he will not gather all his efforts will be in vain. Behold we shall learn from this parable how to worship the Creator, since the Holy One blessed be He, created the sea, which are the fifty gates of *Binah* that were created in the world, so that the men, who are Israel, and their souls, are the sailors [*yordei yam*] sailing in the boats of the body in order to gather pearls and gems, which are the letters/ vocables of the Torah and the commandments and the

extractions [of the sparks] [*berurim*] from the mineral,
vegetable, animal and human [realms], when they eat
... behold when a person is about to perform a commandment or study Torah or pray, he should hint at [the
fact that] he is stored in his entirety within the light of
the divinity."[7]

The first part of passage [d] approximates other teachings of the
Besht about the dwelling of the divinity within a person.[8] However,
again the second part [e], dealing with the storing of men within
the divine light, is unknown in the Beshtian traditions. However,
this second passage [e], which presumably is also intended to be
reported in the name of the Besht in the last quotation, tells us
something about the quotation in the name of the Besht in the
first passage [b]: no one should sit within the divinity but be active
or, in other words, perform the commandments. To use the image
found elsewhere in this book, the persons should behave like
fishes in the sea. Despite the conspicuous oceanic imagery, there
is no passivity involved here, since R. Aharon, or his source, is
concerned more with the image of the active diver, who must be
very quick in finding the pearls; otherwise he will die. The parable
adduced in order to illustrate the concept is fitting the style of the
Besht: mystical experiences should be short, as they are part of the
performing of the rituals. A prolonged experience is implicitly seen
as dangerous.

Let me adduce an expansion of the previous treatment found
in the same book immediately afterward without resorting to the
name of the Besht. Someone should imagine, writes R. Aharon,
that he is immersed within the fifty gates of *Binah*, since fifty
amounts numerically to the value of *Yam*, sea, because:

he is as if stored in his entirety within the light of the
divinity, and it is "like the water of the sea that cover"
[Isaiah 11:9], like a drop that fell within the great sea,[9] or
like someone that is roaming in the sea in order to gather

the pearls, as it is written *"neder le-ha-shem"* [Numbers
30:3], as if he dwells [*dar*] within the fifty gates of *Binah*,[10]
which belong to God, and as if he is stored in his entirety
within the light of divinity.[11]

However, the exegetical ingenuity is perhaps even more dramatic.
Dar, the second part of *Neder*, is not only pointing to the dwelling,
namely the storing within the divinity, but also the pearl, since *dar*
is a word found in the scroll of Esther, which has been interpreted
by R. Abraham ibn Ezra as precious stone. Thus, the dwelling
and the pearl are extracted from the same two consonants. What
is however even more fascinating is the fact that *dar*, when read
inversely, is in Hebrew *red*, which means the imperative to descend,
as in the phrase used in the passage to express the concept of the
sailor: *Yordei Yam*, which is another interpretation of *Neder: N =
Yam, dar = red*. A question that is hard to answer is whether there
was an association between the precious stone, *dar*, and the family
name of the author of the book, Perlov—perle—pearl.

Last but not least: we have interpreted the instruction of the
Besht not to sit, in [b] against sitting, as a polemic against the static
contemplator, that would discover the divine presence as a theological or spiritual exercise, while the approach the Besht proposes is
much more active and based on the imperative of performing commandments with alacrity. The issue of alacrity is part of a polemic
with an approach found in R. Gershon of Kutov, who represents
a more extreme form of ecstatic though passive life, an issue that
was discussed in detail elsewhere.[12] However, there is also another
addressee to this polemic. Let me first translate a short passage
from *Keter Shem Tov*, the earliest and most important collection of
Beshtian traditions we have mentioned previously:

On the issue of *devequt* ... there are people who say
that when he performs a commandment or deals with
the Torah and he makes his body a seat to the soul and
the soul [a seat] to the spirit, and the spirit [a seat to] the

higher soul, and the higher soul a seat to the light of the
Shekhinah which is over his head, and it is as if the light is
spreading around him and he is within the light, sitting
and he is rejoycing, trembling [out of awe]. This is the
reason why the heavens are in every place a hemisphere
. . . and it is written in the *Book Haredim*[13]: the righteous
is looking to heaven, which hint at the supernal world
. . . and it is as if the light is spreading around him and
he is in the middle of the light of the splendor of the firmament, and he sits and rejoices, trembling [out of awe],
and this is the perfect *Yihud*.[14]

I see this passage as supplying some of the elements found in the
first quotation adduced previously from R. Aharon Perlov's book.
Extremely important are the shared elements: the embracing light,
the looking to heaven, the theme of *Yihud*, and especially the mentioning of sitting. However, the alacrity theme is missing here altogether. This is the reason why the teaching about not sitting should
be understood as a critique to the address of *via contemplativa* and
a spur to a form of *via activa*. The Besht, or perhaps R. Aharon, is
therefore not only continuing some forms of Safedian spirituality but also criticizing some of its elements. Was the encompass-
ing vision when combined with alacrity, with omnipresence, and
devequt the discovery of the Besht, and its disappearance in the
writings of his disciples the retreat from it?[15] Or is R. Aharon of
Apta the late discoverer of a more radical spirituality, which he
attributes to the Besht for reasons that are not clear?

Though I would like to leave this question open for the time
being, I would nevertheless opt, tentatively, for a Beshtian extraction of the radical omnipresence and of the radical exegesis of the
biblical verses. One of the reasons for my choice is the paramount
importance of the ritual of bathing for the Besht, sometime conceived of as a mystical event.[16] It is already in thirteenth-century
Kabbalah that the ritual bath, the *miqweh*, has been identified in an
explicit manner with the *Shiy'ur Qomah* or the divinity, provided

the importance of the sizes of the two entities.[17] The identification
of God and water is found already in the book of the *Zohar.*[18] In the
Beshtian practice, however, immersion in water, quite a concrete
event, has been imagined to take place within the divinity and was
understood as a moment of temporary self-obliteration for the sake
of renewal, and involves some form of ecstatic experience.[19] Such
an understanding can explain the oceanic feeling reflected in the
texts of R. Aharon of Apta and the comparison of the mystic with
a fish.[20] On the grounds of the previous text, a feeling of divine
omnipresence does not imply passivity.

Let me adduce a passage that summarizes the Besht's perception, though without mentioning him. In the comprehensive encyclopedia of Kabbalistic topics compiled by the Hasidic author R.
Jacob Tzvi Yalish (1778–1825), there is an instructive passage to this
effect:

> The secret of the [ritual] bath is to come to nothing-
> ness, since before creation there was only water, and
> when someone disappears in water he comes to nothing-
> ness. . . . Everything that needs to come to a new dimen-
> sion should come to nothingness, and this is so insofar
> as everything in the world [is concerned], that steresis
> precedes existence,[21] and every seed that is sown, before
> its growth it is necessary that it should be corrupted and
> it will totally dissipate, and come to nothingness,[22] and
> then it receives existence from nothingness, and this is
> the secret of [immersing in] a bath.[23]

The return to the *'Ayin* in order to create something new, or a
renewal, is found explicitly in a collection of teachings of the Great
Maggid, without mentioning the bath-immersion.[24] However,
despite the importance of this theory for the Great Maggid, my
assumption is that it is also congruent with a view found in the
Besht. I have discussed previously a similar view found in *Maggid
Devarav le-Ya'aqov* as reflecting the approach of the Besht to prayer.[25]

However, I would like to elaborate here more on this vision of mysticism as a return to the primordial Nihil as a potentially Beshtian tradition. Menachem Lorberbaum already proposed to see the Great Maggid's resort to the categories of *Yesh* and *'Ayin* as a "theologization of the views of the Besht."[26] This is evident also in R. Efrayim of Sudylkov, the Besht's grandson, who writes as follows:

> For them[27] the Creator, blessed be He, created the world
> and they sustain the world that is called *Yesh* and in their
> hands is to cause the return of *Yesh* to *'Ayin*, and to cause
> the emergence of a new thing, like the hyle in the hand
> of the sculpture,[28] to change a thing into another, and
> to change from the prime hyle a form that differs from
> the first form, and this is referred by the name *Yisra'el*,
> that they bring close the *Yesh* to the three letters *R'al*[29] as
> mentioned beforehand,[30] there the things are sweetened
> in their source and the entire existence [*ha-Yeshut*] is in
> the secret of the *'Ayin*, and this brief [exposition] suffices
> for the wise, since it is necessary to elaborate since there
> is a depth in it.[31]

It is hard to know whether a longer version of this discussion or a more detailed understanding of the transformation by return to *'Ayin* was known to the Rabbi of Sudylkov. The strong parallelism to the view of the Great Maggid may refer to a common source that most plausibly could be the Besht.[32]

APPENDIX B

THE BESHT AND R. ABRAHAM AZULAI'S
HESED LE-'AVRAHAM

In the present appendix and in the next four I shall try to point out affinities between some Beshtian traditions and the Cordoverian Kabbalah, by expatiating on the content of the latter. As we know, only rarely does the Besht quote his sources, with the exception of biblical and Talmudic passages.[1] Detecting his immediate sources may facilitate understanding his wide conceptual panorama and will help to discern how he understood or in many cases how he actually misunderstood these sources. This is especially relevant insofar as the Cordoverian theory of intention of prayer, informed by the reverberation of the astro-magical theory of Cordovero that is so central for the linkage of mysticism and magic of the Besht. As pointed out previously, the direct and indirect influence of the Safedian Kabbalist on early Hasidism has been addressed already by several scholars.[2] Others, purposely, prefer to overlook or to minimize its importance.[3] Here and in the next appendices, I would like to add several additional examples of Cordoverian impact, relevant for our previous discussions concerning the Beshtian traditions. R. Jacob Joseph Katz writes as follows:

There is one great principle,[4] [namely] that it is incumbent to cleave himself to the innermost part[5] of the Torah
and the commandment, namely to adhere his thought
and his soul to the root of the Torah and the commandment that he performs since if he does not do it, God
forbid, he cuts and separates the branches, and just as I
have received it from my teacher, I likewise found it in
Hesed le-'Avraham, river 14.[6]

Here the *Kavvanah* is closer to the theosophical-theurgical
understanding of the term, but it is conceived of as insufficient, and
the *devequt* is conceived of as essential for causing the appropriate
effect.[7] The passage definitely speaks about performance, including
the Tirahm, which would mean vocalization. Interestingly enough,
R. Jacob Joseph claims that what he first received from the Besht
is similar to the tradition stemming from the Cordoverian school
he found later.

The book mentioned here is one of R. Abraham Azulai's
many writings, a short though widespread compendium of basically Cordoverian Kabbalah,[8] where the talismanic elements are
well represented.[9] The book has been in print since 1685, a year in
which it was published both in Sulzbach and Amsterdam. R. Jacob
Joseph claims that what his teacher, the Besht, has taught him concerning *devequt* is already found in this book. This is also the case
elsewhere in which this disciple refers to both his teacher and to R.
Abraham Azulai's work:

[a] Just as there is matter and form in man so too in the
letters of the Torah, there are matter and form, since the
body of the letters is the matter, and the spiritual force
of the *sefirot* together with the light of the Infinite that
are within it and vivify it, is the form and the soul of
the letter.[10] This is the reason why man should intend by
his [study of the] Torah and prayer, [b] as it is explicitly
written in *Hesed le-'Avraham*, river 43[11] and this is his

formulation: "the quintessence of the *Kavvanah* is that it is incumbent to draw down the spiritual force from the supernal ranks to the vocables that one recites so that the vocables will be capable to ascend up to the supreme rank, to do his require" end of quotation, [c] and [also] as I received from my teacher.[12]

In fact the quote from Azulai [b] is no more than a shortened and simplified version of the definition of the *kavvanah* of prayer as found at the end, which is also the apex, of Cordovero's *Pardes Rimmonim* and was referred to beside ch. 4 n. 7 in this volume and translated and discussed beside appendix C n. 30 in this volume. However, while the Safedian Kabbalist presented a very complex theory that assumes that different terms in the texts of prayer refer to different layers within the divine sphere, Azulai's account simplified this theory. His view should be compared to the teaching R. Jacob Joseph received from the Besht [c], and the two earlier parts of the citation are imagined to operate because of the dual theory of letters/vocables. These two citations exemplify the validity of the claim R. Jacob Joseph made elsewhere, in a passage quoted previously, that he received from his master things similar to views where the imprint of Cordovero's terminology is evident.[13] However, paragraph [a] contains much of the ideas in [b] and constitutes part of the Hasidic author's views, which perhaps predated the reading of Azulai's book, and this is also the case of the content of [c].

The passages cited previously are represented in a paraphrastic manner in a longer passage found in the same book that includes the verb "I have received." The name of the Besht is not mentioned there, though *Hesed le-'Avraham* was referred to explicitly.[14] It would be more than plausible to surmise that the Besht is indeed the subject of the verb. All these facts notwithstanding, the impact of this book and of the mystical-magical model have been explicitly denied as part of the denial of the existence of the mystical-magical model as belonging to the worldview of the Besht.[15] What is more than strange is that some of the material dealt with so far

in this appendix is found at the very beginning of the most important book in early Hasidism, *Toledot Yaʿaqov Yosef*, which preserves
traditions of the Besht, a voluminous book that scholars avoided
using, perhaps because they heavily relied on R. Aharon of Apta's
compendium entitled *Keter Shem Tov*, as mentioned previously at
the beginning of appendix A.

In this context we should consider seriously the conceptual contribution of this remark for understanding the Besht, as well as that
of the Ḥabad nineteenth-century author R. Hillel of Paritch, who
described the path of both the Besht and the Great Maggid, as
"they have drawn down the aspect of revelation of the light of the
Infinite into the plurality of the modi of epiphany."[16] This drawing
down is, therefore, conceived of as shared by these two founding
figures of Hasidism, and attempts at drawing a wedge between the
two—as well as between the Besht and R. Jacob Joseph, on these
grounds—is itself groundless.[17]

With the plausible assumption that *Ḥesed le-ʾAvraham* had an
impact not just on R. Jacob Joseph but also on the Besht, let me
turn to another seminal topic in Hasidism, the theory of the *tzaddiq*
as drawing down supernal influxes by means of vocables, well-
represented in this book. That Cordovero's view of the human righteous as a pipeline that transmits the supernal influx to this world
influenced the Besht is undeniable, since the words of Cordovero
or Azulai on this topic have been copied verbatim by the early
masters of Hasidism, and in some cases also in the name of the
Besht, as we shall see in appendix F. According to a Cordoverian
text copied in two of Azulai's books:

> The higher soul is from [the *sefirah* of] *Binah* and the
> Torah from [the *sefirah* of] *Tiferet*, thus the Torah is a
> garment of the higher soul. And when the *tzaddiqim*[18]
> are preoccupied with the Torah in this world, spiritual
> vocables emerge from those voices, that ascend from
> below on high, according to the secret of *ʾABYʿa*, ranks
> after rank, so that they ascend to the Paradise, the place

where God studies with the souls [of the deceased righteous] . . . and when the [deceased] *tzaddiqim* listen to this issue, they clothe themselves in the vocables of the Torah that the lower [*tzaddiqim*] study, and likewise in [the vocables] of what they studied when they were alive. And they ride[19] on the ladder[20] of the ascension of the voices and descend down and they are united with them.[21] And the reason is that the secret of the union with the Holy One, blessed be He, will be in a perfect manner, is by means of the souls of this world and of the supernal world . . . and this is the reason why the *tzaddiqim* that are [found] in the supernal world descend to the lower world in order to participate with the *tzaddiqim* that are below, so that the union will be perfect.[22]

The vocal aspect of the Torah-study is obvious, since the term *qolot*—voices—is mentioned twice. At the same time there is some form of hypostasis of the vocables, since they became the sonorous garment for the soul.[23] However, the gist of the passage has to do with their attainment of perfect union with God by means of loud study. This point is of great importance for understanding the emergence of the concept of union with God in Hasidism. First let me emphasize that the term *Yiḥud* in this passage does not mean the theurgical unification of the divine powers, as in theosophical Kabbalah and also elsewhere in Azulai's books, or the recognition of divine uniqueness, as in Jewish philosophy, but the perfect union of the souls to God.[24] As such, Azulai's passage translated here anticipates the manner in which the Hasidic masters understood *Yiḥud*.[25] Also in his case, the experience of union is dependent on vocal activity, as later on in Hasidism, and also in this case, it is the *tzaddiq* that has been singled out as capable to attain such a sublime union.[26]

APPENDIX C

DRAWING DOWN SPIRITUAL FORCE, AND PALACES IN CORDOVERO

Throughout the present study,[1] as in many other studies of mine, I have stressed the historical and phenomenological affinities between the Kabbalistic thought of R. Moshe Cordovero and his followers and early Hasidism.[2] This is also the case of ideas found in one of the writings of Cordovero's main follower, R. Abraham Azulai, as discussed in appendix B. Though by now it is not a new finding, some of the prevailing studies in the field in the recent years have scarcely adopted it, as the preference has been given to the impact of Lurianic components in Hasidism. However, Hasidism should be seen, *inter alia*, also as a vital part of a larger development that starts with late antiquity astro-magic in the Hellenistic world, has been translated in Arabic, especially in the book *Ghayyat al-Hakhim*, and in the famous Latin *Picatrix* and in some other minor treatises, and then adopted in Hebrew by Jewish thinkers like Abraham ibn Ezra and his followers, and by some Kabbalists, since the end of the thirteenth century.[3] It was present in the writings of R. Shlomo ha-Levi Al-Qabetz, Cordovero's brother-in-law, who most probably capitalized on the views of an early fifteenth-century Spanish Kabbalist.[4] The basic concept of

what I call the astro-magical or talismanic model[5] consists of the
possibility to draw down astral powers by performing some rituals that may also include prayers to various planetary powers. The
topic is vast since this model has to do with a variety of other topics, like the theory of the *sefirot* in Cordovero, or the theory of the
tzaddiq—to be discussed in appendix E as follows—in his thought
and in Hasidism, but for the sake of the present study I shall concentrate on the constellation of themes related to the special status
of the vocables as related to both causing the descent of spiritual
force and the ascent on high by their means.[6] To be sure: it is not
my intention to offer here an exhaustive analysis of Cordoverian
theories of magic, but solely a discussion related to vocables and
the affinities to the spiritual force and vocal palaces.

In his commentary on *Sefer Yetziyrah*, the Safedian Kabbalist
distinguishes between three levels, or what he calls three aspects,
of letters:

> The first one is the material, the second the corporeal
> that turns to the spiritual and the third one is entirely
> spiritual. And they are the written letter that is essen-
> tially material, without doubt, since it is in a body the
> portent and substratum of the letter and the writing. . .
> . And the second [letters] "are fixed in the mouth"[7] and
> transferred from the written to the tongue, and the
> tongue is material and its enunciation is corporeal. And
> it is transferred from there to the secret of spiritual force
> that is the thought. And the third are the thoughtful
> letters, to which is the main intention and this is the
> spiritual force of the letters. And this is the reason why a
> prayer without intention is like a body without a soul.[8,9]

Prima facie, this discussion deals solely with the modes of existence of letters, first in the lower world, and their transition from
one type of dimension to another, the highest being the letters
within the human thought, namely mental letters. According

to such a reading, prayer would be identical to a philosophical exercise that elevates the signs to sounds and to mental content. This is, indeed, the meaning of the widespread medieval dictum about prayer Cordovero quoted. However, immediately after the previous passage, Cordovero mentions the existence of the third dimension, the spiritual one, situated within the "supernal attributes and paths and they are emanated [in a descending manner] from one another."[10] The attributes and the paths are identical to the *sefirot*, as is evident from the context. This statement takes the letters to a thoughtful level, namely to some kind of mental letters on a metaphysical plane. This would mean that while in the case of the human letters/vocables the ascending process is evident, while in the metaphysical sense it is the descending process that is important. Are those two moves just a matter of concatenation, or of a great chain of letters/vocables? Or is the intention of prayer a matter of a mental ascent on high, some form of Platonic contemplation of the supernal, divine source of letters?

It should be emphasized that the term *spiritual force* has at least two meanings in Cordovero: it refers to the entity that emerges out of the pronunciation of the vocables, related as it is to the vapor of the mouth and to human vitality, and thus this is a human force, though it is related to the divine nature of the human soul; the other one is the supernal spiritual force that descends upon the human vocables from a transcendental realm. The two moves are different in principle and are only discussed together very rarely.[11] Let me adduce an important formulation of the ascending move, very similar to what it has been adduced previously by R. Elijah da Vidas in the name of Cordovero:

> The secret of the recitation of the [divine] name by the vocables that are fixed in mouth, and [the manner] it ascends by the spiritual force and seizes the supernal spiritual force and thus stirs the supernal powers. And how is it possible to rule over the subtle spiritual forces, which are the emanated [entity]? This is [possible] by the

mercy of God that fixed the names in the *sefirot* and engraved them in the mouth of man.[12]

Here the two different senses of *ruḥaniyyut* are found in the same passage: the magical spiritual force that stems from the human and ascends on high, and is capable to move the supernal spiritual forces, namely the sefirotic powers, a view that will be discussed as follows in the context of the manner in which prayer operates.

The downward move is related to supernal letters found in the higher *sefirot*, and they descend upon the lower ones as a form of spiritual force, displaying some kind of linguistic ontology situated within the Kabbalistic theosophy.[13] The first move is much closer to the Rabbinic theory of the ontic status of the vapor of the mouths of children while studying Torah, but the second one is clearly related to astro-magical sources that had been adopted by Kabbalists already in the fifteenth century in Spain and in Cordovero's Kabbalah.

In a text immediately following the previous discussions, Cordovero mentions that the Talmudic masters have received the three dimensions of letters, and this time he designates them as "material, spiritual and divine, and they were not permuting a [single] letter without intending to create something, and they emanated [in a descending manner] from a causa to the causatum, down to the coarse matter."[14] Here the meaning of the concatenation of various levels of letters has clearly magical connotations. According to another discussion, Cordovero envisioned any enunciation of sounds/letters as having magical repercussions. So, for example, in a passage that is especially relevant for the analysis here, and in this study in general, it is said that: "by the pronunciation of the letters/vocables, by the moves of tongue and lip in this material world, their supernal soul is aroused on high, and this because the letters/vocables are the palaces of their spiritual force."[15]

The phrase translated as "palaces of their spiritual force" translates the Hebrew *heikhalot ruḥaniyyutam*, when it is predicated on the vocables/letters, just as in the texts adduced previously from the Besht. It is also evident that this passage has a magical implication: recitation of sounds below provokes a move in the supernal roots of the sounds. Spiritual force that dwells within the ritual sounds mediates the transmission of the lower moves of the vocal apparatus to their higher root.[16] Cordovero's image of palace and vessels anticipates therefore the architecture of sound or vocables that we have seen in the Beshtian traditions,[17] as well as that of the linguistic immanence and the continuum between the different levels of reality grounded in the vocal great chain of being, as seen in Cordovero's passage quoted by R. Elijah da Vidas and translated previously.[18]

Like in the Beshtian tradition, especially that which was found in the *Holy Epistle*, Cordovero also embraced a theory of vocables as monads, asserting that "in the spiritual force of each and every letter/vocable several subtle worlds are comprised."[19] The seminal theory of drawing down spiritual force, when using the verb *MShKh* together with *ruḥaniyyut*, is found several times in his writings.[20] Also the existence of two different views as to the relationship between *ruḥaniyyut* and vocables/letters, the inherent power and the attracted one, can be discerned in Cordovero.[21] It is in the writings of the Safedian Kabbalist that cleaving to spiritual force, sometimes mentioning also vocables, is found.[22] He also recommends articulating each vocable separately, in a context dealing with the spiritual force, in a manner reminiscent of Hasidism.[23]

Is the magical aspect also related to the intention of prayer, a prominent vocal activity, as was mentioned previously? Indeed the magic aspect of Cordovero's thought is evident in his most famous presentations of prayer found at the very end of his classic *Pardes Rimmonim*. Provided the centrality of Cordovero's passage for the entire development of Hasidism, let me translate some parts of it:

When someone pronounces and causes one of the letters/ vocables to move, [then] the spiritual force of that [vocable] will necessarily be stirred, and the vapor[s] of [his] mouth, out of which holy forms are formed, will

ascend and be bound with their root, for they are (!) the
root of the emanation[24] . . . From [i.e., the pronunciation
of a word] the vapor of his mouth, appears a spiritual
force and entity, which is as an angel that will ascend
and will be bound with its source and will hasten to
perform its operation in a speedy and rapid way, and this
is the secret of the pronunciation of [Divine] Names and
the *kavvanah* of prayer.[25]

The reference to the "pronunciation of names" is obviously a reference to Abulafia's type of Kabbalah. The affinity between this
technique of Abulafia and the *Kavvanah* of prayer is twofold: both
were, according to Cordovero, methods to draw downward the
spiritual forces; and "the pronunciation of names" is described by
Abulafia in his *'Or ha-Sekhel* in terms very close to the situation of
prayer: for example, the usage of *Talit* and *Tefillin*, and catharsis
of thought from alien thoughts, and so forth.[26] The view of the
ascending spiritual force as an angel emerging from the ritual vocal
activity is reminiscent of the concept of the "Maggid," known as
a tutorial angel, which has also magical sources, as pointed out by
Shlomo Pines.[27]

Here, as in the following passage, the spiritual force is not only
a supernal entity, but also something stemming from the human
vocal activity, in other words an inherent spiritual force. Elsewhere
in the same book, Cordovero elaborates on some aspects of the
previous passage:

The quintessence of the *kavvanah* is that the person that
intends [during prayer] should draw the spiritual force
[*ruḥaniyyut*] from the supernal degrees onto the letters/
vocables that he pronounces so that he will be able to
elevate those vocables up to the high degree so that his
request will be answered quickly. And the intention is
that the vapor of his mouth[28] of the person is not an
insignificant issue . . . but from the vapor of his mouth

appears a spiritual force [*ruḥaniyyut*], and that spiritual force needs power[29] in order to elevate his requests and elevate the vocables up to the degree that he needs. And this is the quintessence of the *kavvanah* to draw power so that because of that power the vocables will ascend on high, they will be generated on the height of the world and his request will be answered speedily.[30]

This passage is the finale of one of the most theological books in Judaism, which creates a detailed framework for the understanding of the efficacity of prayer in the context of those detailed distinctions. Some of them consist of what I see as projections of astro-magical elements into the divine world and combinations with other techniques of intending during prayer. Ending the book in such a manner is part of what I call the linguistic/liturgical turn that is evident in Safed, and Hasidism should be seen in the framework of this turn.[31]

Many of the theosophical details connected to the intention in prayer characteristic of Cordovero's complex theosophy are referred to in his gate from which we quoted previously, but they are missing in the Hasidic metamorphoses of this passage. The Safedian Kabbalist proposed not just an astro-magical theory, represented by the concept of spiritual force that is drawn down, but also a view similar to al-Kindi—what I referred to previously as the inherent spiritual forces—that deals with the ascending spiritual force of the vocables, as we shall see in the next appendix. This is an interesting synthesis between two different types of magic, both stemming from Arabic sources, and plausibly from earlier Hellenistic ones. They contributed to the transformation of prayer into a spell.[32]

Later on his views provided the exegetical grid for understanding other types of traditions, including the Lurianic ones. It should be pointed out that in one case in *Pardes Rimmonim*, he speaks about the letter/vocable as the palace and the seat of the spiritual force,[33] and in the final chapter of this book, Cordovero resorts to the term

Heikhal in order to refer to the divine name presented as the container of the *sefirot*.[34]

Interestingly enough it seems that Cordovero was aware that he was not the innovator of a view of the inherent spiritual force. In his commentary on the *Zohar*, he writes as follows:

> It is known that the secret of holy speech that emerges from the mouth of a person, and it is comprised from the secret of the soul, the spirit and the high soul, in all the aspects of the ladder,[35] since the voices and the vocables/ letters a spiritual source emerges out of them, and that spiritual force ascends from one aspect to another and ascends in accordance to the secret of the link and union of all the degrees.[36, 37]

The opening phrase "it is known" most probably refers to an existing text, most probably of Jewish, perhaps Kabbalistic, origin. What is fascinating is the resort to the syntagma "holy speech" and not to holy language or holy letters. Here the role of the ascending of spiritual force has nothing magical but some form of theurgical operation. This is also the case in another parallel passage:

> The vocables of the Torah that a person pronounces with his lips, literally, and those vapors that emerge from his mouth, are materialized in the air of the world,[38] and out of them spiritual and holy forms are wrought, that dress[39] the person and lead him to the roots of the letters/ vocables of the supernal Torah . . . and literally it is an entity, a spiritual being, in order to advocate his merit.[40]

The resort to the Hebrew *mamash*, translated as "literally," invites more general reflections on Cordovero's thought and on early Hasidism. Oral acts and the *imaginaire* of what happens in this context should be understood in their proper sense and not as symbols. While visual contemplation may help discovering a hidden sense that allegedly should be found beyond letters or verses, which are stable, the vocables are not since they do not subsist in order to allow the contemplative act that may decode the hidden meaning.

Curiously enough, the above previous passages have not informed Cordovero's voluminous commentary on the prayerbook, *Tefillah le-Moshe*, in a substantial manner. Though he uses phrases like the spiritual force of the letters/vocables—*ruḥaniyyut ha-'otiyyot*,[41] the spiritual force of prayer—*ruḥaniyyut ha-tefillah*,[42] the spiritual force of the song, namely the spiritual force that ascends from the performance of the commandments[43]—*ruḥaniyyut ha-shir*,[44] or the drawing down of spiritual force—*hamshakhat ruḥaniyyut*,[45] the astro-magical model is rather marginal in this book. Nevertheless, there is a connection between *ruḥaniyyut* and a supernal palace,[46] and several times he speaks about the spiritual force of the planet and constellations, *ruḥaniyyut ha-kokhav ve-ha-mazzal*, in the context of the praxis of the magicians.[47]

Interestingly enough for the Safedian Kabbalist, it is the spiritual force of the vocable that constitutes the highest form of Kabbalah, even higher than the Zoharic/sefirotic one, a topic to which he devoted most of his literary creativity.[48] It should be mentioned that the phrase *ruḥaniyyut ha-Torah*, the spiritual force of the Torah, is found in the context of the study of the Torah in a Cordoverian text,[49] and so too the "spiritual force of speech"—*ruḥaniyyut ha-dibbur*.[50] I assume that the meaning of this syntagma is referring to the spiritual force inherent in the act of speech, not necessarily the spiritual force attracted or induced by speech or in speech, as we shall see in appendix D in this volume. From this point of view the spiritual force of speech is identical to the spiritual force mentioned more than once in the connection of vapor of the utterance. It is important to point out that Cordovero speaks about cleaving to the spiritual force as a prerequisite that prayer will be answered.[51]

However, the term *ruḥaniyyut* does not stand everywhere in Cordovero's many writings for an astro-magical term, which means a supernal spiritual force that can be drawn down, but in

many cases it refers to the supernal spiritual world, *ruḥaniyyut
'elyon*, versus the material one, in a more Platonic vein, as part of an
opposition between the two realms. The dichotomy between gash-
miyyut—materiality and *ruḥaniyyut*—spirituality, when it stands
for the spiritual world, recur quite widely in Cordovero's writings, and it differs from the astro-magical meaning of *ruḥaniyyut*.
In some few other cases, *ruḥaniyyut* stands for a power inherent
within a variety of other entities, which is not necessarily drawn
down by the human activity, as we shall see in the next appendix.
Also potentially confusing is the fact that in Hebrew the spellings
of *ruḥaniyyut* and *ruḥaniyyot*—the plural form of *ruḥaniyyut*—are
identical. This means that out of the many thousands of occurrences of the term *ruḥaniyyut* in his writings, it is only the meaning
of a relatively small part that stems from magical sources, and
should be translated as "spiritual force" as I did previously in this
study.

In one of those cases, we can see a comprehensive description of
the role of drawing down the spiritual force as defining the nature
of worship as found in his commentary on the *Zohar*:

> Just as the issue of prophecy[52] will differ its drawing the
> higher soul that each and every one will pomp in accor-
> dance to his worship and the drawing of the supernal
> spiritual force by a measure that is characteristic of his
> worshipping God in comparison to his contemporary,
> so also is his cleaving to his Creator in comparison to
> the cleaving of his companion. And so also the worships
> themselves are different from each other, one is [higher]
> than the other, and one is [higher] than the other, in
> accordance to what each and every one seizes a worship,
> so he will receive a [higher] soul and a spiritual force
> from above, since the capacity of the worship is to draw
> to him the spiritual force of the *sefirot*. And the worships
> differ from each other and each of them draws in accor-
> dance to its [the worship's] capacity.[53]

Though the vocal rites are not mentioned here in an explicit manner, they are certainly comprised in the general category of worship, even more so since prayer has been defined in similar terms in the passage quoted previously from Cordovero's *Pardes Rimmonim*. However, what seems to me equally important is the mentioning of the cleaving—*devequt*—as part of the same type of affinity like worship: it depends, like prophecy, on the specific nature of worship: it is the latter that ensures the descent of a soul and spiritual force,[54] and it is determining the result of the human religious experience: prophecy or cleaving to God. In my opinion, here the term *worship* stands for a magical understanding of worship. In any case, the various days of the week are informed by the specific spiritual force of the divine attributes appointed on them, a reverberation of the various spiritual forces of the planets in astromagic, which have been projected by the Safedian Kabbalist on the divine world, as we shall see in the next appendix.

Therefore, both from the terminological and the historical points of view, the concatenation between the various terms stemming from the astral-magical model found in Cordovero's Kabbalistic thought constitutes the closest and most plausible source for one of the major interpretations of the vocal rites in traditions reported in the name of the Besht. Moreover, for the time being I am not acquainted with another Kabbalist prior to Cordovero or later on that is not dependent on him—Alemanno and Al-Qabetz aside—that resorts to all those terms and their specific conjugations, as discussed in this appendix, a fact that posits Cordovero and his followers, especially R. Abraham Azulai's *Hesed le-Avraham*, as the most plausible source for the Beshtian traditions on those issues.

Though much of the previous quotes stem from Cordovero's books that have been printed only in the recent decades, and thus were unknown to the Besht and his followers, the themes found in the previous citations have been adopted in a lengthy discussion of Azulai in his *Hesed le-'Avraham*, and in da Vidas's *Reshit Hokhmah*, and thus made available in print a generation before the floruit of the Besht.[55] Especially interesting is the occurrence of terms like

'otiyyot maḥashaviyyot, which has been adopted by the Besht as we
have seen in appendix B in this volume.

There are many implications of the present proposal to consider
Cordoverian sources of some major topics in the Besht's traditions:
terminological, ideic historical, and sociological. The first one has
been treated earlier in this appendix. The ideic one relating to the
specific concatenation between the same or similar terms in two
phases of Jewish mysticism has also been dealt with especially here.
The historical one is related to the different channels of transmission and the alternative general picture it articulates in comparison
to the Lurianic-Sabbatean line of explanation for the emergence
of Hasidism, *en vogue* in scholarship. And, last but not least: the
sociological implication: the shift from an elite theory in Safedian
Kabbalah to much more popular forms of exposition, informed by
the primacy of voice and utterances, was done by what I call a secondary elite figure: the Beshtian traditions are telling a story about
the dissemination of specific manner of performing ritual practices that in any case were part of the basic framework of Rabbinic
religiosity, but he diminished the need of the full-fledged theologies, adopting instead a variety of theologumena that are part of
what I call the broken theologies. This attitude is especially evident
insofar as the Cordoverian complex theosophy is concerned, which
is the most pertinent one for our purpose here.

Indeed, the Besht was perceived in Hasidism not necessarily as
a theological innovator but as someone that put a new emphasis
on prayer as part of what I call a wider liturgical turn in Rabbinic
Judaism, evident already in Safed, as mentioned previously. The
following description conveys the status of the Besht as part of
what in a Jewish community until him would be a secondary elite:

> The Besht said that the supernal things he merited to
> receive as a revelation [came] not as the result of his
> intense study of the Talmud but only because of the
> prayer he always was praying with a great *kavvanah*, and
> this is the reason why he merited the high degree.[56]

The question is whether the achievement "by prayer" means not just a technique but also "within the vocables of prayer." The Baʿal Shem Tov played therefore the role of a secondary elite figure by the standard of the traditional Rabbinic Judaism, less concerned as he was with the study of the Talmud, which turned much later into a primary elite figure.[57] The paramount role played by him in the apotheosis of prayer was insightfully pointed out two generations after his death, by the well-known R. Qalonimus Qalman ha-Levi Epstein of Krakau:

> The most essential thing is prayer. With the advent of the saintly Baʿal Shem Tov of blessed memory, the holy light of prayer gleamed and shone forth into the world for all those wishing to approach the worship God, blessed be His Name.[58]

Nota bene: it is not the emergence of Hasidism that is mentioned here but an innovation intended to the entire world. What has been initially intended as a wider spiritual phenomenon ended as a much more modest, though quite lasting and influential, spiritual reform that shifted the center of gravitation from study to prayer and from intellectual activities of the elite to the veneration of the holy person by larger audiences.

APPENDIX D

RU<u>H</u>ANIYYUT HA-'OTIYYOT: DRAWN DOWN OR INHERENT?

In several instances previously it has been pointed out that some of Cordovero's sources for his theory of vocal performance are to be found originally in magical treatises and terminology, or others, perhaps Kabbalistic ones, grounded in this magical material. This is a point that can be understood in more than one way: (a) The Safedian Kabbalist selectively adopted magical terminology and some structures related to it, especially the astro-magical one, within a broader and dominant conceptual structure, the theosophical-theurgical one, grounded especially in the Zoharic literature, and by integrating them he necessarily adapted them to this canonized structure; (b) Cordovero regarded those astro-magical elements as somehow relevant to the theosophical-theurgical structure, but nevertheless a system that is inferior to it; (c) And last but not least: He was well-acquainted with the astro-magical system, adopted it, and even adapted elements of the theosophical-theurgical structure to the logic of the astro-magical system. In my opinion, it is the last alternative that reflects best the situation, especially since in an important case Cordovero situated the knowledge of the "spiritual forces of the letters/vocables," *ru<u>h</u>aniyyut ha-'otiyyot*, as an important part of the highest form of Kabbalah, conceived to be even higher than the Zoharic theosophical Kabbalah, as we shall see further on in this appendix. Nevertheless, in some fewer cases the second alternative may also be pertinent.

By adopting the astro-magical structure, Cordovero was not alone in Jewish culture. During the twelfth century R. Abraham ibn Ezra and R. Yehudah ha-Levi adopted important aspects of the astral magical worldviews.[1] Maimonides, who was well-acquainted with a variety of astral magic treatises, dedicated many efforts in describing it in some of his writings solely in order to fiercely refute it.[2] Nevertheless, many followers of ibn Ezra in the fourteenth and fifteenth centuries elaborated in their supercommentaries on his Commentary on the Pentateuch, pointing to some of his sources to be found in some Arabic magical treatises.[3] Especially prominent in this context is the Pseudo-Ibn Ezra *Sefer ha-'Atzamim.*[4] Therefore, long before the time of Cordovero's floruit, various combinations of astral magic and Judaism, and astral magic and Kabbalah, were evident and also available.[5]

Most interesting in this context is the complex, eclectic, and erudite synthesis of R. Yohanan Alemanno, whose floruit was in the late fifteenth and early sixteenth century, who was well-acquainted with those trends in Jewish thought, especially the supercommentaries on ibn Ezra.[6] It is evident from his writings that the astro-magical worldviews had reached Italy already in the third quarter of the fifteenth century. However, so far it is hard to prove Alemanno's impact on Cordovero's thought, and it is more plausible to assume that they drew from common sources. Closer in time and place is the vast opus of R. Joseph ibn Tzayyaḥ, an older contemporary of Cordovero, active in Jerusalem and then in Syria, whose views were very plausibly known in Safed and to Cordovero.[7] His combination of astrology, magic, and Kabbalah is the most conspicuous synthesis in the Middle East, especially in Jerusalem, plausibly independent of the magical version of Kabbalah from the circle of writings belonging to the *Book of Meshiv*, which had been written mainly in Spain.[8]

The Safedian Kabbalist studied and cited at least some of the Hebrew Kabbalistic-magical corpora mentioned previously.

However, though widely regarding astro-magic as referring to an inferior approach in comparison to theosophical-theurgical Kabbalah, he conceived the logic of drawing down as important and very relevant for his understanding of Kabbalah, and it impacted on his vision of the divine world as containing divine powers described as vessels and other spiritual forces that dwell in those sefirotic vessels.[9] A major exception that concerns us in this context will be addressed immediately as follows. Each of the *sefirot* and all of them together are described as possessing a *ruḥaniyyut* of its own,[10] a concept that he adopted from earlier sources, since this syntagma is found already in one of Yohanan Alemanno's writings in quite an astro-magical context.[11] Cordovero adopted two theories of *sefirot* that are found separately, and even competed with each other in earlier Kabbalah,[12] but he offered a synthesis between them by resorting to a term, *ruḥaniyyut*, that stems from the astro-magical theory. What were considered earlier as the *sefirot qua* the essence of divinity he also describes by using the term *ruḥaniyyut* of the *sefirot*, which are conceived of as vessels. This means that the dichotomy of *ruḥaniyyut* and *heikhal*, which started in astro-magical texts as a description of the astral realm, has been translated in Cordovero and his sources in the vocal terms, and it has also been projected on a higher level, the intra-divine one. To the best of my knowledge, the next phase in Kabbalah, the Lurianic one, was much less concerned with the magical cargo found in Cordoverianism, including the terminology we have discussed previously, and thus cannot be seen as a conduit of astro-magical views concerning vocal rites.

However, in addition to the impact of this distinction in the domain of theosophy, Kabbalistic theurgy was also sometimes imagined as drawing down spiritual forces. Cordovero was well aware of the affinity between his theory of the descent of the influx and the magical practices of preparing amulets or talismans.[13] The constellated universe of the astral magic that assumes deep affinities between everything in this world and one of the planets, stars, or zodiacal signs has been transferred to the sefirotic realm.[14] This means that what has been subordinated to a certain planet in the astral type of order sometimes has now been subordinated by him to a certain *sefirah*. So, for example, we read in *Pardes Rimmonim*:

> All these topics are known and evident to those who write amulets,[15] and we have no part in their labor. But we have seen someone who designed amulets that refer to the [attribute] of [stern] judgment using the color red,[16] and those that refer to Grace in white[17] and those which refer to [the attribute of] Compassion in green,[18] and everything [was done] in accordance with what [was revealed] by true [angelic] mentors, who taught to him the preparation of the amulets.[19] All this [was done] in order to introduce him to the subject of the colors and the operations that derive from above.[20]

Elsewhere he described prayers in terms of incantations, in a manner reminiscent of astro-magic.[21] Cordovero, or his sources, combined the magic of colors as part of prayer, known earlier in Kabbalah, with the astral and the sefirotic structures:

> There is no doubt that the colors can introduce you to the operations of the *sefirot* and the drawing down of their overflow. Thus, when a person needs to draw down the overflow of Mercy from the attribute to Grace, let him imagine the name of the *sefirah* with the color that is appropriate to what he needs, in front of him. If he [applies to] Supreme *Hesed*, [let him imagine] the outermost white. . . . Likewise, when he undertakes a certain operation and is in need of the overflow of [the attribute of Judgment], let him then dress in red clothes and imagine the form [of the letters of] the Tetragrammaton in red, and so on in the case of all the operations causing the descent of the overflows. Certainly in this manner [we may explain] the meaning of the amulets. When a

person prepares an amulet for the [*sefirah* of] _Hesed_, let him imagine the [divine] name in a bright white, since then the operation of that name will be augmented.[22]

According to a discussion in his *Pardes Rimmonim*, there was a tradition that has to do with the talismanic understanding of the divine names that had already been received by the prophets.[23] However, not only colors and divine names are related to the *sefirot* in the context of the astral type of thought. This is also the case of letters, namely written letters. We have seen previously the affinities between amulets and colors and implicitly *sefirot*. Cordovero indeed was suspicious of this affinity. However, amulets contain letters in different alphabets, and according to the astral theory, each planet has some form of alphabet that is characteristic of it, just as it had vocal prayers to be addressed to it. This is found in the famous *Picatrix*,[24] and it was known in Hebrew sources since the last quarter of the thirteenth century in a special version of the *Book of Raziel*.[25] So, for example, R. Levi ben Abraham, a late thirteenth century Provencal thinker, wrote that:

> Every planet has special letters, and therefore one born [under that sign of the Zodiac] is disposed to be proficient in reading some letters more than other letters, as appointed to him, and that is the reason for different languages spoken by different nations.[26]

This means that each alphabet, or characters, probably different sets of characters, has another governing planet, which means also another spiritual force.[27] The efficacy of those components depends on many variants: timing, garments and their colors, specific food, incenses, effigies, and the specific prayers and sacrifices, sometimes of animals, addressed to the specific nature of each planet, actually to its spiritual force, and only when properly combined are they activated in a precise manner.[28] One way to envision those operations is to regard them as an attempt by the magician at imitating or assimilating the specific spiritual force of a certain planet.[29] In other words, the astral dichotomy mentioned previously has not only been elevated to a dichotomy in the divine world, probably under the impact of earlier sources, but also to that of language, which has also been conceived of as constituted of a palace and a spiritual power dwelling on or attracted in it.

It is also possible that Alemanno had been acquainted with another type of magic, stemming from Arabic sources too, that included Al-Kindi's theory of rays, which assumes that each entity, not just the astral bodies, emits rays, and can thereby have an impact on each other and the humans can intervene.[30] The role attributed to utterances was central in this magical worldview,[31] an issue reminiscent of some of the discussions in Alemanno, like the assumption that utterances may have an influence on various entities, independent of the dianoetic communication but because of the movement of the vocal apparatus.[32] According to Alemanno, elements have their own spiritual powers, and he uses the syntagma *ruhaniyyut ha-yesodot*, a term that hardly fits the astro-magic worldview.[33] Elsewhere he mentions the *ruhaniyyut* found in or inherent in the song.[34] In any case, Al-Kindi's book on rays has been known to Alemanno's contemporary, Marsilio Ficino, and had an impact on his thought.[35]

On this background let me address the Hebrew syntagma "the spiritual force of the letters/vocables" that was already in existence at least since the end of the fifteenth century, since it is quoted by R. Yohanan Alemanno in the name of the thirteenth century thinker, R. Isaac ibn Latif, that was active in Spain:

> and it is explicit in the writings of ibn Latif, that there is a *ruhaniyyut* to letters, as the rank of the forms to the matters, a spiritual influx, remaining lasting, spiritual and eternal, after its detachment from the matter, and it will adhere to that spiritual sphere, remaining alone, forever.[36]

However, the writings of the latter do not contain such a phrase, neither is his way of thought consonant to it, and I assume that

Alemanno had seen a spurious writing with ibn Latif's name. From the linguistic point of view, the syntagma can be interpreted in two ways: in an astro-magical one, namely the spiritual forces that are drawn dawn on the letters/vocables, or the spiritual powers that are inherent in the letters/vocables. Provided the two views of the "spiritual force" we referred to previously are found in Alemanno's writings, al-Kindi's approach is the most plausible conceptual background for the emergence of the seminal phrase "the spiritual force of the letters/vocables" in the spurious "ibn Latif" source of Alemanno. In any case, this last phrase occurs in a passage of Alemanno's that deals with the magical power of language, mentioning Apollonius' book *Melekhet Muskelet*, Albertus Magnus, and some other magical statements found in Jewish tradition.[37] Causing the descent of the spiritual force is not mentioned in this passage. Thus, an awareness of the al-Kindi theory and astro-magic, which were combined with Kabbalah, is evident in the writings of an important figure in Florence, but one who was scarcely known in mid-sixteenth century Safed.

It is therefore possible that such an al-Kindi type of theory had been known also to Cordovero, whose discussions of the ascending utterances or ascending spiritual forces may stem from the importance of the utterances as having a cosmic effect. He too espoused in many instances the view that each letter/vocable has a "spiritual force" of its own, as we have seen in the previous chapter when dealing with the manner in which prayer is operating.[38] According to one of his statements, each deed has a spiritual force of its own that ascends on high,[39] and this view does not fit an astro-magical interpretation. The same point is made in his understanding of the manner in which the ascent of the study of the Torah on high is depicted.[40] This is particularly evident in an important discussion in Azulai's *Hesed le-'Avraham*, where the vapor, the *kavvanah*, and the spiritual force are related to the pronunciation done by the five places in the human mouth.[41] I have no doubt that this discussion is also a reverberation of a Cordoverian text. We may depict an important trend in Cordovero's Kabbalah as a synthesis between the Zoharic literature—Spanish in its origin—and another conceptual trend found in Spain, the magical one in the sense of astral magic, while Lurianic Kabbalah constitutes a different synthesis between the Zoharic Kabbalah and some forms of Ashkenazi linguistic magic, without significant astral connotations.

Moreover, as Cordovero elaborated in detail in *Pardes Rimmonim*, each Hebrew letter, namely the graphic shape, corresponds to one or more *sefirot*, a topic to which he dedicated an entire gate, where he amalgamated a variety of earlier theosophical interpretations of the letters, whose first two chapters are quintessential for the understanding of the penetration of astral magic in Kabbalah.[42] These symbolic correspondences between letters and *sefirot* assume that the former depend on the latter. However, insofar as the spiritual force of the letters is concerned, Cordovero has another opinion. As seen in the previous appendix, the occurrence of the "spiritual force of speech" may be understood in this manner. In his famous compendium, he distinguishes between four main domains of studies in Judaism, first that of the Torah, then that of the Law and Midrashic lore, the third being that of the "pleasant *Zohar*" and, finally, the fourth and the highest one, constituted by:

> the spiritual force of the letters and their existence and their linkage with each other and their relationship since someone who will fathom this issue will be capable to create worlds[43] and this is called the [higher] soul of the [higher] soul that depends on *Binah* . . . and the fourth category is scarcely found and this is why it does not have a name [title] of its own,[44] and under its scope stand the [divine] names and their operations and the combinations out of the [biblical] verses.[45]

There can be no doubt that the fourth category is the highest, the rarest, and the most powerful, transcending as it does even the study of the "pleasant' *Zohar*, to which he dedicated most of his efforts by collecting the manuscripts and by composing *'Or Yaqar*,

the most voluminous commentary ever. The relationship between
the third and the fourth categories can be described in modern
terms as that between the symbolic and the magical modes: the
former is a much more noetic type of approach, while the latter
is much more performative. In other words, the magic related to
the activation of the inherently dwelling spiritual forces of the letters, most probably pronounced, is elevated to a status higher than
the study of the book of the *Zohar*. This high status of magic, in
comparison to that of the dominant forms of Kabbalah, is evident
already in an ideal curriculum of R. Yohanan Alemanno, several
decades before Cordovero.[46]

When combined the various letters or sounds produce together
another, more complex spiritual force, and this is the case when
words, verses, and whole biblical books emerge.[47] It seems also that
this view dealing with mixtures and greater efficacy has something
to do with astral magic.[48] In other words, what we can discern
in Cordovero is the transfer of the magical situation, anomian in
nature from a Kabbalistic point of view, to the classical nomian
activities in Judaism; namely, the study of the Torah and prayer as
operations capable of attracting supernal powers, be they sefirotic
or astral: The vocables produced by pronounciation are conceived
of as constituting some form of vocal talisman. In one occassion,
the Torah was described as the spiritual force of the world, by
means of which it has been created.[49] It should be mentioned that
Cordovero explicitly compares the situation of the divine realm sitting on the throne of the spiritual force to the stellar force attracted
into the talismans by means of a special type of lore, though he is
careful to mention the difference between them.[50]

In this context it should be pointed out that the Safedian
Kabbalist testifies that he was acquainted with a rather voluminous book of talismans that contained a thousand recipes.[51]
Unfortunately, I could not identify this treatise, though there are
many books in the Middle Ages entitled the *Book of Talismans*. In
the vein of other Kabbalists, Cordovero regards the books of magic
as dealing with an inferior type of lore, though it is conceived of

as an ancient one, a fact that did not prevent him from adopting terms and structures from those books. In other words, the astro-magic rituals have been adapted to the nomian tendency in Judaism, attenuating their obvious magical overtones and at the same time adopted for a search of a contact or union with the divine powers. This tendency is evident when compared to the more eclectic attitude to magic in R. Yohanan Alemanno's or R. Abraham Yagel's rather similar appropriations of astral magic.[52]

In eighteenth century Hasidism, unaware of the history of medieval astro-magical texts and other magical sources, the more mystical aspects of the combinations between Kabbalistic theosophies and theurgies and astro-magic have been enhanced,[53] though the alleged extraordinary power of the performer has not been reduced, as we shall see in appendix F. This is the phenomenology of the mystical-magical model, which differs from the induced spiritual force and its activation.

From Cordovero's classic of Kabbalah, some of those views made their way, directly and indirectly, to early Hasidism.[54] While Cordovero amplified the gamut of Kabbalistic thought by also incorporating modes of astral thought, the Besht went in the opposite direction, simplifying or breaking Cordoverian theology but at the same time emphasizing even more the special status of speech in general. We have seen previously the threefold distinction between *yihudim* performed in a vocal manner.[55] A similar emphasis on speech-acts is found in the Besht's grandson, R. Efrayyim of Sudylkov, when interpreting his grandfather's thought:

> By the presence of the righteous in the world,[56] when they speak the letters/sounds, of prayer and Torah, in awe and love, or words concerning materiality or stories . . . they elevate the letters/sounds.[57]

Here it seems that the inherent power within the utterances is seen as self-evident, and it qualifies the manner in which the righteous is conceived. It is only the latter that is capable of causing

the ascent or the sublimation of utterances in general, most probably in order to obtain some form of extraordinary result, which
I would call magical. The inclusion of stories, one of the main
genres of the Besht's instruction, together with nomian activities,
shows the importance of the vocal dimension of human activity.
So, for example, the theme of praying by telling tales is evident in
In Praise of the Baal Shem Tov,[58] and this may be the background of
the description that I propose to understand in an erotic manner,
found in the so-called *Testament of the Besht*: "When he prolongs
[the pronunciation of the] word this is *devequt*, that he does not
want to separate himself from that word."[59] This is part of the emotional intensification of the regular ritual, in addition to the louder
forms of recitation.

APPENDIX E

SPIRITUAL FORCES, VITALITY, AND IMMANENTISM IN EARLY HASIDISM

As claimed previously, the vestiges of the astro-magical worldview can be discerned not only in the conceptualization of language and its oral performance and, as we shall see in the next appendix, in the view of the righteous and in Cordovero's theosophy and that of his sources and parallels, like that of R. Yohanan Alemanno or R. Shlomo ha-Levi Al-Qabetz. I would like to point here to certain cases of a nexus between a vision of divinity and the possibility to attract it here below, and also of the theory of radical immanentism. It is the claim of some scholars that a pantheistic approach is the message of Hasidism *par excellence*,[1] and this claim deserves an examination also from the perspective of the astro-magical concepts.

Many of the discussions about dealing with the spiritual force present one of two distinct approaches: some of them assume the preexistence of the spiritual force within the linguistic entities, which we have called inherent, which when activated already contain that force stemming from the vapor of the human utterance, and there is no need for an act of drawing down; and a second one, which assumes the possibility to induce, namely to draw down, the supernal forces within the vocables.[2] It is the latter approach that is reflecting the astro-magical worldview. In both cases it is the human vocal activity that activates the emergence of the sounds and thus the possible cleaving to the content of the vocables. Those approaches have been brought together by Cordovero at the end of his *Pardes Rimmonim*, as we have seen in appendix D. The two approaches are found separately in Beshtian traditions.[3]

However, there is also a third approach, which I called "linguistic immanence," which assumes an ontological presence of the divine power in reality by means of the letters/vocables of the divinity. These words, I assume, conceived of as pronounced by God as part of the process of creation, serve as some kind of Platonic ideas, by means of which the world has been created.[4] This is an extension of the first approach, and it is this third approach that is similar to and influential on the immanentist worldview.

First and foremost let me point out that the concept of immanentism, sometimes described as pantheism, has been detected in many discussions in R. Moshe Cordovero, without, however, addressing the linguistic element or that of the spiritual force as a mode of immanence.[5] This does not mean that he had a systematic theology, as Scholem would like to present him, but that one of his many theologies can be described as such.[6] Here I would like not to address the possible affinities between the Besht and Cordovero's immanentism in general, but to refer to immanentism as related to the concept of *ruḥaniyyut*.

The syntagma "the spiritual force," when attributed to gods, is found already in the early thirteenth century in Arabic in a Jewish-Sufi author in Egypt, as pointed out by Shlomo Pines.[7] Moreover, several discussions related to the spiritual force in Arabic sources display a propensity to immanentism.[8] Spiritual force too is sometimes conceived by Cordovero to be present inherently in every material thing, and he uses in these contexts traditional formulas for divine omnipresence. This is predicated on a specific vision of the *Shekhinah*, the feminine divine power as kinetic, namely as understood to ascend to the *'Eyin Sof* and also to descend to this world, creating therefore a continuum. In some cases the term *ruḥaniyyut* is used in these contexts. So, for example, the Safedian Kabbalist wrote:

> It was hinted at [by the *Zohar*] to Her [of the *Shekhinah*] aspects . . . to the entire spiritual force that is spreading downward in the world of the separate entities,[9] and in the world of the spheres and in the material world.[10]

Dealing with the descent of the spiritual force of the *Shekhinah* from the higher divine worlds, Cordovero wrote:

> in the air of this world Her letters/vocables and spiritual force are materializing first, as I pointed out in *Pardes Rimmonim* in the Gate of *'aBY'a*,[11] the secret of the spiritual force of the *Shekhinah*, that rules over the world and the sparks of Her light are spreading, in accordance of the secret of the *Beriy'ah*, and *Yetziyrah* and *'Assiyah*, and in accordance to this the *Shekhinah* is found below descending the ladder and She is found in the lower [worlds] and She is called *Tefillah*, and She is adorned with the jewels of our prayer[12] in order to ascend a degree after degree.[13]

Nota bene: the association of the letters/vocables with the spiritual force, in the context of prayer, as in Cordovero's other discussions dealt with previously.[14] The linguistic immanence is evident, as the letters/vocables are mentioned. Also interesting is the association of the spiritual force and the sparks of the light of the *Shekhinah* that are depicted as found in the lower world. Such sparks are also mentioned elsewhere in Cordovero's writings,[15] and they represent an anticipation of the fall of the divine sparks in Lurianic Kabbalah. In both cases some discreet entities of divine origin are conceived of as descending within the lower world, but for Cordovero the task of the *Shekhinah* is incomparably more important than in Luria. Descending to the lower world and ascending to the highest one, the *Shekhinah* is unifying reality and is present everywhere also in what I would call an interstitial manner.[16] In a quote in the name of Cordovero's disciple, R. Abraham Galante, it is said that "all the things that were created in the world are the spiritual force that are found in all the worlds, the material and the compounded ones."[17]

The Besht has some special type of referring to immanence, by assuming that God is indeed imbuing reality but people are unaware of it. This is referenced by the biblical theme of God hiding his face. R. Jacob Joseph quotes in the name of the Besht the following passage:

> I heard from my teacher blessed be his memory, that if a person knows that the Holy one, blessed be He, hides there, there is no hideness, since [Psalms 92:10][18] "all the workers of inquity shall be scattered," and this is what is written [Deuteronomy 31:18] "and I shall surely hide my face on that day from them" namely that He shall hide from them that they shall not know that the Holy one, blessed be He, is in hidenness there, etc., and the words of mouth of the sage are pleasant.[19]

This is a theoretical assumption that has been exemplified by a parable that is one of the most remarkable pieces quoted in several cases in the name of the Besht:

> "And I shall hide my face from them"[20] etc. In order to understand this it seems to me that it is written in the *Zohar* that there are palaces of prayer, one higher than another, and angels receive the prayer. . . . And behold, the Holy One, blessed be He fills the entire world, and there is no place that is void of His glory, and wherever someone prays His glory, blessed be He, is found there.[21] Therefore, why there is need for the angels to go from a palace to another, in order that his prayer will be accepted? And it seems to me that I wrote elsewhere

> what I heard from my teacher, blessed be his memory, in
> a parable that he told before the blowing of the Shofar:
> There was a great wise king, and he made walls and
> towers and gates by means of an illusion.[22]

The parable mentioned at the end is the famous parable of the king
that created the world as an illusion of the separation of God from
the world, while actually He is found everywhere. This parable,
found in many versions and a piece that enjoyed many analyses,
is one of the most important illustrations of what I call the third
model, the noetic/immanentist one.[23]

In these passages and their parallels, as well as in the texts discussed in appendix A in this volume, there is no trace of astral
concepts, more specifically the term *spiritual force*. However, let
me cite a passage from one of R. Jacob Joseph of Polonnoye's books
where the Besht is not quoted, though on the same page several of
his other traditions have been adduced:

> [a] just as there are twenty-two letters/vocables of the
> speech of Torah and prayer, so there are twenty-two letters/
> vocables in all the existent things of matter and body in
> the world, because the world and everything in it were
> created by their means . . . but the letters/vocables are
> clothed in the matter of the things of the world, by sev-
> eral covers, garments and shells. And within the letters/
> vocables, dwells the spiritual force of the Holy One,
> blessed be He,[24] [b] Therefore, His Glory, blessed be He,
> fills the entire earth[25] and whatever is within it, and there
> is no place void of Him, as it is interpreted in *Tiqqunim*,[26]
> but He is in hiddenness and when the knowledgeable per-
> sons know about this hiddenness, this is no more a hid-
> denness or a change.[27, 28]

Let me turn first to paragraph [a] in this quote. The divine omnipresence is conceived of as being a matter of "the spiritual force of

God" that is inherent within the creative divine vocables. Here the astral term *ruḥaniyyut* is evident, and it is related to the primeval divine linguistic performance. The assumption of the divine presence within the creative sounds is certainly not new in the teachings of the Besht, as they serve as a starting point of one of his lengthiest discussions that I suggest should be dated at the beginning of his activity.[29] However, the astral concept that concerns us in this study is not found there. Nevertheless, I assume that the nexus between the two paragraphs is not his invention, as the affinity between the two topics is reminiscent of a passage of Cordovero's commentary on *Tiqqunei Zohar*, mentioned previously in this appendix. Moreover, such a nexus is found also in a short passage found in R. Nathan-Netaʿ of Siniewa, a mid-eighteenth-century author in Podolia, who asserted that the letter *Yod*, the first letter of the Tetragrammaton, is found in all the other letters, and its presence corresponds to the presence of "the power and the spiritual force [*ruḥani*] from above, in all the things in the world, and His Glory, blessed be He, fills the entire earth and whatever is in it."[30]

The contents of two parts of R. Jacob Joseph's passage are well-represented here, though in a concise manner, in a treatise that is not influenced by Hasidism and preserves, so I assume, earlier views. Moreover, in a treatise of R. Baruch of Kosov, the author invokes the importance of discussions found in Horowitz's *Shelah*[31] and R. Menahem Azaria of Fano's compendium of *Pardes Rimmonim*, *Pelaḥ ha-Rimmon*,[32] which deals with the spiritual forces found within the divine names, that of *ʾAdonai* and that of the Tetragrammaton, most probably referring also to the corresponding *sefirot Malkhut* and *Tiferet* respectively.[33] The latter *sefirah* is designated also as "The Holy One, blessed be He"—and thus the "spiritual force of the Holy One, blessed be He." This term may stand for both a specific divine power and for the divinity in general. In the first sense it is a parallel to the view found in the passage of R. Nathan-Netaʿ, which deals with the letters of the Tetragrammaton. Those parallels, though partial, reflect a Cordoverian association of divine vocables and spiritual force and could encourage a more

immanentist view. Though I do not assume that the Besht's immanentism emerges solely from such types of discussions, and there
are also other important sources which are not astral, this component should not be neglected.

Let me return to paragraph [a] of R. Jacob Joseph's passage.
The divine presence in the world is dependent on the primordial
divine letters or sounds, what I called linguistic immanence. A
similar view is found also in a teaching attributed to the other
main disciple of the Besht: The Great Maggid, who is quoted by R.
Elimelekh of Lysansk as explaining the meaning of the *tzimtzum*
as follows:

> He contracted Himself within the letters/vocables of the
> Torah, by means of which he has created the world[34] . . .
> and the *tzaddiq*, who studies the Torah for its own sake
> in holiness, draws the Creator downward, blessed be
> He, within the letters/vocables of the Torah[35] as in the
> moment of the creation . . . and by the pure utterances
> related to the study of the Torah, he draws down God
> within the letters/vocables.[36]

Drawing down God by a vocal activity is found also in a third
disciple of the Besht, who studied also with the Great Maggid, R.
Menahem Nahum of Chernobyl:

> *Li-shemah [le-shem he']*, for the sake of the letter *H*, i.e. the
> five places, which is Primordial Speech . . . Man has to
> pronounce the letters/vocables while being in a state of
> cleaving to the "Primordial Speech," and thereby it is pos-
> sible to draw downward the "Primordial Speech"—which
> is an aspect of God—to Israel in a general way. Since this
> is the quintessence of the revelation of the Torah, which
> is an aspect of God, and is in His Name, part of God is
> drawn and infused into the Children of Israel by means of
> speech that emanates from the Primordial Speech.[37]

Like Cordovero, the Great Maggid and R. Menahem Nahum also assume that divinity is found within the Torah as a written document that serves as the blueprint and instrument for the creation of the world. Thus, God is present inherently within the Torah. However, in addition to this type of static immanence, it is possible also to draw down God by activating the written letters by means of the vocal study. Here I discern the concept of drawing down a supernal power by means of a certain vocal rite.

These two phases reflect, in my opinion, a view found in Cordovero's *Pardes Rimmonim* when dealing with intention in prayer. The Safedian Kabbalist wrote as follows:

> [a] Each and every letter has a spiritual form [stemming] from the sublime light that is emanated from the very essence of the *sefirah* that is descending from one degree to another on the path of the descending emanation of the *sefirot*. And behold, this letter is a palace and a seat of that spiritual force.[38] [b] And when a person recites and moves one of the letters, by necessity that spiritual force will be aroused . . . and indeed because of the pronunciation that a person pronounces that word that is hinted at by the letters, because of the move of those powers and the collision of one to another by the hammer of the soul, in addition to their arousal in their supernal source in order to act that operation . . . and this is the secret of the pronunciation of the names and the intention of prayer.[39]

The divine presence is related to the descent of the letters [a], and this type of cosmology reflects the linguistic immanence, or the inherent spiritual force. The divinity of the letters refers to the graphical aspect, but it is only their activation [b] that has an impact on the high realms and can obtain some form of magical act in accordance with the words pronounced. This is a close parallel to another text adduced in the name of the Great Maggid:

divine immanence in the written letters is a precondition to their effective oral activation: be it the drawing of God here below or having an impact via the activation of the supernal roots of the vocalized letters. In a way, Cordovero, and perhaps also the Great Maggid, envisioned a circulation of divine power, and the activation of letters by pronunciations create an energetic exchange that is part of the linguistic circuit.

Different as the texts of the two main disciples of the Besht are, they nevertheless agree on the concept of linguistic immanence in the world, a concept that has been elaborated already in the earlier stage of the Besht as mentioned previously, but now two different motifs have been added: the spiritual force in R. Jacob Joseph's passage, and the drawing down in the Great Maggid's passage.

Let me turn to another possible connection between Cordovero, the Besht, and immanence. The Safedian Kabbalist uses the term *Ḥiyyut*, or *Ḥayyut*, which means vitality, as a synonym for influx, spiritual force, luminosity, or divine light, in order to describe the immanence of the divinity within all creatures.[40] For his former student, R. Ḥayyim Vital, the important assumption is that the divine speech is found in every creature as its vitality.[41] It should be mentioned that in quotations in the name of the Besht, the nexus between *ruḥaniyyut* and *ḥiyyut* as descending entities is evident in a series of texts. This is the case in R. Jacob Joseph's *Toledot Ya'aqov Yosef*[42] in his *Tzafnat Pa'aneaḥ*,[43] or in *Keter Shem Tov*.[44] Indeed, the term *ḥiyyut* has a long history in Judaism, since the High Middle Ages, in most cases not necessarily related to astral magic.[45] One explanation for some of the Hasidic uses of this term has been offered by Joseph Weiss, who proposes to see in the Neoplatonic theory of emanation and its Kabbalistic reverberations the source of the Hasidic concept of the supernal *ḥiyyut* as immanent in this world.[46] Though possible, this possibility has to be substantiated by a more detailed analysis.

However, given the occurrence of this term in connection to *ruḥaniyyut*, I am inclined to see as a more plausible source the astro-magical model. Indeed, R. Gedalyah of Linitz, a disciple of

R. Jacob Joseph, mentioned in his *Teshu'ot Ḥen* the term *ḥiyyut* in a conspicuously astrological context when he speaks about drawing down vitality onto the respective zodiacal sign.[47] This is also the case of R. Yehudah Leib ha-Kohen of Hanipoly, who mentions in his *Ve-Zot li-Yihudah* that there is nothing in the world, including minerals, that does not have "vitality, spiritual forces, a zodiac sign and a decan that is governing it."[48] Thus, we may assume a case of contamination of the term vitality by semantic valences found in the term *spiritual force*. The fact that the terms vitality and spiritual force occur together with the astrological terms shows that the affinity between them persisted into the second half of the eighteenth century, including the very end of that century, reflecting a Cordoverian impact. Similar to the views of Cordovero on the *Shekhinah* is a formulation that occurs in R. Menahem Nahum of Chernobyl, where he describes the *Shekhinah* as "the vitality of God, blessed be He, that dwells in every thing"[49] and several times uses the phrase "the vitality of the Creator"—*ḥiyyut ha-Bore*."[50] Especially important is the resort to the term in several discussions in R. Menahem Nahem of Chernobyl, and in some other Hasidic masters. Last but not least in this context: already a contemporary of the Besht, R. Menahem Mendel, the Maggid of Bar, is reported as embracing a form of immanence very similar to that of the Besht. He explained the reason why he was looking down while he prayed, by saying that:

> He is looking for a very low place, because also there is Divinity and His vitality, and there is no place void of Him[51] because in everything there is His vitality, even in the lowest degree.[52]

What is especially pertinent to our discussions is that here immanentism is related to the vocal rite, though the magical aspect is totally absent, in a manner reminiscent of what I call the Besht's third model. It is therefore also evident that the specific formulation of the immanentism theory by resorting to the term *ḥiyyut* was known in a circle very close to the Besht.[53] As seen previously in the case of the creation of vessels by verbal activity, persons active in the immediate surrounding of the Besht expressed ideas identical both conceptually and terminologically to his.[54]

Last but not least: the semantic similarity between vitality and spiritual force, especially when related to vocal activity, is reminiscent of the view of Edmund Husserl, who distinguished between the quality of vitality—*Leiblichkeit* or *Lebendikeit*—and spirituality—*Geistigkeit*—in connection to the vocal dimension, relayed to a living body—*Leib*—versus the graphical level, described as inanimate body—*Koerper*—in the context of the two dimensions of the linguistic units.[55] Moreover, according to Ludwig Wittgenstein, "Every sign *by itself* seems dead. *What* gives it life? In use it is *alive*. Is life breathed into it there? Or is the use its life?"[56] Whether these philosophers could have been acquainted with Hasidic thought about language while inhabitants of Vienna— then hosting a rather significant number of Hasidic circles—or not is an interesting topic that cannot be discussed here.

APPENDIX F

THE CONCEPT OF *TZADDIQ* AND ASTRAL MAGIC

As a profession, the Besht was a practical magician, and there is plenty of magical material attributed to the Besht, in print and in manuscripts, which consists of classical remedies, *seggulot*, and apotropaic amulets.[1] He was designated as *qosem*, namely someone who performs wonders by producing illusions; this is the way that the Gaon of Vilna described the Besht's influence on the Great Maggid, according to the report of R. David of Makow.[2] However, it is not evident that the magical practices were related, certainly not exclusively, with astro-magic, though, as seen previously, the astro-magic terminology has been adopted in his instructions concerning cultic performance. Nevertheless, the manner in which he envisioned the holy man, the *tzaddiq*, bears evidence of vestiges of astro-magic sources.

The special role played by the *tzaddiq* in Hasidism as a seminal concept and as a living leader and mentor has been duly recognized by scholars and analyzed in some important studies.[3] Especially pertinent are Piekarz's remarks concerning the affinities between aspects of the concept of the righteous in early Hasidism and Cordovero's thought, but without elaborating on the astro-magical aspect of the righteous.[4] In some studies I have addressed the connection between astral magic and the role of the *tzaddiq* in more general terms,[5] and I have claimed that the seminal role of the concept of *tzaddiq* in Hasidism is also the result of an unprecedent ascendancy of what I called the mystical-magical model, which also has earlier astral-magical sources.[6] It is, however, obvious that also in this case early Hasidism drew from a variety of sources, and I do not intend here or elsewhere to reduce this variety to solely one type of source. In this context, the important role played by worship of the *tzaddiq* among North-African Jews should be mentioned as the result of the ascent of the holy man under the impact of Arabic culture.[7]

Now I would like to concentrate more on the axis of Cordovero-Besht, in particular insofar as the role of the righteous is concerned, and make the claim that the astro-magic contributed to the new, magical dimensions of this concept, which in principle are found already in Rabbinic sources but without the astral views.[8] The Safedian master wrote as follows:

> There is a righteous whose power is great,[9] so that the Holy One blessed be He, inscribes him on high among the saints, and the issue of his prayers and commandments are not like those of one of the people, but he is inscribed because he excels in comparison of the other people. So also below he is not part of the people but he is a person inscribed for himself . . . and he is the tabernacle for holiness.[10] And despite the fact that the *Shekhinah* is found upon all the people of Israel, the *Shekhinah* is essentially dwelling upon him, and from there She spreads to the entire world.[11] And the reason is that he is a righteous, and despite the fact that the entire world[12] is unifying the [divine] unity, it is his unification that excels over all. This is the reason why the *Shekhinah* will adhere to him in Her [very] essence, while Her branches are upon all. And he is the well of the blessings[13] upon the world, as it is said[14]: "The entire world is

nourished because of Hanina', My son etc.," and he is
the chariot for the *Shekhinah*[15] . . . He causes the existence of the *Yesod* and *Tiferet* in the world,[16] bound with
the *Shekhinah*. And this is the reason why the *Shekhinah*
adheres to him, as She is pursuing [*rodefet*] for *Yesod* and
Tiferet and does not find them but with him.[17]

This is an interesting combination of theurgical acts of the righteous with a magical one, represented by the view of drawing blessings to the entire world because of the extraordinary power he has.
The righteous is an *axis mundi*, because he is the channel of the
transmission of the higher power and its spreading in the world.
As the embodiment of the two male *sefirot*, he attracts the dwelling
of the divine feminine power, the *Shekhinah*, upon him. The drawing down is less prominent, as it is the *Shekhinah* that is spread in
the world and not the influx, but this point is made clearly by the
Safedian Kabbalist elsewhere:

In accordance to the amount of the intention [of the
righteous man in his prayer] if he intended to cause the
influx from one rank to another, in accordance to the
ranks of the ladder,[18] and will adhere to his Creator by
his knowledge concerning the performance of the commandments, his soul will ascend and be elevated from
one degree to another, from one generator to another,
and from one cause to another, until an abundance of
influx will emanate upon him and he will be the place
of the seat and the dwelling for that influx, and from
there it will be distributed to the world . . . and in accordance to those words he will become the dwelling of the
Shekhinah, because the influx comes by his means, so
the righteous is instead of the great pipeline, the foundation of the world, and this is the reason why he merits
that the *Shekhinah* adheres to him . . . when a *tzaddiq*
and a *ḥasid* is present in this world, the entire world is

nourished by him, as it is written[19] "the entire world is
sustained for the sake of R. Ḥanina', My son."[20]

The meritorious deeds of the righteous ensure his ascent in the
divine world and his mediation of influx, though the magic aspect
of drawing down is not explicit here. However, in his treatise on
the angelic powers, Cordovero asserts that:

> Everything depends upon the spiritual force, the influx
> that flows by means of the *tzaddiq* and of his proper
> deeds. . . . The world is blessed by the spiritual force
> flowing because of the merit [of the *tzaddiqim*] . . . and
> all of the worlds and things are subjected[21] to the *tzaddiq*
> . . . and everything depends upon the secret of the Torah
> that is transmitted to him but not to any other creature.[22]

Here the occurrence of the term *ruḥaniyyut* betrays the magical
source of Cordovero's interpretation of the way the righteous operates. According to this Kabbalist's reading of the Rabbinic text, R.
Hanina' is not just the person for whose sake God nourishes the
world, as a father does out of his love for his son, but actually he is
portrayed as the mediating power that transmits the influx to the
world and the reason for the descent of that power "by means of
the *tzaddiq*," namely through his body that functions as a pipeline.
This statement transforms the human righteous into a supreme cosmic figure, an embodiment of the divine, upon whom all things in
this world depend. The role of the theosophical righteous, namely
the phallic divine power, *Yesod*, has been transfered into a human
elitist function, as the mediator and transmitter of divine power to
the lower world. The righteous plays the role of the pontiff between
worlds, of drawing down supernal powers and distributing them,
most probably by his body. However, unlike the Christian vision of
the divine son, the righteous is not a unique human, but it changes
with time, and actually several righteous may coexist. Here, theosophical images have been conjugated with magical aspects of the

human activity. Interesting enough, the feminine divine power is depicted here in search for the two divine masculine powers, embodied by the righteous' body, and She serves as some form of soul for the three of them, supplying as She does the influx to be distributed.

Parts of this theory reverberated in Abraham Azulai's *Hesed le-'Avraham* mentioned many times. His booklet is replete with references to the special status of the *tzaddiq*, proportionally more than any other Kabbalistic book beforehand, as discussed in appendix B in this volume, a fact that may explain its contribution to nascent Hasidism.[23] Let me adduce one more example that seems to me relevant for the later development of this seminal of this concept in Hasidism:

> And behold, by means of the *tzaddiqim* that dwell in the Israel, the influx descend from above. And since the spiritual influx cannot descend to the material land but by means of the *tzaddiqim*, which are "part of God on high," by the preparation of their deeds and their Torah they cause the descent of the influx [even] contrary to its nature, and the purity of the place is helpful to them.[24]

Here, the magical aspect of the activity of the righteous is evident, as Azulai mentions their capacity to change the natural course of the supernal influx, and again the study of Torah, I assume done in a vocal manner, is mentioned in this context. However, Azulai explains the capacity of the righteous men to mediate because they, namely their souls, are part of God, and he uses the phrase from Job 31:2.[25] The juxtaposition between this biblical phrase and righteousness is not unique with Azulai, as it is found already in another widespread book of Kabbalah, which plausibly influenced Azulai, Cordovero's *'Or Ne'erav*,[26] and a few other similar instances, for example in Lurianic Kabbalah.[27] Nevertheless, I see Azulai's passages as one of the major and most plausible sources for the elevated status of the *tzaddiq* in Hasidism. According to the Kabbalist the soul is considered to be divine, a view found already in ancient Greek sources, as mentioned in appendix F n. 25, and thus divinity dwells upon him and the body serves as the conductor and vessel of divine power, but this is also part of the religious behavior that is capable of and intended for drawing down the divine power, a religious structure that I see as impregnated by astro-magical terminology. The body of the righteous is a conduit for divine power, namely from some form of Shamanic behavior, not a matter of incarnation.

This explanation that had not been taken seriously in consideration in scholarship is, in my opinion, an alternative to the recent emphasis, on the theory of incarnation of the divinity in the *tzaddiq*, which is another case of what I call scholarly Christotropia.[28] I hope to elaborate elsewhere on the divinity as dwelling within the *tzaddiq's* soul as part of the widespread theory in Kabbalah that emphasized the divinity of the soul, along the lines discussed here and in appendix A.[29]

In a text important for our discussion here, a treatise *Yad Yosef,* written by R. Joseph Tzarfati at the beginning of the seventeenth century and quoted verbatim by R. Jacob Joseph of Polonnoye, the assumption is that the *tzaddiq* draws down the influx upon "all the people of his generation."[30] It should be mentioned that the text of R. Joseph Tzarfati, probably written before the *Shenei Luḥot ha-Berit* and *Ḥesed le-'Avraham*, reflects Cordovero's terminology. Also in the influential *Shenei Luḥot ha-Berit*, R. Isaiah Horowitz presents the views we found in Cordoverian passages translated previously:

> The tabernacle has been built in Shilo, the part of [the tribe of] Joseph . . . and despite the fact that it has been destroyed, Joseph nevertheless opened the pipe of holiness, and holiness remained afterwards in the eternal edifice, because Joseph was the pipeline as he is the pillar upon which the world stands, in accordance to the secret of his attribute "The Righteous is the foundation of the world"[31] that all the variety of influx are passing through

this pipeline to *Malkhut*, that is called "World" despite
the fact that the kingdom and the temples were removed
from him [namely from Joseph]. And this is the matter
that "the entire world is nourished because of Hanina'
My son, and Hanina' My son is nourished by one kab of
cabot from the eve of Sabbath to the eve of Sabbath." And
the issue is that R. Hanina' was in his generation the great
righteous, the one single pillar upon which the world
stands, and this is the reason why it is said, "For the sake
of Hanina'": *Bi-shevil*, means a pathway and a pipeline.[32]

Here the classical vision of the righteous as the foundation of the
world, exemplified here by the figure of Joseph, some form of Atlas
mythologumenon, has been amalgamated with the active magical person, capable to open the channel and allow the influx to
descend. Here the theosophical elements are quite visible, as was
the case of Cordovero and Azulai.

Apparently an elaboration on the concepts in the previous passages is found in R. Shelomo Rocca, an Italian Kabbalist who
authored *Kavvanat Shelomo*, a short seventeenth-century Lurianic
treatise, where the *tzaddiqim* sitting here below are described as
drawing down the influx upon the supernal *tzaddiq* and then upon
themselves.[33] The language of this passage is especially interesting
because this Kabbalist also uses the phrase "upon us, the *tzaddiqim*
who sit here below and their heart is [directed] above to draw down
the influx," assuming that the magical activity of the *tzaddiq* is
more than an abstract concept accepted from some earlier sources
but possibly practiced, or at least only recommended in the present.
Elsewhere Rocca mentions the lower *tzaddiq* and his activity on
high is discussed, which culminates with the drawing down of
influx.[34] In general, the recurrence of the term *tzaddiq* in this book
more than in other texts, which appears in several magical contexts,
may be a sign of the surge of the importance of this concept in the
seventeenth century, parallel in time to the composition of Azulai's
booklet.

Those sources demonstrate the wide dissemination of Cordovero's views and their availability to the Besht and his contemporaries.[35] The theory that the righteous is a pipeline, together with the Talmudic passage about R. Hanina', a first-century Galilean charismatic wonder-maker, will become a standard portrait of the righteous in the seventeenth century and then in Hasidism. It may be a matter of debate whether the description of someone upon whom the world depends, and at the same time serves as a pipeline, should or must be described as magic. In my opinion, this is the case, and indeed there is an interesting description by a modern scholar of the ancient magician as a vessel and a channel.[36]

These magical dimensions of the righteous did not attract the attention deserved in scholarship. So, for example, the characterization of the Hasidic righteous according to G. Scholem is the conjugation of the mystical element with the ethical one.[37] R. Jacob Joseph adduced in the name of the Besht the following passage:

> In the name of my teacher: "Hanina' my son has done a pathway and a pipeline in order to draw down the influx in the world, and this is the meaning of the [Rabbinic dictum] 'the world is nourished because of Hanina' my son,' and the words of the mouth of the sage are pleasant."[38]

This general approach is indubitably one of the most recurrent views of Beshtian traditions. However, there are different accents in the variants. In the quoted passages, R. Hanina' is not a righteous, nor is he always a pipeline, but just someone who opened a pipeline, which is not necessarily he or a human being, but some form of cosmical entity. Neither are the canonical performances explicitly depicted as the cause of the descent of the influx. Another occurrence of this interpretation of the Talmudic dictum is found also in R. Jacob Joseph's *Toledot Ya'aqov Yosef,* again in the name of the Besht[39] and anonymously elsewhere in this book,[40] and a rather precise reiteration of this text is found, though anonymously, also in R. Jacob Joseph's *Tzafnat Pa'aneaḥ*. However, immediately afterward, he cites the Besht as follows:

> I heard from my teacher that *"shevil* is a pipe that he opened a pipeline and a pathway for the influx, and this is the meaning of what is said: '*bi-shevil* Hanina' my son. And the words of the mouth of sage are pleasant.'"[41]

However, elsewhere, he quotes his master to this effect, in a passage that plausibly contains a much more magical formulation.

> Since the bodies of the letters/vocables are "a ladder fixed on earth" "and its head" namely its spiritual force "reaches heaven" and by means of it "the angels of God," which are the righteous "ascend" on high in order to cleave to Him, blessed be and "descend" on it in order to cause the descent of the influx in the world, in accordance to the secret of "the world is sustained because of [the pathway and pipeline] R. Hanina', My son," as I heard from my teacher about it.[42]

Elsewhere he elaborates on the meaning of the Besht's statement at length, adding theosophical and theurgical dimensions, which are not so evident in the traditions found in the name of the Besht,[43] while elsewhere in the same book the theme of the righteous is introduced.[44] We may consider some of his discussions as an attempt to reconstruct the theologies that were broken by the Besht, though the vocal element has not been diminished.[45] The term *secret* here refers, as in some other cases, to the idea of power, not so much to a recondite topic as in theosophical-theurgical Kabbalah.

However, for our purpose here, it is especially important to refer to a longer version cited in the name of the Besht, including the resort to the verb *mamshikh* that occurs sometime later on in the book of R. Israel ben Shabbatai, the Maggid of Kuznitz, who preserved also some other interesting statements reported in the name

of Ba'al Shem Tov, unknown otherwise, which is consonant with a
magical vision of the activity of R. Hanina':

> ha-Ribash,[46] blessed be his memory said: the meaning
> of the Gemara: [For R. Yehudah said in the name of
> Rav]: "Every day a 'daughter of voice' [goes forth from
> Mount Horev and] proclaims[47]: 'The whole world is sus-
> tained [or nourished] for the sake of My son Hanina',
> and Hanina' My son has to subsist on a kab of carobs
> from one weekend to the next,' since the *tzaddiq* is like a
> pathway and a pipeline that draws liquids[48] so he does by
> his holy deeds he draws good influxes to the entire world.
> And just as the pipeline does not enjoy from what passes
> through it so also the *tzaddiq* has no other will and wish
> than to cause the influx to all the inhabitants of the
> world, and this is [the meaning of what] the daughter of
> voice [said] 'the entire world is nourished for the sake [*bi-
> shevil*] which means the pipeline that R. Hanina' my son
> does, and it is like the pathway and pipeline that does
> not wish good for himself and he is satisfied with a very
> little and subsists on a kab of carobs etc., and the words
> of the mouth of the sage are pleasant."[49]

R. Israel of Kuznitz is a very knowledgeable author, well-
acquainted with Kabbalistic literature and even editing some
small treatises of early Kabbalah. Nevertheless, he does not notice
the Cordoverian source of the Besht. This is a clear example for
the concept of the righteous as a magician, who acts intentionally in order to bring down the influx for the world, more than in
the other Beshtian passages discussed previously. An interesting
parallel to these perceptions of R. Hanina' as opening a channel
for the benefit of other people is found in *Shivehei ha-Besht*.[50] A
similar interpretation is found, anonymously, in the collection of
the teachings edited in the circle of the Great Maggid's disciples.[51]
This is but another example of the appropriation of a Beshtian

interpretation—which indeed also has earlier sources—by the circle of the Great Maggid, though again without mentioning the Besht as the source.[52] Afterward, this interpretation was adopted by a long series of Hasidic masters.[53]

Like Cordovero, the Besht also interprets the Rabbinic statement about the late antiquity charismatic figure R. Hanina' ben Dossa' as both a righteous—a view not mentioned in the Rabbinic source—and as a pipeline for causing the descent of supernal power for the transmission of the supernal power. Both authors explain this role of mediation as the result of the operation of drawing down the supernal influx, which constitutes the magical aspect of this discussion. We may therefore depict Cordovero's literary corpus as a main turning point of the elevation of the concept of the righteous in Jewish thought by adopting the magic valence, and its transmission through a variety of other sources that were mentioned previously to early Hasidism.

It should be emphasized that in the Hasidic passages discussed previously the righteous is not described in symbolic terms, namely as a hint to a divine power, the *sefirah* of Yesod, as happens in so many cases in theosophical Kabbalah and in some cases also in Hasidism, but as a concrete and present entity that operates within this world. Moreover, the entire range of texts mentioned here deal with the entire world, namely with all the people, either in an universalist—namely including also the gentiles—or in particularist manner—namely restricting the discussion to the people of Israel alone—but certainly not with the concept of a leader of a certain defined and limited community of followers, as is going to be the case later on in Hasidism.[54] The theosophical dimension included in the comparison of the human righteous to the corresponding divine male power, dissipated in the Beshtian traditions.

Interestingly enough, when comparing the Cordoverian discussions to the Beshtian ones, it is evident that the latter are shorter and very rarely do the disciples of the Besht recognize earlier sources that inspired their master's views. This means that the disciples were concerned not so much with the history of ideas in

Judaism or, as in Kabbalah, with originality, but with the authority of their revered master, and the Besht's authority alone formulated orally and in various variants was strong enough in order to impose the specific concept of *tzaddiq* on the later generations of Hasidim, more than any occurrence of this statement found in earlier and authoritative written sources. While Cordovero's discussions, and those of his followers, should be better understood on the background of his luxurious theosophy, the Besht is less concerned with depicting the precise nature of the higher extremity of the pipeline and much more with the function of the lower righteous that operates in this world.[55]

This does not mean that the theosophical dimensions did not return later on as Hasidic interpretations of the Beshtian traditions as some form of theologization.[56] On the other hand, it is possible that the concise version of the quotations in the name of the Besht should be understood as some form of stenographic instructions, understood by his entourage on the ground of the shared conceptual heritage of Cordovero and his followers. When, for example, the Besht was understood as dealing with the righteous as a pipeline, the followers would understand the active function of such imagery, without however being aware of the astro-magical background of the Cordoverian sources.

In this context, let me mention a passage of R. Jacob Joseph that is not attributed to the Besht though, according to two modern authors, it may reflect the Besht's view[57]:

> And even in a commandment that concerns [an act of] speech alone, without a deed, it is incumbent to unify and link the letters/vocables in order to combine them into words, and this is imposible [to be done] but by the righteous that draws the influx of the spiritual force of the *sefirot*, together with the light of the Infinite within it, that unifies the letters/vocables and links them to [form] words, as I wrote in the introduction[58] "Anyone that performs one commandment etc.,"[59] check there.

And behold, the letters/vocables of speech are called vessel,[60] possessing a limit and measure that is called *Yesh* [existence] . . . a vessel called *Yesh* and it is incumbent to draw within it the light of spiritual force and vivify it that is called *'Ayin*, since it is the [high] soul that is emanated from the Infinite, the Life of Lives,[61] corresponding to two [things] that the righteous does in this world in his lifetime, he will consume its compensation, and in the world-to-come [there are] two degrees also, and this is the meaning of [Proverbs 8:21][62] "That I may cause those that who love me [*Yesh*] to inherit substance and I will fill their treasures." *'Aniy* [which means I] from my essence I am—as if it is—*'Ayin*, that is the light of the soul, that is found within the treasure and the vessel, which is vivifying them.[63]

This is a dense and comprehensive picture that deserves a detailed analysis. It has a rather close parallel in another text from the same book we have adduced and analyzed in appendix B.[64] Like in that passage there are dualities: the metaphysical one, the divine *'Ayin*, nothingness, and the existence, *Yesh*, the latter identified with *'Aniy*; the vessel and the content; the letters/vocables and the spiritual forces that unify them; this world and the next one. However, unlike the passage under scrutiny here, there the name of the Besht has been mentioned, together with the book of R. Abraham Azulai. The double activity of the righteous is similar to that of the divine power within the sefirotic realm: he creates a vessel by means of performing a commandment or ritual speech, and then he draws the influx, or the spiritual force, within it. Both acts reflect the impact of the astro-magical model.

Three topics deserve special attention: the portrait of the righteous as an astro-magical-theosophical operator, the concept of a linking power, and finally the relationship between the pair of opposites *'Ayin* and *Yesh*, a dialectic that will inspire many Hasidic authors later, especially the Great Maggid.[65] The first topic, which concerns us especially in this appendix, shows once again the Cordoverian synthesis of astro-magic, theurgy, and theosophy as the actual source of the Hasidic author. As seen previously, this is consonant with the views of the Besht, though the nomenclature is much more Cordoverian. Also, the opposition of *'Ayin* and *'Aniy* is found already in Cordovero and da Vidas, and then also in the Besht.[66]

However, the third element, related to the capacity of the righteous to unify the vocables is, to the best of my knowledge, not found earlier, though it occurs many times in the writings of R. Jacob Joseph of Polonnoye, who uses recurrently the term *ha-koah ha-mehabber*, the unifying power.[67] This aspect of the activity of the righteous deserves a separate analysis, which cannot be done in this framework. In any case, the question of the connections between the vocables after they have been pronounced is reminiscent of the Besht, as we have seen previously when discussing the passage from the *Holy Epistle*.[68] Nevertheless, the question as to how much of the Besht's thought has penetrated this discussion, if at all, is a question hard to answer. Is this bringing together of different themes found separately in the Beshtian teachings by the disciples something new with R. Jacob Joseph, or is it one more example of elaborating upon the master's thought in the latter's vein, or the conceptual contribution of the authors? The fact that he refers to his discussion in the introduction to *Toledot Ya'aqov Yosef,* where he confesses that he received this theory, probably from the Besht, tips the balance in the favor of the former alternative, even more so when the same theories are found also in the school of the Great Maggid, in the writing of one of his main disciples, R. Levi Isaac of Berditchev. This master too deals with the concept of the commandments as related to "existence," *Yesh*:

> There are two [types of] worshipers of the Creator: one that worships him with dedication, and one who worships the Creator by means of commandments and good deeds. And the difference between them is that the one who worships the Creator by dedication [but] not by

means of the commandments is nihil indeed, and the
one who worships the Lord by commandments, worships by means of a thing that is existence—since the
commandments are existence. This is the reason why
someone who worships by dedication is nihil and he
cannot draw the influx on himself, since he is nothing,
as he solely cleaves to the Lord, blessed be He, while the
one the worships by the performance of the commandments and good deeds, he cleaves to the existence [*Yesh*],
because the commandments are existence, and by performing them he is drawing upon himself influx from
God, blessed be He.[69]

I wonder whether these two types do not reflect the dichotomy soul/
body. It is the latter type alone that has a possible social repercus-
sion, and it reflects also the view of Great Maggid, the teacher of R.
Levi Isaac.[70] I dwelled on this aspect of the magical dimension of
the righteous not just in order to refer to an important aspect of the
seminal theory of the *tzaddiq*, but because I consider the primacy
of this widespread theory also from the statistical point of view.

Though only some few of the discussions about the figure of
Hanina' ben Dossa' found in early Hasidism have been adduced
here, the impact of the Cordoverian interpretation is evident, and
it remained formative also later on, provided the role played by
the institution of the *tzaddiq* in the Hasidic movement as a whole.
Therefore, without taking into serious consideration the statistical
density of the occurrence of this theme when dealing with the
Hasidic notion of *tzaddiq*, and the concrete preoccupations of the
Hasidic righteous men in history, especially importing blessings
to their followers, the picture offered by scholars may be seriously
flawed.

NOTES

1. Vocables and *Devequt* in Scholarship of Early Hasidism

1 Scholem, "*Devequt* or Communion with God," in his *The Messianic Idea*, p. 211, and the very same formula has been reiterated in Scholem, p. 246, as part of his polemic with Martin Buber's view of Hasidic *yiḥud*. The term *Torah* stands in Scholem's passage for a certain sort of text, and letters conspicuously refer to written letters. However, for the Besht the *yiḥud* is taking place also, and I would say eminently, during prayer. See Scholem, pp. 203–227, which has been translated in Hebrew and reprinted now in the collection of his studies about Hasidism, *ha-Shalav ha-'Aharon*, pp. 237–258. In a somewhat more pertinent manner, he writes in *The Messianic Idea*, p. 247, that "acts of *yiḥud* are achieved by contemplative communion with the inwardness of the 'letters' which are imprinted in all being. In all the sayings of the Israel Ba'al Shem Tov of which I am aware, the term is used in this precise and technical term." I would, however, say that the term *imprint* in Scholem's statement reflects some form of writing, and the whole interpretation of the Besht as precise and technical is quite reductive to a view that is more reminiscent of the view of the famous German mystic Jacob Boehme than of the Hasidic texts to be discussed as follows, though in other contexts it may be more pertinent. See the passage translated and discussed in my *Enchanted Chains*, pp. 142–143. Compare also to Scholem, *Major Trends in Jewish Mysticism*, p. 329, where he deals with the contemporaries of the Besht, the Kabbalists of the academy of Beit El, whose prayer was depicted as a "mystical contemplation of the elect." For the plausible source of this understanding of *Yiḥud*, see appendices A and B in this volume. For the oral dimension of a cosmic view of sounds in one of the Besht's teaching, see my "Your Word Stands in Heaven." For the various meanings of the term *Yiḥud* in Kabbalah and Hasidism, including the Besht, see the exhaustive monograph of Wacks, *The Secret of Unity*. See also also ch. 2 n. 16 and appendix B in this volume.

   See Weiss, "The Kavvanoth of Prayer in Early Hasidism," reprinted in his *Studies*, pp. 103–107, where he writes on p. 107: "All religious passion of the mind in early Hasidism was concentrated in on *this single aspect of mental communion* with God." Emphasis added. And on p. 104, Weiss speaks explicitly about "consonants," which in Hebrew means a written text. See also Weiss, pp. 58–60, 61, and pp. 124–125, nn. 60, 128–129, and 133–136, and see ch. 7 n. 8, ch. 8 n. 11 and ch. 13 n. 4. On p. 83 Weiss mentions together contemplation, introvertive attitude, passivity, and an emphasis on the mental. Interestingly enough, on p. 131 Weiss duly remarks that speech is detracting from the act of concentration and contemplation, but his statement has little to do with Hasidism. See also ch. 13 n. 4. A similar approach is found also in Schatz-Uffenheimer, *Hasidism as Mysticism*, e.g., p. 60: "man contemplates the words of the prayer by visualizing their letters," as well as pp. 168–170, 221–223 and, more recently, Rosman, *The Founder of Hasidism*, pp. 115, 180. This letteristic tendency is evident also in the manner in which the Beshtian texts are dealt with in: Wolfson, *Circle in the Square*, p. 23; Elior, *The Mystical Origins of Hasidism*, p. 211; ch. 4 n. 2, in this volume; the English translation of Etkes, *The Besht: Magician, Mystic, and Leader*, e.g., pp. 148–149, though he duly emphasizes the primacy of the vocal performance; G. Scholem's description of *devequt* according to the Besht; and n. 21 in this chapter, ch. 2 n. 4 and ch. 5 n. 13. In many of his English translations of texts in Jacobs, *Hasidic Prayer*, some to be cited as follows, he resorts also to the term *letters* when the term *'otiyyot* occurs, to a very great extent following the lead of Weiss and Schatz-Uffenheimer. More recently, see also, e.g., Wolfson, *Through a Speculum that Shines*, p. 278, and his "Weeping, Death, and Spiritual Ascent in Sixteenth-Century Jewish Mysticism," in eds. J. J. Collins and M. Fishbane, *Death, Ecstasy, and Other Worldly Journeys* (SUNY Press, Albany, 1995), p. 212, where a Lurianic practice is described as "the soul of the righteous that he has been brought down by contemplative meditation," as well as his "Immanuel Frommann," p. 195, and following him and Scholem, also Magid, *Hasidism Incarnate*, pp. 166, 209, n. 40, but especially on p. 18, where he translates *devequt* as "contemplative worship." See also ch. 13 n. 6. For an obvious penchant to depict Hasidic masters as contemplative even more recently, see in Kallus's *Pillar of Prayer*, whose subtitle is *Guidance in Contemplative Prayer*, *passim*, especially pp. 51, 55, 59; Mayse, *Beyond the Letters*, *passim*, e.g., pp. 10, 12–13, 21, 162; Brody, "Open to Me the Gates of Righteousness," e.g., pp. 15–16, 18, 23, n. 33; or Altshuler, *The Messianic Secret of Hasidism*, p. 206.

2   An incomplete list of studies would contain Gershom Scholem's seminal chapter, "*Devekut*, or Communion with God," in *The Messianic Idea*, pp. 203–227, and in the Hebrew updated version printed in *ha-Shalav ha-'Aharon*, pp. 237–258, and my comments about the possible sources, *ibidem*, pp. 261–262. For an analysis of the history of *devequt* in Jewish thought up to 1270, see Afterman, *Devequt*, especially on pp. 90–95; on *devequt* and prayer in R. Yehudah ha-Levi, and for later discussions, see Idel, *Kabbalah: New Perspectives*, pp. 35–73, especially the Lurianic and Sabbatean texts on *devequt*, discussed on pp. 57–58; Fishbane, *As Light before Dawn*, pp. 272–282; Goetschel, *R. Meir Ibn Gabbay*, pp. 304–315; Pachter, "Devequt in Sixteenth Century Safed," in his *Roots of Faith and Devequt*, pp. 235–316; Idel, *Hasidism*, pp. 53–65, 86–89, 223–225; and for Hasidism, see also Weiss, *Studies*, especially pp. 155–168, and his "The Beginning of the Emergence of the Hasidic Path," pp. 60–65; Rapoport-Albert, "God and the Zaddik," pp. 299–329; Dresner, *The Zaddik*, pp. 128–132; Tishby, *Studies in Kabbalah and Its Branches*, vol. III, pp. 967–994; Etkes, *The Besht: Magician, Mystic, and Leader*, pp. 114–124, 254–256; Mayse, *Beyond the Letters*, pp. 490–493; Pedaya, "Two Types of Ecstatic Experience in Hasidism," pp. 73–108; Margolin, *The Human Temple*, pp. 87–89, 109–110, 205–206, 241, 245–248, 307–327; Gries, *Conduct Literature*, pp. 202–203; Krassen, *Uniter of Heaven and Earth*, pp. 43–80, 107–122, 176–177, 210–211; Stephen Sharot, *Messianism, Mysticism, and Magic* (University of North Carolina Press, Chapel Hill, 1982), pp. 140–141; Wolfson, *Along the Path*, p. 233, n. 44; Elior, *The Mystical Origins of Hasidism*; Kauffman, *In All Your Ways Know Him*, *passim*; Gedalya Nigal, "The Sources of *Devequt* in Early Hasidic Literature," QS, vol. 46 (1970/71),

pp. 343–348 (Hebrew); Nigal, *The Birth of Hasidism*, pp. 129–142, and in his introduction to his edition of R. Jacob Joseph of Polonnoye, *Kutoneth Passim*, pp. 21–30; Tzvi Mark, "Dibbuk and Devekut in *In the Praise of the Baal-Shem Tov*: Notes on the Phenomenology of Madness in Early Hasidism," *Within Hasidic Circles: Studies in Hasidism in Memory of Mordecai Wilensky*, eds. I. Etkes, D. Assaf, I. Bartal, E. Reiner (The Bialik Institute, Jerusalem, 1999), pp. 247–286 (Hebrew); Baumgarten, *La naissance du Hassidisme*, pp. 280–284; Ysander, *Studien*, pp. 199–208; Weiss, *Studies, passim*; Israel Koren, *The Mystery of the Land: Mysticism and Hasidism in Martin Buber's Thought* (Haifa, 2005), pp. 214–232 (Hebrew); Jay Thomas Rock, *Rabbi Moses Hayyim Efraim of Sudlikov, "Degel Mahaneh Ephraim"* (PhD Thesis, Graduate Theological Union, Berkeley, 1986), pp. 55–56; and the introduction and the texts translated by Lamm, *The Religious Thought of Hasidism*, pp. 133–172, especially pp. 136–137, where he proposed an interesting threefold developmental approach to the praxis of *devequt* in the Besht, which is quite different from that to be articulated as follows. See also now Orent, "Mystical Union," pp. 61–92. It should be pointed out that in Weiss, *Studies*, p. 39, n. 3, *devequt* is described as contemplation, in a manner very reminiscent of Scholem, *On the Mystical Shape of the Godhead*, p. 222. For more on the role of contemplation according to scholarship of Jewish mysticism, see n. 1 above and ch. 10 n. 13 and ch. 13 in this volume. For a non-Hasidic interesting parallel contemporary to the Hasidic emphasis on *devequt*, see Sharon Flatto, "*Hasidim* and *Mitnaggedim*: Not a World Apart," JJTP, vol. 12 (2003), pp. 110–111. See also Fishbane, *As Light before Dawn*, especially p. 227. See also now, *Hasidism, A New History*, pp. 163–165.

3   *The Messianic Idea*, p. 213. See also pp. 211–212, 215. See also previously another statement of Scholem adduced in n. 1 of this volume. Scholem's statement, cited without a specific reference, is perhaps a paraphrase of the quote in the name of the Besht as adduced in R. Jacob Joseph of Polonnoye, *Ben Porat Yosef*, fol. 46c:

לדבק מחשבתו בפנימיות האותיות

However, the cleaving of the thought should not be seen necessarily as contemplation or concentration. See also ch. 5 n. 9. This view about the novelty of the Besht's view has been continued by Weiss, Torah Study in Early Hasidism," in *Studies*, pp. 56–61, 107; Jacobs, *Hasidic Prayer*, p. 75; Etkes, *The Besht: Magician, Mystic, and Leader*, pp. 114–115; Lederberg, *Sod ha-Da'at*, pp. 181–184. See, however, Piekarz, *The Beginning of Hasidism*, pp. 354–355, who quotes R. Isaiah Horowitz's book the Shelah as a possible source, and Idel, *Enchanted Chains*, pp. 58–59, where I propose to see in a passage of R. Elijah da Vidas the possible source for the Besht, who was certainly acquainted with this book, since he refers to a story found only in this book, as well as my *Hasidism*, p. 161. We shall adduce a translation of this passage in our discussion in ch. 3 of this volume and will analyze some elements found in Scholem's description also in appendix B.

For the recommendation to cleave to individual letters, see the thirteenth-century theory found in R. Joseph Gikatilla concerning the letters of the Tetragrammaton in a treatise that, in my opinion, could have been known to the Besht. Cf. Idel, "The Kabbalah's 'Window of Opportunities' 1270–1290," in eds., E. Fleischer et al., *Me'ah She'arim; Studies in Medieval Jewish Spiritual Life, in Memory of Isadore Twersky* (Magnes Press, Jerusalem, 2001), p. 184, and *Absorbing*

Perfections, p. 378. It should be pointed out that already in a thirteenth or fourteenth-century anonymous treatise found in a manuscript that belongs to ecstatic Kabbalah, the divine light was conceived of as being stored within the letters of the Tetragrammaton. See the text printed and discussed in Idel, "From "Or Ganuz' to "Or Torah,'" pp. 43–44. On the other hand, it should be noticed that on the basis of the extant material, none of the contemporaries of the Besht who were active in his immediate vicinity, namely in region of Podolia, did adopt this view directly from the earlier sources, to judge by the traditions extant in documents we have, despite a statement that we shall adduce in chap. 3 from R. Meir Ḥarif Margoliot of Ostrog. See the survey of the views of some of the Besht's contemporaries on the topic in Heschel, *The Circle of the Besht*. Some of them were much more interested indeed with contemplation of the written letters of the divine name, but they scarcely contributed to the emergence of Hasidism as a popular movement, at least insofar as the issue of prayer is concerned. See, e.g., the passage about R. Nahman of Kosov, translated in Lamm, *The Religious Thought of Hasidism*, pp. 157–158. However, it is possible to find a similar view to that of the Besht in one of his younger contemporaries, R. Nathan Netaʿ of Sienewa, *'Olat Tamid ha-Shalem*, II, fols. 11a, 15a, who was not a Hasidic author. See also Idel, *Hasidism*, p. 55.

Compare the view of Cordovero on this issue printed in Bracha Sack, "A Fragment from R. Moshe Cordovero's Commentary on *Ra'ya' Mehemna'*," in *Qovetz 'al Yad* [NS], vol. 20 (1982), p. 264: "The purpose of the worship is to cleave to the simple Divinity." See also *ibidem*, p. 269. This view was reiterated verbatim by R. Abraham Azulai, *Ḥesed le-'Avraham*, fol. 10c, and thereby came to the attention of the Hasidic masters. See, especially, appendix B in this volume.

4   See *The Messianic Idea*, pp. 259–260. See also *ibidem*, pp. 194, 204. For the assumption that *devequt* replaced the ideal of *tiqqun*, see *ibidem*, pp. 216–217. See, however, my critique of this view in "The Tsaddik and His Soul's Sparks," pp. 198–200.

5   Scholem, *The Messianic Idea*, pp. 180–202.

6   See Shalom Rosenberg, "The Return to the Garden of Eden—Remarks for the History of the Idea of the Restorative Redemption in the Medieval Jewish Philosophy," in *The Messianic Idea in Jewish Thought: A Study Conference in Honour of the Eightieth Birth Day of Gershom Scholem*, ed. Sh. Reem (Israel Academy for Science, Jerusalem, 1990), pp. 84–86 (Hebrew); Dov Schwartz, "The Neutralization of the Messianic Idea in Medieval Jewish Rationalism," HUCA, vol. 64 (1993), pp. 41–44 (Hebrew); and Idel, "Types of Redemptive Activity in Middle Ages," pp. 254–258; Idel, *Messianic Mystics*, pp. 58–100, 212–247.

7   Scholem, *Major Trends in Jewish Mysticism*, pp. 140–141, and compare to Idel, "Types of Redemptive Activity in Middle Ages," pp. 259–263; Idel, Messianic Mystics, pp. 58–100; Afterman, *Devequt, passim*.

8   See Idel, *Kabbalah: New Perspectives*, pp. 49–51, and see also Rapoport-Albert, "God and the Zaddik," pp. 307–308.

9   See, e.g., in English his "Hasidism as a Socio-religious Movement on the Evidence of Devekut," in *Hasidism Reappraised*, ed. Rapoport-Albert, pp. 225–248, and his *Between Ideology and Reality*, pp. 150–178, 295, as well as Lederberg, *The Gateway*

to Infinity, p. 403, n. 371. See also the reaction to his views in Etkes, *The Besht: Magician, Mystic, and Leader*, pp. 117–118, Margolin, *The Human Temple*, p. 312, n. 93, and Garb, *Shamanic Trance in Modern Kabbalah*, pp. 96–97.

10   See also my remarks printed in Scholem, *ha-Shalav ha-'Aharon*, pp. 265–267.

11   See Aron Gurwitsch, "Phenomenology of Perception: Perceptual Implications," in ed. J. M. Edie, *An Invitation to Phenomenology* (Quadrangle Books, Chicago, 1965), p. 21; Idel, *Kabbalah: New Perspectives*, pp. 51–58, *Hasidism*, pp. 49, 111, 203, 272, n. 15; and "Models of Understanding Prayer," pp. 106–107, n. 265. For the analysis of *devequt* when conjugated together with other forms of activities as connected to each other see Idel, *Kabbalah: New Perspectives*, pp. 51–58; Brody, "Human Hands Dwell in Heavenly Heights," pp. 123–158; and in some articles I wrote on the Besht and in two books of mine, *Enchanted Chains*, cf. index p. 243 under item, Israel Baal Shem Tov, and *Ascensions on High*, pp. 205–209. This more complex approach has been adopted also more recently in a short discussion of Pedaya, "Two Types of Ecstatic Experience in Hasidism," p. 81, who, apparently unaware of my methodological claims to this effect for many years beforehand, asserted that I analyzed isolated concepts in themselves and not in their wider concatenation in the framework of broader models! Compare also to her "The Besht, R. Jacob Joseph of Polonnoye, and the Maggid of Mezeritch," p. 71. This is one more case of inversion of my explicit methodology.

12   See, e.g., Scholem, *ha-Shalav ha-'Aharon*, pp. 127–128, where he sees the emphasis on *devequt* as a phenomenological alternative to magic! Nevertheless, Scholem claimed correctly that the Besht never stopped resorting to magical activities.

13   See Pedaya's phenomenological study "The Besht, R. Jacob Joseph of Polonnoye, and the Maggid of Mezeritch," in which she emphasizes the religious structure of the Besht as a seer on the one hand, but flatly and insistently denies the existence of the drawing down of the influx in the teachings reported in the name of the Besht, see Pedaya, pp. 33, 55, 58, 63, 71, though she accepts the existence of the magic aspect of some of the Besht's discussions in addition to the hagiographical stories. We shall have more to say about this issue later on in this study, especially in chap. 9 and in appendices B and F.

14   See Kauffman, *In All Your Ways Know Him*, pp. 132–133. Compare, however, the more nuanced formulations and even the examples she adduced in Kauffman, pp. 446–447, 482–483.

15   See Idel, *Hasidism*, pp. 103–127 and nn. 18 and 20 below in this chapter.

16   See, e.g., Idel, pp. 154, 161–163, pp. 311–312, n. 49, and "Models of Understanding Prayer," pp. 32–33. Though emphasizing in those discussions the role of the voice in several Hasidic passages, I translated the Hebrew term *'otiyyot* as "pronounced letters," and here I shall change the translation to "letters/sounds" or "letters/vocables" in order to put even more in relief the sonority or the phonemic meaning of *'ot*. See also my studies referred to in n. 21 below in this chapter and especially in appendix D.

17   See Idel, "The Land of Divine Vitality," pp. 256–275, Idel, "From "Or Ganuz' to "Or Torah,'" pp. 46–56, and Wacks, *The Secret of Unity*, pp. 13, 14, 123, 126. For the view that scholarship should take into consideration the organization of knowledge in Kabbalah and Hasidism see, e.g., Idel, *Kabbalah: New Perspectives*, p. 213; Idel, "The Land of a Divine Vitality," pp. 256–258; *Absorbing Perfections*, pp. 22, 50, 117, 248–249, 255, 272–273, 280–284, 442–444; "Some Forms of Order in Kabbalah," *Da'at*, vol. 50–52 (2003), pp. xxxi–lviii; "Interpretations of the Secret of 'Arayyot in Early Kabbalah," *Kabbalah*, vol. 12 (2004), pp. 104–105 (Hebrew); "Leviathan and Its Consort: From Talmudic to Kabbalistic Myth," in eds., I. Gruenwald and M. Idel, *Myths in Judaism: History, Thought, Literature* (Merkaz Shazar, Jerusalem, 2004), pp. 172–173 (Hebrew); Saturn's Jews, pp. 18–19, 25, 36–38, 116; and "Female Beauty," pp. 318–319; "R. Israel Ba'al Shem Tov's Two 'Encounters' with Sabbatai Tzevi," in eds. H. Taragan and N. Gal, *The Beauty of Japheth in the Tents of Shem, Studies in Honour of Mordechai Omer* [= *Assaph, Studies in Art History*, vol. 23–24] (Tel Aviv University, Tel Aviv, 2010), pp. 471–472; and more recently, Daniel Abrams, *Kabbalistic Manuscripts and Textual Theory, Methodologies of Textual Scholarship in the Study of Jewish Mysticism* (Magnes-Cherub, Jerusalem–Los Angeles, 2010), pp. 591–592, and Gondos, *Kabbalah in Print*, pp. 93–94.

18   See Idel, *Hasidism*, pp. 45–145, and "Prayer, Ecstasy, and Alien Thoughts in the Besht's Religious World." For the resort to models for understanding Hasidism, see also Kauffman, *In All Your Ways Know Him*, passim, and for the Besht's different models of worship in corporeality, pp. 401–407, 519–520; and for other topics in Wacks, *The Secret of Unity*, passim.

19   Idem, "Mystical Redemption and Messianism in R. Israel Ba'al Shem Tov's Teachings."

20   Idem, "Models of Understanding Prayers," pp. 10–11.

21   For the fascination with "contemplation," see the titles of several of Weiss's studies collected in *Studies*. Extremely telling is his essay "Contemplative Mysticism and 'Faith' in Hasidic Piety," reprinted in Weiss, pp. 42–55, where he characterizes the Besht, the Great Maggid, and other main Hasidic thinkers as contemplative, the only major exception being R. Nahman of Braslav. See also his *Studies*, pp. 126, 128, 129–141, and the references to some of Weiss's statements in n. 199 of this volume. Given the importance of speech in the Besht's traditions, which does not comply with the primacy of the contemplative trend of which he was so convinced, Weiss sees in the Besht a paradox of a contemplative who nevertheless emphasizes speech! See Weiss, p. 132. See also Scholem, *The Messianic Idea*, p. 179, and Baumgarten, *La naissance du Hassidisme*, pp. 339–345.

      Compare, however, to the emphasis on sounds in Idel, "Die laut gelesen Tora, Stimmengemeinschaft in der juedischen Mystik," *Zwischen Rauschen und Offenbarung, Zur Kultur und Mediengeschichte der Stimme*, eds. Th. Macho, S. Weigel (Berlin 2002), pp. 19–53; Idel, "The Voiced Text of the Torah," pp. 145–166; and Idel, *Enchanted Chains*, pp. 205–212, 221–223. See also Wacks, *The Secret of Unity*, pp. 86–108.

      On the role of speech and voice in medieval Jewish mysticism, see Scholem, *Major Trends in Jewish Mysticism*, pp. 17–18, and as a comprehensive power permeating reality, what I called "linguistic immanence," see also Pedaya, *Vision and Speech*; Afterman, *The Intention of Prayer in Early Kabbalah*, pp. 112–113, 180–181, 196–197, and his "Letter Permutation Techniques, *Kavanah*, and Prayer in Jewish Mysticism," in *Essays in Honor of Moshe Idel*, eds. S. Frunza and M. Frunza (ProvoPress, Cluj,-Napoca, 2008), pp. 84–87, as well as Idel, *The Mystical Experience in Abraham Abulafia*, pp. 83–95 and *Enchanted Chains*, pp. 196–202. See also Steven Katz, "Mystical Speech and Mystical Meaning," in ed. S. Katz, *Mysticism and Language* (Oxford University Press, New York, 1992), pp. 3–41.

For the rather inferior status of speech in Kashmir Shaivism, see Dyczkowski, *The Doctrine of Vibration*, pp. 198–199 and in Tantra, cf., Padoux, *Vac*, pp. 172–173. For a comparison between Hasidic perception of letters and Tantra, see also Jean Canteins, *La Voie des lettres* (Albin Michel, Paris, 1981), pp. 179–180, who, however, compares Schatz-Uffenheimer's interpretation of the traditions from the Great Maggid's school, as if referring to the written letters, to Tantric and Sufi methods. Cf. Idel, *Hasidism*, p. 347, n. 103. See also the important study of Zoran, "Magic, Theurgy, and the Knowledge of Letters," pp. 19–62.

22 *Sefer Tzafnat Pa'aneah*, ed. Nigal, p. 260, ed. Koretz, fol. 60b: על דרך ששמעתי ממורי זלה"ה שיש יחודים בדבור, בין בדבור תורה ותפלה ובין בדבור עם חבירו בשוק, ויוכל לחברו ולה־ עלות לכל אחד לפי דרגתו, יש על ידי דיבור דקדושה ויש על ידי דיבור חול שיש בו כ"ב אותיות וכו'.

Elsewhere in the same book, Koretz, fol. 18b, the Besht is quoted again to the effect of teaching that we should distinguish between three types of speeches, reminiscent of his teaching quoted here, but adding an important dimension: each type causes a form of sexual union of divine powers. In both cases, however, the speech-act, not the contemplation of the written letters in a text, is considered to be the pertinent cause. See also in this volume the Beshtian text cited toward the end of Concluding Remarks. See also Wacks, *The Secret of Unity*, p. 89, and Kauffman, *In All Your Ways Know Him*, pp. 128–129. See also the quote in the name of the Besht in R. Moshe Hayyim Efrayyim of Sudylkov, *Degel Mahaneh 'Efrayyim*, p. 94: "to speak the letters" לדבר האותיות which can hardly refer only to written letters alone. On the nomian acts of "speech" while dealing with Torah and prayer, see also R. Jacob Joseph of Polonnoye, *Kutoneth Passim*, ed. Nigal, p. 247, and *Toledot Ya'aqov Yosef*, fols. 3a, 7a, 190b. For the context of these passages, see also Lederberg, *Sod ha-Da'at*, pp. 186–187 and see also *Hasidism, A New History*, p. 68.

A similar distinction between three forms of speeches as modes of worship is found in a lengthy discussion of R. Aharon of Zhitomir, *Sefer Toledot 'Aharon*, Berditchev, fol. 118ab. See especially here fol. 182ad, where the ideal is to achieve a situation when someone may speak speech in front of God. Compare also to the short but seminal instruction preserved. For the description of *'otiyyot* as found in the mouth of man, conspicuously an instance of sounds, see R. Menahem Nahum of Chernobyl, *Me'or 'Einayyim*, p. 161, and for the speeches of Torah and prayer see R. Menahem Nahum, p. 152. See also in the book of one of the earliest disciples of the Besht, R. Arieh Leib Galiner of Polonnoye, *Qol 'Arieh*, fol. 56d, as well as in his repetition of the triad Torah, Prayer, and Song, which occurs in R. Arieh Leib Galiner, fols. 56d–57a, 57d, and in a quote in the name of a, perhaps the Maggid R. Menahem of Bar, adduced in R. Jacob Joseph of Polonnoye, *Kuthonet Passim*, ed. Nigal, p. 152. There the importance of cleaving to the vocables of the Torah-study and moralistic teachings is highlighted. The identity of this author is not clear, but it is evident that it is a contemporary of the Besht. Compare, however, to the views of Scholem, Weiss, and Schatz-Uffenheimer, quoted in n. 1 of this volume.

In this context let me notice also that the mistranslation of the *'otiyyot* as letters in some instances is not just a philological mistake, but it stems from a strong ideological bias which also inserted concepts that are not found in the specific Hasidic texts like, for example, translating *Yitz'aq be-laḥash*, namely a cry done in a low voice or in a whisper, as if its meaning is "cry out in silence," and thus it is interpreted as an instance of mental prayer, and then additional speculations were built around this sort of false interpretation. See Schatz-Uffenheimer, *Hasidism as Mysticism*, p. 178, 185–186, and her "Contemplative Prayer in Hasidism," pp. 223–225, and compare to what I have mentioned already in my book, *Hasidism*, pp. 164–165, 349, n. 119, and see also ch. 10 n. 17.. This propensity to translate the Hebrew form of *be-laḥash* as silent rather than whisper is a sheer misunderstanding both from the philological point of view and from the point of view of acquaintance with the Jewish tradition, though it is also shared, however, by the English translation of the *Testament of the Besht* as done by Shochet, an orthodox author. See his translation on p. 26, no. 33. For the emphasis on the centrality of the acts of seeing, of texts and letters, rather than of performing utterances that I emphasize, in her phenomenology of the Besht's experience, see Pedaya, "The Besht, R. Jacob Joseph of Polonnoye, and the Maggid of Mezeritch," pp. 27–30, 55–67. The view that pronouncing the sounds obliterates the stark judgments is quoted elsewhere by the grandson in the name of his grandfather. Let me point out that the theory of cleaving to the utterances of Torah and prayer has been extended also to the instructions of the late antiquity Rabbis, in an interesting discussion of R. Aharon of Zhitomir, *Toledot 'Aharon*, fol. 187a. See also ch. 5 n. 9..

It should be pointed out that though in medieval philosophical Hebrew the word for speech, *dibbur*, may sometimes also refer to what was understood to be the "inner speech" or the intellect, and even to the Agent Intellect that is sometimes, though rarely, referred to as primordial speech, *dibbur qadmon* according to Abraham Abulafia, which is reminiscent of the Hindu "supreme speech"— *paravac*—as discussed by Padoux, *Vac*, pp. 166–167, 172–188—this is not the case in any of the Beshtian teachings I am acquainted with. See M. Idel, "Definitions of Prophecy—Maimonides and Abulafia," in eds. A. Elqayam and D. Schwartz, *Maimonides and Mysticism, Presented to Moshe Hallamish* (Bar-Ilan University Press, Ramat Gan, 2009), pp. 14–15, 19–25 (Hebrew).

It should be pointed out that Cordovero, in *'Or Yaqar*, vol. 15, p. 229, describes speech as both the instrument of uniting the *Shekhinah* and *Tiferet*, namely as part of a theurgical technique, and as the symbol of *Shekhinah*.

2. Reconstructing Multiple Modes of Cleaving to Vocables according to the Besht

1   *Sod ha-qatenut.* There is indeed no secret intended here, but the revelation of the meaning of *qatenut*. See also the so-called *Testament of the Besht*, printed in *Liqqutim Yeqarim*, fol. 3b: כשהאדם במדרגה קטנה אז טוב יותר להתפלל מתוך הסידור שמכח שרואה האותיות התפלה מתפלל יותר בכוונה.

"When a person is on a lower rank it is better to prayer from the prayerbook since out of the fact that he sees the letters of prayer, he is prayer with a greater *Kavvanah*." This is one important example for the affinities between some parts of the so-called *Testament* and Beshtian material, which is found in sources that are independent of the circle of the Great Maggid. See also Idel, *Hasidism*, p. 164 and the pertinent footnotes. On the nexus between the printed form and the worship in the state of *qatenut*, see also R. Aharon of Apta, *'Or ha-Ganuz la-Tzaddiqim*, ed. Warsau, fol. 29c. On this book, which will preoccupy us much more especially in appendix A, see Lieberman, *'Ohel RaHeL*, vol. 1, pp. 7–11.

For the occurrence of the expression *sod ha-qatenut* in a similar context, see again in R. Jacob Joseph, *Kutoneth Passim*, ed. Nigal, pp. 74–75: בסוד הקטנות שאין עבודת הש"י מאהבה ומיראה רק על דרך ההכרח וטורח רב, בלי תענוג, שנקרא ימי קטנות, כאשר שמעתי זה ממורי וכתבתי במקום אחר יעו"ש.

"The secret of *qatenut* is when the worship of God is not done out of love and awe, but as an obligation and as a great burden, without delight, as I have heard from my teacher and I wrote elsewhere, and you should check there."

Perhaps this cross-reference points to the previous passage about the Besht. It should be pointed out that the phrase *sod ha-qatenut* recurs in early Hasidic writings. For an interesting parable of the worship by *qatenut* as reflected by seeing the king, namely God, by means of the written letters, and the seeing of God directly, by means of cleaving one's thought to the light of the infinity within the letters/sounds, understood as the state of *gadelut*, see the quote in the name of the Besht quoted in R. Aharon ha-Kohen Perlov of Apta, *'Or ha-Ganuz la-Tzaddiqim*, fol. 29bc. I did not find this parable elsewhere. For the regular praying by heart and not from a written prayerbook, see now Ephraim Kanarfogel, "Levels of Literacy in Ashkenaz and Sepharad as Reflected by the Recitation of Biblical Verse Found in the Liturgy," in eds. J. R. Hacker, Y. Kaplan, and B. Z. Kedar, *From Sages to Savants, Studies Presented to Avraham Grossman* (The Zalman Shazar Center for Jewish History, Jerusalem, 2009), pp. 187–212 (Hebrew). See also the manner in which the Besht's prayer has been described in the hagiography, *In Praise of the Baal Shem Tov*, p. 55.

2   Namely the ability to concentrate, or the state of *gadelut*. The Hebrew formulation here is a little bit awkward.

3   This is a common formula used in R. Jacob Joseph's books in order to designate the end of the quotation from the Besht's words.

4   *Kutoneth Passim*, ed. Nigal, p. 298: החכם עיניו בראשו להבין ולהשכיל אם הזמן גורם שיוכל לכוון בסוד הפנימי ולהתענג . . . מוטב ואם רואה הוא בסוד הקטנות ואינו יכול לכוין, שמתגברין עליו מחשבות זרות, אזי יתפלל כתינוק בן יומא מתוך כתב, כאשר העיד מורי על עצמו שהיה בארץ אחרת זמן מה בבחינה זו שנסתלק ממנו הנ"ל והיה מדבק עצמו אל האותיות וכו' ואמר: כאשר מתפלל מתוך הכתב ומדבק עצמו אל האותיות אזי מעלה בחינת עשייה כי תיבת ב' בינה. וכך ציווה לאיש פרטי שיעשה כך עד שחזר למדרגתו העליונה וכו' ודברי פי חכם חן. On this passage see also Idel, "Models of Understanding Prayer in Early Hasidism," pp. 63–64, and "The Besht as Prophet and Talismanic Magician," pp. 137–138. For another instruction to attach himself to the letters of the written text [ketav] while praying the eighteen benedictions, see again his *Sefer Kutoneth Passim*, ed. Nigal, p. 299. On this latter passage see Idel, "The Besht as Prophet and Talismanic Magician," pp.

138–139, 142. Elevations of the lower worlds or of the fallen sparks found within the *qelippot*, the husks, by means of prayer, are mentioned in the name of the Besht in R. Jacob Joseph's *Toledot Ya'aqov Yosef*, fol. 59b. Compare also to the views found in *Liqqutim Yeqarim*, p. 5, par. 27 and to *Tzawwa'at ha-Ribash* (Warsaw, 1913), fol. 4a, a treatise edited in the circle of the Great Maggid, as well as to R. Aharon Perlov of Apta's *Ner Mitzwah*, fol. 7b. For a translation and analysis of the fuller context of this passage, see Weiss, *Studies*, pp. 103–104, who resorts to the English terms like "letters" and "text" when dealing with prayer in his explanation of the passage. See also Rapoport-Albert, "God and Zaddik," pp. 310–311. For a recommendation to cleave to written letters as well as to utterances of prayer and Torah that was reported in the name of the Besht, see R. Jacob Joseph of Polonnoye, *Ben Porat Yosef*, fol. 41c.

Let me point out that an important instance of attributing to the cleaving to the graphical forms of letters of the Torah, and thus not to utterances, occurs in this author's *Toledot Ya'aqov Yosef*, fol. 131b, as part of an erotic description of the union of the student with the Torah. On this passage see also Wolfson, *Circle in the Square*, p. 23. However, for the time being, I am not acquainted in the extant sources with an explicit attribution of such a view to the Besht himself, though I assume that at least theoretically it may stem from one of his teachings that is no longer extant. See also note 86 in this volume. On the similar position at the beginning of Kabbalah in the context of prayer, see Scholem, *Origins of the Kabbalah*, p. 416.

5   See *In Praise of the Baal Shem Tov*, pp. 237–238, and even more so in the Yiddisch version of the hagiography. The legends related to the stay of the Besht in Istanbul have been collected and discussed recently by Nigal, *The Besht: Legends, Apologetics, and Reality*, pp. 122–128. See also Mondshine, *Shivehei Ha-Baal Shem Tov, A Facsimile of a Unique Manuscript*, pp. 276–277 and the passage adduced in *Keter Shem Tov*, fol. 20c, no. 156. Extemely interesting is the version of the depression of the Besht on his way, whether historical or not, to Istanbul as reported in a late collection of Hasidic stories. See Menaham Mendel Bodek, *Sippurim Hasidiim*, ed. G. Nigal (Yaron Golan, Jerusalem, 1991), pp. 90–91 (Hebrew). The manner in which the Besht is described fits the present analysis of the passage adduced by R. Jacob Joseph. For the possible messianic implications of this journey, see Yehuda Liebes, "The Messiah of the *Zohar*," in ed. Sh. Re'em, *The Messianic Idea in Israel* (Israeli National Academy for Sciences and Humanities, Jerusalem, 1982), pp. 113–114 (Hebrew). See also Wolfson, *Along the Path*, p. 236, n. 77.

6   The Hasidic masters dealt much more than the Lurianic Kabbalists with the state of mind, rather than the growth of the divine configuration known as *Zei'yr 'Anppin*, described as *qatenut*. For an analysis of the Kabbalistic sources, see Pachter, "Smallness and Greatness," reprint, in his *Roots of Faith and Devequt*, pp. 185–233; Yehuda Liebes, "'Two Young Roes of a Doe': The Secret Sermon of Isaac Luria before his Death," in eds. R. Elior and Y. Liebes, *Lurianic Kabbalah* (Jerusalem, 1994), pp. 113–126 (Hebrew); Mark Verman, "*Aliyah* and *Yeridah*: The Journey of the Besht and R. Nachman to Israel," *Approaches to Judaism in Medieval Times III* (Atlanta, 1988), pp. 159–171; Mark, *Mysticism and Madness*, pp. 294–329; and for the different views of Scholem, *The Messianic Idea in Judaism*, pp. 218–222; and Ada Rapoport-Albert, "'*Qatenut*,' '*Peshitut*,' and '*Eini Yode'a*" in R. Nahman of

Brazlav," in eds. S. Stein and R. Loewe, *Studies in Religious and Intellectual History Presented to A. Altmann* (University of Alabama, Alabama, 1979), pp. 7–33 (Hebrew part); Kauffman, *In All Your Ways Know Him*, p. 351; and the passages translated in Lamm, *The Religious Thought of Hasidism*, pp. 403–408.

7   See in chapter 4 of this volume the passage quoted from the *Holy Epistle*: מתקשרים ומתיחדים יחד האותיות This is, in my opinion, one more proof for the Beshtian origin of this passage. See also the next note. See also in another collection of the teachings of the Great Maggid, *'Or ha-'Emmet*, fol. 18b.

8   The Hebrew term is *ruḥaniyyut*, but its meaning here is closer to the philosophical understanding of the supernal world. See the parallel to learning from the material delight about the spiritual one in a tradition of the Besht adduced by R. Jacob Joseph of Polonnoye, *Toledot Ya'aqov Yosef*, fol. 16c. For the possible source for this type of argumentation, see already in a passage known by the Besht, and cited Polonnoye, fol. 45b, whose source is R. Isaac of Acre's lost book, in the way it was preserved solely in a quote found in R. Elijah da Vidas's treatise. See Idel, *Kabbalah and Eros*, pp. 155–177, 298, n. 58. See also ch. 3 n. 7.

9   *Maggid Devarav le-Ya'aqov*, ed. Schatz-Uffenheimer, pp. 85–86; *'Or ha-'Emmet*, fol. 10a; and in *Keter Shem Tov*, fol. 56ab and *Keter Shem Tov ha-Shalem*, pp. 235–236, no. 387:

בתפלה צריך לשים כל כחו בהדיבורים, וילך כך מאות לאות עד שישכח מגופניות, ויחשוב
שהאותיות מצמרפיה ומתחברים זה עם זה, וזהו תענוג גדול. דמה אם בגשמיות הוא תענוג גדול,
מכ"ש ברוחניות, וזהו עולם היצירה. ואח"כ יבוא לאותיות המחשבה ולא ישמע מה שהוא מדבר,
וזהו בא לעולם הבריאה. ואח"כ הוא בא למדת אי"ן שנתבטלו אצלו כל כוחותיו הגשמיים, וזהו
עולם האצילות, מדת חכמה.

A shorter parallel is found in R. Aharon of Apta's later book *'Or ha-Ganuz la-Tzaddiqim*, fol. 6d, without mentioning any source for it. On this passage see Idel, *Hasidism*, p. 306, n. 9, 347 n. 103; Etkes, *The Besht: Magician, Mystic, and Leader*, pp. 149–150, 307, n. 111; Jacobs, *Hasidic Prayer*, pp. 77–78; Margolin, *The Human Temple*, pp. 204, 346–347; Elior, *The Mystical Origins of Hasidism*, p. 78; Dan Merkur, "The Induction of Mystical Unions: Two Hasidic Teachings," *Studia Mystica*, vol. 14, no. 4 (1991), pp. 71–72; and Lorberbaum, "Attaining the Attribute of *'Ayyin*," *passim*; as well as in appendix A in this volume.

For the possible nexus between speech and the world of *Yetziyrah*, see R. Elijah da Vidas, *Reshit Ḥokhmah*, The Gate of Holiness, chap. 4: אמנם התורה עניינה על ידי דבור והדבור מיצירה. "The matter of the Torah is by means of speech and speech is from [the world of] *Yetziyrah*." See also in ch. 3 n. 7. See also the other Beshtian tradition on the connection between divestment and the World of Emanation preserved in *Keter Shem Tov ha-Shalem*, pp. 111–112, no. 199, and especially the important passage from R. Jacob Joseph of Polonnoye, *Toledot Ya'aqov Yosef*, fol. 88c (copied also in *Keter Shem Tov ha-Shalem*, p. 154 no. 259). For the three types of unions induced by three types of human speeches, one affecting the world of *'Assiyah*, induced by speeches during commercial negotiations, one in the world of *Yetziyrah*, induced by spiritual speeches with a spiritual friend—compare to the term *spiritual* in the context of this world in the passage from *Maggid Devarav le-Ya'aqov* and *Keter Shem Tov*—and the highest, most plausible in the world of *'Atziylut*, that is induced by utterances of Torah and prayer when performed out of awe and love, see the view of R. Jacob Joseph of Polonnoye, in *Tzafnat Pa'aneaḥ* [Koretz], fol. 18bc. Also in this discussion the speeches are connected to experiences of *devequt*. See Kauffman, *In All Your Ways Know Him*, p. 458, n. 89. See also the Great Maggid's *'Or ha-'Emmet*, fol. 41b, for the transition from speech to thought and then to Nothing, thus another strong parallel to the teaching I attribute here to the Besht. If the divestment of corporeality is indeed related to passivity, as Weiss and Schatz-Uffenheimer sometimes claimed, the position of the Besht that assumes that this state is achieved at the end of the process does not allow a significant role to passivity as part of the mystical path.

On the prayer of the Besht himself that was extremely loud, see the material referred in Idel, *Hasidism*, p. 351, n. 130, especially *In Praise of the Baal Shem Tov*, pp. 50–53, and ch. 2 n. 1, as well as ch. 6 n. 5. See also *In Praise of the Baal Shem Tov*, p. 57. It seems therefore that some of the instructions quoted in the name of the Besht, and the manner in which he behaved, coincide quite nicely. See also Lamm, *The Religious Thought of Hasidism*, p. 217, n. 8. Compare also the quote in the name of the Besht to be adduced in n. 81 in this volume, from R. Aharon ha-Levi of Zhitomir, *Toledot 'Aharon*, fol. 130a.

For the concept of "letters of thought," see appendices B, C, and D in this volume. For a critique of my reconstruction of the concepts found in these texts see Moseson, *From the Spoken Word to the Discourse of the Academy*, pp. 24–26.

10   Weiss, *Studies*, p. 74. See also in several other early Hasidic sources, e.g., R. Jacob Joseph of Polonnoye, *Toledot Ya'aqov Yosef*, fol. 176d; and the so-called pseudo-Beshtian *Testament of Rivash*, printed in *Liqqutim Yeqarim*, fol. 3a, in which several times he insistence on the investment of all the power is obvious; as well as in Ms. Jerusalem NUL 80 3282, fol. 73a; in R. Menahem Nahum of Chernobyl's *Yismah Lev* printed at the end of his *Me'or 'Einayyim*, p. 307; and later on in this note, as well as in ch. 8 n. 4. Elsewhere, *ibidem Me'or 'Einayyim*, p. 105, this master speaks about the investment of all the vitality in the acts of speech. Also, the Besht's instruction as to the fortification someone has to fortify before prayer points in a more activist direction. See the passages adduced by Weiss himself, elsewhere in his *Studies*, p. 109, when dealing with another topic, the *Kavvanot*. Though it is possible to discern also few quietist statements in early Hasidism, it seems to me that Weiss, and following him also Schatz-Uffenheimer in *Hasidism as Mysticism*, were overwhelmed by the report of the contemporary of the Great Maggid, the idealistic philosopher Solomon Maimon's depicting of the Great Maggid, and extrapolated from his fascinating remarks as to Hasidism in a more general manner. Writing for a Christian audience, Maimon's autobiography resorted to Christian mystical categories. Also, his very presentation may have something to do with his later idealistic philosophical leanings, as Weiss duly pointed out in *Studies*, pp. 70–71. Maimon is therefore the first instance of presenting Hasidism in what I call a Christotropic manner. Interestingly enough, as mentioned previously, Schechter, in "The Chassidism," p. 151 (writing in the last decade of the nineteenth century), already warned against an understanding of Hasidism by scholars "saturated with Western culture."

See also R. Menahem Nahum of Chernobyl, *Me'or 'Einayyim*, p. 153: כל אשר תמצא ידך לעשות ר"ל כל דבר

שתרצה לעשות רצון השם יתברך בכחך עשה צריך לעשות בכח דהיינו כשמשים כל כחו
וחיותו בתוך האותיות התורה ותפלה בזה מעלה אותם לשרשם, אל הבורא יתברך שמו.

"Everything your hand wants to do namely, everything that you want to do
the will of God blessed be He, do it by your strength. It is incumbent to do with
strength, namely as someone puts all his strength and vitality within the letters/
vocables of Torah and prayer and thus he elevates them to their source, to the
Creator, blessed be His name."

On strength and pronunciation in Jewish mysticism in general, see Garb,
"Powers of Language in Kabbalah," pp. 239–240, and Liebes, "The Power of the
Word," pp. 163–177. See also ch. 8 n. 7. For more on investment of power in recitation, see the interesting passages in the Great Maggid's *'Or ha-'Emmet*, fols. 4c,
15a, and R. Aharon of Zhitomir, *Toledot 'Aḥaron*, fol. 118b, both homiletic books
stemming from the circle of the Great Maggid, where the entire body is described
as participating in the utterances and even entering them. Compare especially to
the view of R. Pinḥas of Koretz, in *Liqqutim me-ha-Rav R. Pinḥas mi-Qoretz*, fol.
6b, about entering within God: "since during the entire year someone should cleave
to God, blessed be He, muz ich arain gein in ha-Shem Yitbarakh." The Yiddisch
words mean "He must eneter in God, blessed be He." Also here, enterance in God
is tantamount to cleaving. See also the following texts translated in appendix A.

Compare, especially, to the Hindu tradition about entering letters/sounds and
understanding them as "a particularized sound-embodiment of Shiva-Shakti . . .
Each letter/sound is accordingly surcharged with a vital force and a spiritual meaning . . . Each letter is pronounced with a *bindu* . . . attached to it." Cf., Beck, *Sonic
Theology*, p. 101. For the creative power of divine language in Muslim mysticism, see
Sara Sviri, "*KUN*, The Existence Bestowing Word in Islamic Mysticism: A Survey
of Texts on the Creative Power of Language," in eds. S. La Porta and D. Shulman,
The Poetics of Grammar and the Metaphysics of Sound and Sign (Brill, Leiden, 2007),
pp. 35–67 (especially pp. 45–46); eadem, "Words of Power and the Power of Words:
Mystical Linguistics in the Works of al-H_akim al-Tirmidh," *Jerusalem Studies in
Arabic and Islam*, vol. 27 (2002), pp. 204–244.

11   For the obliteration of the human senses when reaching the realm of *Hokhmah*, see
also the view of the Besht as quoted by R. Efrayyim of Sudylkov, *Degel Mahaneh
'Efrayyim*, p. 202. See also the tradition from the Great Maggid's circle found in
'Or ha-'Emmet, fol. 4c, and especially in *Maggid Devarav le-Ya'aqov*, ed. Schatz-
Uffenheimer, pp. 94–95, where it is evident that sounds are mentioned even when
the supreme experience is related to *Hokhmah*, and see in the passage translated
near n. 94 in this volume. This view of the Besht, though rare, is nevertheless not so
exceptional in the teachings attributed to him, as Scholem assumes in *The Messianic
Idea*, p. 214. Thus, too sharp a distinction between the Besht and the Great Maggid,
who indeed developed this topic much more, is much smaller than assumed by
Scholem and, following him on this point, also by Pedaya, "The Besht, R. Jacob
Joseph of Polonnoye, and the Maggid of Mezeritch." See also ch. 2 n. 26 and ch. 10
n. 26. In my opinion, the Besht himself should be seen as the source of some of the
Great Maggid's discussions of 'Ayin. See the material collected in Idel, *Hasidism*,
pp. 113–114, and 311, n. 46, which should be taken in account before portraying the
experiences of the Besht in what I call a "monotonic" manner, as part of what I call

deceptive simplicity in scholarship. It is deceptive since the assumption is that scholars know the semantic valences of the term used by the Besht, though in fact they ignore important aspects of the meanings found in some key traditions reported in his name, as in the case of *'ot* or *ruḥaniyyut*.

For the Cordoverian sources that deal with the experience of *'Ayin*, see Idel, *Hasidism*, pp. 109–111. For the obliteration of the bad decrees by causing the ascent of *Malkhut* to the realm of *Hokhmah*, see R. Jacob Joseph of Polonnoye, *Tzafnat Pa'aneaḥ*, ed. Nigal, p. 299, and *Keter Shem Tov*, fol. 12d, no. 91: דשמעתי בשם מורי זלל"ה ה ביאור פסוק 'כל אשר תמצא ידך לעשות בכחך עשה', כי חנוך מטטרון היה מייחד על כל תפירה וכו'. וכאשר מלכות עולה בכחך שהיא חכמה, כח מה, אז נתבטלו כל גזירות קשות ודברי פי חכם חן.

"And I have heard in the name of my teacher, blessed be his memory, a commentary on the verse 'Whatever your hand will find it necessary to do by your strength, do it.' Since Enoch Metatron was unifying on each and every wrinkle [he smoothed in the leather], etc., and when *Malkhut* ascends by your strength, which is *Hokhmah, Koaḥ Mah*, then the grave decrees have been obliterated. And the words of the sage are gracious."

On the background of this theme, see also my *The Angelic World: Apotheosis and Theophany* (Yediyyot Aharonot, Tel Aviv, 2008), pp. 9–10, 119–127 (Hebrew). About obliterating decrees by means of *devequt*, see ch. 4 n.2. See also Kauffman, *In All Your Ways Know Him*, pp. 273–274. The active aspect of the Enoch-Metatron episode that was quite important for the Besht does not fit the understanding of early Hasidism and of the Besht, as based on passivity, according to Weiss's approach and to a certain extent also that of Schatz-Uffenheimer.

For the critique of the emphasis on passivity and quietism in early Hasidism, see Piekarz, *Between Ideology and Reality*, pp. 82–103; Margolin, *The Human Temple*, pp. 178–179, 206, 343–378; and Kauffman, *In All Your Ways Know Him*, pp. 436–438. For a distinction between the transcendence of the power to speech, but not of hearing, by the contact with the world of thought, see Green, *Menahem Nahum of Chernobyl, Upright Practices, The Light of the Eyes*, p. 223, note 10. See also the Beshtian passage quoted beside n. 90 from R. Aharon of Apta's *Keter Nehora'*.

On the occurrence of the hint at abbreviations, see also in some of the following cases, and in Idel, "Models of Understanding Prayer," p. 105, note 263.

12   On the concept of "letters of thought" that emanates from the *Hokhmah*, see in the Great Maggid's discussion on the "primordial mind"—*qademut ha-sekhel*. Cf. Scholem, *ha-Shalav ha-'Aharon*, pp. 271, 273–274, and Schatz-Uffenheimer, *Hasidism as Mysticism*, pp. 211–212. For a phrase quite similar to "letters of thought," see in appendix C, in the texts of Cordovero and Azulai.

The situation described here is reminiscent of a description of the Great Maggid, who recommended pronouncing the Torah through being in a state in which someone is not aware of himself. See the passage of R. Ze'ev Wolf of Zhitomir's *'Or ha-Me'ir*, as translated and analyzed by Weiss, *Studies*, p. 79. Thus, we have some form of correspondence between the manner in which the prayer is pronounced as part of a more advanced phase on the spiritual path and the manner in which the Torah should be pronounced: in both cases the oral activity of the person does not cease, but his awareness of doing it is dissipating. This is the reason why I can hardly see in this attitude a case of quietism, as Weiss does in *Studies*.

For the translation of this technical phrase in a quite free manner as the "letters in his thoughts," see Jacobs, *Hasidic Prayer*, pp. 77–78; Jacobs offers there a different interpretation than that offered here. He attributes to the author of the passage acts related to all the four worlds, assuming that the utterances are related to the world of *'Assiyah* alone, despite the fact that the term does not occur in the passage. Likewise in his translation he resorts twice to the phrase "world of formation," while in the second instance the translation should be "world of creation." However, the utterances should be identified with the "world of formation" and not the "world of making." See ch. 2 n. 12. See the manner in which Schatz-Uffenheimer, *Maggid Devarav le-Ya'aqov*, pp. 85–86, interpreted in her footnotes the term *letters* as if referring to visual contours, namely as letters that are seen, rather than articulated orally. This is a sharp example for what I call the biased understanding of early Hasidism as if concerned with visual and contemplative approaches, which is dominant in scholarship in the field.

13 For the concept of delight in Hasidism, with a special emphasis on the views of the Besht, see Idel, "*Ta'anug*: Erotic Delights from Kabbalah to Hasidism," pp. 131–151, and Nigal, *The Birth of Hasidism*, pp. 159–163.

14 The elevation of *Malkhut*—here referred as related to the world of *'Assiyah*—to the *sefirah* of *Binah* is a *leitmotif* in the Beshtian traditions. See, e.g., the quotes in his name in R. Jacob Joseph of Polonnoye, *Kutoneth Passim*, ed. Nigal, pp. 22, 294, in his *Ben Porat Yosef*, fol. 99d, and see also *Keter Shem Tov*, fol. 9b. Sometimes this elevation has to do with the sweetening of the stern judgments, namely some form of transformation of evil into good, on high and below. See also Kallus, *Pillar of Prayer*, p. 56, no. 62. For the sweetening of the stern judgments, while mentioning also the shells, by the contact with the *sefirah* of *Binah*, see R. Moshe Cordovero, *'Or Yaqar*, vol. 7, p. 208. See also Bracha Sack, ed., *R. Moshe Cordovero, Ma'ayan 'Ein Ya'aqov* (Ben Gurion University Press, Beer Sheva, 2009), pp. 16–17 (Hebrew).

For the critique of the Kabbalistic intentions to the four cosmic worlds, see a younger contemporary of the Besht, R. Ezekiel Landa—who was associated in his youth with the kloiz of Brody—as discussed in Maoz Kahana, *From the Noda be-Yehuda to the Chatam Sofer, Halakhah and Thought in Their Historical Moment* (Zalman Shazar Center, Jerusalem, 2015), pp. 85–86 (Hebrew). See also Maoz Kahana, pp. 117–118.

15 For the role of *'Ayin* in Hasidic mysticism in general, see Matt, "*Ayn*," pp. 139–145, and Piekarz, *Between Ideology and Reality*, pp. 55–81. See also *'Or ha-'Emmet*, fol. 38a, from the school of the Great Maggid, and R. Jacob Joseph of Polonnoye, *Toledot Ya'aqov Yosef*, fol. 20a, in two short discussions on *'Ayin* cited in the name of the Besht. Therefore, two of the most important followers of the Besht reported traditions related to annihilation to their common master. See ch. 6 n. 18 for the quote in the name of the Besht found in R. Reuven Horowitz's *Dudayyim ba-Sodeh*, where the phrase *hitpashshetut ha-gashmiyyut*—the divestment of corporeality—occurs in a very similar context; see as well the discussion in ch. 6 n. 8.

The nexus between prayer and the state of divestment of corporeality is well-known since the early fourteenth century. See Idel, "Models of Understanding Prayer in Early Hasidism," pp. 16, 73–74, 101. The plausible existence of such a vision in a teaching of the Besht, as para-mental and described as some form of trance, as well as other instructions attributed to the Besht (see Idel, *Hasidism*, pp. 113–114), problematize Pedaya's description of the Besht as a monotonic figure and as having, unlike the Great Maggid, only extrovert forms of experiences. See her "The Besht, R. Jacob Joseph of Polonnoye, and the Maggid of Mezeritch," pp. 79–82, and compare also to Kauffman, *In All Your Ways Know Him*, p. 106, note 56. On *'Ayin* in the Great Maggid, see now Lorberbaum, "Attain the Attribute of 'Ayyin"; Lederberg, *The Gateway to Infinity*, pp. 251–281; as well as appendices A and F in this volume.

16 See Paul Kraus, "Jâbir et la science grecque," *Memoires de l'Institute d'Egypt*, vol. 45 (1943), part II, pp. 259, 268; Georges Vajda, "Les letters et les sons dans la langue arabe d'après Abu-Hatim al-Razi," *Arabica*, vol. VIII (1961), p. 129, n. 1; Zoran, "Magic, Theurgy, and the Knowledge of Letters"; Idel, *Language, Torah, and Hermeneutics*, pp. 5–6, 139; Idel, *The Mystical Experience in Abraham Abulafia*, pp. 30–32; and *Hasidism*, p. 164.

I cannot now enter into the details concerning the question of the origin of the fourfold distinction mentioned here, as I do not also analyze in this study other sources for the Besht's thought, with the exception of R. Moshe Cordovero, R. Elijah da Vidas, and R. Abraham Azulai, to be discussed as follows, especially in appendices B and C. See, meanwhile, the passage I adduced from an epistle of Abraham Abulafia found in a unique manuscript, and thus practically unknown to the Hasidic elite in Eastern Europe, as to the existence of letters on four levels also here in the context of cleaving, in *Hasidism*, pp. 230–231. For a threefold distinction, which is much more widespread in the Middle Ages, see *Sitrei Torah*, ed. A. Gross (Jerusalem, 2002), p. 8, *Mafteah ha-Shemot* (Jerusalem, 2001), p. 37. See also Weiss, *Studies*, p. 72, who attempts to explain why in some statements of the Great Maggid the first step of the three, the deed, *ha-ma'aseh*, has not been mentioned, because of the quietist approach that characterizes this master's thought, as well as mysticism as such! However, it seems to me that at least insofar as the Besht is concerned, this first step was conceived to be quite low, since in prayer only children or depressed or unlearned people use printed texts, as the words of prayer were known by heart. Moreover, in prayer, speech is the deed. For these three categories in Cordovero, see Bracha Sack, "The Concept of Thought, Speech, and Action," *Da'at*, vol. 50–52 (2003), pp. 221–241 (Hebrew).

For an interesting discussion of the three levels of existence, which includes the performance of the commandments, which is not connected to letters, the utterances, and the letters in thought, in connection to *devequt*, see the passage of R. Elijah da Vidas, quoted in in ch. 3 n. 7, and the interesting discussion of R. Aharon of Zhitomir, *Toledot 'Aharon*, fol. 49cd. See also *Zohar*, I, fol. 100a, and Margolin, *The Human Temple*, pp. 357–361. For cleaving to God by means of deeds, speech, and thought, see the quote in the name of the Great Maggid adduced by R. Abraham Hayyim of Zloczow, in his *Peri Hayyim*, fol. 36bc. It should be pointed out that the quote cited in Schatz-Uffenheimer, *Hasidism as Mysticism*, pp. 189–190, from the admonisher R. Menahem Mendel of Bar, which deals with three different forms of unification, privileges those done by deeds and speeches to those accomplished by thought, flatly contradicting the conclusion she draws as to the sublime status of the mental and the quietist elements. See also another teaching of his at the end of appendix E. For the meaning of *'otiyyot* as sounds or vocables, see, e.g., the use of R. Aharon ha-Cohen of Apta in his introduction to his commentary on the prayerbook, *Keter Nehora'*, pp. 4 and 100.

17   *Keter Shem Tov ha-Shalem*, p. 123, no. 123b:

כשמדבק עצמו ילך בתחילה בעולם עשיה, ואה"כ יפרח במחשבתו למעלה גבוה יותר, ואה"כ
עוד גבוה יותר בעולם המלאכים והאופנים, ואה"כ בעולם הבריאה, עד שירגיש במחשבתו שפרח
במחשבותיו גבוה מאד לעולם האצילות . ..וכמו אדם שמטייל מחדר לחדר, כן יטייל במחשבתו
בעולמות עליונים.

See also *Keter Shem Tov ha-Shalem*, p. 123, no. 216a, where another instance of ascent through the worlds is found, as well as *Keter Shem Tov ha-Shalem*, p. 162, no. 261a. See also *Liqqutim Yeqarim*, fol. 56a, no. 175, and Jacobs, *Hasidic Prayer*, pp. 79–80. This teaching should be compared with what is written in the *Testament of ha-Rivash*, fol. 6a, where there is a gradation of four forms of prayer: by movement of the body, by soul, and then by thought, or mental prayer, and finally a state when someone does not know, namely is in a state of the divestment of corporeality. See also *Testament of ha-Rivash*, fol. 11a. However, in this treatise there is no correspondence between the four stages and the four cosmic worlds. Elsewhere in the same compilation—fol. 17a—there is however a correspondence between aspects of worship, especially prayers and the first three cosmic worlds, though the world of emanation is not mentioned in this passage. See also the two passages translated in Lamm, *The Religious Thought of Hasidism*, pp. 154–157. For the assumption that the utterances of the prayer take someone from one world to another, mentioning the four worlds, see R. Jacob Joseph ben Yehudah, *Sefer Rav Yeivi*, fol. 83c. For the three levels of *devequt*, see the passage from R. Elijah da Vidas, quoted in ch. 3 n. 7.

18   *Toledot Ya'aqov Yosef*, fol. 7a, and copied also in *Keter Shem Tov*, fol. 12bc, par. 86, and *Keter Shem Tov ha-Shalem*, p. 50, where the pertinent Zoharic sources have been noticed: מבעש"ט ז"ל נודע כי אות א' הוא חכמה ומחשבה...כי א' נתלבשה תוך אות ב', כי
ב' ב' אלפין, ג' ג' אלפין [וכו' כמו ששמעתי ממורי זלה"ה וכו']. וראשית הבריאה הי' ע"י אות א'
שהוא חכמה, ובָרָא הכל ע"י חכמה כמ"ש [כולם] בחכמה עשית כו'. הרי רוחניותו ית' בתוך אות א',
ונתעטף בו ובָרָא אור מן אות א', והוא אור אצילות, ואח"כ נתעטף עם א' בתוך אות ב' ובָרָא עולם
הבריאה כו ' Spirituality, which means in some cases in Hasidism a divine power—pointed originally to an astral power, that is caused to descend, according to astro-magical texts in the Middle Ages—see also ch. 5 n. 12. Despite the theory dealing sometimes with the individual letters as having some form of separate identity, I did not find in the main Hasidic writings of the first generation of Hasidic auhtors—R. Barukh of Kosov being an exception—discussions on the distinct quality of each letter. In fact according to two Hasidic masters, the letters are different in their external form but unified in their inner common nature, which is spiritual and is found on high. See R. Jacob Joseph of Polonnoye, *Tzafnat Pa'aneah*, ed. Koretz, fol. 95b; *Keter Shem Tov*, fol. 24c, no. 190; and R. Issakhar Dov Baer of Zloczow's *Mevasser Tzedeq*, fol. 20ab. For letters/sounds and the lights within them, see more in chapter 8 of this volume. On the concept that speech, namely the

pronounced letters, are the boundaries of everything, see the famous teaching of R. Nahman of Braslav, *Liqqutei Moharan*, I, no. 60, par. 3: ־הַדִּבּוּר הוּא הַגְּבוּל שֶׁל כָּל הַדְּ־ בָרִים, כִּי הַגְּבִיל חָכְמָתוֹ בְּהָאוֹתִיּוֹת, שֶׁאוֹתִיּוֹת אֵלּוּ הֵם גְּבוּל לָזֶה, וְאוֹתִיּוֹת אֵלּוּ הֵם גְּבוּל לָזֶה The apotheosis of speech in R. Nahman deserves a special analysis, which cannot be done here. See, e.g., Nahman, I, par. 225, discussed in ch. 14 beside n. 4. See also the view of R. Pinhas of Koretz cited in ch. 5 n. 7. It should be pointed out that though not quoting the Besht, his first disciple, R. Arieh Leib Galiner, the Admonisher of Polonnoye, describes a variety of vocal activities: study, prayer, and song, as equal, as paramount, and strictly necessary for the elevation of sparks. See *Qol 'Arieh*, fol. 57c. See also ch. 3 n. 8. For clothing within letters/sounds, though the garment is that of the souls, see ch. 4 n. 5 and ch. 6 n. 3, and appendix B in this volume.

19 Those are the terms of Abraham Maslow, I, used in *Hasidism*, pp. 130, 169, 376, n. 1. Compare also to the somewhat similar view of Orent, "Unio Mystica," who emphasizes the means-experiences as part of a spiral understanding of the Habad mysticism.

20 *Mevasser Tzedeq*, fol. 1ab.

21 See the passage translated and discussed by Weiss, *Studies*, p. 110, and also the discussion in the following chapter. This does not mean that the Besht was a "true Lurianic" Kabbalist. See *Hasidism: A New History*, p. 68.

3. R. Meir Margoliot Harif's Tradition about the Besht

1 See Rosman, *The Founder of Hasidism*, pp. 135–136, 155–158.

2 According to the analysis of Adam Teller, "The Sluck Tradition Concerning the Early Days of the Besht," in eds. D. Assaf, J. Dan, and I. Etkes, *Studies in Hasidism* (Institute of Jewish Studies, Jerusalem, 1999), pp. 15–38 (Hebrew).

3 Avot 6:1. On this dictum see Idel, *Absorbing Perfections*, pp. 170–171. It should be pointed out that many interpretations on this dictum have been cited in the name of the Besht, and the emphasis on the linguistic performance is quite significant in many of them.

4 Proverbs 6:23. On lights and letters/sounds, see more in chapter 8 in this volume.

5 Psalm 19:9. See the occurrence of this verse in an interesting passage based on Cordovero's views, found in Isaiah Horowitz's *Shenei Luhot ha-Berit*, as discussed by Piekarz, *The Beginning of Hasidism*, pp. 354–355.

6 *Sod Yakhin u-Vo'az*, chap. 2, pp. 41–42: שיחשוב קודם הלימוד במחשבה נכונה וזכה, שמכין את עצמו ללמוד [תורה] לשמה, בלי שום כוונה זרה. וכאשר הזהירו אותי מוריי הגדולים בתורה ובחסידות ובתוכם ידידי הרב החסיד מופת הדור מוהר"ר ישראל בעש"ט זצלה"ה כוונה רצויה בלימוד לשמה, לדבק את עצמו בקדושה וטהרה, עם אותיות, בכח ופועל, בדיבור ובמחשבה, לקשר חלק מנר"ן ח"י [נפש, רוח, נשמה, חיה ויחידה] בקדושת נר מצוה ותורה, אותיות המחכימות, ומשפיעים שפע אורות וחיות אמיתיות נצחיות וכשיזכה להבין ולהתדבק בהאותיות קדושים יוכל להבין מתוך האותיות ממש אפילו עתידות ולכן נקראת התורה "מאירת עיניים" שמאירה עיני המתדבק בהם בקדושה ובטהרה כמו האותיות על אורים ותומים.

This passage has been mentioned and eventually analyzed by several scholars. See Scholem, *ha-Shalav ha-Aharon*, pp. 132–133; Weiss, *Studies*, p. 59; Weiss, "Talmud-Torah le-Shitat R. Israel Besht," pp. 162–167; Piekarz, *The Beginning of Hasidism*, pp. 354–355, Schatz-Uffenheimer, *Hasidism as Mysticism*, pp. 312–313; Rosman, *The Founder of Hasidism*, pp. 135–136, where another English translation is offered, resorting to the term *letters*; Pedaya, "The Besht, R. Jacob Joseph of Polonnoye, and the Maggid of Mezeritch," pp. 33, 58; Lederberg, *Sod ha-Da'at*, p. 185; Gries, *The Hebrew Book*, p. 255; and Idel, *Hasidism*, pp. 176, 178, 184, and p. 356, n. 28, where I already expressed my uneasiness toward Weiss's interpretation. See also more recently what I wrote in my *Absorbing Perfections*, pp. 183–184, "Remembering and Forgetting," pp. 118–119, and *Enchanted Chains*, pp. 108–110. In this context the recurrence of this passage in later Hasidic literature, where much stronger Beshtian elements have been introduced, will not be addressed here. See, especially, Scholem, *The Messianic Idea*, p. 212, where he refers to this passage as teaching, in the line of his approach, a "definite technique of contemplation."

7   R. Elijah da Vidas, *Reshit Hokhmah*, Gate of Holiness, chap. 10, vol. II, p. 247:

ופירש מורי עליו השלום שמלת קבועות בפה הנאמר שם מורה לנו ענין גדול והוא מציאות
ה' מוצאות שורשם למעלה מעלה בראש והם שורש לכל הנמצאות כמבואר באדרא, אמנם הם
יורדים ומתגלים מעולם לעולם בבחינות אבי"ע והקדוש ברוך הוא לאהבתו את האדם קבע בפיו
האותיות האלו כדי שיוכל להדבק בבוראו, כי בהזכירו למטה אותיות אלו בתורתו או בתפלתו מנענע
ומעורר למעלה השרשים העליונים והיינו מלת קבע שהוא קבע כעין התוקע השלשלת ראשה אחד
במקום אחד וראשה השני במקום אחר, כי אף על פי שיהיה המקום ההוא רחוק בנענע אדם ראש
השלשלת שבידו מנענע כל השלשלת אף על פי שתהיה גדולה כל מה שאפשר להיות.

For two types of unification, in thought and in speech, see Moshe Hallamish, *Kabbalah in Liturgy, Halakhah, and Customs* (Bar Ilan Press, Ramat Gan, 2000), p. 51 (Hebrew). Compare also to Cordovero, *Shi'ur Qomah*, fol. 94ac; Cordovero, '*Eilimah Rabbati*, fol. 132d; and his '*Or Yaqar*, vol. 16, p. 70, vol. 17, p. 83; Cordovero, on *Tiqqunei Zohar Hadash*, vol. 3, pp. 7—to be translated in appendix C of this volume—29, 70, 71, 90, 99, 257. See also the passage from *Hesed le-Avraham*, fol. 11cd—translated and discussed in appendix B—and especially *Hesed le-Avraham*, fol. 24cd, as well as the other discussions found in appendix C. One of the possible sources for both Cordovero and da Vidas is the book of the *Zohar*, I, fol. 100ab, whose views have been quoted in da Vidas, *Reshit Hokhmah*, vol. II, pp. 64–65. See also appendix C beside n. 7 in this volume another interpretation of Cordovero's on the same passage from *Sefer Yetzyirah*.

Da Vidas's text was copied verbatim in an influential ethical-Kabbalistic compedium by R. Isaiah Horowitz, *Shenei Luhot ha-Berit*, I, fol. 112b, and in Nathan of Gaza's *Derush ha-Menorah*, printed in ed. Gershom Scholem, *Be-'Iqevot Mashiah* (Schocken Books, Jerusalem, 1944), p. 106 (Hebrew), who gave to the chain motif a peculiar turn. See also Idel, *Enchanted Chains*, pp. 58–59 and *Hasidism*, pp. 161–162, 346, n. 95. For a clear impact of this passage on R. Reuven Horowitz, see *Diduim ba-Sodeh*, fol. 37b, and on a sermon of R. Dov Baer of Medzeritch as it has been reported by R. Meshullam Phoebus of Zbarazh, see *Kitvei Qodesh*, fol. 4b. For the impact of da Vidas's book on early Hasidism, though not specifically on the Besht, see the studies of Mordechai Pachter, "Traces of the Influence of R. Elijah de Vidas's *Reshit Hockhma* upon the Writings of R. Jacob Joseph of Polonnoye," in eds.

J. Dan and J. Hacker, *Studies in Jewish Mysticism, Philosophy, and Ethical Literature
Presented to Isaiah Tishby* (Jerusalem 1986), pp. 569–592 (Hebrew); Bracha Sack,
"The Influence of *Reshit Ḥokhmah* on the Teachings of the Maggid of Mezhirech,"
in ed. Rapoport-Albert, *Hasidism Reappraised*, pp. 251–257 and her "Inquiry in the
Impact of R. Moshe Cordovero on Hasidism," *'Eshel Be'er Sheva'*, vol. 3 (1986), pp.
229–246 (Hebrew); Rapoport-Albert, "God and the Zaddik," pp. 328–329, n. 71;
Krassen, *Uniter of Heaven and Earth*, pp. 82–83, 132, 168, 237–238, n. 46, 261, n. 48;
Margolin, *The Human Temple*, pp. 145–204, especially 202–204; Brody, "Open to
Me the Gates of Righteousness," p. 23, n. 33; as well as the material discussed in
my *Hasidism*, pp. 110, 303, n. 335, 378–379, n. 40. See also ch. 2 n. 9 and ch. 4 n.
6, ch. 5 n. 13, and appendix B in this volume. For other influences of this book on
R. Gershon of Kutov and the Besht, see Idel, "Models of Understanding Prayer
in Early Hasidism," pp. 17–21, 74, n. 202, 108–110 and "Prayer, Ecstasy, and Alien
Thoughts," p. 63, nn. 16, 119. Equally important for understanding the previous
passage of R. Meir Margoliot are the statements found in R. Elijah da Vidas's book,
Gate of Holiness, chap. 4, vol. II, p. 62:

שלהתדבק האדם בקדושה הוא שישתדל לזכות נפש רוח ונשמה, שהם נקנים על ידי מעשה
המצות ודבור תורה וטהרת המחשבות וכוונת התורה והמצוה

"In order that someone will [be able to] cleave to holiness he should make an
effort to merit [the possession of] *Nefesh, Ruaḥ* and *Neshamah*, which are acquired
by the performance of the commandments, and speech of the Torah and the purity
of thought and the *Kavvanah* of Torah and Commandment." Afterward in another
important statement in da Vidas, p. 65 it is said: "The *devequt* is acquired by means
of deed, so there are speech and thought." הדבקות נקנה על ידי מעשה הרי ודבור ומחשבה
Let me point out that though the study of the Torah is mentioned in the
context of cleaving already in the book of the *Zohar*, the utterances were not mentioned there. See the texts discussed in Wolfson, *Through a Speculum that Shines*, p.
333. This is also the case of most of the Safedian sources which follow the path of
the *Zohar*, especially in Cordovero's writings. For other Cordoverian influences on
early Hasidism, see Idel, *Kabbalah: New Perspectives*, p. 351, n. 357; Kauffman, *In All
Your Ways Know Him*, *passim*, especially pp. 37–39, 67–73; and Wacks, *The Secret
of Unity*, p. 226. For an introduction and English translations of excerpts from
this seminal book, see Lawrence Fine, *Safed Spirituality: Rules of Mystical Piety, the
Beginning of Wisdom* (Paulist Press, New York, 1984) and the recent monograph
of Patrick B. Koch, *Human Self-Perfection: A Re-Assessment of Kabbalistic Musar-
Literature of Sixteenth-Century Safed* (Cherub Press, Los Angeles, 2015).
Needless to say that if I am correct as to the impact of da Vidas's view of
devequt on the Besht, Tishby's proposal in *Studies in Kabbalah and Its Branches*,
referred in n. 2 in this volume, which concentrates on his suggested impact of
Kabbalistic manuscripts of R. Moshe Ḥayyim Luzzatto on his contemporary the
Besht, is becoming even more precarious. What is missing in Luzzatto's texts
adduced by Tishby but is found already in da Vidas's passage is the emphasis on
multiple forms of *devequt*, including by mean of sonorous performances. See also
Scholem, *The Messianic Idea*, pp. 207–208.

8   See also the tradition in *Keter Shem Tov ha-Shalem*, p. 121, no. 212 and the many
passages discussed in Weiss, *Studies*, p. 77, and Schatz-Uffenheimer, *Hasidism as*

Mysticism, pp. 204–214. It should be mentioned that according to R. R. Arieh Leib Galiner of Polonnoye, *Qol 'Arieh*, fol. 11a, "thought and speech are one unit" המח־ שבה והדיבור אחדות אחד Such a collision of speech and thought is found also among the Hasidic thinkers related to the Great Maggid. See Idel, "Reification of Language in Jewish Mysticism," pp. 64, 78, n. 92. For the occurrence of the concept of *'Olam ha-Mahashavah* in R. Jacob Joseph see, e.g., his *Ben Porat Yosef*, fol. 6b, *Tzafnat Pa'aneah* [Koretz], fol. 36a, where the assumption is that it is possible to cleave to this supernal world, identical with the *sefirah* of *Binah; Kuthonet Passim*, ed. Nigal, pp. 81, 144, and several times in his *Toledot Ya'aqov Yosef*, e.g., fol. 8a. See, moreover, the interesting passage found in *Keter Shem Tov*, fol. 34d, no. 255, where the name of the Besht is found on a teaching dealing with the "world of thought," and see also *Keter Shem Tov*, fol. 60b, nos. 405–406, fol. 60d, no. 411, and especially fol. 62c, no. 423, and Idel, "Models of Understanding Prayer in Early Hasidism," pp. 74–75. As to an attribution of the phrase "world of speech" to the Besht, see in the compilation of traditions of the Great Maggid, *'Or ha-'Emmet*, fol. 1b, and Schatz-Uffenheimer, *Hasidism as Mysticism*, p. 191 and n. 8. I cannot enter here the analysis of the widespread Beshtian instruction to unify speech to thought, or "the world of speech" to "the world of thought," teachings that represent a different set of questions regarding the coordination of human acts and attaining a unified mode of activity. See, e.g., R. Yissakhar Dov Baer of Zlotchov, *Mevasser Tzedeq*, fol. 15c, and Kallus, *Pillar of Prayer*, pp. 99–101, no. 74–77.

In the context of this unification, we should understand also another Beshtian teaching that deals with the exile of the speech—see also *'Or ha-'Emmet*, fol. 34b—as well as a statement found in R. Menahem Nahum of Chernobyl in *Me'or 'Einayyim*, p. 27, which claims that the aim of the entire Torah is to amend speech. Amending speech is mentioned also in the context of Moses and of the Besht himself. See *In Praise of the Baal Shem Tov*, p. 129, and in R. Jacob Joseph's *Ben Porat Yosef*, ed. Koretz, fol. 99c:

וזהו ענין מעלת מרע"ה שהעלה ותיקן דיבורו ותחלה היו הצאן שהיה ר[נ]עה אותן ואח"כ .בגלגול נעשו תלמידיו שנתן להם את התורה ולמד עמהם וכו' ודפה"ה—translated as a motto—and discussed in my Idel, "The Besht Passed His Hand over His Face," p. 92, and ch. 5 n. 2.

For the importance of utterances and the vapor of the Torah for the elevation of the sparks on high, see R. Arieh Leib Galiner, *Qol 'Arieh*, fol. 56d, and ch. 2 n. 18 and appendix C n. 13 in this volume. For more on the vapor of the mouth, see beside ch. 8 n. 15 and in appendices C and D in this volume.

Let me point out that the tension between the vocal and the mental forms of prayer in Judaism is quite evident since the thirteenth century, when the more noetically inclined forms of Jewish philosophy implicitly sublated, and some of the philosophers even derided, vocal performances. See, e.g., the survey of this issue in Idel, *Enchanted Chains*, pp. 189–190, 192–193.

9 *Sod Yakhin u-Vo'az*, p. 42: ומילדותי מיום שהכרתי בדבקות האהבה עם מורי ידידי הרב מוהר"ר ישראל תנצב"ה הנ"ל ידעתי נאמנה שזה היו התנהגותיו בקדושה ובטהרה בסוד חסידות ופרישות שאותיות תורתינו הקדושה הם כלם קדושים וכשאדם זוכה להתדבק עם אותיות בלומדו לשם שמים שיוכל להבין עתידות

For the Besht's alleged capacity to know future things by listening to the voice of a student who recites the *Mishnah*, see the episode related to his brother-in-law, R. Gershon of Kutov, discussed in Heschel, *The Circle of the Baal Shem Tov*, p. 48; Etkes, *The Besht: Magician, Mystic, and Leader*, p. 295, n. 53; and Mondshine, *Shivehei Ha-Baal Shem Tov*, p. 263; as well as the testimony R. Jacob Joseph of Polonnoye brings in the name of his master in *Ben Porat Yosef*, fol. 122a [copied in *Keter Shem Tov*, no. 67] as to the Besht's capacity to foretell one's future from the manner in which he recites the *Mishnah*, without however, mentioning the name of his brother-in-law, though probably hinting at this event. For the late collection of some legendary reports to this effect, see R. Isaiah Wolf Chikernic, *Ma'asiyyot u-Ma'amarin Yeqarim* (Zhitomir, 1903), fol. 3ab. For the importance of the recitation of the *Mishnah* in Safedian Kabbalah, see Fine, "Recitation of the *Mishnah*," pp. 183–199; Werblowsky, *Joseph Karo, Lawyer and Mystic*, pp. 18–19, 109–111; and Idel, *Hasidism*, p. 173, and *Enchanted Chains*, pp. 162–164. I hope to elaborate on this issue in a separate monograph.

10   See Ysander, *Studien*, pp. 286–297; Rosman, *The Founder of Hasidism*, pp. 30–36, 114–115; and now Kauffman, *In All Your Ways Know Him*, pp. 403–404; and Idel, "Prayer, Ecstasy, and Alien Thoughts," p. 61, n. 251. See also resorting to cleaving to sounds as a surrogate for ascetic practice in the Besht's letter to R. Jacob Joseph, mentioned in ch. 8 n. 15. I assume that such a change indeed took place. Compare, however, another interesting approach articulated in Haviva Pedaya's critique of Rosman's book in *Zion*, vol. 69 (2004), pp. 517–519 (Hebrew), who offers a more consistent image of the Besht's activities as a whole, as a mystic who started practicing some cathartic ways of behavior in order to gain some forms of revelations under the influence of Kabbalistic books. A similar position is found already in Schechter, "The Chassidism," pp. 156–157, and in Scholem, *ha-Shalav ha-'Aharon*, p. 111. Though interesting, this teleological vision of resorting to the ascetic path at the beginning of his career seems to me quite implausible from a historical point of view. In any case Pedaya's approach differs dramatically from the assumptions of Scholem, *On the Kabbalah and Its Symbolis*m, p. 26, and Weiss, *Studies*, pp. 118, n. 12, who described the Besht as semi-literate or as a relatively illiterate, though it is closer to what he wrote in *ha-Shalav ha-'Aharon*, pp. 134–135. It seems that Weiss, like Solomon Schechter beforehand, has been influenced by some positions expressed in the hagiography, and by maskilic critical writers. See, e.g., Etkes, *The Besht: Magician, Mystic, and Leader*, pp. 260–261, and Schechter, "The Chassidism," p. 162. See also the view of Meir Balaban in a discussion of the Besht in his study of Hasidism in *ha-Tequfah*, vol. 18 (1923), pp. 487–502 (Hebrew), who claims that the Besht was a simple man, namely a simpleton. My position is somewhere in the middle, and similar to that of Rosman, *The Founder of Hasidism*, p. 179, which means that the Besht came from a culturally poor background, and in his earlier phases of his life he had only a very modest Jewish education, but in his twenties he was capable of learning in an accelerated manner, a fact that could account for his capability to attract also some learned disciples.

4. Cleaving to Utterances in the Besht's Holy Epistle

1   On the possible source of this statement in *Tiqqunei Zohar*, see Wacks, *The Secret of Unity*, pp. 88–89, 94, and he assumes here that the speeches not only related to prayer and Torah as mentioned, but also ordinary speech, namely some form of worship done in corporeality already in classical Kabbalah. This is quite an important remark, which demonstrates that the Besht had a remarkable source for his proposal he proposes to R. Gershon. It should be pointed out that this statement refers to the manner of performing canonical texts. However, later on in the *Holy Epistle*, ed. Mondshine, p. 237, the Besht reminds his addressee to keep in mind the things he told him several times before he left Podolia, related to ethics, and repeat them, and be careful about their content, since he will "certainly find in each and every speech, many types of sweet things." It is not clear what is, therefore, the relationship between the written instruction adduced here from the same letter, and what the Besht taught his brother-in-law when they were together beforehand. It may well be that there is here some form of loose redaction. Though the canonical texts are envisioned in a monadic manner, endowed with special powers, his own instruction is presented in a much more modest way, but nevertheless using the same phrase: "in each and every speech." It can hardly be a doubt that those instructions delivered while R. Gershon was in Podolia were oral teachings, and the Besht refers to them as "speeches," emphasizing the content much less. Also the use of the Hebrew phrase "minei metiqut" points to the oral activity. Nevertheless, this passage shows that it is not the first time that the Besht informs R. Gershon as to how to behave, but that it was already a pattern, but this time it has to do, as we see in the opening of the passage translated here, with the fact that he is in the Holy Land. On the hieros gamos on the lips during prayer, see Idel, "Models for Understanding Prayer," pp. 56–78, 80, especially pp. 75–76, n. 206. See also below n. 3 in this chapter.

2   For numerous traces of the Besht's triune view of the content of each letter/source, see Idel, "Models of Understanding Prayer in Early Hasidism," p. 23, n. 45. It is especially important to remark that this triune view is described by R. Efrayim of Sudylkov as a teaching that he heard from the Besht, and thus it may stem from the relatively later period of his life, when the *Holy Epistle* had been redacted. This triunity could, as Weiss, *Studies*, p. 188, has judiciously remarked, easily become "the essential basis for a magical theory that envisages the possibility of man's producing changes either in the world or in the sphere of the Divinity." See also R. Pinhas Shapira of Koretz, *Midrash Pinḥas* (Ashdod, 2001), p. 34, n. 49, and p. 110, no. 2. In a way the three elements found within the vocables constitute the parallel to the *ruḥaniyyut*, described as found in the vocables. See appendices C and D in this volume.

    For an important vision of the *'otiyyot* as comprising worlds and all the other letters, see the traditions found in R. Jacob Joseph of Polonnoye, *Ben Porat Yosef*, fols. 42c and 46c, and in R. Menahem Nahum of Chernobyl, *Me'or 'Einayyim*, p. 161, where each letter is conceived of as comprising the entire Torah. It should be mentioned that in several traditions reported in the name of the Besht, the Torah is described as divinity. On the proposal to understand some perceptions of the letters or sounds in pre-Hasidic and Hasidic literatures as monadic, see my various studies, e.g., *Kabbalah: New Perspectives*, p. 235; *Language, Torah, and Hermeneutics,*

p. XV; "Reification of Language in Jewish Mysticism," pp. 59–66; and *Hasidism*, pp. 154–156.

Let me point out the monadic nature of this widespread statement, which may be not only a phenomenological resemblance to Leibnitz's theory about the monads, but also a possible historical impact of this element of his thought on the Besht. See also Allison P. Coudert, *Leibniz and the Kabbalah* (Kluwer Academic Publisher, Dordrecht, 1995), pp 78–98. In any case, Solomon Maimon, a much younger contemporary of the Besht stemming from Eastern Europe, was aware of at least some aspects Leibniz's thought while he was still in Poland. This issue deserves a separate inquiry. See, meanwhile, M. Idel, "Divine Attributes and *Sefirot* in Jewish Theology," in eds. S. O. Heller Willensky and M. Idel, *Studies in Jewish Thought* (Magnes Press, Jerusalem, 1989), pp. 109–111 (Hebrew). Another possibility for explaining the similarity between the two thinkers would be the existence of a common source in Kabbalah. In any case, for the possible Kabbalistic sources of Leibniz's monadology, see Coudert, *Leibniz and the Kabbalah*, pp. 78–98. For a reading of the triune understanding of each letter/sound as if referring to written letters and texts, see Rachel Elior, *Heiruth 'al ha-Luḥot* (Misrad ha-Bitahon, Tel Aviv, 1999), pp. 74–75 (Hebrew), who also proposes, some years after, the possible impact of a non-specified manuscript of Abraham Abulafia on the Besht, without however offering a precise reference or the source for her statement! For the actual source of this statement, see Idel, *Hasidism*, p. 155 and the pertinent footnotes there. Compare also to her recent shift to a more vocal interpretation of the Besht's thought, in Elior, *Israel Ba'al Shem Tov and His Contemporaries*, vol. 1, pp. 455–463, to be compared to what she wrote in her study mentioned in n. 1 in this volume, again without mentioning her scholarly sources for this shift.

3   The question of who combines the vocables that are conceived of as monadic is perhaps solved in a passage of R. Jacob Joseph of Polonnoye, to be discussed in appendix F, as done by the righteous. In the Koretz version it is written *zeh 'im zeh*, while in the early manuscript printed by Mondshine, the version is *zeh ba-zeh*. An attentive reading of the manuscript version shows that it has an inferior formulation here, for reasons I cannot enter into in this framework. Nevertheless, it is this latter version that is reminiscent of the manner in which the text to be adduced as follows from the Great Maggid's *Maggid Devarav le-Ya'aqov* [see ch. 8 n. 12] describes the sparkling of the lights of the letters, which I propose to interpret in a sexual manner. Compare to the Tantric bipolar perceptions of the sounds as the place of the encounter between Shiva and Shakti, namely male and female divinities. Cf. Beck, *Sonic Theology*, p. 101.

4   I.e., the prayer's soul. See also a similar view found in R. Jacob Joseph of Polonnoye, *Ben Porat Yosef*, fol. 41d, without mentioning the name of the Besht. It is at the end of this book that the Besht's *Holy Epistle* has been printed for the first time. Let me point out that the teaching that the soul soars during prayer from one world to another, because of the *Kavvanah*, is found already in R. Moshe Cordovero in a seminal passage that has been copied by his followers many times. See Idel, *Hasidism*, pp. 100–101, and *Enchanted Chains*, pp. 182–189.

5   On the various understandings of the Hebrew verb *KLL* in the context of mystical union, see Idel, "Universalization and Integration," pp. 27–58, as well as the view

found in R. Nathan Steinhartz's *Liqqutei Tefillot*, part I, no. 73, where some form
of mystical union by being eaten is found. Thanks to Prof. Zvi Mark for the last
reference. See also ch. 6 n. 2.

6   *Epistle on the Ascent of the Soul*, or the *Holy Epistle*, in *Shivehei Ha-Baal Shem Tov*,
      ed. Mondshine, pp. 235–236: ובפרט ...אך זאת אני מודיעך והשם יהיה בעזרך לנכח ה' דרכך
      ואות ליחד כי בכל אות בארץ הקדושה בעת תפלתך ולמודך בכל דבור ודבור ומוצא שפתיך תבין
      יש עולמות ונשמות ואלקות ועולים ומתקשרים ומתיחדים זה בזה עם אלקות ואח"כ מתקשרים
      ומתיחדים יחד האותיות ונעשים תיבה ומתיחדים יחוד גמור באלקות ותכלל נשמ'|תך] עמהם בכל
      בחי' ובחי' מהנ"ל, ומתייחדים כל העולמות כאחד ועולים, ונעשה שמחה ותענוג גדול לאין שיעור,
      בהבינך בשמחת חתן וכלה בקטנות וגשמיות, וכ"ש במעלה העליונה כזאת .. See also the version
      quoted in the name of the Besht in *'Or ha-'Emmet*, fol. 18b. On this specific passage
      from the *Holy Epistle*, see Idel, "Models for Understanding Prayer," pp. 23–25; Idel,
      Absorbing Perfections, pp. 194–195, 545, n. 160; and the translations of *'otiyyot* as let-
      ters in both Etkes, *The Besht: Magician, Mystic, and Leader*, pp. 148–149, 171–172;
      and Jacobs, *Hasidic Prayer*, pp. 74–76 (who translates the term *'otiyyot* as letters and
      teivah as worlds!). For other translations of this passage that resort inertially to the
      term *letters*, also after my discussions on sonority in my book of *Hasidism*, see Dan,
      Jewish Mysticism, vol. 3, p. 126; Altshuler, *The Messianic Secret of Hasidism*, pp. 20,
      n. 19, 343; Lederberg, *Sod ha-Da'at*, pp. 168–171; Dauber, "The Baal Shem Tov and
      the Messiah," pp. 232–239; Wolfson, "Immanuel Frommann," pp. 190–191, 215, n.
      135; and following him also Magid, *Hasidism Incarnate*, p. 166. See also the discus-
      sion in Wacks, *The Secret of Unity*, p. 88. See also R. Aharon of Apta, *Sefer Ner
      Mitzwah*, fol. 5a, and especially the passage from his *Keter Shem Tov*, fol. 56a, which
      has been dealt with previously and referred to in ch. 2 n. 13.

      This passage is not found in the Frenkel-Bauminger version of the epistle, and
      some scholars are inclined to see it as a later accretion. See, however, Dan, *Jewish
      Mysticism*, Idel, "Your Word Stands in Heaven," pp. 235–236, n. 69; and Dauber,
      "The Baal Shem Tov and the Messiah"; who argue that it has been authored by the
      Besht. Compare also to the view found in *Ben Porat Yosef*, fol. 42c, cited by the
      author as a tradition he heard to the effect that "in each word [teivah] the entire
      world is comprised etc., כי כל תיבה נכלל מכל העולם וכו' ודפה"ח The end of quotation
      is reminiscent of the manner in which the Besht is quoted.

      For an important description of a mystical union with the utterance, see also
      the so-called *Testament of the Besht*, fol. 11a. However, let me emphasize that even
      in this case, which is presented as a teaching belonging to the Great Maggid's
      instruction, the speech is described explicitly as being the garment of thought, and
      necessary for the acquaintance with the content of the hidden thought. See also the
      interesting discussion to this effect, *Testament of the Besht*, fol. 11b, and see also ch.
      5 n. 13. See also Kallus, *Pillar of Prayer*, p. 90, no. 70. Elsewhere, the Great Maggid
      speaks about the letters/sounds as the vessels where the lights and vitality are found.
      ch. 8 n. 5; Schatz-Uffenheimer, *Hasidism as Mysticism*, p. 173; and especially *Maggid
      Devarav le-Ya'aqov*, ed. Schatz-Uffenheimer, p. 324, where the vessels and lights of
      the letters/sounds are mentioned. For the possible influence of this passage on R.
      Jacob Joseph ben Yehudah, see his *Sefer Rav Yeivi*, fols. 58c, 83c, 95a; and in the
      quite elaborated discussions in R. Aharon of Zhitomir, *Toledot 'Aharon*, fols. 102ac,
      110c; and see also Aharon, fols. 133a, 133d, and 184a. For the possible Cordoverian

source of the juxtaposition of vitality and light, see ch. 10 n. 14, as well as ch. 1 n. 3 and ch. 3 n. 7 and appendix C in this volume. For a view that assumes that by becoming a chariot to the 248 words of the prayer *Shemaʿ Israel* someone is elevated on high, see the quote from the anonymous followers of Luria, found in R. Isaiah Horowitz, *Shaʿar ha-Shamayyim*, fol. 154c. See also my "Models of Understanding Prayer in Early Kabbalah," pp. 30, 33, where I refer to this passage resorting sometimes to the concept of contemplation, though claiming that this term alone is not sufficient for understanding the *Holy Epistle* or other Beshtian parallels.

For another approach to the views of the Besht on the letters/sounds as comprising worlds, souls and divinity see Moseson, *From the Spoken Word to the Discourse of the Academy*, pp. 104–108. On pp. 107–108 n. 304, he overlooks the importance of the difference between the formulation found in the *Holy Epistle* to the manner in which the grandson brings the Beshtian tradition, as oral, and thus later. A return to the texts should not overlook what is found in texts when it does not fit a certain approach.

7   See appendix C in this volume. See also Cordovero, *Pardes Rimmonim*, XVI, chap. 5.

8   To see more on the proposal to regard a lengthy discussion on the letters/sounds that sustain the firmament as the earliest available teaching of the Besht, see Idel, "Your Word Stands Firm in Heaven," p. 226. It should be pointed out that in this teaching, like in the tradition of R. Meir Margoliot, only the letters/sounds of the Torah are mentioned and not those of the prayer. We may therefore propose, tentatively, to see the addition of prayer as a relatively later stage in the thought of the Besht, when the Besht formulated it in the context of a reaction to another quite extreme theory of ecstasy and prayer, as he himself transmitted in a passage in the name of his brother-in-law, R. Gershon of Kutov. See my "Models of Understanding Prayer," pp. 23–33. For another understanding of the function of this text of the epistle as a substitute for the resort of *Yiḥudim* and charms or divine names that the Messiah taught the Besht, see Dauber, "The Baal Shem Tov and the Messiah," pp. 232–233, who follows Joseph Dan's suggestion in *Jewish Mysticism*, vol. 3, p. 126, n. 59. I see this view as problematic for several reasons. R. Gershon of Kutov probably knew the technique of how to ascend on high, as the Besht mentioned explicitly at the beginning of the epistle. Moreover, the teaching under consideration here is not an *ad hoc* resort to a substitute for the ascents on high, but it existed, in my opinon, at least in part before the epistle was written, as we have seen in the case of the tradition of R. Meir Margoliot and in a more comprehensive manner already in the Cordoverian tradition. And last but not least: the resort to *Yiḥudim* has also been recommended by the Besht in other cases, even in connection to the most ordinary forms of talking, as seen previously. Thus, it is hard to see how the assessments of Dauber, "The Baal Shem Tov and the Messiah," p. 240 and Lederberg, *Sod ha-Daʿat*, pp. 169, 178, that the Besht reached his teaching that we discuss in this chapter as an alternative or as a reflection after the experience of the encounter with the Messiah, can be sustained. See also ch. 4 n. 1 in this volume. For more on this issue, see in the next chapter.

It should be pointed out that R. Gershon is far from being the prototype of the pure erudite who differs significantly from the charismatic, or from someone concerned with "divine communication" as assumed by Rosman, *Founder of*

Hasidism, pp. 174–175, since he is quoted by the Besht as someone concerned with some form of continuous sort of ecstasy. See the detailed analysis of the pertinent passages in Idel, "Prayer, Ecstasy, and Alien Thoughts," pp. 57–77, and "Models for Understanding Prayer," pp. 23–31, as well as the various discussions related to him in the hagiography.

9   See *In the Praise of Baal Shem Tov*, pp. 72–73. Compare also to *In the Praise of Baal Shem Tov*, pp. 60–61, and my "Models for Understanding Prayer," pp. 51–53. See also Heschel, *The Circle of the Baal Shem Tov*, pp. 83–89, and the passage translated beside ch. 6 n. 21 in this volume, where there is an implicit polemic with Kabbalistic *kavvanot*.

5. R. Jacob Joseph of Polonnoye's
Beshtian Traditions on Cleaving to Sounds

1   *Toledot Ya'aqov Yosef,* fol. 90d: שמעתי בשם מורי בעניין התפילה וכוונתה וייחודים, שצריך ‏ לקשר א»»ע בהם. וידוע שהוא עולם קטן ובהתעוררות דלמטה יתעוררו למעלה למעלה, וישפיעו ‏ ‹למטה עד מדרגתו של זה האדם המכווין זה ומקבל משפע וכו

The passage is copied in *Keter Shem Tov,* fol. 56b, no. 389. See also Weiss, *Studies,* p. 105. See also the discussion in *Ben Porat Yosef,* fol. 41d, about prayer and its letters/sounds as a stairway elevating the person and linking him on high, which does not mention, however, any source. On prayer as a ladder see also the Great Maggid, *Maggid Devarav le-Ya'aqov,* ed. Schatz-Uffenheimer, p. 167, and in several passages translated and discussed in appendix B in this volume. On the Besht's resort to *Yiḥudim* for solving some problems, see *In the Praise of the Baal Shem Tov,* pp. 60, 72. On the Besht's approaches to *Yiḥudim,* see Wacks, *The Secret of Unity*; and Naftali Loewenthal, "The Baal Shem Tov's *Iggeret Ha-Kodesh* and Contemporary ḤABAD 'Outreach,'" in eds. D. Assaf and A. Rapoport-Albert, *Let the Old Make Way for the New: Studies in the Social and Cultural History of Eastern European Jewry Presented to Immanuel Etkes,* I: *Hasidism and the Musar Movement* (Merkaz Zalman Shazar, Jerusalem, 2009), pp. 98–100.

     Nota bene: the occurrence of the word *etc.*, like in the earlier quotes, points to the existence of a longer version. See also Idel, "Models of Understanding Prayer in Early Hasidism," p. 105, n. 263. See also in *Toledot Ya'aqov Yosef,* fol. 1c, and in his *Ben Porat Yosef,* fol. 15d, where the cleaving to the commandments is compared, in a passage adduced in the name of the Besht, to the cleaving to the words of prayer and Torah.

2   See in *Shiveḥei ha-Besht,* ed. Mondshine, p. 235. If *yiḥud* is a matter of speech, then the connection between human speech and supernal delight is paralleled in a statement found in the Great Maggid, *Maggid Devarav le-Ya'aqov,* ed. Schatz-Uffenheimer, p. 95, where it is said that

שעתה הוא מדבר רק בשביל שעשועי הש"י

     "he speaks now only for the sake of the delight of God, blessed be He." The question is whether this causing of delight by speech is related to the amending speech in the case of Moses and the Besht. See ch. 3 n. 8 in this volume.

     For the different meanings of the term *Yiḥud* in the Besht, see Wacks, *The Secret of Unity,* pp. 86–97, and ch. 1 nn 1, 22 in this volume, and now Dauber,

"The Baal Shem Tov and the Messiah," pp. 232–233. His attempt to offer what he calls a "theosophical" interpretation versus my alleged "ecstatic" interpretation of the Besht is very surprising, since before reading him I thought that I have seen Hasidism as a concatenation between different models, the ecstatic being only one of them, as it is obvious from my book on *Hasidism*, and that I have even described Hasidism as a synthesis between ecstatic and theurgical forms of Kabbalah: See *Kabbalah: New Perspectives*, p. XVII. For an analysis of messianism and theosophy in the teaching of the Besht that was preserved by R. Menahem Nahum of Chernobyl, see my *Messianic Mystics*, pp. 221–234, and for the Besht and different forms of theurgy, see my "Prayer, Ecstasy and Alien Thoughts," pp. 81–82. Moreover, it is not theosophy that Dauber wants to accentuate in his analyses, but actually some form of theurgy, namely of the *Yiḥud* as creating some form of union between sexually polarized entities. For this aim he could better use the Beshtian texts alluded to in ch. 1 nn 1, 22, or Wacks's book on the history of the resort to *Yiḥud* in Hasidism. It should be pointed out that an analysis of the language used in the epistle shows that the same terms are used in more than one manner, *Yiḥud* being just one of them, an issue that still deserves a separate inquiry.

For my distinction between magic, dealing with changes one can make in this world, and theurgy dealing with changes in the divine world, see e.g., "The Magical and Theurgical Interpretation," or *Kabbalah: New Perspectives*, and *Hasidism*, pp. 29–30. For my definition of magic, drawn from Valerie I. J. Flint, *The Rise of Magic in Early Medieval Europe* (Princeton, New Jersey, 1991), p. 3, "Magic may be said to be the exercise of a preternatural control over nature by human beings, with the assistance of forces more powerful than they," see my *Hasidism*, pp. 29–30.

For this specific understanding of theurgy and magic, see Luck, following the lead of E. R. Dodds, in *Arcana Mundi*, p. 21; and more recently, also Georg Luck, "Theurgy and Forms of Worship in Neoplatonism," *Religion, Science, and Magic*, in eds. J. Neusner et al. (Oxford University Press, New York, 1989), p. 186; and Ruth Majercik, *The Chaldean Oracles* (Brill, Leiden, 1989), p. 22, where she adduced also other similar definitions of theurgy. See Majercik, pp. 22–23. For my general assessment of the role of magic in Judaism and Hasidism, see "On Judaism, Jewish Mysticism, and Magic," eds. P. Schaefer and H. G. Kippenberg, *Envisioning Magic* (Brill, Leiden, 1997), pp. 195–214; Idel, "Jewish Magic from the Renaissance Period to Early Hasidism," in eds. J. Neusner et al., *Religion, Science, and Magic* (Oxford University Press, New York, 1989), pp. 82–117.

3   Namely, every consonant and vowel, *Tenu'ah*, the latter referred to as, following many medieval texts, the entities that move the consonant.

4   The Hebrew form is in the plural, and it implies that two entities will lie between the lips of the person in prayer. See more in Idel, "Models of Understanding Prayer in Early Hasidism," pp. 56–78, and the passage in the name of the Besht in R. Jacob Joseph of Polonnoye, *Ben Porat Yosef*, fol. 46c.

5   Probably the *Shekhinah*.

6   *Toledot Ya'aqov Yosef*, fol. 172c (quoted also in R. Aharon Kohen of Apta, *Keter Shem Tov*, fol. 18bc): שמעתי ממורי שרוב ענונותו של האדם גורם שנתרחק מעבודת הש"י, שמצד שפלותו אינו מאמין כי האדם גורם ע"י תפילתו ותורתו שפע אל כל העולמות וגם המלאכים

ניזונין ע"י תורתו ותפילתו שאלו היה מאמין זה, כמה היה עובד ה' בשמחה ובייראה מרוב כל (!)
והיה נזהר בכל אות ותנועה ומילה לאומרה כדקא יאות ואם וגם לתת לב אל מה מה שאמר שלמה ע"ה 'אם
תשכבון בין שפתים', שקב"ה שומר ושוקד על שפתי האדם לנושקה כשהוא אומרה בתורה ותפילה
בדחילו ורחימו,

See also in the mid-nineteenth-century Hasidic master R. Isaac Aizik Yehiel
Safrin of Komarno, *Sefer Netiv Mitzvotekha* (Jerusalem, 1983), p. 29. For discussions of the passage, see Dresner, *The Zaddik*, pp. 163–164; and Idel, "The Besht as
Prophet and as Talismanic Magician," pp. 135–136; and my *Enchanted Chains*, p. 188.
For an important discussion of the *kavvanah* of prayer as consisting of keeping in
one's mind the plain meaning of the words someone pronounces, when this is done
out of joy and fear, see the passage of R. Meshullam Phoebus of Zbarazh, a disciple
of the Great Maggid, translated and discussed in Schatz-Uffenheimer, *Hasidism
as Mysticism*, pp. 239–240. Schatz-Uffenheimer attributes this view to the Great
Maggid, but in fact this is another instance of the Great Maggid's appropriation of
the Beshtian approach. For the centrality of devotion, *Mesirut Nefesh*, as a parallel to or surrogate for *devequt*, see in many instances in R. Aharon of Zhitomir's
Toledot 'Aharon. See, especially, the tradition he adduced from the mouth of his
teacher R. Levi Isaac of Berditchev, in the name of the Great Maggid, that also the
angels are nourished by the activity of the Jews who cause the descent of the influx.
See *Toledot 'Aharon*, fol. 187d. Thus, we have another example where the impact of
the Besht on the Great Maggid is discernable without quoting his name.

7 For the primacy of vocal activity and thus of the mouth, see also the interesting
passage of R. Pinhas of Koretz, where he distinguishes man from the animals by
the dint of the presence of all the twenty-two letters/sounds with him: "this is
the reason why he rules everything and can do with his mouth everything in the
world." *Liqqutim me-ha-Rav R. Pinhas mi-Qoretz*, fols. 4d–5a. For some interesting
discussions on the mouth, see the views from the Besht's family adduced in my
Enchanted Chains, pp. 210–211. Also this type of mystique is found in several passages of Cordovero's. See Idel, *Enchanted Chains*, pp. 58, 73, 182–183.

8 The erotic aspects of this cleaving are obvious. See, however, ch. 2 n. 4.

9 *Ben Porat Yosef*, fol. 59d: ועניין הדביקות בו ית' הוא ע"י אותיות התורה והתפילה שידבק מחשבתו
ופנימיותו רוחניות שבתוך האותיות בסוד 'ישקני מנשיק' פיהו', דביקות רוחא ברוחא, וכמ"ש ממורי
וכו בין שפתים' תשכבון 'אם. See also *Ben Porat Yosef* [Koretz], fol. 25a, without however
mentioning this time the name of the Besht, but referring to R. Abraham Azulai's
Cordoverian view, found in *Hesed le-'Avraham*. See also R. Aharon Kohen of Apta,
Keter Shem Tov, fol. 7a; *Keter Shem Tov ha-Shalem*, pp. 27–28. For cleaving to letters/
sounds, see also R. Jacob Joseph ben Yehudah, *Rav Yeivi*, fol 6c, and also fol. 55b,
where he speaks about "the twenty-two letters by which the Torah is spoken." For the
earlier sources of the cleaving of thought, see Idel, *Kabbalah: New Perspectives*, pp.
46–49; Goetschel, *R. Meir Ibn Gabbay*, pp. 310–311; and Pacher, *Roots of Faith and
Devequt*, pp. 270–271. I translated the Hebrew text as found in *Ben Porat Yosef*, but I
find the version of the passage problematic and would suggest two small changes
related to the words *u-fenimiyyuto*, to *le-penimiyyut*, so the translation would be, like
in the passage from *Toledot Ya'aqov Yosef*, to be adduced immediately below, "he
should cleave his thought to the inner spirituality within the letters/sounds." Let me
point out that an interesting reference to the inner aspect of the sounds, resorting to

the term *penimiyyut*, occurs also in the Great Maggid's traditions, *Maggid Devarav le-Ya'aqov*, ed. Schatz-Uffenheimer, p. 45, a fact to be discussed as follows. See also the discussion found in another disciple of the Besht, R. Menahem Nahum of Chernobyl, *Yismah Lev*, printed together with *Me'or 'Einayyim*, p. 307, but without mentioning the name of the Besht. R. Menahem Nahum's discussion is close to the formulation found in R. Jacob Joseph, more than to that of the Great Maggid, who was his other teacher in addition to the Besht.

The existence of a common denominator between the three disciples of the Besht may constitute a significant proof for the common source of this statement in the Besht. For a vision that is practically identical, though quoted without any reference to any source, see R. Aharon of Zhitomir, *Toledot 'Aharon*, fol. 100a. See also ch. 5 n. 12.

10   On the distinction between the two theories, see my *Hasidism*, p. 94. For more on this concept, see appendix C in this volume.

11   On Hasidic interpretations of this concept and their sources, see Idel, *Hasidism*, pp. 176–185. See also Roland Goetschel, "Torah li-Shmah as a Central Concept in the Degel Mahaneh Efrayim of Moses Hayyim Ephraim of Sudylkov," in ed. Rapoport-Albert, *Hasidism Reappraised*, pp. 258–267. Also, Goetschel understands the term *'Ot* as referring basically to letters, rather than to sounds. See Goetschel, pp. 262–263 and see n. 1 in this volume.

12   *Toledot Ya'aqov Yosef*, fol. 25a:

ולפי מה שקבלתי ממורי שעיקר עסק תורה ותפלה הוא שידבק את עצמו אל פנימיות רוחניות
אור אין סוף שבתוך אותיות התורה והתפלה, שהוא הנקרא לימוד לשמה, שבזה אמר ר׳ מאיר כל
העוסק בתורה לשמה זוכה לדברים הרבה ומגלין לו רזי תורה וכו׳ ‹ ר‹‹אל שידע עתידות וכל
מאורעותיו מתוך התורה, וידע איך יתנהג בתורה ועבודת הש‹‹י, מלבד שרואה עולמות של מעלה,
וכהנה שמעתי מפי מורי ודפה‹‹ח. See also previously the other passage from R. Jacob
Joseph's *Ben Porat Yosef*, and the important parallel, cited again in the name of the Besht, found in *Toledot Ya'aqov Yosef*, fol. 24b, and its translation and notes in Lamm, *The Religious Thought of Hasidism*, pp. 151–152, who also retains the term *letters*, and especially the discussion from *Toledot Ya'aqov Yosef*, fol. 201b. However, the entire discussion is found in *Toledot Ya'aqov Yosef*, fols. 132b and 133c, without, however, mentioning the name of the Besht. See also the same author's *Ben Porat Yosef*, fol. 25a, and see also *Keter Shem Tov*, fol. 13b, no. 96, as well as ch. 2 n. 18. In should be mentioned that in some cases when R. Jacob Joseph quotes passages starting with the verb "I heard"— שמעתי —we find the content quoted in the name of the Besht elsewhere. See also Idel, "Models of Understanding Prayer in Early Hasidism," pp. 29–30, and our discussion in appendix B of this volume.

Compare, however, to Weiss, *Studies*, p. 59, where he translates this text as if it is dealing with "letters (apparently of the open book)." I am also not convinced by his assumption that according to this passage, "the light of the infinite" indeed "emanates from the letters," cf., Weiss. Compare the term *penimiyyut ruhaniyyut* to the term *ha-ruhaniyyut ha-penimiy* in Cordovero's *Pardes Rimmonim* XXXII, chap. 3; II, fol. 79a; in R. Abraham Azulai's *Hesed le-'Avraham*, fol. 9d—a book quoted by R. Jacob Joseph in his books in pertinent contexts, as we shall see in appendix B—and R. Isaiah Horowitz, *Sha'ar ha-Shamayyim*, fol. 25b. See also R. Menahem Nahum of Chernobyl, *Me'or 'Eynayyim*, p. 171. For another use of the term *ruḥaniyyut*, see also R. Aharon of Apta's *Keter Shem Tov*, fol. 60a, no. 412, in a quote adduced in the name of the Besht.

For cleaving to letters of the divine name in late thirteenth-century Kabbalah, see Idel, *Hasidism*, p. 59, and for cleaving to letters in general, which only in some occasions are sounds, see the views of Cordovero, and R. Elijah da Vidas, one of them analyzed in Idel, *Hasidism*, pp. 160–161, and see also ch. 3 n. 7 in this volume. For seeing future events as the result of intense concentration on individual letters, perhaps also vocables, see the view of the Great Maggid as reported by his follower, R. Ze'ev Wolf of Zhitomir, and discussed in Schatz-Uffenheimer, *Hasidism as Mysticism*, p. 203. For traditions about the extraordinary capacities the Besht allegedly reached by his intense prayer, namely a vocal operation, see the Great Maggid of Mezeritch, cited in *'Or ha-'Emmet*, fol. 83a—translated beside appendix C n. 58. See also as follows in our discussion of a text found in several sources, where the lights of the utterances are mentioned. Let me point out that the cleaving to the Torah that recurs so many times in Hasidism follows a series of Safedian texts, just as it does in the case of cleaving to sounds. For cleaving to the Torah in Safedian Kabbalah, see the texts analyzed by Pachter, *Roots of Faith and Devequt*, in e.g., pp. 241–264, 267, 301–305.

13   Cf. the text of the letter printed in *Shiveḥei ha-Besht*, translated in *In Praise of the Baal Shem*, p. 65 (where the passage has been translated as "contemplating the letters"!), and from a manuscript at the end of R. Barukh of Miedzibush, *Butzina' di-Nehora'*:

אייעצך ויהי אלקים עמך גיבור החיל: בכל בוקר ובוקר בעת לימודו ידבק עצמו באותיות
בדבקות גמור לעבודת בוראו ב"ה וב"ש ואז ימתיקו הדינים בשושרן.

About this epistle see Rosman, *Founder of Hasidism*, pp. 114–115, who also resorts to the term *letters*, and Dresner, *The Zaddik*, pp. 50–52. See also the very important passage reported in the name of the Besht in R. Jacob Joseph's *Toledot Ya'aqov Yosef*, fol. 201b: "I have also heard from my teacher and when someone sees that there are some [bad] decrees concerning him he should study in the morning, in the state of cleaving and desire and he will cleave himself to the light of the Infinite which is within the letters/vocables etc."

שמעתי ממורי כשרואה שיש עליו איזה דינין אזי ילמוד בבוקר בדביקה וחשיקה, שידבק
א"ע אל פנימיות אור א"ס שבתוך האותיות וכו'.

It is possible that "etc." stands for the sweetening of the judgments in their source, as in the passage from *Butzinah di-Nehora'*. This statement demonstrates that the epistle addressed to R. Jacob Joseph and printed in the hagiography is very reliable. Here the disciple writes that he heard, rather than wrote, the teaching of the Besht. This is the only sentence I am acquainted with that is corresponding almost verbatim to the hagiography and can be dated to a generation before the compilation of the hagiography. For the source of the couple of terms *deviqah* and *ḥashiqah*, see the text of R. Elijah da Vidas's *Reshit Ḥokhmah*, analyzed in Pachter, *Roots of Faith and Devequt*, pp. 296–297, and see also ch. 3 n. 7 in this volume. See also *Keter Shem Tov*, fol. 13ab, no. 94, and *Ben Porat Yosef* (1781), fol. 46c.

Here too the Besht is recommending the act of cleaving in order to obliterate the evil decrees. On this passage see also Mondshine, *Shiveḥei ha-Besht*, p. 264 and n. 10; Pedaya, "The Besht, R. Jacob Joseph of Polonnoye, and the Maggid of

Mezeritch," pp. 56–57; and Kauffman, *In All Your Ways Know Him*, pp. 419–420.
See also ch. 2 n. 12. Though indeed different, the two strategies of coping with
evil decrees, the one mentioned here and the other reflected in the text referred
to in ch. 2 n. 12, are nevertheless similar in one respect: by bringing something in
contact with a divine entity, the negative decree is sweetened or mitigated. There
is also a quote in R. Efrayyim of Sudylkov's book in the name of his grandfather
as the sweetening of the judgments by reciting the vocables/letters. It should be
mentioned that in *Toledot Ya'aqov Yosef*, fol. 143b, R. Jacob Joseph speaks about
causing the letters/vocables to cleave to their source. Perhaps we have two forms of
cleaving: first to the letters/vocables, and then the causing of the letters/vocables to
elevate and cleave to their source, and thus as a corollary, also the cleaving of the
person, as we find in the passage from the *Holy Epistle*, as was analyzed previously.

6. Beshtian Traditions on Cleaving to Sounds
in the Great Maggid's School

1   On the very significant difference between the Besht and R. Gershon of Kutov on
the issue of the permanent state of ecstasy that predates prayer on the one hand, and
the view that ecstasy is reached in the moment of prayer, according to the Besht,
on the other hand, see Idel, "Models of Understanding Prayer in Early Hasidism,"
pp. 12–34. The position here indeed reflects the view of the Besht as I portrayed
it there. On the Great Maggid's assumption that someone should divest himself
before prayer, see ch. 6 n. 8 in this volume. Thus, I assume that we have here a
Beshtian approach.

2   For the lower awe as the vessel of the higher awe, which is attracted in it as in a temple, see R. Aharon of Zhitomir, *Toledot 'Aharon*, ed. Lemberg, I, fol. 36d. Elsewhere,
in Lemberg, I, fol. 37a, the supernal awe is identified as the median supernal line,
often related to *Tiferet*. In other Beshtian texts there are other sefirotic identifica-
tions. However, especially important is the teaching quoted in the name of the Besht
in R. Jacob Joseph of Polonnoye, *Ben Porat Yosef*, fol. 38c, where ontology of awe is
found as existing on high and emanating within the world the lower forms of awe.
For the role of love, see R. Aharon of Zhitomir, *Toledot 'Aharon*, Lemberg, I, fol.
38a. The mystical-magical model reverberated in several discussions of R. Aharon of
Zhitomir. See, e.g., his *Toledot 'Aharon*, ed. Berditchev, fol. 3c:

ועל ידי הדבקות ממשיך השפע לעולמות התחתונים

"By means of [or because of] *devequt* he draws the influx to the lower worlds."
See Berditchev, fols. 6d–7a, 97b, 97c, 100a. For the image of fire in Hasidism,
the context of a mystical experience in Hasidism, see Idel "Universalization and
Integration," 42–44, and Garb, *Shamanic Trance in Modern Kabbalah*, pp. 80–85,
99. For a description of the Besht as if not found in this world, see *In Praise of the
Baal Shem Tov*, p. 51.

3   R. Yehoshu'a Abraham ben Yisrael, *Ge'ulat Yisrael* (Amsterdam, 1821), part I, fol.
17c : עד [עולם הזה] כי דרך האמת כן הוא שצריך בשעת עבודה להפשיט עצמו מגשמיות עוה"ז
שיחשב בעיניו כאלו אינו בעוה"ז כלום, ולומר האותיות בקול ודיבור פשוט ולדבק ולקשר מחשבתו
באותיות הק[דושות] ולהבין פירוש המילות הק[דושות] ואז ממילא פתאו[ם] יתלקח ויתלהב בו אש
להבת שלהבת הבערה היראה והאהבה עילאין בעוז ועצום עד מאד. וזהו הדרך ישכון ישכון אור

בעבודת הק[ודש] פנימה. On this passage see also Idel, *Hasidism*, p. 177 and R. Shimeon Menahem Mendel Vodnek, the author of *Ba'al Shem Tov*, vol. I, pp. 124–125. See also ch. 4 n. 5 in this volume.

The comparison of the liturgical worhip to the sacrificial one in a similar context is found already in early Kabbalah. See the passage discussed in Idel, *Kabbalah: New Perspectives*, pp. 53–54, in which these Kabbalists were less concerned with the vocables as recipient of the supernal fire. For the divestment of corporeality see, e.g., ch. 2 n. 9.

4   See Idel, "Models of Understanding Prayer in Early Hasidism," pp. 12–34.

5   *Toledot 'Aharon*, ed. Berditchev, fols. 18d–19a, as well as Berditchev, fols. 40a, 42a, fols. 185b–185d, where the mystic is introducing in the utterances and sounds he emits flame and enthusiasm. For the natural inflammation of the soul, see already the Beshtian teaching adduced by R. Jacob Joseph, *Toledot Ya'aqov Yosef*, fol. 83c.

6   *Toledot 'Aharon*, ed. Berditchev, fol. 130a.

ומבואר בספרו של הגאון הקדוש הרב ר' בער ז"ל מ"מ מעזריטש והוא מחכמה של הרב הקדוש והטהור הבעש"ט ז"ל שהעיקר הוא לדבר דבורים של תורה ותפלה בכל כחו, ואז מדבק א"ע לאור א"ס ב"ה השורה בתוך האותיות וזה מכניע כל כחות הגופניות ובא ממש להתפשטות הגשמיות ואז בא לעולמות העליונים ולשכליות ולבהירות חדשות בכל פעם.

I assume that the quote from the Besht stops here, but this is not quite definite, and it may be that also some sentences that follow this passage belong to the Besht. Compare also Berditchev, fol. 130c, and especially to fols. 165a, 172d–173b, and 182d–183a, where statements that are in part parallels to the passage quoted in the name of the Besht are found, without, however, mentioning him. See also ch. 2 n. 9. Compare also to a passage from the circle of the Great Maggid, in *'Or ha-'Emmet*, fol. 34c:

ידבר בכל כחו כי בזה יעשה אחדות עמו ית' כי כחו באות ובאות שורה הקדוש ב"ר נמצא הוא אחדות עמו יתברך שמו ויתעלה.

"He should speak with all his strength since by its means he will do a union with Him, blessed be He, since his strength in the vocable and in that vocable the Holy One, therefore the union with Him blessed and exalted His name be, will take place." Though using a different terminology, conceptually this assessment is very similar to what has been adduced by the Besht in the Great Maggid's school. Therefore, this is another example of an appropriation of the Besht's thought without referring to him as the source. In R. Levi Isaac of Berditchev's book *Qedushat Levi*, p. 407, there is a similar view that is cited in the name of the Great Maggid, without mentioning the Besht. For other examples see ch. 6 n. 22. See also the passage quoted in the name of R. Levi Isaac, in R. Yehudah Arieh Leib Te'omim's compilation *'Oholei Shem* (Belgoria, 1911), fol. 14ab.

See also to the Besht's grandson's *Degel Mahaneh 'Efrayyim*, p. 202, where the experience of *devequt* causes the cessation of all the desires. On this last discussion see Pedaya, "The Besht, R. Jacob Joseph of Polonnoye, and the Maggid of Mezeritch," p. 38. For a view that deals with cleaving to lights found within sounds, see also in R. Levi Isaac of Berditchev, who was a main source of inspiration for R. Aharon, in *Qedushat Levi*, pp. 327–328, as translated and discussed in Idel, *Old Worlds, New Mirrors*, pp. 327–328.

7   See *Maggid Devarav le-Ya'aqov*, ed. Schatz-Uffenheimer, p. 45; the text was quoted
     also in R. Aharon Kohen of Apta, *Keter Shem Tov*, I, fol. 36c and in his Ner
     Mitzwah, fol. 17a. For the occurrence of the phrase "light and vitality" in the Besht
     and in other Hasidic texts and their origins, see Idel, *Hasidism*, pp. 184, 340, n. 56
     and "The Land of Divine Vitality," as well as the next note and nn. 114, 130, 133, 150.
     See also appendix C in this volume.

8   Compare another tradition, adduced also by R. Aharon of Zhitomir, *Toledot
     'Aḥaron* (Lemberg), II, fol. 20c, also in the name of the Besht, as found in a "book"
     of the Great Maggid, where the divestment of corporeality follows the experience
     of cleaving to the letters, unlike our passage, where it precedes it. Also in this quote,
     the mentioning of the divestment is not accompanied by a magical effect. I would
     therefore say that the two traditions quoted by R. Aharon of Zhitomir describe the
     mystical part of the mystical-magical model, while the magic implications are not
     mentioned there but can be conceived of as complementary, as they may occur in a
     later stage. See also ch. 6 n. 18 in this volume.
         Let me point out that in a lengthy discussion found in this book [ed.
     Berditchev], fol. 102ac, many of the elements discussed in this study have been
     brought together, without however referring to any authority as a source, and this
     is the reason I decided not to analyze it here. See also ch. 6 n. 6 in this volume.

9   *Mevasser Tzedeq*, fols. 2ab, 22b. On this rather marginal author, see Yitzhaq Raphael,
     On Hasidism and Hasidim (Mossad ha-Rav Kook, Jerusalem, 1991), pp. 178–179
     (Hebrew); Schatz-Uffenheimer, *Hasidism as Mysticism*, pp. 193–195; Kauffman, *In
     All Your Ways Know Him*, pp. 301–302.

10   See *Mevasser Tzedeq*, fol. 15a:
     "הקדמה בשם הבעש"ט ז"ל: שהדיבורים של התפלה בם נעשה כלים להמשכת השפע. כי
     באמת הלא הקב"ה הוא יודע מחשבות ולמה צריכין להדיבורים רק שהוא להמשכת השפע. והנה
     לפעמים אדם רוצה לעבוד ולהמשיך שפע גדולה ועצומה למעלה ממדרגתו ואין הכלים יכולים
     לסבול גודל ההשפעה נשברים הכלים".
         It should be pointed out that in this book there are also other unidentified
     passages in the name of the Besht. *Nota bene*: Here the verb *MShKh* is attributed
     to the Besht and used in the strong sense of causing the descent of the influx. For
     another instance of a quote attributed to the Besht where the verb *MShKh* is used,
     see Idel, "Models of Understanding Prayer in Early Hasidism," p. 46, n. 128. For
     a similar formulation to the quoted passage, though not an identical one, see the
     quote adduced by R. Jacob Joseph, in the name of R. Nahman of Kosov, in *Toledot
     Ya'aqov Yosef*, fol. 62b; in *Ben Porat Yosef* [Koretz], fol. 17d; and in *Kutoneth Passim*,
     fol. 28d; and referred to by Heschel, *The Circle of the Baal Shem Tov*, p. 136; and
     see also Idel, *Hasidism*, p. 345, n. 89; as well as the passages of the Great Maggid,
     Maggid Devarav le-Ya'aqov, ed. Schatz-Uffenheimer, p. 90 and p. 324, discussed
     in Kauffman, *In All Your Ways Know Him*, p. 447. See also Schatz-Uffenheimer,
     Hasidism as Mysticism, p. 190, an analysis whose appropriateness is quite contest-
     able because of her "pietistic"-oriented bias. See also the tradition that R. Shmerl
     adduces in the name of R. Menahem Mendel of Bar, which has been translated in
     Schatz-Uffenheimer, *Hasidism as Mysticism*, p. 238. In all these cases we have the
     same type of narrative: a rhetorical question, why is the vocal prayer necessary since
     God knows the thought of man, is answered by presuming that the utterances are

palaces or chambers. See also R. Ze'ev Wolf of Zhitomir's claim that the view that the letters are vessels "is well known in the books." See *'Or ha-'Meir*, fol. 14d.

To be sure: the fact that the same teaching was shared also by other figures in the same period does not automatically mean that the Besht could not be the source of the other authors or, alternatively, that he could not adopt it at a certain stage of his career from another source. The verb *mamshikh* is related to magic in *Ben Porat Yosef*, where there is a distinction between drawing down the spiritual and the material influx by the letters/sounds of prayer. See also appendix C in this volume. Pronounced letters are described there as important for securing the descent of the material influx. For the problems related to identifying this R. Nahman see Dresner's note in *The Circle of the Baal Shem Tov*, pp. 149–151, nn. 153, 160. Compare also the important passage from *Shemu'ah Tovah*, edited by R. Levi Isaac of Berditchev, translated and discussed in Idel, *Hasidism*, pp. 194–195, and compare to Schatz-Uffenheimer, *Hasidism as Mysticism*, pp. 170–171. For the occurrence of the theory of drawing down vitality and the spirituality within vessels that are constituted of linguistic sounds without any attribution, though referring to R. Abraham Azulai's book *Ḥesed le-'Abraham*, see Jacob Joseph of Polonnoye, *Ben Porat Yosef*, fol. 61a, and see ch. 5 n. 1 and appendices B and C of this volume. For words as vessels see also the tradition of R. Nahman of Kosov, cited by R. Jacob Joseph of Polonnoye, *Ben Porat Yosef*, fol. 53b; and that of R. Schmerl, a disciple of R. Pinehas of Koretz, adduced by Schatz-Uffenheimer, *Hasidism as Mysticism*, p. 238; as well as the important discussion in *Maggid Devarav le Ya'aqov*, ed. Schatz-Uffenheimer, p. 45 [= *Keter Shem Tov*, fol. 36a], dealing with the breaking of the vessels conceived of as vocables in a manner reminiscent of the tradition adduced here in the name of the Besht. Let me point out that the assumption that utterances limit the infinite power is found in the Great Maggid, see Schatz-Uffenheimer, p. 324. See the passage translated and discussed in Idel, *Hasidism*, p. 166. See also ch. 9 n. 9 in this volume. Are the passages of the Great Maggid referred to here other instances of resorting to Beshtian traditions without mentioning the source? Compare, for example, the view found in R. Jacob Joseph of Polonnoye's *Toledot Ya'aqov Yosef*, fol. 167b: "Indeed, any worthy person who prays cleaves by his thought to Him, may He be blessed, and the drawing down of the influx is not necessary as it is possible that this [kind of] prayer is better [when performed only] in thought . . . since this prayer needs no vessel in order to draw the influx downwards." See also Idel, *Hasidism*, p. 90; Kallus, *Pillar of Prayer*, p. 92, no. 72 and Garb, *Shamanic Trance in Modern Kabbalah*, p. 80.

11   *Keter Shem Tov*, II, fol. 56ab, translated by Jacobs, *Hasidic Prayer*, pp. 77–78; *Keter Shem Tov ha-Shalem*, p. 129, no. 227; and the Great Maggid, *'Or ha-'Emmet*, fol. 10a; and in *Maggid Devarav le-Ya'aqov*, ed. Schatz-Uffenheimer, pp. 13–14, 81 (on this page the name of the Besht is mentioned),

דהבעש"ט ע"ה אמר על מה שאמרו בזוהר שדנין את האדם בכל היכל והיכל ומגרשין אותו מהיכל, פי' כי הדיבורים נקראו היכלות שהשכל שורה בהם, והאדם המתפלל הוא הולך מאות לאות ומתיבה לתיבה. וכשהוא אינו כדאי מגרשין אותו, דהיינו שזורקין לו מחשבה זרה וממילא הוא בחוץ

The version in this collection of traditions of the Great Maggid contains a slight change in comparison to other versions mentioned in this note, to the effect that after the mentioning of the expulsion of the sinner from the palace, it is written *Pi*, a short form of *Peiresh*, which may be understood as "He interpreted." This is the case in the version of *Keter Shem Tov ha-Shalem*, p. 235, where it is written *Peirush*. On the basis of this "addition" Pedaya, "The Besht, R. Jacob Joseph of Polonnoye, and the Maggid of Mezeritch," pp. 66, suggested, hesitantly, to see in the interpreter the Great Maggid, and to attribute to him the understanding of the utterances as palaces, as part of her theory that differentiates rather starkly between the Besht and his disciples. However, in other occurrences of this passage this word does not occur at all, as we shall see in the texts referred to as follows in this note. However, in the version quoted by R. Reuven Horowitz, *Diduim ba-Sodeh*, fol. 115a, this passage, adduced verbatim in the name of the Besht, has ר"ל instead of פי', which is an acronym for *Rotzeh lomar*, that means "namely," and this seems to be the best reading of the passage. Horowitz's interesting elaboration of the Beshtian statement merits an analysis in itself.

Moreover, the vision of the utterances as containers is found in the name of the Besht in many other traditions attributed to him, so that it is no conceptual gain from denying this understanding of the palaces as utterances to the Besht, in order to preclude an understanding of his view as dealing with drawing down influx. Moreover, if we attribute the interpretation to the Great Maggid, nothing meaningful in this passage remains to be attributed to the Besht, who would sound like someone who just quotes the *Zohar* (see *Zohar* II, fol. 245b, and *Zohar Hadash*, fol. 86b), a situation that is unparalleled in Beshtian traditions and also implausible, a fact that Pedaya also hesitantly recognized there. For versions where the concept of interpretation does not occur, see e.g., in another collection of traditions in the name of the Great Maggid, *'Or ha-'Emmet*, fol. 17c, it is written:

שמה שכת' בזוהר שדנין את האדם בכל היכל, היינו הדבורים ואותיות התפלה הנקרא היכ-
לות, שם דנין את האדם אם כדאי הוא לכנס באותיות התפלה ואם אינו כדאי, מגרשין אותו דהיינו
ששולחין לו מחשבה זרה ודוחין אותו.

See also *'Or ha-'Emmet*, fols. 3bcd, 14c, and R. Abraham Hayyim of Zloczow, *'Orah la-Hayyim*, fol. 98a:

ונראה שהנה כתבתי בפ' נח פי"ח הפסוק ופתח התיבה בצדה תשים. כתבתי שם בשם הרב
הק' בוצינא קדי(ש)א מו"ה דוב בער זללה"ה שאמר בשם הבעש"ט זללה"ה שמה שכתב בזוהר
שדנין את האדם בכל היכל היינו הדבורים ואותיות התפילה הנקרא היכלות שם דנין את האדם אם
כדאי הוא לכנס באותיות התפלה ואם אינו כדאי מגרשין אותו דהיינו ששולחין לו מחשבה זרה
ודוחין אותו עכ"ד.

See also Idel, *Hasidism*, p. 162. See also the tradition adduced in *Mayyim Rabbim* (Brooklyn, 1969), fol. 29a; in R. Reuven ha-Levi Horowitz, *Diduim Ba-Sode*, fol. 115a; and Idel, *Hasidism*, p. 347, n. 103.

Compare, however, to Schatz-Uffenheimer, "Contemplative Prayer in Hasidism," pp. 210–211, and her *Hasidism as Mysticism*, pp. 169–170, where this interesting passage of the Besht has been translated and briefly discussed, and see also my remarks in *Hasidism*, p. 347, n. 103. My translation and interpretation differ from the rendering given by Schatz-Uffenheimer, especially because of her systematic [mis-]translation of *'otiyyot* as letters, as part of her vision of prayer as a preeminently a contemplative-meditative activity, influenced by a passage found in a collection of Hasidic traditions, including Beshtian ones, entitled *Shemu'ah Tovah*, which will be mentioned as follows. She translates what I translate as "the letters/sounds of prayer," namely the utterances, as the "letters of prayer" which should be entered, which is depicted as part of the alleged act of contemplation. See also the important passage of the Great Maggid, translated by Schatz-Uffenheimer, *Hasidism as Mysticism*, pp. 216–217, where the entrance to the words of Torah and prayer is mentioned. This is another instance of the impact of the Besht on his disciple, though his name is not mentioned. See also R. Aharon of Zhitomir, *Toledot 'Aḥaron*, I, fol. 46a.

Let me draw attention to the fact that the view of the letters/sounds as palaces recurs several times in the writings of R. Menahem Nahum of Chernobyl, *Me'or 'Einayyim*, but he never mentions in this context the name of either the Besht or that of the Great Maggid. See, e.g., his discussions on pp. 111, 113, 153. Since R. Menahem Nahum studied with both of them, it is hard to draw a significant conclusion from those quite important occurrences. My impression is, however, from the formulations he uses, that he knows some form of Beshtian tradition, but this is an issue that requires a lengthy analysis that cannot be done here. For speeches as palaces, see also R. Aharon of Zhitomir, *Toledot 'Aḥaron*, fol. 139d.

The nexus between resorting to the term *letters* instead of letters/sounds, and contemplation, is obvious also in many cases in the English translations of Hasidic texts, as found in Jacobs, *Hasidic Prayer*. See also Green, "Discovery and Retreat," p. 123.

12   This is the classical formula for the devotional-emotional prayer, which recurs in several of the texts dealt with here and much more in Hasidic literature. Its source is in the book of *Zohar*, see, e.g., I, fol. 24a (RM).

13   Another plausible translation would be "to all people." Compare also to R. Jacob Joseph of Polonnoye, *Ben Porat Yosef*, fol. 42b: "in accordance to his Torah and Tefillah he will receive parnasah." Here the magical aspect of the vocal rites is evident.

14   *'Or ha-Ganuz la-Tzaddiqim*, 1850, col. VI, fol. 1a:

דרוש נפלא מאד מהבעש"ט זלה" ה איש ישראל העומד להתפלל או עוסק בתורה בד"ו יכול לגרום השפעות וברכות ופרנסות לכל העולם מצד הכלילות שהיו כל הנשמות כלולים באדם הראשון.

I find the quote this author brought in the name of the Besht as reliable, though I could not find an earlier formulation of this teaching elsewhere in Hasidic literature. See also ch. 8 n. 6 in this volume for the other quote in the name of the Besht found in this book where the act of drawing down is related to vocal rituals. See the bibliography referred to in ch. 8 n. 9 in this volume. It should be pointed out that the content of this passage is not found in the corresponding discussion in the Warsaw edition of this book, fol. 21b, which mentions nevertheless the name of the Besht. For more on Perlov's writings and Beshtian traditions, see in appendix A of this volume.

15   *Keter Nehora'*, p. 13:

זה הדבר הוא כלל לכל כוונת הסידור ולימוד תורה וזמירות שירות ותשבחות כי הריב"ש זלה"ה אמר כשאדם יש לו דביקות בהש"י יכול להניח הפה כאלו מדבר ברוח"ק ולהשתמש בעומק הכוונה שהוא קול ודיבור מעומק כוונת המוח והלב כי עי"ז הוא מקשר הדיבורים בשרשן העליון בבורא יתברך שכל דיבור יש לו שורש למעלה בספירות הקדושה כי אין אדם יכול לדבר

שום דיבור או לעשות תנועה בלי שפעו וחיותו יתברך וע"ז נאמר [תהלים נא:יג] 'ורוח קדשך אל
תקח ממני.'

See also *Keter Nehora'*, p. 34. See also n. 33 in this volume. This is a case of *oratio infusa*, and for other instances in early Hasidism, see Idel, "Models for Understanding Prayer," pp. 34–49. For divine vitality see appendix C in this volume.

16   *Avot* 2:2. The Besht is reported elsewhere to have interpreted this statement as deal-
      ing with the "speech-acts of Torah and Prayer." Thus, it is obvious that we have here
      a verbalization of the Torah-text, which is conceived also as having repercussions
      on high, namely creating the union between The Holy One Blessed be He, and the
      Shekhinah. The passage is cited also in *Tzafnat Pa'aneah* [Koretz], fol. 18b, and *Keter
      Shem Tov ha-Shalem*, p. 121, par. 213, and pp. 226–227, no. 362.

17   *Lehamshikh hashpa'ot*. On this issue see more in chapter 9 and appendix C in this
      volume. Also, the version adduced in the name of the Besht in *Sefer Kutoneth
      Passim*, ed. Nigal, p. 246, mentions the noun *hamshakhah*. See meanwhile note
      133 in this volume. I hope to analyze this important teaching of the Besht in more
      detail elsewhere.

18   *Diduim ba-Sodeh*, fol. 16a:

      הצדיק כשמתקרב עצמו לעבודת הבורא ב"ה בתורה ובתפילה, ומדבק עצמו בפנימיותו
      שהוא שורש נשמתו וזש"ה יבא הביתה, רומז לפנימיותו, "לעשות מלאכתו". שמעתי בשם
      הבעש"ט 'כל תורה שאין עמה מלאכה' [אבות ב:ב] ר"ל שאינו עושה מעשה פעולה ע"י תורה
      בעולמות העליונים להעלות העלות הניצוצי' ולהמשיך השפעות ז"ש 'לעשות מלאכתו' ובא למדריגה
      גדולה לדביקות גדול להתפשטות הגשמיות.

      See also *Diduim ba-Sodeh*, fol. 73b, where another statement in the name
      of the Besht is adduced which corroborates, to a certain extent, the sequence of
      actions in the quoted passage as I interpreted it here. For a parallel to this state-
      ment, see e.g., the quote of the Besht's teaching commenting on dictum from *'Avot*,
      in R. Jacob Joseph of Polonnoye, *Tzafnat Pa'aneah*, fol. 18b, and *Sefer Kutoneth
      Passim*, ed. Nigal, p. 246, where again the Torah is constituted by the utterance of
      the words, while *mel'akhah* is the impact of that act. For an important discussion of
      the status of the speech in terms very reminiscent of the Besht, see also in *Diduim
      ba-Sodeh*, fol. 8a, though the latter is nevertheless referred to immediately after the
      discussion of speech as palace. See also *ibidem*, fols. 58a, 72b. See also appendix F in
      this volume. As to the divestment of corporeality, see also ch. 6 n. 8 in this volume.

19   *Qedushat Levi*, p. 407:

      כמו ששמעתי ממורי הגאון החסיד המפורסם מוהר"ר דוב בער מ"מ דק"ק מעזריטש, פירוש
      הפסוק (בראשית ז:א) 'בא אתה וכל ביתך אל התיבה' והיינו שישים האדם כל כוחותיו בתורה
      ובתפלה בכל תיבה שאומר ישים כל כוחותיו באופן שיבוטל מכל פעולותיו הגשמיים ועל פי התיבה
      שהוא רוחניות האותיות מדובק ומקושר האדם להבורא יתברך שמו. ואם יזכה האדם על פי
      התמדת עבודת האלקית יהיה האדם מנהיג הדיבורים כפי אוות נפשו הטהור...אבל בהתחלת עבו-
      דתו התיבה מנהיג לאדם להדבק בבורא יתברך שמו על ידי רוחניות האותיות, כי האותיות נמשך
      ברוחניות והמה מנהיגים את האדם ברוחניות. וזה לשון דיבור, כלומר הנהגה שמנהיג האדם ברוח-
      ניות. ודיבור הוא לשון מנהיג...כלומר שמלובש על ידי דיבורו ברוחניות. ולכן אשרי האיש איש
      חי רב פעלים אשר מקושר ברוחניות דיבורים אשר הוגה בתורה ה' יומם ולילה בלימוד ובכח גדול
      כי אי אפשר לקשר את עצמו בו יתברך שמו, כי אם בדיבור תורה ותפלה.

Some aspects of this passage are elaborated in *Qedushat Levi*, pp. 407–408, and see also Idel, *Hasidism*, p. 346, n. 93.

Compare also to the view of a follower of R. Levi Isaac, R. Aharon of Zhitomir, *Toledot Aharon*, I, fol. 6b:

> There are two kinds of *tzaddiqim:* there is the *tzaddiq* who receives luminosity from the vocables of Torah and prayer, and there is another *tzaddiq*, who is greater, who brings the luminosity to the vocables from above, despite the fact that the vocables are in the supernal world. When the great *tzaddiq* brings new luminosity to the world, this luminosity cannot come to the world but by its being clothed in the vocables . . . and when the luminosity comes down the vocables fly upwards whereas the luminosity remains here below. And the [great] rank of this *tzaddiq* is connected to recitation of the speeches with all his power and with dedication and with all the two hundred and forty-eight limbs and then to each and every word that he recites, he brings [down] luminosity.

On similar distinctions related to the nature of the Righteous found in this Hasidic school, see also Idel, *Hasidism*, pp. 118–122, 317–318, n. 111. The term *behirut*, translated here as luminosity, often has in Hasidism a meaning similar to spiritual force.

20 *Be-hitqasherut gadol.* On resorting to this term, which approximates *devequt*, see Weiss, *Studies*, p. 120, n. 34. However, I am not sure that he is correct when assuming that this term is "a more recent coinage," since it appears in many Kabbalistic writings. On the early Hasidic resort to this noun, see also Idel, "Your Word Stands Firm in Heaven," pp. 250–252; "Models of Understanding Prayer in Early Hasidism," pp. 26–28, 107, n. 265; and *Hasidism*, p. 333, n. 18.

21 *Tzava'at ha-Rivash*, printed in *Liqqutim Yeqarim*, fol. 67a, par. 277, ed. Warsaw, fol. 12b:

> המכוין בתפילתו בכל הכוונות הידועות לו, אינו מכוין רק אותן הכוונות הידועות לו. אבל כשאומר התיבה בהתקשרות גדול וכלל בכל תיבה כל הכוונות מעצמן ומאליהן שכל אות ואות הוא עולם שלם. וכשאומר התיבה בהתקשרות גדול בודאי מתעורר אותן העולמות העליונים ועושה פעולות גדולות בזה. לכן יראה האדם להתפלל בהתקשרות ובהתלהבות גדולה, בודאי יעשה פעולות גדולות בעולמות העליונים כי כל אות ואות מעורר למעלה.

On this compilation see Gries, *Conduct Literature*, pp. 149–230, and Rosman, *Founder of Hasidism*, p. 251, n. 11. For another English translation of this text, which privileges the term letters over the utterances or sounds, see Shochet, *Tzava'at ha-Rivash*, p. 108. See also his other translations of the term *'Ot* as letter, in *ibidem*, pp. 61–62, 99, 102–103. This text recurs also in R. Aharon Kohen of Apta's other book *Ner Mitzwah*, fol. 6a. See also Weiss, *Studies*, pp. 106–107; and Buber, *The Origin and Meaning of Hasidism*, p. 137; and Idel, *Hasidism*, pp.152, 334, n. 20. For the specificity of individual letters according to the Besht, see the passage referred to in ch. 2 n. 18. See also the discussion at the end of chap. 4 in this volume.

22 See Idel, "Your Word Stands Firm in Heaven," pp. 235–239, especially pp. 235–236, n. 69. To this conclusion we may arrive also from the analyses in the present study, where I pointed out other instances where the teachings that are Beshtian have been attributed implicitly to the Great Maggid in collections of the latter's

teachings. See, e.g., ch. 4 n. 7, ch. 5 n. 6, ch. 6 nn. 6, 8, and ch. 9 n. 9 in this volume, and Kauffman, *In All Your Ways Know Him*, pp. 448, 474–475. Those examples reinforce what I claim as to the "fatter" Besht.

7. R. Moshe Shoham of Dolina's Quote of the Besht

1   One of those citations has been analyzed in my "Models of Understanding Prayer in Early Hasidism," p. 13, n. 16, and "Prayer, Ecstasy, and Alien Thoughts," pp. 57–60. See also Scholem, *The Messianic Idea*, p. 216.

2   His impact is obvious in the discussions about the strong relation between the name of a person and his vitality. See, e.g., *Divrei Moshe*, part I, fols. 18c, 22a. For the views of R. Yehiel Mikhal, see Altshuler's monograph *The Messianic Secret of Hasidism*.

3   See *Divrei Moshe*, part I, fols. 10a, 14c, 18c. Compare also to R. Efrayyim of Sudylkov, *Degel Maḥaneh 'Efrayyim*, pp. 4–5, and R. Aharon of Apta, *'Or ha-Ganuz la-Tzaddiqim*, ed. Warsau, fol. 33c. The importance of continuous cleaving recurs in R. Joseph Karo's *Maggid Meisharim* several times. See Pachter, *Roots of Faith and Devequt*, pp. 272, 274, 276. On the impact of Karo on the Besht, see Rachel Elior, "R. Joseph Karo, and R. Israel Baʿal Shem Tov—Mystical Metamorphosis, Kabbalistic Inspiration, Spiritual Internalization," *Studies in Spirituality*, vol. 17 (2007), pp. 267–319, and Idel, "Female Beauty," p. 332, n. 52. In this context the paramount role of loud recitation for inducing a revelation, which is also oral, should be mentioned, especially as found in the famous document authored by R. Shlomo ha-Levi Alqabetz, describing a session of the vigil of Shavuʿot, and preserved solely in R. Isaiah Horowitz's *Shenei Luhot ha-Berit*.

On the topic of the cleaving in thought, see also one of the passages of da Vidas adduced in ch. 3 n. 7, and Margolin, *The Human Temple*, pp. 294–302, 313–318. The existence of this form of continuous *devequt* problematizes to a certain extent Etkes's assumption that intermittent *devequt* is the form that characterizes the Besht's contribution as a leader of a community. See his *The Besht: Magician, Mystic, and Leader*, p. 255. For the claim that continuous cleaving reflects an impact of Luzzatto on Hasidism, see Tishby, *Studies in Kabbalah and Its Branches*, III, pp. 967–975, and for early Hasidism see Weiss, "The Beginning of the Emergence of the Hasidic Path," pp. 60–65. On p. 64, he claims that due to the Besht's inability to speak with people because of his *devequt*, he had to be cured by a technique revealed by Ahijah ha-Shiloni, according to the hagiography, that the Besht learned how to be in *devequt* while speaking to people from R. Nahman of Kosov. I would also compare this state of consciousness to what R. Gershon of Kotov has described as a state of continuous ecstasy, in instructions transmitted by the Besht himself. See my "Prayer, Ecstasy, and Alien Thoughts," pp. 57–66.

4   BT., *ʿAvodah Zarah*, fol. 19b. See also another interpretation of this dictum quoted in the name of the Besht in *Divrei Moshe*, part I, fol. 10a. This statement should be seen in the framework of other discussions about stories and conversations in the market. See ch. 1 n. 22 in this volume.

5 See also his *Divrei Moshe*, part I, fols. 16d, 18b, 18c, 19c, 20a–b, 22b, 32d, 35a, 48a, 57c. On I, fol. 50b, the drawing down of the holiness is understood as *devequt*. See also a similar stand found in R. Aharon Perlov of Apta, *'Or ha-Ganuz la-Tzaddiqim*, ed. Warsau, fol. 25c. On the drawing down of holiness by means of thought, see also in another late disciple of the Besht, R. 'Uzziel Meisles, *Tiferet 'Uzziel*, fol. 49d. See also the non-Hasidic text contemporary to the students of the Besht dealing with the descent of holiness during prayer in Idel, *Hasidism*, p. 153, and in *Absorbing Perfections*, pp. 150–155. See also R. Aharon of Zhitomir, in his *Toledot 'Aḥaron*, I, fol. 7d, where the *tzaddiq* that worships God in "purity and holiness" draws down holiness onto the world, and see also a similar approach in *Toledot 'Aḥaron*, fol. 183b. Let me mention that in some of those cases, the verb used to designate the causing of the descent is *MShKh*. On this issue see also ch. 9 n. 9 and appendix C in this volume.

6 *Divrei Moshe*, part I, fol. 12cd:

שמעתי מהרב בוצינא קדישא הבעש"ט ז"ל שזהו כוונת חז"ל שאמרו: שיחת תלמידי חכמים
צריכה לימוד. ור"ל שצריך ללמד שיכול לדבר שחת חולין ושלא יפרד חלילה מהדבקות והנה יש
בזה שני תועלת [!] א' שאינו נפרד מהדביקות כנ"ל ועוד שעי"ז נמשך קדושה להדבר אשר עוסק
בו היינו אם הוא קונה איזה דבר אז כאשר דבורו אשר הוא מדבר בענין עסק הקני' . אז הוא
ממשיך קדושה להחפץ הנ"ל ועי"ז אח"כ כאשר הוא משמש בהחפץ הזה אשר קנה אזי נקל להיות
שמושו בו ג"כ בדבקות.

See also Kauffman, *In All Your Ways Know Him*, pp. 251–252. For analyses of related topics in R. Moshe Shoham's thought, see Kauffman, pp. 265–267. The drawing down of holiness is reminiscent of formulations found in R. Moshe Cordovero's and in Lurianic texts. For drawing down by cleaving of thought, which is considered as superior to vocal prayer, see already the view of R. Jacob Joseph of Polonnoye, *Toledot Ya'aqov Yosef*, fol. 167b, discussed in Idel, *Hasidism*, p. 164.

7 See Idel, "Models of Understanding Prayer in Early Hasidism," pp. 12–23. From some points of view, the passages of R. Moshe of Dolina, and some discussions of the Great Maggid, presuppose a type of consciousness different from the normal one, cultivated already before praying, a view that is reminiscent of that of R. Gershon of Kutov, which turns out to have been even more influential than I assumed in my article mentioned at the beginning of this note.

8 *In Praise of the Baal Shem Tov*, p. 129, and in Weiss, *Studies*, pp. 132–136. It should be pointed out that also in the translations of these traditions, Weiss resorts systematically to the term letters. See also nn. 1 and 120 in this volume. See also Idel, "Female Beauty," p. 317, citing a text of an opponent of the Besht, R. David of Makov, printed in Wilensky, *Hasidim and Mitnagdim*, II, p. 235, dealing with the Besht contemplating the faces of women in the market.

9 See Heschel, *The Circle of the Besht*, pp. 118–119, and Idel, "Prayer, Ecstasy, and Alien Thoughts," p. 64, n. 23.

10 *Divrei Moshe*, part II, fol. 4d. On purification by bathing, see also appendix A in this volume. On delight in Hasidism, see Idel, "*Ta'anug*: Erotic Delights from Kabbalah to Hasidism." See also Lederberg, *Sod ha-Da'at*, pp. 192–203, 301–302.

11 See also the existence of such a nexus in *Divrei Moshe*, part I, fol. 32d.

12 For more about this development, see Idel, "Prayer, Ecstasy, and Alien Thoughts," pp. 96–105 as well as some discussions toward the end of this study.

8. Seeing Lights within Speeches

1 Interestingly enough, another linguistic unit whose consonants are identical to ShWR, namely *Shor*, which means ox, has been interpreted as pointing to looking, in R. Aharon of Zhitomir, *Toledot 'Aharon*, fol. 50c. For an interpretation of the term *Midbbar*, which means desert, as speech, see also R. Jacob Joseph, *Tzafnat Pa'aneah* [Koretz], fol. 35d, in the context of cleaving to letters/sounds.

2 *'Or ha-Me'ir*, fol. 57bc:

עַל דֶּרֶךְ שֶׁשָּׁמַעְתִּי בְּשֵׁם הַבַּעַ"שט זלל"ה שֶׁפֵּירֵשׁ 'צֹהַר תַּעֲשֶׂה לַתֵּיבָה' לַעֲשׂוֹת צֹהַר מִן
הַתֵּיבָה שֶׁל תּוֹרָה וּתְפִלָּה, לִרְאוֹת וּלְהִסְתַּכֵּל עִמָּהּ מֵרֹאשׁ הָעוֹלָם וְעַד סוֹף, וְזֶהוּ 'וְיֵצְאוּ אֶל מִדְבָּר
שׁוֹר' אִסְתַּכְּלוּתָא שָׁם כְּמַדּוּבָּר, וְדוֹ"ק

Compare also to the sermon of the Great Maggid, *Maggid Devarav le-Ya'aqov*, ed. Schatz-Uffenheimer, p. 182; and see also R. Aharon of Apta, *'Or ha-Ganuz la-Tzadiqim*, fol. 7b—where the Besht is quoted—as well as the collection of Beshtian traditions assembled by Mondshine, *Shivehei Ha-Baal Shem Tov*, pp. 261–263; R. Shimeon Menahem Mendel Vodnek, *Ba'al Shem Tov*, vol. I, pp. 119–123; and *Tzava'at Harivash*, tr. Shochet, pp. 64–65 as well as *Liqqutim Yeqarim*, fol. 13a (= *Keter Shem Tov ha-Shalem*, p. 120, no. 211), where the look of God to the speeches has been designated also as *histakkelut*, like in the tradition reported in the name of the Besht, and was explained as dealing with the divine influence, *hashpa'ah*. See also Idel, "Models of Understanding Prayer in Early Hasidism," pp. 102–103, as well as R. Aharon of Zhitomir, *Toledot 'Aharon*, ed. Berditchev, fols. 50c, 51a. See also Jacobs, *Hasidic Prayer*, pp. 76–77.

3 *Degel Mahaneh 'Efrayyim*, p. 58:

עַל פִּי מַה שֶׁהֵאִיר אָא"ז נ"ע תֵּיבָה מְרוּמָּז עַל מִלָּה שֶׁהוּא נִקְרָא תֵּיבָה וּכְמוֹ שֶׁכָּתוּב צֹהַר
תַּעֲשֶׂה לַתֵּיבָה וְאָמַר הוּא ז"ל שֶׁתִּרְאֶה לְהָאִיר הַתֵּיבָה שֶׁתּוֹצִיא מִפִּיךָ וְהַאֲרִיךְ בָּזֶה

See also *Degel Mahaneh 'Efrayyim*, p. 123, for another instance of illumination of the letters, or sounds, without, however, referring to the Besht. See also the parallel found in the name of the Besht in R. Aharon of Apta, *'Or ha-Ganuz la-Tzaddiqim*, ed. Warsau, fols. 7b and 17b. However, in *'Or ha-'Emmet*, fol. 21c, there is a passage that deals with the illumination of the letters or sounds without, however, mentioning the Besht. See also Idel, "Models of Understanding Prayer in Early Hasidism," pp. 102–103, but compare, however, to the view of Lederberg, *Sod ha-Da'at*, p. 170. For the claim of seeing lights within letters, see also Wolfson, "Immanuel Frommann," pp. 190–191, 195, and following him and Scholem, also Magid, *Hasidism Incarnate*, pp. 166, 209, n. 40. However, here there is a phenomenon of synaesthesis. See Sullivan, "Sound and Senses," pp. 7–8. As to the mentioning of the "mouth," which follows the lead of *Sefer Yetziyrah* and da Vidas's *Reshit Hokhmah*, see also R. Menahem Nahum of Chernobyl, *Me'or 'Einayyim*, p. 161.

See also *Tzava'at Harivash*, tr. Shochet, p. 65: "'Come into the *Teivah* with all your family' (Genesis 7:1), with all your body and strength." See also the similar formulations in R. Menahem Nahum of Chernobyl, *Yismah Lev*, in *Me'or 'Einayyim*, p. 307. On strength invested in the recitation of the word, see ch. 2 n. 13. Compare also to the view of another grandson of the Besht, R. Barukh of Miedzibuz, the younger brother of R. Efrayyim, where the issue of illumination of the Torah by the person that studies it is connected to the assumption that the union with God and Torah is achieved thereby. The illumination is preceded by a hearing of the Torah in one's heart. Cf. the passage translated and discussed in Idel, *Absorbing Perfections*, pp. 425–426. See also ch. 8 n. 8 in this volume.

4   *Liqqutim Yeqarim*, fol. 1a:

ריב"ש אמר: אדם שהוא קורא בתורה ורואה האורות של האותיות שבתור[ה], אע"פ שאין
מבין הטעמים כראוי, כיון שהוא קורא באהבה גדולה ובהתלהבות אין השי"ת [השם יתברך]
מדקדק עמו, אף שאין אומרם כראוי.

See also by Pedaya, "The Besht, R. Jacob Joseph of Polonnoye, and the Maggid of Mezeritch," pp. 65–66; Weiss, "Talmud-Torah le-Shitat R. Israel Besht," p. 161; and Idel, *Hasidism*, pp. 163, 178–180; and the pertinent notes as well as the important discussion found in *Maggid Devarav le-Ya'aqov*, ed. Schatz-Uffenheimer, p. 45, where the lights of the letters are identical with their vitality. For interesting connections between lights and letters, see in R. Moshe Cordovero, *Shi'ur Qomah*, fol. 53d–54b; and R. Moshe Hayyim Luzzatto's text translated and discussed in Idel, *Absorbing Perfections*, pp. 97–98; and in the late eighteenth century in R. Hayyim Joseph David Azulai's *Devarim 'Aḥadim*, quoted in Scholem, *On the Kabbalah and Its Symbolism*, p. 76. See also the view of the Great Maggid, who claims that if someone divests himself from corporeality, he will be able to see the lights and the vitality found within the utterances. Cf., the Great Maggid's *Rimzei Torah* (Brooklyn, 2005), p. 113, no. 485, See also Idel, *Hasidism*, pp. 163, 168, and especially p. 184, where a view attributed to the Besht to this effect is discussed. In the previously mentioned R. Issakhar Dov Baer of Zloczow's *Mevasser Tzedeq*, fol. 20ab, there is an interesting discussion, without referring to any authority, about the *'Otiyyot*,— whether letters or sounds it is not clear—as the coagulations of supernal lights. For experiences of light related to the study of the Torah, see the medieval material referred in Idel, *Absorbing Perfections*, p. 540, n. 73. For creating light on high by the performance of commandments, see Idel, *Enchanted Chains*, pp. 218–219. See also Elliot R. Wolfson, "Hermeneutics of Light in Medieval Kabbalah," in ed. M. Kapstein, *The Presence of Light: Divine Radiance and Mystical Experience* (Chicago University Press, Chicago, 2004), pp. 105–107, and his *Through a Speculum that Shines*, pp. 287–288. On the relation between letters, lights, and secrets in late thirteenth-century Kabbalah in the context of the contemplation of the Torah scroll, especially in the Zoharic literature, see Wolfson, *Through a Speculum that Shines*, pp. 375–376 and the pertinent notes, as well as his "From Sealed Book, to Open Text: Time, Memory, and Narrativity in Kabbalistic Hermeneutics," in ed. S. Kepnes, *Interpreting Judaism in a Postmodern Age* (New York University Press, New York, 1996), p. 153. For contemplation of lights and light-apparitions in Hellenistic forms of mysticism, see, e.g., Erwin Goodenough, *By Light, Light, The Mystic Gospel of Hellenistic Judaism* (Yale University Press, New Haven, 1935); E. R. Dodds, *The Greeks and the Irrational* (California University Press, Berkeley, 1951), p. 299; and Gregory Shaw, *Theurgy and the Soul, The Neoplatonism of Iamblichus* (The Pennsylvania State University Press, University Park, Penn. 1995), pp. 170–188.

In this context it should be mentioned that in the neo-hesychastic mysticism, which was widespread in parts of Eastern Europe in the eighteenth century, contemplation of light as well as the continuous vocal prayer were considered paramount religious practices. For the connection between words and light, see David Chidester, *Word and Light: Seeing, Hearing, and Religious Discourse* (University of Illinois Press, Urbana, Ill., 1992), and Eitan P. Fishbane, "The Speech of Being, the Voice of God: Phonetic Mysticism in the Kabbalah of Asher ben David and His Contemporaries," *JQR*, vol. 98 (2008), p. 506. Let me point out that according to the teachings discussed in this chapter, presences of other entities are found within the sound, in addition to the voice displaying the human presence. Compare, however, to the assessment of Ong, *The Presence of the Word*, p. 168: "Voice is not *peopled* with presences." Compare to the Hindu tradition as to the presence of Shiva and Shakti in every letter, basically in every sound. Cf., Beck, *Sonic Theology*, p. 101, and in ch. 8 n. 12 in this volume.

For the loud study of the *Zohar*, see especially the group of R. Moshe Hayyim Luzzatto as well as the recitations of this book in Northern African communities. Cf. Harvey Goldberg, "The Zohar in Southern Morocco: A Study in Ethnography of Texts," *History of Religion*, vol. 29 (1990), pp. 249–251, and Abraham Stahl, "Ritual Reading of the Zohar," *Pe'amim*, vol. 5 (1980), pp. 77–86 (Hebrew).

For voice as hypostasis in ancient Jewish sources, see Azzan Yadin, "לוק as Hypostasis in the Hebrew Bible," *JBL*, 122/4 (2003), pp. 601–626; James H. Charlesworth, "The Jewish Roots of Christology: The Discovery of the Hypostatic Voice," *Scottish Journal of Theology* 39 (1986), pp. 19–41; and Andrei A. Orlov, "Praxis of the Voice: The Divine Name Traditions in the Apocalypse of Abraham," *JBL*, vol. 127, no. 1 (2008), pp. 53–70. For early Hasidic discussions about the importance of voice and some of their sources, see Idel, "Models for Understanding Prayer," pp. 34–38.

5   See *'Or ha-Ganuz la-Tzaddiqim*, Lemberg, col. IV, fol. 1a:

וז"ש בשם הבעש"ט ז"ל: האותיות שבתורה הם כלים וחדרים של הש"י שע"י (שעל ידי) כוונת האדם, ממשיך בהן את אצילות אור העליון

For the view that the utterances illumine by the lights that the person draws within them, see again in the same book, ed. Warsau, fol. 25c. It should be pointed out that according to another discussion found in this book, the lights of the "letters" correspond to the world of thought. See Warsau, fol. 28c and, in a different form, in fol. 36d. See also ch. 6 n. 14. The letters or sounds are conceived to be vessels and chambers in many discussions of R. Jacob Joseph of Polonnoye. See also the passage of the Great Maggid translated and analyzed in Idel, *Hasidism*, pp. 168–169 and Kallus, *Pillar of Prayer*, p. 101, no. 79. It should be mentioned that a view very similar to the quote cited in the name of the Besht is adduced in the name of R. N., perhaps R. Nahman of Kosov, by R. Jacob Joseph of Polonnoye, *Toledot Ya'aqov Yosef*, fol. 62b:

.שע"י הדיבור נעשה כלים שבו יושפע שפע הברכה

"By means of speech vessels have been wrought, that the influx of blessing are emanated." A similar formulation is found again on the same page. Especially interesting is the fact that on fol. 23c of the same book, he quotes the "Hasid R. Y[ehudah]," most probably R. Yehudah Leib of Pistin, in relation to prayer, as follows: "By the combinations of letters and words a vessel is produced to draw down the influx and blessing for [the people of] Israel." Compare also to R. Barukh of Kosov, *Neḥmad ve-Na'yim - Yesod ha-'Emunah*, fol. 96ab. Those are important examples of the impact of Cordoverianism in the entourage of the Besht.

For the claim that the supernal light or illumination is drawn down within the letters/sounds of prayer, see the end of a parable quoted in the name of the Besht by R. Zeev Wolf of Zhitomir, where it is written in the context of prayer: "And he should protect himself not to utter any letter/sound without pure thought, because then the letters/sounds will be dry and without the wetness of the influx of the supernal illumination they do not ascend on high, for man must bring the filling into the letters/sounds by means of his pure thought." Cf. the translation in Schatz-Uffenheimer, *Hasidism as Mysticism*, p. 222, slightly altered. The Hebrew passage is

וישמור עצמו לבלתי הוציא משפתיו אותיות בלא מחשבה טהורה, שאז האותיות המה יבשות בלתי לחלוחית השפעת האורה עליונה, ואינה פורחת לעילא, כי האדם צריך להכניס מילוי האורה באותיות, על ידי מחשבתו הטהורה

If this is indeed a Beshtian passage, then we have again some form of drawing down of influx within utterances. This passage is especially reminiscent of the Cordoverian theory of drawing spirituality down in order to allow the speeches to soar on high, as found at the very end of *Pardes Rimmonim*. See appendix C in this volume. On lights within speeches and the cleaving to them, see also Great Maggid, ed. Schatz-Uffenheimer, *Maggid Devarav le-Ya'aqov*, p. 330.

Let me point out that according to a statement of R. Ḥayyim Vital, his master R. Isaac Luria was gazing at the written letters of the Torah in order to draw down the great light. See *Sha'ar ha-Kavvanot* (Jerusalem, 1902), fol. 48c. The difference between the texts of Cordovero, which deal with utterances, and that of Luria, dealing with the written form of letters, is evident. Compare, however, to the view of the Besht as adduced by his grandson in *Degel Maḥaneh Efrayyim*, p. 77, discussed in my "Models of Understanding Prayer and Early Hasidism," p. 172, according to which the speech is emanated from the lights. For the view that speech is illumining, *ha-dibbur me'ir*, see already R. Moshe Cordovero, *Sefer 'Or Yaqar*, vol. 11, p. 174.

For early cases of an affinity between study of canonical texts and luminosity, see Ignaz Goldziher, "La notion de la Sakina chez les Mahometans," *Revue de l'histoire des religions*, vol. XIV, 1893, pp. 7–8; and M. M. Ayoub, *The Qur'an and Its Interpreters* (SUNY Press, Albany, 1984), vol. I, pp. 8–9; Idel, "The Concept of the Torah in the Heikhalot Literature and Its Metamorphoses in Kabbalah," *JSJT*, vol. I (1981), pp. 36–37 (Hebrew).

6   On the issue of power see also the material referred to in ch. 2 n. 14. Here there is a shift between putting all one's power within the word, as in the text analyzed previously, and putting all one's thought within the power that exists already in the word. Here we have another example of cleaving by thought. See also the discussion of the Cordoverian source for the superiority of the mental prayer over utterances in my *Enchanted Chains*, p. 204, n. 160. For inserting one's power in the utterances, see R. Aharon of Zhitomir, *Toledot 'Aharon*, fol. 46ab, who asserts that this investment is also a purification that allows some form of experience. See also previously, in the text referred to in n. 90. Interestingly enough, thought is related

to power and not to contemplation, and this is also the case in the different manuscript version of this passage, to be printed in ch. 8 n. 11 in this volume.

7   The subject of the verbal phrase *Mamshikh bahem* is not clear, and in the translation
     I opted for God as emanating within the speech acts. However, if the subject of the
     statement is the man in prayer, we have a strong example of the talismanic magic.
     On this seminal verb see more in the next chapter, especially in ch. 9 n. 9 and in
     appendix C. Let me point out that an interesting discussion of the possibility that
     the people of Israel are capable of inducing the dwelling of light on various matters
     in this world, including prayer and study of the Torah, is quoted by R. Barukh of
     Miedzibusz in the name of R. Menaham Mendel of Bar, a contemporary of the
     Besht, with whom he was in contact. See *Butzina' di-Nehora'*, no pagination. See
     also ch. 9 n. 9.

8   On this triune formula see what I wrote in "Models of Understanding Prayer in
     Early Hasidism," pp. 61–62, nn. 161, 162; and beside nn. 89 and 113; and *Enchanted
     Chains*, pp. 155–157. See also Wolfson, *Circle in the Square*, pp. 23–25 and Pachter,
     Roots of Faith and Devequt, p. 244, n. 37. As I shall elaborate elsewhere, I. Tishby's
     assumption, mentioned in my study referred to previously, as to a Sabbatean source
     for this statement that was allegedly copied according to his hypothesis from the
     writings of R. Moshe Hayyim Luzzatto, is unnecessary since it appears some
     decades before Sabbateanism, more eminently in a passage of R. Isaiah Horowitz's
     classic *Shenei Luhot ha-Berit*, vol. I, fols. 4a, 65a. The latter passage has been quoted
     verbatim from *Shenei Luhot ha-Berit* by R. Barukh of Kosov, *'Amudei ha-'Avodah*,
     fol. 39b. This issue deserves a much more detailed analysis, which will attenuate,
     perhaps even obliterate, the insisting claim recurring in Tishby's article as to the
     ultimately Sabbatean source of this widespread formula in Hasidism.

9   The passage in parentheses is not found in the version as printed in *Maggid Devarav
     le-Ya'aqov* or in the manuscript we shall cite in the next note, and it is plausibly an
     accretion added by R. Aharon of Apta.

10   *Maggid Devarav le-Ya'aqov*, ed. Schatz-Uffenheimer, pp. 47–48, and *Keter Shem
     Tov ha-Shalem*, p. 164, no. 284:

ישים כל מחשבתו בכח הת[י]בות שהוא מדבר עד שיראה האורות של הת[י]בות היאך
מתנוצצים זה בזה, ומתוכם נולדים כמה אורות, וזהו (תהלים צז: יא) 'אור זרוע לצדיק ולישרי לב
שמחה', האותיות שבתורה הם חדרים של השם יתברך שהוא ממשיך בהם את אצילות אורו [כמו
שכתב בזוהר הקדוש קודשא בריך הוא ואורייתא כולא חד, ולתוכן צריך אדם לתת כל הכוונה
שהיא הנשמה כי הכוונה הוא הנשמה, וזהו הדבקות, קודשא בריך הוא ואורייתא וישראל כולא
חד, וזהו התפשטות הגשמיות, פירוש שיפשיט נשמתו מגופו, ותהיה נשמתו מלובשת באותן המח־
.שבות שהוא מדבר, ויראה כמה עולמות העליונים יש באדם

For a slightly different version of this passage, which is nevertheless worthwhile to be adduced here, see Ms. Jerusalem NUL 8° 3282, fol. 106b:

"ישים כל מחשבתו באותיות והתיבות שהוא מדבר אף בכח גדול עד שיראה האורות של
התיבות האיך מתנוצצים זה בזה ומתוכם נולדים כמה האורות וזהו 'אור זרוע לצדיק ולישרי לב
שמחה', בסתם וזהו י האורות של האותיות הם חדרים של השי"ת שהוא ממשיך אותן מאצילותו
לתוכם צריך להפשיט נשמתו מגופו ותהיה נשמתו מלובשת באותם המחשבות שהוא מדבר ויראה
.כמה עולמות העליונים שיש באדם

See also Pedaya, "The Besht, R. Jacob Joseph of Polonnoye, and the Maggid of Mezeritch," p. 67, who does not see in this passage a Beshtian tradition. Compare, however, to the different view of Kauffman, *In All Your Ways Know Him*, p. 458, n. 89. See also *Keter Shem Tov*, fol. 60d, no. 411. For the sonorous garment of the soul, see more in appendix B in this volume. For the use of the verb *MShKh*, see more in chapter 9, in the context of a discussion of a passage from R. 'Efrayyim of Sudylkov, and ch. 9 n. 9. For seeing the future because of cleaving, see the passage in the name of the Besht preserved by R. Jacob Joseph and translated at the end of chapter 5 in this volume. Compare, however, to Weiss, *Studies*, p. 61, who speaks about the "lights that shine in the holy texts." See also note 1 in this volume. The passage translated here should be compared to the view found in the Great Maggid's *Maggid Devarav le-Ya'aqov*, ed. Schatz-Uffenheimer, pp. 45–46, no. 28, and copied in *Keter Shem Tov ha-Shalem*, p. 161, no. 279, where the watching of the lights of the letters/sounds as the inner part of the vessels, which are the speeches or the utterances, is conceived of as preceding, perhaps even inferior, to one's enclothing himself with the speeches after he has divested himself of corporeality, and thus has been united with the Creator. Therefore, this is a sequence that differs from what we have seen in the passage translated previously. See also appendix B and appendix B n.13 in this volume. However, beyond this obvious difference, it is important to point out that if we interpret the investment of all the power at the first stage as intending to a form of cleaving, we may discern the existence of two forms of cleaving: one in the pronunciation, the other in the cleaving after covering oneself with the utterances and being united with the Creator.

For the bringing of lights within the utterances or letters/sounds, see also the interesting discussions found in R. Aharon of Zhitomir, *Toledot 'Aharon*, fols. 100a, 110c, 184a, translated and discussed in Idel, "*Torah Hadashah*," pp. 84–85. Let me point out that according to a surprising statement of Scholem, *Kabbalah*, p. 178, he considers the practice of drawing down light within utterances as found in Azulai's *Hesed le-Abraham*, as if it constitutes a Lurianic teaching! However, Azulai copied verbatim many sentences of Cordovero's, who was influenced by the medieval reverberations of the Hermetic tradition. This is just an example of the privileged status accorded to Lurianic Kabbalah in the historical scheme of Scholem, when in fact it was Cordovero's influence. See beside ch. 15 n. 9, and also the two studies of Tishby, *Studies*, vol. 1, pp. 131–267, and Sack, "The Influence of Cordovero on Seventeenth-Century Jewish Thought," pp. 365–379. See also appendix B in this volume.

11 See, e.g., R. Jacob Joseph, *Ben Porat Yosef*, fols. 17d–18a, and *Keter Shem Tov*, fol. 4c, no. 21, as well as the rich Beshtian material about the act of *hieros gamos* taking place on the lips of the person during prayer, adduced in Idel, "Models of Understanding Prayer in Early Hasidism," pp. 56–78. For an important statement that corroborates the sexual understanding of the relationship between the lights, see the teaching of R. Zeev Wolf of Zhitomir, in the context of the *Kavvanot* in prayer, who testifies that "as known from books, there is no letter/sound similar to its fellow, and they allude to unifications and couplings of the supernal lights. And certainly not every mind is able to undertake this." Cf. the translation and discussion of Schatz-Uffenheimer, *Hasidism as Mysticism*, p. 221. The Hebrew original is

שנודע מספרים שאין אות דומה .לחברתה, המרמזים יחודים וזווגים אורות עליונים

Immediately afterward R. Zeev Wolf adduced a parable in the name of the Besht. See Schatz-Uffenheimer, *Hasidism as Mysticism*, pp. 221–222, and note 115 in this volume. See also the interesting use of the verb *mitnotzetzim*, in an explicit sexual context, dealing with the sparkling of the sparks of the *Tiferet* within *Malkhut*, in Cordovero's *Pardes Rimmonim* XII:4, and R. Isaiah Horowitz's *Sha'ar ha-Shamayyim*, fol. 147b. See also Shelomo, *The Mystical Theology of Moses Cordovero*, pp. 277–280. For some forms of union between lights found in the divine sphere, see already in early fourteenth-century influential Kabbalistic book *Sefer Berit Menuḥah* and even more in Lurianic Kabbalah. For the causing of union of the Holy One Blessed be He and the *Shekhinah* by means of speech, see the tradition adduced in *Keter Shem Tov*, fol. 54ab, no. 362, and ch. 1 n. 22 in this volume. For a discussion concerning the sexual union between the letters, caused by the "light of the soul," see R. Efrayyim of Sudylkov, *Degel Maḥaneh 'Efrayyim*, p. 218. For the possibility that a *hieros gamos* is induced by the activity of prayer according to a passage from the *Holy Epistle*, see Dan, *Jewish Mysticism*, vol. 3, pp. 126–127, and Dauber, "The Baal Shem Tov and the Messiah," pp. 235–238. Let me point out that the possibility of watching the *hieros gamos* is assumed as possible in the messianic times, according to R. Meir ibn Gabbai, *'Avodat ha-Qodesh* (Lemberg, 1957), II:38, fol. 70a. See also ch. 8 n. 5 in this volume.

12   See, e.g., Hollenback, *Mysticism, Experience, Response, and Empowerment*, pp. 60–66, and Mircea Eliade, *Shamanism: Archaic Techniques of Ecstasy* (Princeton University Press, Princeton, 1974), pp. 60–61. See also Idel, *Hasidism*, pp. 75, 214, 218, 225, 289. On the possible affinities between the Besht and Shamanic experiences in certain group living in the Carpathian Mountains, see more recently Idel, Ascensions on High, pp. 148–150 or "18th Century Early Hasidism," pp. 61–67, and "Early Hasidism and Altaic Tribes," and Brill, "The Spiritual World of a Master of Awe," pp. 32–35. See already Idel, *Kabbalah: New Perspectives*, p. 321, n. 137, and in my "Your Word Stands Firm in Heaven," pp. 236–237, n. 74. See especially now Garb, *Shamanic Trance in Modern Kabbalah*, especially pp. 47–74. I am pleased to see that the recent scholarship concerning the Besht has resorted more recently to the category of Shamanism in order to describe aspects of the Besht's practices from the phenomenological point of view.

13   *Me'or 'Einayyim*, p. 89:

הבעש"ט נשמתו בגנזי מרומים שסיפרו עליו כשהיה צריך לדעת שום דבר פרטי אפילו
מעניני בני אדם דבר גשמי היה מסתכל בהתורה ולומד בה בדחילו ורחימו ומדבק את עצמו עד
שהגיע לאור הגנוז בתוכה והיה רואה בדבר שצריך לראות ממש...אך לא כל אדם זוכה למדריגה.

See also *Keter Shem Tov*, fol. 53d, no. 360, and fol. 54d, no. 368. For another statement about the lights within vocables, this time without mentioning the Besht, see the view of his son, R. Mordekhai of Chernobyl, *Liqqutei Torah* (Benei Berak, 1983), fol. 29d, and Idel, *Absorbing Perfections*, p. 184:

> palaces for the revelation of the light of *'Eyin Sof*, blessed be He and blessed His name, that is clothed within them. When one studies the Torah and prays, then they [!] take them out of the secret places and their light is revealed here below. . . . By the cleaving of man to the letters/vocables of

the Torah and of the prayer, he draws down onto himself the revelation of the light of 'Eiyn Sof.

On "letters" and lights in the Besht, see Scholem, *The Messianic Idea*, p. 212. On the affinities between the concept of lights and that of spiritual forces—*ruḥaniyyot*—see Pines, "On the Term *Ruḥaniyyut* and Its Sources," pp. 514, 522. For the Rabbinic and Kabbalistic sources of the theory of the hidden light within the Torah, see Idel, "From ''Or Ganuz' to ''Or Torah,'" pp. 23–62, and Brill, "The Spiritual World of a Master of Awe," p. 36. In a way, the late antiquity Rabbinic vision of the light, believed to have been stored by God within the Torah for the sake of the righteous men, has been conjugated with the Hermetically oriented vision of language, not of texts, as containing spiritual force, vitality, or light. This synthesis has been expressed in terms found in Safedian Kabbalah, dealing with the light or the spiritual force of the Infinite, *'Or 'Eiyn Sof.* For the Besht's "exclusive" resort to *Yiḥudim* in order to heal, see the revealing testimony of R. Menahem Nahum of Chernobyl, *Me'or 'Einayyim*, p. 154, discussed by Wacks, *The Secret of Unity*, pp. 199–201, and Kauffman, *In All Your Ways Know Him*, pp. 474–475; and for other instances of the connection between the concepts discussed here and healing, see the passages discussed in Idel, *Hasidism*, pp. 75, 77–78, 169, 214, and 290, n. 194. See also ch. 9 n. 6 of this volume, and in R. Aharon of Zhitomir, *Toledot 'Aharon*, fol. 100b.

It should be noticed that when dealing with some of the texts analyzed in this chapter, Pedaya, "The Besht, R. Jacob Joseph of Polonnoye, and the Maggid of Mezeritch," p. 67, contends that the Besht was portrayed as ascending through the lights found in the letters [*sic*], on high. No specific reference for this interesting claim has been provided, and for the time being, I did not find a single passage that may support this quite fascinating assertion. If this claim will nevertheless sometime be documented, the intellectual figure of the Besht will be even less homogenous than it is depicted now in scholarship. For a connection between the concept of "light of Torah" and the state of *gadelut* in Beshtian traditions, see R. Jacob Joseph of Polonnoye's *Tzafnat Pa'aneaḥ*, ed. Nigal, pp. 108–110, and compare to R. Efrayyim's *Degel Maḥaneh 'Efrayyim*, p. 173, adduced and discussed in Kauffman, *In All Your Ways Know Him*, pp. 351–352. The state of *qatenut* is described as a kind of worship that is void of light. Compare also to Jacobs, *Their Heads in Heaven*, pp. 59–61, who pointed out a parallel to Cordovero in a Beshtian tradition.

For an interesting description where the Besht was conceived of as someone who has seen the divine lights, see the testimony of the famous opponent to Hasidism, the author R. David of Makov's *Zemer 'Aritzim*, printed in Wilensky, *Hasidism and Mitnaggedim*, II, p. 200. See also R. Elimelekh of Lysansk, *No'am 'Elimelekh*, fol. 69a; Louis Jacobs, *Jewish Mystical Testimonies* (Schocken, New York, 1987), pp. 7–8; and R. Qalonymus Qalman Epstein of Krakau, *Ma'or va-Shemesh*, IV, fol. 22c on luminous phenomena. For an interesting description where the Besht was conceived of as someone who has seen the divine lights, see the testimony of the famous opponent to Hasidism, the author R. David of Makov's *Zemer 'Aritzim*, printed in Wilensky, *Hasidism and Mitnaggedim*, II, p. 200. See also R. Elimelekh of Lysansk, *No'am 'Elimelekh*, fol. 69a; Louis Jacobs, *Jewish Mystical Testimonies* (Schocken, New York, 1987), pp. 7–8; and R. Qalonymus Qalman

Epstein of Krakau, *Ma'or va-Shemesh*, IV, fol. 22c on luminous phenomena. See also Garb, *Shamanic Trance*, pp. 82-85.

14   *Shemu'ah Tovah*, p. 73. See Schatz-Uffenheimer, *Hasidism as Mysticism*, pp. 170–171; Margolin, *The Human Temple*, pp. 368–369; and ch. 2 n. 4 in this volume. It should be pointed out that R. Levi Isaac was one of the few Hasidic masters concerned with the shapes of written letters. See also M. Idel, "White Letters: from R. Levi Isaac of Berditchev's Views to Postmodern Hermeneutics," *MJ*, vol. 26, no. 2 (2006), pp. 169–192; *Old Worlds, New Mirrors*, pp. 234–248; *Hasidism*, p. 284, n. 140; and Weiss, *Letters by which Heaven and Earth were Created*, pp. 209–210. For R. Levi Isaac's vision of lights while the Shofar was blown, which presumably means that they were within the voice of the Shofar, another instance of synesthesia, see *In Praise of the Baal Shem Tov*, p. 249. For visual appearances that Abulafia reports in connection to the combinations of vocalized letters of the divine name and their recitations, see my *The Mystical Experience in Abraham Abulafia*, pp. 100–103, and Shahar Arzy and Moshe Idel, *Kabbalah: A Neurocognitive Approach to Mystical Experience* (Yale University Press, New Haven, 2015). For the personal propensity to transform language into a sort of vision, see the testimony of Roland Barthes as discussed by Jay, *Downcast Eyes*, pp. 438–439.

15   *'Or Yaqar*, on *Tiqqunei Zohar*, vol. 6, pp. 160–161:

כמו שיש באדם עצמות הגוף או התוכיות הפנימי שממנו ההבל והנשימה, כך יש בספירות
העליונות רוח החיים ת"ח ומלכות הפועלות הרצון הפנימי בתוכם שדרך בם מתפשט רצון אלהי
עליון, הרצון הפנימי דהיינו קול ודבור דהיינו ת"ח ומלכות הפועלות דהיינו והאדם בהיותו עוסק בתפלה
ותורה בקול ודבור יש מלאכים ממונים על אותו קול ודבור להעלותו למעלה . . . עכ"ז יש לו
תיכון שפועל בו פעולה זו, והם ג' בחינות הא' הב"ל דק, הב' קול דאשתמע, הג' דבור, והענין
שהקול והדבור בת"ח ומלכות, וההבל שבו סוד הכוונה ורוחניות האותיות כשאדם מאריך ומרחיב
המלה בכוונה נותן לב להיות ולשמות, כל הבל והבל שיוצא מפיו עושה להם אש המתעלה למעלה
וסוד להב ה' לב, דהיינו שרומז בחכמה ובבינה, והיינו כעין סוד ההבל העליוני שהוא קול ה' חוצב
להבות אש מצד הבינה כך האדם חוצב להבות אש בסוד הכוונה תוך הקול והדבור ולזה על קול
ודבור רוכב להב .

      Cordovero is indubitably impacted by the discussion in *Tiqqunei Zohar* no. 22, fol. 63b, that he interprets. See also Cordovero's interesting passage quoted in Azulai, *'Or ha-Ḥammah*, III, fol. 15b. A close and quite interesting parallel is found in his *Shiy'ur Qomah*, fols. 18a, 19b, and especially the passage *Shiy'ur Qomah*, fol. 45a, where light and utterances are connected explicitly. For an affinity between the *ruḥaniyyut* and light also in Cordovero, see Cordovero, *Tiqqunei Zohar Ḥadash*, vol. 3, p. 29, and Pines, "On the Term *Ruḥaniyyut* and Its Sources," p. 522, where both lights and enthusiasm are related to the spiritual force. For the so-called "luminous letters" in Islam, see Zoran, "Magic, Theurgy, and the Knowledge of Letters," pp. 41–42.

9. The Besht and the Mystical-Magical Model

1   See *In Praise of the Baal Shem Tov*, pp. 49–50, 89–90. For the Psalm episode, see *In Praise of the Baal Shem Tov*, pp. 45–46. See also Kallus, *Pillar of Prayer*, pp. 93–95.

2   See Idel, *Hasidism*, pp. 19–20, 178–180. See also *Zohar*, vol. I, fol. 100ab, and ch. 3 n. 7 and appendix F in this volume. Compare also to the syntagma of *unio magica*

used, *inter alia*, in Mensching, *Structures and Patterns of Religion*, pp. 9, 62, 106, 108, 109, 160, 207, 261.

3   Compare especially the views of the Great Maggid of Mezerich, translated in my
    Hasidism, pp. 92–93, where the Torah is understood as some form of incantation
    and as a talisman. See, however, the opposite vision of Buber, *Origin and Meaning of
    Hasidism*, pp. 133–135, 179–180, and the different interpretation found in Lederberg,
    Sod ha-Da'at, pp. 170, 181. For accusations that the Hasidim do not recite the text of
    prayer precisely, see the passage adduced by Scholem, *ha-Shalav ha-'Aḥaron*, p. 68.
    For an important text of the Great Maggid that expresses explicitly the formulaic
    nature of the canonical texts in talismanic-magical contexts, mentioning divine
    names, see the passage adduced and discussed in Kauffman, *In All Your Ways Know
    Him*, p. 447. See also *Maggid Devarav le-Ya'aqov*, ed. Schatz-Uffenheimer, p. 26,
    and compare also to R. Nahman of Braslav's view of the formulaic structure of the
    Torah as a form of medication, discussed in Zvi Mark, *Scroll of Secrets, The Hidden
    Messianic Vision of R. Nahman of Bratzlav* (Bar Ilan University Press, Ramat Gan,
    2006), pp. 90–95 (Hebrew).
        See also the parallel between the uttered words of the Torah and medicine
    found in the passage of the famous eighteenth-century famous R. Ḥayyim Joseph
    David Azulai's *Devarim 'Aḥadim*, quoted in Scholem, *On the Kabbalah and Its
    Symbolism*, p. 76, as well as the much more influential *Ḥesed le-'Avraham*, fol. 94d
    by R. Abraham Azulai, a forefather of the former Azulai, a book known to early
    Hasidic masters; and for these and other additional sources for this comparison, see
    the references in Idel, *Hasidism*, p. 293, n. 219. There I proposed the assumption that
    this is a Cordoverian talismanic approach. The perusal of R. Hayyim Joseph David
    Azulai's whole context, which includes the passage adduced by Scholem, demon-
    strates how much Cordovero's theory of language and talismanics, including the ter-
    minology related to *ruḥaniyyut*, was still alive in the eighteenth century, even when
    Cordovero's name was not mentioned. Compare also ch. 6 n. 8, the texts referred
    to in ch. 9 nn. 6, 8, ch. 10 n. 7, and ch. 12 n. 7, and in appendix B in this volume.

4   Later on in this context the Hasidic author claims that the "secret of the divinity"
    is found within the letters/sounds, and this is the meaning of studying the Torah
    for the sake of the letters, attributing such a view to his grandfather. Drawing down
    the divinity occurs in many cases in discussions found also in the school of the
    Great Maggid; see the previous note. See also the Hasidic texts translated in Idel,
    Absorbing Perfections, pp. 155–160, in *'Or ha-'Emmet*, fol. 41b, and in appendix E in
    this volume.

5   *Sod ha-Neviy'u*. This is an Aramaic phrase for the emerging water, which is used by
    the Zoharic literature as a metaphor for emanation. This term recurs in this book
    and in those of R. Jacob Joseph of Polonnoye as *Nevi'a*. See, e.g., *Toledot Ya'aqov
    Yosef*, fol. 201a.

6   *Degel Maḥaneh 'Efrayyim*, p. 103:

    כי אורייתא וקודשא בריך הוא וישראל כולהו חד הוא ואף ורק כשממשיכין סוד אלוה
    בתורה על ידי שלומדים התורה לשמה אז יש בה כח אלוהות ונעשית סוד נביעו להחיות ולרפא

        Let me point out that already on the very first page of this book, the author
    deals with the coexistence within the Torah of the divinity, of divine names, and

of amulets intended to heal, in the context of the triune powers mentioned in this passage. Similar views are found also in other discussions of this author, sometimes in the context of the Besht's view. See also Rock, *Rabbi Moses Hayyim Efraim of Sudlikov*, pp. 60–64, and see also ch. 9 nn. 3, 8 in this volume. See also Brill, "The Spiritual Worlds of a Master of Awe," pp. 27–65, especially for the sake of the passage quoted previously pp. 51–57, which duly emphasized the magical aspects in the book of R. Efrayyim; see also Idel, *Hasidism*, p. 180, and ch. 8 n. 14 in this volume. See also Garb, *Shamanic Trance in Modern Kabbalah*, pp. 91–96. For the affinity between bodily sickness and spiritual healing based on the correspondence between the human limbs and the commandments, see the explanation offered by the Besht in *In Praise of the Baal Shem Tov*, pp. 177–178. The medieval concept of the spiritual healer, which is evident in this episode, occurs many times in early Hasidic literature, especially in the writings of R. Jacob Joseph of Polonnoye, and has a long history since late antiquity and especially in the Middle Ages.

For a lengthy discussion of healing by drawing down vitality from above, resorting several times to the verb *MShKh*, see the late eighteenth-century R. Eliezer of Lysansk's book, *No'am 'Elimelekh*, fol. 57ab. For the Psalms as potentially healing, see later in this chapter the episode of the Besht's attempt to cure the Great Maggid according to *In the Praise of Baal Shem Tov*. For an interesting parallel to Torah as names instrumental in drawing down influxes, see the Great Maggid, *Maggid Devarav le-Ya'aqov*, ed. Schatz-Uffenheimer, pp. 324, 330. See also R. Ze'ev Wolf's view on the activity of the members of the Great Assembly, who established the literary structure of the prayer, in *'Or ha-Me'ir*, fol. 141d. I hope to elaborate on these issues in a study in preparation. The existence of this vision of magical healing problematizes the view of Weiss, *Studies*, pp. 182–183, who assumes that the innovation of the Great Maggid is the attribution of a magical function of the righteous! See also ch. 9 n. 9 and appendices D and F in this volume.

For one of the earliest uses of the verb in the context of drawing down powers by pronunciation of the vocables of the Tetragrammaton, see the passage of R. Jacob ben Sheshet—mid thirteenth century—discussed by Liebes, "The Power of the Word," p. 168.

7   See, e.g., in the previous chapter, the quote from *Keter Shem Tov*. See also the passage of this Hasidic author translated and discussed in Idel, *Hasidism*, p. 182, and compare also to texts discussed in Idel, pp. 71, 97, 99–100, 236. For more on the meaning of *hamshakhah* in Kabbalah and Hasidism, see Idel, pp. 71–74, and Afterman, *The Intention of Prayer in Early Kabbalah*, pp. 104–106. See also Ms. Jerusalem NUL 80 3282, fol. 94a, in which there is a phrase that reflects the earlier magical background: הוריד את השפע בהמשכה which means to cause the descent of the influx by means of hamshakhah. See also Ms. Jerusalem NUL 80 3282, fols. 82b, 89b. For an attempt to explain *hamshakhah* as just a matter of divine immanence, see Kauffman, *In All Your Ways Know Him*, pp. 130–134. On immanence see more in appendix E in this volume. This interpretation is predicated upon the assumption that immanence was a Beshtian theory that was much more dominant in his thought than I presume it was. In my opinion, as I shall suggest as follows, he did not adopt this theological approach early in his career. For an interesting use

of the verb *MShKh* in order to refer to drawing the spiritual force onto a person, see Cordovero's *'Or Yaqar*, vol. 12, p. 187. Compare also Cordovero, vol. 9, p. 55.

8   See my *Absorbing Perfections*, p. 155; *Hasidism*, p. 173; and "Your Word Stands Firm in Heaven," p. 270. See also the view found in the teachings of the Great Maggid, in *'Or ha-'Emmet*, fol. 25a; *Maggid Devarav le-Ya'aqov*, ed. Schatz-Uffenheimer, p. 236; as praying when the liturgical text is understood as having been constituted by divine names. See also ch. 9 nn. 3, 6. See also Weiss, *Studies*, p. 106. For the entire Torah as a divine name, see also R. Aharon of Zhitomir, *Toledot 'Aharon*, fol. 139a, c. For drawing down influx by means of divine names, see *Toledot 'Aharon*, fol. 96b. For its magical and Kabbalistic sources, see *Absorbing Perfections*, pp. 321–340, and "On Angels in Biblical Exegesis in Thirteenth-Century Ashkenaz," in eds. D. A. Green and L. S. Lieber, *Scriptural Exegesis, Shapes of Culture, and Religious Imagination, Essays in Honour of Michael Fishbane* (Oxford University Press, Oxford, 2009), pp. 227–230.

9   *Degel Mahaneh Efrayyim*, p. 6. Compare, especially, to the view of the Great Maggid, in *Maggid Devarav le-Ya'aqov* (Brooklyn, 2005), p. 38, no. 94, where the drawing down of the vitality to all the creatures is done by means of utterances of the Torah, which someone studies out of awe and love. See also *Maggid Devarav le-Ya'aqov*, p. 12, where miracles are performed by means of drawing down influxes, and see also the interesting discussion on p. 22, no. 53. Those are only some of the examples for a clear cut magical meaning of this verb, and they can be easily multiplied. See ch. 6 n. 10, ch 6 n 18, ch.8 n. 6, ch. 8 n. 11 in this volume for the resort to the verb *Mamshikh* in traditions attributed to the Besht.

   Compare, however, to the different opinion of Pedaya, "The Besht, R. Jacob Joseph of Polonnoye, and the Maggid of Mezeritch," pp. 55, 57, 63, 67, 71, who denies rather insistingly and categorically the existence of traditions attributed to the Besht where the drawing down of influx within letters, or drawing down in general, are mentioned, though once on p. 55, she recognizes that sometimes there are such elaborations that are associated with him. From the context of this discussion, this association seems to be considered as artificial capitalization of the Besht's disciples on their master's teachings. This assertion is not holding for the statements we have adduced previously, neither for other statements of R. Jacob Joseph in the name of the Besht, where the verb under scrutiny here indeed appears, despite her denial. Moreover, the previous discussions of the Besht containing the verb *MShKh* should be compared also to the passages where the resort to the verb *ShF'* is found. On the basis of this alleged absence, she even built up a phenomenology of the Besht's thought as representing an eminently "ascending" and "elevating" figure!

   For the problems related to this one-dimensional portrayal, what I call monotonic, which ignores some parts of the salient material, see also Idel, "Your Word Stands Firm in Heaven," pp. 269–270. On the Besht's resort to the verb *mamshikh* in other contexts see, e.g., the quote adduced in R. Jacob Joseph, *Toledot Ya'aqov Yosef*, fol. 201a, and *Keter Shem Tov*, fol. 20d:

   וזהו ענין תחיית המתים ומשיח שהוא סוד הדעת והוא סוד עה"ב. והנה ע"י מעשי האדם הממשיך על עצמו בעה"ז ע"י בינה שלו שמבין לעשות כל מעשיו בבינה ודעת וכו' ודפ"ח.

   "And the matter of resurrection of death and Messiah that is the secret of the *da'at*, it is the secret of the World-to-come. And behold, that by means of the

deeds of man he draws upon himself while in this world, by his understanding that
he understands how to do all his deeds in wisdom and knowledge etc., and the
words of the sage are gracious." See also Mondshine's edition of *Shiveḥei ha-Besht*,
pp. 244–245, and *In Praise of the Baal Shem Tov*, p. 11. See also R. Ze'ev Wolf of
Zhitomir, *'Or ha-Me'ir*, fols. 247d–248a, where the verb occurs in the context of
a quote from the Besht, but it is however difficult to establish where exactly this
quote ends. See also ch. 6 n. 18 in this volume.

For an additional interesting occurrence of the verb *MShKh* as referring to
drawing down supernal influx upon oneself, see R. Efrayyim of Sudylkov, *Degel
Maḥaneh 'Efraiyym*, p. 242. See also Idel, "Messianic Redemption and Messianism,"
nn. 149, 190, 208. I do not refer to the resort to the verb under consideration here
in the *Commentary on Psalm 107*, attributed to the Besht, since I and other scholars
do not accept this attribution. See Schatz-Uffenheimer, *Hasidism as Mysticism*, p.
356. See, e.g., Rosman, *Founder of Hasidism*, pp. 122–123, and for a more cautious
approach, Mark, *The Revealed and the Hidden Writings*, pp. 298–299.

In more general terms, Pedaya's attribution of the mystical-magical model as I
formulated it solely to the disciples of the Besht but claiming that the latter himself
is someone who was a magician but did not think in these terms is, logically speaking, highly implausible. For some of the sources of the magical view of the verb
MShKh, see more in appendices C and E.

10   *'Or ha-Me'ir*, fol. 43d:

> הנה עינינו רואות אשר יש לך אדם שעושה סגופים ומקואות ומרבה בתורה ותפלה, ועיקר
> כוונתו ומגמתו להשיג רוח הקדוש או גילוי אליהו וכדומה, וכאשר שמעתי בימי הבעש"ט זללה"ה
> היה אחד כזה שעשה סגופים והלך למקוה שישיג רוח הקודש, ואמר הבעש"ט זללה"ה בזה הלשון
> אשר בעולם התמורות משחקים עליו, והאמת כן הוא כי מה לאדם לרדוף אחר זאת ולבו חסור
> העיקר דביקות אל, שזהו תכלית העבודה לדבק במדותיו יתברך באמת ובתמים, ואחרי הדביקות
> השלימה יכול להיות שישיג כל משאלות לבו, כי ממילא נולד מזה השגת רוח הקודש וכדומה
> ממעלות המובחרות והמעולות, אמנם לא לזה ישים את לבו ורוחו ונפשו בהעבודה.

See Schatz-Uffenheimer, *Hasidism as Mysticism*, p. 200, n. 38. In some few
cases the term *attributes* is interpreted in this school as dealing with letters/sounds.
See the passage from *'Or Torah*, translated by Weiss, *Studies*, pp. 136–137 as well as
the discussions at the end of appendix A in this volume as to taking a bath as part
of a pursuit of mystical experience.

11   *In the Praise of the Baal Shem Tov*, p. 82. For the Hebrew text, though in a somewhat
different version, see ed. Rubinstein, *Shiveḥei ha-Besht*, p. 127:

> ורצה לרפאות אותו בדיבורים. ושמעתי מרבי גרשון דקהילת קודש פובליץ שהבעל-שם-
> טוב היה הולך אליו כמו שני שבועות וישב כנגדו ואמר תהלים, ואחר-כך אמר הבעל-שם-טוב
> אליו: הייתי רוצה לרפאת אותך בדיבורים כי היא רפואה קימת, ועכשו אני צריך לעסוק עמך
> ברפואות.

Compare also to an interesting parallel, where again speech could play an
important role, related to the manner in which the Besht could have been born,
discussed in my "The Besht Passed His Hand," p. 90.

For medication and the Besht, see his epistle to R. Moshe of Kutov, discussed
in Rosman, *Founder of Hasidism*, pp. 119–122. See also the interesting parallel
between this episode in the life of the Besht and the beginning of R. Efrayyim of
Sudylkov's *Degel Maḥaneh 'Efrayyim*, pp. 1–2, where the Besht is not mentioned,

and I shall elaborate elsewhere on the affinities. For the assumption that the words of the Torah may become a remedy, see the eighteenth-century passage of R. Ḥayyim Joseph David Azulai's *Devarim 'Aḥadim* as quoted in Scholem, *On the Kabbalah and its Symbolism*, p. 76. For the assumption that mystics are acquiring some extraordinary powers as part of their experiences see, e.g., Hollenback, *Mysticism: Experience, Response, and Empowerment.* On drawing down the remedy, *refu'ah*, see R. Meir ha-Levi of Apta, *'Or la-Shamayyim*, fol. 14d. For healing with words in modern Hasidism, see the material referred to by Seeman, "Ritual Efficacy," p. 478, n. 54.

For the view that the Besht cured someone by permuting the letters or the vocables of his name and thus drawing down vitality and existence see the claim of R. Israel of Ryzhin, discussed in my *Hasidism*, pp. 77–78, which is anticipated by a teaching adduced in the name of the Besht himself cited in R. Joseph of Polonnoye, *Ben Porat Yosef*, fol. 13b, and discussed by Lederberg, *Sod ha-Da'at*, pp. 153–154. About the importance of combinations of letters in early Hasidism, see also Mark, *The Revealed and the Hidden Writings*, pp. 14–17.

12   See the references found in Idel, "Models for Understanding Prayer in Early Hasidism," p. 90, n. 234. See also the Great Maggid, *Maggid Devarav le-Ya'aqov*, ed. Schatz-Uffenheimer, p. 325. Compare to Weiss's interesting expression "contemplative magic" that he uses in order to describe the Besht, *Studies*, p. 14. According to Rivka Schatz, "Contemplative prayer became the spiritual message par excellence of Hasidism." See her "Contemplative Prayer," p. 209, and *Hasidism as Mysticism*, p. 168; as well as Jacobs, *Hasidic Prayer*, pp. 18, 70–92. For more about the problems related to the scholarly overemphasis on contemplation, see chapter 13 in this volume.

10. Intensification, Contact, and Effects

1   See the important study of Immanuel Etkes, "The Place of Magic and the Masters of the Name in the Ashkenazi Society at the end of the 17th and 18th Century," *Zion*, vol. 60 (1995), pp. 69–104 (Hebrew), and his *The Besht: Magician, Mystic, and Leader*, pp. 7–45, 259–271. See also Gries, *Conduct Literature*, pp. 93–99; Zvi Mark, "Dybbuk and Devekut in the *Shivhe ha-Besht*: Toward a Phenomenology of Madness in Early Hasidism," in ed. M. Goldish, *Spirit and Spirit Possession in Judaism* (Wayne State University Press, Detroit, 2003), pp. 257–301; Yohanan Petrovsky-Shtern, "'You Will Find It in the Pharmacy,' Practical Kabbalah and Natural Medicine in the Polish-Lithuanian Commonwealth, 1690–1750," in ed. Glenn Dynner, *Holy Dissent: Jewish and Christian Mystics in Eastern Europe* (Wayne University Press, Detroit, 2011), pp. 13–54; Gedalyah Nigal, *Magic, Mysticism, and Hasidism* (Yaron Golan, Tel Aviv, 1992) (Hebrew); and Idel, *Hasidism*, pp. 290, 315, 326, 334–335; and Jonatan Meir, "Marketing Demons: Joseph Perl, Israel Baal Shem Tov, and the History of One Amulet," *Kabbalah*, vol. 28 (2012), pp. 35–66.

I have seen a lengthy manuscript circulating in Hasidic circles, found in a private collection, which includes an attribution of a magical performance of the Besht, unparalleled to what we know from other sources. However, astral magic is not represented there. This is also the case in R. Ḥayyim Vital's lengthy book of magical recipes printed recently as *Sefer ha-Pe'ulot* (N.P., 2010) (Hebrew). On this book see Gerrit Bos, "Hayyim Vital's 'Practical Kabbalah and Alchemy': A Seventeenth Century Book of Secrets," *JJTP*, vol. 4 (1994), pp. 55–112.

2   See Idel, "Performance, Intensification, and Experience in Jewish Mysticism," *Archaeus*, vol. XIII (2009), pp. 93–134, and *Kabbalah in Italy*, pp. 25–26; and Maurizio Mottolese, *The Intensification of Ritual by the Medieval Kabbalah: Mystical Approaches to Bodily Cultic Practices* (PhD diss., La Sapienza, Roma, 2014). See also the important study of Sullivan, "Sound and Senses," pp. 1–33.

3   See Idel, *Hasidism*, pp. 66–67, 158–160. On man as the "palace of God"—actually an ancient theme—see the tradition attributed to the Besht in R. Jacob Joseph of Polonnoye, *Tzafnat Pa'aneah*, fol. 84b, and without his name in R. Jacob Joseph of Polonnoye, *Ben Porat Yosef*, fols. 12a, 42b, 46b, and his *Tzafnat Pa'aneah*, fols. 49b, 95c; and *Keter Shem Tov ha-Shalem*, pp. 188–189. Interestingly enough, a contemporary of the Besht resorted to the term *heikhal* as pointing to righteous men. See R. Nathan Neta' of Sienewa, *'Olat Tamid ha-Shalem*, II, fol. 8a. See also ch. 2 n. 18, ch. 5 n. 13 in this volume. For the use of the term *Heikhal* in the context of the "spiritual force," see Cordovero, *'Or Yaqar*, vol. 4, p. 29: "we below are the palace of the supernal spiritual force."

שאנו למטה היכל אל הרוחניות העליון

and see also Cordovero, vol. 11, p. 174, where the letters/sounds are depicted as the palaces of the supernal spiritual forces. See also Azulai, *Hesed le-'Avraham*, fol. 26c, where the soul is described as the "palace of the *Shekhinah*." These themes are part of the wider and ancient view of man as the temple of God, discussed by Margolin, *The Human Temple*. In several instances divine names were conceived as palaces for the divine forces. See *Pardes Rimmonim*, XX, chap. 1, XIII, chap. 1, and appendix C in this volume.

For the role of speech in Hermeticism, see Garth Fowden, *The Egyptian Hermes* (Princeton University Press, Princeton, 1993), pp. 23–24, 81.

4   See Idel, *Absorbing Perfections*, pp. 470–481, and beside ch. 13 n. 40. in this volume. Let me mention a parable adduced in the name of the Besht as to the loss of one of the crowns the ancient Israelites had: the crown of the na'aseh, which means in the parable reading books in order to know what to do, was lost, and what remained is the crown of nishma', we shall listen, which means to go to the righteous in order to listen to their sermons and know what to do. See *'Imrei Tzaddiqim*, ed. Meir Bornstein of Radom (Warsau, 1896), fol. 18b. According to the explanation offered to the parable, still in the name of the Besht, "when he learns from books . . . there is no power to stir him." I have my great doubts if the entire discussion is indeed Beshtian, since it assumes someone's visit to the righteous as if a main religious activity, but perhaps part of it may be nevertheless related to the Besht. Indeed, most of the material adduced in this passage is found in R. Nahman of Braslav's *Liqqutei Moharan*, I, no. 120, without however, mentioning the name of his great grandfather. The entire issue deserves a special analysis, which should attempt at seeing whether it is possible to validate the existence by now of only a hypothetical Beshtian discussion, which was probably used by the great grandson on the one hand, and by the story as preserved in the name of the Besht in *'Imrei Tzaddiqim* and its source, on the other hand.

5   On the question of ritual efficacy in Kabbalah and Hasidism, see Idel, *Enchanted Chains*, pp. 25, 27, 34, 59, 65, 73, 79, 162, 220, and Seeman, "Ritual Efficacy," *passim*, especially p. 466, n. 4.

6   See Rosman, *The Founder of Hasidism*, and Gries, *The Hebrew Book*, pp. 245–284.

7   See Idel, *Hasidism*, pp. 156–162 and "Your Word Stands Firm in Heaven," pp. 257–258 and n. 161. For the reverberation of astro-magic in eighteenth-century Eastern Europe see, e.g., the passage of Solomon Maimon, cited in *Hasidism*, p. 73. See also appendices C, D and E in this volume.

8   See, e .g., the version of the palace parable in *Ben Porat Yosef*, fol. 70c; *Keter Shem Tov ha-Shalem*, p. 31, par. 51b; and the view of the Besht's grandson, R. Efrayyim of Sudylkov, translated in Lamm, *The Religious Thought of Hasidism*, pp. 31–32. See also Lamm, p. 27, Lederberg, *Sod ha-Da'at*, pp. 188–189, ch. 10 n. 10 in this volume.

9   See ch. 7 n. 12. For an interesting example of "linguistic immanence," see the lengthy discussion of R. Aharon of Zhitomir, *Toledot 'Aharon*, fol. 139ab. For "dispersed linguistic immanence" in early Hasidism, see Kauffman, *In All Your Ways Know Him*, pp. 511–512. See also my *Kabbalah in Italy*, pp. 333–335, and Azulai's *'Or ha-Hammah*, III, fol. 1a. For a combination of linguistic immanence with the second and the third models of the Besht, without however, mentioning him, see the synthesis of R. Menahem Nahum of Chernobyl, *Me'or 'Einayyim*, pp. 284–285, and Kauffman, *In All Your Ways Know Him*, pp. 307–308. See also appendix E in this volume.

10   For different analyses of the various versions of this parable and its interpretations in the Besht's family, see Scholem, *The Messianic Idea*, pp. 224–225; Green, "Discovery and Retreat," pp. 107–110; my *Ben*, pp. 543–559; and Kauffman, *In All Your Ways Know Him*, pp. 102–117. See also ch.10 n. 8 in this volume. I hope to return to the significance of this parable in the context of another one used by the Besht in a future, more detailed study. See, meanwhile, Gries, *The Hebrew Book*, p. 269, and n. 69.

11   In my opinion, traditions that the grandson describes as received directly from his grandfather, opening with the verb *shama'ti*, I heard, reflect the views of the later Besht. This does not mean that in his books there are not many elements that reflect the earlier stages of the Besht's thought, with which he was acquainted from the printed books of R. Jacob Joseph of Polonnoye. Let me point out that a very short version of the parable is found again at the end of *Ben Porat Yosef*, fol. 99b, in the context of a response to a philosopher, namely in a more general context of omnipresence, without however, any reference to a ritual. See also appendix E in this volume.

12   See his *The Origin and Meaning of Hasidism*, pp. 167, 170–171; and Schatz-Uffenheimer, *Hasidism as Mysticism*, pp. 30–31; Idel, *Enchanted Chains*, pp. 63-64; *Hasidism*, p. 179, n. 43; and Kauffman, *In All Your Ways Know Him*, pp. 65–162, 395–523.

13   For this distinction concerning the views and the sources of *devequt* in Kabbalah and Hasidism, see Idel, *Kabbalah: New Perspectives*, pp. 38–46; *Hasidism*, pp.

86–89; and n. 2 in this volume. For astro-magic and Hermeticism in Judaism in general and especially in Kabbalah, see Pines, "Le *Sefer ha-Tamar* et les *Maggidim* des Kabbalists," pp. 333–363, and his "On the Term *Ruḥaniyyut* and Its Sources," pp. 511–540; Schwartz, *Studies on Astral Magic*; Fabrizio Lelli, "Le Version Ebraiche di un Testo Ermetico: Il *Sefer Ha-Levanah*," *Henoch*, 12 (1990), pp. 147–164; Idel, "The Magical and Neoplatonic Interpretations," pp. 192–193, 199, 202–205; Idel, "Hermeticism and Judaism," in eds. I. Merkel and A. Debus, *Hermeticism and the Renaissance* (Cranbury, NJ, 1988), pp. 59–76; Idel, "Hermeticism and Kabbalah," in eds. P. Lucentini, I. Parri, and V. P. Compagni, *Hermeticism from Late Antiquity to Humanism* (Brespols, 2004), pp. 389–408; Idel, "An Astral-Magical Pneumatic Anthropoid," *Incognita*, 2 (1991), pp. 12–14; and Idel, "Astral Dreams in Judaism: Twelfth to Fourteenth Centuries," in eds. D. Shulman and G. G. Stroumsa, *Dream Cultures, Explorations in the Comparative History of Dreaming* (Oxford University Press, New York, 1999), pp. 235–250.

The theory of drawing down the supernal pneuma by means of incantations is quite early. See Hans Lewy, *Chaldaean Oracles and Theurgy*, ed. M. Tardieu (Vrin, Paris, 1978), p. 47. See also ch. 11 n. 9 in this volume.

For my view as to the primacy of the Muslim sources for understanding many phases of Jewish mysticism, including Hasidism, see my "Mystique juive et pensèe musulmane," *Perspectives*, no. 9 (2002), pp. 138–157; Idel, *Studies in Ecstatic Kabbalah*; Idel, *Hasidism, passim*; Idel, "Orienting, Orientalizing, or Disorienting the Study of Kabbalah: 'An Almost Absolutely Unique' Case of Occidentalism," *Kabbalah*, vol. 2 (1997), pp. 13–48.

14 See my "Female Beauty," p. 332. See also Idel, *Hasidism*, p. 378–379, n. 40; ch. 3 n. 7, ch. 4 n. 6, ch. 6 n. 15 in this volume; and Azulai's *'Or ha-Ḥammah*, II, fol. 246a. I assume that this is an impact of Cordovero's view. See also Margolin, *The Human Temple*, p. 32 and n. 118. It should be mentioned that the omnipresence of the vitality and light of the Infinite is elaborated in a Cordoverian passage quoted in Azulai's *Ḥesed le-'Avraham*, fol. 2cd.

For a brave effort to continue Scholem's thesis that connected Hasidism so firmly to the Lurianic-Sabbatean forms of Kabbalah, marginalizing both Cordovero's seminal contributions and the magical aspects of this movement, see Rachel Elior, "Hasidism—Historical Continuity and Spiritual Change," in eds. J. Dan and P. Schaefer, *Gershom Scholem's Major Trends in Jewish Mysticism, 50 Years Later* (JCB Mohr, Tuebingen, 1993), pp. 303–323. See especially ch. 3 n. 7 and appendix B in this volume. On omnipresence or immanence in early Hasidism, see Etkes, *The Besht: Magician, Mystic, and Leader*, pp. 135–138; Idel, *Hasidism*, pp. 107–111; *Kabbalah and Eros*, p. 298, n. 38; and Kauffman, *In All Your Ways Know Him, passim*.

15 For discussions of these early Hasidic views, see Idel, "Models of Understanding Prayer in Early Hasidism," p. 51, "Prayer, Ecstasy, and Alien Thoughts," pp. 87–93, and "Your Word Stands Firm in Heaven," pp. 250–252, 268–269.

16 See Gershom Scholem, "Martin Buber's Interpretation of Hasidism," in his *The Messianic Idea*, pp. 228–250, especially pp. 240–241. On this controversy in general,

there is a vast scholarly literature. See the bibliography I compiled in my *Old Worlds, New Mirrors*, pp. 205–216, and in ch. 15 n. 14 in this volume.

17 See e.g., Schatz-Uffenheimer, *Hasidism as Mysticism*, pp. 43, 111–143, and beside n. 3 and in ch. 8 n. 11 in this volume. Especially telling is her formulation on p. 43: "Hasidism was the first mystical movement in Judaism to create a true conflict with action." This is the case also of Joseph Weiss's preference for *via passiva*. See his *Studies*, pp. 67–94. For Weiss's use of the term "contemplation" also in Hebrew, see his important early essay "The Beginning of the Emergence of the Hasidic Path," *Zion*, p. 61. The term "contemplation" recurs in many instances in the context of prayer in Jacobs, *Hasidic Prayer*, pp. 70–92, and in Arthur I. Green's presentation of the thought of R. Menahem Nahum of Chernobyl. See his *Menahem Nahum of Chernobyl, Upright Practices*, pp. 17, 38–39, 203–204, 258. I cannot enter here into a more elaborated discussion of the nexus between orality and the non-symbolic approach. See, meanwhile, Ong, *The Presence of the Word*, p. 323, and James R. Russel, "Sounds as Symbol: The Case in Pagan and Christian Armenian Poetics," in his *Armenian and Iranian Studies* (Harvard University Press, Cambridge, MA, 2004), pp. 713–726.

The written form of language was privileged by Scholem as part of his pan-symbolic approach to mysticism in general, whereas human voice has been given only a very modest role in what he considered to be the mystical phase of religion, as he envisioned it. I hope to return to this issue in a separate study. For Scholem's drastic reduction of the role of the divine voice in the Sinaitic revelation as part of his understanding of the categories of revelation and tradition in Hasidism, see Idel, *Old Worlds, New Mirrors*, pp. 119–125, and "Transfers of Categories," pp. 15–43, where I discussed an example of reading a hypothetical Hasidic text against its meaning, which assumes a vocal activity. See also ch. 1 n. 22 and ch. 11 n. 14 and in appendix B in this volume.

18 See, especially, my "Prayer, Ecstasy, and Alien Thoughts," *passim*.

19 Idel, "Prayer, Ecstasy, and Alien Thoughts," pp. 87–93, and for the analysis of some of the Beshtian traditions to this effect, see Kauffman, *In All Your Ways Know Him*, pp. 351–355.

20 A quite interesting attempt to describe three stages in the development of the Besht's theory of *devequt* in general, without in fact mentioning the cleaving to sounds, is found in Lamm, *The Religious Thought of Hasidism*, pp. 136–137. Methodologically speaking this is indeed a very laudable effort, but its proponent is reluctant to take in consideration the magical aspects of the Besht's praxis and thought and their reverberations in Hasidic literature.

21 See also the pertinent remarks of Rosman, *Founder of Hasidism*, pp. 27, 34–36, 38–39, 173–174.

22 This tendency is found, in one way or another, in the conceptualization of Martin Buber, who prefers to speak about the "message of Hasidism" in his *The Origin and Meaning of Hasidism*, pp. 111, 127, though he was much less concerned with theology but regarded Hasidism as a special way of religious life. See also Buber, p. 70, where he speaks about a "simple and united" voice that can be reconstructed

from the Besht's teachings. On the omnipresence of God as the defining "key-note" of the Besht's thought see, e.g., Schechter, "The Chassidism," p. 167, and Simon Dubnow, *Toledot ha-Hasidut* (Devir, Tel Aviv, 1966), p. 53. See also Green, *Menahem Nahum of Chernobyl, Upright Practices, The Light of the Eyes*, p. 175, n. 3; Elior, *The Mystical Origins of Hasidism*, pp. 37–38; and Moshe Hallamish, "The Teachings of R. Menahem Mendel of Vitebsk," ed. A. Rapoport-Albert, *Hasidism Reappraised* (Littman Library, London, Portland, 1996), p. 268. See also in n. 1 in this volume Scholem's claim that the Besht has used a certain term in a "precise and technical sense." Also Israel Zinberg's introduction to J. Opatoshu, *Fun Unsere Oitzer, Mayses fun Baal Shem Tov* ("Cico" Bicher Farlag, New York, 1957), p. 20 (Yiddisch), speaks about the Besht's "system" as based upon the Zoharic assumption that the supernal and the terrestrial worlds can be brought together; see Etkes, *The Besht: Magician, Mystic, and Leader*, pp. 151, 195, who speaks about "a path" or "a mode of worhip" and, on p. 152, about a message.

23   See note 1 in this volume. Let me point out that this assumption as to the existence of a single message may have something to do with Weiss's perception of mysticism as a monolithic religious modality in general including Jewish mysticism, see his *Studies*, pp. 69–71, characterized by the alleged omnipresence of moments of passivity in mysticism as a whole. This essentialist approach, in which the Besht's approach was also included, cf. Weiss, pp. 74–76, ignores the activist elements in the Besht's tradition as discussed previously, especially the recurrent instructions to put all the strength within the recitation. See however, Weiss, p. 132, where he describes what he considers being a "paradoxical" situation related to the Besht. See n. 21 in this volume. *En passant*, I do not know what the source is of the interesting phrase "atomization of devequt," which Lamm attributes to Weiss, in *The Religious Thought of Hasidism*, p. 377, n. 12. More on scholars' claims as to the presence of a message in Hasidism see Idel, "Early Hasidism and Altaic Tribes," pp. 31–32.

24   See ch. 9 n. 12 in this volume.

25   See, respectively, *Hasidism as Mysticism*, and *Hasidic Prayer*, pp. 31–32. Their formulations follow basically Scholem. See the quotes of his statements in ch. 1 nn. 1 and 3 in this volume. For the assumption that there is a pietistic "ideal" related to what is described as contemplation, asceticism, and letters, see Wolfson, "Immanuel Frommann," p. 195.

26   See her "The Besht, R. Jacob Joseph of Polonnoye, and the Maggid of Mezeritch" and also "Two Types of Ecstatic Experience in Hasidism," pp. 95–98, 105–108, where another "quintessential" principle of Hasidism *par excellence* is proposed: the centrality of the personality, which is not lost in the ecstatic experience, and also her review of Etkes's Hebrew version of his book, in *Zion*, vol. 70 (2005), p. 260 (Hebrew). In some few cases she also mentions the importance of speech in the Besht. See her "The Besht, R. Jacob Joseph of Polonnoye, and the Maggid of Mezeritch," p. 30. See also her *Vision and Speech*, p. 99. Compare, however, to ch. 9 nn. 9, 12 in this volume. See also Nigal, *The Besht: Legends, Apologetics, and Reality*, pp. 39–41.

27   On this issue see Idel, "The Land of Divine Vitality," pp. 256–259.

28 I cannot enter again here into the important methodological questions raised by
    Rosman, *The Founder of Hasidism*, as to the reliability of Beshtian traditions, since
    I addressed some of them in other studies of mine. See, e.g., "The Besht as Prophet
    and Talismanic Magician." Here we have just another example as to the many
    passages adduced in the name of the Besht that reinforce each other's content and
    allow the drawing of a picture that seems to me historically and phenomenologi-
    cally more plausible. This is the answer that someone can offer to some of Rosman's
    quandaries regarding the questions of the authenticity of the diverse material
    reported in the name of the Besht: by widening the compass of the sources which
    report traditions in the name of the Besht, we can ascertain better than earlier the
    eventual convergences between these traditions, without subscribing, however, to
    a one-dimensional approach to his thought that attempts to harmonize between
    them.

29 See Idel, *Hasidism*, pp. 69, 136, 218–221, 224. See also Jay, *Downcast Eyes*, pp. 36–41.
    I hope to return elsewhere at length to the issue of what is the best background for
    the understanding the Besht, Cordoverian Kabbalistic magic, or the concept of
    quietism. See, for the time being, appendices B–F in this volume.

30 Idel, *Hasidism*, pp. 41, 206. As I mentioned from time to time previously, the ques-
    tion of the Besht's sources has been addressed here in a tangent manner, since
    some of the sources had already been discussed elsewhere, especially in my book
    on *Hasidism*, In appendices B and C, and some others will be discussed on other
    occasions.

11. Between Letters' Shapes and Their Sounds

1   *In the Praise of the Baal Shem Tov*, p. 198.

2   See Idel, "Prayer, Ecstasy, and Alien Thoughts," p. 58, n. 3, and the passage from
    Liqqutim Yeqarim, translated and discussed in Schatz-Uffenheimer, *Hasidism as
    Mysticism*, p. 245. See also a text to this effect in appendix A of this volume.

3   See his *Studies*, p. 104.

4   Idel, *The Mystical Experience in Abraham Abulafia*, pp. 83–95. For concentration in
    Yoga techniques dealing with sounds, see Eliade, *Yoga*, p. 133, where he assesses:
    "obtaining ecstasy through concentration on sounds," and Beck, *Sonic Theology*, p.
    100.

5   Idel, *The Mystical Experience in Abraham Abulafia*, pp. 83–86; Idel, *Hasidism*, pp.
    35, 265, n. 13; and Idel, *Absorbing Perfections*, pp. 470–481. That does not mean that
    Abulafia, who was a prolific author, refrained from disseminating his Kabbalah in
    an oral manner, in "every city and market" as he once formulated it, to both Jews
    and Christians. In both cases we may speak about a popularization of Kabbalah by
    means of intense oral dissemination, done by resorting to psychological interpreta-
    tions of theosophical terms. For some more detail of this trend of understanding
    elements found in the theosophical Kabbalah, see Idel, *Hasidism*, pp. 227–238, and
    for the Besht see especially pp. 235–236. See also the text translated around ch. 6 n.
    15 in this volume.

6   See Idel, "On Prophecy and Early Hasidism," pp. 65–70. See also my *Hasidism*, pp. 53–65.

7   See my study "R. Menahem Mendel of Shklov and R. Avraham Abulafia," in eds. M. Hallamish, Y. Rivlin, and R. Shuhat, *The Vilna Gaon, and his Disciples* (Bar Ilan University Press, Ramat Gan, 2003), pp. 173–183 (Hebrew); Bezalel Naor, "The Song of Songs, Abulafia and the Alter Rebbe," *Jewish Review*, April–May (1990), pp. 10–11; and Naor, "*Hotam Bolet Hotam Shoqe'a*, in the Teaching of Abraham Abulafia and the Doctrine of Habad," *Sinai*, vol. 107 (1991), pp. 54–57 (Hebrew); and in more general terms, see Idel, *Hasidism*, pp. 137–140.

8   For this complex approach to *devequt* in Hasidism as reflecting a synthesis, see Idel, *Kabbalah: New Perspectives*, p. 58.

9   See Idel, *The Mystical Experience in Abraham Abulafia*, pp. 77–83. For the few talismanic elements in Abulafia, which is an interesting component that still needs a special study, see meanwhile, Idel, *Kabbalah: New Perspectives*, pp. 169–170, and *Hasidism*, p. 302, n. 322. For the *Zohar* see especially I, fols. 43a, 100ab, II, fol. 69a. See also Idel, *Hasidism*, pp. 97–98, and Yehudah Liebes, *The Cult of the Dawn, the Attitude of the Zohar toward Idolatry* (Carmel, Jerusalem, 2011) (Hebrew), and in more general terms, Dorit Cohen-Aloro, *Magic and Sorcery in the Zohar* (PhD Thesis, Hebrew University, Jerusalem, 1989) (Hebrew). See also ch. 10 n. 13 in this volume.

10 See Idel, *Studies in Ecstatic Kabbalah*, pp. 103–112. See also Ong, *The Presence of the Word*, p. 310.

11 See Schatz-Uffenheimer, *Hasidism as Mysticism*, pp. 243–244, and Altshuler, *The Messianic Secret of Hasidism*, pp. 338–343. This does not mean that R. Nahman of Kosov was not aware of the primacy of the community for praying together, but that he did not create such a community despite his wandering from one place to another in order to teach people how to pray. See Heschel, *The Circle of the Baal Shem Tov*, pp. 134–135.

12 See, especially, the recent approach of Pedaya, "The Besht, R. Jacob Joseph of Polonnoye, and the Maggid of Mezeritch." On the significant difference between clientele and a religious community in the context of different types of magician-figures, see my remarks in *Hasidism*, pp. 212–215. On an instance when the Besht sees images of figures who reveal to him in oral manner information as to how to answer a question of one of his acquaintances, see *In Praise of the Baal Shem Tov*, pp. 136–137. On magic and community see Gustav Mensching's interesting remark on the relationship between magic and communal life as part of a coherent vision of reality in his *Structures and Patterns of Religion*, p. 10.

13 Gershom Scholem, "Mysticism and Society," *Diogenes*, vol. 58 (1967), pp. 17–19, and following him, Schatz-Uffenheimer, *Hasidism as Mysticism*, p. 244. See also ch. 9 n. 11 in this volume. For instructions for loud prayer, see R. Jacob Joseph of Polonnoye, *Toledot Ya'aqov Yosef*, fols. 6a and 28b. For shouting during prayer see the early testimony of R. Ze'ev Wolf of Zhitomir, *'Or ha-Me'ir*, fol. 68d—a phenomenon that he actually criticizes—as translated in Jacobs, *Hasidic Prayer*, p. 63:

We can see for ourselves that many are to be found who, at the time of Torah study or prayer, raise their voices too much so that they are heard at a distance. They smite palm to palm and make similar gestures with their limbs and dance on their feet as is the custom. Many of them are ignoramuses who imagine that the main idea of prayer depends on this. The truth is otherwise.

See also Idel, *Hasidism*, p. 168. This is a fine example of what I consider to be a domestication of early Hasidism toward the end of the eighteenth century. Nevertheless, the very loud type of prayer has been preserved in the Karlin-Stolin Hasidic sect to this day in Jerusalem. See also Lederberg, *Sod ha-Da'at*, pp. 189–190.

14   *In Praise of the Baal Shem Tov*, p. 51. Compare also to Etkes, *The Besht: Magician, Mystic, and Leader*, pp. 126–127. See also the other, more characterological differences between the Besht and this disciple of his, as well as some doctrinal divergences that were pointed out by Pedaya, "The Besht, R. Jacob Joseph of Polonnoye, and the Maggid of Mezeritch," especially pp. 30–32.

15   See also Scholem, *Major Trends in Jewish Mysticism*, p. 348; Weiss, *Studies*, p. 122, n. 50; Idel, "Female Beauty," pp. 317–334; and Mark, *Mysticism and Madness*. See also Piekarz, *Between Ideology and Reality*, pp. 231–264. Compare to the belated critique of Scholem's view in Schatz-Uffenheimer, *Hasidism as Mysticism*, pp. 35, 51. See also ch. 13 n. 33 in this volume. It should be mentioned that already in the book of the *Zohar*, III, fol. 191a, shouting is conceived to have some form of theurgical valence. See Idel, *Enchanted Chains*, pp. 207–208.

16   For the high status of silence in comparison to voice according to Scholem's understanding of religion, see his very early statement in one of his youth theses no. 58: "Teaching is transmitted in silence—not by silence." Though this may indeed fit a Zen type of teaching, I hardly see it to be pertinent for the activity of the Besht as formulated in the traditions about him, though his great grandson, R. Nahman of Braslav, whose impact on Scholem's own theological thought was significant, would adopt the importance of silence. In the teachings that are reported in the name of the Besht there is, to the best of my knowledge, only one teaching that speaks about performing a *Yihud* by silence in the *Testament of the Besht*, and from there it was copied in R. Aharon Perlov of Apta, *'Or ha-Ganuz la-Tzaddiqim*, ed. Warsau, fol. 37b. See also nn. 22, 153, and Seeman, "Ritual Efficacy," p. 496, n. 124. See also the assumption that at the beginning of the process of emanation, there is a stage where the early Kabbalists assumed the necessity of what he calls a "contemplation without language" or "mute contemplation." Cf., Scholem, *Origins of the Kabbalah*, p. 280, and his "The Name of God and the Linguistic Theory of the Kabbalah," pp. 167–168. On contemplation see also chap. 13 in this volume. On silence as being consonant with contemplation, see Weiss, *Studies*, pp. 131–132. On R. Nahman of Braslav on silence, see Yehuda Liebes, "Nahman of Braslav and Ludwig Wittgenstein," *Dimmui*, vol. 19 (2001), pp. 10–13 (Hebrew). See also Moshe Hallamish, "On Silence in Kabbalah and Hasidism," in eds. M. Hallamish and A. Kasher, *Religion and Language: Essays in General and Jewish Philosophy* (Tel Aviv, 1982), pp. 79–90 (Hebrew). On silence in Christianity see Breck, *La puissance de la parole*, pp. 13–14. See, especially, Breck, p. 14 for the connection between silence

and contemplation. For silence and the ancient Temple cult, see Israel Knohl, *The Sanctuary of Silence, The Priestly Torah, and the Holiness School* (Fortress Press, Minneapolis, 1995), and Knohl, "Between Voice and Silence: The Relationship between Prayer and Temple Cult," JBL, vol. 115 (1996), pp. 17–30.

17   *In Praise of the Baal Shem Tov*, p. 83, and Idel, *Hasidism*, pp. 172–174, 353, n. 8; Idel, *Absorbing Perfections*, pp. 182–183; and Etkes, *The Besht: Magician, Mystic, and Leader*, pp. 182–183.

12. The Apotheosis of Speech and the Complexity of the Besht's Thought

1   *In Praise of the Baal Shem Tov*, pp. 83–84. See also the Great Maggid's text translated in Idel, *Hasidism*, pp. 167–168, and also Sullivan, "Sound and Senses," pp. 24–26.

2   See, e.g., the view of the Great Maggid and his followers that sometimes prefer the worship by means of utterances over that done by means of thought. Cf., the collection of texts translated and discussed in Idel, *Hasidism*, pp. 118–120. According to their view that fits that of the Besht, only the righteous, namely the *tzaddiq*, is capable to draw down influxes. In my opinion, some of the complexities found in the Besht's teachings reverberated in the writings of his disciples not only because they have preserved his diverse teachings, but also because they themselves were complex personalities.

For the dominance of the oral performance over the sight in some forms of Kabbalah, see already my "Reification of Language in Jewish Mysticism," pp. 61–63. See also the view of Eugen Rosenstock-Huessy to the effect that "Experiences of the first order, of the first rank, are never realized through the eye," as discussed by Ong, *The Presence of the Word*, p. 167, and Martin Heidegger's critique of the primacy of pictures in the modern world, as stemming from ancient Greek philosophical sources, as discussed by Christopher Fynsk, *Language & Relation . . . that there is language* (Stanford University Press, Stanford, 1996), pp. 17–134, and Jay, *Downcast Eyes*, pp. 269–275. However, Heidegger was concerned more with hearing versus seeing, than with speech versus vision. See however, ch. 10 n. 13 in this volume. For more on these issues, see chap. 13 in this volume.

3   See Buber, *The Origin and Meaning of Hasidism*, pp. 245–254.

4   See Yehuda Liebes, *Studies in the Zohar* (SUNY Press, Albany, 1993), and his "New Directions in the Study of Kabbalah," *Pe'amim*, vol. 50 (1992), pp. 150–170 (Hebrew).

5   See Rapoport-Albert, "God and the Tzaddiq," and appendix F in this volume.

6   Let me point out that though early Hasidic literature as a whole was relatively not so much interested in astronomy and astrology in the strict sense of these terms, and does not mention specific examples of non-Kabbalistic astro-magic as found in the Middle Ages and the Renaissance, the situation is different in the book of one of the earliest disciples of the Besht, R. Arieh Leib Galiner, the admonisher of Polonnoye. See, e.g., in *Qol 'Arieh*, fols. 3b–d, 4b, 9a, 10d, 11a, 52c, and in a quote

of the Besht adduced in this book, *Qol 'Arieh*, fol. 6b, as well as in the different writings of R. Nahman of Braslav, where speech-acts and shouting reached another apotheotic moment. I hope to deal with this issue again in more detail elsewhere. See, meanwhile, the material adduced in Idel, *Hasidism*, pp. 75–81. See also the pertinent material referred to in ch. 9 n. 3, ch. 10 n. 7 in this volume. For the phenomenon of the same author's quoting anonymously a statement that was adduced elsewhere in the name of the Besht, see Idel, "Models of Understanding Prayer in Early Hasidism," pp. 105–106, n. 264.

7   See Dresner, *The Zaddik*, pp. 125–128, and Idel, *Hasidism*, pp. 189–207. As we know, the specific interpretation of the Rabbinic saying about R. Hanina ben Dossa, which has been mentioned in ch. 9 n. 9 in this volume, is a Cordoverian astro-magical interpretation of the Talmudic dictum concerning the late antiquity thaumaturgic figure active in the Galilee, which recurs in different forms in the writings of those who followed Cordovero and in the books of R. Jacob Joseph, and it became a major proof-text for the subsequent theory of *tzaddiq* in Hasidism as the leader that supplies sustenance to the community. See also Arthur Y. Green, "Typologies of Leadership and the Hasidic *Zaddiq*," in ed. A. Green, Jewish Spirituality, vol. 2, p. 131; Green, "The *Zaddiq* as *Axis Mundi*," pp. 328–347; Green, "Around the Maggid's Table"; Margolin, *The Human Temple*, pp. 385–386; Piekarz, *Between Ideology and Reality*, pp. 174–175; as well as in appendix E in this volume.

      See also Scholem, *On the Mystical Shape of the Godhead*, pp. 88–139; Dresner, *The Zaddik*; Rapoport-Albert, "God and the Zaddik"; Green, "Typologies of Leadership and the Hasidic Zaddiq," pp. 127–156; Azriel Shohat, "Ha-Tzaddiq in the Hasidic Doctrine," in *Yaacob Gil Jubilee Volume* (Jerusalem, 1979), pp. 299–306 (Hebrew); Jacobs, *Their Heads in Heaven*, pp. 73–89, 160–169; Idel, *Ascensions on High*, pp. 143–166; Idel, *Ben*, pp. 534–537; or Idel, "The Tsaddik and His Soul's Sparks."

8   See, e.g., R. Barukh of Miedzibush, *Butzina' di-Nehora'*, no pagination, in a quote in the name of the Besht which describes the righteous as a gate to heaven, and that all should believe in the righteous as such, and another quote in the same context in the name of his brother, R. Efrayyim of Sudylkov, who adds to the metaphor of gate also the view of the *tzaddiq* as a door.

9   See Dresner, *The Zaddik*, and Idel, *Hasidism*, p. 345, n. 88.

10   On the approach referring to the panorama of a wider range of Jewish sources that should be preferred over the unilinear Scholemian reading of the history of Jewish mysticism that alleged it to be free of cross-currents, as indispensable for a better understanding of Hasidism, see Idel, *Hasidism*, pp. 9–15; Pedaya, "The Besht, R. Jacob Joseph of Polonnoye, and the Maggid of Mezeritch," pp. 35–45; and for the non-Jewish elements, see Igor Tourov, "Hasidism and Christianity of the Eastern Territory of the Polish-Lithuanian Commonwealth: Possible Contacts and Mutual Influences," Kabbalah, vol. 10 (2004), pp. 73–105; as well as Rosman, *Founder of Hasidism*, p. 58; Idel, *Ben*, pp. 544–545; and my study "R. Israel Ba'al Shem Tov 'In the State of Walachia,'" where I proposed affinities between the Besht and Neo-hesychasm, including the possible resonance of the centrality of prayer in the two forms of mysticism. See also ch. 4 n. 3 in this volume. Let me point out that my

panoramic approach is not intended to offer an alternative to a historical approach, as some scholars mistakenly claim, but to a simplistic historicist one. See Etkes, *The Besht: Magician, Mystic, and Leader*, p. 119.

11   See, especially, the manner in which teachings of the Besht, which were cited in R. Jacob Joseph's *Toledot Ya'aqov Yosef,* have been copied anonymously in the anthological compilation *Sefer Darkhei Tzedeq*. On this book and its Hasidic sources, especially the Beshtian teachings quoted anonymously, see the detailed analysis in Gries, *Conduct Literature*, pp. 322–353. As mentioned previously, as late as the early nineteenth century, when R. Aharon of Zhitomir wrote his *Toledot 'Aharon*, the Beshtian approach regarding the role and the nature of the ritual speeches is quite evident in many of his discussions that have been referred to in many notes in this volume. This is also the case with many discussions of R. Aharon Perlov of Apta, in his own writings. I decided to resort many times to their views, as they exemplify the strong impact of the linguistic type of mysticism of the Besht, even two generations after his death. See, e.g., the passage of the latter author translated in my *Enchanted Chains*, pp. 155–156 and, in a different context, appendix A in this volume.

12   For an illuminating passage portraying the greatness of the Besht, combined with the emphasis on the fact that his students went in different directions, see a late Hasidic text adduced by Ada Rapoport-Albert, "The Hasidism after 1772: Structural Continuity and Change," in Hasidism Reappraised, ed. Rapoport-Albert, p. 80.

13. On Contemplation, Symbolism, and Scholarship of Jewish Mysticism

1   For Plato's theory see A. J. Festugiere, *Contemplation et vie contemplative selon Platon* (J. Vrin, Paris, 1950); and for Neoplatonic forms of contemplation, see Bernard McGinn, *Foundations of Mysticism* (Crossroad, New York, 1991), pp. 23–61, and David Winston, "Philo and the Contemplative Life," ed. Arthur Green, *Jewish Spirituality* (Crossroad, New York, 1986), vol. I, pp. 198–231. For several sustained discussions of later Christian understandings of contemplation see, e.g., McGinn, *The Growth of Mysticism* (Crossroad, New York, 1994), especially 50–79, 345–347; Cuthbert Butler, *Western Mysticism: The Teachings of Saints Augustine, Gregory, and Bernard on Contemplation and the Contemplative Life: Neglected Chapters in the History of Religion* (Dutton, New York, 1923); Friedrich Heiler, *Prayer*, tr. S. McComb (Oxford University Press, Oxford, 1932), pp. 184–190; Heiler, "Contemplation in Christian Mysticism," in ed. J. Campbell, *Spiritual Disciplines* (Princeton University Press, Princeton, 1960), pp. 186–238, especially on p. 221: "Christianity is a contemplative religion in the full sense of the word"; or Breck, *La puissance de la parole*, p. 113, n. 25. See also Hollenback, *Mysticism, Experience, Response, and Empowerment*, pp. 535–536; Breck, *La puissance de la parole*, pp. 92–113; and see more recently William Harmless, SJ, *Mystics* (Oxford University Press, New York, 2008), *passim*. For the nexus between contemplation and stasis, see Ernst Cassirer, *The Philosophy of Symbolic Forms* (Yale University Press, New Haven, 1971), vol. 2, pp. 104–105, discussed in my *Ascensions on High*, pp. 122–123.

For some remarks on contemplation in Kabbalah and Hasidism, see Scholem, *Major Trends in Jewish Mysticism*, pp. 328–329; Elior, *The Paradoxical Ascent to God*, *passim*; Idel, *Absorbing Perfections*, pp. 555–556, n. 126; *Ascensions on High*, *passim*; Margolin, *The Human Temple*, pp. 193–198; the introduction of Louis Jacobs, *On Ecstasy, A Tract by Dobh Baer of Lubavitch* (Rossel Books, 1963); or Green, *Menahem Nahum of Chernobyl, Upright Practices*, pp. 17, 38–39, 203–204, 258. See also ch. 8 n. 11 in this volume.

2   He refers here to his article on *devequt* that we have discussed at the beginning of this study, see n. 1. In this article he wrote also as follows: "*Devekut* is clearly a contemplative value without Messianic implications and can be realized everywhere and at any time." See *The Messianic Idea*, p. 185. See also *The Messianic Idea*, p. 216 for a similar statement; and the Hebrew formulation of this view as "inner contemplation" in his description of *devequt* in the thought of the Great Maggid in *Devarim be-Go* ('Am 'Oved, Tel Aviv, 1976), p. 340 (Hebrew); and now in *ha-Shalav ha-'Aharon*, p. 249; and especially in his critique of Buber, reprinted in *The Messianic Idea*, pp. 238–239. Compare also to Krassen, *Uniter of Heaven and Earth*, p. 82. See also Idel, *Messianic Mystics*, pp. 279–280. In any case, Abraham Abulafia's approach to *devequt* does have redemptive and messianic implications. See, e.g., his *Mafteah ha-Tokhehot*, ed. A. Gross (Jerusalem, 2001), p. 78.

3   *On the Mystical Shape of the Godhead*, p. 216. Emphases added. See also his "Sin and Punishment: Some Remarks Concerning Biblical and Rabbinical Ethics," in eds. J. Kitagawa and C. Long, *Myth and Symbols, Studies in Honor of Mircea Eliade* (Chicago, 1969), pp. 175–176. See the concept of "active contemplation" attributed by Scholem, in his *On the Kabbalah and Its Symbolism*, p. 18, correctly in my opinion, to Habad meditation. See also ch. 13 n. 1 in this volume. The distinction between active contemplation, conceived to be lower, and passive contemplation, conceived of as higher, is found in Christian mysticism. For another example of the combination of contemplation with what is called "aspiritual activism" as a general description of Hasidism, see Rachel Elior, "HaBaD: The Contemplative Ascent to God," in ed. A. Green, *Jewish Spirituality* (Crossroad, New York, 1989), vol. II, p. 158; her *The Paradoxical Ascent to God*, *passim*, especially pp. 30–31; Naftali Loewenthal, "Habad Approaches to Contemplative Prayer, 1790–1920," in *Hasidism Reappraised*, ed. Rapoport-Albert, pp. 288–300; and Loewenthal, *Communicating the Infinite: The Emergence of the Habad School* (Chicago University Press, Chicago, 1990), especially pp. 154–163. See, however, my *Kabbalah: New Perspectives*, p. 57, where the *tiqqun* is predicated upon *devequt* according to a Lurianic and in a Sabbatean text, and now "The Tsadik and His Soul's Sparks." See also the interesting passage attributed to R. Abraham ha-Levi Berukhin, a follower of Luria, in Vital's *Liqqutei Torah* (Amsterdam, 1802), fol. 107a.

4   *Studies*, p. 58 (emphases added). Later on the same page, Weiss speaks in the same context about the "external shapes of letters." See also the sharp formulations in Weiss, pp. 69–71. The Besht is described alsewhere as immersed in contemplation in Weiss, p. 32. See also pp. 130–141, where he distinguishes between the Besht and the Great Maggid, and especially p. 59, where the contemplative exercise of the first Hasidim is mentioned in the context of letters and *devequt*. See also for another reference, Weiss, p. 183, to "contemplative techniques for bringing them to

repentance." See also n. 120 in this volume. Weiss was indubitably influenced also by Shlomo Maimon's description of early Hasidism. See ch. 9 n. 8 in this volume. For a survey of the *devequt*, understood explicitly as contemplation, in the circle of early masters with whom the Besht was in close relation, see Weiss, "The Beginning of the Emergence of the Hasidic Path," pp. 60–69. Compare also to the more recent reiteration of the nexus between the Besht, contemplation, graphical letters, and quietism in Wolfson, "Immanuel Frommann," p. 195, as if it is a fact found in the analyzed material and not a construct of scholars before him. See also Krassen, *Uniter of Heaven and Earth*, p. 83, and Arthur Green and Barry Holtz, *"Your Word is Fire": The Hasidic Masters and Contemplative Prayer* (Paulist Press, New York, 1977). Insofar as Jewish mysticism in general is concerned, contemplation is considered to be an essential topic in the various books of Elliot R. Wolfson, as can be seen sometimes even from the titles and indexes of some of his studies cited in ch. 13 nn. 6, 17, 19.

5   For Lurianism as an enrichment of the contemplative aspects of early Kabbalah, as part of a linear history of Kabbalah, see Scholem, *Major Trends in Jewish Mysticism*, p. 287. See also ch. 13 n. 22 in this volume. For him, the elevation of sparks has been understood as quite an important aspect of Hasidism, unlike Buber's emphasis on the worship in corporeality. See Scholem's treatments in *The Messianic Idea*, pp. 186–195, 241–244, but compare to the proposal of a multilinearity in Idel, "On Prophecy and Early Hasidism," pp. 46–47.

6   See *Major Trends in Jewish Mysticism*, pp. 132–133, 137–138, 155, and *On the Possibility of Jewish Mysticism*, p. 137. See also ch. 13 n. 5 in this volume. See also the item Meditation in *The Encyclopedia of Religion*, ed. M. Eliade, vol. 9 (MacMillan, New York, London, 1987), pp. 325–326. See a similar approach to this Kabbalist that emphasizes the importance of contemplation in Elliot R. Wolfson, *Abraham Abulafia: Hermeneutics, Theosophy, and Theurgy* (The Cherub Press, Los Angeles, 2000), index *sub voce, contemplation*, for the numerous resorts to this term.

7   See Idel, *The Mystical Experience in Abraham Abulafia*, pp. 20, 111; *Enchanted Chains*, pp. 103–104; and *Studies in Ecstatic Kabbalah*, pp. 2, 99, n. 26. See also Idel, *Kabbalah: New Perspectives*, pp. 50–51. Abulafia allowed some form of contemplative activity, mainly in the context of allegorical interpretation of the Bible, conceived of as a lower activity than the Kabbalistic one. See Idel, *Absorbing Perfections*, pp. 326, 342–344, and see also Idel, pp. 444–445. However, I would say that another ecstatic Kabbalist, R. Isaac of Acre, was much more inclined toward what can be designated as contemplation, basically under the impact of ultimately Platonic or Neoplatonic sources. See Idel, *Kabbalah & Eros*, pp. 155–168, and Fishbane, *As Light before Dawn, passim*.

8   Fine, "Recitation of Mishnah," pp. 183–199, and his "The Contemplative Practice of Yihudim in Lurianic Kabbalah," in ed. A. Green, *Jewish Spirituality*, vol. 2 (Crossroad, New York, 1989), pp. 64–98. See also ch. 13 n. 20 in this volume. See also the view of R. J. Zwy Werblowsky, "The Safed Revival," *Jewish Spirituality*, p. 24, who speaks in the context of R. Ḥayyim Vital about contemplative *devequt*, and about *scala contemplationis*. See also Idel, *Hasidism*, pp. 99–100.

9 *Kabbalah*, pp. 88–89, emphases added, and see also, e.g., *Kabbalah*, pp. 3, 32–33, 35, 44, 46, 47. See also *Major Trends in Jewish Mysticism*, pp. 116, 122, 132–133; and Werblowsky, *Joseph Karo, Lawyer and Mystic*, p. 189. For a critique of this approach, see Idel, *Enchanted Chains*, pp. 10–11. For an interesting discussion of Jewish mysticism in general as a matter of contemplation, written in 1944 in Hebrew, where Scholem uses the phrase *histakkelut penimit*, in my opinion to be translated as inner contemplation, see Gershom Scholem, "Ha-Mistorin ha-Yehudi ve-ha-Qabbalah," reprinted in his collection of studies *Explications and Implications, Writings on Jewish Heritage and Renaissance* (entitled in Hebrew *Devarim be-Go*) ('Am 'Oved, Tel Aviv, 1975), p. 230 (Hebrew). This more general description, like the one quoted previously, neglects the traditional awareness of many of the Jewish mystics that they are part of a tradition and that they inherited transmitted esoteric knowledge. See also Arthur Green, *Devotion and Commandment, The Faith of Abraham in Hasidic Imagination* (HUC Press, Cincinnati, 1989), p. 81, n. 42, where an interesting link between symbols and contemplation is surmised in Hasidism.

10 *On the Kabbalah and Its Symbolism*, p. 99. Compare to my reactions to this view in *Ascensions on High*, p. 17, and *Absorbing Perfections*, p. 293.

11 *On the Possibility of Jewish Mysticism*, pp. 178, 181. For another approach to the study of the Torah as a contemplative form of activity, almost a Platonic approach, attributed again to Rabbinic Judaism, see the claims of Arnaldo Momigliano, as discussed in Idel, *Old Worlds, New Mirrors*, pp. 19–20.

12 Edward Caird, *The Evolution of Theology in the Greek Philosophers* (James MacLehose and Sons, Glasgow, 1904), vol. II, pp. 188–189. Emphases added. See also my *Enchanted Chains*, pp. 18–19.

13 Caird distinguishes between different forms of contemplation. See his views in Caird, pp. 2, 8–10.

14 Martin Buber, *On Judaism*, ed. Nahum N. Glazer (Schocken Books, New York, 1972), pp. 57–60.

15 See Idel, *Ascensions on High*, pp. 30–35, and *Absorbing Perfections*, pp. 173–175.

16 See Adena Tanenbaum, *The Contemplative Soul: Hebrew Poetry and Philosophical Theory in Medieval Spain* (Brill, Leiden, 2002), *passim*; and Afterman, *Devequt*, pp. 102–168.

17 See, e.g., Scholem, *Origins of the Kabbalah*, pp. 126–131, 244–245, 268, 270–275, and ch. 11 n. 16 in this volume. See also Elliot R. Wolfson, in his "Megillat 'Emmet ve-'Emunah: Contemplative Visualization and Mystical Unknowing," *Kabbalah* vol. 5 (2005), pp. 55–110; and Afterman, *Devequt*, pp. 176–332.

18 See Idel, *Ascensions on High*, pp. 112–113.

19 See Elliot R. Wolfson, "Sacred Space and Mental Iconography: 'imago templi' and Contemplation in Rhineland Jewish Pietism," in eds. Robert Chazan, William W. Hallo, and Lawrence H. Schiffman, *Ki Baruch Hu: Ancient Near Eastern, Biblical, and Judaic Studies in Honor of Baruch A. Levine* (Winona Lake, IN: Eisenbrauns, 1999), pp. 593–634.

20   See Lawrence Fine, "The Study of Torah as a Rite of Theurgical Contemplation in
       Lurianic Kabbalah," *Approaches to Judaism in Medieval Times* III (1988), pp. 29–40,
       and his *Physician of the Soul, Healer of the Cosmos, Isaac Luria and His Kabbalistic
       Fellowship* (Stanford University Press, Stanford, 2003), p. 34. See also ch. 13 n. 8 in
       this volume. It should be pointed out that in some cases, Scholem uses the term
       meditation in order to describe the spiritual intention that accompanies the perfor-
       mance of the commandments in Lurianic Kabbalah. See his *On the Kabbalah and
       Its Symbolism*, pp. 126–127.

21   For the description of R. Isaac the Blind as a "pure contemplative mystic", see
       Scholem, *On the Kabbalah and Its Symbolism*, p. 21, and for this Kabbalist as resort-
       ing to a prophetic contemplation of the *sefirot*, see Wolfson, *Through a Speculum
       that Shines*, p. 293, and of R. Ezra as self-contemplating, see Wolfson, p. 295 and his
       Language, Eros, Being: Kabbalistic Hermeneutics and Poetic Imagination (Fordham
       University Press, New York, 2005), pp. 209–212, 521, n. 131. See especially Wolfson,
       p. xii, where he announces that he is "theorizing a poetics of kabbalah by investigat-
       ing the phenomenological contours of the contemplative envisioning of the divine
       in the history of Jewish mysticism."
           However, Scholem's vision of "pure contemplation" as Wolfson's comprehen-
       sive vision of contemplation are both problematic, in my opinion, since what is
       depicted as contemplative is part of a wider sequence of activities, which include
       theurgy and magic as main components. See Idel, "On R. Isaac Sagi Nahor's
       Mystical Intention of the Eighteen Benedictions," eds. Michal Oron and Amos
       Goldreich, *Massu'ot, Studies in Kabbalistic Literature and Jewish Philosophy in
       Memory of Prof. Ephraim Gottlieb* (Mossad Bialik, Jerusalem, 1994), pp. 25–52
       (Hebrew), and Brody, "Human Hands Dwell in Heavenly Heights," pp. 123–158.
       For contemplating the structure of the letters of the Torah as iconic, reflecting
       the divine structure mainly in some texts stemming from thirteenth- and early
       fourteenth-century forms of Kabbalah, see also, e.g., Idel, *Absorbing Perfections*, pp.
       66–75, 82, 101, 119, 120–121, and my "Jewish Kabbalah and Platonism in the Middle
       Ages and Renaissance," in ed. Lenn E. Goodman, *Neoplatonism and Jewish Thought*
       (SUNY Press, Albany, 1993), pp. 320–321, and Afterman, *Devequt*, pp. 169–285. See
       also ch. 13 n. 17 in this volume.
           It should be mentioned that the contemplative "metamorphosis" of Kabbalah
       has been adopted also by Aryeh Kaplan, *Meditation and the Bible* (Weiser, New
       York, 1978), especially pp. 133–137. See also my remarks in *Hasidism*, p. 347, n. 103
       and in "Visualization of Colors, 2: Implications of David ben Yehudah he-Hasid's
       Diagram for the History of Kabbalah," *Ars Judaica*, vol. 12 (2016), pp. 47–51. See
       also ch. 13 n. 8 in this volume.

22   See Idel, *Kabbalah: New Perspectives*, p. 233, and see also Idel, p. 254. See also my
       "Transfer of Categories," pp. 24–27. For Scholem's claim that contemplation in
       Judaism is related to more abstract issues than in Christianity, see ch. 13 n. 35 in this
       volume. In fact, our emphasis on the importance of magical aspects of Hasidism
       substantially attenuates the contemplative components. See Idel, *Hasidism*, p. 170.

23   See n. 136 in this volume, and *Joseph Karo: Lawyer and Mystic*, pp. 38–83. The source
       of this concept is found in the seventeenth-century Christian Kabbalist Athanasius
       Kircher. See in Mark A. Waddell, *Jesuit Science and the End of Nature's Secrets*

(Routledge, London, New York, 2015), p. 100, that it is adumbrated by a passage in Marsilio Ficino's writings. See Ruderman, *Kabbalah, Magic, and Science*, p. 111.

24   See Reuchlin, *On the Art of Kabbalah*, p. 63. See also my introduction to this edition, pp. xxi–xxiii, as well as *Ascensions on High*, pp. 13–14. The "separated forms" reflect the concept of *sefirot*, which were described as forms but also of philosophical terminology, where the cosmic intellects were described as separated from matter.

25   Reuchlin, *On the Art of Kabbalah*, p. 111.

26   Reuchlin, pp. 97–99. This distinction is reminiscent, *mutatis mutandis*, of the difference between Neoplatonism and Hermeticism. A similar approach is found in a discussion between the Besht and the Great Maggid, as part of their distinction between Kabbalah and Hasidism. See the discussion of R. Hillel of Parich, an author related to Habad Hasidism, *Pelah ha-Rimmon* (Brooklyn, 1957), vol. II, p. 78, translated in my *Hasidism*, pp. 235–236.

27   Reuchlin, *On the Art of Kabbalah*, pp. 237–239. See also pp. 111–113, 241, and especially p. 45.

28   Paulus Riccius, printed in ed. Johan Pistorius, *Ars Cabalistica* (Minerva, Frankfurt, 1970), p. 116; as translated in Wilhelm Schmidt-Biggeman, "Christian Kabbala: Joseph Gikatilla (1247–1305), Johannes Reuchlin (Wilhelm 1455–1522), Paulus Riccius (d. 1541), and Jacob Boehme (1575–1624)," in ed. A. Coudert, *The Language of Adam/Die Sprache Adams* (Harassowitz Verlag, Wiesbaden, 1999), p. 101, emphases added. See also Idel, *Kabbalah in Italy*, pp. 295–296. On this Christian Kabbalist see the fine monograph of Bernd Roling, *Aristotelische Naturphilosophie und christliche Kabbalah im Werk des Paulus Ritius* (Niemeyer, Tuebingen, 2007), especially pp. 26–27, 232–239 for the discussion of symbolism, and pp. 325–326, where the impact of Abraham Abulafia's Kabbalah has been put in relief.

29   Reuchlin, *On the Art of Kabbalah*, p. 145.

30   On contemplation in Marsilio Ficino, see Paul O. Kristeller, *The Philosophy of Marsilio Ficino*, tr. V. Conant (Columbia University Press, New York, 1943), *passim*. To be sure: though I emphasize the Florentine thinker as a main source of inspiration for Christian Kabbalists, I do not assume that there were not interesting examples of Neoplatonic and Pythagorean themes in Kabbalah long beforehand. See, e.g., my "Anamnesis and Music, or Kabbalah as Renaissance before the Renaissance," *Rivista di storia e letteratura religiosa*, XLIX (2013), pp. 389–412. It should also be mentioned that Ficino operated with some form of astral theory, influenced by *Picatrix* and al-Kindi, when he sang songs, in order to attract the planetary influxes upon himself inspired by the Hermetic sources he translated in Latin, though he was much more inspired by Platonic and Neoplatonic sources. See also Couliano, *Eros and Magic*, pp. 137–143.

31   See Scholem's unqualified claim that for mystics in general, language possesses a symbolic dimension, in his article "The Name of God and the Linguistic Theory of the Kabbalah," p. 60, and see also the similar view of Elliot R. Wolfson, as discussed in my *Kabbalah in Italy*, p. 312, or his "Letter Symbolism and Merkavah Imagery in the Zohar," in ed. M. Hallamish, *Alei Shefer: Studies in the Literature of Jewish*

Thought Presented to Rabbi Dr. Alexandre Safran (Ramat-Gan: Bar-Ilan Press, 1990), pp. 195–236, (English section). Compare, however, the different view of Abraham J. Heschel that proposed to minimize the role of symbolism in Judaism, including in Jewish mysticism, as discussed Idel, *Old Worlds, New Mirrors*, pp. 225–226. In my opinion, without allowing the existence of different schools, of cross-currents, of various theories of what can be described as symbolism, and of more comprehensive models, which differ from each other substantially, both in Kabbalah and Hasidism, or in mysticism in the broader sense, even the most accomplished scholars may fall prey to simplification and essentialism. The approach to the Ba'al Shem Tov in scholarship can be depicted as "deceptive simplicity."

Compare, however, to the other tendency found in some other essays of Weiss's, like, for example, the one dealing with the differences between the Braslav and Ḥabad schools as two distinct forms of Hasidism, or in another instance, between different, non-essentialist approaches to Judaism, found in the same collection, Weiss, *Studies*, pp. 43–55 and 249–269 respectively.

32   See the discussions in Idel, *Old Worlds, New Mirrors*, pp. 83–107, 111, especially p. 84, and *Absorbing Perfections*, pp. 272–304. See also my "Johannes Reuchlin: Kabbalah, Pythagorean Philosophy, and Modern Scholarship," *Studia Judaica*, vol. 16 (2008), pp. 30–55. It should be mentioned that Reuchlin, following Giovanni Pico della Mirandola, was aware of the importance of voice, following some Kabbalists, but he connects it to magic and to the divine name, not to the daily liturgical rites. See, e.g., his *On the Art of Kabbalah*, pp. 271, 309, 341 337.

33   See *Kabbalah*, p. 371. As seen previously, abstraction is not the term that would fit the Besht's recommendation to cleave to utterances. In general I propose to see in the concrete aspects of Jewish mysticism fundamental aspects that should not be ignored. See also Idel, "Models of Understanding Prayer in Early Hasidism," p. 88 and ch. 11 n. 15 in this volume.

34   See Idel, *Kabbalah: New Perspectives*, pp. 231–232, and *The Mystical Experience in Abraham Abulafia*, pp. 39–40. Compare, however, to the descriptions of the states of samadhi, translated as levels of contemplation, in Dyczkowski, *The Doctrine of Vibration*, pp. 153, 156, 264, n. 263, 265, n. 279. For the resort to the term of contemplation in order to describe Yoga practices, see Eliade, *Yoga, passim*.

35   For a description of the practice and of the sharp acceleration of one's thoughts it produces, see the passage by R. Nathan ben Sa'adyah Harar, a student of Abulafia's, as translated in Scholem, *Major Trends in Jewish Mysticism*, pp. 147–155, and Idel, *Natan ben Sa'adyah Har'ar, Le Porte della Giustizia*, pp. 414–418.

36   Idel, *Kabbalah: New Perspectives*, pp. 224–225, 233.

37   On this topic see, meanwhile, Idel, *Hasidism*, pp. 46–57, Idel, *"Torah Ḥadashah,"* p. 77, and Kauffman, *In All Your Ways Know Him*, pp. 152–154.

38   *Keter Shem Tov*, fol. 18b; See also Jacobs, *Hasidic Prayer*, pp. 93–94.

39   For the need to take into consideration both types of elements in Hasidism, pre-axial and axial altogether, see Idel, *Hasidism*, p. 225, and *Ascensions on High*, pp. 153–154.

40 See, e.g., Idel, "Female Beauty," *passim, Kabbalah and Eros*, pp. 168–177, and *Absorbing Perfections*, pp. 198–199.

41 See her "Contemplative Prayer," p. 209, and *Hasidism as Mysticism*, p. 168. Elsewhere in her book, pp. 62–64, she distinguishes between activism and quietism in Hasidism, but nevertheless she writes (p. 63): "we must not be misled by the spirit of that activism which rejoices over realization. Since it is based in Hasidism upon an acosmic world-view, it is unable to have a fully 'realistic' tendency . . . The 'real' is an illusion." This statement is based on an essentialist vision of Hasidism as a whole as theologically acosmic, a view that is totalizing and, in my opinion, not representative of the first two models of the Besht I described previously, but only of the third one. Strong theistic views can be easily found in Hasidic literature side by side with immanentistic attitudes. On the other hand, Etkes, in *The Besht: Magician, Mystic, and Leader*, conceived the core of Hasidism to be ecstatic prayer.

42 See Idel, *Old Worlds, New Mirrors*, pp. 110–113.

43 For the time being see the discussions of some of those issues in my *Ben*, pp. 58–62, 99–101, 329–330.

44 For another quite dramatic misunderstanding of the Lurianic theory of elevating sparks, as if not including the elevation of personals sparks, as proposed by Scholem and followed by all the scholars writing on this topic, see my "The Tsadik and His Soul's Sparks."

45 See ch. 8 n. 13 in this volume, and Idel, "Prayer, Ecstasy, and Alien Thoughts," p. 5. See also Mircea Eliade's claim that in the Carpathian Mountains, some form of pre-Christian cosmic religiosity has been preserved. Cf., my *Mircea Eliade*, pp. 226–228, 231–236.

46 See my most recent studies "R. Israel Ba'al Shem Tov 'In the State of Walachia,'" and "18th Century Early Hasidism," as well as the earlier *Kabbalah: New Perspectives*, pp. 321, nn. 133, 137, or *Ascensions on High*, pp. 148–150, 154, 160; Arthur Green, *Speaking Torah* (Jewish Lights, Woodstock, VT, 2013), vol. 1, p. 9; and Magid, *Hasidism Incarnate*, pp. 19, 96. For a comparison between Hasidim's oral activation of the text and Shamanesque approaches, see Garb, *Shamanic Trance in Modern Kabbalah*, pp. 128–130.

47 See my "18th Century Early Hasidism," and "Early Hasidism and Altaic Tribes."

14. Orality and the Emergence of Hasidism as a Popular Movement

1 On orality in Hasidism, see now also Mayse, *Beyond the Letters*, pp. 40–51. See also Shaul Stampfer, "How and Why Did Hasidism Spread?" *Jewish History*, 27 (2013), pp. 201–219, for the importance of the small synagogues, the *schtiblech*, in the dissemination of Hasidism. For more general remarks, see the views of Levinas as discussed in Jay, *Downcast Eyes*, pp. 555–556.

2 *In Praise of the Baal Shem Tov*, p. 179. See also ch. 10 n. 4 in this volume. The distinction in spelling between "Torah" and "torah" is that of the translators. See also

the important parallel adduced by Scholem, *ha-Shalav ha-'Aharon*, pp. 123–125, and discussed again by Rosman, *The Founder of Hasidism*, pp. 146–147. See also Jacobs, *Their Heads in Heaven*, pp. 26–42. About *dibbur* see also nn. 22 and 246.

3 Compare also to Idel, *Absorbing Perfections*, pp. 461–469, on the Lurianic discussions about the sparks of the Torah that are found within the realm of evil.

4 *Liqqutei Moharan* I, no. 225:

וזהו בחינת מה שמספרין על הבעל שם טוב זכרונו לברכה, שהיה שומע דבורים מקול הכנור, כי היה עושה מצפצופים דבורים.

Compare also to the tradition adduced in the name of R. Nahman that was cited in the motto as well as to ch. 1 n. 22, ch. 14 n. 2 in this volume. See also the statements about the understanding of the language of birds in R. Efrayim of Sudylkov, *Degel Mahaneh Efrayim*, p. 39, and *In Praise of the Baal Shem Tov*, pp. 242–244. See also Schwartz, *Music in Jewish Thought*, pp. 79, 81. Compare however, to the different attitude to the alleged knowledge of the language of birds attributed to R. Isaac Luria, in R. Hayyim Vital's *Sha'ar Ruah ha-Qodesh*, derush III, fol. 5b, where the assumption is that secrets of the Torah are hidden there.

Compare, however, to the view of the Great Maggid, as to the danger that chirping of birds may interrupt one's concentration, cf., *Liqqutim Yeqarim*, p. 56, no. 175 and Mayse, *Beyond the Letters*, pp. 107–108, 233–234. See also Mayse, pp. 177–178, and n. 646.

5 See the study of Lieberman on the attitude of Hasidim to Yiddisch in *'Ohel RaHel*, vol. III, pp. 1–13. For Yiddisch material reported in the name of the Besht and preserved mainly in the Habad Hasidism, see Abraham Hanokh Glizenstein, *Rabbi Israel Baal-Shem-Tov* (Kehot, Brooklyn, NY, 1960), pp. 142–165 (Hebrew), and in some statements adduced by R. Pinhas Shapira of Koretz.

6 *In Praise of the Baal Shem Tov*, pp. 124–125.

7 Indeed, R. Israel Ba'al Shem Tov's thought and that of his followers was informed by the threefold distinction, widespread in the Middle Ages, between letters in their written, vocal, and mental manifestations. See ch. 2 n. 16 and appendix C in this volume for some of Cordovero's discussions of this topic.

See, however, the claim of Schatz-Uffenheimer, *Hasidism as Mysticism*, p. 43: "Hasidism was the first mystical movement in Judaism to create a true conflict with action." Compare, however, to Jerome Gellman, "Hasidic Mysticism as an Activism," *Religious Studies*, vol. 42, no. 3 (2006), pp. 343–349.

8 See, especially, Idel, "Your Word Stands Firmly in Heaven." I intend to discuss elsewhere in greater detail the identity of the utterances that are in exile with the *Shekhinah* as it appears in some teachings of Israel Ba'al Shem Tov. See, for the time, R. Pinchas Shapira of Koretz, *Likutim me-ha-rav R. Pinhas mi-korets*, fol. 6a. R. Moses Hayim Ephraim of Sudylkov, in *Degel Mahaneh 'Efrayim*, p. 101, discusses an interpretation of the notion of "seeing the voices" in the Sinaitic revelation as a sort of contemplation; the passage mentions the Ba'al Shem Tov, but whether this is his own view or that of his grandson is not clear from the context. In any case, from this discussion it seems that the sense of hearing is more important than that of sight. In a parallel discussion on p. 62, it is clear that it is the

interpretation of the Rabbi of Sudylkov that is offered. See also the passage attributed to the Ba'al Shem Tov in R. Dov Ber of Mezeritch, *'Or ha-'Emmet*, fol. 1b, and R. Reuven Horowitz, *Diduim ba-Sodeh*, fol. 8a, in a passage quoting the Besht. Another example of the hypostatization of utterances is related to the Beshtian assumption that sins committed in speech are incarnated as enemies of the sinner, and they must be repaired by means of utterances in prayer. See, e.g., the quotes in R. Jacob Joseph of Polonnoye, *Ben Porat Yosef*, fol. 99bc, and R. Jacob Joseph of Polonnoye, *Toledot Ya'aqov Yosef*, fol. 15a, as well as the more detailed analysis of this issue in my study "The Tsadik and His Soul's Sparks." See also the image of prayers that "shone as the bright dawn" and spoke to the Ba'al Shem Tov, in *In Praise of the Baal Shem Tov*, p. 56.

9   Discussions of the verse from Psalm 16:8 played an important role in many texts related to the Besht as preserved, for example, in *Toledot Ya'aqov Yosef*, fols. 114d, 165d, and in the Rabbi of Sudylkov's *Degel Maḥaneh 'Efrayim*. See more in my "Remembering and Forgetting," pp. 126–127, and Schatz-Uffenheimer, *Hasidism as Mysticism*, p. 104. For the Kabbalistic background, see Idel, *Kabbalah: New Perspectives*, pp. 50–51.

10   Schatz-Uffenheimer, "Gershom Scholem's Interpretation of Hasidism." For the existence of Platonic elements in early Hasidism, see also my "Female Beauty."

11   Eadem, "Man's Relationship to God and World in Buber."

12   See my "The Hasidic Revival."

13   See my *Ascensions on High*, pp. 113–119, *Ben*, pp. 58–62, 99–101, 329–330, and appendix B in this volume.

15. Concluding Remarks

1   See, e.g., S. R. Driver, *An Introduction to the Literature of the Old Testament* (Charles Scribner's Sons, New York, 1950), 3rd ed.; Jon D. Levenson, *The Hebrew Bible, the Old Testament, and Historical Criticism* (Westminster/John Knox Press, Louisville, 1993); Israel Knohl, *The Sanctuary of Silence, The Priestly Torah, and the Holiness School* (Fortress, Minneapolis, 1995), pp. 124–125, 168–172, 227; Knohl, *The Divine Symphony, The Bibles' Many Voices* (Jewish Publication Society, Philadelphia, 2003); Baruch J. Schwartz, "The Pentateuch as Scripture and the Challenge of Biblical Criticism: Responses among Modern Jewish Thinkers and Scholars," in ed. B. D. Sommer, *Jewish Concepts of Scripture: A Comparative Introduction* (New York University Press, New York, 2012), pp. 203–229; and Michael Carasik, *The Bible's Many Voices* (Jewish Publication Society, Philadelphia, 2014).

2   See my *Primeval Evil*, ch. 5 pars. 5–11, and *"Male and Female" Equality, Female's Theurgy, and Eros—R. Moshe Cordovero's Dual Ontology* (in preparation).

3   See the depiction of Diotalevi in Umberto Eco, *Foucault's Pendulum*, tr. W. Weaver (Janovich, San Diego, 1989), pp. 564–566 as to the secularization of Kabbalah.

4   "Immanuel Frommann," p. 195, cited verbatim by Magid, *Hasidism Incarnate*, p. 166. See also ch. 13 n. 41 in this volume.

5   See also Wolfson, "Immanuel Fromman," p. 196, where he mentions the iconic aspects of letters.

6   See Idel, "Transfers of Categories."

7   See in Idel my analysis of the scholarly imposition of Maimonides's thought on a Hasidic statement dealing with God's utterance at Sinai, as if it refers actually to silence, and its reverberations in Gershom Scholem's view of revelation and following him many other more recent interpretations of Judaism.

8   See my *Ascensions on High*, pp. 11–13, and some of the following chapters of the book deal with such an approach.

9   See my "Mystique juive et pensèe musulmane," *Perspectives*, no. 9 (2002), pp. 138–157; Idel, *Studies in Ecstatic Kabbalah*; Idel, *Hasidism, passim*; and Idel, "Orienting, Orientalizing, or Disorienting the Study of Kabbalah: 'An Almost Absolutely Unique' Case of Occidentalism," *Kabbalah*, vol. 2 (1997), pp. 13–48. See also ch. 8 n. 11 in this volume.

10 See Warburg, *The Renewal of Pagan Antiquity;* Edgar Wind, *Pagan Mysteries in the Renaissance* (Faber & Faber, Harmondsworth, 1967); the studies of Frances A. Yates and Daniel Pikering Walker; and my *Saturn's Jews* and *Hasidism*, pp. 78–79 and pp. 246, 391, n. 10. In more general terms see the approach of Moses Gaster, *Ilchester Lectures on Greeko-Slavonic Literature* (Truebner & Co., Ludgate Hill, London, 1887); and Gaster, *Literatura populara romana*, ed. M. Angelescu (Minerva, Bucuresti, 1883). On his views of the history of Jewish mysticism in general, see M. Idel, "Moses Gaster on Jewish Mysticism and the Book of the Zohar," in ed. R. Meroz, *New Developments in Zohar Studies* (Te'udah, XXI–XXII) (Tel Aviv, Tel Aviv University, 2007), pp. 111–127; my "'In a Whisper': On Transmission of *Shi'ur Qomah* and Kabbalistic Secrets in Jewish Mysticism," *Rivista di storia e letteratura religiosa*, 47, no. 3 (2011) [*Il mantello di Elia: Tradizione, innovazione nella cabala*], 477–522; and *Ben*, pp. 8–15, 51–57.

11 See my *Hasidism*, p. 21, and *Enchanted Chains*, pp. 5–7.

12 See also appendix B in this volume.

13 See Lieberman, *'Ohel RaHel*, vol. 1, pp. 1–49. For Scholem's response to some of the critiques, see his *ha-Shalav ha-'Aharon*, pp. 92–94, 98–99, 101–105. For Piekarz, see *Between Ideology and Reality*, pp. 29–31.

14 See, e.g., Michael Oppenheim, "The Meaning of Hasidut: Martin Buber and Gershom Scholem," *Journal of the American Academy of Religion*, vol. 49, no. 3 (1981), pp. 409–421; Steven D. Kepnes, "A Hermeneutic Approach to the Buber-Scholem Controversy," *JJS*, vol. 38 (1987), pp. 81–98; Jerome [Yehudah] Gellman, "Buber's Blunder: Buber's Replies to Scholem and Schatz-Uffenheimer," *MJ*, vol. 20 (2000), pp. 20–40; the introduction of Samuel H. Dresner, to Heschel, *The Circle of the Besht*, pp. XVI–XIX; David Biale, *Gershom Scholem, Kabbalah, and Counter-History* (Harvard University Press, Cambridge, MA, London, 1982), 2nd ed., pp. 89–93; as well as Harold Bloom, *Poetics of Influence* (Henry R. Schwab, New Haven, 1988), pp. 325–346. Buber's view of Hasidism, including the description of the criticism of Scholem, has been extensively discussed in Grete Schaeder,

The Hebrew Humanism of Martin Buber, tr. N. J. Jacobs (Wayne State University Press, Detroit, 1973), pp. 287–338; see also Margolin, *The Human Temple, passim*. See also ch. 10 n. 16 in this volume.

15 See his claim in *The Origin and Meaning of Hasidism*, p. 70.

16 See Idel, *Mircea Eliade, passim*, esp. pp. 241–245.

17 See Werblowsky, *Joseph Karo, Lawyer and Mystic*, pp. 18–19, 109–111; Fine, "Recitation of the Mishnah," pp. 183–199; Garb, *Shamanic Trance in Modern Kabbalah*; Daniel Reiser, *Vision as a Mirror: Imagery Techniques in Twentieth Century Jewish Mysticism* (Cherub Press, Los Angeles, 2014) (Hebrew); and the expanded English version *Imagery Techniques in Modern Jewish Mysticism* tr. Eugene D. Matanky, (de Gruyter, Magnes, Berlin, Boston 2018), Ron Wacks, *The Flame and the Holy Fire: Perspectives on the Teachings of Rabbi Kalonymus Kalmish Shapiro of Piaczena* (Tevunot, Alon Shevut, 2010) (Hebrew); Zvi Leshem, "Flipping into Ecstasy: Towards a Syncopal Understanding of Mystical Hasidic Somersaults," *Studia Judaica*, vol. 17 (2014), pp. 157–183; and Tomer Persico, *Jewish Meditation: The Development of Spiritual Practices in Contemporary Judaism* (Tel Aviv University Press, Tel Aviv, 2016) (Hebrew).

18 See my *Enchanted Chains*, pp. 31–41.

19 See *Enchanted Chains*, pp. 26–30.

20 See his *Beginning of Hasidism, passim*; Idel, *Hasidism*, pp. 190–191; and see ch. 5 n. 12 and appendix B in this volume.

21 See, e.g., Scholem, *Major Trends in Jewish Mysticism*, pp. 330–334; Buber, *The Origin and Meaning of Hasidism*, pp. 60–83, 170; Elior, *Israel Ba'al Shem Tov and His Contemporaries*; as well as the approaches of historians like S. Dubnow and B. Z. Dinur. Discussions of historical crises may sometimes be important for understanding the emergence of a social movement, but much less for understanding the forging of conceptual themes by individuals, especially when their sources are evident. Compare, however, my "The Diffusion of Lurianic Kabbala and Sabbateanism: A Re-examination," *Jewish History*, vol. 7, no. 2 (1993), pp. 79–104, and Gries, *Hebrew Book*, p. 48. For a critique of the explanation of Hasidism grounded on crises, see Immanuel Etkes, "Hasidism as a Movement: The First Stage," in ed. B. Safran, *Hasidism: Continuity or Innovation?* (Harvard University Press, Cambridge, MA, 1988), especially p. 23, and Rosman, *Founder of Hasidism*, pp. 82, 178.

22 Compare ch. 8 nn. 9, 11 and appendices B and F in this volume.

23 *Testament of the Besht*, fol. 1b, and *Keter Shem Tov*, fol. 28d, no. 220:

צריך לעבוד את השם יתברך בכל כחו, שהכל הוא צורך, מפני שהשם יתברך רוצה שיעבדו
אותו בכל האופנים, והכוונה כי לפעמים האדם הולך ומדבר עם בני אדם, ואז אינו יכול ללמוד,
וצריך להיות דבוק בהשם יתברך וליייחד יחודים, וכן כשהאדם הולך בדרך, ואינו יכול להתפלל
וללמוד כדרכו, וצריך לעבוד אותו יתברך שמו באופנים אחרים, ואל יצער את עצמו בזה, כי השם
יתברך רוצה שיעבדוהו בכל האופנים, פעמים באופן זה ופעמים באופן זה, לכך הזדמן לפניו לילך
לדרך, או לדבר עם בני אדם, בכדי לעבוד אותו באופן הזה.

Emphases added. See also Idel, "Models for Understanding Prayer," p. 90 and n. 234. There, in Idel, pp. 96–97, a Beshtian tradition dealing with the ongoing changes in creation and in the Torah has been discussed.

24   See Idel, "The Besht Passed the Hand," pp. 89–90. See also ch 3. n. 8, ch. 5 n. 2 in this volume.

25   See also R. Menahem Nahum of Chernobyl, *Me'or 'Einayyim*, p. 250.

26   See Idel, *Saturn's Jews*, pp. 186–187, and Lederberg, *Sod ha-Da'at*, pp. 154–155.

27   See, e.g., Dresner, *The Zaddik*, pp. 125-128.

28   See his *The Origin and Meaning of Hasidism*, pp. 170, 173, 179–180.

29   See the end of chap. 9 in this volume.

30   See his response to the critiques of Scholem and Schatz-Uffenheimer, in Buber, "Interpreting Hasidism," pp. 218, 219.

31   See Arthur Green, "Abraham Yoshua Heschel: Recasting Hasidism for Moderns," *MJ*, vol. 29 (2009), pp. 60–79.

Appendix A: Forlorn Unitive Views of the Besht?

1   Gedalyah Nigal, "A Primary Source for Early Hasidic Story Literature: About *Keter Shem Tov* and Its Sources," *Sinai*, vol. 79 (1976), pp. 132–146 (Hebrew); Gries, *Conduct Literature*, p. 125, n. 84; Mayse, *Beyond the Letters*, pp. 61–64; and Garb, *Shamanic Trance in Modern Kabbalah*, pp. 44, 87, 101, 108, 114, 120, 122–123, 135.

2   Tishby, *Studies*, vol. III, p. 945, n. 22. See also ch. 6 n. 14 in this volume.

3   The letters of the Tetragrammaton have been conceived of as the soul of the other letters in many Kabbalistic and Hasidic texts. On *ruḥaniyyut* and divine names, see appendix D in this volume. On innerness see also appendix C. We witness here a series of terms that are found together also in R. Moshe Cordovero's writings.

4   Warsau, ed., fol. 8c. See also Idel, *Hasidism*, p. 63, and *The Mystical Experience in Abraham Abulafia*, p. 124. On *Yiḥud* as union with God see n. 1 and appendix B in this volume. For immersion of the soul of the mystic within the divine light, see the late thirteenth- and early fourteenth-century material discussed in my *R. Natan ben Sa'adya Har'ar, Le Porte della Giustizia*, pp. 189–200.

5   For a linkage between *ruḥaniyyut* and omnipresence, see more in appendix E.

6   See my "Female Beauty."

7   *'Or ha-Ganuz la-Tzaddiqim*, fol. 40b.

8   On this issue see more in appendix B.

9   On this image for mystical union, see Idel, *Kabbalah: New Perspectives*, pp. 67–70. See also Orent, "Mystical Union." See, especially, this imagery in the collection of traditions from the circle of the Great Maggid, *'Or ha-'Emmet*, fols. 39 a, 39c discussed in Idel, *Hasidism*, p. 168.

10   See, e.g., *BT, Nedarim*, 38a.

11   *'Or ha-Ganuz la-Tzaddiqim*, fol. 40c.

12   Idel, "Prayer, Ecstasy, and Alien Thoughts in the Besht's Religious World," pp. 66–77.

13   For R. Eleazar Aziqri's views on *devequt* see, especially, Pachter, *Roots of Faith and Devequt*, pp. 278–279.

14   *Keter Shem Tov*, pars. 192–193, discussed by Scholem, *The Messianic Idea*, pp. 207–208.

15   See Green, "Hasidism: Discovery and Retreat," pp. 104–130.

16   Kauffman, "Ritual Immersion," pp. 409–425, especially pp. 423–425, and Menachem Kallus, "The Relation of the Baal Shem Tov to the Practice of Lurianic Kavvanot in Light of his Comments on the Siddur Rashkov," *Kabbalah*, vol. 2 (1997), pp. 151–167. For the importance of taking bath for attaining extraordinary experiences, see previously the passage translated from R. Zeev Wolf of Zithomir's book, beside n. 134. See also *In Praise of the Ba'al Shem Tov*, p. 206, as well as other discussions therein, and Garb, *Shamanic Trance in Modern Kabbalah*, pp. 125–128.

17   See my "Sefirot above Sefirot," *Tarbiz*, vol. 51 (1982), pp 250–251 (Hebrew).

18   Kauffman, "Ritual Immersion," p. 422.

19   Kauffman, pp. 423–425.

20   About mysticism and oceanic feelings, see Wiliam B. Parsons, *The Enigma of the Oceanic Feeling, Revisioning the Psychoanalytic Theory of Mysticism* (Oxford University Press, New York-Oxford, 1999).

21   Compare to R. Menachem Nahum of Chernobyl, *Me'or 'Einayyim*, p. 215. On this dictum see my *Primeval Evil*.

22   See R. Yehudah ha-Levi, Kuzari, 4:23. This theme occurs already in quite an explicit manner in the Great Maggid's *Maggid Devarav le-Ya'aqov*, ed. Schatz-Uffenheimer, p. 134. On the development of this theme in earlier Jewish sources, see Dov Sdan, *"Hittah she-Niqberah,"* in *Proceedings of the Israeli Academy for Sciences and Humanities* (Jerusalem, 1963), pp. 1–21 (Hebrew); Morton Smith, "Transformation by Burial (I Cor. 15.35–49; Rom 6.3–5 and 8.9–11)," *Eranos Jahrbuch*, vol. 52 (1983), pp. 87–112; Scholem, *Major Trends in Jewish Mysticism*, pp. 268, 412, n. 72; Krassen, *Uniter of Heaven and Earth*, pp. 169–171; Idel, *Kabbalah & Eros*, p. 165; and Lorberbaum, "Attain the Attribute of *'Ayyin*," pp. 198–200.

23   *Qehilat Ya'aqov* (Jerusalem, 1971), part III, fol. 9a.

24   See, e.g.,*'Or ha-'Emmet*, fol. 39ab, Lorberbaum, "Attain the Attribute of 'Ayyin." See also Idel, *Hasidism*, pp. 140–142.

25   See chap. 2 in this volume.

26   Lorberbaum, "Attain the Attribute of *'Ayyin*," p. 234; Krassen, *Uniter of Heaven and Earth*, pp. 170–171; and see also Lederberg, *The Gateway to Infinity*, pp. 251–281; and Mayse, *Beyond the Letters*, pp. 30–31. This is also the case in some discussions

of R. Jacob Joseph. See appendix F in this volume. For the theologization in the academic interpretations of Jewish mysticism, see M. Idel, "On the Theologization of Kabbalah in Modern Scholarship," in eds. Y. Schwartz and V. Krech, *Religious Apologetics—Philosophical Argumentation* (Tübingen, 2004), pp. 123–173. As to Hasidism see the assumption that there is just one pertinent theology, the divine immanence, in *Hasidism: A New History*, pp. 161-163.

27   For the people of Israel.

28   Cf. Jeremiah 18:6. See already the parable of the artisan in the Besht's tradition analyzed in my "Your Word Stands Firm in Heaven."

29   The division between the five consonants of *Yisra'el* into two units is found much earlier in Kabbalah, though the interpretations of the two units differ somewhat. In all the cases the unit of three letters *Ra'al*, amounting in gematria to 231, refers to the number of the combinations of two letters by means of which the world was created, according to some interpretations of *Sefer Yetziyrah*. This is part of a wider vision of creation by means of letters in late antiquity Judaism. See Weiss, *Letters by which Heaven and Earth Were Created*, pp. 84–146.

30   *Degel Maḥaneh 'Efrayyim*, p. 212.

31   *Degel Maḥaneh 'Efrayyim*, p. 213:

כי בשבילם ברא הבורא ברוך הוא את העולם והם המחזיקים את העולם הנקרא יש ובידם
להחזיר היש לאין ולהוציא דבר חדש כמו חומר ביד היוצר להפך דבר מדבר ולהפוך מחומר
ראשון לצורה אחרת מצורה ראשונה וזהו מורה בשם ישראל כי כשמקרבים הי"ש לתלת אותיות
רא"ל, כנ"ל שם נמתקים הדברים בשרשם כל הישות בסוד האין ודי בזה, ולחכם יספיק הקיצור,
כי יש בזה צורך להאריך כי יש בזה עמקות.

For R. Jacob Joseph's own assessment that there are esoteric issues on a certain topics which are related to speech, see his *Kutoneth Passim*, ed. Nigal, p. 250.

32   Whether the Braslavian view of mystical union referred in ch. 4 n. 5 in this volume reflects a Beshtian source is an issue that cannot be discussed here. See previously the Beshtian passage cited in ch. 6 n. 3 in this volume from R. Yehoshu'a Abraham ben Yisrael, *Ge'ulat Yisrael*.

Appendix B: The Besht and R. Abraham Azulai's *Ḥesed le-'Avraham*

1   See Scholem, *Ha-Shalav ha-'Aharon*, p. 134.

2   See Idel, *Hasidism*, pp. 218–219, 220–221, and ch. 3 n. 7 in this volume.

3   See, e.g., Elior, *Israel Ba'al Shem Tov and His Contemporaries*, or Magid, *Hasidism Incarnate*. See also ch. 10 n. 14 in this volume.

4   On principles see also, e.g., the passage adduced in ch. 6 n. 15 in this volume.

5   On the term *penimiyyut*, which appears many times also in this book, see, e.g., fols. 14a, 18a; see also ch. 5 nn. 9, 12, ch. 6 n. 8 in this volume.

6   *Ben Porat Yosef*, fol. 21a:

יש כלל אחד גדול, שצריך לדבק עצמו לפנימיות התורה והמצוה, דהיינו לקשר מחשבתו
ונשמתו אל שורש התורה והמצוה אשר הוא עושה דאם לא כן עושה ח"ו קיצוץ ופירוד בנטיעות,
'וכאשר קבלתי ממורי וכן מצאתי בחסד לאברהם נהר י"ד וכו

I assume that this is the passage that Scholem, *The Messianic Idea*, p. 211, sum-
marized in his description of Hasidism adduced in n. 1. Compare also to a similar
view in *Ben Porat Yosef*, fols. 16c, 25a, 25b, 46c, and see also Piekarz, "Devekuth,"
p. 141.

7   For the passage of Azulai and its Cordoverian background, see in more detail, Idel,
    Enchanted Chains, pp. 182–187, as well as my *Hasidism*, pp 192–193. See also Azulai's
    'Or ha-Hammah, II, fols. 110b, 110c, and Cordovero's passage quoted in Azulai, fol.
    133d. See also R. Aharon of Zhitomir, in his *Toledot 'Aharon*, fol. 6d, which claims
    that "by means of the speech he reaches the *devequt*." Let me mention here that a
    theurgy of sound, namely the sending of the sounds to the body of Indra, is found
    in the Upanishads. See Beck, *Sonic Theology*, p. 27.

8   See Bracha Sack, "Toward the Sources of the Book *Hesed le-'Avraham* by R.
    Abraham Azulai," *QS*, 56 (1981), pp. 164–175 (Hebrew). On this Kabbalist see Ronit
    Meroz, "*Sefer 'Or Ganuz* by R. Abraham Azulai," *QS*, vol. 60 (1985), pp. 310–324
    (Hebrew).

9   Idel, *Hasidism*, pp. 65–66, 179, 192, 200–201.

10 Compare to Cordovero, *'Or Yaqar*, on *Tiqqunei Zohar*, vol. 6, p. 303, where the
    phrase "spiritual force of the *sefirot*" occurs together with a discussion of nature of
    the Torah. See also Cordovero, p. 320. Compare also to Horowitz, *Ha-Shelah*, I, fol.
    5a, and in the passage from *Toldedot Ya'aqov Yosef*, fol. 136a translated in appendix F.

11 *Hesed le-'Avraham*, fol. 14a. This passage is found also in his *Ben Porat Yosef*, fol.
    21a, where he refers to *Hesed le-'Avraham* several times on the same page, without
    mentioning, however, the Besht in this context. Moreover, on fol. 21b, he points out
    again to an affinity between what he received from the Besht and Azulai's book.

12 *Toledot Ya'aqov Yosef*, fol. 6a:

כמו שיש באדם חומר וצורה כך יש באותיות התורה חומר וצורה. כי גוף האותיות הוא
החומר, ורוחניות הספירות עם אור אין סוף שבתוכו המחיה, הוא הצורה ונשמה אל האותיות, ואל
זה יכוון האדם בתורתו ותפלתו, וכמו שכתב בחסד לאברהם נהר מ"ג מפורש וזה לשונו, עיקר
הכוונה, כי צריך להמשיך הרוחניות מן מדרגות עליונות אל האותיות שהוא מזכיר, כדי שיוכלו
.האותיות לעלות עד מדרגה העליונה לעשות שאלתו עד כאן לשונו, וכאשר קבלתי ממורי

See also his very important reiteration of the theory of Cordovero and Azulai
    in *Ben Porat Yosef*, fol. 15d, which is again juxtaposed to the view of the Besht.
    About elevation of the sounds, see also ch. 1 n. 22 in this volume. For the juxtaposi-
    tion of a passage from another follower of Cordovero's, R. Elijah da Vidas's *Reshit
    Hokhmah*, and the Besht, see R. Jacob Joseph's *Toledot Ya'aqov Yosef*, fol. 5b. For the
    centrality of speech in a text of Cordovero, see his *'Or Yaqar*, vol. 6, p. 203.

13 See the passage from the same book translated around ch. 5 n. 12 in this volume and
    compare to the content of the following note. For the term *'Otiyyot mahashaviyyot* in
    the Besht, Cordovero, and Azulai, see in the text beside ch. 2 n. 9 and in appendices
    C and D in this volume.

14 See *Toledot Ya'aqov Yosef*, fol. 3a.

15 Pedaya, "The Besht, R. Jacob Joseph of Polonnoye, and the Maggid of Mezeritch," p. 63. See also appendix F in this volume.

16 See Idel, *Hasidism*, pp. 235–236.

17 Pedaya, "The Besht, R. Jacob Joseph of Polonnoye, and the Maggid of Mezeritch," p. 61.

18 For more on *Tzaddiqim*, see appendix F in this volume.

19 On words as horses in early Hasidism see, e.g., *Maggid Devarav Le-Ya'aqov*, ed. Schatz-Uffenheimer, pp. 80–82; *'Or ha-'Emmet*, fol. 51a; and *Liqqutim Yeqarim*, 109b. Though this is a riding downward, Azulai's version of Cordovero contains also rising upward by means of vocables. Compare also to a similar view found in R. Ḥayyim Vital's *Sha'ar Ruaḥ ha-Qodesh*, pp. 9–10.

20 Indubitably this is a hint at the vision of Jacob's ladder where angels ascend and descend, recurring in early Hasidism, though now both the souls and the vocables do so. See also *Ben Porat Yosef* (Brooklyn, 1976), fol. 53d:

> The letters/vocables of the Torah and prayer are a ladder to attach his soul and ascend by means of the letters/vocables because the body of the letters' vocables is found on earth, in the corporeal realm and the head, namely the *Kavvanah* of letters reaches heaven, on high.

See also *Ben Porat Yosef*, fol. 59d, to be discussed in appendix F and as addressed in appendix C in this volume. About the *tzaddiqim* as the angels of God in a similar context, see *Ben Porat Yosef*, fol. 45d. See also ch. 5 n. 1 in this volume. On Jacob's dream and the ladder in Hasidism, see Jacobs, *Their Heads in Heaven*, pp. 56–72.

21 I assume that with the lower righteous. See also Azulai, *'Or ha-Ḥammah*, I, fol. 54a.

22 *Hesed le-Avraham*, fol. 11c, 11d:

העניין הוא כי הנשמה היא מבינה, והתורה מת"ת, ונמצאת התורה לבוש אל הנשמה, ובעת
היות הצדיקים עוסקים בעולם הזה בתורה, אותם הקולות מתהוים מהם אותיות רוחניות משתלשֿ-
לות ממטה למעלה בסוד אבי"ע ממדריגה למדריגה עד עלייתם לג"ע מקום הקב"ה עם הנשמות,
כאומרו חבירים מקשיבים לקולך השמיעני, וכשמוע הצדיקים עניין זה מתלבשים בסוד אותיות
התורה שהתחתונים עוסקים, ומה גם אם הוא דבר שהם עסקו בו בהיותם בחיים, ובסולם מדריגות
עליות הקולות רוכבים הם ויורדים למטה ומזדווגין עמהם, והטעם כי סוד הייחוד לקב"ה בשלימות
הוא ע"י נשמות עולם זה ועולם העליון כנזכר בזוהר תרומה, ולזה הצדיקים שהם בעולם העליון
יורדים לעולם התחתון להשתתף עם הצדיקים שהם למטה כדי שיהיה היחוד שלם.

An almost identical passage is found in Azulai's *'Or ha-Ḥammah*, I, fol. 8d. See a partial parallel in Cordovero's *'Or Yaqar*, vol. 16, p. 70. See also Cordovero, fols. 9b, 9c, 38a, and 47a. See also previously the text of R. Elijah da Vidas as well as the texts mentioned in n. 50, and the interesting passage in *Hesed le-'Avraham*, fol. 30b, which is referenced in R. Jacob Joseph of Polonnoye, *Toledot Ya'aqov Yosef*, fol. 66c. For several references to *Hesed le-'Avraham*, see the eighteenth-century Kabbalist close to Hasidism, R. Barukh of Kosov, *'Amudei ha-'Avodah*, fols. 2b, 20b–21a, 39a, 98b. See also Garb, "Powers of Language," pp. 258–249. Those Cordoverian texts served as an exegetical grid for understanding the ideal manner of prayer and study of the Torah. See Idel, "Female Beauty," pp. 332–333, n. 53.

Elsewhere I have suggested that the Besht has marginalized a Lurianic view in favor of a Cordoverian one. See my "Models of Understanding Prayer," p. 52.

23   Compare to Cordovero's *'Or Yaqar*, vol. 13, p. 57; *Tefillah le-Moshe*, fol. 4a; *Shi'ur Qomah*, fol. 18a; and especially to Azulai's *'Or ha-Ḥammah*, I, fol. 170a, and II, fol. 71d. On the garment of the souls in the world-to-come as constituted of the commandments performed during one's life, see Gershom Scholem, "The Paradisic Garb of the Souls and the Origin of the Concept of *Ḥaluqa' de-Rabbanan*," *Tarbiz*, vol. 24 (1955), pp. 297–306 (Hebrew); Scholem, *On the Mystical Shape of the Godhead*, pp. 264–273; and Avishai bar Asher, "Kabbalistic Commentaries on the Secret of the Garment in the sixteenth century," *Da'at*, vol. 76 (2014), pp. 191–213 (Hebrew); and *In Praise of the Baal Shem Tov*, p. 206. For the view that one can dress himself with the utterances after he has divested himself during prayer, see the Great Maggid's *Maggid Devarav le-Ya'aqov*, ed. Schatz-Uffenheimer, pp. 45–46, and in ch. 8 n. 11 in this volume. See also *Toledot Ya'aqov Yosef*, fol. 3a, where letters/vocables of a commandment are described as vessels and garments when dealing specifically with letters of the divine name:

באותיות מצוה כי ה' הוא הכלי והלבוש

This sonorous garment seems to be a synthesis between the Rabbinic theme of the garment of the soul and its medieval metamorphoses on the one hand, and the magical theory of putting the garment upon which the divine name is written on the other. About the latter garment see, e.g., Scholem, *Major Trends in Jewish Mysticism*, p. 77. Azulai's passage seems to be the closest theory to the Hasidic instruction to enter the vocables, which have been discussed previously. See also the views of the garment in the fifteenth-century Kabbalistic-magical *Book of Meshiv*, discussed in Idel, *Enchanted Chains*, pp. 114–118.

See the view found in *Ge'ulat Yisra'el*, ed. Y. M. Rasfeld (Warsau, 1908), fol. 20a, where the speeches of prayer and Torah are described as creating *maqqifim*, namely circles that circumvent the body, and are described as garments. This is a Lurianic term. Later on in fol. 20c, the utterances are described as comprising all the worlds, angels, and souls.

24   Compare also to his use of the verb *meyaḥed*, in fol. 10d.

25   See n. 1 in this volume.

26   See also appendix F in this volume.

Appendix C: Palaces and Drawing Down of Spiritual Force in Cordovero

1   See, especially, ch. 1 n. 22, ch. 3 n. 7, ch. 8 n. 11, ch. 10 n. 3, and the previous appendix.

2   See, e.g., *Hasidism*, *Enchanted Chains*, and "The Besht as Prophet and Talismanic Magician."

3   See ch. 10 n. 13 in this volume.

4   See Idel, *Hasidism*, p. 159.

5   See Idel, pp. 65–81.

6   For the medieval magical sources that informed Cordovero's understanding of language see Idel, pp. 156–162.

7   Cf. *Sefer Yetziyrah* II:3. See also beside ch. 3 n. 7 in this volume.

8   See, e.g., the view of R. Bahyah ibn Paquda, adduced in Jacobs, *Hasidic Prayer*, pp. 71–72. See also Cordovero's important discussion of *kavvanah* in prayer, resorting to this dictum, in *Pardes Rimmonim*, XXXI, chap. 5. In Hasidism this dictum occurs many times. See, e.g., R. Jacob Joseph, *Kutoneth Passim*, ed. Nigal, p. 162.

9   *Commentary on Sefer Yetziyrah*, chap. 2, p. 89:

העניין כי אל האותיות שלשה בחינות, האחד גשמית, והשני גשמי יוצא אל הרוחני, והשלישי רוחני כולו. והם האחת האות בכתב היא גשמית בעצם בלי ספק, שהיא בגשם נושא ונשוא האות והכתב...השנית הם האותיות הקבועות בפה, והם נעתקות מכתב אל לשון, והלשון גשמית וזכירתה גשמית, אבל נעתקת משם אל סוד הרוחניות שהיא המחשבה. השלישית, הם האותיות המחשביות שאליהם עיקר הכוונה, והוא רוחניות האותיות. ולכך תפלה בלא כוונה כגוף בלא נשמה.

A similar discussion is found also *Commentary on Sefer Yetziyrah*, chap. 3, pp. 163–164; in *Pardes Rimmonim*, XXXII, chap. 2, XVII, chap. 2; and in *'Or Yaqar*, vol. 15, p. 31, where he refers to his *Commentary on Sefer Yetziyrah*. The syntagma אותיות מחשביות is found already in R. Nathan ben Sa'adyah Har'ar's *Sha'arei Tzedeq*, a book that was known to Cordovero. See Idel, *Le Porte della Giustizia*, p. 411.

10   *Commentary on Sefer Yetziyrah*, chap. 2, p. 89:

הרוחניות שהם במדות והנתיבות העליונות, והם משתלשלים אלו מאלו. . . .

11   The most explicit discussion is found in *'Or Yaqar*, vol. 2, p. 93; and see also *'Or Yaqar*, vol. 1, pp. 44, 68, 81; and *'Or Yaqar*, on *Tiqqunei Zohar*, vol. 6, pp. 318–319.

12   *'Or Yaqar*, on *Tiqqunei Zohar Hadash*, vol. 3, p. 7:

סוד ביטויי השם הקבוע באותיות בפה, ועולה ברוחניות ותופס עד רוחניות העליון, ועל ידי כך מנענע הכחות העליונים שהייאך היה אדם יכול לשלוט ברוחניים הדקים הם הנאצלים, אם לא בחסדי השם שקבע השמות בספירות וחקקם בפי האדם.

For the assumption that there are spiritual forces of divine names, see *'Or Yaqar*, pp. 105, 112.

13   *'Or Yaqar*, vol. 3, p. 149.

14   *Commentary* on *Sefer Yetziyrah*, chap. 2, p. 90:

גשמיו"ת ורוחניו"ת ואלהיו"ת, ולא היו מגלגלים אות שלא היו מכוונים בהמצאת הדבר והשתלשלו מעלה לעלול עד הגשם העב This is a different distinction than the earlier one, part of what I call Cordovero's conceptual fluidity.

Compare also to *Commentary on Sefer Yetziyrah*, chap. 3, p. 164, where the entire concatenation is mentioned in the context of the creation of the Golem according to the Talmudic account. See also *Commentary on Sefer Yetziyrah*, p. 92, and Idel, *Golem*, pp. 196–203.

15   *'Or Yaqar*, vol. 10, p. 142:

ומהזכרת האותיות מתעוררים בהנעת לשון ושפה בעולם הגשמי הזה יעוררו נשמתם העליונה למעלה, וכל זה מטעם שהאותיות הם היכלות לרוחניותם.

Compare also *'Or Yaqar*:

כי האותיות הם היכלות וכלים המחזיקים ברמיזתם האורות העליונים

"Since the sounds/letters are palaces and vessels that contain in their alluded [sense] the supernal lights."

A very similar view is found in Azulai's *'Or ha-Ḥammah*, I, fol. 10c:

וכפי חיוב אותם הבחינות מקיבוץ אותיות הקדושות שהם היכלות לרוחניות.

This passage stems from Cordovero's important passage in *'Or Yaqar*, vol. 1, p. 78. See also the important discussion in *Pardes Rimmonim*, Gate XXVII, chap. 2, and *'Or Yaqar* on *Tiqqunei Zohar Ḥadash*, vol. 3, p. 116.

16   See also Cordovero, *'Or Yaqar*, vol. 10, p. 172. This view is found in rather similar terms in Azulai's *Ḥesed le-'Avraham*, fol. 9d. For spiritual vocables that are created by recitation or from the spiritual force emerging from the performance of the commandments and ascend on high, see the passages preserved in Azulai, *'Or ha-Ḥammah*, I, fols. 38a, 47a, 54a. For the view that the spiritual forces connect the different levels of reality, see *'Or Yaqar*, vol. 4, p. 50.

17   For the material things and deeds as the vessels for the spiritual force, see the passage from Azulai, *'Or ha-Ḥammah*, I, fol. 63b. For the spiritual force of the house, namely the temple, see *'Or ha-Ḥammah*, fol. 68a. See also R. Reuven Horowitz, *Diduim ba-Sodeh*, fol. 21b, who also uses the image "house"—*Bait*, while elsewhere in fol. 86a, he adds also the image of the tent for human utterances, and perhaps also sanctuary or tabernacle, according to 117a. For the relationship between sanctuary and the dwelling of the spiritual force, see, e.g., Cordovero, *'Or Yaqar*, vol. 1, p. 62; Cordovero, vol. 4, p. 95; and Cordovero, vol. 17, p. 84, where he also mentions the two temples. See also Idel, *Hasidism*, pp. 295–296, n. 242, and Schwartz, *Studies on Astral Magic*, pp. 106–109. For the image of labyrinth for the phoneme, see Derrida, *La voix et le phénomène*, p. 117.

      For the righteous as the palace of God, see Horowitz, *Diduim ba-Sodeh*, fol. 121b. This latter theme deserves a more detailed consideration for understanding one of the main sources of early Hasidic understanding of the divine nature of the *Tzaddiq*. See also appendix B n. 18 in this volume.

18   See beside ch. 3 n. 7 in this volume. Compare also to Cordovero's *Tefillah le-Moshe*, fol. 4a.

19   Cordovero, *'Or Yaqar*, vol. 5, p. 214:

שבכל אות ואות ברוחניותה נכללים כמה עולמות דקים.

      See also Cordovero, vol. 8, p. 36:

שכל אות ואות הוא עולם ורוחניות ומאור נפלא.

      "Since each and every sound/letter is a world, a spiritual force and a wondrous light." A similar view is found also elsewhere in Cordovero's *'Or Yaqar*, vol. 11, p. 48, and in Cordovero, *Tiqqunei Zohar Ḥadash*, vol. 3, p. 99. See also *Pardes Rimmonim*, XXVII:2, in a passage to be quoted in the next appendix. For the existence of all the letters in each letter, just as each *sefirot* comprises all of them, see *Pardes Rimmonim*, and *Commentary on Sefer Yetziyrah*, p. 104. This is quite an old theme in Kabbalah. For an interesting discussion where the term *'otiyyot* stands for the separation of the amorphous voice into speeches, see Cordovero, *'Or Yaqar*, vol. 11, p. 174.

20   See Idel, *Hasidism*, pp. 70–71 and, e.g., Cordovero, *'Or Yaqar*, vol. 11, p. 283, and his
      texts cited by Azulai's *'Or ha-Ḥammah*, vol. II, fols. 171c, 249d, vol. III, fol. 85d. For
      the occurrence of *'Otiyyot* together with drawing down, see Cordovero, *'Or Yaqar*,
      vol. 7, pp. 17–18, and see also *Pardes Rimmonim*, XXXII, chap. 2.

21   See Idel, "The Besht as Prophet and Talismanic Magician," pp. 135–136, beside ch.
      8 n. 15 in this volume, and the more elaborate treatment in the next appendix.

22   See also the passage of Cordovero, *'Or Yaqar*, vol. 9, p. 144, on the cleaving of the
      soul to the "inner spiritual force"—הרוחניות הפנימי—without, however, mentioning
      vocal rituals. See also Cordovero on *Tiqqunei Zohar*, vol. 5, p. 33. See also *Pardes
      Rimmonim*, XXXII, chap. 3; *'Or Yaqar*, vol. 10, p. 166; *'Or Yaqar*, vol. 11, p. 286; *'Or
      Yaqar*, on *Tiqqunei Zohar*, vol. 4, pp. 42, 210; and *Tiqqunei Zohar*, vol. 5, p. 17,
      and several times in *Derishot*. In many cases in his writings, Cordovero resorts
      to the term penimiyyut as referring to the sefirot as the essence of divinity. The
      phrase "inner spiritual force" was taken over by Azulai, *Ḥesed le-'Avraham*, fol. 9d.
      Compare also to R. Abraham Yehoshua Heschel, *'Ohev Israel* (New York, 1956),
      fols. 34c, 47a, and especially 72d.
      It should be mentioned that in Cordovero, *'Or Yaqar* on *Tiqqunei Zohar*, vol.
      5, p. 33, there is an interesting discussion concerning the cleaving to the spiritual
      forces and *sefirot* that are drawn down during prayer. See also Cordovero, *ibidem*, p.
      68, and *ibidem*, p. 85, on the descent of the spiritual force on the letters.

23   See *'Or Yaqar*, vol. 2, p. 247:
      וצריך לחתך האותיות בתפלתו ותורתו להורות חילוק בין אות לאות, כדי שיהיה אבנים
      שלימות.
      "It is necessary to divide the vocables in his prayer and his Torah [study] in
      order to evince the distinction between vocable and vocable, so that the stones will
      be perfect." *Nota bene:* the instruction that puts together prayer and study of the
      Torah, as the early Hasidic masters will do, on the ground of the common denomi-
      nator: the primacy of pronunciation.

24   This is part of the linguistic ontology.

25   Cordovero, *Pardes Rimmonim* XXVII, chap. 2; II, fol. 59cd:
      ובהיות האדם מזכיר ומניע אות מהאותיות בהכרח יתעורר הרוחניות ההוא והבל הפה ממנו
      יתהוו צורות קדושות יתעלו ויתקשרו בשרשם שהם שרש האצילות...עוד יתהווה ממנה מהבל
      פיו רוחניות ומציאות יהי' כמו מלאך שיעלה ויתקשר בשורשו שימהר להפעיל פעולתו בזריזות
      ומהירות וזהו סוד הזכרת השמות וכוונת התפלה.
      See Bracha Sack, "A Fragment of R. Moshe Cordovero's *Commentary on Ra'aya
      Meheimna*," *Qobetz 'al Yad (Minora Manuscripta Hebraica)* X (XX) (Jerusalem,
      1982), pp. 270–271. Therefore, the ascent of the vocables of prayer is meant to bind
      the prayer to God in a way similar to that indicated by some Hasidic masters. See
      also Sack, "A Fragment," p. 270, n. 52. The Cordoverian nexus between combina-
      tions of letters and *kavvanah* was paraphrased in Azulai's *Ḥesed le-'Avraham*, fol.
      10a.

26   See my introduction to my edition of *R. Natan ben Sa'adyah Har'ar, Le Porte della
      Giustizia*, pp. 147–153.

27 See also *'Or Yaqar*, vol. 2, p. 247; Cordovero,, *Derishot*, p. 55; and Pines, "Le *Sefer ha-Tamar* et les *Maggidim* des Kabbalists," pp. 333–363; and "On the Term *Ruḥaniyyut* and Its Sources," pp. 511–540. For the concept of "Maggid" in more general terms in Safedian Kabbalah, see Werblowsky, *Joseph Karo, Lawyer and Mystic*, cf., index under item Maggid, Maggidism; and for a different view see M. Idel, "Joseph Karo and His Revelations: On the Apotheosis of the Feminine in Safedian Kabbalah," *Tikvah Center Working Paper Series* (NYU School of Law, New York, 2010), pp: 1–50. See also my "Astral Dreams in R. Yohanan Alemanno's Writings," pp. 120–121. See also appendix B. n. 23 in this volume.

28 See also *'Or Yaqar*, vol. 14, p. 177; *'Or Yaqar*, vol. 15, p. 2; and *'Or Yaqar*, vol. 17, p. 114. Compare to Or Yaqar on *Tiqqunei Zohar*, vol. 4, p. 205:

סוד התפלה שהיא רוחניות הבל הנשמה .

"The secret of prayer is the spiritual force of the vapor of the [higher] soul." See also Cordovero's seminal passage translated beside ch. 8 n. 15 in this volume.

29 See also in appendix F in this volume.

30 Cordovero, *Pardes Rimmonim*, XXXII, chap. 3,

עיקר הכוונה צריך המכוון להמשיך רוחניות מהמדרגות העליונות אל האותיות שהוא מזכיר
כדי שיוכל להפריח האותיות ההם עד המדרגה העליונה ההיא למהר שאלתו. והכוונה כי הבל פיו
של אדם לא דבר רק הוא... אמנם היא רוחניות מתהווה מהבל פיו של אדם. וצריך אל הרוחניות
ההוא כח להפריח שאלותיו ולהעלות האותיות עד המדרגות הנרצות לו. וזהו עיקר הכוונה להמ־
שיך כח כדי שבכח ההוא יעלו האותיות למעלה ויתחוו במקום רומו של עו/'ט וימהרו בקשתו

I checked this seminal passage against one of the earliest manuscripts of Cordovero's book, Ms. Vatican-Neofiti 28, and the printed version corresponds to the manuscript.

See also my discussion in Idel, *Hasidism*, pp. 165–166, where I pointed out to an impact of this passage on early Hasidic masters, via the mediation of Horowitz's *Sha'ar ha-Shamayyim*. See, e.g., R. Meshullam Phoebus of Zbarazh, *Kitvei Qodesh*, fol. 18a (= *Yosher Divrei 'Emmet*, fol. 132a). For this theory see also Azulai, *Ḥesed le-'Avraham*, fol. 24c, 24d, and his *'Or ha-Ḥammah*, I, fol. 170a; Garb, "Powers of Language in Kabbalah," pp. 245–249; and now Yoed Kadary, *The Angelology of Rabbi Moses Cordovero* (PhD Thesis, University of Ben Gurion, Beer Sheva, 2014), pp. 281–283 (Hebrew).

This seminal passage should be compared to what Cordovero wrote in *Pardes Rimmonim*, XVI, chap. 5, and XXVII, chap. 2—the latter cited previously—and in his *'Or Yaqar*, vol. 11, p. 296, vol. 12, p. 92; and *'Or Yaqar* on *Tiqqunei Zohar*, vol. 4, pp. 185, 205;, and *'Or Yaqar* on *Tiqqunei Zohar*, vol. 5, p. 296, that deals with causing of ascent in the context of the "spiritual force," and see also the parallels mentioned in the previous note. See also Ben Shlomo, *The Mystical Theology of Moses Cordovero*, p. 42.

Though in some cases Cordovero's "letters" indeed stand for vocables, in some others it stand for the signs, namely graphical representations. See, e.g., *Pardes Rimmonim* XXVII, chap. 2.

For Cordovero's views on prayer, see Bracha Sack, "Prayer in the Thought of R. Moshe Cordovero," *Da'at* vol. 9 (1982), pp. 5–12 (Hebrew), and her *The Kabbalah of Rabbi Moshe Cordovero*, pp. 193–202; Margolin, *The Human Temple*, pp. 298–302; and my *Hasidism*, pp. 149–188. It should be pointed out that this ascent on high by means of letters/sounds was described on the basis of the Heikhalot literature alone, without mentioning in this context the Cordoverian ascensional material regarding the utterances, cf., Pedaya, "The Besht, R. Jacob Joseph of Polonnoye, and the Maggid of Mezeritch," p. 53, and especially Pedaya, pp. 55ff., whereas the Beshtian views surveyed are actually of Cordoverian extraction! See also my "The Besht as Prophet and Talismanic Magician," pp. 135–136. For the ascent of the role played by letters/sounds in Jewish mysticism, see my "Reification of Language in Jewish Mysticism," pp. 66–69.

31   See my "Models of Understanding Prayer," and "The Liturgical Turn: From the Spanish Kabbalas, to the Kabbalas of Safed, and to Hasidism," in ed. U. Erlich, *Jewish Prayer: New Perspectives* (Ben Gurion University Press, Beer Sheva, 2016), pp. 9–50 (Hebrew).

32   See my *Hasidism*, p. 147.

33   Cordovero, *Pardes Rimmonim* XXVII, chap. 2:

והנה האות היכל ומכון לרוחניות ההוא.

     In fact in *'Or Yaqar*, vol. 14, p. 11, Cordovero speaks also about a variety of ritual acts, not only vocal, that constitute palaces for higher entities.

34   Idem, *Pardes Rimmonim*, XXXII, chap. 3.

35   See in appendix B in this volume.

36   Compare to a similar discussion in *Derishot*, p. 28:

שהוא מושך להם השפע מרוחניותו ודקותו והם משפיעים אליו בבחינת עביותם, כיצד האדם מייחד וקושר הספירות באין סוף על ידי נשמה דאצילות.

37   Cordovero, *'Or Yaqar*, vol. 16, p. 70:

ונודע שסוד הדבור הקדוש היוצא מפי האדם הוא כליל מסוד הנפ"ש והרו"ח והנשמ"ה בכל בחינות סולם, מפני שהקולות והאותיות מתהוה מהם רוחניות והרוחניות ההיא מסתלק מבחינה אל בחינה ועולה בסוד קשר וייחוד כל המדרגות.

38   Compare to the very similar language found in the Cordoverian passage adduced in Azulai's *'Or ha-Ḥammah*, I, fol. 106c, where it is said that the "lower powers that are demons, materialize in the air and draw the powers of the stars [=planets]."

כי הכחות התחתונים שהם השדים המתגלמים באויר מושכים כחות הכככים.

     Both the positive and negative powers are depicted as materializing in the air, using the same verb derived from *GLM*.

39   On the garment of vocables, see in appendix B in this volume.

40   Azulai, *'Or ha-Ḥammah*, I, p. 170:

שממש אותיות התורה שהאדם יבטא בשפתיו ואותם ההבלים היוצאים מפיו מתגלמין באויר העולי ויעשה מהם צורות רוחניות קדושות שהם המלבישי' האדם ומוליכות אותו לשורשי האותיות ואותיות התורה העליונה שהיא חיי העולם הבא והיא ממש יש מציאות רוחני ללמד זכותו.

     Those themes reverberate on the same page later on. Similar views are found in Isaiah Horowitz's *Shenei Luḥot ha-Berit*, see, e.g., I, fols. 6b, 9b, 16b, 19ab, III, fol. 183b.

41   See, e.g, *'Or Yaqar*, vol. 12, pp. 1, 92, and a more elaborated analysis of this crucial term in appendix D in this volume.

42   *Tefillah le-Moshe*, fol. 79b. See also the quote in the name of R. Abraham Galante, Cordovero's disciple, in Azulai's *'Or ha-Hammah*, II, fol. 72b.

43   *Derishot*, p. 55.

44   *Tefillah le-Moshe*, fol. 64a, and see also his *Shi'ur Qomah*, fol. 16c. It seems plausible that the meaning is that there is an inherent spiritual force in the song.

45   *Tefillah le-Moshe*, fol. 4a, and also fols. 213a, 360a, and for drawing down, see also fol. 57b.

46   *Tefillah le-Moshe*, fol. 63a.

47   *Tefillah le-Moshe*, fol. 190b. See also *'Or Yaqar*, vol. 17, p. 14; *'Or Yaqar*, vol. 6, p. 36; and appendix D in this volume.

48   See Idel, *Studies in Ecstatic Kabbalah*, pp. 139–140, and appendix D in this volume.

49   Cordovero, *'Or Yaqar*, vol. 17, pp. 20, 25, 67; *Derishot*, p. 70; and Azulai, *'Or ha-Hammah*, I, fols. 10c, 11b. See also *'Or Yaqar*, vol. 1, pp. 76, 81; *'Or Yaqar*, vol. 12, p. 2; Idel, *Absorbing Perfections*, pp. 130–131; and appendix D in this volume.

50   *'Or Yaqar*, vol. 14, p. 213.

51   *'Or Yaqar*, p. 209.

52   See also Cordovero's *Commentary on Sefer Yetziyrah*, p. 177; *'Or Yaqar*, on *Tiqqunei Zohar*, vol. 5, p. 17; and the quote in his name in Azulai's *'Or ha-Hammah*, II, fol. 26d; as well as two other discussions about prophecy in Cordovero in my "On Prophecy and Early Hasidism," pp. 53–54. See, especially, my discussion in "The Besht as a Prophet and Talismanic Magician," pp. 142–143. Prophecy is discussed in many instances also in astro-magical contexts. See, e.g., Schwartz, *Studies on Astral Magic*, index, p. 260, under item prophecy, or Yohanan Alemanno, who continued some of the Spanish astro-magical trends. See his *Hesheq Shlomo*, Ms. Moscow-Ginzburg 140, fols. 100a and 287a, and Idel, *Golem*, pp. 171–172.

53   *'Or Yaqar, Tiqqunei Zohar Hadash*, vol. 2, p. 9:

וכעין ממש שישתנה ענין הנבואה מצד המשכתה על ידה נשמה שכל אחד ואחד ישאב כפי
כח עבודתו והמשכת רוחניות עליון עליו, במדה שיתייחד עבוד' לבורא מעבודת בן גילו, כך יתייחד
דבקותו בבוראו מדבקות חברו. וכן העבודות בעצמן הם משונות זו מזו, זה עבודה על עבודה,ועבודה
על עבודה כפי מה שיאחוז כל אחד ואחד בעבודה כך יקנה לעצמו נשמה ורוחניות מלמעלה, מפני
שסגולת העבודה להמשך אליו רוחניות הספירות, והעבודות ישתנו וימשיכו כל אחד ואחד כפי
סגולתה.

See also his discussion in *Pardes Rimmonim*, XXI, chap. 1, I, fol. 96d, and Cordovero's view cited in Azulai's *'Or ha-Hammah*, II, fols. 82c, 89c.

54   *'Or Yaqar*, vol. 15, p. 31, and Azulai, *'Or ha-Hammah*, II, fol. 100a. See also R. Jacob Joseph ben Judah, *Rav Yeivi*, fol. 40b, where the same two terms *neshamah* and *ruhaniyyut* occur together.

55   Fols. 94d–95a, and see in some of the notes in this appendix.

56   See the Great Maggid cited in *'Or ha-Emmet*, fol. 83a, and R. Menahem Mendel of Rimanov's book *'Ilana' de-Hayyei* (Pietrkov, 1908), fol. 56b. See also at the end of ch. 5 n. 12 in this volume.

57   For the Besht's self-awareness as an elite figure see, e.g., the balanced discussions of Rosman, *Founder of Hasidism*, pp. 176–177, 179–180, 182–183. See also ch. 3 n. 10 in this volume. However, his transformation from secondary to primary elite is part of his transitional social status, mentioned by Rosman, *Founder of Hasidism*, pp. 182–183, but also of the inner conceptual transitions I mentioned many times previously.

58   R. Qalonymus Qalman Ha-Levi Epstein, *Ma'or va-Shemesh*, I, fol. 38a:

העיקר הוא התפלה מעת שבא הבעש"ט הקדוש זצוק"ל הציץ וזרח אור התנוצצות קדושת
התפלה בעולם אל כל מי שרוצה לגשת לעבודת השי"ת. אבל צריך לזה לבוא לתפלה זכה שימוש
חכמים הרבה ליגיעה יומם ולילה בתורה ובמעשים טובים עד שעל ידי זה יכולים לבוא באמת
לידע להתפלל ביראה ואהבה רבה, כידוע למבינים.

        For an earlier discussion that emphasizes the high status of prayer and *devequt* and not of theological topics, see the fascinating passage of R. Meshullam Phoebus of Zbarazh, *Derekh 'Emmet* (Zhitomir, 1855), fol. 3cd. See also Pedaya, "The Besht, R. Jacob Joseph of Polonoy, and the Maggid of Mezeritch," pp. 43–45, 48–49.

Appendix D: *Ruḥaniyyut ha-'Otiyyot*: Drawn Down or Inherent?

1   See Pines, "On the Term *Ruḥaniyyut* and its Sources"; Schwartz, *Studies on Astral Magic*, pp. 1–26; Elliot Wolfson, "Merkavah Traditions in Philosophical Garb: Judah Halevi Reconsidered," *PAAJR*, vol. 57 (1991), pp. 190–192; and Idel, "Universalization and Integration," pp. 28–30.

2   See e.g., Schwartz, *Studies on Astral Magic*, pp. 28–54; Bezalel Safran, "Maimonides' Attitude to Magic and to Related Types of Thinking," in eds. B. Safran and E. Safran, *Porat Yosef: Studies Presented to Rabbi Dr. Joseph Safran* (Ktav, Hoboken, NJ, 1992), pp. 93–110; and Aviezer Ravitzky, *Maimonidean Studies* (Schocken, Jerusalem, Tel Aviv, 2006), pp. 181–203 (Hebrew).

3   Schwartz, *Studies on Astral Magic*, *passim*, contributed many important studies to the conceptual content of those supercommentaries. See, e.g., his "La magie astrale dans la pensée juive rationaliste en Provence au XIVe siecle," *AHDLMA*, vol. 61 (1994), pp. 31–34; Schwartz, "Worship of God or of Star? The Controversy of R. Abraham al-Tabib and R. Solomon Franco," *Kabbalah*, vol. 1 (1996), pp. 205–270 (Hebrew); "Astrology and Astral Magic in the Writings of R. Salomon Alconstantin," *JSJF*, vol. 15 (1993), pp. 37–82 (Hebrew); Schwartz, "Various Forms of Magic in 14th Century Spanish Jewish Thought," *PAAJR*, vol. 57 (1991), pp. 17–47 (Hebrew); and also the most updated list of supercommentaries on ibn Ezra found in Uriel Simon, *The Ear Discerns Words, Studies in Ibn Ezra's Exegetical Methodology* (Bar Ilan University Press, Ramat Gan, 2013), pp. 465–473 (Hebrew), contains 73 different items.

4   See, especially, *Sefer ha-'Atzamim*, ed. M. Grossberg (London, 1901), p. 21.

5   Schwartz, *Studies on Astral Magic*, pp. 56–178; and Idel, "The Magical and Neoplatonic Interpretations," p. 233, n. 68, *Hasidism*, pp. 158–159, and *Kabbalah in Italy*, pp. 279–280.

6   See, especially, his introduction to <u>Hesheq</u> *Shelomo*, the Commentary on the Song of Songs, printed as *Sha'ar ha-<u>H</u>esheq*, fol. 38b; and for astro-magic in the writings of Alemanno and his sources see, e.g., my *Absorbing Perfections*, pp. 146–150; *Kabbalah in Italy*, pp. 184–189, 255–256, 259, 261, 281–286, 294, 333–335, 344–347, 419, n. 41, 425, n. 74; Idel, "Talismanic Language"; Idel, "Astral Dreams in R. Yohanan Alemanno's Writings," pp. 111–128; *Saturn's Jews*, pp. 24–28, and the endnotes pp. 130–134; "The Magical and Theurgical Interpretation," pp. 33–63; Idel, *Hasidism*, pp. 157–158; and Stéphane Toussaint, "Ficino's Orphic Magic or Jewish Astrology and Oriental Philosophy? A Note on Spiritus, the Three Books on Life, Ibn Tufayl and Ibn Zarza," *Accademia*, vol. 2 (2000), pp. 19–21. For sound and magic in Renaissance Italy, see Daniel P. Walker, *Spiritual and Demonic Magic from Ficino to Campanella* (London, 1958), pp. 8–10, and now the detailed analysis of Marsilio Ficino's appropriation of Plotinus, Proclus, and Hermeticism in matters of magic in Copenhaver, *Magic in Western Culture, passim*. See also the working paper of Flavia Buzzetta, "Adaptations de thèmes magico-cabalistiques juifs médievaux par le Quattrocento italien," FMSH-WP-2014-68, May 2014.

7   See Jonathan Garb, *Manifestations of Power from Rabbinic Literature to Safedian Kabbalah* (Magnes Press, Jerusalem, 2004), pp. 187–200 (Hebrew); Garb, "The Kabbalah of Rabbi Joseph ibn Sayyah as a Source for the Understanding of Safedian Kabbalah," *Kabbalah*, vol. 4 (1999), pp. 255–313 (Hebrew); Garb, "Techniques of Trance in the Jerusalem Kabbalah," *Pe'amim*, 70 (1997), pp. 47–67 (Hebrew); Garb, *Shamanic Trance in Modern Kabbalah*, pp. 63–64; Sachi Ogimoto, *The Concept of the Ascent of Prayer by Sixteenth-Century Jerusalem Kabbalist, R. Joseph ibn Zayyah* (PhD Thesis, Hebrew University of Jerusalem, 2011); M. Idel, "The Relationship of the Jerusalem Kabbalists and Israel Sarug of Safed," *Shalem*, vol. 6 (1992), pp. 165–173 (Hebrew).

8   See, e.g., my "Magic and Kabbalah in the Book of the Responding Entity," in ed. M. Gruber, *The Solomon Goldman Lectures*, vol. VI (Spertus College, Chicago, 1993), pp. 125–138.

9   See ben Shlomo, *The Mystical Theology of Moses Cordovero*, pp. 87–169.

10   See *'Or Yaqar*, vol. 13, p. 118, and *'Or Yaqar*, vol. 16, p. 83. The phrase and the concept of the spiritual force found in each of the *sefirot* are widespread in Cordovero. See, e.g., *ibidem*, pp. 57, 133; *ibidem*, vol. 14, pp. 4, 78, 177, 222; *ibidem*, vol. 16, pp. 70, 83; *ibidem*, on *Tiqqunei Zohar*, vol. 5, pp. 74, 105. This term occurs several times in R. Jacob Joseph of Polonnoye's *Toledot Ya'aqov Yosef*.

11   See his untitled treatise extant solely in Ms. Paris BN 849, fol. 77b, and Idel, *Hasidism*, p. 158. It should be mentioned that discussions of spiritual force in the astral sense are found in Alemanno's earlier writings, but they are quite rare in his later ones.

12   See, e.g., Idel, *Kabbalah: New Perspectives*, pp. 137–144, and "Between the View of Sefirot as Essence and Instruments in Renaissance Period," *Italia*, vol. 3 (1982), pp. 89–111 (Hebrew), *R. Menahem Recanati, the Kabbalist* (Schocken, Jerusalem, Tel Aviv, 1998), I, pp. 175–214 (Hebrew).

13 See the passages from *Pardes Rimmonim* and *Tefillah le-Moshe*, fols. 189b, 190b, and in other Cordoverian treatises, e.g., his *'Or Yaqar*, vol. 7, p. 20, and in the quote from Cordovero in Azulai's *'Or ha-Ḥammah*, II, fol. 248d, and that of R. Abraham Galante, quoted in Azulai, fol. 5a.

14 See also Idel, *Saturn's Jews*, pp. 80–81.

15 I am not sure whether all the references to amulets are indeed related to this category and not to talismans. On the terms "talisman" and "amulet," see the literature metioned in Roy Kotansky, "Incantations and Prayers for Salvation on Inscribed Greek Amulets," in eds. C. A. Faraone and D. Obbink, *Magika Hiera, Ancient Greek Magic & Religion* (Oxford University Press, New York, Oxford, 1911), p. 124, n. 5; and Tewfik Canaan, "The Decipherment of Arabic Talismans," in ed. E. Savage-Smith, *Magic and Divination in Early Islam* (Ashgate Variorum, Aldershot, UK, 2004), 125–177, a reprint of the original article, which first appeared in *Berytus Archaeological Studies*, vol. 4 (1937), pp. 69–110 and *Berytus Archaeological Studies*, vol. 5 (1938), pp. 141–151.

16 The *sefirah* of *Gevurah*.

17 Namely the *sefirah* of *Hesed*.

18 Namely the *sefirah* of *Tiferet*.

19 I assume that it is the Kabbalists that belong to the circle of R. David ben Yehudah he-Hasid or to the circle of Kabbalists related to *Sefer ha-Meshiv*. See M. Idel, "Nehemiah ben Shlomo the Prophet on *Magen David*, pp. 28–32; Idel, *Kabbalah: New Perspectives*, pp. 103–111; Idel, "Kabbalistic Prayer and Colors," in ed. D. R. Blumenthal, *Approaches to Judaism in Medieval Times*, vol. III (Atlanta, GA, c1988), pp. 17–27; Idel, "Kavvanah and Colors: A Neglected Kabbalistic Responsum," in eds. M. Idel, D. Dimant, and S. Rosenberg, *Tribute to Sara: Studies in Jewish Philosophy and Kabbalah Presented to Professor Sara O. Heller Wilensky* (Magnes Press, Jerusalem, 1994), pp. 1–14 (Hebrew); and in the next note.

20 *Pardes Rimmonim* X, chap. 1, I, fol. 59bc. See also my *Kabbalah, New Perspectives*, pp. 110–111; Nicholas Sed, "La 'kawanah' selon le XXXII, chapitre du '*Pardes Rimmonim*' de R. Moise Cordovero," in ed. R. Goetschel, *Priere Mystique et Judaisme* (Coll. Strasbourg, 1984), pp. 187–207; Idel, "Visualization of Colors, 1: David ben Yehudah he-Hasid's Kabbalistic Diagram," *Ars Judaica*, vol. 11 (2015), pp. 31–54; "Visualisation of Colors 2: Implications of David ben Yehudah he-Hasid's Diagram for the History of Kabbalah," *Ars Judaica*, vol. 12 (2016), pp. 39–52.

21 *'Or Yaqar* on *Tiqqunei Zohar Ḥadash*, vol. 3, p. 90.

22 *Pardes Rimmonim*, X, chap. 1, I, fol. 59b.

23 XXI, chap. 1, I, fol. 96d. For the capacity of the divine names to draw down the "spiritual force on earth" in the context of the "spiritual force of the stars/planet," see the anonymous Hebrew translation of *Picatrix*, Ms. Munchen 214, fol. 51a, where Aristotle, evidently a Pseudo-Aristotelian text, is cited as follows:

בזמן הקדום היה בשמות האלוהיות דבר מה כשתוריד בו הרוחניות אל הארץ ירדו לשפל ולפעמים יהרגו למוריד כשלא יהיה בטבע רוחניות הכוכב היורד.

In the ancient time there was in the divine names something that when one causes the descent of the spiritual forces, they will descend to the terrestrial world, and sometimes they will kill the person that causes the descent, when he will not be of the nature of the spiritual force of the star that descends.

See also *Picatrix*, Ms. Munchen 214, fol. 71d. In *Sha'ar ha-Hesheq*, Yohanan Alemanno quoted this passage almost verbatim. For one's *ruhaniyyut* as revealing to him, see also the Hebrew version of *Picatrix*, Ms. Munchen 214, fol. 62a. See also Idel, "The Magical and Neoplatonic Interpretations," pp. 200, 233, n. 68, and in *Hasidism*, pp. 287–288, n. 178 as well as the references in n. 371.

About the Hebrew versions of the book of *Picatrix*, see Leicht, *Astrologumena Judaica*, pp. 316–322. For the impact of *Picatrix* in the Middle Ages and Renaissance in Christian thought, see Warburg, *The Renewal of Ancient Paganism*, pp. 643, 687, 691, 701–702, 734, 735, 736, 753; Eugenio Garin, *Astrology in the Renaissance, The Zodiac of Life* (Arkana, London, 1983), pp. 29–55; Frances A. Yates, *Giordano Bruno and the Hermetic Tradition* (The University of Chicago Press, Chicago and London, 1979), pp. 49–57, 69–72, 80–82, 107–108, 141–142, 370–371; Couliano, *Eros and Magic*, pp. 142–143. For extant editions and translations of this book, see *Picatrix. Das Ziel des Weisen von Pseudo-Magriti*, eds. and trs. H. Ritter and M. Plessner (Warburg Institute, London, 1962), and *Picatrix. The Latin Version of the Ghayat Al-Hakim*, ed. D. Pingree (Warburg Institute, London, 1986).

24 *Picatrix* III, chap. 4, and see David Pingree, "Some of the Sources of the *Ghayat al-Hakim*," *JWCI*, vol. 43 (1980), pp. 10–11, and Bert Hansen, "Science and Magic," in ed. D. C. Lindberg, *Science in the Middle Ages* (University of Chicago Press, Chicago, 1978), pp. 487–488. See also Pingree's very important survey "The Diffusion of Arabic Magical Texts in Western Europe," in *La diffusione delle Scienze Islamiche nel Medio Evo Europeo* (Accademia dei Lincei, Roma, 1987), pp. 57–101.

25 See Alejandro Garcia Avilés, "Alfonso X y el *Liber Razielis*: imágenes de la magia astral judía en el scriptorium alfonsí," *Bulletin of Hispanic Studies*, vol. LXXIV (1997), pp. 21–39; Avilés, "Two Astromagical Manuscripts of Alfonso X," *JWCI*, vol. LIX (1996), pp. 14–23; and Leicht, *Astrologumena Judaica*, pp. 187–293, 331–341. This book differs from the much more well-known compilation of Hebrew sources entitled *Sefer Raziel ha-Malakh*, which does not contain astro-magical themes. See Bern Rebiger, "Zur Redakziongeschichte des Sefer Raziel ha-Malach," *Frankfurter Judaistischer Beitraege*, vol. 32 (2005), pp. 1–32. On this latter book and early Hasidism, see Jonatan Meir, "Enlightenment and Esotericism in Galitzia: The Writings of Elyakim Getzl Milzhagi," *Kabbalah*, vol. 33 (2015), pp. 306–309 (Hebrew), and my "On Prophecy and Early Hasidism," pp. 65–70. See also now my "*Sefer Razi'el ha-Mal'akh*, New Inquiries," in E. Abate (ed.), *L'eredità di Salomone la magia ebraica in Italia e nel Mediterraneo, "Testi e Studi del Meis,"* (Giuntina, Firenze 2019), pp. 143–168.

26 *Livyat Hen*, Ms. Paris BN 1066, fol. 7b, as translated and discussed in Schwartz, *Studies on Astral Magic*, p. 139, n. 39.

27 See, e.g., Gideon Bohak, "The *CHARAKTÊRES* in Ancient and Medieval Jewish Magic," *Acta Classica*, vol. XLVII (2011), pp. 25–44; Hans A. Winkler, *Siegel und*

Charaktere in der Mohammedanischen Zauberei (GeheimesWissen, Graz, Austria, 2006), pp. 76–195; M. Idel, "The Anonymous *Commentary on the Alphabet of Metatron*: A Treatise by R Nehemiah ben Shlomo," *Tarbiz*, vol. 76 (2007), pp. 255–264 (Hebrew); Flavia Buzzetta, "Il simbolismo della 'scrittura ad occhi' nel *Liber misteriorum venerabilium (Shimmushei Torah)*, Aspetti di un peculiar retaggio della magia ebraica medieval," *Aries*, vol. 14 (2014), pp. 129–164. For a testimony as to the Besht's acquaintance with the angelic characters, see the introduction of R. Shlomo of Lutzk to *Maggid Devarav le-Ya'aqov*, ed. Schatz-Uffenheimer, pp. 2–3.

28   See, e.g., Henry Kahane, Renée R. Kahane, and Angela Pietrangle, "*Picatrix* and the Talismans," *Romance Philology*, vol. 19 (1965–1966), pp. 574–593; or Maribel Fierro, "Bāṭinism in al-Andalus, Maslama b. Qāsim al-Qurṭubī (d. 353/964), Author of the *Rutbat al-Ḥakīm* and the *Ghāyat al-Ḥakīm (Picatrix)*," *Studia Islamica*, vol. 84 (1996), pp. 87–112. For the earlier sources of such views, see Henry Corbin, "Rituel Sabeen et Exegese Ismailienne du rituel," *Eranos Jahrbuch*, vol. 19 (1951), pp. 194–197, n. 41, p. 214.

29   See Pingree, "Some of the Sources of the *Ghayat al-Ḥakim*," p. 4.

30   See M. T. d'Alverny and F. Hudry, "Alkindi—De radiis," *AHDLMA*, vol. 42 (1974), pp. 139–260, and the bibliography collected in *Al-Kindi, De radiis*, tr. Didier Ottaviani (Editions Allia, Paris, 2003); and Pinella Travaglia, *Magic, Causality, and Intentionality: The Doctrine of Rays in Al-Kindi (Micrologus' Library)* (Edizioni del Galluzzo, Florence, 1999); Peter Adamson, *Al-Kindi* (Oxford University Press, Oxford, New York, 2007); and Copenhaven, *Magic in Western Culture*, pp. 253–256.

31   *Al-Kindi, De radiis*, tr. Ottaviani, pp. 40–70. Al-Kindi's book that survived only in its Latin translation, *De Radiis*. Al-Kindi wrote also a *Treatise on the Spirituality of the Planets*. One of his epistles on astrology has been translated in Hebrew and was quite widespread. See Schwartz, *Studies on Astral Magic*, p. 153, n. 76. Al-Kindi influenced the famous encyclopedia of the Sincere Brethren, of Ismaiyylia extraction, a part of which was known in the Middle Ages in Europe in a Hebrew translation. For the possible impact of *De Radiis* in medieval Judaism, see the suggestion of Colette Sirat, "La Qabbale d'apres Juda b. Salomon Ha-Cohen," in eds. George Nahon and Charles Touati, *Hommage à Georges Vajda* (Peeters, Louvain, 1980), p. 202.

32   See *Sha'ar ha-Ḥesheq*, fol. 38b.

33   See his *Untitled Treatise*, Ms. Paris BN 849, fol. 28a, discussed in Idel, "Astral Dreams in R. Yohanan Alemanno's Writings," pp. 117–118, 125.

34   See the text printed and discussed in Idel, "The Magical and Theurgical Interpretation," pp. 38–39:

הנגון החומרי מפני יחסיו יוכל לפעול פעליו המיוחסי' אליו מפני הרוחניות שבו.

For magical interpretations of music in Hasidism, see Idel, "The Magical and Theurgical Interpretation," pp. 60–62, and also Schwartz, *Music in Jewish Thought*, pp. 159–161.

35 Couliano, *Eros and Magic*, pp. 118–123, 126–128, and Gary Toumlison, *Music in Renaissance Magic, Toward a Historiography of Others* (Chicago University Press, Chicago, 1993), pp. 79–82, 118–119, 122–123.

36 *Sha'ar ha-Hesheq*, fol. 38b:

והמבואר לספרי אבן לטיף כי יש רוחניות לאותיות כמדרגת הצורות לחמרים , שפע רוחני
נשאר קיים ורוחני ונצחי אחרי הפרדו מהחמר ויתדבק באותו הגלגל הרוחני נשאר לבד לעולם.

See also the discussion of the "world of letters" as collecting supernal influxes in Alemanno. Cf., Idel, *Golem*, p. 169. For this concept and its possible origin in Islam, see Zoran, "Magic, Theurgy, and the Knowledge of Letters," p. 43 and n. 107.

37 See my "Magical and Neoplatonic Interpretations."

38 For some of the occurrences of the phrase רוחניות האותיות see, e.g., Cordovero's passage translated and discussed beside ch. 8 n. 15 in this volume; in *Tefillah le-Moshe*, fol. 57b; *Shiy'ur Qomah*, fol. 18a; Cordovero, *'Or Yaqar*, vol. 5, p. 215; Cordovero, vol. 10, pp. 16, 17, 137, 142; Cordovero, vol. 11, p. 48; Cordovero, vol. 12, p. 92; Cordovero, vol. 16, p. 70; Cordovero, vol. 17, pp. 83, 172; and Cordovero, on *Tiqqunei Zohar*, vol. 4, p. 185; Cordovero, on *Tiqqunei Zohar*, vol. 5, p. 85; or Azulai, *'Or ha-Ḥammah*, II, fols. 189d, 227c; as well as the several occurrences in *Pardes Rimmonim*, some of which will be discussed immediately as follows. See also Horowitz, *Shenei Luhot ha-Berit*, I, fol. 16b.

39 *Shiy'ur Qomah*, fol. 18a.

40 *Derishot*, p. 71.

41 *Hesed le-'Avraham*, fol. 24c:

וזה ענין שמים חדשים שנעשים מחדושי התורה כנז' בזוהר בראשית ובפר' קדושים, כי ע"י
עסק בתורה אותן האותיות המתהוות ומצטרפות בפיו יתהוה מהם רוחניות וענין נחמד, וזו היא
ענין התפלה שאכתריא"ל מקבל וקושר קשרים לרבו, ולזה כאשר לא תהיה למצוה כוונה הרי היא
כגוף בלי נשמה, וכפי שעור הכוונה כן יגדל רוחניות המצוה ותעלה מעלה מעלה, ולכן ארז"ל
מצות צריכות כוונה אם כיון שלא לצאת לא יצא.

A comparison between the interesting discussion about voice, speech, and vapor, found in the very first page of R. Ḥayyim Vital, *Sha'ar Ruaḥ ha-Qodesh*, to Cordovero's views shows the difference between them, as Vital does not resort to the term *ruḥaniyyut*.

42 *Pardes Rimmonim*, Gate XXVII. This is a very important part of this book from the point of view of the development of topics we have discussed previously. See especially *Pardes Rimmonim*, XXXII, chap. 2.

43 See also Cordovero's *Derishot*, p. 5, and Idel, *Golem*, pp. 27, 67, 108.

44 In the Zoharic literature, that is mentioned beforehand.

45 *Pardes Rimmonim*, XXVII, chap. 1, II, fol. 59c:

החלוקה הרביעית היא רוחניות האותיות ומציאותם וחיבורם אלו באלו והתייחסם כך מי
שירד לעומק הענין הזה יוכל לברוא עולמות וזה נקרא נשמה לנשמה שהוא תלוי בבינה...והחלוקה
הרביעית אינה נמצא כמעט, ולכן לא באה בשם. ותחתיה תעמוד השמות ופעולותם וצרופם מתוך
הפסוקים.

See also the important parallel found in his *'Or Yaqar*, vol. 14, p. 11; Idel, *Studies in Ecstatic Kabbalah*, pp. 139–140; and *Hasidism*, pp. 159–160. See also Gondos, *Kabbalah in Print*, p. 91.

Compare to the view of R. Nathan ben Sa'adyah Har'ar, *Le Porte della Giustizia*, p. 472, a book he was acquainted with and which seems to be the direct source of the Safedian Kabbalist.

46 See Idel, *Kabbalah in Italy*, pp. 340–343.

47 See Cordovero, *'Or Yaqar*, vol. 15, pp. 15, 31; Cordovero, on *Tiqqunei Zohar*, vol. 3, p. 99; and the passage of R. Abraham Azulai's *Ḥesed le-'Avraham*, fol. 9d. See also the important passage found in Azulai, *'Or ha-Ḥammah*, III, fol. 15a. ammah, Hammah, II, fol. 15a. This view has reverberated in R. Isaiah Horowitz and then in Hasidism. See Lederberg, *Sod ha-Da'at*, p. 292, n. 235. The various combinations of letters and sounds are compared to a medicine. In fact, after quoting almost verbatim two passages from *Ḥesed le-'Avraham*, his famous descendant R. Hayyim Yoseph David Azulai, (HYDA') offers another passage which reiterates the analogy between combinations of letters and medicine in a very interesting manner. See his Shem Gedolim, I, fol. 54b. I have not yet found the source of the last passage. See also *Ḥesed le-'Avraham*, fol. 10d, in a text obviously influenced by the aforementioned passage from *Pardes Rimmonim*, where the mixtures of the letters and words of the Torah reflect the supernal spiritual force, *ruḥaniyyut*. See also the occurrence of this passage in another book of HYDA' entitled Devash le-Fi, as discussed by Scholem, On the Kabbalah and Its Symbolism, p. 76.

It should be mentioned that R. Yehudah ha-Levi, one of the earliest and most important exponents of the astro-talismatic theory in Judaism, uses the metaphor of medicine several times in order to point out the necessity of worshipping God in a precise manner. See, e.g., *Kuzari* I, par. 97; Pines, "On the Term *Ruḥaniyyut* and Its Sources," pp. 527–528, 529; H. J. Zimmels, *Magicians, Theologians, and Doctors* (Feldheim, NY, 1952), pp. 137–139, 250, nn. 153–154; and see also Karl-Erich Groezinger, "Ba'al Shem oder Ba'al Hazon: Wunderdoctor oder charismatiker, zur Fruhen Legenden bildung um den Stifter des Hasidismus," *Frankfurter Judaistische Beitrage*, vol. 6 (1978), pp. 71–90.

48 Pingree, "Some of the Sources of the *Ghayat al-Ḥakim*," pp. 13–14. For mixtures as part of quasi-Hermetic magic and their influence in the Middle Ages and Renaissance, see also my *Golem*, pp. 166, 170, 179, 302, n. 10, and *Kabbalah in Italy*, p. 282.

49 *'Or Yaqar*, vol. 6, p. 31. See also *'Or Yaqar*, on *Tiqqunei Zohar*, vol. 4, p. 185.

50 *'Or Yaqar*, vol. 9, p. 128.

51 See, especially, Cordovero's reference to a certain *Book of Talismans, Sefer ha-Talisma'ot*, in his *'Or Yaqar*, on *Tiqqunei Zohar*, vol. 6, pp. 385–386, where, as he testified, he has seen it and offers some general astro-magical principles. See also *'Or Yaqar*, on *Tiqqunei Zohar*, p. 384, and his *Derishot*, p. 63. According to another discussion he sees the science of talisman as "an ancient wisdom." See the quote in the name of Cordovero in Azulai, *'Or ha-Ḥammah*, I, fol. 106c. According to another discussion, found in Azulai, fol. 150c, following a very important discussion in

Cordovero's *'Or Yaqar*, vol. 8, pp. 107–108, 109, the drawing down of the spiritual force of the planets is not necessarily a forbidden type of knowledge. See also the view of R. Abraham Galante's view, cited by Azulai, *'Or ha-Ḥammah*, vol. I, fol. 89a, and Cordovero's view cited in Azulai, *'Or ha-Ḥammah*, vol. II, fol. 234a, where he speaks about the "science of the talismanics." See also references to earlier material on talismans I collected in *Hasidism*, pp. 341–342, n. 73.

52   R. Abraham Yagel defines the preparations of matters to receive spiritual force as "natural magic." See Ruderman, *Kabbalah, Magic, and Science*, pp. 110–111. See also my "Jewish Magic in Renaissance and Hasidism," p. 85, and *Saturn's Jews*, pp. 27–29, 62–63, 135–136, 152–153.

53   See in the first passage quoted in the next appendix.

54   See, e.g., R. Barukh of Kosov, *Nehmad ve-Na'yim—Yesod ha-'Emunah*, fols. 96a–c, or R. Meshullam Phaebus of Zbarazh, *Yosher Divrei 'Emmet*, fol. 132a.

55   See beside ch. 1 n. 22 in this volume.

56   For the special status of the righteous as a magician, see appendix F.

57   See his *Degel Maḥaneh 'Efrayyim*, p. 123. See also *Degel Maḥaneh 'Efrayyim*, p. 164; and R. Jacob Joseph's *Ben Porat Yosef*, fol. 11c, the tradition cited in the name of the Besht; and *Ben Porat Yosef*, fol. 27c; Scholem, *On the Mystical Shape of the Godhead*, pp. 128–129; Weiss, *Studies*, pp. 132 133; Kauffman, *In all Your Ways Know Him*, pp. 511–512; and Lederberg, *The Gateway to Infinity*, p. 88. On this explanation see also Mark, *The Revealed and the Hidden Writing*s, pp. 14–17.

      The ascent of the vocables by means of the speech of the righteous differs from the other types of ascent on high of the vocables because of the spiritual force, as discussed previously. See also my Idel, "Models of Understanding Prayer," p. 51, n. 129.

58   pp. 136–137. See also previously the passage referred to by n. 278. See also Lederberg, *Sod ha-Da'at*, pp. 182–183 and ch. 7 n. 4 in this volume. For prayer as speech with God, see the story cited in the name of the Besht in R. Jacob Joseph of Polonnoye, *Toledot Ya'aqov Yosef*, fols. 169b and 196c.

59   See the *Testament of the Besht*, and in R. Aharon of Apta's *Keter Shem Tov ha-Shalem*, p. 28 (and again *Keter Shem Tov ha-Shalem*, p. 106): וכשמאריך בתיבה הוא דביקות שאינו רוצה ליפרד מאותה תיבה See also his *'Or ha-Ganuz la-Tzaddiqim*, fol. 6b; and also R. Gedalyahu of Lunitz, *Teshu'ot Hen*, fol. 39a; Idel, "Models of Understanding Prayer," pp. 61–62; and ch. 5 n. 9 in this volume. For other erotic imagery in early Hasidism concerning prayer, see the material discussed in Jacobs, *Hasidic Prayer*, pp. 59–60.

Appendix E: Spiritual Forces, Vitality, and Immanentism in Early Hasidism

1   See the references adduced in Idel, *Hasidism*, pp. 17–18.

2   See Idel, p. 94, and appendix D.

3   See appendix D.

4   See my "Your Word Stands Firm in Heaven," *passim.*

5   See the many discussions of pantheism and panentheism in Cordovero in Ben Shlomo, *The Mystical Theology of Moses Cordovero*, under those items, especially pp. 295–296; or Scholem, *The Messianic Idea*, pp. 223–227; Scholem, *Major Trends in Jewish Mysticism*, pp. 252–253; and Piekarz, *Between Ideology and Reality*, p. 102.

6   See Scholem, *Major Trends in Jewish Mysticism*, p. 252: "Cordovero is essentially a systematic thinker."

7   "On the Term *Ruḥaniyyut* and Its Sources," p. 512.

8   "On the Term *Ruḥaniyyut* and Its Sources," pp. 513, 515.

9   Probably the angelic world. See *'Or Yaqar*, vol. 9, p. 104.

10   *'Or Yaqar*, vol. 15, p. 73:

שרמז בחינותיה רמזו באומרם כותל מערכי הוא כלל הרוחניות המתפשט למטה בעולם הנפרדים ועולם הגלגלים ועולם הגשמי.

11   Gate XVI.

12   This is a Zoharic, theurgical theme adopted by Cordovero.

13   *'Or Yaqar, Tiqqunim*, vol. 3, p. 70:

ובאוירא דעלמא דין מתגלמין ראשונה אותיותיה ורוחניותה וכבר פירשנו בספ"ר בשער אבי"ע סוד רוחניות השכינה המנהגת
העולם המתפשטת ניצוצות אורה בסוד הבריאה והיצירה והעשיה, וא"כ לפי זה נמצאת
שכינה למטה יורדת בדרך הסולם, והיא נמצאת בתחתונים, היא היא נקראת תפלה מתקשטת בתכ־
שיטי תפלותינו להסתלק מדרגה אחר מדרגה.

14   See appendix C in this volume.

15   See, e.g., *'Or Yaqar*, vol. 9, pp. 51, 150, 155, vol. 11, pp. 15, 34, 251, 304, vol. 13, pp. 186–187, and see also vol. 14, pp. 193–194, 209, vol. 17, pp. 24, 36, *'Or Yaqar*, on *Tiqqunim*, vol. 2, p. 168, vol. 4, p. 224.

16   On the presence of the divinity within the entire realm of reality, see *'Or Yaqar*, vol. 8, p. 235, *'Or Yaqar*, on *Tiqqunim*, vol. 3, p. 217. About the continuous nature of reality in Cordovero, see the discussion of ben-Shlomo, *The Mystical Theology of Moses Cordovero*, pp. 283–290. See also Idel, *"Male and Female,"* passim, and *Enchanted Chains.*

17   In Azulai's *'Or ha-Ḥammah*, II, fol. 29a:

שכל הדברים שנבראו בעולם הן רוחניות שבכל העולמות הן גשמיות הן מורכבים.

See also Azulai, fol. 86d, and especially the discussion in *Derishot*, pp. 37–38.

18   This verse occurs in many teachings of the Besht. The wrongdoers are reminiscent of the shells in the first part of the first passage quoted previously.

19   *Toledot Ya'aqov Yosef*, fol. 7a:

דשמעתי ממורי זלה»ה שאם ידע האדם שהקדוש ברוך הוא מסתתר שם אין זה הסתרה,
[תהילים צב:ין] ‹כי נתפרדו כל פועלי און,› וז«ש ואנכי הסתר אסתיר פני מהם [דברים לא:יח] ר»ל
שיסתיר מהם שלא ידעו שהקדוש ברוך הוא שם בהסתרה זו וכו› ודפה»ח.›

20   See also the short quotes in the name of the Besht in *Tzafnat Pa'aneaḥ*, fol. 2a.

21 Compare to the view of the Besht quoted in R. Jacob Joseph of Polonnoye, *Tzafnat Pa'aneah*, fol. 2c, according to which prayer is called *Shekhinah*. For prayer as a name for God in Kabbalah and Hasidism, see Idel, *Enchanted Chains*, pp. 172–180.

22 *Ben Porat Yosef*, fol 70c, quoted with some few changes in R. Aharon Kohen of Apta, *Keter Shem Tov*, I, fol. 8a. A parallel to this variant, quoted again in the name of the Besht, is found elsewhere in *Ben Porat Yosef*, fol. 111a.

23 On this parable and its variants, see Idel, *Ben*, pp. 543–567.

24 This syntagma occurs again later on the same page.

25 See also Cordovero, *Derishot*, p. 74.

26 *Tiqqunei Zohar*, no. 70, fol. 122b.

27 The denial of a change in divinity has to do with the inherent omnipresence, and the revelation of divinity in a certain place does not mean a change.

28 *Toledot Ya'aqov Yosef*, fol. 7a:

הנה כמו שיש כ"ב אותיות בדבור תורה ותפלה, כך יש בכל עניני החומר והגשמי שבעולם
ג"כ כ"ב אותיות שבהם נברא העולם וכל אשר בו...רק שהאותיות מלובש בחומר עניני העולם
בכמה כסויין ולבושין וקליפות, ובתוך האותיות שורה רוחניות הקדוש ברוך הוא, הרי שכבודו ית'
מלא כל הארץ וכל אשר בה, לית אתר פנוי מניה כמבואר בתיקונים, רק שהוא בהסתרה. וכאשר
אנשי הדעת יודעין מזה ההסתרה אינו אצלם המחרה ושיוני,

29 Idel, "Your Word Stands Firm in Heaven."

30 *'Olat ha-Tamid*, fol. 11a.

31 See e.g., *Shenei Luhot ha-Berit*, I, fols. 4b–5a, 6b–7a, 19a–20a. The opening of this book is replete with significant quotes from Cordovero dealing with language. See also appendix F in this volume.

32 See Menahem 'Azariyah of Fano, quoted already in *Shenei Luhot ha-Berit*, I, fols. 4b–5a, 6a.

33 *'Ammud ha-'Avodah*, fol. 113cd, and compare also to *'Ammud ha-'Avodah*, fol. 47ab.

34 See a similar view in R. Aharon of Zhitomir, *Toledot 'Aharon* II, fols. la, 36b.

35 Compare also *Toledot 'Aharon*, fol. 7d, where the *tzaddiq* draws the Creator down within the worlds.

36 *No'am 'Elimelekh*, fol. 8a. See also *Maggid Devarav le-Ya'aqov*, ed. Schatz-Uffenheimer, pp. 227, 324, and my *Hasidism*, pp. 162–170. See also the very interesting passage of R. Shlomo Lutzker, *Dibrat Shelomo* (Zolkiew, 1848), fol. 6a, dealt with by Schatz-Uffenheimer in *Hasidism as Mysticism*, pp. 219–221.

The drawing down of the Godhead into the worlds is a leitmotif of R. Eliezer Lippa, the son of R. Elimelekh, in his *'Orah le-Tzaddiq*. See also Elliot Wolfson, "Beautiful Maiden Without Eyes," in ed. M. Fishbane, *The Midrashic Imagination* (SUNY Press, Albany, 1993), pp. 189–190.

37 *Me'or 'Einayyim*, p. 171, and my *Hasidism*, pp. 183–184.

38 See the other text of Cordovero, translated and analyzed in my *Hasidism*, pp. 200–201, that depicts the righteous in exactly the same terms.

39 *Pardes Rimmonim*, XXVII: 2:

וכל אות ואות יש לה צורה רוחניות ומאור נכבד מעצם מעצם הספי' משתלשל ממדרגה
למדרגה דרך השתלשלות הספירות. והנה האות היכל ומכון לרוחניות ההוא ובהיות האדם מזכיר
ומניע אות מאותיות, כהכרח יתעורר הרוחניות ההוא... והנה בהזכרת האדם התיבה ההיא הרומזת
באותיות בסבת תנועת הכחות ההם והכאתם זה בזה על ידי פטיש הנשמה בזולת שיתעוררו הם
בשרשם העליון לפעול הפעול' ההיא... וזהו סוד הזכרת השמות וכוונת התפלה.

See also R. Meshullam Phaebus of Zbarazh, *Yosher Divrei 'Emmet*, fol. 132a.

40 See, e.g., in *Pardes Rimmonim*, III chap. 5, the expression "the vitality of all the creatures" as describing the *sefirah* of Keter. See also *Pardes Rimmonim*, VIII: 2,3, IX:5, XXI:10, XXIV:10, II, fol. 50b, XXVII:1, XXVII:11, where vitality is related to a letter; and Derishot, p. 47. See also Azulai's *'Or ha-Ḥammah* vol. I, fol. 63d, and the interesting discussions to this effect in R. Isaiah Horowitz's *Sha'ar ha-Shamayyim*, fol. 91b, as well as Ben Shlomo, *The Mystical Theology*, pp. 288–290, and Idel, *Golem*, p. 197.

The omnipresent vitality is reminiscent of the theory of consanguinity of all beings in what was conceived of as the mentality of primitive man, cf., Ernst Cassirer, *The Philosophy of the Symbolic Form*, tr. Ralph Manheim (Yale University Press, New Haven, 1955), vol. I, p. 118, and his *Essay on Man* (New York, 1960), p. 108; Julia Kristeva, *Language, the Unknown, an Initiation in Linguistics*, tr. Anne M. Menke (Columbia University Press, New York, 1989), p. 50. See, however, the interesting criticism of Stanley J. Tambiah, "The Magical Power of Words," *Man* [NS], vol. III (1968), pp. 175–208.

41 *Liqqutei Torah* (Vilnius, 1880), fols. 96a–97a, but compare to the view of Jakob Boehme, mentioned in n. 1 in this volume.

42 *Toledot Ya'aqov Yosef*, fol. 171c:

הקשה מורי מה זה לו ית' לתועלת שנאהבנו, יתוש כמונו אם יאהב למלך גדול ונורא מה זה
נחשב לכלום. הגם דשמעתי ממנו פירוש נפלא על קו' זה לבד, כי בריאות העולם היה על ידי דין,
שהוא סוד הצימצום כנודע. לכך דיני ויסורי האדם הם גוף אל הנשמה וחיות הרוחניות, וכשאדם
מקבל היסורין באהבה ובשמחה שהוא בחינת החיות והרוחניות, הוא מקרב ומקשר ומדבק הגוף
אל הנשמה שהוא החיות החיות והרוחני, ונתבטל הדין. וח"ו בהיפך, דוחה הגוף שלו מן החיות. לכך א'
עצה היעוצה לאדם, ואהבת את ה' אלהיך שהוא בחי' דין, לקבלו בשמחה ולקשרו אל הויה שהוא
הנשמה ע"י ואה"בת והבן ודפח"ח.

43 fol. 2c.

44 I, fol. 59b. See also R. Arieh Leib Galiner of Polonnoye, *Qol Arieh*, fols. 1d, 11a, 57b; R. Jacob Joseph ben Judah, *Sefer Rav Yeivi*, fol. 10a. See also Idel, *Hasidism*, pp. 63, 350–351, n. 126.

45 See Idel, "The Land of Divine Vitality," and *Golem*, index, p. 358 under item "Vitality," and compare also to my "The Besht Passed His Hand over His Face," p. 103, n. 95, and "Remembering and Forgetting," p. 118, n. 26.

46 See his *Studies*, p. 46, where he proposes to see in the Neoplatonic theory of emanation and its Kabbalistic reverberations the source of the Hasidic concept of *ḥiyyut*.

On ẖiyyut as the divine immanence in Cordovero and Horowitz's *Shenei Luhot ha-Berit*, see Sack, "The Influence of Cordovero in the Seventeenth Century," p. 369. See also the quote from Cordovero in Horowitz's Sha'ar ha-Shamayim, p. 18.

47 (Brooklyn, 1982), p. 98.

48 R. Yehudah Leib ha-Kohen of Hanipoly, *'Or ha-Ganuz* (Zolkiew, 1899), fol. 23a. Another astrological interpretation of this Midrashic passage from *Genesis Rabbah*, X:6 is found in R. Qalonimus Qalman Epstein, *Ma'or va-Shemesh* II, fol. 6b. A less astrological formulation, apparently an attenuation of the quoted interpretation to the Midrash, is found in *'Or ha-'Emmet*, fol. 52a. See also R. Israel of Kuznitz, *'Avodat Yisrael*, fol. 76d.

49 *Me'or 'Einayyim*, pp. 96, pp. 16, 34, 35, 37–38, 105, 102–103, 105. See also the later Hasidic view discussed in Idel, *Golem*, pp. 248–249.

50 *Me'or 'Einayyim*, pp. 16, 34, 35, 37–38, 105, 102–103, 105; and for another example of using the phrase "vitality of the Creator" in the context of immanentism, see Brody, "Open to Me the Gates of Righteousness," pp. 15–16, when dealing with an interesting passage of the disciple of the Great Maggid, R. Shlomo of Lutzk. See also Vital's *Sha'ar Ruah ha-Qodesh*, pp. 14, 112, where ẖiyyut occurs several times.

51 This Zoharic formula was used as a slogan for immanentism in Hasidic writings; of many discussions see, e.g., Weiss, in ed. A. Rubenstein, *Studies in Hasidism* (Jerusalem, 1977), pp. 173–174 (Hebrew); R. Menahem Nahum of Chernobyl, *Me'or 'Einayim*, p. 105; and Norman Lamm, *Torah Lishmah* (New York and New Jersey, 1989), p. 19.

52 Quoted in *Siddur Beit 'Aharon ve-Yisrael*, by R. Aharon of Karlin (Brooklyn, 1952), no pagination, in the discussion on *Sukkot*. See already my *Hasidism*, pp. 17–18. See also Menahem Mendel Viznitzer, *Sefer Mishnat Hasidim* (Benei Beraq, 1981), p. 319; and the way the teaching of the Great Maggid was described in R. Israel ben Isaac Simẖah, *'Eser 'Orot*, printed in Zekhut 'Avraham (Jerusalem, 1973), fol. 12a.

53 See n. 38 in this volume. On this figure, known mainly from the quotations cited by R. Jacob Joseph of Polonnoye, see Nigal, *The Birth of Hasidism*, pp. 39–42. His few extant teachings are a good example for the katabatic model in Hasidism, which I mentioned in my *Hasidism*, pp. 100, 103–104, 106–107, 122, 206, 212.

54 See n. 114 in this volume.

55 Cf. Francoise Dastur, "Husserl and the Problem of Dualism," in ed. Anna-Teresa Tymieniecka, *Soul and Body in Husserlian Phenomenology: Man and Nature, Analecta Husserliana*, vol. 16 (Springer, New York, 2013), pp. 68–71. See also the critique of Derrida, *La voix et le phénomène*, pp. 15–16, 91, and his introduction to the translation of Husserl's, *L'origine de la géométrie* (Presses Universitaires de France, Paris, 1995), pp. 83–100.

56 Ludwig Wittgenstein, *Philosophical Investigations*, tr. G. E. M. Anscombe (Basil Blackwell, Oxford, 1967), p. 128, sec. 432. See also secs. 1–37, 65–67, 304.

Appendix F: The Concept of *Tzaddiq* and Astral Magic

1   See the bibliography at n. 137 in this volume and Aharon Wertheim, *Law and Custom in Hassidism* (Jerusalem, 1960), pp. 235–236 (Hebrew).

2   See Wilensky, *Hasidim and Mitnaggedim*, vol. 2, p. 236. Compare also to p. 209. See also my proposal to explain the manner in which the Besht attracted his disciple by some form of hypnosis, "The Besht Passed His Hand over His Face," pp. 79–106.

3   See ch. 12 n. 7 in this volume.

4   The affinities between some of the texts to be discussed as follows have been duly pointed out by Piekarz, *The Beginning of Hasidism*, pp. 16–17, and Sack, *The Kabbalah of Rabbi Moshe Cordovero*, pp. 53, 218–219.

5   See the discussions of this issue in Idel, *Hasidism*, p. 70; Idel, "Models of Understanding Prayer in Early Hasidism," pp. 47–48, especially n. 126; Idel, "Your Word Stands Firm in Heaven," pp. 272–273; and *Ben*, pp. 534–537. See also ch. 5 n. 6, ch. 8 n. 6, ch. 12 n. 7 in this volume. On the basis of these cases adduced in the name of the Besht, the resort to this verb *MShKh* in a passage from *Keter Shem Tov*—adduced in n. 117 in this volume—does not constitute a problem from the point of view of attribution to the Besht. See also the passage analyzed in Idel, *Hasidism*, pp. 235–236. The attribution to me of the view that this concept is the only innovation in Hasidism by Magid, *Hasidism Incarnate*, p. 184, n. 14, does not specify any study of mine where did he find it, and it is actually an inversion of my approach, which is read against what I declared, perhaps in the vein of his more general approach to texts, to be mentioned later on in this appendix.

6   See, for example, in my *Hasidism*, especially pp. 189–190; *Ascensions on High*, pp. 143–160; and as discussed in chap. 9 in this volume.

7   See, e.g., Yissakhar Ben 'Ammi, *Culte des saints et pèlerinages judéo-musulmans au Maroc* (Maisonneuve & Larose, Paris, 1990), and my *Hasidism*, p. 209.

8   See my *Ben*, pp. 152–153.

9   For power see already in Cordovero's description of ideal prayer in appendix C, and Idel, *Hasidism*, p. 148.

10 See the references adduced in ch. 6 n. 2, ch. 10 n. 3, appendix C n. 17 in this volume.

11 This is an extension of the view of the righteous as a sanctuary.

12 Namely all the people.

13 See Nahmanides' Commentary in Genesis 2:3.

14 *BT, Berakhot*, fol. 17a.

15 *Merkavah la-Shekhinah*. See *Genesis Rabbah*, 47:6, 87:6. In fact, Cordovero speaks elsewhere in the commentary on the *Zohar* about the human righteous as becoming the chariot for the *sefirah* of Yesod. See *'Or Yaqar*, vol. 4, pp. 1–2, 4–5. See also Idel, *Hasidism*, pp. 91, 364, n. 109; Idel, *Messianic Mystics*, pp. 317–319; and Eitan P. Fishbane, "A Chariot for the Shekhinah: Identity and the Ideal Life in Sixteenth-Century Kabbalah," *Journal of Religious Ethics*, vol. 37 (2009), pp. 385–418.

16   The image of the pipeline for the human righteous stems from early Kabbalah, where the ninth *sefirah* has been conceived of phallically, and as such a pipeline for the divine influx or semen virile. See, e.g., the material assembled by Cordovero, *Pardes Rimmonim*, Gate VII, chap. 2.

17   *'Or Yaqar*, vol. 12, pp. 192–193, already quoted and discussed in Sack, *The Kabbalah of Rabbi Moshe Cordovero*, pp. 53, 218–219.

18   The images of ladder and chain recur in Cordovero's writings. See Idel, *Enchanted Chains*, chap. 1; Idel, *Ascension on High*; as well as in appendix B in this volume.

19   *BT Berakhot*, fol. 17a.

20   Cordovero, *Pardes Rimmonim*, XXXII:1; II, fol. 78bc:

מדרגת האיש החסיד בתפילתו לפי שיעור כוונתו כי אם יכוון להשפיע ממדרגה למדרגה
כמדרגות הסולם וידבק בקונו בידיעותיו בעשיית מצוותיו תעלה ותתעלה נשמתו ממדרגה למדרגה
ומסיבה לסיבה ומעלה לעלה עד ישפיע עליו שפע רב ויהיה הוא מקום מושב ומכון להשפעה וממנו
יתחלק לכל העולם... ולכן על פי הדברים האלה יהיה מכון לשכינה מאחר שהשפע בא על ידו
נמצא שהצדיק הוא במקום הצנור הגדול יסוד עולם ולכן ראוי שידבק בו השכינה ונקרא שושבין
למלכא ואשריו ואשרי חלקו כי זכה וזיכה וכל העולם נידון לכף זכות בעבורו. ועד"ז נמצא כי
בשעה שיש צדיק וחסיד בעולם בעולם כל העולם נזון על ידו כאמרם ז"ל (ברכות דף יז) כל העולם נזון
בשביל חנינא בני וכו'.

The passage was copied also in the preface to Vital's *Peri 'Etz Hayyim* by R. Nathan Shapira of Jerusalem and in his own *Me'orot Nathan*. See Idel, *Hasidism*, pp. 235–236; Ben, pp. 440–446, 531–532, 534–539; and the material referenced in nn. 107, 133, 190 in this volume. Compare also the text of Cordovero, quoted in my *Hasidism*, pp. 100–101.

21   *Meshu'abbadim*. See also *Derishot*, pp. 75, 77. This verb can be translated as as subordinated.

22   *Derishot*, p. 76.

שהכל תלוי ברוחניות השפע הנשפע על ידי הצדיק ומעשיו הכשרים...והיה העולם מתברך
בזכותם מהרוחניות הנשפע בעולם בזכותם...שכל העולמות והעניינים משועבדים לצדיק...והכל
תלוי בסוד התורה הנמסרת אליו ולא לשאר הנבראים

See also *Pardes Rimmonim*, XXIV, chaps. 10–11; II, fols. 50d–51b; XXX, chap. 3; II, fol. 69b; *'Or 'Yaqar*, vol. 14, p. 194; and my *Hasidism*, pp. 65–72.

23   See also Cordovero's *Pardes Rimmonim* XXXII, chap. 1, and Azulai's *Massekhet 'Avot* (Jerusalem, 1986), fol. 3a. The theme of the *tzaddiq* recurs many times also in the latter's *'Or ha-Hammah*.

24   *Hesed le-'Avraham*, fol. 22bc:

והנה הצדיקים היושבים בארץ ישראל באמצעותם השפע יורד מלמעלה, וזה אחר שהשפע
רוחני א"א שירד למטה לארץ הגשמית אלא על ידי הצדיקים שהם 'חלק אלוה ממעל' ובהכנת
מעשיהם ותורתם יורידו השפע הפך טבעו, ויעזור להם טהרת המקום.

For the importance of the Land of Israel for theurgical operation, see Cordovero, *'Or Yaqar*, vol. 7, p. 20.

25   See my "Nishmat 'Eloha, The Divinity of the Soul in Nahmanides and His School," in eds. S. Arzy, M. Fachler, and B. Kahana, *Life as a Midrash: Perspectives in Jewish Philosophy* (Yediot Aharonot, Tel Aviv, 2004), pp. 338–382 (Hebrew); and

"The Tsadik and His Soul's Sparks." For the earlier sources see Michel Tardieu, "ΨΥΧΑΙΟΣ ΣΠΙΝΘΗΡ: Histoire d'une metaphore dans la tradition platonicienne jusqu'a Eckhart," *Revue des Études Augustiniennes*, vol. XXI (1975), pp. 227–232; Lucia Saudelli, *"Lux sicca*, Marsile Ficin exégète d'Heraclite," *Accademia*, vol. X (2008), pp. 29–42; Louis Jacobs, "The Doctrine of the 'Divine Spark' in Man in Jewish Sources," in *Rationalism, Judaism, Universalism in Memory of Leon Roth* (New York, 1966), pp. 87–114.

Compare also the texts of R. Shneur Zalman of Liady from the book of *Tanya* copied in R. Aharon of Apta's *'Or ha-Ganuz la-Tzaddiqim*, discussed by Lieberman, *'Ohel Ra_Hel*, vol. 1, p. 10, to the effect that the divine light dwells on the human soul, depicted as the part of God on high. See also R. Menahem Nahum of Chernobyl, *Yisma_h Lev*, fol. 1b, where the dwelling of the divine vitality is conceived of as found everywhere but also on the "part of God on high." On this text see Wacks, *The Secret of Unity*, p. 195, and compare also to the resort to this phrase in a similar context in R. Shneor Zalman of Lyadi, *Sefer ha-Tanya, Liqqutei 'Amarim*, chap. 41, fol. 56b. See also the discussions of R. Jacob Joseph ben Yehudah, a student of the Great Maggid, in his *Rav Yeivi*, fols. 4a, 10a, 32c, 43b, 48a, 65b, 123c.

This theme is the proper framework for understanding the Hasidic vision of divine presence in man. See also previously in a passage discussed in appendix A and in Jonathan Garb, "The Psychological Turn in Sixteenth Century Kabbalah," in eds. G. Cecere, M. Loubet, and S. Pagani, *Les mystiques juives, chretienes et musulmanes dans l'Egypte médiévale (7.–16. siècles): interculturalités et contextes historiques* (Institut français d'archéologie orientale, Le Caire, 2013), p. 119; and his *Yearnings of the Soul, Psychological Thought in Modern Kabbalah* (Chicago University Press, Chicago, 2015), pp. 29–30. See also the Beshtian text translated in appendix A as to the awareness of the existence of divinity within oneself, without using the prooftext from Job. See also the important passage of the Vidas, *Reshit _Hokhmah*, "Gate of Holiness," chap. 6; II, p. 87, to the effect that the pure soul becomes "a seat for the supernal spiritual force [ru_haniyyut]." See also Vidas, p. 110, and the text from *Pardes Rimmonim*, XXXII, chap. 1; II, fol. 78bc. See also Green, "The *Zaddiq* as *Axis Mundi*." Needless to say that I do not consider texts where the divine power is attracted within a person, stemming from the astro-magical worldview, to represent cases of incarnation.

26 Part I, chap. 3.

27 See, e.g., R. _Hayyim Vital's *Liqqutei Torah* (Vilnius, 1880), fol. 108b.

28 Magid, *Hasidism Incarnate*, especially p. 181, n. 20, where the author proposes, claiming that he follows the lead of Scholem—actually quoting a sentence of Walter Benjamin—to read the texts "against their declared intention," namely Benjamin's "grain." This is indeed what he does. However, scholarship starts only when someone reads the texts against the grain of the scholar and his cultural ambiance. I wonder what the criteria are for offering one interpretation or another that may contradict the interpreted text. There is, to be sure, more than one way of going against the text. I propose however, to read them against their most plausible Kabbalistic backgrounds, especially the Safedian ones, before projecting the phenomenological category of incarnation in texts whose meaning can be explored

with some philological effort. In such a manner of reading, any possible interpretation that differs from the intention of the text is possible, generating what can be called a disincarnate scholarship.

Moreover, the awareness of the possible implications of the existence of a strong Christian mystical renascence in the immediate vicinity of the centers of early Hasidism, the Neo-hesychasm, is hardly mentioned, though not discussed in his rather superficial depiction of Eastern Christianity. For more on this issue see Idel, "R. Israel Ba'al Shem Tov 'In the State of Walachia,'" a study that he conveniently overlooked, though he was aware of the book itself and quoted from it. This is part of a broader phenomenon in recent scholarship that speculates about possible sources without actually investing time in serious study of the specific pertinent backgrounds, while it is possible to discern the actual sources in widespread Kabbalistic books and in the religious life in the surroundings of early Hasidism, an issue that still deserves a longer treatment. See, meanwhile, also my "18th Century Early Hasidism." The religious background of the emergence of Hasidism was much more complex from the religious point of view than it transpires from the Eurocentric type of Christotropia so evident in recent scholarship of Hasidism. See also, Idel, *Ben*, pp. 523–524, 567–570. See also the interesting remark of Morton W. Bloomfield, *Essays and Explorations, Studies in Ideas, Language, and Literature* (Harvard University Press, Cambridge, 1970), p. 83: "Unless the significance of a literary work can be subsumed in a system of interpretation—usually Christian, though not always—it is assumed to have no meaning." See also my "Early Hasidism and Altaic Tribes," p. 33.

29 See, meanwhile, my *Hasidism*, p. 246.

30 See Mendel Piekarz, "The Devekuth as Reflecting the Socio-Religious Character of the Hasidic Movement," *Da'at*, vol. 24 (1990), pp. 140–141 (Hebrew), where he referred to *Yad Yosef* (Amsterdam, 1680), fol. 12b. Compare also the very important discussion of R. Elijah ha-Itamari of Smyrna, in his widespread *Sefer Shevet Musar*, chap. 39 (Jerusalem, n.d.), pp. 318–319. This book had been translated in Yiddish and printed several times at the middle of the eighteenth century.

31 See the view found in the *Book of Bahir* and discussed by Scholem, *On the Mystical Shape of the Godhead*, p. 94.

32 Shenei Luhot ha-Berit, III, fol. 59b:

מכל מקום פתח יוסף צנור הקדושה ואח"כ נשאר הקדושה בבית עולמים. כי יוסף הוא הצנור, כי הוא העמוד שהעולם עומד עליו, בסוד המדה שלו צדיק יסוד עולם, שכל מיני שפע הולכים דרך צינור זה למלכות הנקרא עולם. ואע"פ שנסתלק אח"כ המלכות והמקדש ממנו. והוא כענין כל העולם ניזון בשביל חנינא בני וחנינא בני די לו בקב חרובין מערב שבת לערב שבת והענין כי ר' חנינא היה בדורו הצדיק הגדול עמד אחד שהעולם עומד עליו, וזה שאמרו בשביל חנינא, ובשביל פירושו לשון שביל וצינור.

Horowitz was very much interested in this legend about R. Hanina', which he mentions briefly several times. See also Sack, *The Kabbalah of R. Moshe Cordo*vero, p. 53, n. 108.

33 (Venice, 1770), fol. 78d. On the possible Sabbatean background of this Kabbalist, see Bezalel Naor, *Post-Sabbatian Sabbatianism* (New York, 1999), pp. 71–73. See also my "Nehemiah ben Shlomo the Prophet on *Magen David*," pp. 58–59.

34 *Kavvanat Shelomo*, fol. 75cd.

35 See ch. 8 n. 5 in this volume.

36 See Luck, *Arcana Mundi*, p. 3. I find his introductory discussions on ancient magic quite helpful for understanding aspects of magic also in the texts to be discussed as follows, as well as previously in this study.

37 *On the Mystical Shape of the Godhead*, pp. 133–134.

38 *Ben Porat Yosef*, fol. 63b:

בשם מורי: כי חנינא בני עשה שביל וצינור להמשיך שפע בעולם וזה שאמר העולם ניזון
בשביל חנינא בני ודפח"ח.

Another variant of this statement, again in the name of the Besht, occurs in *Ben Porat Yosef*, fol. 59d, and in this context the *tzaddiq* is mentioned explicitly. For a survey of the many occurrences of this dictum in R. Jacob Joseph's writings, see Dresner, *The Zaddik*, pp. 125–128, and see also Scholem, *On the Mystical Shape of the Godhead*, pp. 136–137, who dealt with the Ba'al Shem Tov's views and those of his followers, without discussing their source in Cordovero and his followers.

39 *Toledot Ya'aqov Yosef*, fol. 167b, 167c.

40 *Toledot Ya'aqov Yosef*, fol. 299d.

41 Fol. 7b, 7c:

וממורי שמעתי כי שביל הוא צנור שפתח צנור ושביל השפע וז"ש בשביל חנינא בני
ודפח"ח.

See also *Toledot Ya'aqov Yosef*, fol. 1c, where the Besht is mentioned. On fol. 7c, 7d, R. Jacob Joseph elaborates on the meaning of the Besht's statement at length, adding theosophical and theurgical dimensions not alluded to in the traditions found in the name of the Besht. See also *Toledot Ya'aqov Yosef*, fol. 46d, where the theme of the righteous is introduced.

42 *Toledot Ya'aqov Yosef*, fol. 59d:

כי האותיות הם 'סולם מוצב ארצה' - גופי האותיות 'וראשו' דהיינו רוחניותו ופנימיותו
- 'מגיע השמימה' ועי"ז 'מלאכי אלהים' - הם הצדיקי' 'עולים' למעלה לדבק ב' ית' 'ויורדים' בו
להוריד השפע בעולם בסוד 'העולם ניזון בשביל' וצינור ר"ח בני וכמו ששמעתי ממורי בזה.

43 See *Toledot Ya'aqov Yosef*, fol. 7c, 7d.

44 *Toledot Ya'aqov Yosef*, fol. 46d.

45 See Derrida, *La voix et le phénomène*, p. 115, who draws a strong nexus between metaphysics and orality, or Derrida, p. 87, between phoneme and phenomenon, since the former, according to his view, masters the latter.

46 A common acronym for R. Israel Ba'al Shem. It should be mentioned that this acronym is used also in a magical recipe attributed to another magician, a generation before the Besht, R. Joel Ba'al Shem. See my "Nehemiah ben Shlomo the Prophet on *Magen David*," p. 50.

47 This structure is found also elsewhere in Rabbinic literature. See Avot 6:2, and see the discussion of this issue in chap. 6 of this volume

48 I suggest seeing here the trace of an astral theme: the liquids, nozelim, are some-times related to the concept of *mazzal*, the zodiacal sign. See, e.g., R. Joseph Gikatilla's introduction to *Sha'arei Orah*.

49 *'Avodat Yisra'el*, fol. 66b:

הריב"ש ז"ל אמר פירוש הגמרא יצאה בת קול ואמרה כל העולם ניזון בשביל חנינא בני
וחנינא בני די לו בקב חרובין מערב שבת לערב שבת, דהצדיק הוא כמו שביל וצינור הממשיך
נוזלים, כן הוא על ידי מעשיו הקדושים ממשיך השפעות טובות לעולם, וכמו שהצינור אינו נהנה
במה שעובר עליו, כן הצדיק אין רצונו וחפצו כי אם להשפיע לכל באי העולם, וזהו הבת קול כל
העולם ניזון בשבי"ל, פירוש, בצינור שעושה חנינא בני, והוא כמו השביל והצינור שאין חפץ
בטובת עצמו, ומסתפק במועט ודי לו בקב חרובין וכו' ודפה"ח.

See also *'Avodat Yisra'el*, fols. 66b, 66c, 78c. Compare also to the Rabbi of Gur's *Sefer Sefat 'Emmet* (Jerusalem, n.p., 1871), vol. 4, fol. 75c, where he describes the drawing down of the vitality to this world as being a teaching of the Besht:

ופי' הבעש"ט אוכלין בעוה"ז ובזה עצמו נוחלין לעוה"ב מלשון נחל שממשיכין חיות
השי"ת גם לעניני עוה"ז.

50 Ed. Rubinstein, p. 290.

51 Ms. Jerusalem NUL 80 3282, fol. 82b:

כל העולמות ניזון [!] בשביל חנינא בני דהיינו שהצדיק הוא ממשיך שפע לכל העולמות.

52 See ch. 6 n. 22 in this volume.

53 See *'Or Torah*, p. 12; see also *'Or Torah*, p. 13: "The *tzaddiqim* sustained and nourished the world" and the numerous discussions on pp. 28, 118, 148; cf. Green, "*Zaddiq as Axis Mundi*," p. 338, and Idel, *Hasidism*, p. 115. Similar views occur in R. Elimelekh's *No'am 'Elimelekh*. R. Menahem Nahum of Chernobyl refers several times to this image. See also R. Jacob Josef ben Yehudah, *Sefer Rav Yeivi*, fol. 51d. On the subject of man as a pipeline in another context, based on the theory of *oratio infusa*, see Schatz-Uffenheimer, *Hasidism as Mysticism*, pp. 201–202, without referring to the material discussed previously, and for later Hasidic discussions, Elior, "Between *Yesh* and *Ayin*," pp. 426–427, 448, n. 48.

54 See beside ch. 6 n. 18 in this volume.

55 See also the different view found in *Ben Porat Yosef*, fol. 18d, where the assumption is that by exercising an influence in the mundane world, the *tzaddiq* causes an abundance of influx in the higher world. In other words, in some cases a magical activity has also a theurgical aspect.

56 See appendix A in this volume.

57 On this text as a potential tradition of the Besht, see the footnote of Shimeon Menahem Mendel Vodnek, ed. *Ba'al Shem Tov*, p. 142, n. 59; Pedaya, "Outlines for a Religious-Typological Approach," p. 57; and Idel, "The Besht as a Prophet and a Talismanic Magician," p. 141.

58 See indeed, the interesting discussion in *Toledot Ya'aqov Yosef*, fol. 3a.

59 See *Mishnah, Qiddushin*, chap. I, Halakhah 10.

60 About this theme in the lifetime of the Besht see chap. 10.

61   This is a designation for the divinity found in traditions of the Besht. See Idel, *Hasidism*, pp. 126, 364 n. 113.

62   For a very similar understanding of this verse, see *Ben Porat Yosef*, fol. 59d, where he mentions a tradition he heard.

63   *Toledot Ya'aqov Yosef*, fol. 136a:

ואפילו במצו' הנוגע לדיבור לבד בלי מעשה צריך יחוד וחיבור אותיות לצרפ' לתיבות וזה
א"א כי אם ע"י צדיק הממשיך שפע רוחניות הספירות עם אור א"ס שבתוכו שהוא המיוחד
האותיות לחברן לתיבות וכמו שכתבתי בהקדמה 'כל העושה מצוות אחת וכו" יעו"ש. והנה
האותיות של הדיבור נק' כלי כלי בעלי גבול ומידה הנק' יש ומכ"ש במצוות מעשיות כמו תפילין וטלית
הכלי נק' יש וצריך להמשיך בתוכו אור הרוחניות המחי' אותו הנק' אין כי הוא נשמה הנמשך
מא"ס חיי החיים נגד ב' שעושה הצדיק בעה"ז בחייו יאכל שכרו ובעה"ב ב' מדרגות ג"כ וז"ס
"להנחיל אוהבי י"ש ואוצרותיה אמלא". אני מעצמותי אין כביכול שהוא אור הנשמה שבתוך
האוצר והכלי המחי' אותן.

64   *Toledot Ya'aqov Yosef*, fol. 6a.

65   See Weiss, *Studies*, p. 150; Weiss, *Studies in Braslav Hasidism*, ed. M. Piekarz (Magnes Press, Jerusalem, 1974), pp. 121–125 (Hebrew); Elior, *The Paradoxical Ascent to God, passim*; Elior, "Between *Yesh* and *Ayin*," pp. 393–445; Elior, "*Yesh* and '*Ayin* as Fundamental Paradigms in Hasidic Thought," in eds. A. Goldreich and M. Oron, *Massu'ot: Prof. Ephrayim Gottlieb Memorial Volume* (Mossad Bialik, Jerusalem, 1994), pp. 53–76 (Hebrew); and Mayse, *Beyond the Letters*, pp. 15–16, 177–178. About '*Ayin* in Jewish mysticism, see Matt, "Ayin," pp. 121–159.

66   See Idel, *Hasidism*, pp. 109–111, 113–114.

67   See, e.g., *Toledot Ya'aqov Yosef*, fols. 1c, 4c, etc., and in the school of the Great Maggid see in *'Or ha-'Emmet*, fol. 52c: מדת התחברות and see also fol. 29a.

68   See chap. 4, n. 56.

69   *Qedushat Levi*, p. 15:

יש שני עובדי הבורא, אחד שעובד הבורא במסירות נפש ואחד שעובד הבורא במצות ובמע־
שים. טובים והההפרש שזה העובד את הבורא במסירת נפש לא על ידי מצות ומעשים טובים הוא
כאין ממש וזה העובד את ה' במצות הוא עובד על ידי דבר היש כי המצות הם יש ולכן זה שעובד
במסירות נפש דהוא כאין אינו יכול להמשיך על עצמו שפע כי הוא אינו כלום רק שמדבק את
עצמו להשם יתברך וזה שעובד על ידי מצות ומעשים טובים הוא על ידי דבר יש לכן יכול להמ־
שיך על עצמו שפע מהשם יתברך.

       See also the view of Cordovero, adduced in my *Hasidism*, p. 71, as well as *Hasidism*, pp. 127–128.

70   See, e.g., Kauffman, *In all Your Ways Know Him*, pp. 426–466; Mayse, *Beyond the Letters*, p. 12; and compare also to a view of the Great Maggid discussed in Brody, "Open to Me the Gates of Righteousness," p. 20.

ABBREVIATIONS

Journals

AHDLMA	Archives d'histoire doctrinal et litteraire du moyen age
HTR	Harvard Theological Review
HUCA	Hebrew Union College Annual
JBL	Journal of Biblical Literature
JJR	Journal of Jewish Studies
JJTP	Journal of Jewish Thought and Philosophy
JQR	Jewish Quarterly Review
JSJF	Jerusalem Studies in Jewish Folklore
JSQ	Jewish Studies Quarterly
JWCI	Journal of the Warburg and Courtland Institutes
MJ	Modern Judaism
PAAJR	Proceedings of the American Academy of Jewish Research
QS	Qiryat Sefer

SOURCES

R. Abraham Azulai, *Hesed le-'Avraham* (Lemberg, 1863).

R. Abraham Azulai, *'Or ha-Hammah* (Premislany, 1896), 3 volumes.

R. Abraham Hayyim of Zloczow, *'Orah la-Hayyim* (Jerusalem, 1960).

R. Aharon ha-Kohen Perlov of Apta, *'Or ha-Ganuz la-Tzaddiqim* (Lemberg, 1850).

R. Aharon ha-Kohen Perlov of Apta, *'Or ha-Ganuz la-Tzaddiqim* (Warsaw, 1887).

R. Aharon ha-Kohen Perlov of Apta, *Ner Mitzwah* (Pietrkov, 1881).

R. Aharon ha-Kohen Perlov of Apta, *Keter Nehora'* (New York, 2011).

R. Aharon ha-Kohen Perlov of Apta, *Keter Shem Tov* (Brooklyn, 1974).

R. Aharon ha-Kohen Perlov of Apta, *Keter Shem Tov ha-Shalem* (Brooklyn, 2004).

R. Aharon of Zhitomir, *Sefer Toledot 'Aharon* (Berditchev, 1817).

R. Arieh Leib Galiner, the Admonisher of Polonnoye, *Qol 'Arieh* (Koretz, 1798).

R. Barukh of Kosov, *Nehmad ve-Na'yim—Yesod ha-'Emunah* (New York, 1931).

R. Barukh of Kosov, *'Amud ha-'Avodah* (Chernovitz, 1863).

R. Barukh of Miedzibush, *Butzina' di-Nehora'* (Jerusalem, n.d.).

R. Dov Ber of Mezeritch, *Liqqutim Yeqarim* (Jerusalem, 1974).

R. Dov Ber of Mezeritch, *'Or ha-'Emmet* (Zhitomir, 1900); reprinted Benei Beraq, 1967.

R. Dov Ber of Mezeritch (the Great Maggid), *Maggid Devarav le-Ya'aqov*, ed. R. Schatz-Uffenheimer, 2nd ed. (Magnes, Jerusalem, 2000).

R. Eliezer of Lysansk, *No'am 'Elimelekh* (Lemberg, 1865).

R. Elijah da Vidas, *Reshit Hokhmah*, ed. H. Y. Waldman (Jerusalem, 1984), 3 volumes.

R. Gedalyahu of Lunitz, *Teshu'ot Hen*, (Berditchev, 1816).

R. Hayyim Vital, *Sha'ar Ruah ha-Qodesh* (Jerusalem, 1984).

In Praise of the Baal Shem Tov—In Praise of the Baal Shem Tov (Shivḥe haBesht), eds. and English tr. by D. Ben-Amos and J. R. Mintz (Schocken Books, New York, 1984).

R. Isaiah Horowitz, *Sha'ar ha-Shamayyim* (Amsterdam, 1717).

R. Isaiah Horowitz, *Shenei Luḥot ha-Berit* I–III (Jerusalem, 1969).

R. Israel of ben Sabbatai, the Maggid of Kuznitz, *'Avodat Yisra'el* (Warsaw, 1875).

R. Issakhar Dov Baer of Zloczow, *Mevasser Tzedeq* (Dubna, 1798).

R. Jacob Joseph ben Judah, *Sefer Rav Yeivi* (Ostrog, 1806).

R. Jacob Joseph of Polonnoye, *Ben Porat Yosef* (Koretz, 1781) and (Lemberg, 1866).

R. Jacob Joseph of Polonnoye, *Sefer Kutoneth Pasim*, ed. G. Nigal (Jerusalem, 1985).

R. Jacob Joseph of Polonnoye, *Sefer Tzafenat Pa'neaḥ* (Koretz, 1782).

R. Jacob Joseph of Polonnoye, *Sefer Tzafnat Pa'aneaḫ*, ed. G. Nigal (Jerusalem, 1989).

R. Jacob Joseph of Polonnoye, *Toledot Ya'aqov Yosef* (Koretz, 1780).

R. Levi Isaac of Berditchev, *Qedushat Levi* (Jerusalem, 1993).

R. Meir Ḥarif Margoliot of Ostrog, *Sod Yakhin u-Vo'az*, ed. Nathan Margoliot (Jerusalem, 1990).

R. Menahem Mendel of Rimanov, *'Ilana' de-Ḥayyei* (Pietrkov, 1908).

R. Menahem Nahum of Chernobyl, *Me'or 'Eynayim* (Jerusalem, 1975).

R. Meshullam Phaebus of Zbarazh, ed. A. Dov Baer, *Kitvei Qodesh* (Herskovits, Dej, 1933).

R. Meshullam Phaebus of Zbarazh, *Yosher Divrei 'Emmet*, printed together with *Liqqutim Yeqarim*.

Mondshine, ed., *Shivehei Ha-Baal Shem Tov*—Yehoshua Mondshine, ed. *Shivehei Ha-Baal Shem Tov, A Facsimile of a Unique Manuscript* (Jerusalem, 1982).

R. Moshe Cordovero, *Derishot be-'Inianei Mal'akhim*, printed as an appendix in *Mal'akhei 'Elyon*, ed. R. Margoliot (Mosad ha-Rav Kook, Jerusalem, 1945).

R. Moshe Cordovero, *'Eilimah Rabbati* (Lemberg, 1881).

R. Moshe Cordovero, *'Or Yaqar*, vol. 1 (Jerusalem, 1962).

R. Moshe Cordovero, *'Or Yaqar*, vol. 2 (Jerusalem, 1963).

R. Moshe Cordovero, *'Or Yaqar*, vol. 4 (Jerusalem, 1967).

R. Moshe Cordovero, *'Or Yaqar*, vol. 5 (Jerusalem, 1970).

R. Moshe Cordovero, *'Or Yaqar*, vol. 6 (Jerusalem, 1974).

R. Moshe Cordovero, *'Or Yaqar*, vol. 7 (Jerusalem, 1975).

R. Moshe Cordovero, *'Or Yaqar*, vol. 8 (Jerusalem, 1976).

R. Moshe Cordovero, *'Or Yaqar*, vol. 9 (Jerusalem, 1976).

R. Moshe Cordovero, *'Or Yaqar*, vol. 10 (Jerusalem, 1979).

R. Moshe Cordovero, *'Or Yaqar*, vol. 11 (Jerusalem, 1981).

R. Moshe Cordovero, *'Or Yaqar*, vol. 12 (Jerusalem, 1983).

R. Moshe Cordovero, *'Or Yaqar*, vol. 13 (Jerusalem, 1985).

R. Moshe Cordovero, *'Or Yaqar*, vol. 14 (Jerusalem, 1986).

R. Moshe Cordovero, *'Or Yaqar*, vol. 15 (Jerusalem, 1987).

R. Moshe Cordovero, *'Or Yaqar*, vol. 16 (Jerusalem, 1989).

R. Moshe Cordovero, *'Or Yaqar*, vol. 17 (Jerusalem, 1989).

R. Moshe Cordovero, *'Or Yaqar* on *Tiqqunei Zohar Ḥadash*, vol. 3 (Jerusalem, 1975).

R. Moshe Cordovero, *'Or Yaqar* on *Tiqqunei Zohar*, vol. 3 (Jerusalem, 1981).

R. Moshe Cordovero, *'Or Yaqar* on *Tiqqunei Zohar*, vol. 4 (Jerusalem, 2004).

R. Moshe Cordovero, *'Or Yaqar* on *Tiqqunei Zohar*, vol. 5 (Jerusalem, 2007).

R. Moshe Cordovero, *'Or Yaqar* on *Tiqqunei Zohar*, vol. 6 (Jerusalem, 2009).

R. Moshe Cordovero, *Pardes Rimonim* (Muncasz, reprint, Jerusalem, 1962), two parts.

R. Moshe Cordovero, *Perush Sefer Yetziyrah* (Jerusalem, 1989).

R. Moshe Cordovero, *Shi'ur Qomah* (Warsaw, 1883).

R. Moshe Cordovero, *Tefillah le-Moshe* (Premislany, 1892).

R. Moshe Ḥayim Ephraim of Sudylkov, *Degel Maḥane Efrayim* (Jerusalem, 1995).

R. Moshe Shoham of Dolina, *Divrei Moshe* (Polonnoye, 1801), two parts.

R. Nahman of Braslav, *Liqqutei Moharan* (Benei Beraq, 1992), two parts.

Natan ben Sa'adya Har'ar, Le Porte della Giustizia, ed. M. Idel, tr. M. Mottolese, *Natan ben Sa'adya Har'ar, Le Porte della Giustizia* (Adelphi, Milano, 2001).

R. Nathan Neta' of Sienewa, *Sefer 'Olat Tamid ha-Shalem* (Premislany, 1895).

R. Pinchas Shapira of Koretz, *Liqqutim Me-ha-rav R. Pinḥas mi-koretz* (Pietrkov, 1914).

R. Qalonymus Qalman Ha-Levi Epstein of Krakau, *Ma'or va-Shemesh* (Warsaw, 1877).

R. Reuven ha-Levi Horowitz, *Diduim Basode* (Lemberg, 1859).

A. Rubinstein, ed., *Shivhei ha-Besht* (Reuven Mass, Jerusalem, 1991).

Shemu'ah Tovah (Warsaw, 1938).

R. Shimeon Menahem Mendel Vodnek, ed. *Ba'al Shem Tov* (Lodge, 1938), 2 volumes.

Tzava'at Ha-Rivash, printed together with *Liqqutim Yeqarim* by R. Dov Ber of Mezerich (Jerusalem, 1981).

Tzava'at Ha-Rivash: The Testament of Rabbi Israel Baal Shem Tov, tr. Jacob Immanuel Schochet (New York, 1998).

R. 'Uzziel Meisles, *Tiferet 'Uzziel* (Warsaw, 1863).

R. Yohanan Alemanno, *Sha'ar ha-Ḥesheq* (Halberstadt, 1860).

R. Ze'ev Wolf of Zhitomir, *'Or ha-Me'ir* (Parichi, 1815).

STUDIES

Afterman, *Devequt* — Adam Afterman, *Devequt: Mystical Intimacy in Medieval Jewish Thought* (Cherub Press, Los Angeles, 2011) (Hebrew).

Afterman, *The Intention of Prayer in Early Kabbalah* — Adam Afterman, *The Intention of Prayer in Early Kabbalah, A Study and Critical Edition of an Anonymous Commentary to the Prayers* (Cherub Press, Los Angeles, 2004) (Hebrew).

Altshuler, *The Messianic Secret of Hasidism* — Mor Altshuler, *The Messianic Secret of Hasidism* (Brill, Leiden, 2006).

Baumgarten, *La naissance de Hasidism* — Jean Baumgarten, *La naissance de Hasidism, Mystique, rituel, société (XVIIIe–XIXe siècle)*, (Albin Michel, Paris, 2005).

Beck, *Sonic Theology* — Guy L. Beck, *Sonic Theology, Hinduism, and Sacred Sound* (Motilai Banarsidass Publisher, Delhi, 1995).

Ben Shlomo, *The Mystical Theology of Moses Cordovero* — Joseph ben Shlomo, *The Mystical Theology of Moses Cordovero* (Mossad Bialik, Jerusalem, 1965) (Hebrew).

Breck, *La puissance de la parole* — Jean Breck, *La puissance de la parole, Une introduction à l'herméneutique orthodoxe* (Le Cerf, Paris, 1996).

Brill, "The Spiritual World of a Master of Awe" — Alan Brill, "The Spiritual World of a Master of Awe: Divine Vitality, Theosis, and Healing in the *Degel Mahaneh Ephraim*," *JSQ*, vol. 8, no. 1 (2001), pp. 27–65.

Brody, 'Human Hands Dwell in Heavenly Heights" — Seth Brody, "'Human Hands Dwell in Heavenly Heights': Contemplative Ascent and Theurgic Power in Thirteenth Century Kabbalah," in ed. R. A. Herrera, *Mystics of the Book: Themes, Topics, & Typology* (Peter Lang, New York, 1992), pp. 123–158.

Brody, "'Open to Me the Gates of Righteousness' — Seth Brody, "'Open to Me the Gates of Righteousness': The Pursuit of Holiness and Non-Duality in Early Hasidic Teaching," *JQR*, vol. LXXXIX (1998), pp. 3–44.

Buber, *Hasidism and Modern Man* — Martin Buber, *Hasidism and Modern Man*, ed. and English tr. Maurice Friedman (Schocken, New York, 1958).

Buber, "Interpreting Hasidism" — Martin Buber, "Interpreting Hasidism," *Commentary*, vol. 36, no. 9 (September 1963), pp. 218–225.

Buber, *The Origin and Meaning of Hasidism* — Martin Buber, *The Origin and Meaning of Hasidism*, ed. and English tr. by Maurice Freedman; introduction by D. B. Burrell (Atlantic Highlands, NJ, 1988).

Copenhaver, *Magic in Western Culture* — Brian P. Copenhaver, *Magic in Western Culture, from Antiquity to the Enlightenment* (Cambridge University Press, New York, 2015).

Couliano, *Eros and Magic* — Ioan P. Couliano, *Eros and Magic in the Renaissance* (Chicago University Press, Chicago, London, 1987).

Dan, *Jewish Mysticism* — Joseph Dan, *Jewish Mysticism*, vol. III (Jason Aronson, Northvale, NJ, 1999).

Dauber, "The Baal Shem Tov and the Messiah" — Jonathan V. Dauber, "The Baal Shem Tov and the Messiah: A Reappraisal of the Baal Shem Tov's Letter to R. Gershon of Kutov," *JSQ*, 16 (2009), pp. 210–241.

Derrida, *La voix et le phénomène* — Jacques Derrida, *La voix et le phénomène* (PUF, Paris, 1993).

Dresner, *The Zaddik* — Samuel H. Dresner, *The Zaddik, The Doctrine of the Zaddik according to the Writings of Rabbi Yaakov Yosef of Polnoy* (Schocken Books, New York, 1974).

Dyczkowski, *The Doctrine of Vibration* — Mark S. G. Dyczkowski, *The Doctrine of Vibration: An Analysis of the Doctrines and Practices of Kashmir Shaivism* (SUNY Press, Albany, 1987).

Eliade, *Yoga* — Mircea Eliade, *Yoga: Immortality and Freedom*, tr. W. R. Trask (Princeton, University Press, Princeton, 1958).

Elior, "Between *Yesh* and *Ayin*" — Rachel Elior, "Between *Yesh* and *Ayin:* The Doctrine of the Zaddik in the Works of Jacob Isaac, the Seer of Lublin," in eds. A. Rapoport-Albert and S. J. Zipperstein, *Jewish History: Essays in Honour of Chimen Abramsky* (London, 1988), pp. 393–445.

Elior, *Israel Ba'al Shem Tov and His Contemporaries* — Rachel Elior, *Israel Ba'al Shem Tov and His Contemporaries* (Carmel, Jerusalem, 2014), two volumes (Hebrew).

Elior, *The Mystical Origins of Hasidism* — Rachel Elior, *The Mystical Origins of Hasidism*, tr. S. Carmy (Littman Library, Oxford, UK-Portland, OR, 2008).

Elior, *The Paradoxical Ascent to God* — Rachel Elior, *The Paradoxical Ascent to God*, tr. J. M. Green (SUNY Press, Albany, 1993), pp. 393–445.

Etkes, *The Besht: Magician, Mystic, and Leader* — Immanuel Etkes, *The Besht: Magician, Mystic, and Leader*, tr. S. Sternberg (New England University Press, Waltham, MA-Hanover, NH, 2004).

Fine, "Recitation of Mishnah" — Lawrence Fine, "Recitation of Mishnah as a Vehicle for Mystical Inspiration: a Contemplative Technique Taught by Hayyim Vital," *REJ*, vol. CXVI (1982), pp. 183–199.

Fishbane, *As Light before Dawn* — Eitan P. Fishbane, *As Light before Dawn: The Inner World of a Medieval Kabbalist* (Stanford University Press, Stanford, 2009).

Garb, "Powers of Language in Kabbalah" — Jonathan Garb, "Powers of Language in Kabbalah: Comparative Reflections," in eds. S. La Porta and D. Shulman, *The Poetics of Grammar and the Metaphysics of Sound and Sign* (Brill, Leiden, 2007), pp. 233–269.

Garb, *Shamanic Trance in Modern Kabbalah* — Jonathan Garb, *Shamanic Trance in Modern Kabbalah* (Chicago University Press, Chicago, 2011).

Glazer, "Afterword" — Aubrey L. Glazer, "Afterword," in Kallus, *Pillar of Prayer*, pp. 227–245.

Goetschel, *R. Meir Ibn Gabbay* — Roland Goetschel, *R. Meir Ibn Gabbay; Le Discours de la Kabbale espagnole* (Peeters, Leuven, 1981).

Gondos, *Kabbalah in Print* — Andrea Gondos, *Kabbalah in Print, Literary Strategies of Popular Mysticism in Early Modernity* (PhD Thesis, Concordia University, Montreal, 2013).

Green, "Around the Maggid's Table" — Arthur Y. Green, "Around the Maggid's Table: Tzaddiq, Leadership, and Popularization in the Circle of R. Dov Baer of Medzerich," *Zion*, vol. 78 (2013), pp. 73–106 (Hebrew).

Green, "Hasidism: Discovery and Retreat" — Arthur Green, "Hasidism: Discovery and Retreat," in ed. P. L. Berger, *The Other Side of God, A Polarity in World Religions* (New York, 1981), pp. 104–130.

Green, *Menahem Nahum of Chernobyl* — Arthur Green, *Menahem Nahum of Chernobyl: Upright Practices, The Light of the Eyes* (Paulist Press, New York, 1982).

Green, "Typologies of Leadership and the Hasidic *Zaddiq*" — Arthur Green, "Typologies of Leadership and the Hasidic *Zaddiq*," in ed. A. Green, *Jewish Spirituality*, vol. 2 (Crossroad, New York, 1989), pp. 127–156.

Green, "*Zaddiq* as *Axis Mundi*" — Arthur I. Green, "The *Zaddiq* as *Axis Mundi* in Later Judaism," *Journal of the American Academy of Religion*, vol. 45 (1977), pp. 328–347.

Gries, *Conduct Literature* — Ze'ev Gries, *Conduct Literature (Regimen Vitae), Its History and Place in the Life of the Beshtian Hasidism* (Mossad Bialik, Jerusalem, 1989) (Hebrew).

Gries, *The Hebrew Book* — Ze'ev Gries, *The Hebrew Book, an Outline of Its History* (Mossad Bialik, Jerusalem, 2015) (Hebrew).

Hasidism, a New History—*Hasidism, a New History*, by D. Biale & alia, with an afterword by A. Green (Princeton University Press, Princeton and Oxford, 2018).

Heschel, *The Circle of the Baal Shem Tov* — Abraham J. Heschel, *The Circle of the Baal Shem Tov: Studies in Hasidism*, ed. S. H. Dresner (Chicago University Press, Chicago-London, 1985).

Hollenback, *Mysticism, Experience, Response* — Jess Byron Hollenback, *Mysticism, Experience, Response, and Empowerment* (Penn State University, University Park, 1996).

Idel, "18th Century Early Hasidism" — M. Idel, "18th Century Early Hasidism: Between Europe and Asia," *Studia & Acta Historiae Iudaeorum Romaniae*, vol. XX (2015), pp. 49–76.

Idel, *Absorbing Perfections* — M. Idel, *Absorbing Perfections: Kabbalah and Interpretation* (Yale University Press, New Haven, CT-London, 2002).

Idel, *Ascensions on High* — M. Idel, *Ascensions on High in Jewish Mysticism: Pillars, Lines, Ladders* (CEU Press, Budapest, New York, 2005).

Idel, "Astral Dreams in R. Yohanan Alemanno's Writings" — M. Idel, "Astral Dreams in R. Yohanan Alemanno's Writings," *Accademia*, vol. 1 (1999), pp. 111–128.

Idel, *Ben* — M. Idel, *Ben: Sonship and Jewish Mysticism* (Continuum, London-New York, 2008).

Idel, "The Besht as Prophet and Talismanic Magician" — M. Idel, "The Besht as Prophet and Talismanic Magician," in eds. A. Lipsker and R. Kushelevsky, *Studies in Jewish Narrative: Ma'aseh Sippur*,

Presented to Yoav Elstein (Bar Ilan University Press, Ramat Gan, 2006), pp. 122–133 (Hebrew).

Idel, "The Besht Passed His Hand over His Face" — M. Idel, "'The Besht Passed His Hand over His Face': On the Besht's Influence on His Followers: Some Remarks," in eds. Ph. Wexler and J. Garb, *After Spirituality, Studies in Mystical Traditions* (Peter Lang, New York, 2012), pp. 79–106.

Idel, "Die laut gelesen Tora" — M. Idel, "Die laut gelesen Tora: Stimmengemeinschaft in der juedischen Mystik," in eds. Th. Macho and S. Weigel, *Zwischen Rauschen und Offenbarung: Zur Kultur und Mediengeschichte der Stimme* (Berlin, 2002), pp. 19–53.

Idel, "Early Hasidism and Altaic Tribes"—M. Idel, "Early Hasidism and Altaic Tribes, Between Europe and Asia," *Kabbalah*, vol. 39 (2017), pp. 7–51

Idel, *Enchanted Chains* — M. Idel, *Enchanted Chains: Techniques and Rituals in Jewish Mysticism* (Cherub Press, Los Angeles, 2005).

Idel, "Female Beauty" — M. Idel, "Female Beauty: A Chapter in the History of Jewish Mysticism," in eds. I. Etkes, D. Assaf, I. Bartal, and E. Reiner, *Within Hasidic Circles, Studies in Hasidism in Memory of Mordecai Wilensky* (The Bialik Institute, Jerusalem, 1999), pp. 317–334 (Hebrew).

Idel, "From ''Or Ganuz' to ''Or Torah'" — M. Idel, "From ''Or Ganuz' to ''Or Torah': A Chapter in the Phenomenology of Jewish Mysticism," *Migvvan De'ot be-Yisrael*, vol. 11 (2002), pp. 23–62 (Hebrew).

Idel, *Hasidism* — M. Idel, *Hasidism: Between Ecstasy and Magic* (SUNY Press, Albany, 1995).

Idel, "The Hasidic Revival" — M. Idel, "The Hasidic Revival: An Interpretation of the Emergence of a Spiritual Movement," in ed. Y. Friedmann, *Religious Movements and Transformations in Judaism, Christianity, and Islam* (The Israel Academy in Sciences and Humanities, Jerusalem, 2016), pp. 51–82.

Idel, *Kabbalah & Eros* — M. Idel, *Kabbalah & Eros* (Yale University Press, New Haven, CT, 2005).

Idel, *Kabbalah in Italy* — M. Idel, *Kabbalah in Italy: 1280–1510, A Survey* (Yale University Press, New Haven, 2011).

Idel, *Kabbalah: New Perspectives* — M. Idel, *Kabbalah: New Perspectives* (Yale University Press, New Haven, CT, 1988).

Idel, "The Land of Divine Vitality" — M. Idel, "The Land of Divine Vitality," in ed. A. Ravitzky, *The Land of Israel in Modern Jewish Thought* (Yad ben Zvi, Jerusalem, 1998), pp. 256–275 (Hebrew).

Idel, *Language, Torah, and Hermeneutics* — M. Idel, *Language, Torah, and Hermeneutics in Abraham Abulafia*, tr. M. Kallus (SUNY Press, Albany, NY, 1989).

Idel, "The Magical and Neoplatonic Interpretations of the Kabbalah" — M. Idel, "The Magical and Neoplatonic Interpretations of the Kabbalah in the Renaissance," in ed. B. D. Cooperman, *Jewish Thought in the Sixteenth Century* (Harvard University Press, Cambridge, MA, 1983), pp. 186–242.

Idel, "The Magical and Theurgical Interpretation" — M. Idel, "The Magical and Theurgical Interpretation of Music in Jewish Texts: Renaissance to Hasidism," *Yuval*, vol. 4 (1982), pp. 33–63 (Hebrew).

Idel, *Messianic Mystics* — M. Idel, *Messianic Mystics* (Yale University Press, New Haven, 1998).

Idel, *Mircea Eliade* — M. Idel, *Mircea Eliade, from Magic to Myth* (Peter Lang, New York, 2014).

Idel, "Models of Understanding Prayer" — M. Idel, "*Adonay Sefatay Tiftaḥ*: Models of Understanding Prayer in Early Hasidism," *Kabbalah*, vol. 18 (2008), pp. 7–111.

Idel, *The Mystical Experience in Abraham Abulafia* — M. Idel, *The Mystical Experience in Abraham Abulafia*, tr. J. Chipman (SUNY Press, Albany, 1987).

Idel, 'Mystical Redemption and Messianism in R. Israel Baʻal Shem Tov's Teachings' — M. Idel, "Mystical Redemption and Messianism in R. Israel Baʻal Shem Tov's Teachings," *Kabbalah*, vol. 24 (2011), pp. 7–121.

Idel, "Nehemiah ben Shlomo the Prophet on *Magen David*" — M. Idel, "Nehemiah ben Shlomo the Prophet on *Magen David* and the Name *Taftafiah*, from Jewish Magic to Practical and Theoretical Kabbalah," in eds. A. Reiner et al., *Ta Shma, Studies in Judaica in Memory of Israel M. Ta Shma* (Tevunot Press, Alon Shvut, 2011), pp. 1–76 (Hebrew).

Idel, *Old Worlds, New Mirrors* — M. Idel, *Old Worlds, New Mirrors: On Jewish Mysticism and Twentieth-Century Thought* (Pennsylvania University Press, Philadelphia, 2010).

Idel, "On Prophecy and Early Hasidism" — Moshe Idel, "On Prophecy and Early Hasidism," in ed. M. Sharon, *Studies in Modern Religions, Religious Movements, and the Babi-Baha'i Faiths* (Brill, Leiden, 2004), pp. 41–75.

Idel, "On Talismanic Language" — M. Idel, "On Talismatic Language in Jewish Mysticism," *Diogenes*, vol. 43, no. 2 (1995), pp. 23–41.

Idel, "Prayer, Ecstasy, and Alien Thoughts in the Besht's Religious World" — M. Idel, "Prayer, Ecstasy, and Alien Thoughts in the Besht's Religious World," in eds. D. Assaf and A. Rapoport-Albert, *Let the Old Make Way for the New: Studies in the Social and Cultural History of Eastern European Jewry Presented to Immanuel Etkes*, I: *Hasidism and the Musar Movement* (Merkaz Shazar, Jerusalem, 2009), pp. 57–120 (Hebrew).

Idel, *Primeval Evil* — M. Idel, *Primeval Evil: Totality, Perfection, and Perfectibility* (forthcoming).

Idel, "R. Israel Ba'al Shem Tov 'In the State of Walachia'" — M. Idel, "R. Israel Ba'al Shem Tov 'In the State of Walachia': Widening the Besht's Cultural Panorama," in ed. G. Dynner, *Holy Dissent. Jewish and Christian Mystics in Eastern Europe* (Wayne University Press, Detroit, 2011), pp. 104–130.

Idel, "Reification of Language in Jewish Mysticism" — M. Idel, "Reification of Language in Jewish Mysticism," in ed. S. T. Katz, *Mysticism and Language* (Oxford University Press, New York, 1992), pp. 42–79.

Idel, "Remembering and Forgetting" — M. Idel, "Remembering and Forgetting as Redemption and Exile in Early Hasidism," in eds. M. C. Frank and G. Ripple, *Arbeit am Gedaechtnis* (Fink, Muenchen, 2007), pp. 111–129.

Idel, *Studies in Ecstatic Kabbalah* — M. Idel, *Studies in Ecstatic Kabbalah* (SUNY Press, Albany, 1988).

Idel, "*Ta'anug*: Erotic Delights from Kabbalah to Hasidism" — M. Idel, "*Ta'anug*: Erotic Delights from Kabbalah to Hasidism," in eds. W. J. Hanegraaf and J. J. Kripal, *Hidden Intercourses: Eros and Sexuality in the History of Western Esotericism* (Brill, Leiden-Boston, 2009), pp. 131–151.

Idel, "*Torah ḥadashah*" — M. Idel, "*Torah ḥadashah*: Messiah and the New Torah in Jewish Mysticism and Modern Scholarship," *Kabbalah*, vol. 21 (2010), pp. 57–109.

Idel, "Transfers of Categories" — M. Idel, "Transfers of Categories: The German-Jewish Experience and Beyond," in eds. S. Aschheim and V. Liska, *The German-Jewish Experience Revisited* (de Gruyter, Berlin, 2015), pp. 15–43.

Idel, "The Tsaddik and His Soul's Sparks" — M. Idel, "The Tsaddik and His Soul's Sparks: From Kabbalah to Hasidism," *JQR*, vol. 103, no. 2 (Spring 2013), pp. 196–240.

Idel, "Types of Redemptive Activity in Middle Ages" — M. Idel, "Types of Redemptive Activity in Middle Ages," in ed. Z. Baras, *Messianism and Eschatology* (Merkaz Shazar, Jerusalem, 1983), pp. 253–279 (Hebrew).

Idel, "The Voiced Text of the Torah" — M. Idel, "The Voiced Text of the Torah," *Deutsche Vierteljahrsschrift für Literaturwissenschaft und Geistesgeschichte*, vol. 68 (1994), pp. 145–166.

Idel, "Universalization and Integration" — M. Idel, "Universalization and Integration: Two Conceptions of Mystical Union in Jewish Mysticism," in eds. M. Idel and B. McGinn, *Mystical Union and Monotheistic Faith, an Ecumenical Dialogue* (Macmillan, New York, 1989), pp. 27–58.

Idel, "Your Word Stands Firm in Heaven" — M. Idel, "'Your Word Stands Firm in Heaven': An Inquiry into the Early Traditions of R. Israel Baal Shem Tov and Their Reverberations in Hasidism," *Kabbalah*, vol. 20 (2009), pp. 219–286 (Hebrew).

Jacobs, *Hasidic Prayer* — Louis Jacobs, *Hasidic Prayer* (Schocken Books, New York, 1978).

Jacobs, *Their Heads in Heaven* — Louis Jacobs, *Their Heads in Heaven: Unfamiliar Aspects of Hasidism* (Vallentine Mitchell, London, 2005).

Jay, *Downcast Eyes* — Martin Jay, *Downcast Eyes: The Denigration of Vision in Twentieth-Century French Thought* (University of California Press, Berkeley, 1994).

Kallus, *Pillar of Prayer* — *Pillar of Prayer: Teachings of Contemplative Guidance in Prayer, Sacred Study, and the Spiritual Life from the Baal Shem Tov and his Circle*, tr. and annot. by Menachem Kallus (Louisville, KY, 2011).

Krassen, *Uniter of Heaven and Earth* — Miles Krassen, *Uniter of Heaven and Earth: Rabbi Meshullam Feibush Heller of Zbarazh and the Rise of Hasidism in Eastern Galicia* (SUNY Press, Albany, 1998).

Kauffman, *In All Your Ways Know Him* — Tsippi Kauffman, *In All Your Ways Know Him: The Concept of God and the 'Avodah Begashmiyut in the Early Stages of Hasidism* (Bar Ilan University Press, Ramat Gan, 2009) (Hebrew).

Kauffman, "Ritual Immersion" — Tsippi Kauffman, "Ritual Immersion at the Beginning of Hasidism," *Tarbiz*, vol. 80 (2012), pp. 409–425 (Hebrew).

Lamm, *The Religious Thought of Hasidism* — Norman Lamm, with contributions of Allan Brill and Shalom Carmy, *The Religious Thought of Hasidism* (Yeshivah University Press, New York, 1999).

Lederberg, *The Gateway to Infinity* — Netanel Lederberg, *The Gateway to Infinity, R. Dov Bear, the Magid Meisharim of Mezhirich* (Reuven Mass, Jerusalem, 2011) (Hebrew).

Lederberg, *Sod ha-Da'at* — Netanel Lederberg, *Sod ha-Da'at: Rabbi Israel Baal Shem Tov—His Spiritual Character and Social Leadership* (Reuven Mass, Jerusalem, 2007) (Hebrew).

Leicht, *Astrologumena Judaica* — Reimund Leicht, *Astrologumena Judaica* (Mohr, Tübingen, 2006).

Lieberman, *'Ohel RaHeL* — Hayyim Lieberman, *'Ohel RaHeL* (Author's printing, New York, 1980–1984), 3 volumes (Hebrew and Yiddisch).

Liebes, "The Power of the Word" — Yehuda Liebes, "The Power of the Word as the Foundation of Its Meaning in Kabbalah," in eds. M. M. Bar–Asher et al., *Davar davur 'al ofanav mehkarim be-farshanut ha-Mikra ve-ha-Ḳur'an bi-yeme ha-benayim mugashim le-Ḥagai Ben-Shamai* (Yad ben Zvi and Hebrew University, Jerusalem, 2007), pp. 163–177 (Hebrew).

Lorberbaum, "Attain the Attribute of *'Ayyin*" — Menachem Lorberbaum, "'Attain the Attribute of *'Ayyin*': The Mystical Religiosity of *Maggid Devarav Le-Ya'aqov*," *Kabbalah*, vol. 31 (2014), pp. 169–235 (Hebrew).

Luck, *Arcana Mundi* — Georg Luck, *Arcana Mundi, Magic and the Occult in the Greek and Roman Worlds* (Crucible, Great Britain, 1987).

Magid, *Hasidism Incarnate* — Shaul Magid, *Hasidism Incarnate: Hasidism, Christianity, and the Construction of Modern Judaism* (Stanford University Press, Stanford, 2014).

Margolin, *The Human Temple* — Ron Margolin, *The Human Temple: Religious Interiorization and the Inner Life in Early Hasidism* (Magnes Press, Jerusalem. 2004) (Hebrew).

Mark, *Mysticism and Madness* — Zvi Mark, *Mysticism and Madness in the Work of R. Nahman of Braslav* (Hartman Institute, Jerusalem-Tel Aviv, 2003) (Hebrew).

Mark, *The Revealed and the Hidden Writings* — Zvi Mark, *The Revealed and the Hidden Writings of Rabbi Nachman of Bratslav, His Worlds of Revelation and Rectification*, tr. Y. D. Shulman (De Gruyter, Magnes, Berlin, 2015).

Matt, "Ayin" — Daniel Matt, "Ayin: The Concept of Nothingness in Jewish Mysticism," in ed. R. K. C. Forman, *The Problem of Pure Consciousness, Mysticism, and Philosophy* (Oxford University Press, New York, Oxford, 1990), pp. 121–159.

Mayse, *Beyond the Letters* — Evan Drescher Mayse, *Beyond the Letters: The Question of Language in the Teachings of Rabbi Dov Baer of Mezrich* (PhD Dissertation, Harvard University, Cambridge, 2015).

Mensching, *Structures and Patterns of Religion* — Gustav Mensching, *Structures and Patterns of Religion*, tr. H. F. Klimkeit and V. Srinivara Sarma (Banarsidass, Delhi, 1976).

Moseson, *From the Spoken Word to the Discourse of the Academy* — Chaim Elly Moseson, *From the Spoken Word to the Discourse of the Academy: Reading the Sources for the Teachings of the Besht* (PhD Thesis, Boston University, 2017).

Nigal, *The Baal Shem Tov: Legends, Apologetics, and Reality* — Gedalyah Nigal, *The Baal Shem Tov: Legends, Apologetics, and Reality* (Jerusalem, 2007) (Hebrew).

Nigal, *The Birth of Hasidism* — Gedalyah Nigal, *The Birth of Hasidism* (Jerusalem, 2004) (Hebrew).

Nigal, "Sources of 'Devekut'" — Gedalyah Nigal, "Sources of 'Devekut' in Early Hasidic Literature," *QS*, vol. 66 (1970–1971), pp. 343–348 (Hebrew).

Ong, *The Presence of the Word* — Walter J. Ong, SJ, *The Presence of the Word, Some Prolegomena for Cultural and Religious History* (University of Minneapolis Press, Minneapolis, 1981).

Orent, "Mystical Union" — Leah Orent, "Mystical Union in the Writings of the Hasidic Master, R. Shneur Zalman of Lyady," *Studies in Spirituality*, vol. 18 (2008), pp. 61–92.

Pachter, *Roots of Faith and Devequt* — Mordechai Pachter, *Roots of Faith and Devequt: Studies in the History of Kabbalistic Ideas* (The Cherub Press, Los Angeles, 2004).

Padoux, *Vac* — André Padoux, *Vac: The Concept of the Word in Selected Hindu Tantras*, tr. J. Gontier (SUNY Press, Albany, 1990).

Pedaya, "The Baal Shem Tov, R. Jacob Joseph of Polonnoye, and the Maggid of Mezeritch" — Haviva Pedaya, "The Baal Shem Tov, R. Jacob Joseph of Polonnoye, and the Maggid of Mezeritch: Outlines for a Religious-Typological Approach," *Daat*, vol. 45 (2000), pp. 25–73 (Hebrew).

Pedaya, "Two Types of Ecstatic Experience in Hasidism" — Haviva Pedaya, "Two Types of Ecstatic Experience in Hasidism," *Daat*, vol. 55 (2005), pp. 73–108 (Hebrew).

Pedaya, *Vision and Speech* — Haviva Pedaya, *Vision and Speech: Models of Revelatory Experience in Jewish Mysticism* (Cherub Press, Los Angeles, 2002) (Hebrew).

Piekarz, *The Beginning of Hasidism* — Mendel Piekarz, *The Beginning of Hasidism, Ideological Trends in Derush and Musar Literature* (Mossad Bialik, Jerusalem, 1978) (Hebrew).

Piekarz, *Between Ideology and Reality* — Mendel Piekarz, *Between Ideology and Reality: Humility, Ayn, Self-Negation, and Devekut in Hasidic Thought* (Mossad Bialik, Jerusalem, 1994) (Hebrew).

Pines, "Le *Sefer ha-Tamar* et les *Maggidim* des Kabbalists" — Shlomo Pines, "Le *Sefer ha-Tamar* et les *Maggidim* des Kabbalists," in eds. G. Nahon and Ch. Touati, *Hommage à Georges Vajda* (Peeters, Louvain, 1980), pp. 333–363.

Pines, "On the Term *Ruḥaniyyut* and Its Sources" — Shlomo Pines, "On the Term *Ruḥaniyyut* and Its Sources and On Judah Halevi's Doctrine," *Tarbiz*, vol. 57 (1988), pp. 511–540 (Hebrew).

Pingree, "Some of the Sources of the *Ghayat al-Hakim*" — David Pingree, "Some of the Sources of the *Ghayat al-Hakim*," *JWCI*, vol. 43 (1980), pp. 1–15.

Rapoport-Albert, "God and the Zaddik" — Ada Rapoport-Albert, "God and the Zaddik as the Two Focal Points of Hasidic Worship," *History of Religions*, vol. 18 (1979), pp. 296–325, reprinted in ed. G. D. Hundert, *Essential Papers on Hasidism* (New York University Press, New York, 1991), pp. 299–329 (the references will be to this reprinting).

Rapoport-Albert, ed., *Hasidism Reappraised* — *Hasidism Reappraised*, ed. A. Rapoport-Albert (The Littman Library, London, Portland, 1996).

Reuchlin, *On the Art of Kabbalah* — Johann Reuchlin, *On the Art of Kabbalah, De Arte Cabalistica*, tr. M. Goodman and S. Goodman (Nebraska University Press, Lincoln, 1993).

Rosman, *The Founder of Hasidism* — Moshe Rosman, *The Founder of Hasidism: A Quest for the Historical Ba'al Shem Tov* (California University Press, Berkeley-Los Angeles-London, 1996).

Ruderman, *Kabbalah, Magic, and Science* — David Ruderman, *Kabbalah, Magic, and Science, The Cultural Universe of a Sixteenth-Century Jewish Physician* (Harvard University Press, Cambridge, MA, London, 1988).

Sack, "The Influence of Cordovero on Seventeenth-Century Jewish Thought" — Bracha Sack, "The Influence of Cordovero on Seventeenth-Century Jewish Thought," in eds. I. Twersky and B. Septimus, *Jewish Thought in the Seventeenth Century* (Cambridge, MA, 1987), pp. 365–379.

Sack, *The Kabbalah of R. Moshe Cordovero* — Bracha Sack, *The Kabbalah of R. Moshe Cordovero* (Magnes Press, Jerusalem, 1995) (Hebrew).

Schaeder, *The Hebrew Humanism of Martin Buber* — Grete Schaeder, *The Hebrew Humanism of Martin Buber*, tr. N. J. Jacobs (Wayne University Press, Detroit, 1973).

Schatz, "Contemplative Prayer in Hasidism" — Rivka Schatz, "Contemplative Prayer in Hasidism," in eds. E. E. Urbach, R. J. Zwi Werblowsky, and Ch. Wirszubski, *Studies in Mysticism and Religion Presented to Gershom G. Scholem* (Magnes Press, Jerusalem, 1967), pp. 209–226.

Schatz-Uffenheimer, "Gershom Scholem's Interpretation of Hasidism" — Rivka Schatz-Uffenheimer, "Gershom Scholem's Interpretation of Hasidism as an Expression of His Idealism," in ed. P. Mendes-Flohr, *Gershom Scholem: The Man and His Work* (SUNY Press, Jerusalem-Albany, 1994), pp. 87–103.

Schatz-Uffenheimer, *Hasidism as Mysticism* — Rivka Schatz-Uffenheimer, *Hasidism as Mysticism: Quietistic Elements in Eighteenth-Century Hasidic Thought*, tr. J. Chipman (Princeton University Press, Princeton-Jerusalem, 1993).

Schatz-Uffenheimer, "Man's Relationship to God and World in Buber" — Rivka Schatz-Uffenheimer, "Man's Relationship to God and World in Buber's Rendering of Hasidic Teachings," in eds. P.

Schilpp and M. Friedman, *The Philosophy of Martin Buber* (La Salle, IL, 1967), pp. 403–435.

Schechter, "The Chassidim" — Solomon Schechter, "The Chassidim," reprinted in his *Studies in Judaism: Essays on Persons, Concepts, and Movements of Thought in Jewish Tradition* (Atheneum, New York, 1970), pp. 150–189.

Scholem, *ha-Shalav ha-'Aḥaron* — Gershom Scholem, *The Latest Phase: Essays on Hasidism*, eds. D. Assaf and E. Liebes (Magnes Press, Jerusalem, 2008) (Hebrew).

Scholem, *Kabbalah* — Gershom Scholem, *Kabbalah* (Keter Publishing, Jerusalem, 1974).

Scholem, *Major Trends in Jewish Mysticism* — Gershom Scholem, *Major Trends in Jewish Mysticism* (Schocken Books, New York, 1960).

Scholem, "Martin Buber's Interpretation of Hasidism" — Scholem, *The Messianic Idea*, pp. 228–250 (expanded version of his article originally published in *Commentary*, vol. 32, no. 10 [October 1961], pp. 305–316).

Scholem, *The Messianic Idea* — Gershom Scholem, *The Messianic Idea in Judaism and Other Essays on Jewish Spirituality*, tr. M. Meyer (Schocken Books, New York, 1971).

Scholem, "The Name of God and the Linguistic Theory of the Kabbalah" — Gershom Scholem, "The Name of God and the Linguistic Theory of the Kabbalah," *Diogenes*, vol. 79 (1972), pp. 59–80; vol. 80, pp. 164–194.

Scholem, *On the Kabbalah and Its Symbolism* — Gershom G. Scholem, *On the Kabbalah and Its Symbolism*, tr. R. Manheim (Schocken Books, New York, 1969).

Scholem, *On the Mystical Shape of the Godhead* — Gershom Scholem, *On the Mystical Shape of the Godhead*, tr. J. Neugroschel, ed. J. Chipman (Schocken Books, New York, 1991).

Scholem, *On the Possibility of Jewish Mysticism* — Gershom Scholem, *On the Possibility of Jewish Mysticism in Our Time and Other Essays*, ed. A. Shapira, tr. J. Chipman (Jewish Publication Society, Philadelphia, 1997).

Scholem, *Origins of the Kabbalah* — Gershom Scholem, *Origins of the Kabbalah*, tr. A. Arkush, ed. R. J. Zwi Werblowsky (Princeton University Press, Princeton, 1987).

Schwartz, *Music in Jewish Thought* — Dov Schwartz, *Music in Jewish Thought* (Bar Ilan University Press, Ramat Gan, 2013) (Hebrew).

Schwartz, *Studies on Astral Magic* — Dov Schwartz, *Studies on Astral Magic in Medieval Jewish Thought*, trs. D. Louvish and B. Stein (Brill, Leiden, 2005).

Seeman, "Ritual Efficacy" — Don Seeman, "Ritual Efficacy, Hasidic Mysticism, and 'Useless Suffering' in the Warsaw Ghetto," *HTR*, vol. 101, no. 3–4 (2008), pp. 465–505.

Sullivan, "Sound and Senses" — Lawrence E. Sullivan, "Sound and Senses: Toward a Hermeneutics of Performance," *History of Religion*, vol. 26 (1986), pp. 1–33.

Tishby, *Studies* — Isaiah Tishby, *Studies in Kabbalah and Its Branches, Researches, and Sources* (The Magnes Press, Jerusalem, 1993), 3 volumes (Hebrew).

Wacks, *The Secret of Unity* — Ron Wacks, *The Secret of Unity: Unifications in the Kabbalistic and Hasidic Thought of R. Ḥayim ben Solomon Tyrer of Czernowitz* (Cherub Press, Los Angeles, 2006) (Hebrew).

Warburg, *The Renewal of Pagan Antiquity* — Aby Warburg, *The Renewal of Pagan Antiquity*, tr. David Britt (Getty Research Institute, Los Angeles, 1999).

Weiss, "The Beginning of the Emergence of the Hasidic Path" — Joseph Weiss, "The Beginning of the Emergence of the Hasidic Path," *Zion*, vol. 16 (1951), pp. 46–105 (Hebrew).

Weiss, *Letters by which Heaven and Earth Were Created* — Tzahi Weiss, *Letters by which Heaven and Earth Were Created: The Origins and the Meaning of the Perceptions of Alphabetic Letters as Independent Units in Jewish Sources in Late Antiquity* (Mossad Bialik, Jerusalem, 2014) (Hebrew).

Weiss, *Studies* — Joseph Weiss, *Studies in Eastern European Jewish Mysticism*, ed. D. Goldstein (Littman Library, Oxford, 1997).

Weiss, "Talmud-Torah le-Shitat R. Israel Besht" — Joseph Weiss, "Study of the Torah in R. Israel Baal Shem Tov's Doctrine," in eds. H. J. Zimmels, J. Rabbinowitz, and I. Finestein, *Essays Presented to Chief Rabbi Israel Brodie* (London, 1967), pp. 162–167 (Hebrew).

Werblowsky, *Joseph Karo, Lawyer and Mystic* — R. J. Zwi Werblowsky, *Joseph Karo, Lawyer and Mystic* (Oxford University Press, Oxford, 1962).

Wilensky, *Hasidim and Mitnaggedim* — Mordecai Wilensky, *Hasidim and Mitnaggedim* (Mossad Bialik, Jerusalem, 1970), 2 volumes (Hebrew).

Wolfson, *Along the Path* — Elliot R. Wolfson, *Along the Path, Studies in Kabbalistic Myth, Symbolism, and Hermeneutics* (SUNY Press, Albany, 1995).

Wolfson, *Circle in the Square* — Elliot R. Wolfson, *Circle in the Square: Studies in the Use of Gender in Kabbalistic Symbolism* (SUNY Press, Albany, 1995).

Wolfson, "Immanuel Frommann" — Elliot R. Wolfson, "Immanuel Frommann's Commentary on Luke and the Christianizing of Kabbalah: Some Sabbatean and Hasidic Affinities," in ed. G. Dynner, *Holy Dissent: Jewish and Christian Mystics in Eastern Europe* (Wayne University Press, Detroit, 2011), pp. 171–222.

Wolfson, *Language, Eros, Being* — Elliot R. Wolfson, *Language, Eros, Being: Kabbalistic Hermeneutics and Poetic Imagination* (Fordham University Press, New York, 2005).

Wolfson, *Through a Speculum that Shines* — Elliot R. Wolfson, *Through a Speculum that Shines* (Princeton University Press, Princeton, 1995).

Ysander, *Studien* — Torsten Ysander, *Studien zum B'estshten Hasidismus* (Lundeqistka Bokhandeln, Upsala, 1933).

Zoran, "Magic, Theurgy, and the Knowledge of Letters" — Yair Zoran, "Magic, Theurgy, and the Knowledge of Letters in Islam and Their Parallels in Jewish Literature," *JSJF*, vol. 18 (1997), pp. 19–62 (Hebrew).